Communication Yearbook 32

Communication Yearbook 32

Edited by
Christina S. Beck

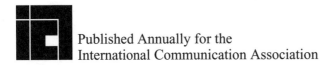

Published Annually for the
International Communication Association

Routledge
Taylor & Francis Group

NEW YORK AND LONDON

First published 2008
by Routledge
270 Madison Ave, New York, NY 10016

Simultaneously published in the UK
by Routledge
2 Park Square, Milton Park, Abingdon, Oxon OX14 4RN

Routledge is an imprint of the Taylor & Francis Group, an informa business

© 2008 Taylor & Francis

Typeset in Times by
HWA Text and Data Management, London
Printed and bound in the United States of America on acid-free paper by
Edwards Brothers, Inc.

ISSN: 0147-4642

ISBN10 HB: 0-415-98859-4
ISBN10 EB: 0-203-93128-9

ISBN13 HB: 978-0-415-98859-9
ISBN13 EB: 978-0-203-93128-8

Contents

The International Communication Association

The International Communication Association (ICA) was formed in 1950, bringing together academics and other professionals whose interests focus on human communication. The Association maintains an active membership of more than 4,000 individuals, of whom some two-thirds teach and conduct research in colleges, universities, and schools around the world. Other members are in government, law, medicine, and other professions. The wide professional and geographic distribution of the membership provides the basic strength of the ICA. The Association serves as a meeting ground for sharing research and useful dialogue about communication interests.

Through its divisions and interest groups, publications, annual conferences, and relations with other associations around the world, ICA promotes the systemic study of communication theories, processes, and skills. In addition to *Communication Yearbook*, the association publishes the *Journal of Communication, Human Communication Research, Communication Theory, Journal of Computer-Mediated Communication, A Guide to Publishing in Scholarly Communication Journals*, and the *ICA Newsletter*.

For additional information about ICA and its activities, visit online at www. icahdq.org or contact Michael L. Haley, Executive Director, International Communication Association, 1730 Rhode Island Ave. NW, Suite 300, Washington, D.C. 20036 USA. Phone: 202-530-9855; Fax: 202-530-9851; E-mail ica@icahdq.org.

Editors of the *Communication Yearbook* series:

Volumes 1 and 2, Brent D. Ruben
Volumes 3 and 4, Dan Nimmo
Volumes 5 and 6, Michael Burgoon
Volumes 7 and 8, Robert N. Bostrom
Volumes 9 and 10, Margaret L. McLaughlin
Volumes 11, 12, 13, and 14, James A. Anderson
Volumes 15, 16, and 17, Stanley A. Deetz
Volumes 18, 19, and 20, Brant R. Burleson
Volumes 21, 22, and 23, Michael E. Roloff
Volumes 24, 25, and 26, William B. Gudykunst
Volumes 27, 28, and 29, Pamela J. Kalbfleisch
Volumes 30, 31, and 32, Christina S. Beck

Information Systems
Paul David Bolls, *University of Missouri-Columbia*

Interpersonal Communication
Pamela Kalbfleisch, *University of North Dakota*

Health Communication
Douglas Storey, *Johns Hopkins Bloomberg*

Philosophy of Communication
Ingrid Volkmer, *University of Melbourne*

Communication & Technology
Jan A.G.M. Van Dijk, *University of Twente*

Popular Communication
Lynn Schofield Clark, *University of Denver*

Public Relations
A.A. Betke Van Ruler, *University of Amsterdam*

Feminist Scholarship
Vicki Mayer, *Tulane University*

Communication Law & Policy
Sharon Strover, *University of Texas–Austin*

Instructional/Development
Amy Nathanson, *Ohio State University*

Language & Social Interaction
Mark Aakhus, *Rutgers University*

Visual Communication Studies
Marion G. Mueller, *Jacobs University – Bremen*

Global Communication/Social Change
Oliver Boyd-Barrett, *Bowling Green State University*

Journalism Studies
John E. Newhagen, *University of Maryland*

SPECIAL INTEREST GROUP CHAIRS

Gay, Lesbian, Bisexual, and Transgender Studies
David Phillips, *University of Toronto*; Lynn A. Comella, *University of Nevada–Las Vegas*

Communication History
David W. Park, *Lake Forest College*

Intergroup Communication
Bernadette Maria Watson, *University of Queensland*

Ethnicity and Race in Communication
Kumarini Silva, *Northeastern University*

Game Studies
John L. Sherry, *Michigan State University*

Children, Adolescents, and the Media
Patti M. Valkenburg, *University of Amsterdam*

Editorial Board

Eric Kramer   University of Oklahoma
Ronald L. Jackson II   Pennsylvania State University
Michael Kent   University of Oklahoma
Wendy Leeds-Hurwitz   University of Wisconsin-Parkside
Dafna Lemish   Tel-Aviv University
Leah A. Lievrouw   University of California, Los Angeles
John Lucaites   Indiana University
Gianpietro Mazzoleni   University of Milano
Raymie McKerrow   Ohio University
Caryn Medved   Baruch College–City University of New York
Paul Messaris   University of Pennsylvania
Michaela D. E. Meyer   Christopher Newport University
Renee Meyers   University of Wisconsin-Milwaukee
Dennis Mumby   University of North Carolina-Chapel Hill
Susan Ohmer   University of Notre Dame
Daniel J. O'Keefe   Northwestern University
Michael J. Papa   Central Michigan University
Ronald Pelias   Southern Illinois University
Elizabeth Perse   University of Delaware
W. James Potter   University of California, Santa Barbara
Brian Quick   University of Illinois at Urbana-Champaign
Sandra Ragan   University of Oklahoma
Jeffery D. Robinson   Rutgers University
Matthew W. Seeger   Wayne State University
Barbara Sharf   Texas A&M University
Christina Slade   Macquarie University
J. Michael Sproule   Saint Louis University
Jeffrey St. John   Ohio University
Maureen Taylor   University of Oklahoma
Teresa Thompson   University of Dayton
Nick Trujillo   California State University, Sacramento
Patti M. Valkenburg   University of Amsterdam
Robert Westerfelhaus   College of Charleston
Andrew Wood   San José State University
Gust A. Yep   San Francisco State University
Barbie Zelizer   University of Pennsylvania

Guest Reviewers

Alison Alexander	University of Georgia
Jens Allwood	University of Göteborg
Greg G. Armfield	Angelo State University
Margaret Baker Graham	Iowa State University
Dawna Ballard	University of Texas at Austin
Michael D. Basil	University of Lethbridge
David Beard	University of Minnesota-Duluth
Zane Berge	University of Maryland, Baltimore County
Lori Bergen	Texas State University
Joseph Bonito	University of Arizona
Melanie Booth-Butterfield	West Virginia University
Hans-Bernd Brosius	Ludwig-Maximilians-Universität, Munich
Rose G. Campbell	Butler University
Simone Chambers	University of Toronto
April Chatham-Carpenter	University of Northern Iowa
Jay P. Childers	University of Kansas
Rebecca M. Chory	West Virginia University
Jonathan Cohen	Haifa University
Anne Cooper-Chen	Ohio University
John Cotton	Marquette University
Douglas E. Cowan	University of Waterloo
Brenda Danet	Hebrew University of Jerusalem/Yale University
Prabu David	Ohio State University
John Davies	University of North Florida
Diana Davis	James Cook University
Victoria DeFrancisco	University of Northern Iowa
Susan Dente Ross	Washington State University
Renee Edwards	Louisiana State University
John Eighmey	University of Minnesota-Twin Cities
Laura L. Ellingson	Santa Clara University
Jesper Falkheimer	Lund University
James Floyd	University of Central Missouri
Shiv Ganesh	University of Waikato
Kenneth Gergen	Swarthmore College
Gloria Galanes	Missouri State University
Elizaeth Graham	Ohio University
Bradley Greenberg	Michigan State University
Glenn J. Hansen	University of Oklahoma
Jeremy Harris Lipschultz	University of Nebraska, Omaha
Greg Hearn	Queensland University of Technology
David Henningsen	Northern Illinois University

Krishnamurthy Sriramesh   Nanyang Technological University
Cynthia Stohl   University of California, Santa Barbara
Charles R. Taylor   Villanova University
C. Erik Timmerman   University of Wisconsin-Milwaukee
Diane-Gabrielle Tremblay   University of Quebec, Montreal
Steven Venette   University of Southern Mississippi
Dejan Verčič   University of Ljubljana
Courtney Waite Miller   Elmhurst College
H. Allen White   Murray State University
Danielle R. Wiese   Grand Valley State University
Hugh Willmott   University of Cardiff
Roger Wimmer   Wimmer Research
Roy Wood   University of Denver
Xu Wu   Arizona State University
Niki Young   Western Oregon University
Jensen Zhao   Ball State University
Shuhua Zhou   University of Alabama

Editor's Introduction

Christina S. Beck

*C*ommunication Yearbook 32 (*CY*) marks the third volume under my editorship, and chapters in this book reflect my continued commitment to comprehensive literature reviews of communication research that advance our theoretical and/or empirical understanding of a topic, highlight potential connections across our discipline, and pursue perspectives from communication professionals from around the globe. The contributions to *Communication Yearbook 32* do more than summarize and analyze works on a particular issue, although each certainly excels in that capacity. They also strive to spark dialogues about the ways in which that research could be potentially insightful to and valuable for others in our international community of communication scholars.

When I issued the call for *Communication Yearbook 32*, I cast a wide net, inviting submissions on any communication topic as long as the author could explain why a certain body of research might be pertinent for a diverse audience of international communication scholars. Of course, writers should always acknowledge and engage their varied readership, especially when their work appears in international publications. Additionally, I believe that *Communication Yearbook*, as a premier outlet for state-of-the-art commu-nication literature reviews, should prompt ideas for collaborations across our discipline and inspire conversations about the theoretical, empirical, and/ or methodological usefulness of concepts that may come from one area of research but hold possible relevance for others as well.

Owing to the broad call, the nine chapters in this volume may appear, at first glance, to be very different. In fact, they do represent a cross-section of our discipline, ranging from a chapter that emphasizes theory to one with a focus on methodology to reviews of literature on resistance, meaningful work, virtual teams, media coverage of terrorism, and constructions of whiteness, media literacy, and supportive messages. In so doing, the chapters span disciplinary interests in interpersonal communication, health communication, organizational communication, spiritual communication, group commun-ication, communication and technology, intercultural communication, rhetoric, and mass media. Despite this contextual diversity, two general themes echo through this volume, and I highlight them briefly before previewing each of the chapters.

First, the chapters in this volume position communication as socially co-constructed and, moreover, as the means through which members/ stakeholders/ interactants discursively co-negotiate emergent definitions, roles, and relationships. In our lead chapter, Bartesaghi and Castor tackle this matter in great detail, but this appreciation for (and acknowledgment of) the constitutive nature of communication appears (to varying extents) in each subsequent chapter. As social actors, we co-define actions that constitute "resistance" (see Pal & Dutta, this volume), "terrorism" (see Keränen & Sanprie, this volume), "support" (see Bodie & Burleson, this volume), and the like. As individuals and, concurrently, co-participants in social interactions, we continually determine (and often reconsider, in light of the era, experiences, media influences, spiritual perspectives, and perhaps even unfolding economic, social, and technological conditions and constraints) what counts as "work" (see Cheney, Zorn, Planalp, & Lair, this volume), "successful" team experiences (see Gibbs, Nekrassova, Grushina, & Wahab, this volume), and racism (see Lacy, this volume). Even in our scholarly dialogues, we debate the "effectiveness" of research approaches (see Zoller & Kline, this volume) and dispute definitions of important terms such as "media literacy" (see Rosenbaum, Beentjes, & Konig, this volume).

As the chapters in this book attest, we struggle to discern "reality" on a daily basis, not just as scholars but as health care participants, organizational members, media consumers, members of a culture, and individuals in relationships. For example, I was in the final stages of polishing this book when I took a short holiday break. I share my daughters' passion for Disney movies, and we went to see the recently released movie, *Enchanted*. The film begins as an animated feature in the classic Disney tradition, and it takes a jarring turn when the evil stepmother pushes Giselle, a beautiful fairy-tale princess, into a magical well. When the no-longer-animated princess pops up in New York City (through a sewer hole), the live-action comedy commences as Giselle literally falls into the arms of Robert, a cynical New York divorce attorney. After spending the night on Robert's couch, Giselle repays his kindness by summoning animal friends (albeit more dingy cousins to their bright and clean counterparts in her homeland forest) to help with tidying his apartment and then by singing through (and creating a spectacle in) Central Park. In Giselle's fairy-tale world, nothing matters more than love's first kiss. To Robert, the "real world" seems doomed with certain disappointment, especially in terms of potential long-term commitment. Robert resists an initial impulse to dismiss Giselle as "confused," and their subsequent interactions enable them to appreciate (and, ultimately, believe) their different life vistas and to create a "new normal," wherein "happily ever after" means something far different (yet profoundly better) than either ever imagined.

Alas, perhaps, fairy-tale endings (especially in the tradition of Walt Disney films) may hold little similarity to others, but the movie mirrored "real life" in that we never conclusively "set" or "define" static realities. They emerge as we collectively co-construct, co-negotiate, and occasionally dispute them, and this orientation to the world (and to scholarship) impacts our pursuit of understandings about communication—as well as what we create and accomplish through it.

Indeed, second, the chapters in this book demonstrate the consequential and potentially liberating nature of communication. The ways in which we interact with others quite simply matter, as do our decisions not to communicate at all. To belabor the movie example for just one more moment, I was struck by the male lead's choice to help Giselle instead of passively ignoring her plight. Obviously, the movie depended on that fateful act of getting involved, yet how much more lingers with our own everyday willingness to interact with someone a tad different, to add voice to a cause, to make the extra effort to contribute to a team or support a friend, or to consider the ramifications of a mediated message or stereotypical comment.

The chapters in *Communication Yearbook 32* reveal how communication can liberate stakeholders to redefine or reposition circumstances or perspectives (see especially Cheney et al., this volume; Gibbs et al., this volume; Pal & Dutta, this volume; Zoller & Kline, this volume). This book highlights the ways in which invested individuals can communicate to resist problematic policies or practices (Pal & Dutta, this volume; Zoller & Kline, this volume), and it contains important examples of the ways in which communication proves consequential, on an everyday basis, in terms of how we treat others as we construct, interpret, and reify messages (see Bodie & Burleson, this volume; Cheney et al., this volume; Gibbs et al., this volume; Keränen & Sanprie, this volume; Lacy, this volume; Rosenbaum et al., this volume). These chapters remind us that our editorial and scholarly choices implicitly position research as "valuable," methods as "appropriate" (see Zoller & Kline, this volume), or definitions as "adequate" (see Rosenbaum et al., this volume).

Such characterizations do not simply reflect social constructions; they indicate agency to spark or deter change in how we view each other, our lives, our organizations, our media, our scholarship, and our world. Thus, they matter greatly, and I applaud the chapters in this volume for reminding us about the consequentiality of communication in a variety of intriguing contexts.

Overview of Chapters

As I indicated earlier, we begin *Communication Yearbook 32* with a compelling chapter on social construction from a communication perspective. Mariaelena Bartesaghi and Theresa Castor revisit prior conversations on social construction, and they describe various approaches to it within the communication discipline. This chapter holds considerable relevance for a broad array of communication scholars, and it provides a strong theoretical foundation for several of the other chapters in this volume.

In their chapter, Mahuya Pal and Mohan J. Dutta explore resistance, especially in light of globalization. Pal and Dutta highlight research from across the globe, detailing current approaches to resistance as well as affirming the need to examine resistance in a global context. Though this chapter relates most clearly to scholars in the areas of organizational communication and health communication, others in interpersonal communication, intercultural communication, communication and technology, and rhetoric would also benefit from reading this insightful chapter.

Heather M. Zoller and Kimberly N. Kline provide an excellent companion chapter to the first two in the volume. They begin by tracing the traditions of interpretive and critical scholarship, and they underscore the many theoretical contributions of research from this framework. This chapter provides valuable information for scholars across the discipline in terms of its careful treatment of interpretative and critical approaches to research. Further, its discussion of resistance continues the conversation on that topic from Chapter 2, and it could be especially useful for organizational communication scholars as well as individuals in health communication.

Similarly, George Cheney, Theodore E. Zorn, Sally Planalp, and Daniel J. Lair offer a review that transcends disciplinary boundaries with a thoughtful exploration of the meanings of work. Though we may traditionally link "work" with organizational communication, our views of (and discourses about) work extend from (and reflexively impact) our culture, our families, our individual identities, spiritual beliefs, available technology, and so on. As such, this chapter could be very relevant for scholars in interpersonal communication, family communication, intercultural communication, communication and technology, and spiritual communication, in addition to organizational communication.

Indeed, as Jennifer L. Gibbs, Dina Nekrassova, Svetlana V. Grushina, and Sally Abdul Wahab observe, the advent of technology and globalization greatly impacts the ways in which individuals accomplish work around the world, especially as members of virtual teams. Providing a powerful extension to preceding arguments in this volume on social construction and resistance, Gibbs et al. challenge earlier depictions of communication as a variable, and they argue that we should pursue understandings of virtual teams from a constitutive perspective. This chapter will be particularly pertinent to scholars in the areas of communication and technology, organizational communication, small-group communication, interpersonal communication, and intercultural communication.

As we consider our increasingly global community, we realize that technology connects us more than ever before in board rooms as well as news rooms. In Chapter 6, Lisa Keränen and Virginia Sanprie detail media coverage of terrorism. They delineate the relationship between media and acts of terrorism, and they review the ways in which stakeholders construct and challenge representations of terrorism through television, print, and the Internet. Although this chapter will be especially salient for media scholars and those in the specific area of terrorism and communication, it also holds relevance for scholars in the areas of interpersonal communication, group communication, organizational communication, spiritual communication, intercultural communication, and communication and technology.

Bridging from Keränen and Sanprie's discussion of representations of others in terms of terrorism, in his chapter, Michael Lacy explores rhetorical constructions of "white absolutism." Lacy describes how rhetors employed language to present themselves as "pure" while casting others as "evil." This chapter invites reflection on taken-for-granted social constructions of self and other in terms of race. As such, this chapter provides key insights for scholars across our discipline as they pursue enactments of race and identity in interpersonal exchanges, organizational or group communication, media representation, and intercultural dialogues.

Chapters 6 and 7 point strongly to the need for media literacy and, in Chapter 8, Judith E. Rosenbaum, Johannes W. J. Beentjes, and Ruben P. Konig review the literature on this important topic. Notably, definitions vary across this area of research as scholars construct this term (and their responses to it) differently, and Rosenbaum et al. synthesize this research by providing a model with key aspects of media literacy. Media scholars will benefit from this chapter as well as researchers in interpersonal communication, family communication, instructional communication, intercultural communication, and communication and technology.

We conclude *Communication Yearbook 32* with a chapter on supportive messages. As we reflect on the issues addressed in this volume of *CY*, our global community could benefit from signs of support—when we're struggling with health, family, or relational problems…when we're over-burdened with work or work conflicts…when we're afraid due to threats of violence or personal attacks on core parts of our identity. Bodie and Burleson review existing literature on supportive messages and offer a dual-process theory for explaining the impact of such messages in light of various moderators. This chapter will be particularly valuable for scholars in the areas of interpersonal communication, health communication, and intercultural communication.

Summary of Process

I received 60 submissions to *Communication Yearbook 32*. Overall, reviewers applauded the outstanding quality of submissions, and competition for the possible chapter slots was incredibly intense. I selected 10 proposals for development into chapters for this volume, based on reviewer feedback (during a blind, peer-review process) about the strong quality of those potential literature reviews and their fit with the theme of *Communication Yearbook 32*. Unfortunately, schedule conflicts eventually prevented the author of one accepted proposal from completing his work, and that individual did not withdraw early enough in the process to allow me to replace his chapter.

Thus, this volume of *Communication Yearbook* features nine chapters by scholars from the United States, the Netherlands, and New Zealand, representing diverse areas in our discipline. Each selected chapter received input during at least two rounds of review from peer reviewers as well as feedback from the editor. Further, all accepted authors benefited from receiving a CD with early drafts of all chapters that were targeted for publication in this volume, and I encouraged cross-referencing to facilitate a more cohesive volume.

Grateful Acknowledgments

As I conclude work on this third volume under my editorship, I remain incredibly grateful to the Publications Committee of the International Communication Association for this wonderful opportunity to interact with scholars across the globe through this work on *Communication Yearbook*. I have truly enjoyed my interactions with potential contributors and reviewers, and I appreciate the very positive ways in which this editorial journey has impacted my life.

I also thank and acknowledge members of my editorial board for their dedicated service to this publication. Further, given that I received the bulk of these diverse submissions around the same time in November, 2006, I also turned to several guest reviewers for input and counsel. I am deeply grateful to all of these editorial board members and guest reviewers for their excellent and prompt feedback. I know that the chapters in this volume benefited immensely from their insights, and I appreciate their time, energy, and willingness to serve.

Furthermore, I thank my senior editorial associate, Jennifer Scott, for her uplifting support, generous spirit, and wise input. She truly possesses the spiritual gift of encouragement, and I appreciate all of her continued support and assistance during my editorial journey.

I am also grateful for my editorial assistants, Stephanie Young and Michael Pfahl, and an undergraduate research assistant, Brittany Pangburn. Stephanie and Brittany assisted with identifying possible reviewers for this volume, and Michael took over the helm in the spring by compiling data for reports and confirming vital information in the front of this book.

Finally, I must conclude by thanking my family for their ongoing patience with my editorial responsibilities. Although my academic lifestyle provides me with much flexibility, little exists during the rush of finding reviewers around the Christmas holidays or finalizing each edition in November right before Thanksgiving. Though I know that the promise of a trip to DisneyWorld after another volume goes to press cushions the lack of time during special seasons, I'm very grateful to my husband, Roger Aden, and our daughters—Emmy Grace (age 6), Chelsea Meagan (age 13), and Brittany Nicole (age 21)—for their ongoing understanding, patience, and unconditional love. In them, I have found my own "happily ever after," and I dedicate this book to each of them.

Communication Yearbook 32

CHAPTER CONTENTS

1 Social Construction in Communication

Re-Constituting the Conversation

Mariaelena Bartesaghi
University of South Florida

Theresa Castor
University of Wisconsin

In this chapter, we offer a response to Shotter and Gergen's (1994) proposal in *Communication Yearbook* for social construction (SC) as a framework for communication by reconstituting its impact in our field. We provide an overview of SC research in the communication discipline to illustrate the ways in which scholars have developed specifically communication-oriented SC approaches. After wresting SC from the realm of epistemology and placing it into that of practical theory, we select three areas of research and praxis where social constructionist thinking about communication makes a dramatic difference in thinking and practice. These areas—gender, crisis, and therapy— allow us to move beyond the confines of an American academic forum and engage the concerns of an audience of practitioners in a more global exchange. Additionally, these three topics give us the opportunity to address relevant and still pressing critiques that we take to be consequential to both SC and communication: materiality, agency, and critical applications of practical theory that allow social construction scholars to speak politically on matters heretofore considered extradiscursive. A section on future directions for and challenges to social constructionism concludes our reflection.

In their 1994 *Communication Yearbook* chapter, psychologists John Shotter and Kenneth Gergen rejoined an ongoing exchange about SC (P. L. Berger & Luckmann, 1966; Gergen, 1985; Gilbert & Mulkay, 1984; Goolishian & Anderson, 2002; McNamee & Gergen, 1999; Potter & Wetherell, 1987; Shotter & Gergen, 1989, among others), staking a claim to its paradigmatic vision as a framework for communication. Delineating the merits of a conversational epistemology and arguing for the centrality of conversation as both a site

Correspondence: Mariaelena Bartesaghi, University of South Florida, CIS 1040, 4202 E. Fowler Avenue, Tampa, FL 33620; Phone: 813-974-6822; E-mail: mbartesa@cas.usf.edu and a generative metaphor for communication study, the authors pressed for a relational, situated, and reflexive space for communication research. As a rejoinder to Shotter & Gergen (1994), this review of SC in communication itself comprises a conversational move: an act of and into communication (W. B. Pearce, 1994) from a particular positioning and, by its very performance, strategic (Bernstein, 1992).

The timing for our rejoinder seems right. Our desire to write this chapter partially results from a strong, resurgent interest of SC in the discipline as evidenced through the Summer Institute "Catching Ourselves in the Act" sponsored in the summer of 2006 by the National Communication Association (NCA; see Galanes & Leeds-Hurwitz, forthcoming) and the ensuing formation of the Social Construction Division in the NCA. As academics who were graduate students in the 1990s and, as scholars of language and social interaction, we were raised conversant in the language of SC and identify with its sentiment and research praxis. In our exchanges with other scholars, we remark how ideas about the narrative construction of identity and the constructed nature of gender, problems, and even our own relationships have settled as curricular dust that seems neither worthy of stirring nor cleaning up. Yet, like Edwards, Ashmore, and Potter (1995), we find that others continue to express misgivings about rampant relativism and implied moral turpitude that begin with furniture thumping (the reality of furniture cannot be denied!) and ultimately equate SC with an immaterial (Penman, 2000) and inconsequential (Sigman, 1995) view of communication. However, social constructionism offers little critical reflection of its own presence on the academic stage, appearing as a magically driven enterprise, "an image more consistent with the scientism it sought to overthrow" (Stam, 2001, p. 295).

We choose this forum to rejoin Shotter and Gergen's (1994) conversational proposal by taking their contribution as a marker in time and asking how we can appreciate its impact within the discipline in terms of creating spaces for new vocabularies, research practices, theoretical applications, and challenges. Our move is aligned with Craig's (1999) outline for a metadiscursive appreciation of communication as composed of a set of self-contained, yet dialectically coherent traditions, each with its taken-for-granted assumptions, inner complexity, and practical outcomes. In turn, we understand and evaluate SC in communication not as a theory but as a metatheoretical position and aim not for deconstruction but for reconstruction and reconstitution, in the spirit of searching for possibility.

Our review chapter unfolds as follows. Recognizing the constructed nature of SC (Bernstein, 1992; W. B. Pearce, 1995; Potter, 1996), we begin by providing an overview of communication SC approaches to illustrate the ways in which scholars have developed a specifically communication-oriented SC thinking. Wresting SC from the realm of epistemology and placing it into that of practical theory (Cronen, 1995b), which allows us, in Wittgenstein's sense, to create the knowledge of "how to go on" (1980, p. 875), we then select three areas of research and praxis where social constructionist thinking about communication makes a dramatic difference in thinking and practice. A section on future directions for and challenges to social constructionism concludes our chapter.

SOCIAL CONSTRUCTION IN COMMUNICATION: A REVIEW OF THE LITERATURE[1]

A key word search for "social constructionism" in the Communication and Mass Media Index database yielded only 86 references, with the broader search term of "social construction" yielding 213 references. While promising, these numbers pale in comparison to the overall research output in the discipline. Thus, we felt that this first view belied a more complex picture of the status of SC in communication. Indeed, the ongoing interest in SC in the field, as evidenced by the 2006 NCA Summer Institute, the new NCA Social Construction Division, and the ease with which communication scholars acknowledge the influence of social constructionism in their work, attests to the position of SC in the communication discipline.

In this section, we argue that a vibrant SC program in communication exists—one that has reconstituted SC as a specifically communication process. We refer to this enterprise as communication social construction (CSC) to distinguish it from the development of SC in other fields.

Craig (1999) noted that many theories of communication are "borrowed from other disciplines" (p. 123). For example, the very phrase "social construction" comes from P. L. Berger and Luckmann's (1966) sociological treatise, while probably the most recognized social constructionist, Kenneth J. Gergen, primarily addressed psychology (Gergen, 1985, 1991, 1994, 1998, 1999, 2001). Our review focuses on interdiscursive connections—the specific nuances with which researchers have adapted, built on and refined SC ideas from a communication perspective. Inspired by Craig's metamodel of communication theories, we address the following three questions:

1. What is the metadiscursive vocabulary for describing and applying CSC?
2. What are specific CSC approaches?
3. How has CSC research addressed the issues of materiality, agency, and consequentiality?

Metadiscursive vocabulary constitutes terminology related to communication (Craig, 1999). We identify the terms that CSC researchers utilize to describe and apply a SC perspective. As Leeds-Hurwitz (forthcoming) noted, a great deal of CSC research is implicitly rather than explicitly identified as such (i.e., scholars apply the metatheoretical framework afforded by social constructionism, but they do not necessarily invoke the specific term "social construction"). In posing our first question, we wish to underscore the alternative ways that communication scholars employ to describe SC.

For our second question, rather than ask what SC thinking has done for communication, we reverse the relationship and emphasize what communication has contributed to understanding SC processes. Hence, we selectively identify and describe communication theories and approaches that are social constructionist or draw from this tradition.

Finally, we provide a commentary on three areas of CSC research—gender, therapy, and crisis—to illustrate how contemporary CSC work has addressed the problematics of materiality, agency, and consequentiality that have typically been used to level critiques against SC.

Metadiscursive Vocabulary

Four vocabularies frame SC research: (1) *interpretive* approaches, (2) *social approaches*, (3) a *constitutive* perspective, and (4) *construction* with modifiers. Our selection of order is approximately chronological. As we discuss each variation, we also note cautions in the application of this vocabulary to understanding CSC.

Interpretive Approaches

The term *interpretive approaches* became popular with Putnam and Pacanowsky (1983). As a counter to the dominant functionalist perspectives of organizational communication that treat communication in an instrumental fashion (i.e., as a "tool" to understand more significant phenomena), "interpretivists believe that reality is *socially constructed* through the words, symbols, and behaviors of its members" (emphasis added, Putnam, 1983, p. 35). Putnam further elaborated that an interpretive perspective focuses on symbolic processes and a pluralistic approach.

Though scholars widely use interpretive approaches in communication, Cheney (2000) is critical of how the use of the term *interpretive* mystifies more than it reveals. Cheney's own interpretation of "interpretive" identified strategies of allegiance (against functionalists), methodological identification ("a simplistic synonym for qualitative data analysis"), and deflection within a conversation ("never having to explain your methodology," p. 25; see also Hacking, 1999).

Social Approaches

Explicitly drawing a parallel to Putnam and Pacanowsky's (1983) introduction of interpretive approaches to organizational communication, Leeds-Hurwitz (1995) introduced *social approaches* as an alternative to social scientific approaches to the study of interpersonal communication. In contrast to an "objectivist" position, social approaches are methodologically interpretive and focus on the dynamics of interpersonal communication (e.g., Baxter, 2004; Baxter & Montgomery, 1996; Varey, 2000). Though several differences exist across social approaches, Leeds-Hurwitz identified 11 themes: (1) a focus on the social rather than cognitive, (2) communication as process as well as product, (3) a social construction of reality perspective, (4) the creation of social meanings, (5) identity as socially constructed, (6) culture, (7) the significance of context, (8) the use of direct observation in research, (9) symbols, (10) reflexivity in research, and (11) a holistic approach. Examples of social approaches that Leeds-Hurwitz specified include discourse analysis, ethnography of communication, ethnomethodology, conversation analysis, pragmatics, coordinated management of meaning, symbolic interactionism, cultural studies, critical theory, and narrative analysis, to name a few.

Lucaites and Fitch (1997) cautioned that the rubric "social approaches" risks collapsing important differences between the specific approaches. In this respect, we must consider the differences among social approaches that W. B. Pearce (1995) outlined at a metatheoretical level, notably seeking certainty versus exercising "curiosity," a monadic versus pluralistic view of the world, and a representational versus practical view of knowledge. Though communication scholars do not widely utilize the term *social approaches*, the more specific approaches described within this area have been applied regularly in research, most notably in language and social interaction (see Fitch & Sanders, 2005).

Constitutive Perspective

The term *constitutive* has rippled throughout conversations of communication (e.g., Dixon, 2000; Goldsmith & Baxter, 1996; Mumby, 1989; Mumby & Stohl, 1996; Trethewey, 2000), with Deetz (1994) providing one of the most explicit articulations of this perspective and its connection to social construction (see also Stewart, 1995). Standing for the place of communication as a mode of explanation, "constitutive" evokes a reflexive relationship between theory and culture as well as Deetz's stake for a disciplinary effort to reconstruct practices of deliberation, democracy, and negotiation (see also Craig, 1999). Deetz's articulation of a constitutive view of communication is an ontological one. Deetz explained:

> *If we are to make our full social contribution, we have to move from studying 'communication' phenomena as formed and explained psychologically, sociologically, and economically, and produce studies that study psychological, sociological, and economic phenomena as formed and explained communicationally.* (p. 568; emphasis in original)

How to understand communication as constitutive is still under exploration, particularly in the field of organizational communication (e.g., Dixon, 2000).

Some areas of research include the relationship between discourse and organizing (Fairhurst & Putnam, 2004), identity (S. J. Tracy & Trethewey, 2005), messages (McPhee & Zaug, 2000), embodiment (Trethewey, 2000), and resistance (Mumby, 2005).

Construction with Modifiers

Rather than SC, several projects have used variations such as *discursive construction, co-construction, joint construction,* and *joint action.* For example, some studies examined discursive constructions in organizations (Fairhurst & Putnam, 2004), problems (Buttny, 1996, 2004), information (Terranova, 2006), and gender in interpersonal (Pienaar & Bekker, 2006) as well as organizational contexts (Ashcraft & Mumby, 2004b; Buzzanell & Liu, 2005). Others coined the term *co-construction* (e.g., Jacoby & Ochs, 1995; McVittie, 2004), and some described joint construction (e.g., Georgakopoulou, 2002). Authors who employed the terminology of joint action include Cronen (1995a) in detailing the coordinated management of meaning perspective, and Castor (2005), Shotter (2005), and Holman and Thorpe (2003) in explicating SC processes in organizational contexts.

The variations on construction underline the importance of language in the case of discursive construction and the salience of interaction in the cases of co-construction, joint construction, and joint action. These variations highlight how "construction" modified by "social" does not necessarily offer the key way to capture an SC approach in communication. Instead, researchers emphasize the linguistic and interactive aspects of SC processes. To identify social constructionist research in communication, one must go beyond the specific term of *social construction* and evaluate research by how it furthers SC's metatheoretical possibilities, rather than paying lip service to its terminology.

Communication Social Construction Approaches

Many approaches have influenced CSC research such as the dramaturgical approach (e.g., Goffman, 1959), ethnomethodology (e.g., Garfinkel, 1967), poststructuralism (e.g., Foucault, 1980), philosophy of language (e.g., Wittgenstein, 1953), literacy criticism (e.g., Bakhtin, 1981, 1984, 1986; Volosinov, 1986) and others (e.g., Vygotsky, 1986). Several communication approaches advance an SC perspective. Some are explicitly social constructionist; whereas, others hold SC assumptions but do not necessarily emphasize SC as a primary frame. We present four approaches that provide a specifically communication perspective on SC[2] and that were selected according to their emphasis on a practical, relational, and/or questioning perspective of communication and social construction. In this section, we emphasize the coordinated management of meaning, relationally-responsive social constructionism, action-implicative discourse analysis, and dialogic approaches. As we examine each orientation to research, we explain why we chose it for inclusion, review its key assumptions, describe example studies, and specify contributions of each to understanding the relationship between communication and SC.

Coordinated Management of Meaning

W. B. Pearce and Cronen (W. B. Pearce, 1976, 1989; W. B. Pearce & Cronen, 1980; Philipsen, 1995) developed the coordinated management of meaning (CMM), initially known as a "rules" approach (Berger, 2005; Pearce, 1976), in the late 1970s and early 1980s. CMM has undergone a great deal of development and transformation. According to Barge and W. B. Pearce (2004, p. 25), "Its evolution can be charted in several ways: from purely academic to thoroughly integrated in various sorts of practice; from scientific to social constructionist/ pragmatic; and from explanatory/predictive to a practical theory." CMM has progressed from an interpretive theory to one with a critical edge and, currently, a practical theory (W. B. Pearce, 2004). This theory also has been identified as a communication theory influenced by social construction (e.g., Barge & Pearce, 2004; Dillon & Galanes, 2002; Griffin, 2006).

Shailor (1997) argued that "[t]he basic premise of CMM is that our social realities are continually created, maintained and transformed in a reflexive process of action and interpretation" (p. 97). Because CMM constitutes a very broad and "ambitious" (Philipsen, 1995, p. 14) theory and research program, we address only four of its key concepts: *persons in conversation, the hierarchy of meaning, rules,* and *loops*. Persons in conversation constitutes the primary unit of observation in CMM (Cronen, 1995a). This idea foregrounds interaction in the construction of social reality and the ongoing negotiation of meaning in conversation. In the CMM perspective, interlocutors construct meaning through their stories, which themselves exist within the context of episodes. Conversational partners may point to one level among a multilevel hierarchy of contexts, such as episodes, relationships, identity, and culture (W. B. Pearce, 2004). Also, as Shailor emphasized, "contexts are not found things, but are interpretive achievements" (p. 97).

Rules were a key aspect of initial articulations of CMM (C. R. Berger, 2005; W. B. Pearce, 1976). CMM identifies two types of rules: *regulative* and *constitutive*. Regulative rules direct actions by specifying what kind of behavior should or should not occur. Constitutive rules serve as guides for interpretation. A *loop* refers to a cycle of interaction and how interlocutors respond to each other. Loops may be charmed, subversive, or strange—which terms refer, respectively, to when levels of meaning in the hierarchy are consistent with each other, when levels of meaning differ (perhaps irreparably so), and when a change of level entails a shift in meaning.

Barge and W. B. Pearce (2004) described five research "streams" in CMM: interpersonal and intercultural communication; organizational communication and management; public communication; therapy and consultation, and conflict, mediation, and dialogue.[3] For example, Shailor (1994) analyzed transcripts and video recordings of dispute mediation sessions and identified how mediators who tended to use a "problem-solving approach" were less successful in helping the disputants and even worsened the problems in some cases. Alternatively, mediators who utilized approaches that were similar to some of the key ideas in CMM tended to be more successful in assisting clients. Shailor's analysis applied CMM by examining the kinds of communication occurring in relation to the CMM model and the interrelationship of communication with disputants' abilities to coordinate their meanings. In a cultural and health context, Bruss et al. (2005) applied CMM to understanding childhood obesity in the Commonwealth of the Northern Mariana Islands. Also, Bruss et al. focused on what acceptable eating habits meant for the community of focus to understand cultural assumptions related to health. As with Shailor's project, Bruss et al. had a practical orientation in trying to understand how to bring about social change.

As a social constructionist approach that draws from American pragmatists such as James and Dewey (Barge, 2004; Cronen, 1995a; W. B. Pearce, 2004; Shailor, 1997), CMM addresses communication practices and their moral implications. Thus, CMM takes a "realistic" position with regard to ontology, in contrast to an objectivist or relativist stance. Key to this orientation, as Cronen explained, is the notion of being able to "go on"—for which a response must enable a next step. Cronen provided the example of someone trying to test a theory of bouncing a bag of potato chips—the world will not respond in a way to enable such a theory. If theories have (moral) careers, then it is interesting to note how CMM was one of the first to be explicitly characterized as social constructionist, while gradually evolving to align with the realistic-ontological and practical voices in social construction.

Relationally Responsive Social Constructionism

"To understand human communication better," wrote Shotter (2000a), "we do not need any new theories. We need to elaborate critically the spontaneous theory of language we already possess" (p. 129). Set against Shotter's (1999) progressive disaffection with "the way of theory" in communication as a belief in unifying principles, the relationally responsive social constructionist perspective (Cunliffe, 2002; Shotter, 1993, 1998, 2000b, 2004, 2005) weaves together the work of various scholars, including Bakhtin, Garfinkel, Vico, Volosinov, Vygotsky, and Wittgenstein.[4] Because Shotter (1993) resisted the characterization of theory, he referred to his work as providing a "critical tool box" of sensitizing concepts for researchers to apply (p. 206). Here, we describe his "tools" of joint actions, persons-in-conversation, responsiveness, and unique events.

Like CMM, the relationally responsive approach describes social construction as based on the joint actions of persons-in-conversation. Shotter's (1993) conversational world is one of unintended consequences, not fully explainable processes, and unpredictable outcomes. As Shotter (2005) explained, "for, whether we like it or not, the fact is that we are always 'entangled' or 'entwined' in a ceaseless flow of relational background activity going on between ourselves and the realities of the others and othernesses around us" (p. 114).

Drawing from Bakhtin, Shotter (1993) desired to capture the unselfconscious presence of human beings in spontaneous interaction with each other. According to Shotter, the idea of responsiveness relates to the enablements and constraints of communication in social accountability where people's words and actions are intelligible within an already specified interactional context of moral implications and answerability. Shotter's recent work on Bakhtinian "once-occurrent events of Being" develops responsiveness away from "theory" toward a Wittgensteinan notion of "social poetics" (see, for e.g., Shotter, 2000b). Like the "dialogical moments" recognized by Martin Buber and Carl Rogers (as we detail later in this chapter), once-occurrent events comprise unique, unfinished moments of connection in communication that render possible other connections, in unique and unexpected ways. For example, Shotter and Katz's (1998) discussion of the work of therapist Tom Andersen focused on his ability to transcend notions of therapy as change—born of theories and of reframes—by acting within fleeting aspects of a conversation to create new openings for practical re-direction.

In addition to Katz and Shotter's work in therapeutic settings (1996; see also Shotter & Katz, 1998), the relationally responsive approach has been utilized to understand interactions involving reported speech (Buttny, 2004) and accounts (Castor, 2005; Shotter, 1984). More recent discussions of relationally responsive social constructionism have addressed organizational contexts (e.g., Castor, 2005; Cunliffe, 2001, 2002; Holman & Thorpe, 2003; Shotter, 1998, 2004, 2005, 2006).

The relationally responsive approach highlights SC as a relational process. As such, this approach privileges understanding communication phenomena (i.e., accounts, reported speech) in actual, moment-to-moment interactions in which interlocutors are accountable to a past, present, anticipated future, and each other. In this respect, the relationally responsive approach contributes to an understanding of CSC as practical and relational.

Action-implicative Discourse Analysis

Blending various interaction-centered approaches, AIDA (Action-implicative Discourse Analysis) is based on Craig and K. Tracy's (1995) explication of grounded practical theory and focuses on the interconnection between theory and practice, or how practice can inform and shape theory. AIDA argues for the interconnection of three levels of analysis—communication practice, problems, and situated ideals. By using problems as a nexus, researchers applying AIDA seek to describe the communication practices that function to shape problems and the situated ideals of participants as discerned through problem analysis.

Adopting grounded practical theory (see Craig & K. Tracy, 1995) as a metatheoretical perspective, AIDA constitutes a *normative* approach. Its analysis draws from participants' descriptions to make explicit their situated ideals for communication practices. In situating knowledge in the practice of communication and viewing discursive construction as constitutive and consequential, AIDA works to describe what *should be* as opposed to the "what-is" descriptions of empiricist discourse approaches (K. Tracy, 1995, p. 196).

AIDA concentrates on problems because it permits exploration of challenging situations that participants most likely reflect on and make explicit their expectations of what should be. Craig and K. Tracy (1995) explained that "[a] working assumption of our model is that communication problems typically arise because communicators pursue multiple, competing goals or purposes such that conflicts among goals often emerge to block ongoing discourse and require reflective thinking" (p. 254).

Craig and K. Tracy (1995) elaborated on the following three levels of analysis for AIDA:

1. *The technical level:* At the most concrete level, a practice can be reconstructed as a repertory of specific communicative strategies and techniques that are routinely available to be employed within the practice. (p. 253)
2. *The problem level:* Intrinsic to every practice are certain problems or dilemmas that affect the use of specific techniques. (p. 253)
3. *The philosophical level:* At the most abstract level, a practice can be reconstructed in the form of elaborated normative ideals and overarching principles that provide a rationale for the resolution of problems...A practice can thus be reconstructed by articulating these situated ideals as explicit philosophical positions. (pp. 253-254)

Each of these levels pinpoints different foci for description and analysis. The foci at the technical level are concrete communication activities. For example, Craig and K. Tracy described the providing of background information and question formulations as technical moves. For this level, K. Tracy (1995) advocated the use of naturally occurring discourse data to identify the repertory of communication practices utilized by social actors. This level, in particular, reflects the discourse analytic roots of AIDA in examining naturally occurring communicative interactions with attention to the interconnection between language use and context.

At the problem level, questions such as "What are the problems actors see as they seek to communicate appropriately? What concerns do actors themselves have?" guide analysis (Craig & K. Tracy, 1995, p. 255). For example, in detailing the problems that participants encounter during academic intellectual discussions, K. Tracy (1995) described the competing goals of idea development and building community (see also K. Tracy & Baratz, 1993). Craig and K. Tracy also positioned the level of problems as central to their approach in that this level implicates the level below (the technical level) and the level above (the philosophical level) in terms of abstraction. The problem level functions as a nexus for understanding the interconnection between micro-practices, in the forms of interactions and specific communication actions, and the macro-level, in the form of generalizeable, situated ideals. Craig and K. Tracy also referred to this latter level as the philosophical level.

At the philosophical level, researchers reconceptualize a practice in terms of the ideals that participants have for that practice or, as Craig and K. Tracy (1995) suggested, the "theoretical reconstruction" or "rational reconstruction" (p. 252) of a practice. The ideals formulated through rational reconstruction go beyond the immediate situation (e.g., a school board policy debate; K. Tracy & Ashcraft, 2001) and contribute to a more general normative theory (i.e., the understanding of how large groups manage dilemmas). Emphasizing the mutual interplay between theory and practice, Craig and K. Tracy explained:

> The ultimate test of such a practical theory is not, then, like scientific theory, its capacity to explain an existing reality but rather its usefulness for practice and reflection. The underlying philosophy is not realism (theory describes the world) or idealism (theory constitutes the world) but rather a reflective pragmatism (theory informs praxis). (p. 252)

Though K. Tracy (1995) does not explicitly identify AIDA as social construction research, in its ability to connect the discursive construction of problems to the situated ideals of participants and especially in its way of proposing new grammars of practice, we consider AIDA to be a practical social construction theory.

Dialogic Approaches

As "one key concept that helped...scholars guide their research with more constructionist epistemologies" (R. Anderson, Baxter, & Cissna, 2004, p. 10), *dialogue* appears as both philosophical idea and practical theory in CSC. Dialogic perspectives can be descriptive or prescriptive (Stewart, Zediker, & Black, 2004). Stewart et al. characterized "all human life" as dialogical (p. 21). In prescriptive approaches, such as that described by Buber (1970), the term *dialogue* refers to a unique circumstance of connections between people. In addition to providing basic background information on dialogue, we examine dialogic approaches that address constructionist concerns: McNamee and Gergen's (1999) conception of relational responsibility, Baxter and Montgomery's (1996) relational dialectics, and practical, community applications of dialogue. Each of these perspectives addresses the dialogical nature of communication and social constructionist concerns of practicality of theory, the consequential and constitutive nature of communication, and the relational nature of knowledge.

R. Anderson et al. (2004) noted that "readers surveying the historical literature on dialogue within communication (in interpersonal communication, rhetoric, and media studies especially) encounter four names with regularity: Buber, Gadamer, Habermas, and Bakhtin" (p. 3). Collectively, these authors contribute the following ideas to our understanding of dialogue. Dialogue, as an ideal, constitutes a relational process in which self and other (I-thou) are interconnected and both altered in the process of dialogue (Buber, 1970; Gadamer, 1975). As Wood (2004) explained, dialogue "means that interlocutors are immersed in a process that shapes and forms them even as they shape and form it and one another in ways that are not entirely predictable or finalizable" (p. xvii). Habermas (1984) stressed the interconnection between situation or public context and conditions that facilitate dialogue. The work of Russian literary scholar Bakhtin (1981, 1984) emphasized the "multivocal" nature of social life. Theorizing about dialogue also involves theorizing about the socially constructed nature of self and the social world (see also Lucaites & Fitch, 1997).

Cissna and R. Anderson's (1998) analysis of the transcribed conversation between therapist Carl Rogers and Martin Buber offers a way to bridge notions of dialogue as ideal and as situated relational knowing by means of the concept of dialogic moments—"both a quality of relationships, that arises, however briefly, between two or more people and [also] a way of thinking about human affairs that highlights their dialogic quality" (p. 64). According to Cissna and R. Anderson, dialogic moments occur when structural inequalities (presumed by the helping relationship of therapy) or asymmetry between I and Thou do not matter. They asserted that moments of dialogue permit the creative connections whereby dialogic partners "turn toward the other and both mutually perceive the impact of each other's turning" (p. 74).[5]

Criticizing traditional notions of responsibility that locate blame and deviance at the individual level, McNamee and Gergen (1999) argued for a perspective of responsibility as relational in which the "joint-action" of social actors is featured in considering responsibility. Responsibility in relationships, then, involves "... a dialogic process with two transformative functions: first, in transforming the interlocutors' understanding of the action in question (the fault, failing, crime, etc.) and second, in altering the relations among the interlocutors themselves" (p. 5). The concept of relational responsibility provides a re-conceptualization of a significant concept (responsibility) through a social constructionist lens.

Baxter and Montgomery's (1996) theory of relational dialectics under-scored the contradictory tensions present in interpersonal relationships. Using an analogy with the concept of the yin and the yang from Chinese culture, Baxter and Montgomery asserted that these contradictions are not necessarily undesirable aspects of relationships but, rather, inherent in relationships. Examples of relational contradictions include the competing desires to be autonomous yet connected to another, to maintain privacy and share, and to experience certainty and surprise. Each of these dialectics may operate in terms of how self and relational partner interact, or how a relational grouping (i.e., the couple as a unit) interacts with outsiders. Relational dialectics focuses on the constitutive role of communication in constructing relationship; drawing heavily from Bakhtin's (1981) idea of polyphony, it also calls attention to the multiplicity of voices involved in constructing social relationships.

Building bridges both within the discipline and into practical theory, the approach of dialogue has combined assumptions from the coordinated management of meaning theory to open up a new space for interaction in communities (e.g., Dillon & Galanes, 2002; K. A. Pearce & W. B. Pearce, 2001; W. B. Pearce & K. A. Pearce, 2000; Spano, 2001). Endeavors such as the *Public Conversations Project* (Family Institute of Cambridge, MA) have taken dialogue as practical theory to the public arena, where shifts in modes of accounting affect relationships between people who disagreed strongly on issues of public significance, such as abortion, the Israeli–Palestinian crisis, or the events of September 11, 2001 (Herzig & Chasin, 2006). Though they did not necessarily achieve agreement, they co-constructed a new awareness of the others' accounts as a possibility to coexist as long as the conversation continues. This idea of a continuing conversation reflects Bakhtin's (1986) notion of dialogue as infinite process, or indeed, as a ripple effect of relational configurations that transcend the self-other dyad to create a conversational multilogue, or polyphony. H. Anderson (1997) summarized that "each conversation is embedded within and will become a part of, will be influenced by and will influence myriad other past and future conversations" (p. 111).

Summary

We have identified several ways in which social constructionist ideas have been applied in communication. First, we noted how communication scholars use different terms (i.e., *interpretive, social, constitutive*) to articulate a social constructionist stance. Second, we outlined a sample of communication approaches that apply social constructionist assumptions. In identifying them, we called attention to specific ways in which communication scholars have developed social constructionist perspectives. In analyzing SC in communication research, we have identified it as embodied (e.g., Bruss et al., 2005; Cronen, 1995a; Shailor, 1994; Shotter & Katz, 1998), practical and grounded (e.g., Holman & Thorpe, 2003; Castor, 2005; Craig & K. Tracy, 1995), ontologically oriented (e.g., Deetz, 1994; W. B. Pearce & K. A. Pearce, 2000; Stewart, 1995; Tracy & Baratz, 1993), and experiential in terms of real phenomena in our everyday life (Edley, 2001).

PRACTICING SOCIAL CONSTRUCTION IN GENDER, CRISIS, AND THERAPY: ADDRESSING MATERIALITY, AGENCY, AND CONSEQUENTIALITY

In this section, we strive to take our presentation further and address one (as yet unresolved) misunderstanding both within and without social construction—which equates an SC view as relativist and offers realism as its alternative (see Burr, 2003; Edley, 2001; Edwards et al., 1995; Gergen, 2001; Shotter & Lannamann, 2002, for voices within the debate)—and show how practical applications of it have allowed stepping outside this knot. As social constructionists, Shotter and Lannamann, as well as Burr, recognized that SC has gradually become a source of disenchantment if not "personal paralysis" (Burr, p. 14). Shotter and Lannamann also observed how the epistemologically elegant ritual of theory, criticism, and debate in social constructionist discussions fail to engage the messy, embodied, and accountable ontology of living beings.

More specifically, Burr (2003) found that the construct of agency put forth by SC indicates no more than "an effect of discourse" that pulls "the rug... out under our feet" (p. 14), leaving no notion of the choosing person intact. A second problematic deals with SC's limitations in matters of materiality (Lannamann, 1998). Ultimately, this dilemma grapples with how social constructionists account for the physical world without denying it through a strict relativist argument or subordinating their own position to a realist and representational rather than constitutive notion. Finally, social constructionists have had to address the belief that social action (or change, or oppression, or liberation) happens outside of discourse. We refer to this belief as an *issue of consequentiality*.

We borrow Gergen's (1998) Wittgensteinian question and "go on" to offer a contribution to SC dilemmas from communication practice. We focus our review now on CSC research in the three topic areas of gender, crisis, and therapy. These three research areas address the limitations identified by SC critics and supporters in matters of materiality, agency, and consequentiality. Research on gender highlights issues of identity, agency, and materiality by describing the different ways in which people construct identity in light of various circumstances. We also concentrate on two areas of practice. By selecting crisis and therapy, we consider the concerns of practitioners in everyday life situations who apply the propositions of CSC to make decisions with long-lasting consequences in the lives of others. Especially with the situation of crisis, we illustrate that SC can speak meaningfully on the issue of material circumstances. Crises are as real in material terms as they are in the visceral reaction of seeing death; both crises and therapy can be productively understood by means of a SC perspective.

Our choice of three topic areas is strategic because gender, crisis, and therapy provide ways to understand differences across cultures, nations, and socioeconomic circumstances. We hope that our three areas of focus allow readers to imagine building conversational connections between social constructionist work that pushes boundaries not only across practices but across national communities, recognizing SC's potential to reconstitute conversations in the many embodied responses of scholars and practitioners internationally.

Social Construction and Gender: Re-constituting Identity and Materiality

"All feminist theory since Simone de Beauvoir ('one is not born but becomes a woman')," argued Cameron (2005), "could aptly be described as 'social constructionist': the whole concept of gender, as distinct from sex, is inherently social constructionist" (pp. 332-333). By locating gender in the dynamic of interaction and in the accomplishments of performance, a CSC approach illustrates how identity is not pre-set but a matter of discursively constructed physical presence. While gender and communication research has traditionally focused on women's experiences and the construction of female identity, more recent work has called attention to the construction of masculine identity (e.g., Ashcraft & Mumby, 2004b; Dow & Condit, 2005) as well as transgendered identity (Papoulias, 2006).

We must distinguish between "second wave" and "third wave" approaches. Cameron (2005) characterized second wave as a modernist or essentialist approach that treats gender as a stable and binary category that focuses on differences of communication between males and females. Studies that describe gender in terms of "dominance" or "difference" fall within this category in that these terms imply an "essentialist" assumption regarding gender. The third wave approach, as explained by Cameron, comprises a postmodernist or social constructionist approach that examines gender as performed (Butler, 1990)[6] and locally enacted through communication. However, notably, the third wave can be divided even further into two main categories: interaction-focused and poststructuralist.

Interaction-focused studies draw from traditions such as symbolic interactionism, Goffman's (1959) dramaturgical perspective, Garfinkel's (1967) ethnomethodological approach, conversation analysis (e.g., Sacks, 1995), and sociolinguistics (e.g., Gumperz, 1982). Poststructuralist projects draw from philosophers of language (Bakhtin, 1981, 1984, 1986; Vygotsky, 1986) and critical theorists such as, most notably, Foucault (1980). Both approaches assume that gender encompasses a social practice, constituted in and through interactions and discursive constructions. However, differences exist in the type of research conducted under the umbrella of each approach.

Among interaction-oriented approaches, two key perspectives include ethnomethodology (e.g., Hansen, 2006; Papoulias, 2006; see also Garfinkel, 1967, for his classic analysis of Agnes) and narrative (i.e., Gubrium, 2006). Interaction-oriented approaches may also focus on various levels of discourse.

For example, Guerin (1994) examined gender bias at the level of verbs and adjectives. Stapleton (2003) described the practice of swearing and its interrelationship with gender. Madsen (2003) analyzed the negotiation of power among bilingual Turkish-Danish children. Addressing the interrelationship between power and everyday language practices, Kitzinger (2005) and Land and Kitzinger (2005) studied the discursive display of heterosexual and homosexual identity. Schiffrin (1996) explored the use of narrative by Jewish American women to exercise agency and construct identity. In a similar project, Gubrium detailed the use of narrative by African American women to construct their own "American Dream" story as a form of empowerment. As Gubrium explained, her main interviewee "talked herself into being" (p. 231) through the stories she told about her life. Pienaar and Bekker (2006) applied critical discourse analysis and Butler's theory of performance to explain how young South African women constructed and performed notions of an ideal feminine physique in their everyday conversations. Using an ethnographic approach, Hansen focused on the interconnection between gender and dance in constructing Mexican identity. Hansen's study highlighted communication in the form of personal address and reference terms as well as costuming and accessories, thus including both the discursive and material in his analysis.

Gender CSC researchers have considered the interconnection between communication and materiality in other ways as well. Brush (1997), using historical data starting from the 1900s, described how "expert talk" constructs single mother identity and the implications of those constructions for social policy. Ryan (1994) focused on space, city life, social class, and gendered identities. Literally addressing the body, Papoulias (2006) provided a conceptual piece on transgendered identity:

> Transgender is one of the latest in a series of terms which, in the social sciences, have sought to name counter-normative materializations of gender on individual bodies, through practices of gender-crossing either in matters of dress and presentation, and/or in terms of body modification. (p. 231)

As mentioned earlier, increasingly, scholars attend to the construction of masculine identities. Meân (2001) concentrated on sports and how the discourse of male football referees constructs gendered (both male and female) identities. Harter (2004) examined masculine identity and the agrarian frontier in a cooperative organization.

A growing number of organizational communication scholars draw from postmodern and poststructuralist traditions (e.g., Ashcraft & Mumby, 2004a; Buzzanell & Liu, 2005). Buzzanell (1995) explicitly took a social constructionist perspective in her analysis of the glass ceiling. Trethewey (2000) detailed how communication constitutes organizations through culture and embodied identity. Interactionist and poststructuralist do not encompass all of the approaches; others include sense-making (Buzzanell et al., 2005), communities of practice (Stapleton, 2003), and critical legal theory (Hasian, 2004). Scholars use Butler's gender as performance work as a primary basis for theoretical framing (Pienaar & Bekker, 2006) and in gender and communication research (e.g., Bell & Blaeuer, 2006). Also, some scholars have begun to develop uniquely communication approaches that theorize about gender (Ashcraft & Mumby, 2004a, 2004b; see also Harter, 2004) Ashcraft and Mumby, in particular, developed a feminist communicology of organization that argues for the interconnection of the SC of gendered identity and organizations. Ashcraft and Mumby's project also explicitly featured the discursive construction of identity, power, resistance, history, and materiality.

Several gender and communication scholars have stressed the contradiction and irony in the construction of gendered identities. For example, Harter (2004) highlighted the incongruities involved with constructions of gender in her organizational site with the typically feminine notion of cooperation being connected to masculine notions of the frontier. Buzzanell and Liu (2005) analyzed the inconsistencies involved with maternity leave policies. S. J. Tracy and Trethewey (2005) provided a very insightful argument for re-conceptualizing the organizational self in terms of a "crystallized" identity. Critiquing popular and scholarly research that discusses "fake selves" and "real selves," S. J. Tracy and Trethewey noted that such a dichotomy serves the managerial interests of the organization. In contrast, "[t]he crystallized self is multidimensional--the more facets, the more beautiful and complex.....crystallized selves have different shapes depending on the various discourses through which they are constructed and constrained" (p. 186). S. J. Tracy and Trethewey recognized that identity is socially constructed; in their proposal, they emphasized agency by advocating a change in how organizational members, popular writers, and organizational scholars conceptualize organizational identities. Refracted through a social constructionist lens, researchers position gender in communication in terms of the discursive construction of identity, where communication both enables and constrains identity and always responds to social and material circumstances.

Crisis: The Consequentiality of Social Construction

Crisis, argued Edelman (1974), is nothing if not a discursive construction that serves the political aims of those who can benefit from events being enacted as crisis (see also Altheide, 2001). Envisioning a disaster such as Hurricane Katrina or the Southeast Asian tsunami as a crisis involves considering the consequentiality of certain discursive constructions by particular people in certain ways on the lives of impacted individuals (see related discussion on trauma by Grey, 2007). Notions of risk, vulnerability, preparedness, and nature itself are all forms of accounting that coordinate action in crisis situations, making the difference between life and death. Stallings (1990, p. 92) noted that "[r]isk is not the *outcome* of media and public discourse, but exists *in and through* processes of discourse. Hence, risk is never constant. It is created and recreated in discussion of events that are seen to undermine a world taken for granted."

We proceed from an overview of problems as social constructions to discussing the significance of understanding social problems and natural disaster crises in social constructionist terms.

Schön (1983) argued that problems are not described, but rather "set." He explained that "problem setting is a process in which, interactively, we *name* the things to which we will attend and *frame* the context in which we will attend to them" (p. 40). In this view, problems are not 'givens' but, instead, constructed as such through communication. Buttny (2004) provided a very explicit discussion of the social (discursive) construction of problems in various contexts, including therapy discussions (see also Buttny, 1996) and campus discussions of race. K. Tracy's work also addressed the construction of problems in areas such as school board meetings (K. Tracy & Muller, 2001) and emergency service requests (K. Tracy, 1997). Castor (2007) described the construction of problems in school board meetings as well as during a university budget crisis (Castor & Cooren, 2006). Collectively, these projects illustrate how various discursive practices such as reported speech (Buttny, 1996, 2004), problem formulation (Tracy), metacommunication (Castor), and accounting (Castor & Cooren) function to define and construct what counts as a problem and the consequences of those definitions to the actors involved.

Studies on the SC of crises have usefully drawn from examinations of social problems (Best, 1995; Spector & Kitsuse, 1977) to highlight the role of the media in the discursive construction of problem accounts. For example, Altheide (2001) argued in the title of his book that the media constructs crisis by "creating fear." Abu-Laban and Garber (2005) and Greenberg and Hier (2001) each detailed the SC of immigrants and refugees as social problems in Canada by using textual analyses of newspapers. Mazzarella and Pecora (2007) described the construction of "girls in crisis," and, also considering the construction of youth, Staller (2003) focused on runaways in the U.S. media in the 1960s and 1970s. Pride (1999) pursued the construction of race in the south. Finally, exploring a global context, Tacke (2001) addressed the SC of BSE (mad cow disease) as a problem.

In a recent online interdisciplinary forum on Hurricane Katrina, anthropologists, environmentalists, management, and geography experts among others discussed how disasters constitute *un*natural phenomena (Smith, 2006), dictated by social forces as much as by nature. Tracing the shift between constructs of preparedness and vulnerability in knowledge about disaster, Bankoff (2006) argued that the latter seemed to provide a notion of embodied first person as opposed to the third person scientific knowledge of the former. Vulnerability evokes the relative position of a body to another and the image of how a body might be left behind. However, the way in which the particular form of accounting materialized revealed very different stakes at work for those so categorized. Bodies considered "vulnerable" were isolated from those considered safe, with help transferred to the safe zone and the "vulnerable" zone declared "unsafe." This practice, as Bankoff concluded, revealed that vulnerability and preparedness, while seemingly different at the level of representation, practically materialized as flip sides of the same coin. As Smith observed, a similar fate seems destined to the account of "reconstruction" offered to the zone hit by the Indian Ocean tsunami, where the rebuilding project privileges oceanfront wealth.

These studies of crisis from CSC perspectives illustrate the discursive accomplishment of problems. Of course, events such as immigration, hurricanes, and the like are not exclusively forms of discourse, but their meanings and treatment as "problems" or "crises" mark a communicative achievement. Significantly, whether and what kind of action is taken as follow-up depends on how stakeholders construct them as such.

Reconstituting Therapy: From Narrative to Performance, from Representation to Action

In its manifestations of Fred Newman's social therapy, narrative therapy, and dialogical therapy, social constructionist constitutions of therapy reflect discursive *differences that make a difference* (Bateson, 1972); they continue to add significance to the embeddedness of mind in communication established by Bateson and the Palo Alto Group (e.g., Watzlawick, Bavelas, & Jackson, 1967).

Lannamann (1998) cautioned against the danger of an immaterial, abstract version of SC in therapeutic practice:

[A] social constructionist approach [should]…be *a political approach*, not in the sense of imposing a particular arrangement of authority, but rather in the sense of identifying the material practices in which certain forms of relational embodiment are enabled while others are constrained (emphasis added). (p. 411)

In presenting the following examples, we believe that applications of forms of SC in therapeutic practice constitute political acts of discursive re-embodiment, reconfiguring relationships, experiences of the material world, past constraints, and future enablements. The work of philosopher Fred Newman and psychologist Lois Holzman at the East Side Center for Social Therapy in New York City makes a crucial political distinction between "power" and "authority" (Holzman, 2004). Whereas authority, as Lannamann (1998) described it, is imposed by individuals (authors) in the form of knowledge, power comprises the bottom-up activity by stakeholders able to creatively resist it. One form of creative resistance to authority involves the refusal to adopt the knowledge of specialized vocabulary of expert description (Newman, 1991). Working within a Marxist awareness on myths as social control and Vygotsky's perspective about enacting social change in everyday settings, Newman and Holzman attack the social potential of diagnosis and other forms of expert mythology—addiction, deviancy, panic, depression—that maintain the authority of psychiatric nomenclature. In its place, they practice community therapy, which is actually not therapy in the traditional sense at all but the overseeing of open-ended group performances organized around therapeutic themes and terms. By recontextualizing an expert practice such as diagnosing into "a radically democratic, performatory environment" (Holzman, 1999, p. 85), Newman seeks to "create new forms of life" by exploiting gaps in Wittgensteinian language games. Newman aims to demystify psychological classification and authority and to move toward a collaborative, participatory, and truly embodied practice of psychology.

In the United Kingdom, practitioners employ both social constructionist and narrative therapies of White and Epston (1990) politically to serve clients in the lesbian, gay, bisexual, and queer community (www.thepinkpractice. com.uk). Paying attention to how the stories that we tell about ourselves trap us into cultural and relational plots that hurt us, practitioners at The Pink Practice apply the ideas of White and Epston to challenge assumptions about pathology, sexuality, gender, and life choices. They replace stories of oppression with ones of possibility. As Lotringer said, one does not cure neurosis; one changes a society which cannot do without it (as cited in Holtzman, 1999, p. 83).

No less political is the material change affected by Norwegian therapist Tom Andersen (1990) by introducing the practice of the reflecting team to family therapy. Traditionally, the one-way mirror divided therapist and family (Hoffman, 2001) so as to permit two kinds of observation and two kinds of accounting: the first in the moment, by the therapist in the room with the family; the second, detached, by the therapists of the team hidden behind the looking glass, always informing the first. A hierarchical construction of knowledge would, therefore, be set up between levels of therapist accounting and family accounts (Bartesaghi, 2004). By tearing down the reflecting barrier between the first-person knowledge of the family's experience and the third-person theoretical assumptions of the therapist, Tom Andersen's approach works by allowing the two kinds of accounting to continuously feed into each other, rejecting the secrecy of therapeutic strategy in favor of an accountable exchange between viewpoints (see discussion by H. Anderson, 1997). This strategy makes room for a third kind of knowing, collaborative and emergent in the between. Katz and Shotter (1996) noted how Andersen makes connections in the moment during a session of therapy that a client finds striking, arresting, moving.

Therapy entails communication that is constitutive and consequential; a client's reality can shift dramatically in the course of a fifty-minute session, reconstructing versions of past, present, and possible future. A therapist can create this shift through strategic questioning. Questions comprise powerful discursive resources. In everyday conversation, they both open and constrain a space for the other's answer (Wang, 2006); in therapy, they intervene in the client's world by forcing a common ground with the therapist's presuppositions (McGee, Del Vento, & Beavin Bavelas, 2005). "Every time we ask a question," remarked narrative therapist David Epston, "we're generating a possible version of a life" (in Freedman & Combs, 1996, p. 113). Constructionist therapists Freedman and Combs generate new experience for their clients by opening up a space for accounting that defies problems, even in the midst of problematic life accounts. For instance, the therapist(s) might ask, "You've said that, even though moods of hopelessness often lead you to suicidal thoughts, you know that you don't really want to die. When was the last time this knowledge helped you turn suicidal thoughts away?" (p. 101).

Alternatively, the therapist(s) may show the client how to "go on" by inviting them to step into someone else's accounting position, by asking such questions as "Can you understand how from my point of view you are ready to take on this responsibility? What do you think I've noticed that makes me think so?" (Freedman & Combs, 1996, p. 127). We see these questions pushing for SC as a practice that is, as Keillor (1987) suggested, "not for the timid" (p. xv).

Harlene Anderson[7] posed a stern counter-proposition to the traditional assumption of the therapist's ability to exert authority through theoretical, non-conversationally generated knowledge. Rejecting all notions of strategy and intervention as unproductive for therapeutic conversation as a joint process between therapist and client, H. Anderson (1997) proposed that the therapist approach interaction from a perspective of *not knowing*. What the therapist should not know, and should try to prevent herself from knowing, encompasses anything for which she cannot be directly accountable to the client from within the conversation. Thus, according to H. Anderson, they should reject common practices such as reading the client's record prior to a session, being aware of a patient's diagnosis, or all ideas pertaining to manuals and phases of the session because the therapist is inside, and not outside, the process (she) is trying to create. Drawing on the idea of dialogue as reciprocal, accountable interaction between multiple voices elaborated by Bakhtin (1981, 1984, 1986), H. Anderson described the not-knowing stance as one of freedom. Once the therapist is liberated from the ideological bind to control the conversation and the trappings (and potential entrapments) of authority, s/he clears space for creativity, trust, and problems to be resolved through the emergence of a new way of telling the story of self.

However, how much can a dialogical therapist truly be free from the hierarchal demands of power and still be a therapist (Guilfoyle, 2003)? The question belies a view of communication as strategy and of authority (or power) as, once again, something outside of it (H. Anderson, 2005). According to H. Anderson, the answer, as social construction in its therapeutic applications suggests, lies in taking communication as practical theory and therapy as a conversation of "everyday life" (p. 503), rife with ambiguity, difficult questions, shifting asymmetries, and moments of connection (or not), that can, at best, be addressed as life in conversation.

Summary

In reviewing CSC research in gender, crisis, and therapy, we highlighted the specific ways in which communication researchers have applied an SC perspective. As we stated earlier, our choice of topical areas was strategic in that these topics address key issues and dilemmas in SC research such as identity, agency, materiality, and power.

FUTURE DIRECTIONS: WHERE TO THE CONVERSATION?

In rejoining Shotter and Gergen's (1994) contribution to *Communication Yearbook*, we wished to explore the place of SC research in communication. The variety of theories that attribute their development to SC and practical research in areas such as gender, crisis, and therapy point to the significant interrelationship between communication and SC. While this theorizing and research is promising, we advance specific future issues and directions for CSC research.

The Role of Criticism and Contemporary Social and Political Issues

A central premise of SC, we believe, is to raise questions about tacit knowledge (Burr, 2003; Gergen, 1999; see also related discussion by Garfinkel, 1967, regarding the taken-for-granted in ethnomethodology). As such, we conceive of SC as a critical position, for when stakeholders make visible taken-for-granted assumptions and perspectives, they can realize that previously accepted orientations "could have been different—and, in taking something for granted, we forget that it could have been different" (Phillips & Jørgensen, 2002, pp. 185-186). Contemporary issues (such as terrorism, the growing disparity between the rich and the poor, lack of adequate health care, genocide with the accompanying systematic raping of women, and civil wars with children soldiers) constitute circumstances that "could" and *should* be different. SC researchers are well-poised to interrogate how participants discursively co-construct these situations and to explore alternatives.

On May 26, 2004, editors of the *New York Times*, including Howell Raines and Gerald Boyd, published an apology for the newspaper's sloppy coverage of the events leading up to the Iraq war prior to Raines' and Boyd's resignations (see Mnookin, 2004). The editors cited numerous examples in which the paper as a whole (reporters and editors) failed to question constructions of the situation in Iraq presented by various officials and their sources. Perhaps the most significant evidence dealt with Saddam Hussein's capacity to develop nuclear weapons and the controversy of the "aluminum tubes" as evidence for that capacity. As the *New York Times* editors explained, "There were hints that the usefulness of the tubes in making nuclear fuel was not a sure thing, but the hints were buried deep, 1,700 words into a 3,600-word article. Administration officials were allowed to hold forth at length on why this evidence of Iraq's nuclear intentions demanded that Saddam Hussein be dislodged from power" (p. 2). The editorial letter from the *New York Times* illustrates the need to ask questions. In retrospect, the editors recognized their own taken-for-granted assumptions (see also Arsenault & Castells, 2006).

Estimates suggest that hundreds of thousands of people have been killed in the Darfur region of the Sudan over the past few years ("Hundreds Killed in Attacks in Eastern Chad," 2007). This situation has been constructed in diverse ways, from a need for humanitarian efforts to a crisis, genocide, and ethnic cleansing; each account leads to a different consequence in terms of action. In September, 2004, U.S. President George Bush declared the situation "genocide" and authorized aid to the region (Bush, 2004). However, the United Nations, while providing support, has declined to label the situation genocide ("Report of the International Commission of Inquiry on Darfur to the United Nations Secretary-General," 2005). About this matter, Reeves (2006) explained:

> [N]one of this would be more than a debate about nomenclature if a finding of genocide did not hold the potential to dictate the need for humanitarian intervention in Darfur ... Genocide should not, of course, be the threshold for humanitarian intervention; but in the world as we find it, in the wake of genocides in the Balkans and Rwanda, the g-word has come increasingly to constitute a ghastly gold standard for international action. (¶ 37)

A social constructionist position does not deny dead bodies. However, a CSC position (which we have captured here as it is articulated in its theoretical universe as practical, consequential, and constitutive) would interrogate the discursive constructions, the consequences of those constructions, the alternatives, and the entailments of future responses.

Conceptual Issues

For CSC to be relevant and practical, social constructionists must engage the interrelationship between *d*iscourse and *D*iscourse, or communication and what is now largely (mis)understood as residing in the universe of the extra-discursive: power and agency, respectively (Burr, 2003; Lannamann, 1998; Phillips & Jørgensen, 2002). This perceived split between what social construction can offer and the (realities of the) material world is born from a pragmatic, representational, and purely epistemological version of SC (Gergen,

1992, 1994, 1998, 2001) that sets aside ontological matters for the purpose of selecting among available forms of communication. However, practical communication choices cannot be performed from ontological disengagement but only from within the moral and social constraints that allow them and the consequences that will follow (Held, 2002). When thinking in terms of our responsibility and of the consequences with respect to our decisions, choices, and actions within the larger political and social frame, it is impossible to extricate discourse and Discourse. To avoid the potential paralysis of an "ontologically mute" (Gergen, 1992, p. 171) social constructionism, we should attend to the concerns of the material world in our discursive reconstitution of SC. Though CSC researchers have dealt with the (so-called) extra-discursive (i.e., in studies of gender and crisis), the extra-discursive needs to be more thoroughly and explicitly addressed as consequential and inextricable from the discursive so that we may break out of—rather than avoid or circumvent—arguments that begin with furniture thumping and lead us nowhere.

Alvesson and Karreman (2000) described four "levels" of discourse that, for the sake of simplicity, we collapse into the categories of "discourse" (with a lower-case d) and "Discourse" (with an upper-case D). The former refers to language use in specific contexts or micro-practices. The latter refers to enduring patterns across contexts. Variations exist in terms of how communication social constructionists address $d$iscourse and Discourse. Those of us with roots in ethnography, ethnomethodology, and other language and social interaction approaches (Fitch & Sanders, 2005) tend to focus on discourse. As Alvesson and Karreman observed, social construction researchers who emphasize poststructural analysis tend to concentrate on Discourse, viewing data as a manifestation of broader systems or patterns. One conceptual issue that communication social constructionists need to address involves finding ways to make our theoretical accounts of the world relevant both in $d$iscourse and Discourse, bridging micro- and macro-universes of analysis; in so doing, communication theories will critically reflect on the material reality of those theorized about and, as a result, constituted in its practical applications (Krippendorff, 1996, 1997; Parker, 1999). This issue is considered to a degree through the study of accounting and social accountability (e.g., Buttny, 1993, 1996, 2004; Shotter, 1984). Organizational communication scholars, in particular, have done a thorough job of showing the problematics involved with interrelating discourse and Discourse (e.g., Cooren & Fairhurst, in press; Dixon, 2000; Fairhurst & Putnam, 2004).

Notions of power and agency warrant additional attention from a CSC perspective. By constituting communication as an ontological discipline that makes a difference in practice, social constructionist scholarship cannot eschew political considerations in its research and applications (Lannamann, 1998; Phillips & Jørgensen, 2002). It cannot, for example, abstain from addressing power by arguing that making claims regarding power privileges one position (usually, the researchers') over others, as if such a practice comprised an avoidable (or undesirable) condition of doing research. Nor can researchers or practitioners within an SC communication tradition presume that power exists "outside of" our SCs, as institutions or abstract social structures.

The work of Foucault (1980), among other theorists examining the role of language as a form of social and institutional power (e.g., Bakhtin, 1981, 1986; Habermas, 1984; Volosinov, 1986), is largely credited for illuminating the social consequentiality of communication. Ironically, however, Foucault's work abstracted power rather than materialized it because he did not offer a clear conceptual map to locate power within the embodied communication of relationships (Thornborrow, 2002). Foucaultian power, being everywhere, is (for practical purposes) nowhere at all (Krippendorff, 1995) and remains empirically unavailable.

In communication, scholars of language and social interaction (Fitch & Sanders, 2005) have grounded a notion of discursive power in everyday discourse, linking interaction with the broader social and institutional framework that enables and constrains it, thus showing how power is empirically accessible and visibly co-constructed in the constantly shifting asymmetry of moment-to-moment conversational relationships. An example of how power is made visible as embodied communication is the study of questioning by various scholars in both conversation and discourse analysis across various institutional settings. Sacks (1995) noted that asking questions within a conversation constitutes a powerful discursive act (see also Wang, 2006, for an overview of questioning research) that delineates different rights and obligations for participants in an exchange. Further, Mehan (1996) detailed how the definition of a student as learning disabled results from a decision-making process that not all involved parties can dispute or understand. Power, argued Mehan (1990, 1996), entails the ability of some to define the reality of others by deciding on the meaning of a situation; asking questions is a powerful way to define reality within an institution.

If questions constitute powerful discursive resources, the study of questioning practices illuminates the difference between those who are able to use the resource for their advantage and those who cannot and interrogates the material consequences of such difference. Zimmerman's (1992) as well and K. Tracy's (K. Tracy, 1997; K. Tracy & S. J. Tracy, 1998) research on 911 emergency call centers examines the co-construction of problems between callers and dispatchers, which can make the difference between getting and not getting help. Hutchby (2002) examined how a child in counseling responds to the therapist's questioning in a baffling and noncooperative way (according to the therapist!), somewhat upsetting the therapeutic asymmetry and causing the therapist to seek novel discursive strategies.

Thornborrow's (2002) analysis of institutional talk offers another example of how CSC can address power by making it visible in processes of co-construction. By blending conversation analysis and critical discourse analysis, Thornborrow specified how members structurally accomplish institutions through the everyday orderliness of conversational turn-taking, while all the time leaving cracks open at the level of conversational order for upheavals in structure to occur. Empirical work such as Thornborrow's demystifies the notion of power as everywhere, or even structural and invisible, (Krippendorff, 1995), citing its material consequences in the dynamics of communication.

The issue of agency encompasses another problematic for SC researchers. A traditional notion of agency objectifies this construct as a property of the individual, in that individuals make choices, have responsibility, and can be blamed. However, this notion over-presumes the role of an individual in an interaction (see McNamee & Gergen, 1999). An alternative conception of agency as relational is more consistent with SC research (see Robichaud, 2005). In the notion of agency as relational, one's agency is established or based in relationship with others, as we position ourselves as the "I," as actors in our own self-discourse (Harré, 1999). In conversation, others grant us agency by validating our first-person constructions. In turn, a relationally situated agency calls for a moral notion of self (Lewis, 2003) as a co-constituted account that we claim, and others can deny or validate, in everyday negotiations of the self. What the self can or should be or what it can accomplish as agent is situated in the discursive accomplishments of our speech acts, accounts, and narratives (e.g., Potter & Wetherell, 1987).

CONCLUSION

In his response to their proposal for social construction as a framework for communication, W. B. Pearce (1994) critiqued Shotter and Gergen (1994) for not being sufficiently radical and instead identifying propositions of SC grounded in psychology conversations, best suited for a critique of Enlightenment thinking. We agree with W. B. Pearce's sentiment and assert that communication has a greater role to play in constructing SC than that originally put forth by Shotter and Gergen.

In re-constituting SC in this chapter, we provided a different starting point for discussing SC from a communication perspective. We described the metadiscursive vocabulary in use by researchers who do social constructionist research; these terms include *interpretive research, social approaches, constitutive perspective*, and *construction* with various modifiers. The existence of this vocabulary indicates a great deal of SC research in communication, but this research may not be easily identified under the *nom de plume* of "social construction." Our review also identified a selection of approaches in communication that reflects a social constructionist orientation. These approaches illustrate how communication scholars have made unique contributions to understanding SC. In highlighting research on gender, crisis, and therapy, we selected topics of relevance for researchers and practitioners.

Our selected topic areas illustrated how SC research in communication has fruitfully engaged a dialogue within challenging conceptual areas such as identity, agency, and materiality in the tug-of-war of two monological dead ends represented by relativism on the one hand and realism on the other.

While research and theorizing in CSC have been promising, additional issues and future directions should be considered by CSC researchers to increase relevance to the discipline and to practitioners. First, CSC researchers should deal with social and political issues. CSC researchers have a unique voice to lend in examining how certain circumstances came to be as part of a communication process. A next step from a social constructionist perspective involves further interrogating how things could be otherwise.

At a more general, conceptual level, CSC researchers should address issues of (what is now perceived as) the extra-discursive: power and agency. These topics pose particular challenges to SC researchers, and they have been discussed and debated in other fields such as psychology and sociology. Despite some discussion (notably, in the area of organizational communication), we feel that CSC as an enterprise can develop more sophisticated ways of conceptualizing and researching communication through further dialogue on these issues.

*   *   *

It is impossible 'for us to imagine a conversation about communication without the ideas, tensions, or possibilities set forth by SC. At the conclusion of our contribution, we are humbled to have created an opportunity for the conversation to continue.

ACKNOWLEDGMENTS

We thank Ken Cissna and Karen Tracy for their feedback on our chapter proposal. Additionally, Mariaelena thanks Klaus Krippendorff, and Theresa thanks John Stewart for introducing us to SC.

NOTES

1. We wish to note this chapter is not unique in providing a review of communication social constructionist work (e.g., Allen, 2005; W. B. Pearce, 1992, 1994). Leeds-Hurwitz (forthcoming), which covers SC research in the last decade, is the most recent project that provides an extensive analysis of social construction research in communication. Other relevant reviews include Wicks' (2005) review of constructionism in mass communication framing research, and the Jackson, Poole, and Kuhn's (2002) review of the social construction of technology in the workplace. As we write this chapter, another forthcoming work deserves notice as a marker that SC is alive and well as a framework in the social sciences: *The Handbook of Social Constructionist Research*, edited by Holstein & Gubrium (2007).

2. Acknowledging that our review is not exhaustive, we also note what we did not include, namely, rhetorical perspectives (Billig, 1987; Potter, 1996) and technological perspectives (Dayton, 2006; Fulk, 1993; Jackson et al., 2002).
3. For a more thorough discussion of research in CMM, we recommend Barge & W. B. Pearce (2004).
4. Shotter has used various terms for his work including a "rhetorical-responsive version of social constructionism" (1993, p. 1), a "dialogical-relational-responsive form of practical understanding" (1998, p. 140), "expressive responsive" (2004, p. 205), and "relationally-responsive" (2006, p. 590). We utilize the phrasing *relationally responsive* in accordance to Shotter's most recent choice.
5. This notion of mutual impact in dialogue resembles Shotter's (2000b) description of knowing of the third kind and Lannamann's (1998) idea of presence.
6. Some scholars described Butler's work as social constructionist; whereas, others (e.g., Bell & Blaeuer, 2006) characterized Butler's work as distinct from social constructionism.
7. A close collaborator of the late Harold Goolishian (see, e.g., Anderson & Goolishian, 1988, 1992; Goolishian & Anderson, 2002).

REFERENCES

Abu-Laban, Y., & Garber, J. A. (2005). The construction of the geography of immigration as a policy problem. *Urban Affairs Review, 40*, 520-561.

Allen, B. J. (2005). Social constructionism. In S. May & D. K. Mumby (Eds.), *Engaging organizational communication theory and research: Multiple perspectives* (pp. 35-53). Thousand Oaks, CA: Sage.

Altheide, D. L. (2001). *Creating fear: News and the construction of crisis.* New York: Aldine de Gruyter.

Alvesson, M., & Karreman, D. (2000). Varieties of discourse: On the study of organizations through discourse analysis. *Human Relations, 53*, 1125-1149.

Andersen, T. (1990). *The reflecting team: Dialogues and dialogues about the dialogues.* New York: Borgmann.

Anderson, H. (1997). *Conversation, language, and possibilities.* New York: Basic Books.

Anderson, H. (2005). Myths about "not knowing." *Family Process, 44*, 497-504.

Anderson, H., & Goolishian, H. (1988). Human systems as linguistic systems: Preliminary and evolving ideas about the implications for clinical theory. *Family Process, 27*, 371-393.

Anderson, H., & Goolishian, H. (1992). The client is the expert: A not-knowing approach to therapy. In. S. McNamee & K. Gergen (Eds.), *Social construction and the therapeutic process* (pp. 25-39). Newbury Park, CA: Sage.

Anderson, R., Baxter, L. A., & Cissna, K. N. (2004). Texts and contexts of dialogue. In R. Anderson, L. A. Baxter, & K. N. Cissna (Eds.), *Dialogue: Theorizing difference in communication studies* (pp. 1-17). Thousand Oaks, CA: Sage.

Arsenault, A., & Castells, M. (2006). Conquering the minds, conquering Iraq: The social production of misinformation in the United States--a case study. *Information, Communication & Society, 9*, 284-307.

Ashcraft, K. L., & Mumby, D. K. (2004a). Organizing a critical communicology of gender and work. *International Journal of the Sociology of Language, 166*(1), 19-43.

Ashcraft, K. L., & Mumby, D. K. (2004b). *Reworking gender: A feminist communicology of organization*. Thousand Oaks, CA: Sage.

Bakhtin, M. M. (1981). *The dialogic imagination* (M. Holquist, Trans.). Austin: University of Texas Press.

Bakhtin, M. M. (1984). *Problems of Dostoevsky's poetics* (C. Emerson, Trans.). Minneapolis: University of Minnesota Press.

Bakhtin, M. M. (1986). The problem of speech genres. In M. H. C. Emerson (Ed.), *Speech genres and other late essays* (pp. 60-102) Austin: University of Texas Press.

Bankoff, G. (2006). The tale of the three pigs: Taking another look at vulnerability in the light of the Indian Ocean Tsunami and Hurricane Katrina. *Understanding Katrina: Perspectives from the social sciences*. Retrieved April 5, 2007, from http://understandingkatrina.ssrc.org

Barge, J. K. (2004). Articulating CMM as a practical theory. *Human Systems, 15*, 193-204.

Barge, J. K., & Pearce, W. B. (2004). A reconnaissance of CMM research. *Human Systems, 15*, 13-32.

Bartesaghi, M. (2004). *Explanatory paths, therapeutic directions, conversational destinations: Accountability and authority in therapeutic interaction*. Unpublished dissertation, University of Pennsylvania, Philadelphia, PA.

Bateson, G. (1972). *Steps to an ecology of mind: Collected essays in anthropology, psychiatry, evolution, and epistemology*. Chicago: University of Chicago Press.

Baxter, L. A. (2004). Relationships as dialogues. *Personal Relationships, 11*(1), 1-22.

Baxter, L. A., & Montgomery, B. M. (1996). *Relating: Dialogues and dialectics*. New York: Guilford Press.

Bell, E., & Blaeuer, D. (in press). Performing gender and interpersonal communication research. In B. Dow & J. Wood (Eds.), *The gender and communication handbook* (pp. 9-23). Thousand Oaks, CA: Sage.

Berger, C. R. (2005). Interpersonal communication: Theoretical perspectives, future prospects. *Journal of Communication, 55*, 415-447.

Berger, P. L., & Luckmann, T. (1966). *The social construction of reality*. Garden City, NY: Double Day.

Bernstein, R. J. (1992). *The new constellation: The political horizons of modernity/postmodernity*. Cambridge, MA: MIT Press.

Best, J. (1995). *Images of issues: Typifying contemporary social problems*. Hawthorne, NY: Aldine de Gruyter.

Billig, M. (1987). *Arguing and thinking: A rhetorical approach to social psychology*. Cambridge, England: Cambridge University Press.

Brush, L. D. (1997). Worthy widows, welfare cheats: Proper womanhood in expert needs talk about single mothers in the United States, 1900 to 1988. *Gender & Society, 11*, 720-746.

Bruss, M. B., Morris, J. R., Dannison, L. L., Orbe, M. P., Quitugua, J. A., & Palacios, R. T. (2005). Food, culture, and family: Exploring the coordinated management of meaning regarding childhood obesity. *Health Communication, 18*, 155-175.

Buber, M. (1970). *I and thou* (W. Kauffman, Trans.). New York: Scribner's.

Burr, V. (2003). *Social constructionism* (2nd ed.). London: Routledge.

Bush, G. W. (2004). President's statement on violence in Darfur, Sudan. Retrieved April 29, 2007, from http://www.whitehouse.gov/news/releases/2004/09/20040909-10.html

Butler, J. (1990). *Gender trouble*. New York: Routledge.

Buttny, R. (1993). *Social accountability in communication.* London: Sage.

Buttny, R. (1996). Clients' and therapist's joint construction of the clients' problems. *Research on Language and Social Interaction, 29,* 125-153.

Buttny, R. (2004). *Talking problems: Studies of discursive construction.* Albany: State University of New York Press.

Buzzanell, P. M. (1995). Reframing the glass ceiling as a socially constructed process: Implications for understanding and change. *Communication Monographs, 62,* 327-354.

Buzzanell, P. M., & Liu, M. (2005). Struggling with maternity leave policies and practices: A poststructuralist feminist analysis of gendered organizing. *Journal of Applied Communication Research, 33,* 1-25.

Buzzanell, P. M., Meisenbach, R., Remke, R., Liu, M., Bowers, V., & Conn, C. (2005). The good working mother: Managerial women's sensemaking and feelings about work-family issues. *Communication Studies, 56,* 261-285.

Cameron, D. (2005). Relativity and its discontents: Language, gender and pragmatics. *Intercultural Pragmatics, 2,* 321-334.

Castor, T. R. (2005). Constructing social reality in organizational decision making: Account vocabularies in a diversity discussion. *Management Communication Quarterly, 18,* 479-508.

Castor, T. R. (2007). Language use during school board meetings: Understanding controversies of and about communication. *Journal of Business Communication, 44,* 111-136.

Castor, T. R., & Cooren, F. (2006). Organizations as hybrid forms of life. *Management Communication Quarterly, 19,* 570-600.

Cheney, G. (2000). Interpreting interpretive research: Toward perspectivism without relativism. In S. R. Corman & M. S. Poole (Eds.), *Perspectives on organizational communication: Finding common ground* (pp. 17-45). New York: Guilford.

Cissna, K. N., & Anderson, R. (1998). Theorizing about dialogic moments: The Buber-Rogers position and postmodern themes. *Communication Theory, 8,* 63-104.

Cooren, F., & Fairhurst, G. T. (in press). Dislocation and stabilization: How to scale up from interactions to organizations. In L. L. Putnam & A. M. Nicotera (Eds.), *The communicative constitution of organization: Centering organizational communication.* Mahwah, NJ: Erlbaum.

Craig, R. T. (1999). Communication theory as a field. *Communication Theory, 9,* 119-161.

Craig, R. T., & Tracy, K. (1995). Grounded practical theory: The case of intellectual discussion. *Communication Theory, 5,* 248-272.

Cronen, V. E. (1995a). Coordinated management of meaning: The consequentiality of communication and the recapturing of experience. In S. J. Sigman (Ed.), *The consequentiality of communication* (pp. 17-65). Hillsdale, NJ: Erlbaum.

Cronen, V. E. (1995b). Practical theory and the tasks ahead for social approaches to communication. In W. Leeds-Hurwitz (Ed.), *Social approaches to communication* (pp. 217-242). New York: Guilford.

Cunliffe, A. L. (2001). Managers as practical authors: Reconstructing our understanding of management practices. *Journal of Management Studies, 38,* 351-371.

Cunliffe, A. L. (2002). Social poetics as management inquiry: A dialogical approach. *Journal of Management Inquiry, 11,* 128-146.

Dayton, D. (2006). A hybrid analytical framework to guide studies of innovative IT adoption by work groups. *Technical Communication Quarterly, 15,* 355-382.

Deetz, S. (1994). Future of the discipline: The challenges, the research, and the social contribution. In S. Deetz (Ed.) *Communication yearbook 17* (pp. 565-600). Thousand Oaks, CA: Sage.

Dillon, R. K., & Galanes, G. J. (2002). Public dialogue: Communication theory as public affairs praxis. *Journal of Public Affairs, 6*, 79-90.

Dixon, T. C. (2000). Communication as a constitutive process in organizing and organizations [Special issue]. *Electronic Journal of Communication, 10* (1-2) Retrieved on July 3, 2007, from http://www.cios.org/www/ejc/v10n1200.htm#Introduction

Dow, B. J., & Condit, C. M. (2005). The state of the art in feminist scholarship in communication. *Journal of Communication, 55*, 448-478.

Editors. (2004). The Times and Iraq. *New York Times.* Retrieved April 29, 2007, from http://www.nytimes.com/2004/05/26/international/middleeast/26FTE_NOTE.html ?ex=1400990400&en=94c17fcffad92ca9&ei=5007&partner=USERLAND

Edelman, M. (1974). The political language of the helping professions. *Politics and Society, 4*, 295-310.

Edley, N. (2001). Unravelling social constructionism. *Theory and Psychology, 11*, 433-411.

Edwards, D., Ashmore, M., & Potter, J. (1995). Death and furniture: The rhetoric, politics and theology of bottom line arguments against relativism. *History of the Human Sciences, 8*(2), 25-49.

Fairhurst, G. T., & Putnam, L. L. (2004). Organizations as discursive constructions. *Communication Theory, 14*, 5-26.

Fitch, K. L., & Sanders, R. E. (Eds.). (2005). *Handbook of language and social interaction.* Mahwah, NJ: Erlbaum.

Foucault, M. (1980). *Power/knowledge: Selected interviews and other writings, 1972-1977* (C. Gordon, L. Marshall, J. Mepham, & K. Soper, Trans.). New York: Pantheon Books.

Freedman, J., & Combs, G. (1996). *Narrative therapy: The social construction of preferred realities.* New York: W.W. Norton.

Fulk, J. (1993). Social construction of communication technology. *Academy of Management Journal, 36*, 921-950.

Gadamer, H. G. (1975). *Truth and method.* New York: Seabury.

Galanes, G. J., & Leeds-Hurwitz, W. (Eds.). (forthcoming). *Socially constructing communication.* Creskill, NJ: Hampton.

Garfinkel, H. (1967). *Studies in ethnomethodology.* Englewood Cliffs, NJ: Prentice-Hall.

Georgakopoulou, A. (2002). Narrative and identity management: Discourse and social identities in a tale of tomorrow. *Research on Language and Social Interaction, 35*, 427-451.

Gergen, K. J. (1985). The social constructionist movement in modern psychology. *American Psychologist, 40*, 266-275.

Gergen, K. J. (1991). *The saturated self: Dilemmas of identity in contemporary life.* New York: Basic Books.

Gergen, K. J. (1992). Social construction in question. *Human Systems, 3,* 163-182.

Gergen, K. J. (1994). *Realities and relationships: Soundings in social construction.* Cambridge, MA: Harvard University Press.

Gergen, K. J. (1998). Constructionism and realism: How are we to go on. In I. Parker (Ed.), *Social constructionism, discourse and realism* (pp. 147-155). London: Sage.

Gergen, K. J. (1999). *An invitation to social construction.* London: Sage.

Gergen, K. J. (2001). Construction in contention: Toward consequential resolutions. *Theory & Psychology, 11*, 419-432.

Gilbert, G., & Mulkay, M. (1984). *Opening Pandora's box: A sociological analysis of scientists' discourse.* Cambridge, England: Cambridge University Press.

Goffman, E. (1959). *The presentation of self in everyday life.* New York: Doubleday.

Goldsmith, D. J., & Baxter, L. A. (1996). Constituting relationships in talk. *Human Communication Research, 23*, 87-114.

Goolishian, H.A., & Anderson, H. (2002). Narrative and self: Some postmodern dilemmas of psychotherapy. In D. S. Fried Schnitman & J. Schnitman (Eds.), *New paradigms, culture and subjectivities* (pp. 217-228). New York: Hampton Press.

Greenberg, J., & Hier, S. (2001). Crisis, mobilization and collective problematization: "Illegal" Chinese migrants and the Canadian news media. *Journalism Studies, 2*, 563-583.

Grey, S. H. (2007). Wounds not easily healed: Exploring trauma in communication studies. In C. S. Beck (Ed.), *Communication yearbook 31* (pp. 174-223). Mahwah, NJ: Erlbaum.

Griffin, E. (2006). *A first look at communication theory* (6th ed.). New York: McGraw Hill.

Gubrium, A. (2006). "I was my momma baby. I was my daddy gal": Strategic stories of success. *Narrative Inquiry, 16*, 231-253.

Guerin, B. (1994). Gender bias in the abstractness of verbs and adjectives. *Journal of Social Psychology, 134*, 421-428.

Gumperz, J. J. (1982). *Discourse strategies: Studies in interactional sociolinguistics.* Cambridge, England: Cambridge University Press.

Guilfoyle, M. (2003). Dialogue and power: A critical analysis of power in dialogical therapy. *Family Process, 42*, 331-343.

Habermas, J. (1984). *The theory of communicative action.* Boston: Beacon Press.

Hacking, I. (1999). *The social construction of what?* Cambridge, MA: Harvard University Press.

Hansen, A. D. (2006). On the construction and performance of gender in Mexican folkloric dance. *Texas Speech Communication Journal, 30*, 170-186.

Harré, R. (1999). Discourse and the embodied person. In D. Nightingale & J. Cromby (Eds.) *Social constructionist psychology* (pp. 97-112). Buckingham, England: Open University Press.

Harter, L. M. (2004). Masculinity(s), the agrarian frontier myth, and cooperative ways of organizing: Contradictions and tensions in the experience and enactment of democracy. *Journal of Applied Communication Research, 32*, 89-118

Hasian, M., Jr. (2004). Critical legal theorizing, rhetorical intersectionalities, and the multiple transgressions of the "tragic mullata," Anastasie Desarzant. *Women's Studies in Communication, 27*, 119-148.

Held, B. (2002). What follows?: Mind fallibility, and transcendence according to (strong) constructionism's realist and quasi-realist critics. *Theory & Psychology, 12*, 651-669.

Herzig, M., & Chasin, L. (2006). *Fostering dialogue across divides.* Watertown, MA: Public Conversations Project.

Hoffman, L. (2001). *Family therapy: An intimate history.* New York: W. W. Norton & Company.

Holman, D. J., & Thorpe, R. (2003). Introduction. In D. J. Holman & R. Thorpe (Eds.), *Management and language: The manager as practical author* (pp. 1-12). London: Sage.

Holstein, J. A., & Gubrium, J. F. (Eds.). (2007). *Handbook of social constructionist research.* New York: Guilford Press.

Holzman, L. (1999). *Performing psychology: A postmodern culture of the mind.* New York: Routledge.

Holzman, L. (2004). Power, authority, and pointless activity. In T. Strong & D. Pare (Eds.), *Furthering talk: Advances in discursive therapies* (pp. 73-86). New York: Springer-Verlag.

Hundreds Killed in Attacks in Eastern Chad (2007). [Electronic version]. *The Washington Post*. Retrieved April 29, 2007, from http://www.washingtonpost.com/ wp-dyn/content/ article/ 2007/ 04/ 10/ AR2007041001775.html

Hutchby, I. (2002). Resisting the incitement to talk in child counseling: Aspects of the utterance 'I don't know'. *Discourse Studies, 4*, 147-168.

Jackson, M. H., Poole, M. S., & Kuhn, T. (2002). The social construction of technology in studies of the workplace. In L. Lievrouw & S. Livingstone (Eds.), *The handbook of new media* (pp. 236-253). Newbury Park, CA: Sage.

Jacoby, S., & Ochs, E. (1995). Co-construction: An introduction. *Research on Language & Social Interaction, 28*, 171-183.

Katz, A. M., & Shotter, J. (1996). Hearing the patient's 'voice': Toward a social poetics in diagnostic interviews. *Social Science Medicine, 46*, 919-931.

Keillor, G. (1987). *Leaving home*. New York: Vintage Penguin.

Kitzinger, C. (2005). "Speaking as a heterosexual": (How) does sexuality matter for talk-in-interaction? *Research on Language & Social Interaction, 38*, 221-265.

Krippendorff, K. (1995). Undoing power. *Critical Studies in Mass Communication, 12*, 101-132.

Krippendorff, K. (1996). A second-order cybernetics of otherness. *Systems Research, 13*, 311-328.

Krippendorff, K. (1997). Seeing oneself through others' eyes in social inquiry. In M. Huspek & G. P. Radford (Eds.), *Trangressing discourses: Communication and the voice of other* (pp. 47-72). Albany: State University of New York Press.

Land, V., & Kitzinger, C. (2005). Speaking as a lesbian: Correcting the heterosexist presumption. *Research on Language & Social Interaction, 38*, 371-416.

Lannamann, J. (1998). Social construction and materiality: The limits of in-determinacy in therapeutic settings. *Family Process*, 37, 393-413.

Leeds-Hurwitz, W. (1995). Introducing social approaches. In W. Leeds-Hurwitz (Ed.), *Social approaches to communication* (pp. 3-20). New York: Guilford.

Leeds-Hurwitz, W. (forthcoming). Social constructionism: Moving from theory to research (and back again). In G. J. Galanes & W. Leeds-Hurwitz (Eds.), *Socially constructing communication*. Creskill, NJ: Hampton.

Lewis, Y. (2003). The self as a moral concept. *British Journal of Social Psychology, 42*, 225-237.

Lucaites, J. L., & Fitch, K. L. (1997). Book reviews. *Quarterly Journal of Speech, 83*, 262.

Madsen, L. M. (2003). Power relationships, interactional dominance and manipulation strategies in group conversations of Turkish-Danish children. *Journal of Multilingual & Multicultural Development, 24*(1/2), 90-101.

Mazzarella, S. R., & Pecora, N. O. (2007). Girls in crisis. *Journal of Communication Inquiry, 31*(1), 6-27.

McGee, D., Del Vento, A., & Beavin Bavelas, J. (2005). An interactional model of questions as therapeutic interventions. *Journal of Marital and Family Therapy, 31*, 371-384.

McNamee, S., & Gergen, K. J. (1999). *Relational responsibility: Resources for sustainable dialogue*. Thousand Oaks, CA: Sage.

McPhee, R. D., & Zaug, P. (2000). The communicative constitution of organizations: A framework for explanation. *Electronic Journal of Communication,*

10 (1-2). Retrieved on March 15, 2007, from http://www.cios.org/ EJCPUBLIC$$4677329331206$$/010/1/01017.html.

McVittie, J. (2004). Discourse communities, student selves and learning. *Language & Education, 18*, 488-503.

Meân, L. (2001). Identity and discursive practice: Doing gender on the football pitch. *Discourse & Society, 12*, 789-815.

Mehan, H. (1990). Oracular reasoning in a psychiatric exam: The resolution of conflict in language. In A. D. Grimshaw (Ed.), *Conflict talk: Sociolinguistic investigations of arguments in conversation* (pp. 160-177). Cambridge, MA: Cambridge University Press.

Mehan, H. (1996). The construction of an LD student: A case study in the politics of representation. In M. Silverstein & G. Urban (Eds.), *Natural histories of discourse* (pp. 253-276). Chicago: University of Chicago Press

Mnookin, S. (2004). *The scandals at The New York Times and what it means for the American media*. New York: Random House.

Mumby, D. K. (1989). Ideology and the social construction of meaning: A communication perspective. *Communication Quarterly, 37*, 291-304.

Mumby, D. K. (2005). Theorizing resistance in organization studies: A dialectical approach. *Management Communication Quarterly, 19*, 19-44.

Mumby, D. K., & Stohl, C. (1996). Disciplining organizational communication studies. *Management Communication Quarterly, 10*, 50-72.

Newman, F. (1991). *The myth of psychology*. New York: Castillo International.

Papoulias, C. (2006). Transgender. *Theory, Culture & Society, 23*, 231-233.

Parker, I. (1999). Critical reflexive humanism and critical constructionist psychology. In D. J. Nightingale & J. Cromby (Eds.), *Social constructionist psychology* (pp. 23-36). Buckingham, England: Open University.

Pearce, K. A., & Pearce, W. B. (2001). The public dialogue consortium's school-wide dialogue process: A communicative approach to develop citizenship skills and enhance school climate. *Communication Theory, 11*, 105-123.

Pearce, W. B. (1976). The coordinated management of meaning: A rules-based theory of interpersonal communication. In G. R. Miller (Ed.), *Explorations in interpersonal communication* (Vol. 5, pp. 17-35). Beverly Hills, CA: Sage.

Pearce, W. B. (1989). *Communication and the human condition*. Carbondale: Southern Illinois University.

Pearce, W. B. (1992). A "camper's guide" to constructionisms. *Human Systems, 3*, 139-161.

Pearce, W. B. (1994). Recovering agency. In S. Deetz (Ed.), *Communication yearbook 17* (pp. 34-41). Thousand Oaks, CA: Sage.

Pearce, W. B. (1995). A sailing guide for social constructionists. In W. Leeds-Hurwitz (Ed.), *Social approaches to communication* (pp. 88-113). New York: Guilford.

Pearce, W. B. (2004). The coordinated management of meaning (CMM). In W. Gudykunst (Ed.), *Theorizing communication and culture* (pp. 35-54). Thousand Oaks, CA: Sage.

Pearce, W. B., & Cronen, V. E. (1980). *Communication, action, and meaning: The creation of social realities*. New York: Praeger.

Pearce, W. B., & Pearce, K. A. (2000). Extending the theory of the Coordinated Management of Meaning (CMM) through a community dialogue process. *Communication Theory, 10*, 405-424.

Penman, R. (2000). *Reconstructing communicating: Looking to a future*. Mahwah, NJ: Erlbaum.

Philipsen, G. (1995). The coordinated management of meaning theory of Pearce, Cronen, and associates. In D. P. Cushman & B. Kovačić (Eds.), *Watershed research traditions in human communication theory* (pp. 14-43). Albany: State University of New York Press.

Phillips, L., & Jørgensen, M. W. (2002). *Discourse analysis as theory and method.* London: Sage.

Pienaar, K., & Bekker, I. (2006). Invoking the feminine physical ideal: Bitch-slapping, she-men and butch girls. *Southern African Linguistics & Applied Language Studies, 24*, 437-447.

Potter, J. (1996). *Representing reality: Discourse, rhetoric and social construction.* London: Sage.

Potter, J., & Wetherell, M. (1987). *Discourse and social psychology: Beyond attitudes and behaviours.* London: Sage.

Pride, R. A. (1999). Redefining the problem of racial inequality. *Political Communication, 16*, 147-167.

Putnam, L. L. (1983). The interpretive perspective: An alternative to functionalism. In L. L. Putnam & M. E. Pacanowsky (Eds.), *Communication and organizations: An interpretive approach* (pp. 31-54). Beverly Hills, CA: Sage.

Putnam, L. L., & Pacanowsky, M. E. (Eds.). (1983). *Communication and organizations: An interpretive approach.* Beverly Hills, CA: Sage.

Reeves, E. (2006). Darfur 101. *The New Republic Online.* Retrieved April 29, 2007, from http://www.tnr.com/doc.mhtml?i=w060501&s=reeves050506#8

Report of the International Commission of Inquiry on Darfur to the United Nations Secretary-General. (2005). Retrieved April 29, 2007, from http://www.un.org/News/dh/sudan/com_inq_darfur.pdf

Robichaud, D. (2005). Steps toward a relational view of agency. In F. Cooren, J. R. Taylor, & E. J. Van Every (Eds.), *Communication as organizing: Practical approaches to research into the dynamic of text and conversation* (pp. 101-114). Mahwah, NJ: Erlbaum.

Ryan, J. (1994). Women, modernity and the city. *Theory, Culture & Society, 11*(4), 35-63.

Sacks, H. (1995). *Lectures on conversation: Volumes I & II.* Oxford, England: Blackwell.

Schiffrin, D. (1996). Narrative as self-portrait: Sociolinguistic constructions of identity. *Language in Society, 25*, 167-203.

Schön, D. A. (1983). *The reflective practitioner: How professionals think in action.* New York: Basic Books.

Shailor, J. G. (1994). *Empowerment in dispute mediation: A critical analysis of communication.* Westport, CT: Praeger.

Shailor, J. G. (1997). The meaning and use of "context" in the theory of the Coordinated Management of Meaning. In J. L. Owens (Ed.), *Context and communication behavior* (pp. 97-110). Reno, NV: Context Press.

Shotter, J. (1984). *Social accountability and selfhood.* Oxford, England: Basil Blackwell.

Shotter, J. (1993). *Cultural politics of everyday life: Social constructionism, rhetoric and knowing of the third kind.* Toronto, Canada: University of Toronto Press.

Shotter, J. (1998). An organization's internal public sphere: Its nature and its supplementation. In O. Palshaugen, B. Gustavsen, D. Ostergerg, & J. Shotter (Eds.), *The end of organizational theory?: Language as a tool in action research and organizational development* (pp. 131-146). Amsterdam: John Benjamins.

Shotter, J. (1999). Problems with the "The way of theory." In B. Maiers. B. D. Bayer, R. Esgalhado, R. Jorna, & E. Schraube (Eds.), *Challenges to theoretical psychology* (pp. 27-34). Toronto, Canada: Captus University Press.

Shotter, J. (2000a). Inside dialogical realities: From an abstract-systematic to a participatory-holistic understanding of communication. *Southern Communication Journal, 65*, 119-132.

Shotter, J. (2000b). Wittgenstein and the everyday: From radical hiddenness to "nothing is hidden": From representation to participation. *Journal of Mundane Behavior, 1*(2). Retrieved on April 3, 2007, from http://www.mundanebehavior.org/index2.htm

Shotter, J. (2004). Expressing and legitimating 'actionable knowledge' from within 'the moment of acting.' *Concepts and Transformation, 9*, 205-229.

Shotter, J. (2005). 'Inside the moment of managing': Wittgenstein and the everyday dynamics of our expressive-responsive activities. *Organization Studies, 26*, 113-135.

Shotter, J. (2006). Understanding process from within: An argument for "withness"--thinking. *Organization Studies, 27*, 585-604.

Shotter, J., & Gergen, K. J. (1989). *Texts of identity.* London: Sage.

Shotter, J., & Gergen, K. J. (1994). Social construction: Knowledge, self, others, and continuing the conversation. In S. Deetz (Ed.), *Communication yearbook 17* (pp. 3-33). Thousand Oaks, CA: Sage.

Shotter, J., & Katz, A. (1998). 'Living moments' in dialogical exchanges. *Human Systems, 9*, 81-93.

Shotter, J., & Lannamann, J. (2002). The situation of social constructionism: Its' imprisonment within the ritual of theory-criticism-and-debate. *Theory & Psychology, 12*, 577-609.

Sigman, S. J. (Ed.). (1995b). *The consequentiality of communication.* Hillsdale, NJ: Erlbaum.

Smith, N. (2006). There's no such thing as a natural disaster. *Understanding Katrina: Perspectives from the social sciences.* Retrieved April 5, 2007, from http://understandingkatrina.ssrc.org

Spano, S. J. (2001). *Public dialogue and participatory democracy: The Cupertino community project.* Creskill, NJ: Hampton Press.

Spector, M., & Kitsuse, J. I. (1977). *Constructing social problems.* Menlo Park, CA: Cummings.

Staller, K. M. (2003). Constructing the runaway youth problem: Boy adventurers to girl prostitutes, 1960-1978. *Journal of Communication, 53*, 330-346.

Stallings, R. A. (1990). Media discourse and the social construction of risk. *Social Problems, 37* (1), 80-95.

Stam, H. J. (2001). Introduction: Social constructionism and its critics. *Theory & Psychology, 11*, 291-296.

Stapleton, K. (2003). Gender and swearing: A community practice. *Women & Language, 26*(2), 22-33.

Stewart, J. (1995). *Language as articulate contact: Toward a post-semiotic philosophy of communication.* Albany: State University of New York Press.

Stewart, J., Zediker, K. E., & Black, L. (2004). Relationships among philosophies of dialogue. In R. Anderson, L. A. Baxter, & K. N. Cissna (Eds.), *Dialogue: Theorizing difference in communication studies* (pp. 21-38). Thousand Oaks, CA: Sage.

Tacke, V. (2001). BSE as an organizational construction: A case study on the globalization of risk. *British Journal of Sociology, 52*, 293-312.

Terranova, T. (2006). The concept of information. *Theory, Culture & Society, 23*, 286-288.

Thornborrow, J. (2002). *Power talk: Language and interaction in institutional discourse.* London: Longman.

Tracy, K. (1995). Action-implicative discourse analysis. *Journal of Language & Social Psychology, 14*, 195-215.

Tracy, K. (1997). Interactional trouble in emergency service requests: A problem of frames. *Research on Language and Social Interaction, 30*, 315-343.

Tracy, K., & Ashcraft, K. (2001). Crafting policies about controversial values: How wording disputes manage a group dilemma. *Journal of Applied Communication Research, 29*, 297-316.

Tracy, K., & Baratz, S. (1993). Intellectual discussion in the academy as situated discourse. *Communication Monographs, 60*, 300-320.

Tracy, K., & Muller, H. (2001). Diagnosing a school board's interactional trouble: Theorizing problem formulating. *Communication Theory, 11*, 84-104.

Tracy, K., & Tracy, S. J. (1998). Rudeness at 911: Reconceptualizing face and face attack. *Human Communication Research, 25*, 225-251.

Tracy, S. J., & Trethewey, A. (2005). Fracturing the real-self fake-self dichotomy: Moving toward "crystallized" organizational discourses and identities. *Communication Theory, 15*, 168-195.

Trethewey, A. (2000). Cultured bodies: Communication as constitutive of culture and embodied identity. *Electronic Journal of Communication, 10*(1/2). Retrieved March 15 2007, from http://www.cios.org/EJCPUBLIC$$111732947644$$/010/1/01016. html.

Varey, R. J. (2000). A critical review of conceptions of communication evident in contemporary business and management literature. *Journal of Communication Management, 4*, 328-340.

Volosinov, V. (1986). *Marxism and the philosophy of language* (L. Matejka & I. R. Titunik, Trans.). Cambridge, MA: Harvard University Press.

Vygotsky, L. (1986). *Thought and Language* (Alex Kozulin, Trans.). Cambridge, MA: MIT Press.

Wang, J. (2006). Questions and the exercise of power. *Discourse & Society, 17*, 529-548.

Watzlawick, P., Beavin Bavelas J. B., & Jackson, D. D. (1967). *Pragmatics of human communication: A study of interactional patterns, pathologies, and paradoxes.* New York: Norton.

White, M. K., & Epston, D. (1990). *Narrative means to therapeutic ends.* New York: Norton.

Wicks, R. H. (2005). Message framing and constructing meaning: An emerging paradigm in mass communication research. In P. Kalbfleisch (Ed.), *Communication yearbook 29* (pp. 333-361). Mahwah, NJ: Erlbaum.

Wittgenstein, L. (1953). *Philosophical investigations.* (G. E. M. Anscombe, Trans.) Oxford, England: Blackwell.

Wittgenstein, L. (1980). *Culture and value* (P. Winch, Trans.). Oxford, England: Blackwell.

Wood, J. T. (2004). Foreword: Entering into dialogue. In R. Anderson, L. A. Baxter, & K. N. Cissna (Eds.), *Dialogue: Theorizing difference in communication studies* (pp. xv-xxiii). Thousand Oaks, CA: Sage.

Zimmerman, D. H. (1992). The interactional organization of calls for emergency assistance. In P. Drew & J. Heritage (Eds.), *Talk at work* (pp. 418- 469). New York: Cambridge University Press.

CHAPTER CONTENTS

2 Theorizing Resistance in a Global Context

Processes, Strategies, and Tactics in Communication Scholarship

Mahuya Pal
Purdue University

Mohan J. Dutta
Purdue University

In recent years, we have witnessed an increase in scholarship documenting the relevance of theorizing resistance in communication scholarship in globalization contexts. Historically, communication scholars have studied resistance in organizational communication, public relations, health communication, gender, and rhetoric. Our review of this research documents the common threads among distinct yet interdependent lines of scholarship, and we identify additional ways in which communication theorists have explored resistance (and processes for communicating resistance) in the contexts of power, ideology, and hegemony. We conclude our chapter by discussing the need to theorize power, subordination, and resistance as complex and intertwined processes in light of globalization that play out in the complicated terrains of transnational hegemony. In so doing, we suggest an overarching framework for locating studies of resistance in the realm of globalization politics and connecting resistance theories in communication to the possibilities for transformative politics.

The processes of globalization have widened the disparities between the developed and developing nations. The flow of capital determined by the pro-market economy—which protects the interest of transnational corporations—remains central to these disparities (Miyoshi, 1995). However, the flow of capital intersects with resistance efforts that counter the hegemonic forces and system (Tarrow, 2005). Enactment of such resistance within

Correspondence: Mahuya Pal and Mohan J. Dutta, Department of Communication, Steven C. Beering Hall of Liberal Arts and Education 2114, Purdue University, 100 North University Street, West Lafayette, IN 47907-2098; Phone: 765-494-3429; Fax: 765-496-1394; E-mail: mpal@purdue.edu; mdutta@purdue.edu dominant configuration of capital holds the potential to advance social change by emphasizing an equitable structure of development.

Increasingly, communication scholars have started attending to the concept of resistance as a communicative strategy in the realm of globalization (Cloud, 2001; Cox, 2004; Ganesh, Zoller, & Cheney, 2005; Grossberg, 1993; Holmer Nadesan, 2001) As globalization opens up the doors of nation states to the dominant configurations of transnational capitalism accompanied by the dramatic rise in global inequalities (Lyotard, 1984; Millen & Holtz, 2000; Millen, Irwin, & Kim, 2000), they also generate new avenues for theorizing resistance as enacted in the context of the rapid diffusion of global capitalism. Against the backdrop of this divide between "North" (wealthy countries in the northern hemisphere) and "South" (poorer developing countries; see Melkote & Steeves, 2001), scholars conceptualize resistance in terms of the communicative processes and messages that seek to counter the dominant structures of power (i.e., efforts to maintain the status quo in transnational configurations); they treat resistance as active and manifest in the form of communicative practices (Cheney & Cloud, 2006). Theorizing about resistance offers opportunities for conceptualizing and enacting social change in the global arena, challenging the dominant structures of power that create and sustain the conditions of marginalization, and presenting the voices of marginalized cultural and economic sectors of the global complex that have historically been silenced by powerful actors. In our review of communication scholarship, we pay particular attention to those areas within the discipline of communication that have explored this active communicative nature of resistance, specifically considering communicative practices that oppose dominant structures.

The significance of examining communicative processes through which stakeholders enact resistance has become particularly relevant in the realm of globalization processes that have brought the role of resistance in challenging the dominant structures to the forefront (Ganesh et al., 2005). In the communication literature, scholars have investigated resistance in the areas of organizational communication, public relations, health communication, gender, and rhetoric. Organizational communication scholars have traditionally focused on resistance with regard to internal organizational publics (Larson & Tompkins, 2005; Mumby, 1993a, 1993b; Tracy, 2000; Tretheway, 1997); public relations researchers have explored resistance by activist groups (see Dozier & Lauzen, 2000; Dutta & Pal, 2007; Murphy & Dee, 1992); health communication scholars have studied individual practices within the physician-patient relationship and participatory processes that challenge unhealthy structures (Dutta-Bergman, 2004a, 2004b; Zoller, 2005). Moreover, the literature on resistance and gender has detailed the ways in which social actors challenge patriarchal practices through their everyday practices as well as through their participation in transformative politics (Ashcraft & Mumby, 2004; Buzzanell, 1994, 1995), and rhetoricians have historically analyzed message strategies utilized by social movements to mobilize action and the discursive spheres for political action (Stewart, Smith, & Denton, 2006).

This chapter theorizes about the possibilities of conceptualizing resistance to the dominant structures in the realm of globalization politics, explores the empirical research on resistance, and creates strategic opportunities for action, situating these discussions in light of the globalization processes that maintain and propagate the domination of transnational hegemony (Krugman, 2002). This examination of resistance also establishes a foundation for future scholarship on resistance, particularly in the context of globalization processes. Such theorizing about resistance offers entry points for new theory building that acknowledges the multiple processes and ways through which individuals, groups, and communities come to organize themselves and challenge the dominant structures that constrain their lives and to spark change. These processes create the substratum for understanding the ways in which individual and collective entities seek to transform the ideologies, practices, and institutions that serve as sites of the dominant hegemony in the realm of transnationalism (Ganesh et al., 2005). This review begins by describing the literature on globalization, following with a discussion of the common threads and tensions that connect the current literature on resistance in a variety of communication contexts, and concluding with an exploration of the gaps in the literature on resistance in the realm of globalization processes. Locating our conversation about resistance in the context of globalization provides both pragmatic and theoretical value by suggesting new arenas for research and practice by communication scholars.

THEORIZING GLOBALIZATION

The increasing speed and flow of people, capital, ideas, goods, and services that connect actors across national borders remains central to many definitions of globalization (Keohane, 2002; McMichael, 2003). The creation of the World Trade Organization (WTO) in the 1990s (accompanied by the formation of the many regional and trans-regional blocs such as North American Free Trade Agreement [NAFTA], The European Union, Asia Pacific Economic Corporation, and Asia-Europe Meeting [ASEM]) marked the decade as the harbinger of globalization, reflected in significant increases in cross-national trading and communication, expanding operational scope of transnational corporations (TNCs), and increasingly evident inequalities between the North and South. Simultaneously, the various avenues through which globally dispersed publics resist these dominant structures became more clear (Sriramesh & Vercic, 2003; Tarrow, 2005). According to Tarrow, the interplay between the global and the local, the complicated interconnections among the five *scapes* of globalization, and the nature of time–space distanciation play an important role in activist publics' resistive practices. The complex and continuous interconnections between local spaces and global agendas mark globalization; the local constitutes (yet continually becomes defined by) the global. Globalization also reflects the increasingly multi-layered interpenetrations of identities, mediated communications, technology flows, economic flows and flow of ideas, prompted by the compressions in dimensions of time and space (Giddens, 2000; Harvey, 2000). These key concepts developed from the globalization literature (Dutta & Pal, 2007) offer theoretical entry points for connecting collective resistance in the global realm with the opportunities for transformation in global politics that define the parameters for global organizations (transnational corporations, WTO, World Bank, IMF, etc.) and global organizing (i.e., activist organizing).

Connecting the Local and Global

The mobilization of local issues in the global arena and externally originating conflicts locally challenge the modernist discourse of organizational management and facilitates the articulation of hitherto silenced voices on key issues (typically performed by powerful social actors in traditional domains located at the center; Dutta & Pal, 2007). Particularly given globalization, the surge in activist movements demonstrates the need to focus on the diffusion of movements across borders and the opportunities for international mobilization (Della Porta & Tarrow, 2005). Activist movements draw our attention to the necessity of theorizing about the ways in which stakeholders enact resistance in complexly connected sites that weave the global with the local. Resistance becomes a communicative space connected with individual and collective practice through which the interplay of the global and local becomes situated in the realm of transformative politics (Mittelman & Chin, 2000). On one hand, according to Dutta and Pal, local economies and livelihoods are embedded within global politics; on the other hand, locally situated practices challenge global politics and organize globally with other locally dispersed actors to mobilize for change. For instance, the recent Argentine protests were triggered by the pressures of international financial institutions but directed at local institutions (Auyero, 2003). Simultaneously, movement organizations often become involved supranationally in order to create international alliances for nationally weak social movements. With their Eurostrike in 1997, Spanish, French, and Belgian Renault workers protested the closing of the Renault factory of Vilvorde in Belgium at the EU level (Drache, 2001).

In the domain of global organizations, issues of workplace practices in locally situated sites intersect with the global politics surrounding these practices (Cheney & Cloud, 2006). Though dominant cultural practices become imposed as the acceptable practices within globally dispersed organizations, they can also spark resistance in the everyday strategies of local actors and the transformative cultural politics in which they participate. The globalization of communicative platforms also create new spaces for organized resistance that connect the local with the global (Herod, 1997; Juravich & Bronfenbrenner, 2000; Moody, 1988); new media such as the Internet prompt offline activism that connects locally dispersed workers on globally situated workplace policies (Juris, 2004). Movements in global labor demonstrate the possibilities of international solidarity; issues of workplace organizing aimed at specific organizational practices locally draw on the collective involvement of globally dispersed stakeholders and simultaneously seek to impact global policies. For instance, the protests against the Free Trade Agreement of Americas (FTAA) in Miami in 2003 brought out labor leaders who stressed the relevance of international solidarity in labor organizing (Cheney & Cloud, 2006). In addition to resisting the specific unhealthy and worker unfriendly practices of organizations at the local level that directly impact worker rights and working environment, international movements of solidarity also challenge the hegemonic global structures that promote and upkeep unhealthy workplace policies.

The practice of global activism underscores the global connectivity of issues, demonstrating that issues are no longer simply situated within locally isolated spaces but rather interrelate globally with global processes and practices (Smith, 2001). The WTO protests, for example, reveal the ways in which global policies impact local actors and the processes through which participation by geographically dispersed local actors bring about globally situated resistance to powerful social actors (in this instance, the WTO) (Routledge, 2000). Global events impact local ones and vice versa. Global policies inform and constrain local issues and potential reactions.

For instance, the articulation and implementation of global health policies (especially those that govern the innovation, dissemination, and use of health products) impacts the framing of local policies related to the pharmaceutical industry. Drawing on this emphasis on transnational resistance, critical public relations scholars (Bardhan, 2003; Curtin & Gaither, 2005; Dutta-Bergman, 2005a; Karlberg, 1996; McKie & Munshi, 2005; Pal & Dutta, in press) explore the ways in which the public relations strategies of powerful global actors affect global and local policies, the lives of locally situated publics, and opportunities for resistance. Furthermore, this line of critical scholarship interrogates how the framing of global issues emerges from the flow of power and control in the realm of globalization. Global HIV/AIDS activist groups have emerged that mobilize locally as well as globally to shape global HIV/AIDS policies (see DeSouza & Dutta, in press). DeSouza and Dutta detailed discourses of resistance that circulate in the e-forum of Saathi, a not-for-profit organization that "was founded in response to numerous requests to create a neutral platform for multi-sectoral dialogue among people living with HIV/AIDS (PLWHA), health care providers, policy makers, educators and volunteers." They described the ways in which local HIV/AIDS activists throughout various parts of India use the forum to align with each other, to connect and co-organize with other HIV/AIDS organizations in other parts of the world, and to mobilize both offline and online around key issues such as patent acts and WTO policies that affect PLWHAs globally.

This example suggests the relevance for engaging in globally situated issues management that is sensitized to the continuous interpenetration of the local and the global. This critical standpoint affirms the importance of pursuing the global power structures within which stakeholders frame issues and manage policies. Time–space compression in global organizations accompanies this local-global interflow and impacts the complex interplay among the various scapes of social life within which people organize experiences and human activism becomes possible.

Time–Space Compression and Scapes

Time–space compression has disrupted and disoriented political-economic practices as well as cultural and social life (Harvey, 2000). Harvey asserted that accelerating turnover time (coupled with speed-up in exchanges and consumption, outsourcing and sub-contracting, and improved systems of techniques of distribution) has "accentuated volatility and ephemerality of fashion, production, techniques, labour processes, ideas and ideologies, values and established practices" (p. 83). This time–space compression underscores the complexity of global processes within which members communicate. Strategies and tactics employed by organizations in the global landscape occur amid these dynamic intersections of identities, mediated communications, technology flows, economic flows, and sharing of ideas.

Giddens (2000) advanced his conceptual framework of "time–space distanciation" (p. 92), noting the complicated relations between "local involvements" (p. 92), and "interaction across distance" (p. 92). Globalization comprises a "stretching" process that represents the interconnectivity between different social contexts or regions across the world. The action in a "distanciated" location influences events in another place through economic, political, or media processes. For instance, Giddens explained how prosperity of an urban area in Singapore could be causally linked to the impoverishment of a neighborhood in Pittsburgh, whose local products have become globally uncompetitive. The outcomes of "distanciated" influence do not act in a homogenized manner, nor are they in sync with the happenings of distant locales. Local happenings caused by an infinite distance may move in a reverse direction. As noted in the previous example, the decline in the economy of a neighborhood in Pittsburgh enables the economy in an urban locale in Singapore to flourish and, hence, influences it to move in a reverse direction. While the globalized social relationships diminish nationalist sentiments linked to the nation-state, it also simultaneously intensifies localized identities. For instance, call center employees in India catering to the clients in the United States display a tension in their interactions as they experience possibilities of cultural erosion at their workplace (Pal & Buzzanell, 2008).

Globalization also suggests rapid deployment of new organizational forms, new technologies, and revolution of communication systems. Altering Fordist tendencies of vertical integration, globalization emphasizes flexible accumulation and accelerating turnover time by speedy production system involving sub-contracting and outsourcing, quick delivery system and intense labor processes. Within these satellite networks of global organizations, new opportunities for resistance arise. The emergence of the Internet as a powerful medium in facilitating activist movements validates the phenomenon (Juris, 2004; Routledge, 2000).

Reflecting on this complexity of global processes, Appadurai (2000) argued that "the new global cultural economy has to be understood as a complex, overlapping, disjunctive order" (p. 230). He offered five dimensions of global cultural flow: ethnoscapes, mediascapes, technospaces, finanscapes, and ideoscapes. According to Appadurai, *ethnoscape* essentially consists of diasporic community moving in a fluid world constituted in the realm of the politics of nations. This global flow of diasporic communities is central to the ways in which organizations conceptualize and communicate with their internal and external stakeholders. For instance, according to Appadurai, the off-shoring of jobs in developing countries, the flow of technology-based expertise across nation states, and the fluid movement of knowledge managers across national boundaries critically affects how organizations develop, implement, and communicate such policies. Similarly, the idea of ethnoscapes also suggests that organizational communication with external stakeholders is continually fragmented and interwoven across multiple spaces.

According to Appadurai (2000), *technoscape* refers to the fluidity of technology that makes tangible and intangible knowledge flows possible across boundaries. For public relations practice, this possibility of knowledge flow across boundaries significantly impacts the ways in which organizations craft and target information toward various publics. For instance, the growing reach and penetration of the Internet have fostered new challenges for public relations practitioners regarding the ways in which practitioners communicate with their publics within the rich intersections of time and space (Lordan, 2001; M. Taylor, Kent, & White, 2001). The use of the Internet as a medium for exchange of information globally within short time frames suggests that an organization might need to communicate with geographically dispersed publics pretty rapidly during a crisis (Coombs, 2007; Heath, 2001; Springston, 2001). From a critical standpoint, Heath asserted that the mobilizing power of the Internet in organizing local communities into global platforms has resulted in an emancipatory role of public relations. Critical public relations scholars examine the ways in which technology serves as a site of contestation and framing of global issues and the processes through which power and ideology emerge through technologically mediated sites (Dutta & Pal, 2007). As Appadurai explained, the growth of technologically mediated activism brings forth the importance of theorizing the communication of resistance in the realm of technoscapes.

Appadurai (2000) defined *finanscape* as the inter-linkage of capital with monetary and commodity flows across boundaries; it enables stakeholders to challenge the political economy of public relations practice in the context of globalization. According to Appadurai, the practice of public relations conceptualized within the dominant framework of managerial utilitarianism takes the economic functions served by powerful social actors for granted. From a critical standpoint, finanscape offers a theoretical lens for examining the complex interflow of economic interests and the political processes through which participants pursue economic interests in the global arena. In doing so, it takes discussions of political economy from beyond the realm of locally situated actors and relationships into one of complexly interconnected webs of global actors, situated both locally and globally. For example, a criticism of the public relations strategies used by Nike in its "sweatshop" dilemma may be considered through a political economic lens that interrogates the financial interests of the various stakeholders at the local and global levels (Bullert, 2000).

According to Appadurai (2000), *mediascape* carries the information across borders by providing images that depend on several interests of global actors. Appadurai observed that the way in which consumerism has fuelled across the world for new commodities attests to the power of media.

Appadurai (2000) asserted that *ideoscape* refers to the conflict of often political ideologies due to clashes with perspectives of nation states. A critical approach examines the contestation of ideologies and the hegemonic processes through which certain ideologies are privileged over others in global discursive framing and implementation of global policies. Ultimately, ideoscapes provides a link into the interrogation of the intricately complex processes through which multiple local and global actors interact to shape communicative practices. Explaining the phenomenon, Appadurai wrote:

> So, while an Indian audience may be attentive to the resonances of a political speech in terms of some key words and phrases reminiscent of Hindi cinema, a Korean audience may respond to the subtle codings of Buddhist or neo-Confucian rhetorical strategy encoded in a political document. (p. 233)

In summary, the global shift associated with the creation of world markets and with international communication and media flows holds profound implications for how people make sense of their lives, the changing world, and the ways in which they resist the dominant global configurations (Robins, 2000). According to Robins, "It is provoking new senses of disorientation and of orientation, giving rise to new experiences of both placeless and placed identity" (p. 198). In essence, most of the globalization theories (such as Appadurai's *scapes*, Giddens' time–space *distanciation*, or Harvey's time–space *compression*) explain globalization in terms of diversity and difference rather than in terms of homogenization. National identities are no longer marked by simplistic concepts such as collectivism and individualism that offer polar opposites to locate national cultures as static and delimited within the geographical definitions of nation states (Appadurai, 2000; Giddens, 2000; Harvey, 2000) Cultures exist in continuous flux, constantly interpreted and reinterpreted through human interactions, and embedded within the context of the lives of members (Dutta-Bergman, 2004a, 2004b).

Within this dialectical tension between tradition and transformation, identities and relationships become meaningful, suggesting the necessity of conceptualizing communication within an organic framework of evolving relationships, rather than within a simplistic modernist frame that seeks to develop the best strategy for a national culture based on predefined markers such as individualism/collectivism, power distance, uncertainty avoidance, and masculinity/femininity (see Curtin & Gaither, 2006; Pal & Dutta, in press). The complex interplay of the global-local tension, accompanied by dynamic interactions among the five scapes, offer theoretical and pragmatic entry points for exploring the ways in which parties enact resistance through global activism.

EXISTING APPROACHES TO RESISTANCE

The communication literature has explored and theorized the concept of resistance in multiple ways in a variety of contexts, ranging from organizations to small groups to relationships to individuals. Whereas a bulk of the scholarship on resistance has occurred in organizational communication, with its emphasis on resistive strategies utilized by workers (Murphy, 1998; Tracy, 2000; Tretheway, 1997), other areas of the communication discipline (such as public relations, health communication, gender, performance studies and rhetoric) have also explored resistance, either implicitly or explicitly. Several epistemological pursuits and a wide array of methodological tools with an impetus on critical inquiry have opened up vistas of research in resistive politics (Mumby, 2005). Along with issues related to macro- and micro-level interplays of power, control, and domination, critical communication studies have also pursued different possibilities for resistance (Boal, 1985, 1998; Chatterjea, 2004; Hashmi, 2007). In this section, we map four different approaches to and concepts of resistance in communication—traditional, postmodern, discourse-centered, and feminist—before discussing resistance from a postcolonial perspective. Notably, these four categories extend from diverse epistemological, ontological, and axiological foundations, though we note overlaps between them throughout this section.

Traditional Approaches

Marx's (1867/1967) labor process theory provides a historical backdrop to different philosophical traditions that primarily draw from or contend with the former. For Marx, the concept of resistance revolves around one key source: revolutionary class consciousness. In this case, resistance opposes the capitalist mode of production and the exploitation of labor through surplus value and remains firmly rooted in a material base (Cheney & Cloud, 2006). This postulate assumes inevitability of antagonism between the capitalist class and the working class, and resistance embodies the mobilization of a collective identity that opposes the exploitative goals of dominant social actors. Estranged from the ownership of production, laborers must abolish private ownership of production by organizing labor solidarity and "class-based resistance" (Jermier, Knights, & Nord, 1994, p. 3). Members exert control through economically sustained access to discursive spaces and processes that serve as sites of power and control; resistance, therefore, is constituted in the realm of the opposition to the materially located economic disparities within the system (Cloud, 1994; Marx, 1867/1967). In public relations scholarship, the material substratum of traditional critical theory offers the basis for critique of dominant models (such as the symmetrical model of public relations) that does not account for the material nature of structural inequities that are fundamental to the communicative processes, strategies and outcomes (Grunig, 2001).

The material and symbolic closely interpenetrate each other; for instance, Cheney and Cloud (2006) observed:

> Class is both material and symbolic, especially if one understands Marx's distinction between a 'class in itself'--the material existence of a mass of people who share in common the experience of exploitation under capitalism--and a 'class for itself'--understood as the rhetorically shaped and motivated movement of workers organized to demand both greater voice and greater control of their economic lives. (pp. 517-518)

For instance, Clair and Thompson (1996) argued that pay inequity exists both as discursive and material practices that are interdependent and intertwined. According to Cheney and Cloud, this relationship between the symbolic and the material becomes particularly evident in light of globalization as dominant discursive strategies create climates of support for neo-liberal policies that contribute to the economic disparities across the globe, and these economic disparities serve simultaneously as the material bases on which the discursive strategies are constituted through access to dominant public spheres.

Notably, the ideology of liberal democracy emphasizes privacy and autonomy and does not entertain the possibilities of economic self-rule of workers and the redistribution of wealth as the bases for democratic participation in work and in society as a whole (Cheney & Cloud, 2006; Dutta-Bergman, 2005b); therefore, drawing on Marxist notions of revolutionary class consciousness, Cheney and Cloud suggested that global efforts of resistance ought to be theorized in terms of a revolutionary model of democratic change that draws from the fundamental structural antagonism between employer and worker in capitalism and builds on the transformative capacity of worker solidarity. We witnessed this solidarity in the varied forms of labor participation in global justice movements against corporate globalization such as the Seattle protests against the WTO in 1999 and the mass protests against the FTAA in Miami in 2003 (Turner, 2006).

Resistance in the traditional sense has a distinctly material component that draws on the antagonistic relationship between employers and labor (Marx, 1975). The role of labor in the production process is both materially and rhetorically significant; production of goods and services stops when workers collectively refuse to work (J. Freeman & Rogers, 1999; R. B. Freeman & Medoff, 1984). Unions have historically afforded one of the best avenues for negotiating favorable conditions for workers through their ability to collectively refuse to work. Cheney and Cloud (2006) asserted that "it is the economic force of the strike or threatened strike that provides workers with leverage to reach agreements on their terms, rather than just those of the bosses" (p. 524). Through materially driven strategies, in addition to the use of symbols, workers can bring about changes in the structure. For instance, in the Justice for Janitors case in Houston, Texas, workers gained union victory through their use of collective refusal to work (Greenhouse, 2000). The strike of drivers against the United Parcel Service (UPS) for full-time jobs led to an estimated $30 million loss each day in profits, ultimately forcing UPS to create 10,000 full time jobs, to limit the use of subcontracted labor, and to increase the pay of both part-time and full-time workers.

In health communication, the local politics of marginalized groups with limited access to basic resources reveal the material basis of resistance, and efforts such as *gheraos* (collectively blocking a health service facility) and sit-ins seek to disrupt the very materiality of the production/service process (see Dutta-Bergman, 2004a, 2004b). Disrupting the materiality of hegemonic spaces historically has been at the heart of performative avenues such as street theater, described by Hashmi (2007) as a "militant political theater of protest" (p. 13) that employs performance to raise consciousness, bringing forth the closely connected relationship between the material and the symbolic.

Scholars of labor movements maintain that this sort of collective action is increasingly difficult to organize in the realm of globalization, given the loss of power by states to protect domestic labor and the increased disjunction between the mobility of capital and the localization of labor (Silver, 2003; Tilly, 1995). In the global economy, access to labor is cheap, and capital can move to wherever companies can pay less for labor, leading to the increasing tendency of weak governments eager to attract foreign capital to side with the interests of foreign capital and repress labor on their behalf. Tarrow (2005) noted:

> [The] basic gap is strengthened by several structural features of the current wave of globalization: sharply lowered costs of transportation; the internationalization of finance; a dominant ideology of neoliberalism; and the segmentation of production, which makes it possible for multilateral companies to subcontract important stages of their production process to firms for which they bear no legal responsibility. (p. 154)

Given these structural barriers in globalization processes, workers increasingly turn to domestic direct action that draws on their rights as citizens, operating with the assistance of external allies and international institutions; issues of worker's rights have spilled over to the public sphere and become starting points for community action. In addition to utilizing traditional forms such as protests, direct action also involves community-wide events that are difficult for authorities to repress without drawing public attention; resources supplied by international allies and institutional access gained through cross-border collaborations fit with the local direct action of workers (Gentile, 2003). The case of the Coalition for Justice in *Maquiladoras* exemplifies how local actions by workers to defend their rights were complemented by cross-border institutional support in the form of publicizing the local movement globally, drawing on international solidarity networks to put international pressures on corporations, and coalition building to challenge free trade policies such as NAFTA, Central America Free Trade Agreement (CAFTA), and Korea–U.S. Free Trade Agreement (KORUS) (Williams, 1999). As *Maquiladoras* demonstrates, forms of direct action in the realm of globalization are no longer simply localized but, rather, realized at the interstices of the local and the global. Furthermore, local-global resistance simultaneously operates in terms of identities, mediated communications, technology flows, economic flows, and flow of ideas, as local cultural identities interweave within complex global networks that connect the local politics with a global audience and challenge global policies.

Discussing the material foundations of resistance and suggesting the necessity to theorize about the various contexts within which resistance plays out, Edwards (1984) offered a typology of control—simple control, technical control, and bureaucratic control—with the rationale that social and historical contexts shape the forms of control. For simple control, capitalists exercise power obtrusively; for technical control, they assert power through machines or technology; and, for bureaucratic control, power emerges through the social relations of production. For the latter two, the systems of control are institutionalized and operate through structures. Edwards explained that this typology of control reflects the historical process of organizing work. Each form marks a definite stage of the capitalist era by reflecting different stages in the process of the development of the firms. Also, because of the uneven progress of capitalism, all types of control co-exist in the economy.

Contrary to Marx (1867/1967) and Braverman (1974, 1984) who did not acknowledge resistance beyond revolution, Edwards (1984) suggested that the objective behind such systems of control is to combat resistance. Stakeholders reorganize work to establish structures to minimize resistance and maximize profits. Each system exploits wage-labor and shapes the working class accordingly, which, in turn, has its implications for resistance. As Edwards explained, in simple control, workers struggle to oppose the despotic control; in technical control, workers resist the mechanized pace of production and fight for rights collectively; and in bureaucratic control, workers demand workplace democracy. Thus, the modes, strategies, and tactics of resistances are influenced by the different forms of exploitation that, in turn, impact the needs and demands of the workers.

Critics of the traditional approach argue that Marx's (1867/1967) and Braverman's (1974, 1984) explanation of capitalist interest undermines subjective consciousness and its role in reinforcing resistance to capitalist labor processes. To the contrary, labor becomes a normative category of universal human nature. Understanding resistance objectively (i.e., labor as a universal category) does not account for subjective experiences and the meanings that stakeholders attach to resistance. Jermier et al. (1994) observed:

> Marx and Braverman were aware of the importance of subjective consciousness and the part it plays in resistance to capitalist labour processes. Neither could escape these issues, even when their work consciously attempted to limit the scope of analysis to a more [objectivist position]. However, neither chose to theorize subjectivity and resistance. (p. 6)

Subsequently, scholars (Edwards, 1984; Friedman, 1977) called for the need to theorize resistance and made necessary contributions by emphasizing the importance of the concept through documenting various class struggles and other labor processes. However, this literature focuses more on the managerial control rather than on specific resistance practices. Overall, the traditional idea of resistance hinges on the grand narratives of class conflict and revolutionary struggle. It refers to any kind of organized collective opposition such as organized worker protests, strikes, grievances, unionized movements, etc. (Jermier et al., 1994; P. Prasad & A. Prasad, 2000). Early uses of resistance concentrated on the reaction of employees primarily in factories to specific changes in management practices. As Jermier et al. noted, within the United States, for example, much of the previous empirical work explained resistance as "actions of a seemingly homogeneous group of male blue-collar factory workers fighting an assumed, common identifiable cause" (p. 9). Such an understanding has its theoretical limitations because it suggests a simplistic relation of power between the subordinated and the dominant. Overlooking human subjectivity, the traditional conception of resistance also does not account for its multifaceted nature and the influence of time and space in resistive practices.

This orientation toward resistance as "fixed" can be located in critical social science. Alvesson and Deetz (2000) explained that critical social science addresses how cultural traditions and practices of powerful members "freeze social reality" (p. 9) to the advantage of certain sectional interests at the expense of others, consistent with the modernist assumptions embedded in organizations and the dominant research traditions of either a positivist or Marxist thinking. For instance, F. Taylor's (1947) and Weber's (1921) concepts of rationalization and bureaucratization follow the modernist logic of instrumentalization of people through scientific-technical knowledge. In a similar light, the unitary view of resistance as overt and cohesive, aimed at forming a class-based struggle to abolish private ownership also follows a deterministic and predictable logic of positivism (Jermier et al., 1994). Inspired by Marxist sensibilities, the traditional approach tends to treat workers' opposition as a natural reaction that emanates from the structural economic relations of production. Fleming and Sewell (2002) rightly observed that this dialectics of class relations implies workers are bound to resist to neutralize the capitalist forces and to champion their real interests.

Postmodern Approaches

The emergence of critical theory and postmodernism in communication coincided with the changing organizational contexts in a more turbulent economy and the critique of modernism in communication scholarship as more and more scholars became interested in the limits of the modernist project (Mumby, 1997). Whereas critical theory traditionally sought to critique modernism from within, still espousing some of the ideals of the enlightenment project such as emancipation and progress, Mumby noted that postmodernism typically situated itself in opposition to modernity as an external critique of the modernist project. Alvesson and Deetz (2000) asserted:

> The increased-size of organizations, rapid implementation of communication/information technologies, globalization, the changing nature of work, reduction of the working class, less salient class conflicts, professionalization of the workforce, stagnant economies, widespread ecological problems and turbulent markets are all parts of the contemporary context demanding a research response. (p. 9)

These changes shifted the focus to service industries as the most dominant economic form over and above the manufacturing industries in the post-industrial Western world. Elucidating the implications of these shifts, Alvesson and Deetz (2000) argued that these changes challenged instrumental rationality by imposing structural limits on control and emphasizing new themes such as culture, identity, mind power instead of labor power, and recognizing subjectivities of employees. Stakeholders constitute individual identities in ways that support the power and control of the dominant social actors, through the stories that circulate in the culture narrated through organizations (schools, workplaces etc.), media, and other dominant cultural systems (Kellner, 1989; Rosen, 1985, 1988; Witten, 1993).

In health communication, as grand narratives of the biomedical model came under scrutiny, scholars became increasingly interested in the role of identities as entry points for understanding health meanings, circulating and resisting dominant meanings of health (Ellingson, 2005; Frey, Adelman, Flint, & Query, 2000; see related arguments by Zoller & Kline, this volume). Similarly, interpersonal communication scholars became interested in the subjective human experience as an entry point for resisting dominant meanings that circulated in cultures. Mumby (1997) characterized postmodernism with the phrase "discourse of vulnerability" which not only questions the notion of "a Truth," but also depicts "… the ways in which the postmodern intellectual has given up the 'authority game' as a uniquely positioned arbiter of knowledge claims, exchanging a priori and elitist assumptions for a more emergent and context-bound notion of what counts as knowledge" (p. 14). The postmodern individual is constituted and constructed through knowledge structures (Foucault, 1979, 1980a, 1980b); according to Mumby, s/he comprises a product of discursive practices and processes that operate to "normalize and institutionalize our subjectivity" (p. 15).

In the absence of totalizing, collective consciousness under critical postmodernism, the focus shifted more to localized forms of resistance and subjectivity. Social construction of reality remains central to critical postmodernism; as individuals socially constituted identities through discursive apparatuses, these discursive formations also facilitate resistance (Collinson, 2002; Murphy, 2001; Tretheway, 1997; see also related arguments by Bartesaghi & Castor, this volume). Participants create and recreate meaning in discursive spaces, thus rendering communication problematic (Mumby, 1997). Mumby suggested that communication is simultaneously stable and unstable as some challenge centered communicative practices (or those that emerge from centers of power) from the margins.

Postmodern communication scholars continue to explore the ways in which apparently seamless communicative processes and discourses at the center are resisted from the margins and simultaneously transformed (Mumby, 1997). For instance, Bell and Forbes (1994) described the ways in which female secretaries utilize official bureaucratic structures for the purposes of creating resistive spaces to bureaucracy. Questioning the grand metanarratives of class consciousness, critical postmodernism disputes the taken-for-granted and conventional wisdom that circulate in cultures. Critical postmodernism strives to disrupt the status quo and support silenced or marginalized voices (Alvesson & Deetz, 2000; Kilduff & Mehra, 1997; Mumby, 1997). Hence, resistance intersects with subjectivity and, since individuals create subject positions in a number of competing discourses, self-identity is always fragmented and ruptured.

Burawoy's (1984) critical ethnography drew early attention to subjectivity by exploring development of consent among shop floor factory workers engaged in the "game of making out" (Jermier et al., 1994, p. 7; see also Mumby, 2005). Burawoy detailed constitution of the labor process, which works toward obscuring and securing surplus labor. While Burawoy's research highlights the subjective constitution of the labor process, where workers compete and mask their common membership, it also reflects how construction of employee identities fulfills the dominant interest. His research does not have a direct implication for understanding shop floor resistance. However, the workers' practices indicate presence of resistance when they consent to the rules on their own terms. According to Burawoy, such actions exemplify an emancipated society with people consciously making history for themselves.

Health communication scholars also emphasize subjectivity as an entry point for resistance, especially scholars who examine the ways in which individuals navigate their identities in response to the control exerted by the biomedical model and its dominant practices (Frank, 1991, 1995; Sharf, 2005). Sharf detailed the role of identity in the context of the physician-patient relationship. In her chapter, Sharf discussed the way in which she fired her surgeon. In this instance, the individual identity of the patient and her negotiation of this identity in the context of a health care interaction provided a starting point for interrogating the traditional doctor-patient relationship and fundamentally resisting the normative ideals of the accepted biomedical model even as she participated in the biomedical framework. Her identity impacted her relationship with the physician and, in turn, the relationship shaped how she negotiated her identity through the interaction. Sharf's negotiation and renegotiation of her identity challenged the dominant discursive framing of physician-patient relationships even as she participated within the traditional framework of the relationship. By firing her surgeon, Sharf renegotiated the traditional power dynamic that places physicians at the center of the physician-patient relationship.

Drawing from Foucault (1980a), the constitution of subjectivity suggests the complex relation of power that is tied to knowledge production and information. Collinson (1994) illustrated resistances shaped by certain subjective orientations to power, knowledge and information. While Collinson's "resistance through distance" (p. 50) indicates how employees in an engineering factory concealed their knowledge to minimize involvement with the company, "resistance through persistence" (p. 40) demonstrates how employees in an insurance case study acquired knowledge to challenge managerial practices. However, resistance is always intricately linked to organizational discipline, power, and control such that oppositional practices often mutually facilitate control and resistance. Hence, resistance forms do not represent institutionalized labor conflict but take place on a "local, immediate and often informal level" (Gottfried, 1994, p. 107). This everyday form of resistance includes covert and subtle forms like even "sabotage and theft" (p. 107) that outsiders may not easily recognize as resistance. James Scott (1985) regarded such occasions as mundane resistance. Such routine and creative forms of resistance serve as hidden agenda because others do not perceive them in dominant spheres that play out articulations of power. They are neither documented in any public record nor do they involve any collective action. Scott offered the following definition of resistance:

> At a first approximation, I might claim that class resistance includes any act(s) by members(s) of a subordinate class that is or are intended either to mitigate or deny claims...made on that class by superordinate classes... Finally, it focuses on intentions rather than consequences, recognizing that many acts of resistance may fail to achieve their intended result. (p. 290)

Routine resistance has been described to some extent in organizational communication as informal organization (P. Prasad & A. Prasad, 2000). P. Prasad and A. Prasad developed a four-fold typology to categorize resistance as (1) open confrontations, (2) subtle subversions of control systems through gossip, (3) employee distance, and (4) ambiguous accommodations. Most of these resistances are ubiquitous and manifest in mundane practices. In sociology, Fleming and Sewell (2002) created the concept of *svejkism*. They conceptualized svejkism after the character in Jaroslav Hasek's (1973) novel, *The good soldier, svejk*, who actively disengages and complies without conforming to resist the army practices. Gottfried (1994) suggested that withdrawal of cooperation can take symbolic expressions such as subverting dress codes. Viewing cooperation and accommodation by employees as absence of resistance undermines human agency in the context of power relations. Gottfried asserted that "resistance implies human agency in the context of power relations, where agency can be understood in terms of consciousness or action, whether structurally or subjectively determined, either collectively or individually engaged" (p. 105).

Hence, the everydayness of struggle demonstrates ways in which social relations of daily existence are enmeshed in resistance, thereby rendering power tenuous (Haynes & Prakash, 1992). It dislocates power and resistance from the monolithic and autonomous form of social structure that people challenge only at dramatic moments of revolt. This commonplace idea of struggle need not result in any material or structural transformation. In this sense, according to Haynes and Prakash, resistance becomes innocuous practices of subordinate groups that contest hegemonic social formations, where presence of consciousness is not necessary. This daily act of resistance rearticulates and renegotiates the position of the subordinate with respect to the dominant and continues to disrupt and fragment power. Haynes and Praksash contended that "[i]n sum, neither domination nor resistance is autonomous" (p. 3). The intertwined nature of domination and resistance fragments the singular conception of power and renders it fluid, particularly lending itself to the complexly layered and intertwined nature of globalization politics (Appadurai, 2000). Everyday forms of resistance emerge, for instance, in the culturally situated practices of workers in call centers that simultaneously reify and challenge the dominant U.S.–centric ideology of the workplace (Pal & Buzzanell, 2008). Similarly, Dutta-Bergman (2004a, 2004b) articulated the everyday resistive practices of Santalis in rural Bengal as they participate in their health care decision making, simultaneously using biomedicine with homeopathic and Ayurvedic medicines and resisting the Cartesian dualistic framework of the biomedical model. Critical postmodernism draws attention to the fractured and fragmented nature of global public spheres within which interested parties debate, contest, and articulate issues and policies; the discursive formations around such policies are embedded with the possibilities of change as stakeholders construct and articulate new meanings and interpretations (Dutta & Pal, 2007).

Discourse-centered Approach

The everydayness of resistance shifts focus from what Mumby (2005) called the dualistic to a dialectical relationship between control and resistance, foregrounding the discursive nature of resistance. The discourse-centered approach to resistance emphasizes talk and language in social interaction and pursues discourse at the site of the dialectical relationship between control and resistance (Fairhurst & Putnam, 2004). Research on dialectics of control and resistance in organizational communication literature has been inadequate in conceptualizing the interactive and dynamic nature of resistance (Clegg, 1994; Jermier et al., 1994; Mumby, 2005; P. Prasad & A. Prasad, 2000). Much of the critical literature tends to privilege one over the other without really looking at the discursive spaces in which they continually constitute each other. Inspired by post-structuralism, primarily Foucault (1980a, 1980b), critical research in organizational communication predominantly examines how organizations, similar to Foucault's prisons, establish disciplinary mechanisms to produce docile bodies and sustain managerial interest (Barker, 1993; Burawoy, 1984; Deetz, 1992; Holmer Nadesan, 1997; Kunda, 1992). This body of research focuses on discursive construction of control that perpetuates hegemony and normalizes domination.

For instance, Holmer Nadesan (1997) argued that the discourse of personality exams functions as a form of government by providing authorities with a technique for engineering the workplace and disciplining the employees. Kunda's (1992) "tech culture" pays attention to construction of a culture that fulfills company goals. In other words, management compels people to behave in ways that a company finds rewarding. This emphasis on managerial control that works to perpetuate hegemony obscures the presence of resistance. In opposition, a significant body of research on resistance has romanticized it, treating it in a theoretical lacuna that doesn't acknowledge its relationship with methods of control (Mumby, 2005). Because of this polarized perspective, Mumby deemed this literature on control and resistance as dualistic. Much of the critical literature on employee behavior tends to "overstate either consent or resistance and to separate one from the other...Rather they are usually inextricably and simultaneously linked, often in contradictory ways within particular organizational cultures, discourses and practices" (Collinson, 1994, p. 29).

Elucidating Foucault's philosophy, Clegg (1994) wrote that certain practices through state institutions discipline the body and regulate the mind to privilege institutionalized bodies of knowledge. Since such knowledge emerges through institutional and organizational practices, it constitutes "discursive practice." Discourse becomes the means to institute power. Even when members invoke resistance, it becomes subsumed within the system that acts to reaffirm the disciplinary practices of power. Foucault (1980a) observed:

> I would say that the State consists in the codification of a whole number of power relations which render its functioning possible, and that Revolution is a different type of codification of the same relations. This implies that there are many different kinds of revolution, roughly speaking as many kinds as there are possible subversive recodifications of power relations, and further that one can perfectly well conceive of revolutions which leave essentially untouched the power relations which form the basis for the functioning of the State. (p. 123)

Suggesting the notion of power as a process rather than a possession and stressing the role of discourse in power relationships, Foucault (1980a) further argued that "there are manifold relations of power which cannot themselves be established, consolidated nor implemented without the production, accumulation, circulation and functioning of discourse" (p. 93). Power is simultaneously both productive and repressive, and participants create, perpetuate, and contest it through discourse. Discourses become sites of legitimizing as well as challenging the dominant structures of power. Foucault noted that "[d]iscourses are not once and for all subservient to power or raised up against it, any more than silences are...Discourse transmits and produces power; it reinforces it, but also undermines and exposes it, renders it fragile and makes it possible to thwart it" (pp. 100-101). Discursive formations can also fluctuate (Broadfoot, Deetz, & Anderson, 2004; Laclau & Mouffe, 2001). Noting this transitivity of discourse, Broadfoot et al. observed:

> [B]ecause discourses are systems of signification the meanings of any objects and subjects constructed discursively are necessarily vulnerable, fleeting and temporary as they depend on the sustenance and longevity

of the specific discourses through and by which they are constituted...
thus, discursive formations as articulated series or collages of discourses
always carry the seeds of their own transformation and restructuring in the
form of alternative others that lie latent, awaiting the necessary social and
historical context in which to become dominant. (p. 196)

Emphasizing this discursive shift in studies of resistance, Mumby (2005)
called for a more dialectical approach to studying resistance that simultaneously
interrogates the complex interplay of control and resistance. The dualistic
approach can recognize the dialectical relationship between control and
resistance; however, critics dispute its underlying assumption that power and
control upstage resistance, thereby undermining the intricacies of the power-
resistance dynamic (Jermier et al., 1994; Knights & Vurdubakis, 1994; Kondo,
1990; Mumby, 2005). According to Mumby, poststructural analyses need
to analyze work place resistance as a discursive practice that is "complex,
often contradictory, and socially situated attempts to construct meanings and
identities" (p. 36). In this dialectical relationship, resistance is neither an
authentic nor a pristine form of opposition, nor is it perpetually reproducing
dominant interest. Within this poststructuralist framework, scholars primarily
consider resistance in organizational communication to be embedded in the
routine discourses, the meaning of which depends on the context in which
disciplinary power gets normalized (Tretheway, 2000; Weedon, 1997, 1999).
     As Mumby (2005) noted, much of the current resistance literature in
organizational communication (Buzzanell & Liu, 2005; Clair, 1994; Collinson,
2002; Murphy, 2001; Tretheway, 1997) examines the discursive practices in
organizations to understand resistance as a routine yet complex social process
that draws its meaning from the contextual aspects of organizing. Scholars have
studied a variety of discursive practices such as humor and joking (Ezzamel,
Wilmott, & Worthington, 2001), "bitching" and gossip (Sotirin & Gottfried,
1999), modes of dress (Gottfried, 1994), and discursive distancing as forms
of resistance (Collinson, 1994). Collinson's study of discursive construction
of humor suggests that the ambiguity in humor facilitates effective forms of
resistance. Manufacture of humor as a form of managerial control through
discursive constructions of joking relations does not necessarily invoke social
cohesion or dialogic communication. It can prompt tensions, conflicts, and
power inequalities, thereby underpinning the possibility of resistance. Humor
by subordinates can be expressed in satire by mocking managerial practices,
silence by distancing from managerial humor, or cynicism by not trusting the
managerial joking practices. Murphy described how flight attendants enact
agency on flight and disrupt their historically feminized roles. Similarly, in
their analysis of maternity leave discourse, Buzzanell and Liu observed the
ways in which women productively negotiated their identities and determined
what courses of action to take as they complied with and resisted the dominant
interpretations of maternity leave.

Other scholars, drawing from structuration and dramaturgical perspectives, articulate the storied nature of resistance (Harter, Kirby, Edwards, & McClanahan, 2005; Harter, Scott, Novak, Leeman, & Morris, 2006; Morgan & Krone, 2001). For instance, in their ethnographic fieldwork with Passion Works, a nonprofit collaborative art studio that serves approximately 160 adults with mental retardation and developmental disabilities, Harter et al. (2006) detailed how the narrative of freedom through flight disrupt and transcend the dominant interpretations of disability, and artistic self-expression "thrives as embodied performance" (p. 14). Examining the self-story of Cathy Hainer, a journalist whose reflections on her journey with cancer were published in the *USA Today* in the late 1990s, Beck (2005) explored the capacity of narrative to prompt alternative meanings and provide new languages for talking about illness experiences. Similarly, in Dutta-Bergman's (2004b) research conducted in the Santali communities of rural India, peasant members of marginalized communities that have minimal access to resources discussed the ways in which structural constraints impede their health choices, and they resisted dominant meanings of health by narrating stories as one of the key markers of their lived experience. The narratives of health articulated by the participants draw attention away from the dominant stories that construct health as a matter of individual choice and instead locate it in the context of structural constraints and economic resources (see related arguments by Zoller & Kline, this volume).

Resistance renegotiates and redefines the same practices that it confronts and, in doing so, facilitates a point of change. It validates the belief that, despite power being omnipresent, space remains for resistance. These resistances occur through covert, non-confrontational, routine discursive practices. Hence, studies examine the processes through which subjects engage in meaning making in their daily experience of organizing. Understanding such meanings suggests possibilities for constructing alternative, resistant, counterhegemonic accounts of organizing (Mumby, 2005).

Another key development in the discursive approach involves an emphasis on identity. Foucault (1980a, 1980b) suggested that identities comprise continuous outcomes of subjectivities since self-formation is a complex consequence of subjugation. According to Jermier et al. (1994, p. 8), "Power then does not directly determine identity but merely provides the conditions of possibility for its self-formation—a process involving perpetual tension between power and resistance or subjectivity and identity." Holmer Nadesan (1997) proposed that personality exams become a government mechanism to subjugate employees by articulating the desired identity in the workplace in terms of race, class, and gender-based norms.

This tension between identity and power is clearly evident in the study by Ezzamel et al. (2001). They explored the resistance strategies utilized by workers at an engineering plant, where opposition by the workers stemmed from experiences with the new identity formations. The workers opposed new methods of production introduced by managers because the identities invoked by the new practices made them value the experiences that they enjoyed earlier. The conflict with the self-identity and the new methods imposed by power relations sparked resistance. Though the new methods were discursively constructed as "empowering" and "involving," the workers did not passively accommodate but exercised their agency and challenged the discourse that was made available to them. Thus, intricately tied to resistance and discourse, identities are multidimensional and emergent through discursive practices (Ashcraft, 2005). Health communication scholars also demonstrate the ways in which the negotiation of identity becomes the entry point for re-constituting alternative narratives in the realm of illness; these narratives resist the dominant stories of health that circulate in the culture and are reified by the dominant social institutions (Frank, 1995).

The interconnections among discourses, identities, and resistance enable individuals to challenge dominant positions in global politics as discourses from marginalized contexts circulate in counter-public spheres and eventually navigate mainstream public spheres through overt and covert organizing strategies; counter-publics find their ways in dominant discursive spaces by setting themselves in opposition to some other, wider public (Asen, 2000). Suggesting a dual character of counter-publics, Fraser (1992, pp. 123-124) articulated that, on the one hand, counter-publics "function as spaces of withdrawal and regroupment; on the other hand, they function as bases and training grounds for agitational activities directed toward wider publics." The discursive location of counter-publics in relationship with a wider public fosters resistive politics. These discourses and communicative strategies provide new possibilities for thinking about global policies and resisting policies that marginalize.

These studies illustrate that, while discourse can be an instrument to perpetuate power, it can also be an act of resistance, drawing attention to the simultaneity of power and resistance. Furthermore, studies of the rhetoric of social movements highlight the role of discourse in collective mobilization for transformative politics (Stewart et al., 2006). According to Stewart et al., strategies such as identification, polarization, and power in language (accompanied by discursive tactics such as slogans, songs, labeling, ridicule, obscenity, and symbolic acts) build and mobilize collective identities for the purposes of the movement. For instance, in the 1900s, the Industrial Workers of the World produced the little red book of *Songs of the Workers to Fan the Flames of Discontent*, and songs such as "We Shall Overcome" helped African Americans during the civil rights movement confront institutional violence and hatred. Similarly, slogans such as "Freedom, freedom, freedom" (civil rights movement in the United States), "We will remember in November" (women's liberation movement in the United States), and "Inquilaab Zindabad" (movement of the Left in India) facilitate both identification and polarizing functions, offering the discursive basis for collective mobilization. Symbols such as the red flag embodying the solidarity of workers not only mark the identity of the collective for the members of the collective but communicate the fundamental message of the collective to external stakeholders. The power of discourses and symbols to organize and activate collective identities also occur in performative avenues of change such as street theater, protest theater, resistance songs, and resistance dance (Boal, 1985, 1998; Chatterjea, 2004; Hashmi, 2007). Zoller (2005) referred to this organizing function of discourse and its collective mobilizing capacity in the health care sector when she stressed the need for critical and multisectoral communication scholarship in health activism.

Feminist Approaches

Conceptualization of resistance with respect to identity also appears in a growing body of research on gender in communication, particularly in the context of the patriarchal values and norms that gender organizational practices and the ways in which such values and norms might be challenged (Allen, 2005; Mumby, 2005). In the introduction to the book, *Reworking Gender,* Ashcraft and Mumby (2004) detailed the premises for studying the gendered nature of organizations: (1) gender is constitutive of organizing; (2) gendering of organizations that involves a struggle over meaning, identity, and difference is embodied in a discursive struggle, and (3) these discursive struggles privilege certain interests. Ashcraft and Mumby argued that struggle for gendered meaning entails a deeply material matter, for it produces preferred truths and selves as well as tangible systems of advantages and disadvantages. Feminist authors have illustrated the constitution of gendered subjectivities in organizational contexts within relations of power. Over previous decades, feminist research has either examined the interplay between gender, organizing, identity, and power or explored these issues individually (Allen, 2000; Ashcraft, 2000; Buzzanell, 1994, 1995, 2000; Murphy, 1998; Tretheway, 1997, 2000). This body of work advances the idea that organizations comprise the "site of gendered communication practices" (Mumby, 2000, p. 3). In the preface of *Rethinking Organizational and Managerial Communication From Feminist Perspectives*, Buzzanell (2000) wrote that the book sought to stimulate greater thinking about how organizing itself can be "gendered and exclusionary" (p. x). Hence, the theme of resistance is central to feminist approaches as it aims to "prompt continued change toward greater equality, dignity, and justice for women and men...an equitable and ethical vision for organizational lives and processes" (p. x). According to Allen, this body of research suggests that social discourse about gender influences gender relations within organizations and vice versa.

Inspired by this belief, a significant portion of the literature on resistance in feminist approach extends from the discursive logic, critiquing the communicative processes in organizations. For instance, challenging the conceptions of glass ceiling, Buzzanell (1995) urged rethinking about the practice. Buzzanell argued that defining the glass ceiling merely as an invisible barrier for women's advancement to the top makes us lose sight of gender as an organizing aspect of our lives. Instead, it oversimplifies the issue and offers superficial solutions.

Collinson (1988) revealed how workers in a trucking industry discursively used humor to conform and resist managerial power, where one of the key elements of discursive practices of identity formation encompassed producing a strong masculine culture on the shop floor. Ezzamel et al. (2001) advanced similar observations. Also, Ashcraft and Mumby (2004) explored the discursive legacy of the airline industry that is mired in gender, race and class formations. As Ashcraft and Mumby inquired, "How did the aviator become symbolically and materially involved, nestled in a white male body, and how did he secure unprecedented professional standing?" (p. 132). Ashcraft and Mumby argued that these gendered identities are institutionalized with specific interests in the political economy. Company officials strategically invoke the "dashing male" image associated with pilots to maintain a gendered nature of commercial flying, a perception as important to pilots as to the consumers. Since the occupation constitutes a discursive struggle over the right for occupational control, Ashcraft and Mumby contended that diversifying pilot identity means resisting the system.

However, diversification of pilot identity brings up another way of thinking about resistance. Ashcraft (2005) examined how pilots employ discursive strategies to incorporate instructions to empower crew members and to oppose the threats of feminization associated with such instructions. Through this analysis, Ashcraft asserted that resistance can come from the threat of identity loss and also from privileged voices.

The human body as a site of struggle has been another feature of resistance in the discursive feminist approach. Inspired by a poststructuralist Foucauldian analysis, Tretheway (2000) and Murphy (1998) specified bodies as a site of struggle. Women's embodied identities work toward resisting gender domination rather than normalizing it. Though women's bodies are subordinated and tend to accommodate the norms, women still resists control and discipline by disrupting dress, style, and other signifying gendered practices. Murphy's work on flight attendants demonstrates the panopticon conditions under which they operate. Flight attendants disrupt the gendered expectations of having to wear high heels and wear lipstick by not doing so except on days of appearance checks or while flying through cities that have supervisors. As Tretheway explained, these embodied resistance practices that reverse the panopticon reveal the different subject positions that women may assume.

In health communication, the narrativization of identity as a resistive strategy is evident in the writings of the feminist writer Audre Lorde (1980) as she reflected on her experiences with cancer. She described the necessity to reclaim oneself by making the self available after her mastectomy. Lorde explained that "[i]n order to keep me available to myself, and be able to concentrate my energies on the challenges of those worlds through which I move, I must consider what my body means to me" (p. 65). Through her story, Lorde sought to find a language that allowed her to speak as a one-breasted woman, thus not only connecting with her self but with other women who have experienced mastectomy. As Lorde argued, making oneself available to oneself not only necessitates reconnecting with the body after the illness experience but also finding a connection with others who share the condition, thus resisting the dominant patriarchal articulations of the feminine and the definitions of feminine normalcy imposed by the biomedical model.

Overall, these studies encourage reflection about resistance as emerging from the interconnection between knowledge, power, and subjectivity. Kondo's (1990) ethnographic study of a family-owned Japanese confectionary factory revealed the embedded nature of discourse, identity, compliance, and resistance. Kondo's account of resistance demonstrates the ambiguities and shifting nature of power, providing conditions for multiple, gendered, fragmented selves. The female workers' resistance is discursively constructed from their gendered role in Japan and their position in the workplace. Despite their marginalized status at the workplace, their traditional identity as caregiver prompts them to consider themselves superior to men in the workplace. Hence, the discursive construction of their resistive space embodies a dialectical tension that represents simultaneous coexistence of subjugation and resistance. As Mumby (2005, p. 35) concluded, "Such a tension is not resolvable but is central to the ongoing management of meaning in this workplace."

Discourses contribute to individual identities as sites of contestation as well as organize collectives and signal the capacities of collective organizing in bringing about social change (Luthra, 2003). Chatterjea (2004) described the political capacity of performance, suggesting that women's groups in India:

> … aware of the constant breakdown of the judicial and legal system, often perform the social ostracizing of a wife batterer or dowry demander. Surrounding the house of such a person (a practice known as gherao), the women would sing songs articulating incriminating evidence any time a member of the offending household would emerge from the house. Grass-roots women's organizations like the Stree Shakti Shangathana would also perform plays in the streets, using a great deal of ritualistic movement, about dowry deaths, women's nutrition and other issues. (p. 90)

This approach predominantly focuses on centrality of languages, movements, and images that become sites of contestation for male domination as they reconfigure new ways of thinking and looking at the world. In performance, resistance occurs through the materialization of new meanings in public discursive spaces (Conquergood, 1982a, 1982b, 1988, 1989, 1991). Collective movements of solidarity addressing oppressive patriarchal structures have been constituted discursively and materially through collective organizing of globally dispersed local groups utilizing a variety of performative avenues that connect the body to the public sphere and place it as a disruption of the hegemonic structure (Chatterjea, 2004).

Another important body of scholarship that examines the centrality of language and materiality in constituting the self and the other in cultural terms is postcolonial theory (Narayan & Harding, 2000). Postcolonial theory is particularly relevant for the ways in which we theorize and understand resistance in a global context. The histories of colonialism define the relationships among geographically distributed spaces, creating openings for new spaces for constituting alternative discourses to dominant narratives of development and modernity. In the context of global organizing, these postcolonial narratives underscore the interplays of power in the definitions of nation states, civil societies, transnational corporations, and global publics.

Postcolonialism and Subaltern Studies

In his *Orientalism*, Edward Said (1978), one of the most influential postcolonial thinkers, stressed how the construction of the Orient comprises a systematic discursive production by the West. Arguing that Orient is not Oriental in a commonplace sense but was made to be Oriental, Said dislocated the "familiar" concept of the Orient. The Orient helps to define the West with its contrasting languages, images and experiences. According to Said, "The relationship between Occident and Orient is a relationship of power, of domination, of varying degrees of a complex hegemony…" (p. 5). Said's *Orientalism* suggested a postcolonial approach that facilitates understanding how certain Western labor and management practices become dominant as an act of "othering" non-Western practices. According to A. Prasad (2003, p. 32), "The postcolonial perspective can be helpful in understanding such ethnocentricism, and thereby, developing an alternative understanding of non-Western management."

Postcolonial theory focuses on a Eurocentric colonial past and examines how practices in the non-Western locations negotiate Western domination. Challenging the universality of Western modernity, postcolonial theory encompasses an ongoing resistance to colonial experience (Narayan & Harding, 2000; Spivak, 1987). While colonialism involves an overt coercion taking the form of occupation of territories, imperialism comprises an act of economic and political domination. American imperialism operates through its control over institutions such as World Trade Organization, the World Bank, and International Monetary Fund (IMF) (A. Prasad, 2003). The economic and political control cannot function without cultural control. For instance, in his analysis of public relations efforts of U.S. democracy promotion in nations of the South, Dutta-Bergman (2005a) detailed how the concept of democracy serves undemocratic agendas that co-opt the participatory capacity of citizens and instead seek to promote pro-U.S., pro-market, neoliberal logics. In yet another analysis of health promotion efforts, Dutta (2007) demonstrated the ways in which stakeholders utilize dominant articulations of health promotion abroad in order to serve U.S. geo-strategic, military, and market interests, thus exposing the links between the cultural constructions of development and the material benefits of such constructions to the colonial agenda.

Hence, the endeavor of postcolonialism requires a "genuine global decolonization at political, economic and cultural levels" (A. Prasad, 2003, p. 7). A. Prasad explained that, unlike poststructuralism, where scholars emphasize the interconnected nature of ideology and discourse, postcolonialism highlights the linkages between material and the ideological. Postcolonial theory enables organizational scholars to critically engage with practices that are instituted through disciplinary mechanisms to perpetuate Western domination (Munshi & Kurian, 2005). For instance, Dutta and Basnyat (2006) interrogated the very logic of development and participatory democratic processes embedded in a USAID-sponsored radio drama in Nepal that seeks to promote family planning; promoters employed the veil of democratic audience participation as a co-optive strategy to push the family-planning agenda of campaign planners and to further advance the hegemonic logic of dominant social actors who frame questions of poor health in subaltern sectors in terms of individual lifestyle instead of addressing structural issues surrounding health inequities.

This line of work further demonstrates that discourses of development often serve the political economy of dominant social actors; the missionary zeal embodied in the rhetoric of emancipation ultimately serves as a façade for colonial and imperial agendas (Dutta, 2006; Dutta & Basnyat, 2006). Suggesting the relevance of understanding the workings of images during the U.S. war with Afghanistan in the backdrop of the actual economic and geopolitical aims of the United States, Cloud (2004) asserted that mercenary motives to control the world oil supply were couched under the rhetoric of saving the people and, more specifically, the women of Afghanistan. In a similar vein, Dutta-Bergman (2006) observed that the rhetoric of liberating Iraqi people from dictatorship and bringing democracy to Iraq served as the chador for U.S. neo-imperialism embodied in Operation Iraqi Freedom. By its endeavor to engage with and give legitimacy to non-Western experiences, postcolonial scholarship remains peripheral to Western modernity as a resistive act (Dutta-Bergman, 2004a, 2004b). A. Prasad (2003) argued that, since "defamiliarization" constitutes one of the primary interests of critical organizational scholarship, postcolonial theory provides opportunities for perpetual surprises. Just as feminism offers a new meaning of organization by explaining it as a gendered site, postcolonial theory suggests defamiliarization in new ways.

Postcolonialism is relevant for the study of management and organizations, especially given rapidly changing global political and economic activities. Instead of a dominant single center over the peripheries forming the global processes, a number of competing centers bring about shifts in the global balance of power between nation-states "forging new sets of interdependencies" (Featherstone, 1995, p. 13). As more players participate in the game, they demand the access and the right to be heard. Much earlier, Said (1978) suggested that the West cannot now avoid listening to the other or assume that the latter is at an earlier stage of development. Under these changing conditions, postcolonial insights can provide understanding of the implications of these changes (A. Prasad, 2003). These changes raise the following questions that merit examination. How does global culture produce differences, power struggles, domination, and resistances? How is the colonialist other reformulated through new formations of transnational relations of capital and culture? In other words, what is the new form of the other (Shome & Hegde, 2002)?

Some of the tensions at the workplace in the global economy can be seen in a new light using a postcolonial lens. For instance, Bhabha's (1994) notion of *ambivalence* holds the potential to open up new vistas of research (A. Prasad, 2003). Ambivalence represents the empowering intentions of the colonizer by way of civilizing the primitive, and it also speaks of violent colonization of the other. Hence, ambivalence ruptures the monolithic discourse of colonization by revealing the cracks and fissures for potential resistance by the colonized. Bhabha advanced the ideas of *mimicry* and *hybridity* to enumerate the potential for resistance through ambivalence. Bhabha's conceptualization of the colonized's mimicry of the colonizer's discourse rearticulates existential heterogeneities as the colonized's copy of the colonizer displaces the established dominations. Mimicry upsets the stasis between the original and the copy as mimicry is "almost same, but not quite" (p. 127). According to A. Prasad, while mimicry has been traditionally viewed as continuation of the colonizer's hegemony with the perpetual dependence of the colonized, Bhabha noted that mimicry can also be viewed as a space for resistance.

Bhabha's (1994) concept of hybridity is the other robust idea that enables the rise of postcolonial resistance. Hybridity, similar to mimicry, refers to a process of cultural assimilation that is never congruous or complete. According to Bhabha, the process of hybridization ruptures colonizer's discourse with differential knowledge and positionalities, enabling a "strategic reversal of the process of domination" (p. 114). Also, hybridity comprises an act of resistance because it disrupts the colonizer's intentions and expectations by misappropriating the colonizer's demands. Bhabha's ideas of mimicry and hybridity also reject the essentialist and singular construction of social subjects and problematize the totalizing notion of power. It coincides with critical organizational scholars who reject the "triumph of hegemony" (A. Prasad & P. Prasad, 2003, p. 110).

A. Prasad (2003) elucidated applicability of ambivalence in managerial discourses. Managerial discourses emphasize workers' autonomy and empowerment, while simultaneously inscribing strategies of surveillance and control at the workplace. More specifically, the existence of multiple subcultures in individual organizations replete with cultural differences exemplifies the possibility of hybridity in postcolonial theory. Application of these concepts has the potential to open up new areas of inquiry. A. Prasad and P. Prasad (2003) noted:

For instance, management researchers might investigate the ways in which differences (e.g. of cultural categories, their meanings, their prioritization etc.) across organizational subcultures often distort processes of planned organizational change... (p. 113)

Establishing the relevance of such thinking, A. Prasad called for postcolonial intervention in organizational research that can expand the scope of workplace resistance.

A. Prasad (2003) introduced the relevance of postcolonial studies for organizational communication; however, he merely touched on the tenets of subaltern studies. Subaltern studies involve writing history from below (Guha, 1981), thus challenging dominant constructions of knowledge. Subaltern studies, as an intervention in South Asian scholarship, came into existence to interrupt the Indian historiography dominated by "colonialist elitism and bourgeois-nationalist elitism" (p. 1). The Subaltern Studies project chronicles the historiography of the people by documenting their agency and politics, which had always been left out of dominant discursive spaces of knowledge. Subaltern studies were launched with the initiative and inspiration of Ranajit Guha, "an extraordinarily brilliant Indian historian and political economist" (Said, 1988, p. v). Guha, along with five other scholars from South Asia, published several volumes of an editorial collective, entitled *Subaltern Studies: Writings on South Asian History and Society*, with Guha editing the first six volumes (see e.g., Guha, 1983).

Drawing from Gramsci (1971), the themes of subaltern studies pay considerable attention to the dominant class, as the subaltern exists in a binary relationship with the dominant. Subaltern studies offer a complex critique of modernity. Said (1988) argued:

As an alternative discourse then, the work of the Subaltern scholars can be seen as an analogue of all those recent attempts in the West and throughout the rest of the world to articulate the hidden or suppressed accounts of numerous groups—women, minorities, disadvantaged or disposed groups, refugees, exiles, etc... This is another way of underlining the concern with politics and power. (p. vi-vii)

Subaltern studies radically challenge modernist epistemologies and monolithic notions of modernity, inspired by postcolonial thinking (Beverly, 2004; Prakash, 1994). Since subaltern scholars strive to recover the history of the marginalized "other" against the institutionalized system of knowledge constructed by the West and the national elite in postcolonial states, it becomes a critique of the dominant system of knowledge production itself, legitimized by the West. At the same time, Beverly characterized it as postmodern because it endeavors to bring about "epistemological rupture" (p. 15) or what Lyotard (1984) regarded as interrupting grand metanarratives. Dynamic in their multidisciplinarity, subaltern studies allows for investigations of different colonial situations. Establishing its relevance across territories, Guha (2001) elucidated that, though subaltern studies extend from South Asian experience, it informs the experiences of any silenced subordination. Though it relies on postcolonialism, Prakash argued that it remains distinct in its scholarly inquiry because it preserves the record of colonial domination and tracks the "(subaltern) positions that could not be properly recognized and named" (p. 1486). Hence, Guha positioned it as a study to destabilize issues of power from the elitist agenda by drawing attention to the "other." The postcolonial strand plays out in global movements such as the Narmada Bachao Andolan and the Chipko movement that articulate alternative meanings of development based on diverse ways of knowing that directly contradict Eurocentric bases of knowledge (Dutta & Pal, 2007).

The study of resistance presented in these different strands of communication scholarship offer opportunities for exploring both micro- and macropolitics of resistance. Whereas the traditional approach to resistance involves collective practices of resistance, critical postmodernism and discourse-based approaches emphasize more of the individualized forms. Both feminist and postcolonial approaches explore the intersections between the individualized and collective forms of resistance as they simultaneously engage with possibilities of individualized narratives of resistance through the crafting of alternative discourses and the possibilities of collective organizing that challenge the dominant structures. Critics of postmodern and discourse-centered approaches claim that the emphasis on individualized forms of resistance is antithetical to the agendas of collective struggle (Ganesh et al., 2005). With the increasing disparities between the haves and have-nots in the recent past, a marginal reemergence of interest in the traditional genre of resistance has occurred (Cloud, 2001; Ganesh et al., 2005). Ganesh et al. expressed concern over research on resistance in organizational communication which, they argue, has been explored in largely individualized terms. With much work focusing on a dialectical model of resistance and control, resistance gets conceptualized as "individual awareness of power inequities" (p. 174) or "individual's ability to articulate alternative meanings to that of dominant constructions" (p. 174).

Also, given the focus on U.S. organizations, the organizational literature perhaps overlooks instances of collective resistances in other parts of the world. Ganesh et al. (2005) cautioned that the emphasis on individual strategies does not get connected to the realm of collective resistances, thus limiting the possibilities for transformational politics in the context of neoliberalism. Similarly, Cloud (2001) argued that current critical organizational communi-cation theorizing predominantly focuses on identity politics without really exploring the transformative aspects of communication. However, though the conceptualization of traditional resistance in this neo-liberal age gets redefined in many ways, much of its essence remains the same in terms of its goal and collective appeal. Ganesh et al. characterized resistance as effort with transformation potential, which attempts to "affect large-scale, collective changes in the domains of state policy, corporate practice, social structure, cultural norms, and daily lived experience" (p. 177).

Furthermore, the study of resistance in public relations practice offers an opportunity for exploring the role of resistance in the realm of collective organizing as it engages with issues of global activism (see Holtzhausen, 2005; Pal & Dutta, in press). The interrogation of the ways in which activist publics organize themselves in a global landscape offers an entry point to theorize collective organizing that connects the local sites of resistance with global support through digital media.

RESISTANCE IN A GLOBAL CONTEXT

Each of the existing approaches to resistance provides possibilities for theoretically engaging with the concept in the realm of globalization. In this section, we identify key elements in global resistance that draw on the existing communication literature on resistance and specify new vistas for exploration.

Transnational Activism: The New Global Movement

As Harvey (2000) observed, globalization has particular bearing on postmodern thinking that necessitates theorizing in new directions. Transnational activism connects the structural and cultural dimensions of global resistance, demonstrating the dialectical tension between control and resistance (M. J. Papa, Singhal, & W. Papa, 2006). Global resistance, the authors suggested, is at once modern and postmodern; it draws on the impetus of critical theory to explore the material roots of global inequities and simultaneously foregrounds the temporality of discourse that continuously shifts amid complexly layered global structures. According to Papa et al., the "complex interplay of economic and cultural dynamics" (p. 201) in transnational activism necessitates an understanding of its implications for communication research. For instance, scapes, detailed earlier in this chapter, demonstrate that public consciousness no longer stretches across national spaces but "ignites the micro-politics of a nation-state" (Appadurai, 2000, p. 236).

Hence, what are the challenges for communication research in view of these complex global shifts? While working in a community-based setting, grassroots organizers increasingly network with transnational activists to affect changes in specific communities, thereby connecting the local and the global (Naples & Desai, 2002). According to Tarrow (2005), though transnational activism is not a new phenomenon, it is particularly striking given its connection to the current wave of globalization and its relation to the changing structure of international politics. The latter provides activists with focal points for collective action, expanded resources, and unity in transnational coalitions and campaigns.

Tarrow (2005) suggested that transnational activists link nonstate actors, their states, and international politics with the potential to create a new political arena. Tarrow and Della Porta (2005) explained such linkages by posing the concept of *complex internationalization* that involves "expansion of international institutions, international regimes, and the transfer of the resources of local and national actors to the international stage, producing threats, opportunities and resources for international NGOs, transnational social movements and, indirectly, grassroots social movements" (p. 235). These actors possess varying levels of power. The state constitutes the central actor; international institutions represent state interests and their bureaucratic claims; some NGOs gain direct access to both states and institutions, and social movements operate from outside this structure to influence its policies.

Della Porta and Tarrow (2005) summarized five key changes that have expanded the scope of contemporary wave of transnational contention: (1) the institutions representing neoliberalism (IMF, WB, and the WTO) have become central to targets of resistance; (2) these institutions provide a focal point for the global framing of a variety of domestic and international conflicts; (3) new electronic technologies enhance the organizing of movements in many venues at once; (4) within transnational contention, tendencies can be seen toward formation of transnational campaigns and coalitions, and (5) partial but highly visible successes of campaigns by non-state actors such as the international support for the liberation movement in South Africa, the anti-landmine campaign, the international solidarity movement with the Zapatista rebellion among others. However, development of conflicts over global issues is not necessarily organized around transnational social movement organizations. Instead, they are rooted at the local and national levels, turning simultaneously to various governmental agencies and making linkages between different social and political actors.

In addition to active interaction between domestic and international populations of movement organizations, members form local and global coalitions. A local coalition can occur by changing the framing of domestic political conflicts. However, Della Porta and Tarrow (2005) characterized global social justice as a masterframe of new mobilizations. In turn, this framework creates loosely coupled transnational networks that organize around particular campaigns or series of campaigns, using varied forms of protests. In other words, Della Porta and Tarrow argued that local issues of such struggles remain distinct even though they get connected by sharing a common global agenda. They explained:

> Specific concerns with women's rights, labor issues, the defense of the environment, and opposition to war survive, but are bridged together in opposition against 'neoliberal globalization.' In order to keep different groups together, 'tolerant' inclusive identities develop, stressing differences as a positive quality of the movement. (p. 12)

Awareness about local phenomena getting increasingly linked with broader global processes gained immense importance in the 20th century (Seidman, 2000). The new global perspective on identities, networks, and communities (and the way in which international processes shape and redefine local ones) prompted social movement theorists to reconsider many of their basic assumptions. Some of the questions, Seidman summarized, evoke special interests: (1) when does a social process become a global one; (2) when does a local social movement become linked enough with the global processes to be considered a global social movement; (3) what do global processes mean for the very local processes through which movements create collective identities; (4) who represents movements on the global stage, and how are those representations redesigned internationally; (5) how do local movements change in response to global resources or audiences, and (6) what roles do global organizations play in provoking local movements?

In terms of mobilization of resources, Della Porta and Tarrow (2005) identified two emerging challenges for movements. First, the fragmentation in the social structure has expanded social heterogeneity affecting formation of social groups that used to be an important basis for many social movements. Second, increasing individualization of cultures has led to declining solidarity in the society. However, Della Porta and Tarrow asserted that transnational mobilization embraces different movement strategies as a means of coping with such changes. For instance, flexible networks allow heterogeneous social forces to become part of one movement.

These networks of groups and activists imbibe an emerging identity, involve in conflictual issues, and follow non-traditional forms of participation. A large majority of the activists who participate in demonstrations against international summits identify themselves with movement related to globalization. Different names have been proposed for it (no global, Seattle people, globalization from below, global justice, etc.), indicating that its core goals remain to be crystallized. Tarrow (2005) suggested that availability of resources and opportunities facilitate this era of transnational activism. Greater access to higher education, emergence of English as the main language of international trade and services, and evidence of formulation of decisions that affect people's lives at international avenues contribute to generating activist interest.

Generating Issues and Mobilizing Resources

While considerable attention has been paid to global protests, scholars have attended less to how global issues affect the civic and political life at the local level. Diani (2005) specifically inquired about the impact of global issues on grassroots political organizations' strategies and orientations. Diani espoused that stakeholders generally perceive environmental conditions, labor rights, and migrants' rights as global issues. Yet, such perceptions largely depend on the interpretations attributed to issues by social actors. Sometimes involved parties treat issues as existing agendas, such as ones related to developing countries' debts are considered to be agendas of traditional Leftist politics. Diani provided an analysis of issue structures that explains the new global movement and argued that presence of a distinctive set of issues does not necessarily imply that the protest activities and other forms of collective actions on such issues will be promoted. Social movements comprise sustained series of campaigns that may be linked to broader chains of protests through framing and discursive practices, and also through multiple attachments of actors. Diani's study of two different local U.K. settings suggests mobilization of global issues relies on specific alliances based on identity bonds within British civil society. Global issues are pervasive and distinctive and, thus, not always equally appealing to civic bodies. Global issues resonate with organizations with networks and share a common identity.

Smith, Pagnucco, and Chatfield (1997) contended that issue networks aid communication and strategic coordination facilitating movement activity when linked by a common interest in advancing a particular value. Coalitions among actors in issue networks typically form around campaigns, which involve attempts to coordinate movement actions around a particular policy.

McCarthy (1997) argued that case studies in locations outside the United States provide six core concepts that are central to these movements: strategic framing processes, activist identities, mobilizing structures, resource mobilization, political opportunity structures, and repertoires of contention. Activist groups draw from institutional structures in mobilizing around issues of concern. For instance, support of the church guarantees providing personnel, access to technology and financial resources.

Alger (1997) identified five categories of transnational social movement activity: creating and mobilizing global networks, participating in multilateral political arenas, facilitating in interstate cooperation, acting within states, and enhancing public participation. Tarrow and Della Porta (2005) explained transnational social activism through three broad categories of diffusion, internalization, and externalization that encompass many of the factors enunciated by international relations scholars. Diffusion concerns adoption or adaptation of organizational forms of one country in another. In this sense, particular practices or frames can be transferred from one country to another through cheap travel, knowledge of common languages, and access to Internet. According to Tarrow and Della Porta, internalization refers to addressing issues that originate externally, and externalization means organized interests looking for alliances with international institutions for mobilization of resources.

Though these models and categories of mobilization of issues and resources comprise a step forward in approaching social movements as rational responses rather than as examples of deviancy (Mayo, 2005), they still remain limited to rational functionalist models that are inadequate for addressing some of the concerns that have emerged with globalization. Focusing on actors' choices, these models provide a top-down approach that does not take the wider structural context into account. For instance, as Mayo noted, availability of resources, such as the political freedom to organize, needs to be considered. Also, we should craft space for movements that organize on the peripheries of civil societies. Bound within the limits of rationality and reason, the categories operate within the dominant episteme without encouraging marginalized subaltern voices.

Transformative Potential

To understand the promise of the new social movements, we must illustrate the features that distinguish the new from the old. According to Mayo (2005), new social movements represent a new form of transformative politics. The old social movements represent class-based politics struggling to gain control of the state. On the contrary, Mayo argued, new social movements involve multiple social actors establishing their presence in a fragmented social and political space. Old social movements focused on the working class, especially industrial projects that struggled for improvements and wages and conditions. The old movements were also problematic because of their bureaucratic forms that resulted in professional leaderships rather than grassroots level action. In contrast, new social movements comprise a transformational politics that fosters new forms of life and decentralized and non-bureaucratic politics.

In this sense, resistance in the context of globalization occurs amid fragmented communicative processes that challenge globally situated politics from local contexts. Local communities become the sites of mobilizing and yet intersect with multiple local communities elsewhere in the globe. This complexly intertwined and fragmented nature of transnational activism suggests the necessity for new theorizing of resistance that simultaneously connects the local and the global, discusses structurally situated politics, and yet attends to global influences through local narratives and locally situated forms of organizing (Dutta & Pal, 2007; Juris, 2004). In articulating the processes through which global activist publics offer resistance to the dominant hegemonic configurations, the literature on transnational activism demonstrates the relevance of theorizing about the discursive openings and material strategies through which stakeholders initiate shifts in the macro-level structures (Tarrow, 2005)

CONCLUSION

As we close this chapter, we offer a few suggestions for further exploration in terms of theory building, empirical investigation, and development of praxis in terms of global resistance. First, we note the relevance of future theorizing in global resistance that studies the intersections between the global-local and material-symbolic dialectics. This intersection is both practically and theoretically relevant as globally dispersed local publics engage in material and symbolic practices of resistance. What are the instances of local direct action where material practices become meaningful, and what are the ways in which these material practices connect with symbolic practices both locally and globally? How do local symbolic practices impact globally situated material ones? How do stakeholders mobilize global material practices for purposes of local resistance? These questions also hold pragmatic value in terms of suggesting guidelines for organizing that connects the local with the global and develops a matrix of symbolic and material practices.

Second, the intersections of workplace practices of resistance and community-based practices of resistance in the realm of mainstream public spheres and subaltern public spheres should be studied further. What are the possibilities for labor politics of resistance in the realm of the public spheres of community life? What are the possibilities for the politics of citizenship in the realm of access to work? How does access to work play out in the realm of access to political platforms? What resistive strategies are available for transforming these very platforms to which subaltern groups have limited access because of their limited economic resources?

Third, future scholarship on resistance ought to explore the linkages between the individual and collective aspects of resistance. What are the ways in which individual identities play out in terms of collective mobilization? What roles do individualized discourses play in collective mobilizations of resistance? Emphasizing the individual *and* the collective provides a valuable alternative to examining them separately. Instead, narratives articulating individual identities become entry points for interpreting and mobilizing collective resistance.

Fourth, globalization processes simultaneously impact various aspects and contexts of human life, ranging from workplace practices to mediated practices to health practices. Simultaneously, our review of resistance demonstrates the multiple contextual settings within which resistance is played out. Therefore, future empirical work on resistance in the context of globalization ought to explore the intersections among the different contexts of communication, calling for more interdisciplinary work on resistance. For instance, workplace practices of resistance are simultaneously intertwined with resistive practices of healthcare that seek to transform unhealthy workplace practices. Similarly, resistive practices in the realm of securing access to affordable health care are often intertwined with questions of work and income.

Fifth, this review argues that postcolonialism has immense potential to offer new ways of thinking about power, domination and resistance, particularly in the context of globalization. Central to postcolonialism is repudiation of Eurocentric knowledge and identities instituted through Western domination. While it ruptures and resists Eurocentric metanarratives by articulating conditions of marginality created by Western domination, its theme of ambivalence also provides a space for resistance in the new age global economy.

Communication scholars should further explore the sensibilities of postcolonial scholarship for their work on global resistance.

Sixth, this literature review suggests the relevance of creating discursive openings in the literature on resistance for the voices of cultural participants who have typically been erased from the dominant modes of inquiry and mainstream civil society platforms. Subaltern studies scholarship is particularly suitable in answering questions of erasure and voice in the realm of global hegemony. Subaltern voices find new avenues in the realm of transformative politics as we look at various movements of global activism that connect positions of subalternity with the globally situated movements (as demonstrated in the case of the Narmada Bachao Andolan discussed earlier; Dutta & Pal, 2007; Grosfoguel, 2005; Kriesberg, 1997). This review documents the communicative possibilities for resistance in terms of the new social movements as responses to global forces of domination. Future theorizing and research ought to explore the ways in which subaltern strategies capture mainstream public spheres and bring about discursive and material shifts in these structures. Furthermore, much work is needed in exploring the ways in which deep-seated structures of knowledge are resisted by alternative ways of knowing that emerge from subaltern spaces? How do these forms of knowing simultaneously get co-opted by dominant structures, impact dominant epistemic structures, and open up transformative avenues for changing these structures?

Seventh, although the various existing approaches to resistance outlined in this review have been presented separately as seemingly mutually exclusive categories, the materially situated and discursively constituted nature of global resistance suggests the necessity of exploring the boundaries and shared spaces among these approaches (see also Broadfoot et al., 2004). For instance, with the increasing material disparities across the globe, how can traditional approaches to resistance be coupled with critical postmodern approaches to understand the ways in which identities are negotiated through material practices and simultaneously offer spaces for transforming these material practices?

We began this review with the goal of being as comprehensive as possible in reviewing the literatures on resistance in communication. To this extent, we surveyed the existing scholarship in organizational communication, public relations, health communication, gender studies, rhetoric, and performance studies, with the greatest focus on organizational communication because of the wide treatment of resistance within this sub-discipline. Though we could not include related works from interpersonal communication, family communication, critical media studies, or cultural studies owing to space constraints, we acknowledge their importance and encourage future examinations of linkages between those bodies of work and the ones discussed in this chapter.

Future communication scholarship might explore the intersections between the concepts of interpretations as resistance and practices of resistance in mediated contexts. We also note the need for communication scholarship that bridges the current and growing scholarship on resistance in areas such as social movement studies, sociology, philosophy, geography, women's studies, and political science; communication scholars might contribute to the discussions in these areas by seeking to understand the meaning-making processes underlying various forms of resistance and the communicative practices through which resistance is articulated (Cheney, 1998; Ganesh et al., 2005). Though we have attempted to be international in our scope of the review, we have perhaps omitted some of the increasingly available literature on global resistance beyond Europe, North America, and South Asia. We hope that this review will spark additional theorizing of global resistance that draws on other cultural contexts and particularly attends to issues of subalternity in postcolonial contexts. In conclusion, we hope that this review offers the basis for additional communication scholarship that celebrates and engages with opportunities for resistive politics in the realm of the neoliberal agendas of globalization.

REFERENCES

Alger, C. F. (1997). Transnational social movements, world politics, and global governance. In J. Smith, C. Chatfield, & R. Pagnucco (Eds.), *Transnational social movements and global politics* (pp. 260-275). Syracuse, NY: Syracuse University Press.

Allen, B. (2000). "Learning the ropes": A black feminist standpoint analysis. In P. M. Buzzanell (Ed.), *Rethinking organizational and managerial communication from feminist perspectives* (pp.177-208). Thousand Oaks, CA: Sage.

Allen, B. (2005). Social constructionism. In S. May & D. K. Mumby (Eds.), *Engaging organizational communication theory and research: Multiple perspectives* (pp. 35-53). Thousand Oaks, CA: Sage.

Alvesson, M., & Deetz, S. (2000). *Doing critical management research.* Thousand Oaks, CA: Sage.

Appadurai, A. (2000). Disjuncture and difference in the global cultural economy. In D. Held & A. McGrew (Eds.), *The global transformations reader: An introduction to the globalization debate* (pp. 230-238). Malden, MA: Blackwell.

Asen, R. (2000). Seeking the "counter" in counterpublics. *Communication Theory, 10*, 424-446.

Ashcraft, K. L. (2000). Empowering "professional" relationships: Organizational communication meets feminist practice. *Management Communication Quarterly, 13*, 347-392.

Ashcraft, K. L. (2005). Resistance through consent? Occupational identity, organizational form, and the maintenance of masculinity among commercial airline pilots. *Management Communication Quarterly, 19*, 67-90.

Ashcraft, K. L., & Mumby, D. K. (2004). *Reworking gender: A feminist communicology of organization.* Thousand Oaks, CA: Sage.

Auyero, J. (2003). *Contentious lives: Two Argentine women, two protests, and the quest for recognition.* Durham, NC: Duke University Press.

Bardhan, N. (2003). Rupturing public relations metanarratives: The example of India. *Journal of Public Relations Research, 15*, 225-248.

Barker, J. R. (1993). Tightening the iron cage: Concertive control in self-managing teams. *Administrative Science Quarterly, 38*, 408-437.

Bartesaghi, M., & Castor, T. (2008). Social construction in communication: Reconstituting the conversation. In C. S. Beck (Ed.), *Communication yearbook 32* (pp. 3-39). New York: Routledge.

Beck, C. S. (2005). Becoming the story: Narratives as collaborative, social enactments of individual, relational and public identities. In L. M. Harter, P. M. Japp, & C. S. Beck (Eds.), *Narratives, health and healing: Communication theory, research, and practice* (pp. 61-81). Mahwah, NJ: Erlbaum.

Bell, E. L., & Forbes, L. C. (1994). Office folklore in the academic paperwork empire. The interstitial space of gendered (con)texts. *Text and Performance Quarterly, 14*, 181-196.

Beverly, J. (2004). *Subalternity and representation: Arguments in cultural theory.* Durham, NC: Duke University Press.

Bhabha, H. K. (1994). *The location of culture.* New York: Routledge.

Boal, A. (1985). *Theater of the oppressed* (C. A. McBride & M. L. McBride, Trans.). New York: Theater Communications Group.

Boal, A. (1998). *Legislative theatre* (A. Jackson, Trans.). London: Routledge.

Braverman, H. (1974). *Labor and monopoly capital.* New York: Monthly Review Press.

Braverman, H. (1984). The real meaning of Taylorism. In F. Fischer & C. Sirianni (Eds.), *Critical studies in organization and bureaucracy* (pp. 55-61). Philadelphia: Temple University Press.

Broadfoot, K., Deetz, S., & Anderson, D. (2004). Multi-leveled, multi-method approaches in organizational discourses. In D. Grant, C. Hardy, C. Oswick, & L. Putnam (Eds.), *The Sage handbook of organizational discourse* (pp. 193-211). Thousand Oaks, CA: Sage.

Bullert, B. J. (2000). Progressive public relations, sweatshops and the net. *Political Communication, 17*, 403-407.

Burawoy, M. (1984). Organizing consent on the shop floor: The game of making out. In F. Fischer & C. Sirianni (Eds.), *Critical studies in organization and bureaucracy* (pp. 134-143). Philadelphia: Temple University Press.

Buzzanell, P. M. (1994). Gaining a voice: Feminist organizational communication theorizing. *Management Communication Quarterly, 7*, 339-383.

Buzzanell, P. M. (1995). Reframing the glass ceiling as a socially constructed process: Implications for understanding and change. *Communication Monographs, 64*, 327-354.

Buzzanell, P. M. (2000). Preface. In P. M. Buzzanell (Ed.), *Rethinking organizational and managerial communication from feminist perspectives* (pp. ix - xii). Thousand Oaks, CA: Sage.

Buzzanell, P. M., & Liu, M. (2005). Struggling with maternity leave policies and practices: A poststructuralist feminist analysis of gendered organizing. *Journal of Applied Communication Research, 33*, 1-25.

Chatterjea, A. (2004). *Butting out: Reading resistive choreographies through works by Jawole Willa Jo Zollar and Chandralekha.* Middletown, CT: Wesleyan University Press.

Cheney, G. (1998). *Values at work: Employee participation meets market pressure at Mondragon.* Ithaca, NY: Cornell University Press.

Cheney, G., & Cloud, D. (2006). Doing democracy, engaging the material: Employee participation and labor activity in an age of market globalization. *Management Communication Quarterly, 19,* 501-540.

Clair, R. P. (1994). The use of framing devices to sequester organizational narratives: Hegemony and harassment. *Communication Monographs, 60,* 113-136.

Clair, R. P., & Thompson, K. (1996). Pay discrimination as a discursive and material practice: A case of extended housework. *Journal of Applied Communication Research, 24,* 1-20.

Clegg, S. (1994). Power relations and the constitution of the resistant subject. In F. Fischer & C. Sirianni (Eds.), *Critical studies in organization and bureaucracy* (pp. 274-325). Philadelphia: Temple University Press.

Cloud, D. (1994). The materiality of discourse as oxymoron: A challenge to critical rhetoric. *Western Journal of Communication, 58,* 141-163.

Cloud, D. (2001). Laboring under the sign of the new. *Management Communication Quarterly, 15,* 268-278.

Cloud, D. (2004). "To veil the threat of terror": Afghan women and the <clash of civilization> in the imagery of the U.S. war on terrorism. *Quarterly Journal of Speech, 90,* 285-306.

Collinson, D. (1988). Engineering humor: Masculinity, joking and conflict in shop-floor relations. *Organizational Studies, 9,* 181-199.

Collinson, D. (1994). Strategies of resistance: Power, knowledge and subjectivity in the workplace. In J. M. Jermier, D. Knights, & W. R. Nord (Eds.), *Resistance and power* (pp. 25-68). New York: Routledge.

Collinson, D. (2002). Managing humor. *Journal of Management Studies, 39,* 269-288.

Conquergood, D. (1982a). Communication as performance: Dramaturgical dimensions of everyday life. In J. I. Sisco (Ed.), *The Jensin lectures: Contemporary communication studies* (pp. 24-43). Tampa: University of South Florida Press.

Conquergood, D. (1982b). Performing as a moral act: Ethical dimensions of the ethnography of performance. *Literature in Performance, 5,* 1-13.

Conquergood, D. (1988). Health theater in a Hmong refugee camp. *The Drama Review, 32,* 174-208.

Conquergood, D. (1989). Poetics, play, process, and power: The performative turn in anthropology. *Text and Performance Quarterly, 9,* 82-88.

Conquergood, D. (1991). Rethinking ethnography: Towards a critical cultural politics. *Communication Monographs, 58,* 179-194.

Coombs, T. W. (2007). *Ongoing crisis communication: Planning, managing, and responding.* Thousand Oaks, CA: Sage.

Cox, J. R. (2004). "Free Trade" and the eclipse of civil society: Barriers to transparency and public participation in NAFTA and the Free Trade Area of the Americas. In S. P. Depoe, J. W. Delicath, & M-F. Aepli Elsenbeer (Eds.), *Communication and public participation in environmental decision making* (pp. 201-219). Albany: State University of New York Press.

Curtin, P. A., & Gaither, K. T. (2005). Privileging identity, difference, and power: The circuit of culture as a basis for public relations theory. *Journal of Public Relations Research, 17,* 91-115.

Curtin, P. A., & Gaither, K.T. (2006). Contested notions of issue identity in international public relations: A case study. *Journal of Public Relations Research, 18*, 67-89.

Deetz, S. A. (1992). *Democracy in an age of corporate colonization: Developments in communication and the politics of everyday life.* Albany: State University of New York Press.

Della Porta, D., & Tarrow, S. (2005). Transnational processes and social activism. In D. Della Porta & S. Tarrow (Eds.), *Transnational protest and global activism* (pp. 1-17). New York: Rowman & Littlefield.

DeSouza, R., & Dutta, M. (in press). Global and local networking for HIV/AIDS: The case of the *Saathii* E-Forum. *Journal of Health Communication.*

Diani, M. (2005). Cities in the world: Local civil society and global issues in Britain. In D. Della Porta & S. Tarrow (Eds.), *Transnational protest and global activism* (pp. 45-67). New York: Rowman & Littlefield.

Dozier, D. M., & Lauzen, M. M. (2000). Liberating the intellectual domain from the practice: Public relations, activism and the role of the scholar. *Journal of Public Relations Research, 12*, 3-22.

Drache, D. (2001). *The market or the public domain: Global governance and the asymmetry of power.* New York: Routledge

Dutta, M. (2006). Theoretical approaches to entertainment education campaigns: A subaltern critique. *Health Communication, 20*, 221-231.

Dutta, M. (2007). Communicating about culture and health: Theorizing culture-centered and cultural sensitivity approaches. *Communication Theory, 17*, 304-328.

Dutta, M., & Basnyat, I. (2006). The radio communication project in Nepal: A culture-centered approach to participation. *Health Education and Behavior, XX*, 1-13.

Dutta, M., & Pal, M. (2007). The Internet as a site of resistance: The case of the Narmada Bachao Andolan (Save the river Narmada movement). In S. Duhe (Ed.), *New media and public relations* (pp. 203-215). New York: Peter Lang.

Dutta-Bergman, M. (2004a). The unheard voices of Santalis: Communicating about health from the margins of India. *Communication Theory, 14*, 237-263.

Dutta-Bergman, M. (2004b). Poverty, structural barriers and health: A Santali narrative of health communication. *Qualitative Health Research, 14*, 1-16.

Dutta-Bergman, M. (2005a). Civil society and public relations: Not so civil after all. *Journal of Public Relations Research, 17*, 267-289.

Dutta-Bergman, M. (2005b). Theory and practice in health communication campaigns: A critical interrogation. *Health Communication, 18*, 103-112.

Dutta-Bergman, M. (2006). U.S. public diplomacy in the Middle East: A critical cultural approach. *Journal of Communication Inquiry, 30*, 102-124.

Edwards, R. C. (1984). Forms of control in the labor process: An historical analysis. In F. Fischer & C. Sirianni (Eds.), *Critical studies in organization and bureaucracy* (pp. 86-119). Philadelphia: Temple University Press.

Ellingson, L. L. (2005). *Communicating in the clinic: Negotiating frontstage and backstage teamwork.* Cresskill, NJ: Hampton Press.

Ezzamel, M., Wilmott, H., & Worthington, F. (2001). Power, control and resistance in the factory that time forgot. *Journal of Management Studies, 38*, 1053-1079.

Fairhurst, G., & Putnam, L. (2004). Organizations as discursive constructions. *Communication Theory, 14*, 5-26.

Featherstone, M. (1995). *Undoing culture.* London: Sage.

Fleming, P., & Sewell, G. (2002). Looking for the good soldier, *svejk*: Alternative modalities of resistance in the contemporary workplace. *Sociology, 36*, 857-873.

Foucault, M. (1979). *Discipline and punish: The birth of the prison* (A. Sheridan, Trans.). New York: Vintage.

Foucault, M. (1980a). *Power/knowledge. Selected interviews and other writings 1972-1977* (C. Gordon, L. Marshall, J. Mepham, & K. Soper, Trans.). New York: Pantheon Books.

Foucault, M. (1980b). *The history of sexuality: Volume 1* (R. Hurley, Trans). New York: Vintage Books/Random House.

Frank, A. (1991). *At the will of the body: Reflections on illness.* Boston: Houghton Mifflin.

Frank, A. (1995). *The wounded storyteller: Body, illness, and ethics.* Chicago: University of Chicago Press.

Fraser, N. (1992). Rethinking the public sphere: A contribution to the critique of actually existing democracy. In C. Calhoun (Ed.), *Habermas and the public sphere* (pp. 109-142). Cambridge, MA: MIT Press.

Freeman, J., & Rogers, J. (1999). *What workers want.* Ithaca, NY: Cornell University Press.

Freeman, R. B., & Medoff, J. L. (1984). *What do unions do?* New York: Basic Books.

Frey, L., Adelman, M., Flint, L., & Query, J. (2000). Weaving meanings together in an AIDS residence: Communicative practices, perceived health outcomes, and the symbolic construction of community. *Journal of Health Communication, 5*, 53-72.

Friedman, A. L. (1977). *Industry and labor: Class struggle at work and monopoly capitalism.* London: Macmillan.

Ganesh, S., Zoller, H., & Cheney, G. (2005). Transforming resistance, broadening our boundaries: Critical organizational communication meets globalization from below. *Communication Monographs, 72*, 169-191.

Gentile, A. (2003, August). *Workers with citizens; workers as citizens: Dockers contending neoliberal globalization and post-Sept. 11 statism.* Paper presented at the annual meeting of the American Political Science Association, Boston.

Giddens, A. (2000). The globalization of modernity. In D. Held & A. McGrew (Eds.), *The global transformations reader: An introduction to the globalization debate* (pp. 92-103). Malden, MA: Blackwell.

Gottfried, H. (1994). Learning the score: The duality of control and everyday resistance in the temporary-help service industry. In J. M. Jermier, D. Knights, & W. R. Nord (Eds.), *Resistance and power* (pp. 102-127). New York: Routledge.

Gramsci, A. (1971). *Selections from the prison notebooks* (Q. Hoare & G. N. Smith, Trans.). New York: International Publishers.

Greenhouse, S. (2000, February 26). Labor, in switch, urges amnesty for all illegal immigrants. *The New York Times* [national edition], p. A1.

Grosfoguel, R. (2005). The implications of subaltern epistemologies for global capitalism: transmodernity, border thinking, and global coloniality. In R. P. Appelbaum & W. I. Robinson (Eds.), *Critical globalization studies* (pp. 283-292). New York: Routledge.

Grossberg, L. (1993). Cultural studies and/in new worlds. *Critical Studies in Mass Communication, 10*, 1-22.

Grunig, J. E. (2001). Two-way symmetrical public relations: Past, present and future. In R. L. Heath (Ed.), *Handbook of public relations* (pp. 11-30). London: Sage.

Guha, R. (1981). Preface. In R. Guha (Ed.), *Subaltern studies: Writings on South Asian history and society* (Vol. 1, pp. vii-viii). Delhi, India: Oxford University Press.

Guha, R. (Ed.). (1983). *Subaltern studies: Writings on South Asian history and society* (Vol. 2). Delhi, India: Oxford University Press.

Guha, R. (2001). Subaltern studies: Projects of our time and their convergence. In I. Rodriguez (Ed.), *The Latin American subaltern studies reader* (pp. 35-46). Durham, NC: Duke University Press.

Harter, L. M., Kirby, E., Edwards, A., & McClanahan, A. (2005). Time, technology and meritocracy: The disciplining of women's bodies in narrative constructions of age-related infertility. In L. M. Harter, P. M. Japp, & C. S. Beck (Eds.), *Narratives, health, and healing: Communication theory, research, and practice* (pp. 83-106). Mahwah, NJ: Erlbaum.

Harter, L. M., Scott, J. A., Novak, D., Leeman, M., & Morris, J. (2006). Freedom through flight: Performing a counter-narrative of disability. *Journal of Applied Communication Research, 34*, 3-29.

Harvey, D. (2000). Time-space compression and the postmodern condition. In D. Held & McGrew (Eds.), *The global transformations reader: An introduction to the globalization debate* (pp. 82-91). Malden, MA: Blackwell.

Hasek, J. (1973). *The good soldier, svejk* (Cecil Parrott, Trans.). London: Heinemann.

Hashmi, S. (2007). The first ten years of street theater. In S. Deshpande (Ed.), *Theater of the streets: The Jana Natya Manch experience* (pp 11-16). New Delhi, India: Janam.

Haynes, D., & Prakash, G. (1992). Introduction: The entanglement of power and resistance. In D. Haynes & G. Prakash (Eds.), *Contesting power: Resistance and everyday social relations in South Asia* (pp. 1-22). Berkeley: University of California Press.

Heath, R. L. (2001). Public relations in cyberspace. The frontier of new communication technologies. In R. L. Heath (Ed.) *Handbook of public relations* (pp. 579-581). Thousand Oaks, CA: Sage.

Herod, A. (1997). From a geography of labor to a labor geography: Labor's spatial fix and the geography of capitalism. *Antipode, 29*, 1-31.

Holmer Nadesan, M. (1997). Constructing paper dolls: The discourse of personality testing in organizational practice. *Communication Theory, 7*, 189-218.

Holmer Nadesan, M. (2001). Fortune on globalization and the new economy. *Management Communication Quarterly, 14*, 498-506

Holtzhausen, D. R. (2005). Public relations practice and political change in South Africa. *Public Relations Review, 31*, 407-416.

Jermier, J. M., Knights, D., & Nord, W. R. (1994). Introduction. In J. M. Jermier, D. Knights, & W. R. Nord (Eds.), *Resistance and power in organizations* (pp. 1-24). New York: Routledge.

Juravich, T., & Bronfenbrenner, K. (2000). *Ravenswood: The steelworkers' victory and the revival of American labor.* Ithaca, NY: Cornell University Press.

Juris, J. S. (2004). Networked social movements: Global movements for global justice. In M. Castells (Ed.), *The network society* (pp. 341-362). Northampton, MA: Edward Elgar.

Karlberg, M. (1996). Remembering the public in public relations research: From theoretical to operational symmetry. *Journal of Public Relations Research, 8*, 263-278.

Kellner, D. (1989). *Critical theory, Marxism and modernity.* Cambridge, England: Polity.

Keohane, R. O. (2002). *Power and governance in a partially globalized world.* New York: Routledge.

Kilduff, M., & Mehra, A. (1997). Postmodernism and organizational research. *The Academy of Management Review, 22,* 453-481.

Knights, D., & Vurdubakis, T. (1994). Foucault, power, resistance and all that. In J. M. Jermier, D. Knights, & W. R. Nord (Eds.), *Resistance and power* (pp. 102-127). New York: Routledge.

Kondo, D. K. (1990). *Crafting selves: Power, gender, and discourses of identity in a Japanese workplace.* Chicago: University of Chicago Press.

Kriesberg, L. (1997). Social movements and global transformation. In J. Smith, C. Chatfield, & R. Pagnucco (Eds.), *Transnational social movements and global politics: Solidarity beyond the state* (pp. 3-18). Syracuse, NY: Syracuse University Press.

Krugman, P. (2002). *The great unraveling: Losing our way in the new century.* New York: W. W. Norton.

Kunda, G. (1992). *Engineering culture: Control and communication in a high-tech corporation.* Philadelphia: Temple University Press.

Laclau, E., & Mouffe, C. (2001). *Hegemony and socialist strategy: Towards a radical democratic politics.* New York: Verso.

Larson, G., & Tompkins, P. (2005). Ambivalence and resistance: A study of management in a concertive control system. *Communication Monographs, 72,* 1-21.

Lordan, E. J. (2001). Cyberspin: The use of new technologies in public relations. In R. L. Heath (Ed.), *Handbook of public relations* (pp. 583-589). Thousand Oaks, CA: Sage

Lorde, A. (1980). *The cancer journals.* San Francisco: Aunt Lute Books.

Luthra, R. (2003). Recovering women's voice: Communicative empowerment of women of the South. In P. J. Kalbfleisch (Ed.), *Communication yearbook 27* (pp. 45-65) Mahwah, NJ: Erlbaum.

Lyotard, J. (1984). *The postmodern condition: A report on knowledge.* (G. Bennington & B. Massouri, trans.). Minneapolis: University of Minnesota Press.

Marx, K. (1967). *Capital.* New York: Dutton. (Original work published 1867)

Marx, K. (1975). *Early writings.* London: Penguin Books. (Original work published in 1833-1834)

Mayo, M. (2005). *Global citizens: Social movements and the challenge of globalization.* Toronto, Canada: Canadian Scholars' Press Inc.

McCarthy, J. D. (1997). The globalization of social movement theory. In J. Smith, C. Chatfield, & R. Pagnucco (Eds.), *Transnational social movements and global politics* (pp. 243-259). Syracuse, NY: Syracuse University Press.

McKie, D., & Munshi, D. (2005). Tracking trends: peripheral visions and public relations. *Public Relations Review, 31,* 453-457.

McMichael, D. P. (2003). *Development and social change: A global perspective.* Newbury Park, CA: Pine Forge Press.

Melkote, S. M., & Steeves, H. L. (2001). *Communication for development in the third world: Theory and practice for empowerment.* Thousand Oaks, CA: Sage.

Millen, J., & Holtz, T. (2000). Dying for growth, Part I: Transnational corporations and the health of the poor. In J. Kim, J. Millen, A. Irwin, & J. Gershman (Eds.), *Dying for growth: Global inequality and the health of the poor* (pp. 177-223). Monroe, ME: Common Courage Press.

Millen, J., Irwin, A., & Kim, J. (2000). Introduction: What is growing? Who is dying? In J. Kim, J. Millen, A. Irwin, & J. Gershman (Eds.), *Dying for growth: Global inequality and the health of the poor* (pp. 3-10). Monroe, ME: Common Courage Press.

Mittelman, J. H., & Chin, C. (2000). Conceptualizing resistance to globalization. In J. H. Mittelman (Ed.), *The globalization syndrome: Transformation and resistance* (pp. 165-178). Princeton, NJ: Princeton University Press.

Miyoshi, M. (1995). A borderless world? From colonialism to transnationalism and the decline of the nation-state. *Critical Inquiry, 19*, 726-751.

Moody, K. (1988). *An injury to all: The decline of American unionism.* New York: Verso.

Morgan, J., & Krone, K. J. (2001). Bending the rules of professional display: Emotional improvisation in caregiver performances. *Journal of Applied Communication Research, 29*, 317-340.

Mumby, D. K. (1993a). Critical organizational communication studies. The next ten years. *Communication Monographs, 60*, 18-25.

Mumby, D. K. (Ed.). (1993b). *Narrative and social control: Critical perspectives.* Newbury Park, CA: Sage

Mumby, D. K. (1997). Modernism, postmodernism, and communication studies: A rereading of an ongoing debate. *Communication Theory, 7*, 1-28.

Mumby, D. K. (2000). Communication, organization, and the public sphere: A feminist perspective. In P. M. Buzzanell (Ed.), *Rethinking organizational and managerial communication from feminist perspectives* (pp. 3-23). Thousand Oaks, CA: Sage.

Mumby, D. K. (2005). Theorizing resistance in organizational studies: A dialectical approach. *Management Communication Quarterly, 19*, 19-44.

Munshi, D., & Kurian, P. (2005). Imperializing spin cycles: A postcolonial look at public relations, greenwashing and the separation of publics. *Public Relations Review, 31*, 513-520.

Murphy, A. G. (1998). Hidden transcripts of flight attendant resistance. *Management Communication Quarterly, 11*, 499-535.

Murphy, A. G. (2001). The flight attendant dilemma: An analysis of communication and sensemaking during in-flight emergencies. *Journal of Applied Communication Research, 29*, 30-53.

Murphy, P., & Dee, J. (1992). DuPont and Greenpeace: The dynamics of conflict between corporations and activist groups. *Journal of Public Relations Research, 4*, 3-20.

Naples, N. A., & Desai, M. (2002). Women's local and translocal responses. An introduction to the chapters. In N. A. Naples & M. Desai (Eds.), *Women's activism and globalization* (pp. 34-41). New York: Routledge.

Narayan, U., & Harding, S. (Eds.). (2000). *Decentering the center: Philosophy for a multicultural, postcolonial, and feminist world.* Bloomington: Indiana University Press.

Pal, M., & Buzzanell, P. M. (2008). The Indian call center experience: A case study in changing discourses of identity, identification, and career in a global context. *Journal of Business Communication, 45*, 31-60.

Pal, M., & Dutta, M. (in press). Public relations in a global context: The relevance of critical modernism as a theoretical lens. *Journal of Public Relations Research.*

Papa, M. J., Singhal, A., & Papa, W. (2006). *Organizing for social change: A dialectic journey of theory and praxis.* New Delhi, India: Sage.

Prakash, G. (1994). Subaltern studies as postcolonial criticism. *The American Historical Review, 99*, 1475-1490.

Prasad, A. (2003). The gaze of the other: Postcolonial theory and organizational analysis. In A. Prasad (Ed.), *Postcolonial theory and organizational analysis: A critical engagement* (pp. 3-43). New York: Palgrave Macmillan.

Prasad, A., & Prasad, P. (2003). The empire of organizations and the organization of empires: Postcolonial considerations on theorizing workplace resistance. In A. Prasad (Ed.), *Postcolonial theory and organizational analysis: A critical engagement* (pp. 95-119). New York: Palgrave Macmillan.

Prasad, P., & Prasad, A. (2000). Stretching the iron cage: The constitution and implications of routine workplace resistance. *Organizational Science, 11*, 387-403.

Robins, K. (2000). Encountering globalization. In D. Held & A. McGrew (Eds.), *The global transformations reader. An introduction to the globalization debate* (pp. 195-201). Malden, MA: Blackwell.

Rosen, M. (1985). Breakfast at Spiro's: Dramaturgy and dominance. *Journal of Management, 11*, 31-48.

Rosen, M. (1988). You asked for it: Christmas at the bosses' expense. *Journal of Management Studies, 25*, 463-480.

Routledge, P. (2000). Our resistance will be as transnational as capital: Convergence space and strategy in globalizing resistance. *GeoJournal, 52*, 25-33.

Said, E. W. (1978). *Orientalism.* Harmondsworth, England: Penguin.

Said, E. W. (1988). Foreword. In R. Guha & G. C. Spivak (Eds.), *Selected subaltern studies* (pp. v-xii). New York: Oxford University Press.

Scott, J. (1985). *Weapons of the weak: Everyday forms of peasant resistance.* New Haven, CT: Yale University Press.

Seidman, G. W. (2000). Adjusting the lens: What do globalizations, transnationalism, and the anti-apartheid movement mean for social movement theory? In J. A. Guidry, M. D. Kennedy, & M. N. Zald (Eds.), *Globalizations and social movements: Culture, power, and the transnational public sphere* (pp. 339-357). Ann Arbor: The University of Michigan Press.

Sharf, B. F. (2005). How I fired my surgeon and embraced an alternative narrative. In L. M. Harter, P. M. Japp, & C. S. Beck (Eds.), *Narratives, health, and healing: Communication theory, research, and practice* (pp. 325-342). Mahwah, NJ: Erlbaum.

Shome, R., & Hegde, S. R. (2002). Postcolonial approaches to communication: Charting the terrain, engaging the intersections. *Communication Theory, 12*, 249-270.

Silver, B. J. (2003). *Forces of labor: Workers' movements and globalization since 1870.* New York: Cambridge University Press.

Smith, J. (2001). Globalizing resistance: The battle of Seattle and the future of social movements. *Mobilisation, 6*, 1-20.

Smith, J., Pagnucco, R., & Chatfield, C. (1997). Social movements and world politics. In J. Smith, C. Chatfield, & R. Pagnucco (Eds.), *Transnational social movements and global politics* (pp. 59-77). Syracuse, NY: Syracuse University Press.

Sotirin, P., & Gottfried, H. (1999). The ambivalent dynamics of secretarial "bitching": Control, resistance, and the construction of identity. *Organization, 6*, 57-80.

Spivak, G. (1987). *In other worlds: Essays in cultural politics.* New York: Methuen.

Springston, J. K. (2001). Public relations and new media technology: The impact of the Internet. In R. L. Heath (Ed.) *Handbook of public relations* (pp. 603-614). Thousand Oaks, CA: Sage.

Sriramesh, K., & Vercic, D. (2003). A theoretical framework for global public relations research and practice. In K. Sriramesh & D. Vercic (Eds.), *The global public relations handbook* (pp. 1-19). Mahwah, NJ: Earlbaum

Stewart, C., Smith, C., & Denton, R. (2006). *Persuasion and social movements.* Long Grove, IL: Waveland Press.

Tarrow, S. (2005). *The new transnational activism.* New York: Cambridge University Press.

Tarrow, S., & Della Porta, D. (2005). Conclusion: "Globalization," complex internationalism, and transnational contention. In D. Della Porta & S. Tarrow (Eds.), *Transnational protest and global activism* (pp. 227-246). New York: Rowman & Littlefield.

Taylor, F. (1947). *Scientific management.* New York: Harper & Row.

Taylor, M., Kent, L. M., & White, J. W. (2001). How activist organizations are using the Internet to build relationships. *Public Relations Review, 27,* 263-284.

Tilly, C. (1995). Globalization threatens labor's rights. *International Labor and Working-Class History, 47,* 1-23.

Tracy, S. J. (2000). Becoming a character for commerce: Emotion labor, self subordination, and discursive construction of identity in a total institution. *Management Communication Quarterly, 14,* 90-128.

Tretheway, A. (1997). Resistance, identity, and empowerment: A postmodern feminist analysis of clients in a human service organization. *Communication Monographs, 64,* 281-301.

Tretheway, A. (2000). A feminist critique of disciplined bodies. In P. M. Buzzanell (Ed.), *Rethinking organizational and managerial communication from feminist perspectives* (pp. 177-208). Thousand Oaks, CA: Sage.

Turner, L. (2006). Globalization and the logic of participation: Unions and the politics of coalition building. *Journal of Industrial Relations, 48,* 83-97.

Weber, M. (1921). *Economy and society.* Totowa, NJ: Bedminster.

Weedon, C. (1997). *Feminist practice and poststructuralist theory.* Malden, MA: Blackwell.

Weedon, C. (1999). *Feminism, theory and the politics of difference.* Malden, MA: Blackwell.

Williams, H. L. (1999). Mobile capital and transborder labor rights mobilization. *Politics and Society, 6,* 55-68.

Witten, M. (1993). Narrative and the culture of obedience at the workplace. In D. K. Mumby (Ed.), *Narrative and social control: Critical perspectives* (pp. 97-118). London: Sage.

Zoller, H. (2005). Health activism: Communication theory and action for social change. *Communication Theory, 14,* 341-364.

Zoller, H., & Kline, K. (2008). Theoretical contributions of interpretive and critical research in health communication. In C. S. Beck (Ed.), *Communication yearbook 32* (pp. 89-135). New York: Routledge.

CHAPTER CONTENTS

3 Theoretical Contributions of Interpretive and Critical Research in Health Communication

Heather M. Zoller
University of Cincinnati

Kimberly N. Kline
University of Texas at San Antonio

Health communication researchers have made great strides in developing theoretically grounded research, resulting in more complex understandings of communication in health contexts. Integral to these developments has been the burgeoning use of interpretive and critical perspectives. Yet, we still lack a broader description and assessment of the contributions of interpretive and critical research to theory and practice in health communication. Such an assessment is important, given that the nature of these contributions differ at times from post-positivist research (in some cases overlapping, in others acting complementarily, and still others antagonistically). Thus, in this chapter, we describe the unique elements of interpretive and critical contributions in the extant literature and assess these contributions to identify ways in which they can be strengthened. Though we primarily draw on U.S. literature, this scholarship comprises interdisciplinary, international, multi-methodological, and cross-cultural research in an array of communication contexts (intra- and interpersonal, small group, organizational, mass-mediated). Thus, this chapter not only provides a comprehensive review of the ways in which interpretive/ critical approaches have been utilized in health communication research across a range of global contexts and concerns; it also builds an overarching argument with regard to the contribution of interpretive and critical approaches that is germane to the study of communication in general.

In the 1980s, many scholars in the field of health communication complained of a lack of theory-driven work and simplistic views of communication (Thompson, 2003). In the 1989 inaugural issue of the journal *Health*

Correspondence: Heather M. Zoller, University of Cincinnati, Cincinnati OH 45221-0184; Phone: 513-556-4468; Fax: 513-556-0899; E-mail: Heather.Zoller@uc.edu. Kimberly N. Kline, University of Texas at San Antonio MB 2.312, One UTSA Circle, San Antonio, TX 78249-0643; Phone: 210-458-5990; E-mail: kim.kline@utsa.edu

Communication, Editor Teresa Thompson (1989) also noted the need for health communication research to be more socially relevant and useful to practitioners. Health communication was, at that time, a relatively new area of scholarship stemming from research in other academic disciplines, especially behavioral science, (social) psychology, but also sociology, anthropology, political science, and even history (Rogers, 1996; Thompson, 2003). Within the field of communication studies, health communication scholars often got their start in interpersonal and mass communication studies (Ratzan, Payne, & Bishop, 1996). Essentially, these scholars drew from their disciplinary commitments, but they were particularly interested in health-related issues and contexts. Since then, health communication researchers have made great strides in developing theoretically guided research grounded in more complex understandings of communication.

We believe the burgeoning use of interpretive and critical perspectives in health communication research has been integral to these advancements. Only a decade ago, John Tulloch and Deborah Lupton (1997) lamented that "the field of health communication could potentially incorporate social and cultural theory in understanding how individuals make sense of and experience medicine, health and disease" and opined that "such theory has received little attention" (p. 16). We argue that, in just 10 short years, these perspectives have become more mainstream rather than "alternative" in contemporary research practices.

We feel that a delineation and assessment of the contributions of interpretive/ critical research is important, given that the nature of these contributions often differs from post-positivist research (in some cases overlapping, in others acting complementarily, and still others antagonistically), and that what counts as a theoretical contribution depends on one's worldview.[1] In this chapter, we describe the nature of interpretive and critical contributions, assess these contributions to understand how these perspectives are being applied, and identify ways in which they can be strengthened.

Though this chapter focuses on health communication, it also speaks to the communication discipline more generally. First, health communication provides a useful example of the growth of intra- and inter-disciplinary research in the field of communication. Health communication clearly intersects with other areas of communication. For example, scholars may study interpersonal health issues, health organizations, mediated health messages, and the like. Further, it draws from and contributes to other disciplines as well (e.g., biological sciences, sociology, public health). Indeed, in this chapter, we refer to scholarship that others may not necessarily consider to be "health communication;" we include this research because it employs interpretive/critical approaches to address issues of health and illness along with communication. (Conversations with colleagues suggest that some scholars working on health issues do not label their research as health communication because of lingering perceptions of the field as a post-positivist domain.) This chapter highlights interrelationships between health and issues and concerns across the discipline.

Second, health communication constitutes a model for areas of the discipline that have not yet grappled with the application of theories and concepts across cultures. The field addresses international health concerns and, as a result, works across national boundaries. Indeed, U.S.-based journals and publications give escalating attention to health concerns in multiple countries, particularly Africa, Australia, India, and Mexico (Diop, 2000; Dutta & Basu, 2007; Harter, Sharma, Pant, Singhal, & Sharma, 2007; D. Johnson, Flora, & Rimal, 1997; Storey, Boulay, Karki, Heckert, & Karmacha, 1999; Witte, 1998). Third, because we argue that the theoretical contributions of interpretive research should be evaluated differently than post-positivist research, this examination itself may act as a model for the broader discipline. This chapter provides a comprehensive review of the ways in which interdisciplinary interpretive and critical approaches have been utilized in health communication research across a range of international contexts and concerns; in doing so, it speaks to the role that these perspectives play in the study of communication in general.

We begin this chapter with the historical development of interpretive/ critical research in health communication, and we then describe the theoretical underpinnings of this research and the perspectives that contribute to these paradigms. In our analysis, we articulate how interpretive and critical research has contributed to our understanding of health communication theory and praxis using research exemplars. We conclude by evaluating these contributions and describing how future research can expand them.

DEVELOPMENT OF MULTIPLE PERSPECTIVES IN HEALTH COMMUNICATION

Like other areas in communication, early research in health communication was marked by mostly post-positivist (often quantitative) studies of cognitive-behavioral variables. The discipline was motivated by its roots in epidemiological research to determine the "behavioral and psychological variables important to the process of prevention and adopting healthier behaviors" (Finnegan & Viswanath, 1990, p. 17) as well as the psychological orientation of interpersonal research (Ratzan et al., 1996) and the scientific perspective of medical research (Rogers, 1996). As a result, quantitative/cognitive-behavioral approaches came to be understood as the "traditional" approach and qualitative/interpretive-critical approaches as the "alternative" approach (Burgoon, 1995).

Many early insights into social constructionist approaches to communication issues in health came from outside the discipline. Even before communication scholars recognized health communication as an important sub-area of the discipline, historian-philosophers Michel Foucault (1973) and Ivan Illich (1976) and medical sociologist Irving Zola (1972) interrogated the sociopolitical discourses of health, illness, and medicine that led all three to critique the powerful influence of the so-called medical establishment in disciplining the individual body and, thus, members of society. Around the same time, Susan Sontag's (1978) pioneering book, *Illness as Metaphor* (see also Sontag, 1990), delineated the moralizing function of cultural metaphors for illness. Medical journalist Lynn Payer (1992) described the promotional discourses of medicine in her book, *Disease-Mongers: How Doctors, Drug Companies, and Insurers Are Making You Feel Sick*. Physician-sociologist Howard Waitzkin (1991) had an important influence, introducing a critical analysis of doctor-patient communication that described how these interactions reinforce dominant ideologies. Sociologist Lupton (1994c) addressed the role of culture in the experience of health, and her article in *Health Communication* (1994d) called for researchers to address systematic issues of power related to the practice of health communication.

Within the discipline, a special issue of the *Journal of Applied Communication Research* edited by David Smith (1988b) included articles that discussed the central role of communication in understanding the relationship between health and values (see D. H. Smith, 1988a) and critiqued health campaigns for their failure to address issues of power (McKnight, 1988). Later, Patricia Geist and Jennifer Dreyer (1993) introduced a dialogic framework to understand provider–patient interactions. In media studies, Barbara Sharf and colleagues (Sharf & Freimuth, 1993; Sharf, Freimuth, Greespon, & Plotnick, 1996) sought to understand the rhetorical construction of illness in primetime television, offering an audience analysis of viewer interpretations and a textual analysis of media messages.

These publications created pathways for additional inquiries into relationships among communication, meaning, and health from interpretive and critical perspectives. In our chapter, we highlight the immense growth in this area of research. First, we define and describe the philosophical and methodological underpinnings of these approaches.

Defining our Terms: What do we Mean by Interpretive and Critical Approaches?

Most broadly, at the metatheoretical level, approaches to research can be positioned on a paradigmatic continuum that takes into account variations in ontological, epistemological, axiological, and methodological assumptions. Numerous examinations of paradigmatic differences exist; scholars compare and contrast in the context of organizational (Burrell & Morgan, 1979), cultural (Martin & Nakayama, 1999), and interpersonal (Leeds-Hurwitz, 1995) studies; some make the case for complementarity of associated qualitative and quantitative methodologies (Deetz, 2001), and still others challenge their compatibility (J. K. Smith & Heshusius, 2004). Rather than reiterate these discussions, this section sets the parameters of research considered in this chapter. Notwithstanding their differences, discussions of meta-theoretical paradigms generally acknowledge post-positivism (or, at its most extreme, positivism) at one end of the continuum and interpretive/critical at the other. Though we do not want to reify dichotomies or reinvigorate tensions, these paradigms define contributions to the field differently because definitions of theory, research goals, and practical orientations often vary.

Both interpretive and critical approaches start with the most basic ontological assumption that our perceptions of reality are constituted as subjects attach meaning to phenomena and that these meanings arise through interactions. The concomitant epistemological assumption affirms that we come to agreement about what is real intersubjectively. As Lupton (2000) described, "[F]or most social constructionists, the types of knowledges that are developed and brought to bear upon health, illness, and medical care may be regarded as assemblages of beliefs that are created through human interaction and preexisting meanings" (p. 50).

Because of their foundational, ontological, and epistemological assumptions, interpretive scholars strive to better understand interpretation and the process of meaning making. Scholars consider such research to be interpretive because they "are concerned with…describing the subjective, creative communication of individuals, usually using qualitative research methods" (Martin & Nakayama, 1999, p. 5). This perspective seeks to provide in-depth understanding of lived experience or a unique, well-argued and defended interpretation of a discourse to impart some insight into the multiple ways in which communication fosters particular meanings. Interpretive/critical scholars do not necessarily attend to (in)accuracy or rightness/wrongness of messages as measured against some objective reality. Rather, they engage in the double hermeneutic (Giddens, 1984) of interpreting others' interpretations, remembering that the phenomena we study in the social sciences are socially constructed (see related review by Bartesaghi & Castor, this volume).

Where interpretive scholarship offers "thick description" of communicative activity (see Geertz, 1973), critical scholarship also asks us to take an ethical position with regard to the implications of that communicative activity. We can distinguish between interpretive and critical research by employing the concepts of "consensus" and "dissensus" (Deetz, 2001). According to Deetz, researchers orienting near the "consensus" pole— interpretive scholars—"seek order and treat order production as the dominant feature of natural and social systems" (p. 14); trust and concerns with harmony characterize this approach. Researchers associated with the "dissensus" pole—critical scholars—"consider struggle, conflict and tensions to be the natural state" (p. 15); the approach features concern with the privileging of interests by particular constructions of reality. Thus, both approaches assume socially constructed realities, but interpretive perspectives tend to focus on describing and understanding those realities; whereas, critical ones challenge dominant orders and aim to unmask and reclaim hidden conflicts. With regard to health communication, "the critical perspective takes an overtly political approach, questioning the values of biomedicine and focusing on the identification of political, economic, and historical factors that shape a culture's responses to and concepts of health, disease, and treatment issues" (Lupton, 1994d, p. 58).

Critical theorizing involves deconstructing dominant, taken-for-granted assumptions about health, often with the hope of introducing possibilities for alternative, more inclusive meaning systems. These perspectives emphasize the role of human-made systems of meaning but link these systems to material consequences for people's lives (Waitzkin, 1991). This scholarship serves a crucial function for the field of health communication, which sometimes assumes that researchers' goals of health improvements are an "unquestioned good" (Rogers, 1996, p. 18). Critical research gives attention to issues of power, inequality, class, and other differences that may be overlooked in more functionalist research (Deetz, 2001; Lupton, 1994d; Mumby, 1997). Theorizing proceeds by examining how communication in health contexts creates, reproduces, or challenges dominant power relations.

The criteria for judging the credibility and validity of interpretive/critical scholarship are distinctive from post-positivist research (Patton, 2002). Whereas post-positivist scholars hold that theories must be predictive and generalizeable, interpretive scholars tend to view theory as more contextually bound, as a dialectic between local and more general understanding (Martin & Nakayama, 1999). With regard to ethnography, for instance, "the essential task of theory building here is not to codify abstract regularities but to make thick description possible, not to generalize across cases but to generalize within them" (Geertz, 1973, p. 56). Thus, depth of insight into local constructions constitutes a key way to assess interpretive research. As Patton noted, we can evaluate interpretive research in terms of process, such as the openness of researchers' relationships with subjects and their reflexivity in addressing their own role in data gathering and analysis. Patton contended that contributions to praxis, or theoretically informed social change, mark another important means of evaluating "alternative" research. For critical scholarship, praxis involves pursuing connections between local practices and larger systems of power to facilitate change (Lupton, 1994d).

Despite the emphasis on local knowledge, we argue that interpretive/ critical researchers should maintain a systematic approach to building health communication theory. The focus on contextualization does not rule out some level of generalization or the need for theories that cut across individual contexts. Geertz (1973) suggested that theory building can be seen as an activity "[b]etween setting down the meaning particular social actions have for the actors whose actions they are, and stating, as explicitly as we can manage, what the knowledge thus attained demonstrates about the society in which it is found and, beyond that, about social life as such" (p. 57). Thus, in interpretive/critical studies, "[p]articular persons and situations are artifacts used to understand the system of meanings through which particular persons and situations are composed and connected to the larger sociocultural context" (Deetz, 1992, p. 85).

This view is consistent with Austin Babrow and Marifran Mattson's (2003) description of theorizing as, in part, "an inherently communicative process by which we attempt to formulate a consciously elaborated and justified understanding of the world" (p. 37). As we examine the contributions of individual studies, we discuss the degree to which research, individually or taken as a body of literature, contributes to broader issues of health and illness as well as insight into the case under study.

Three caveats are in order regarding comparisons between interpretive/critical theorizing and post-positivist theorizing. First, interpretive/critical approaches may seem synonymous with qualitative methodologies (and, alternatively, post-positivist approaches synonymous with quantitative methodologies); in research practice, however, they are not always the same.[2] In our view, the approach to analyzing and understanding data, not the strategy for *collecting* data, distinguishes between post-positivist and interpretive/critical research. Second, the focus on local, in-depth knowledge in interpretive methodologies leads some to view this research as pre-scientific, as hypothesis generators that require validation and generalization (Bowers, 1972; J. B. Brown, Stewart, & Ryan, 2003). However, it could just as well be argued that quantitative research is pre-interpretive, given that generalized findings require investigation of local interpretations of elite operational definitions and conclusions. In other words, the goals of generalizability and depth of insight can work in complementary ways among various research traditions, and no single approach needs to be privileged. Third, we described a dialectic between local understanding and more general insights in interpretive/critical research; we note similar tensions in post-positivist research that aims towards generalization through atomistic methods. Social-scientific scholars often criticize variable analytic research when it does not attempt to build and test communication theories (Witte et al., 1996). So, despite differences, the paradigms share some similar concerns.

In sum, this section illustrates useful distinctions between interpretive and post-positivist research (metatheoretical commitments, goals, and assessment criteria) as well as parallel concerns (methodology and legitimacy). This understanding of differences and commonalities can help to maintain a cohesive discipline in the face of heterogeneous approaches. In the next section, we describe the various research traditions that constitute interpretive/critical studies.

Research Traditions in Interpretive/Critical Research

The multi-disciplinary, multi-conceptual, multi-methodological, multi-topical —indeed, the multi-theoretical—approaches in the studies to which we refer make it challenging to parse them in terms of their theoretical lens. A single study often represents several different theoretical commitments. (For example, one study might be social constructionist, grounded, and employ a particular theory for analysis.) Even within a philosophical paradigm, numerous, sometimes overlapping, foci garner the attention of researchers and serve to direct attention to different aspects of communication phenomena (Craig, 1999; Patton, 2002). Moreover, the research to which we refer often did not overtly state a theoretical perspective. For instance, Bartesaghi and Castor (this volume) noted that social constructionist research routinely reflects the tenets but does not invoke the specific term. As we review relevant research, we infer the theoretical approach from authors' discussion. In this section, we briefly describe these perspectives to provide background for our discussion of their contributions.

Rhetorical perspectives are largely concerned with the suasory potential of communication. Whether subscribing to a more Aristotelian conceptualization of rhetoric (i.e., rhetoric as the available means of persuasion of logos, ethos, and pathos) or a Burkean conceptualization (i.e., rhetoric as a means of inducing cooperation through identification), research in this vein concentrates on rhetorical situations and, hence, the *appeals used* by rhetors (Lupton, 1992; Signorielli, 1990). The suasory implications of a text/discourse may be the result of the carefully crafted and consciously strategic efforts of the rhetor (as in advertising or health campaigns) or the unconscious but implicitly persuasive actions of rhetors (as in journalism or entertainment media) (Kline, 2003, 2006). In either case, the rhetorical scholar presumes that a rhetor "has selected certain material and certain arrangements to accomplish a purpose" (Andrews, 1990, p. 47). Rhetorical research usually involves textual analytic methods.

Narrative research is often, though not always, aligned with the rhetorical perspectives (Fisher, 1987). Narrative perspectives in health communication comprise one of the strongest trends in current interpretive research (Frank, 1995; Greenhalgh & Hurwitz, 1998; Kleinman, 1988; Sharf & Vanderford, 2003). As evidenced by the edited book *Narratives, Health, and Healing* (Harter, Japp, & Beck, 2005a) and other research, narrative can be used as a method for analyzing discourse (Arrington & Goodier, 2004) and interpersonal dialogue (Rice & Ezzy, 1999), a methodology for communicating personal experience (Rawlins, 2005; Sharf, 2005), and a theoretical perspective that focuses on the ways that humans construct the meaning of objects, on-going events, and personal and social identity through plotting and use of storytelling (Babrow, Kasch, & Ford, 1998). Narrative theories point us away from transmission models of communication and assumptions of rational logics as they show us how people make sense of and explain their world through the use of narrative logics. In this view, stories constitute "both mundane and extraordinary ritual symbolic forms," and they provide "sites for action and agency" (Harter, Japp, & Beck, 2005b, p. 9).

Grounded theorizing is another important trend in health communication (Beck et al., 2004). It emphasizes allowing the themes, categories, and issues of concern to emerge from research participants themselves rather than beginning research with issues and concepts defined by the researcher (Charmaz, 2002; Glaser & Strauss, 1967). Ethnographic perspectives are also grounded, but they arise from hermeneutic and phenomenological commitments that emphasize human interpretation of local meanings as a methodology (Geertz, 1983; Rawlins, 1998). Ethnographic work seeks to learn about culture by attempting, as much as possible, to understand the construction of meaning from the perspective of cultural members through observation and participation (Geertz, 1983). The perspective provides insight into everyday communicative health practices and relationships between culture and health (DeSantis, 2002; Ellingson, 2005; J. L. Johnson et al., 2004).

Dialogic perspectives have helped to bring a relational focus to a field often focused on messages. Research from a dialogic perspective investigates the co-construction of meaning through the flow of ongoing interaction (Cissna & Anderson, 1994). Dialogue is rooted in voicing otherness and acknowledging differences, and it involves genuine listening and willingness to be changed in interaction (Bakhtin, 1981, 1993; Buber, 1958; Cissna & Anderson, 1994). Health communication scholarship examines practical attempts at dialogue such as community health planning (Zoller, 2000) as well as evaluates discourse and interaction such as provider–patient interactions by comparing it to the ideals of dialogue (Geist & Dreyer, 1993).

Critical perspectives in communication include several traditions. The cultural studies tradition emphasizes the culturally situated nature of health communication interactions and processes and locates culture in the realm of structure and power (Dutta, 2008). For example, critical studies of media illustrate how ideologies of health and illness produce social knowledge in ways that reflect dominant cultural constructions that legitimize dominant power relationships (Lupton, 1995). Likewise, scholars using the label critical or critical-interpretive investigate how everyday taken-for-granted assumptions about reality reinforce dominant power relationships and how communication may resist or alter those power relationships (Mokros & Deetz, 1996). Both cultural studies and critical interpretive scholars are influenced by the Marxist tradition, including Frankfurt school theorists, Italian theorist Antonio Gramsci, as well as Stuart Hall and the Centre for Contemporary Cultural Studies (Mumby, 1988). Other branches include postcolonial theory (Spivak, 1999), feminist studies (Dow & Condit, 2005), and queer theory (Yep, Lovaas, & Elia, 2003).

Critical approaches may draw from postmodern theories as well. *Postmodernism* is a contested term that itself represents a number of potential research orientations. Here, we reference work that shares a suspicion of meta-narratives, including a questioning of unified conceptions of the self (Lupton, 1995; Mumby, 1997). Postmodern theorizing interrogates the relationship between power and the construction of knowledge, often focusing on the micropolitical level, understanding everyday instances of power and resistance (Deetz, 2001). Postmodern theorists tend to focus on deconstruction, reclaiming and celebrating conflict, rather than articulating a preferred ideology or social configuration as those with more Marxist commitments might (Deetz, 2001; Waitzkin, 1991). Despite differences in both labels and approaches, critical scholars share concern with issues of power, ideology, and domination, as well as resistance and emancipation. With this understanding of what constitutes interpretive/critical research, we now describe how we developed our discussion of the theoretical contributions that extant work makes to the field of health communication. We then describe these contributions using research exemplars.

THEORETICAL CONTRIBUTIONS OF INTERPRETIVE/CRITICAL RESEARCH

Rather than sets of predictive theories, theoretical contributions from interpretive/critical research focus on the development of insight. In their description of social constructionist research, Babrow and Mattson (2003) argued that it contextualizes discourse, identifies contrasting perspectives, incorporates cultural sensitivity, and reveals what is rhetorical. We used these ideas as guides, expanding, altering, and adding categories as we gathered significant examples of interpretive/critical work from various theoretical traditions. These inductive categories illustrate theoretical advancements represented in the work. Of course, these categories are interconnected and overlapping, but each sheds light on a different value imparted by the research. Our list focuses directly on issues of health, but we believe the contributions themselves can be applied in the broader discipline. We discuss this application in the conclusion.

Uncovering Everyday, Contextualized Experiences of Health and Illness

Interpretive research (including grounded theory, ethnographic, case study, discourse analysis, and narrative methodologies) expands our understanding of the everyday experience of health communication processes. Interpretive scholarship demonstrates the ways that individuals define and make sense of health and illness through factors such as personal experiences, interpersonal negotiations, cultural backgrounds, and class frameworks, much more so than by some externally defined biomedical criterion. These personal views of health provide important foundations for how people interpret health information and directives. Critical perspectives contextualize these everyday constructions within social and political structures. In this section, we provide exemplars in the areas of the interpretation of health, the experience of illness, and medical interactions.

Everyday Definitions of Health and Illness

Before we can promote "health," we need to understand how diverse groups and individuals define and experience the concept in every day life. Grounded and ethnographic perspectives shed light on this process by acknowledging differences in what constitutes health and healthy living, particularly when considering gender, social class, and culture. For example, Australian women viewed their children's health and well-being (and even intelligence and other outcomes) almost exclusively in terms of their own vigilance, planning, and effort (Lupton, 2008). These beliefs reflect dominant health promotion messages aimed at mothers and do not consider notions of luck or fate that might also play a role in defining health. Critical research can uncover the class assumptions in definitions of health; Zoller (2004) found that some members of the working class may be more likely to define health as release (i.e., doing what one enjoys) (see also Crawford, 1984), focusing on sports and fun and ignoring disciplinary approaches associated with middle-class values that define health in terms of hard work and self-control.

Culture-centered research elucidates how Western, often biomedical, health concepts fail to address the perspectives of non-Western cultural groups that may place more value on family, society, spirit, and nature than individual biology. For instance, Latina women on the Texas-Mexico border describe the importance of family to their conceptions of health and illness (Villagran, Collins, & Garcia, 2008). Dutta-Bergman (2004) used ethnography to understand the polymorphic health beliefs of the Santalis in India, describing the tensions that they experienced between maintaining traditional views of health as a balance with nature and accepting dominant scientific frameworks.

Contextualized research into health constructions among social groups helps us to understand how deeply rooted norms for health values and behaviors may develop, and they highlight the "non-rational" ways that health promotion messages may be interpreted in light of emotional and social needs. For instance, patrons in a cigar shop collectively rationalized smoking behavior through their shared narratives and, in doing so, created barriers to anti-smoking arguments (DeSantis, 2002). Health promotion campaigners must account for these group stories and the needs that they meet, which are not met by PSAs and other education material.

Illness Experiences

Interpretive researchers also illuminate everyday communication processes related to illness experience. Ethnographic work examines the experience of social support for people with illnesses in hospice situations (Adelman & Frey, 1997) and support groups (Arrington, 2005). Narrative perspectives, in particular, build knowledge of how people negotiate and make sense of illness experiences (Frank, 1995; Gibbs & Franks, 2002; Greenhalgh & Hurwitz, 1998; Harter et al., 2005b; Kleinman, 1988; Ott Anderson & Geist Martin, 2003; Sharf & Vanderford, 2003; Vanderford, Jenks, & Sharf, 1997; A. J. Young & Rodriguez, 2006). Narrative approaches do not formulate a singular theory of illness experience because, as Harter et al. asserted, "[e]ngaging in narratives require scholars to delve more deeply into murky, cluttered, and complicated interrelationships between sometimes incompatible issues" (p. 8). This narrative engagement shows us *how* humans construct meanings associated with illness through plotting and use of storytelling. Ott Anderson and Geist Martin detailed how one couple's narrative after a cancer diagnosis elucidated the processes through which they constituted supportive relationships and established the central role of family communication in forming and altering illness identities. Their study revises the discrete illness identities proffered in emotion and identity management theories (victim, warrior, survivor), finding a "continuous, multifaceted process" (p. 141) of identity formation. Building on this insight, Christina Beck's (2005) analysis of Cathy Hainer's news columns about her breast cancer experience concluded that "health narratives are necessarily embodied rhetoric—powerful, persuasive, deeply personal yet inherently social," theorizing that people make choices about how they talk about their illness "in the relational context of what others might think or how they want to construct individual or relational identities in light of such others" (p. 79).

By grounding theory about illness in the experience of those who are ill, interpretive perspectives generate new understanding of social problems. McGrath (2005), a researcher from an Australian school of nursing, sought to "deepen our understanding of how individuals construct their spirituality in the face of life-threatening illness" (p. 217). She found that the nonreligious lack a shared language to describe illness but also determined that shared experiences could form the basis for such language. This study is noteworthy because this absence would be difficult to measure using postpositivist research methods. Critical perspectives challenge elite definitions of social problems, allowing marginalized groups to define their experience, such as the unique problems of sick people who face economic barriers to care (Gillespie, 2001).

Medical Interactions

Research into the everyday experience of medical care and provider–patient communication illustrates how participants accomplish issues of illness, identity, and compliance through interaction. Also, interpretive/critical research often broadens our theorizing by including less powerful participants in the medical process. Interpretive and critical work addresses effectiveness, but, because it does not privilege provider perspectives, it also introduces other concerns, such as whose agenda prevails in interaction (Sharf & Freimuth, 1993), how provider communication is interpreted (Dillard, Carson, Bernard, Laxova, & Farrell, 2004; Hines, Babrow, Badzek, & Moss, 1997), or how technological discourse influences decision making (Keränen, 2007).

Sharf (1990) paved the way for approaching the interpersonal dialogue between a doctor and a patient as a rhetorical situation in which each participant has a rhetorical agenda. Subsequent work has used narrative (Eggly, 2002; Ellingson & Buzzanell, 1999; Greenhalgh & Hurwitz, 1998; Sharf & Vanderford,

2003) and dialogic lenses (Ellingson & Buzzanell, 1999; Geist & Dreyer, 1993) to investigate the complexities of interaction and the possibility of more open and mutual agenda formations. This research may revise dominant models of medical communication; for example, narrative-based medicine could transform palliative care by focusing on the situational, emotional, cultural, and moral needs of patients (Ragan, Mindt, & Wittenberg-Lyles, 2005). Likewise, physician communication about end-of-life decisions among the elderly would be improved using the theory of problematic integration (Hines et al., 1997).

Interpretive perspectives foster attention to actual, everyday communication and interactions among multiple health care workers (Geist & Hardesty, 1992). In a year-long qualitative observation of emergency departments, Eisenberg et al. (2005) found that departments consistently substituted technical rationality for patients' narrative rationalities in ways that contributed to medical mistakes (see also Keränen, 2007). Ellingson (2003) used Goffman's theory of dramaturgy to research the "backstage" teamwork of an interdisciplinary geriatric oncology team at a cancer center (see also Ellingson, 2005). She concluded that studies of interdisciplinary health teams fail to account for informal interaction by focusing on formal meetings (thereby privileging public, "masculine" forms of communication). Backstage communication about patients can influence caregiver perceptions of patients before they meet them in both positive and negative ways.

In sum, interpretive perspectives focus on communication in everyday life, thereby providing rich accounts of health communication processes as people constitute and interpret the meaning of health and illness and negotiate medical care from interpersonal to organizational settings. These studies capture moments of ongoing interactions and, as such, they are not generalizeable or predictive in any simple fashion. Yet, these studies add complexity to our understanding of health behaviors, including the role of culture, values, and emotion, and they offer a counter-balance to the individualizing tendencies of post-positivist research. We should strengthen connections across these works to build systematic theorizing about the implications of meaning construction in health interactions.

Understanding the Mediated Construction of Health Meanings

Interpretive/critical research attends to the manner in which *discourse* is constitutive of personal, social, political, and economic influences (and, in this case, health and illness). In part, discourse includes intra- and interpersonal dialogue but, in this section, we refer to the messages and meanings produced for "the masses" that mediate understandings. Interpretive/critical scholars pursue the ways in which media representations produce and reproduce social knowledge (Hall, Hobson, Lowe, & Willis, 1980; Seale, 2004b). Notably, such scholars assume that media producers frame social (health) "problems" and "solutions" in such a way as to privilege certain interests while deflecting attention from other (marginalized) interests. Interpretive/critical media research presumes that mass media messages influence, maintain, perpetuate—indeed, constitute—knowledge and values (Kline, 2003). Understanding this production of knowledge requires close interrogation of the implied meanings in all forms of mass media.

Like most interpretive/critical research, media research is frequently interdisciplinary, combining rhetorical, semiotic (Knuf & Caughlin, 1993), linguistic, media theory and method, the rhetoric of science, medical anthropology, sociology, and historiography. In health communication, the preponderance of interpretive/critical media research is textual analytic (for reviews, see Kline, 2003, 2006). In contrast to quantitative content analysis (esp. Signorielli, 1990)[3] which attends more to manifest meaning in mediated texts, interpretive/critical textual analysis delves into latent meanings, centering "attention upon the rhetorical devices and linguistic structure, the 'style' as well as the subject matter of verbal communications, and the manner in which ideology is reproduced in them" (Lupton, 1992, p. 145). Juanne Clarke's (1999) textual analysis of mediated representations of prostate cancer distinguished between manifest and latent content, assessing the manifest messages by gauging the number of messages that referred to early detection, cancer incidence, or treatment. Analysis of latent content, though, revealed a "gender wars" theme wherein the discourse expressed not just the need for more funding but frustration that breast cancer received so much attention (p. 67)—an insight that could have been missed in the initial assessment.

Interpretive/critical textual analysis attempts to identify thematic consistency in rhetorical choices and then consider possible implications (though not necessarily actual effects) given relevant information about the audience and/or social context of the rhetorical act. For instance, pointing out that popular media acts as an "unobtrusive source of health information for vast numbers of people" (p. 141), Sharf and Freimuth (1993) analyzed the ongoing storyline in the television show *thirtysomething* wherein a major character suffers from ovarian cancer to "construct [their] own reading of this text in the context of contemporary biomedical and cultural information regarding ovarian cancer" (p. 145). The authors described how the representations addressed various issues of information-seeking choices, self-image, sexuality, relationships with family and friends, relationships with doctors, and spirituality, and they noted missed opportunities for presenting additional information and perspectives that might be useful to a diverse audience. In other words, media researchers may make their case with regard to their interpretations of a text by citing evidence that media messages have, indeed, had an effect on social policies and individual experiences, but the primary research question focuses on how certain textual messages *invite* audience members to make meanings from a text. In the next section, we describe micro-analytic and macro-analytic studies of popular media (entertainment, journalistic, advertising) texts and then discuss the emerging use of textual analytic methods to assess and revise health promotion texts.

Micro Analyses of Popular Media

Much of the interpretive/critical health media research addresses the micro-meaning of discourse in that it "emphasizes specific textual (spoken, written, visual or multimodel) practices and regularly isolates extracts of text for in-depth analysis" (Gwyn, 2002, p. 26). That is, scholars attend to a specific health topic as represented in specific (set of) media representations. For instance, Lupton detailed the ways in which such health issues as HIV/AIDS (1998, 1999), cholesterol (1994b), and condom use (1994a) are socially constructed in Australian newspapers. Notably, her discursive approach allowed her to focus on different aspects of the representations even as she analyzed the same topic/set of texts. In one study, Lupton (1998) discussed topical themes and found that the media generally portrayed HIV/AIDS as a biomedical, rather than public health problem, that affected gay men, as opposed to the general population. She suggested that, as a consequence of these issue frames, the press became less interested in the topic of HIV/AIDS (with concomitant implications for general attitudes toward the syndrome as well as public policy and funding decisions). In another analysis of the same news articles, Lupton (1999) identified three dominant archetypes used in reports of individuals with HIV/AIDS—the victim, survivor, and carrier. Her discussion of implications focused on what these representations revealed about "more general moral notions regarding the body, medicine, health and illness" (p. 41). Theoretically, each of these studies provides a contextualized understanding of how mediated messages create or reinforce knowledge about health issues and their potential influences on how individuals might think and act with regard to those issues.

Macro Analyses of Popular Media

Though investigations of "specific 'discursive' practices cannot fail to throw light on the wider cultural practices in which they are embedded" (Gwyn, 2002, p. 30), we also found interpretive/critical research that has more directly addressed the implications of mediated texts for broader discourses or macro meanings—that is, according to Gwyn, "entire modes of representation in culture" (p. 26). In his book, *Media & Health*, Clive Seale (2004b) concentrated on how the aggregate representations cohere in an overarching social narrative. He reviewed extant health media research and identified a meta-narrative in health media that emphasizes risks to the audiences, perpetuates the notions of villains and freaks (i.e., stigma), innocent victims (i.e., children), professional and ordinary heroes, and implicates gender in almost all aspects of the story. Thus, Seale demonstrated how mediated texts contribute to a broader social discourse of health, illness, and medicine.

Macro-level interpretive/critical research also recognizes the intertextuality of mediated communication (Ott & Walter, 2000), investigating its links with intra- and interpersonal, group, and organizational communication in the social/ discursive construction of a health issue. Vanderford and Smith's (1996) book on the silicone breast implant controversy cogently illustrated the complex and dynamic communicative forces that impinge on health-related sense making and uncertainty. In chapters that employed a variety of methodologies, they described the experiences of women who were satisfied and unsatisfied with silicone breast implants, conflicting and conflicted personal stories of physicians, mass-mediated representations and public perceptions of the issue, organizational discourse in the form of press releases issued by Dow Corning, and even their own narrative of pursuing the project. Thus, macro-level interpretive/ critical approaches to mass-mediated messages generally share an interest in the confluence of medium production values, hegemonic ideologies, and material influences that impinge on representational choices, as well as the audience power to negotiate understandings of the mediated messages, that combine for possible particular constructions and (mis)understandings of discursive acts (see also Baglia, 2005; Elwood, 1999; Gwyn, 2002; Scott, 2003).

Reformative Analysis of Health Promotion Campaign Messages

While most interpretive/critical health media research prioritizes the mediated production of social knowledge, some health communication researchers seek to explicitly identify, and then remedy, weaknesses in persuasive arguments. At the core, such researchers maintain that health promotion specialists must understand cognitive and behavioral variables that impinge on how individuals process health messages, but we must also attend to how health promotion specialists use audience-analytic findings to craft health information and promotion messages. Perloff and Ray (1991) content-analyzed HIV/AIDS educational literature directed at IV drug users and their partners and concluded that messages focused on risk and prevention but failed to address issues of self-efficacy. Likewise, Kline and Mattson (2000) noted the lack of self-efficacy messages in breast cancer early detection pamphlets. More recently, Kline (2007) used qualitative methods to assess the cultural sensitivity of breast cancer education materials designed for African American women. Using the PEN-3 model of cultural sensitivity as a theoretical framework to assess whether audience specific breast cancer education pamphlets incorporate messages and message framing that reflected a profound understanding of African American cultural values, she found that the pamphlets could be made more culturally sensitive in a number of ways.

Whereas many of the theories and models that ensue from cognitive/ behavioral approaches often position mass media messages as an intervening variable in decision-making, interpretive/critical approaches treat mass media as phenomena worthy of extended analysis in its own right (Kline, 2003).

In doing so, this research also adds to the broader project of interpretive/ critical research by deconstructing taken-for-granted assumptions reflected and constituted in mass-mediated representations of health, illness, and medicine. Thus, it expands and explicates the role of mass-mediated messages in fostering and/or inhibiting social knowledge about health and often seeks to redress problematic constructions. Much of this research engages extant mass media theories in the study of health communication, though it could do so more explicitly. Hazelton's (1997) study of Australian news reporting of mental health referred to the "media's capacity…to construct preferred reading positions through the use of particular discourses and genres" (p. 76). Reference to the idea of a preferred reading invokes a whole host of theorizing about audience meaning-making and pleasure (Hall, 1997); however, like many other media scholars, Hazelton's goal was not so much to extend this theory but to identify the preferred reading suggested by the representations. Overall, though, this review suggests that interpretive/critical mass media research responds to the call for theory-driven, complex views of health communication that are socially relevant and potentially useful to practitioners.

Understanding the Ideological Implications of Health Discourse for Identity and Social Power

Interpretive scholarship has prompted a turn from reductionist understandings of health and illness and highlighted the social production of knowledge. This work has stimulated attention to the role of ideology as shared sets of social beliefs, and critical perspectives have begun to investigate its role in shaping identity and the social relations of power that influence health and illness. We now describe work that connects ideology to identity construction and relationships of domination and resistance.

Constructing Identity

Interpretive/critical perspectives have brought attention to the ways that health discourses construct, reinforce, or resist social identities. Interpretive research views the self as dynamically constructed and identity as an ongoing communicative process rather than a fixed category or a variable that influences message "reception," an important revision of post-positivist assumptions (see related review by N. Young, 2007). We described identity issues in illness and disability research above; in this section, we discuss the politics of identity construction in health discourse.

Critical work draws attention to strategic and unintended identity construction in health social marketing campaigns and biomedical discourse. Lupton (1995) argued that campaigns typically represent the public as apathetic and in need of shocks and "stern warnings" (p. 115), such as AIDS campaigns that use fear appeals based around a discourse of punishment for sexual sins and denial of pleasure. According to Lupton, campaigns draw on body image concerns, so, for example, overweight bodies are depicted as disgusting and out of control. Her textual analysis built the theoretical argument that the consumerist tenets of social marketing fail to apply to the ascetic and top-down approach of most illness prevention campaigns. Critical work in biomedical discourse similarly addresses embodiment as it describes relationships between diagnosis and identity. Nadesan's (2005) genealogy of autism examined how multiple historical and contemporary discourses (psychiatric, psychological, and biogenetic) have constituted autism as a diagnosable "disorder" and delimited therapeutic authorities and protocols. She described the implications for the autistic self, when diagnosis can both produce stigma but also reduce "responsibility" for behavior "problems" and investigated how high functioning autistics such as those with Asperger's inhabit, alter, and resist ascribed identities. Nadesan identified a theoretical challenge for the field in finding ways to address relationships among materiality/biology, culture, and identity, without reifying these complex concepts.

Health and biomedical discourse also reflects and reinforces social stereotypes about marginalized social groups. Paula Treichler (1987, 1999) illustrated how stereotypes of gay identity deeply influenced both public and biomedical discourse about the emerging AIDS epidemic and which then contributed greatly to the stigma associated with both homosexuality and HIV/AIDS.

Influencing Social Power Relations

Treichler's (1987) study makes clear that issues of identity and marginalization are intimately connected to the constitution and perpetuation of social power differentials. Critical/interpretive scholars have begun to address relationships among health discourse, power, and economic, gender, and racial hierarchies.

Critical perspectives that investigate ideology and identity in health promotion initiatives have described the social and economic interests that they privilege. In an early articulation, McKnight (1988) argued that lifestyle campaign messages themselves actually may be "unhealthy" for those who need political power to change their social circumstances. He asked, "Could it be that for those in greatest need, their health does not depend upon receiving messages? Could it be that their health depends upon controlling the microphone?" (p. 43). Follow-up has been somewhat slow but is emerging. Zoller (2003b) described how the seemingly value-neutral health promotion program at a workplace fitness center established norms for the body and employee identity that reinforced managerial values of hard work, self-denial, and self-control. These identity constructions actually promoted employee consent to occupational health hazards. More broadly, critical approaches demonstrate how the individualistic and scientific ideologies of the "new public health," with its emphasis on self-care, directly contradict the stated goals of redressing inequality and promoting democratic participation (A. Peterson & Lupton, 2000).

In terms of medical hegemony, a wealth of interdisciplinary research describes the power of physicians, managed-care representatives, and pharmaceutical interests. Payer (1992) described how promotional discourses contribute to medical power and profits as they promote (over)treatment and (unnecessary) testing by "making you feel sick." Waitzkin (1991) detailed bias in physicians' talk with patients through critical analysis of actual transcripts of medical visits, finding that physicians reinforce dominant gender and class assumptions. Scholars exhibit growing interest in issues of communication, power, and economics in health care, including the ability to influence medical decision making and diagnosis, health policy, and prescription drug usage (Conrad & McIntush, 2003; Geist & Hardesty, 1992; Lammers & Geist, 1997; Stokes, 2005).

Feminist and cultural researchers have made great strides in specifying the roles of gender, sexuality, and ethnicity in organizing social power differentiation in the domain of health and communication. Though feminist research addresses multiple forms of oppression (K. A. Foss, S. K. Foss, & Griffin, 1999), it concentrates on how health discourses both reflect and construct gender roles (and are, therefore, both gender*ed* and gender*ing*). Feminist researchers have contributed to health communication by systematically focusing on health issues unique to women, including fertility, pregnancy and childbirth (Davis-Floyd, 1992; Treichler, 1990); cervical (Posner, 1991), ovarian (Sharf et al., 1996), uterine and breast health (Ellingson & Buzzanell, 1999; Kline, 2003) and menstruation and menopause (Gannon & Stevens, 1998). This work corrects the assumption that women's health can be understood through research based primarily on men's bodies and health experiences (Tavris, 1992) and challenges a history of women's marginalization in the biomedical sciences.

Theoretically, interpretive/critical scholars have shown how medical hegemony in Western cultures reflects and reinforces gender and racial hierarchies. As Barbara Ehrenreich and Deirdre English (1978) convincingly detailed, in Western societies, the socialization of women has been intimately tied to the hegemonic status of the medical institution and vice versa (see also Corea, 1985; Daly, 1990; Davis-Floyd, 1992; Dreifus, 1977; Hubbard, 1990; Jacobus, Keller, & Shuttleworth, 1990; Oakley, 1984; Ratcliff, 2002; Rothman, 1989; Vanderford & Smith, 1996). Thus, interpretive/critical research on women's health has elaborated broader theories of professionalization (legitimation of authority and medical hegemony) (Ehrenreich & English, 1978), the technological imperative of medical practices (Harter & Japp, 2001; Pineau, 2000), and the pathologizing and medicalization of normal body processes (Crawford, 1980; Zola, 1972).

Health discourses both reflect and construct gender roles. For instance, Lantz and Booth (1998) critiqued the mass media for suggesting that "it is those women who are behaving less traditionally (e.g., those who are delaying childbearing or not having children, those who control their fertility with birth control pills, those women who drink alcohol, etc.) who are experiencing an increased risk of breast cancer" (p. 916) and are, therefore, to blame for the breast cancer epidemic. Arrington (2005) described how men's post-prostate cancer stories illustrated changes in their family roles, communication, and relationships. Interestingly, research about men's health often discusses how men's social roles are socially constructed in dialectal tension with the social construction of women's roles (Courtenay, 2000; Coyle & Morgan-Sykes, 1998; Lyons & Willott, 1999). For instance, myths of paternity have absolved men of responsibility for lifestyle choices that might cause fetal harm in contrast to cultural myths of maternity that blame women for fetal harm (Daniels & Parrott, 1996).

With increasing attention to queer theory in the broader discipline of communication (Yep, Lovaas, et al., 2003), we also note at least some research concerned with the health experiences of, if not the full range of "queer" individuals, at least gay men and lesbians (see also Harcourt, 2006; Northridge, 2001). Much of this research refers to gay men and HIV/AIDS (noted throughout this chapter, but also G. Brown & Maycock, 2005; De Moor, 2005; Farrell, 2006; Stone, 1999); however, some researchers have explored lesbian health care experiences (Chao, 2000; Feinberg, 2001; Stevens & Hall, 2002). Research related to sexuality often comments on how relevant discourses reinscribe heteronormative values (Braun, 2005) in ways that reinforce the stigma and "deviance" associated with gay, bisexual, transsexual (or queer[4]) identities. In sum, interpretive/critical research investigates the interrelationships of power and gender construction, contrasting with approaches that treat gender as a variable, which tend to focus on measuring (relatively stable) differences (Mumby, 1996).

A growing body of research also addresses how health-related ideologies reinforce racially and ethnically based health disparities, nationally and transnationally. For instance, cultural research situates marginalization and stigmatization of illnesses, such as AIDS, within existing power relations and a nexus of racial, national, sexual, and religious hierarchies (Petros, Airhihenbuwa, Simbayi, Ramlagan, & Brown, 2006). This research addresses the communicative processes that construct and maintain hegemony. A study by J. L. Johnson et al. (2004) of the experience of discriminatory medical treatment by South Asian immigrant women articulated *how* othering (as a communicative practice of constructing identities in opposition and magnifying differences) takes places in medical interactions through the use of essentialist, culturalist, and racialized medical explanations. Research describes how othering processes in health care further contribute to health disparities, such as the historical and sociopolitical issues that lead to African American distrust toward the biomedical community (Gamble, 1997; Harter, Stephens, & Japp, 2000). The culture-centered perspective explicitly links cultural constructions with structures of power. For instance, top-down health messages in a radio program in Nepal fail to respect cultural beliefs and reinscribe colonialist assumptions, suggesting that family size should be determined by one's income (Dutta & Basnyat, in press).

Extant interpretive/critical work has challenged the basic theoretical orientation of health communication by moving from a representational view of communication as instrumental in achieving effectiveness to a constitutive view that envisions health, identities, and power relations as mutually constructed (for discussion, see Ford & Yep, 2003). This research addresses linkages between health experiences and social and economic power structures. Feminist and cultural research seeks understanding of unique social standpoints that elucidate multiple and overlapping forms of hegemony. Continued research should guard against essentialism, such as equating gender with (women's) sexual health or treating cultural groups as homogenous. This emerging body of work on identity and social power, which expands the goals of health communication research to include exposing and subverting systems of domination, merits further development. Much of this research also sheds light on the biases of the discipline as well, which we detail in the following section.

Deconstructing Biases in Dominant Approaches to Health Communication

Along with the recognition that health discourses are not politically neutral for individuals came attention to our own academic commitments and the ways that they are influenced by hegemonic power arrangements. Interpretive/critical research has promoted reflexivity regarding our own assumptions about health education and promotion. Interdisciplinary scholars like Lupton (1994c, 1995), Payer (1996), Gwyn (2002), Seale (2004b), and Airhihenbuwa and Obregon (2000) have investigated biases in health communication practices, including our own scholarly endeavors. Interpretive/critical researchers increasingly recognize and alter biases toward ideologies of objectivity and uncertainty, individualism and victim blaming, Western culture, and elite definitions of effectiveness.

Biased Methodological Assumptions

Interpretive/critical research deconstructs the values hidden in the "objective" voice of both medical and social sciences. One of the earliest works in the field to address health-related themes rhetorically, Martha Solomon (1985) conducted a Burkean analysis of medical reports in the Tuskegee Syphilis project to demonstrate the ideology of what is assumed to be objective medical reporting. The analysis showed how the very language of objectivity exposes a value that encourages the dehumanization of medical subjects, and how the goals of science can be driven by racist assumptions that contribute to human suffering. She illustrated the connection between medical communication and its influence on actions (inactions) among health professionals and the larger public. This work implicates the presumption in our own research that medical decision-making comprises a neutral and scientific process that should be aided by better (clearer) communication. It also challenges the idea that objectivity constitutes either a possible or significant goal for communication researchers.

Additionally, as Babrow and Kline (2000) asserted, dominant views of objectivity and scientific medical knowledge have encouraged an "ideology of uncertainty reduction" in health communication (p. 1806). Babrow and Kline explained that "the ideology of uncertainty reduction is also attractive for its compatibility with the hoary biomedical or mechanistic paradigm" so that, "ultimately, the biomedical-mechanistic paradigm fosters the idea that uncertainty can—and should—be reduced and eradicated" (p. 1806). They used the mass mediated discourse of breast self-examination as an exemplar of the cultural construction of the ideology of uncertainty reduction and elaborate on the often problematic implications of these differences for health understandings. A study by Eisenberg et al. (2005) of emergency rooms supports this point, as the authors argued for the need for medical practitioners and scholars to better understand uncertainty in emergency medicine because it is central to this type of work. Thus, interpretive/critical research challenges views of communication borne of information theories that equate communication with objectivity and the reduction of uncertainty and encourages attention to the complexities of communicating in the face of multiple uncertainties.

Biased Approaches to Health and Illness

Research also underscores the bias toward individualistic definitions of health and illness and the failure of these definitions to account for the socio-political and even biological determinants of health (Crawford, 1977, 1980). Interpretive/ critical communication researchers have challenged the ideology of victim blaming inherent in many dominant behavioral models of health promotion theory and practice. Kirkwood and Brown (1995) used rhetorical analysis to theorize about the latent messages of victim-blaming in disease prevention discourse perceived by already-diagnosed publics. Messages that focus on individual efforts to prevent disease contribute to assumptions that illness is an individual's fault. Zoller (2003a) found support for this claim as she noted that auto workers interpreted the lifestyle messages in their workplace health promotion program in ways that promoted blaming injured workers rather than changing workplace-generated sources of ill health, including stress, injury, and toxic exposure.

Kline's (1999) analysis of newspaper and magazine representations revealed that women were blamed for not "doing their part to reduce high breast cancer mortality statistics" and that they "established the locus of all reasons for refraining from the activity with the woman, and chastised these women for failing to engage in the activity" (p. 135). As this research deconstructs the problems of individualistic, lifestyle discourses of public health and medicine, it clearly problematizes many of the dominant models of health promotion and medical interaction in the field of health communication itself. The Health Belief Model and the Theory of Reasoned Action, for example, focus on motivating individual behavior change, and they remain largely silent about addressing the socio-economic barriers that audiences may face in complying with such messages (Ashing-Giwa, 1999).

Biased Theories of Culture

Cultural research plays an important role in deconstructing both the presumption of objectivity and the focus on individualism. To begin, cultural research has indicated how apparently generalizable health promotion theories are culturally biased toward the U.S. middle-class context in which they are created. Dutta-Bergman (2005) used culture-centered and structural-centered approaches to critique dominant theories of health promotion for their individual, cognitive orientation. Dutta-Bergman illustrated how these theories overlook the role of the community in more collectivist cultures, the role of local meaning and customs, and material barriers to health. Airhihenbuwa and Obregon (2000) criticized the tendency to conflate "barrier" with "culture" when applying health promotion in contexts for which they were not created (p. 10). Kline's (2007) qualitative textual analysis of breast cancer education pamphlets designed for African American women revealed that pamphlets utilized rhetorical strategies that were consistent with dominant Western rationales. She argued that these rhetorical strategies undermined cultural sensitivity since they emphasized personal responsibility and empowerment contrary to African American spiritual and religious beliefs. Even research on interpersonal issues such as social support often stresses and assumes the communicative norms of European Americans. Addressing this gap, Yep, Reece, and Negron (2003) found that members in an AIDS support group for Asian Americans endorsed alternative treatments, paid greater attention to the "face needs" of members by avoiding conflict, and dealt with culturally based biases against homosexuality and HIV.

Critical-interpretive research facilitates a wider range of voices in health communication, deconstructing cultural biases and broadening the theoretical reach of the field to address those outside of dominant white, European groups, such as Asians, African Americans, Hispanic/Latino, and Native Americans (Airhihenbuwa, 1995; Aull & Lewis, 2004; Casas, Wagenheim, Banchero, & Menoza-Romero, 1994; J. L. Johnson et al., 2004; Lynch & Dubriwny, 2006; McLean, 1997; Vargas, 2000; Whaley, 1999; Yep, Reece, et al., 2003). The critique of cultural bias in many of these works calls us to go beyond "cultural sensitivity" responses because such approaches may promote static and stereotypical views of individuals and social groups. They may do so by failing to theorize culture as a network of meanings tied to sociopolitical processes and by ignoring individual variation within groups (Dutta, 2007; J. L. Johnson et al., 2004). Owing to its in-depth engagement with cultural members, interpretive/critical research adds complexity to our understanding of cultural beliefs. This nuanced approach is evident in the Yep, Reese, et al. study described above, where they stated at the outset that the support group was marked by heterogeneity (multiple differences), hybridity (negotiation of dominant and traditional culture), and multiplicity (influenced by multiple power relationships).

Biased Definitions of Effectiveness

The concept of *effectiveness* in health communication often refers to gaining compliance with campaign or health provider messages (Witte, 1994). Commonly, communication strategies focus on promoting health by crafting interpersonal or mediated interventions that motivate individuals to engage in health-protective behaviors (see Cline, 2003; Salmon & Atkin, 2003). However, as Cline observed, the preceding critiques from interpretive/critical studies encourage us to significantly alter definitions of effectiveness by grounding practice-related research goals in the experiences and needs of those involved. For instance, Ellingson and Buzzanell (1999) examined women's narratives of breast cancer treatment to understand how these women defined and experienced satisfaction with physician communication. They contrasted these views with traditional communication satisfaction research, noting that these women's views of effectiveness included dialogic relationships and preferences for feminine communication styles.

In terms of campaign research, post-positivistic research tends to measure effectiveness in terms of behavior or attitudinal change, such as altered nutritional or sexual habits (Dutta-Bergman, 2005). Researchers have used grounded inquiry to investigate how different groups define effectiveness based on their own cultural and material circumstances (Cline, 2003). Critical scholars, in particular, recognize that interventions and effectiveness should be evaluated in part on their potential for facilitating agency among research participants themselves (Dutta-Bergman, 2004; Melkote, Muppidi, & Goswami, 2000) and emancipatory social change (McKnight, 1988; Zoller, 2005a). More work remains to be done in addressing biases in others' practices and our own. As Airhihenbuwa and Ludwig (1997) noted, even critical work in the tradition of Freire that promotes critical consciousness often focuses on the consciousness of the targeted rather than the interventionist.

Developing Context-sensitive Models of Health Promotion Communication

We have shared how interpretive/critical research has contributed to the deconstruction of biases in our presumptions and models. To move toward praxis, we describe how some interpretive/critical scholars have begun to develop context-sensitive models of health promotion. Many of these alternative theories have arisen from scholars who address the role of health in the global south among marginalized groups and critique the lingering colonialist assumption of many Western campaigns. Other context-based research promotes participatory methodology for creating campaigns with marginalized groups, where the gaps between top-down approaches and local needs also are quite evident.

Culture-centered Models

Concerned that most health promotion programs are guided by the "Western so-called scientific culture" (p. 27), and based on his research in South Africa, Airhihenbuwa (1995) developed the PEN-3 model of communication to "offer a space within which cultural codes and meanings can be centralized in the development, implementation, and evaluation of health promotion programs" (p. 28). The model accounts for cultural identity, relationships, and expectations, and it conceives of cultural empowerment as a key health intervention objective. The model also emphasizes the need to consider cultural motivations and reward "positive" behaviors rather than focusing on "negative" (individualized) behaviors or benign behaviors indigenous to the group that some blame for failure to adopt recommendations (see also Airhihenbuwa & Obregon, 2000; Airhihenbuwa & Webster, 2004).

Dutta-Bergman (2004) articulated the culture-centered approach to health communication. The culture-centered approach treats culture as dynamically constitutive of health meanings, "with an emphasis on speaking from the margins, on building epistemologies from the margins, and on creating alternative discursive spaces for the conceptualization of health" (p. 1108). The perspective foregrounds agency by "acknowledging marginalized people's capacity to determine their own life course, model their own behaviors, and develop epistemologies based on self-understanding" (p. 1108). Clearly, this model radically reconceptualizes the role of the researcher in health campaigns, from creating messages to providing spaces for marginalized groups to articulate their own needs and formulate solutions (Dutta, 2007). The model differs sharply from the traditional, top-down approach of health campaign scholars.

Participatory Methodologies

A growing number of interpretive and critical studies have begun to adopt participatory research methods to improve the appropriateness and effectiveness of campaigns and health delivery and to promote more democratic models of health interventions (Harter et al., 2007; Melkote et al., 2000). Community organizers on the Warm Springs Indian Reservation chose health projects based on the needs of residents as articulated during dialogue and trust-building sessions (McLean, 1997). Even the increasing use of focus groups demonstrates the growing awareness of the importance of understanding how audiences define problems and interpret promotional messages; for example, Bull, Cohen, Ortiz, and Evans (2002) engaged focus groups to develop a targeted media campaign to promote condom use among women. Scholars have also employed narratives as a participatory intervention. Workman (2001) gathered narratives from fraternity members about drinking alcohol and then distributed these local narratives on campus to change social norms and challenge dominant perceptions about binge-drinking.

Interpretive/critical research has helped to demonstrate the need for health promotion methodologies that involve dialogue and practical engagement with health campaign audiences in the formation of both the goals and methods of interventions, and it has promoted alternative, context-sensitive models. We look to the growth of rigorous assessment across studies with the growth of these methods.

Investigating Health Policymaking as a Communicative Process

Interpretive/critical research also expands the potential for health communication intervention by linking health discourse to health policymaking processes. In the early years, health communication scholars generally did not address policy as an element of health communication. Sharf (1999) discussed the absence of policy research as one of the most important oversights in the field, given its influence on public health. Though policy is by no means the sole province of interpretive/critical perspectives, these paradigms bring insight to the interpretation and influence of existing policies as well as the negotiation of new ones. Work addresses agenda setting, elite policy processes, and the experience of health policy.

Agenda Setting

A central concern among critical scholars involves understanding the ability of different groups to set public agendas and to frame debates. Interpretive and critical research examines how stakeholders frame issues as groups compete to define concerns as social problems as a way to advance particular responses and solutions. In doing so, it questions taken-for-granted assumptions about social participation in political debates, emphasizing meaning formation as well as expression.

Rhetorical analyses such as Perez and Dionisopoulos' (1995) study of the Surgeon General's report on AIDS illustrate the role of policy reports in setting public agendas such as Reagan's rhetorical management of the AIDS crisis. Dejong and Wallack (1999) criticized the discourse of the U.S. anti-drug media campaign for promoting simplistic messages against drug use in the face of its failure to promote drug treatment. Zoller (2005b) used feminist analysis to examine how the language of the U.S. Public Health Service's *Healthy People 2000*, despite explicit attention to health disparity, guides public health policies in ways that may reinforce inequities among women (particularly minorities) by failing to prioritize their social and material circumstances in its "multi-causal web" approach to health (p. 179). These analyses demonstrate that policies hinge on rhetoric about health that always involves value-laden theories of disease causation and prioritization, which the public may presume are scientific rather than political decisions.

Law-making Processes

Conrad and McIntush (2003) provided a number of theories for understanding health care policy making as a process marked by complex interactions among rhetoric, ideology, and structure. They noted that functionalist presumptions of rationality and equitable participation in policymaking are problematic from a communication perspective. Their chapter illustrates the interdisciplinary nature of health policy research by drawing from organizational theories including "garbage can" approaches to decision-making, mobilization, and community-power debates. Conrad and Jodlowski (2008) also articulated the role of rhetoric in elites' ability to outflank the public in policymaking, using de Certeau's (1984) and Mann's (1986) theories of strategic action and outflanking/counteroutflanking. At the micro-level of interaction, textual analysis of public transcripts of Congressional testimony shows framing devices employed in unfolding communication during policy debates over nicotine (Murphy, 2001).

Health communication researchers help to demonstrate how health policy discourse is unique from other policy contexts. For instance, Sharf (2001) explained that the powerful influence of personal breast cancer narratives on legislators and other health policy leaders put breast cancer on the agenda, but this kind of funding often occurs at the expense of other health spending. Other unique issues include the privileging of "conservative medical-psychiatric and health bureaucratic solutions to policy 'problems'" (Hazelton, 1997, p. 88), and the promotion of "biofantasies"—mass-mediated stories that play up the medical benefits of genetic research—in deflecting public attention from systemic problems, social conditions, and the environment (A. Peterson, 2001).

Policy and Health Experiences

Critical perspectives, in particular, can address the power-laden contexts of policy making and their influence on the lived experience of different publics. Though not specifically oriented toward health communication, Gillespie's (2001) use of feminist and postmodern lenses to examine "asthma as a symbolic site of struggle over definitions of appropriate health care resource utilization in the wake of Medicaid's move to managed care" (p. 98) illustrated the value of interpretive/critical policy research. She described how the disciplinary practices constituting managed care encourage patient self-care and responsibility. These expectations guiding physician communication about asthma failed to address material, class-based barriers (such as lack of control over living conditions, transportation, etc.) and social barriers (e.g., depression), leading to "non-compliance" classifications. She found that capitation also creates unrealistic bureaucratic barriers for marginalized groups. The project highlights the experience of lower-income patients in managing these policies, providing an important corrective to health communication that, along with the field at large, can be accused of focusing on issues of importance to middle-class audiences. It also redresses the problem of client-provider communication that concentrates on "patients" only while they are in the provider's office.

Growth in policy research is fundamental to the goals of emancipation central to critical research. Notably, eight years after Sharf's (1999) call for more policy research, researchers still need to build advocacy to improve health policies and the communicative processes that produce them.

Highlighting Possibilities of Resistance and Social Change at the Margins

We have discussed the role of interpretive/critical theories in facilitating social change by developing context-sensitive health promotion models and examining policy mechanisms. Additionally, by building theories about the political implications of health discourse, interpretive and critical researchers have begun to create space within the discipline for the study of resistance and social change among marginalized groups. The deconstruction of taken-for-granted assumptions about what counts as health (e.g., bio-medical) and how it should be achieved (e.g., physician compliance and lifestyle directives) creates the possibility of resisting dominant relations of power reinforced by those assumptions and altering social arrangements. Perhaps because of the relative lack of critical perspectives in health communication, much existing research into health-related resistance and social change comes from rhetoric, cultural studies, and other areas of communication. We now describe what health communication research contributes to this body of knowledge through a focus on agency and resistance as well as advocacy and activism.

Agency and Resistance

We have noted that, in contrast to the view of patients and health communication audiences as passive, interpretive/critical researchers have brought attention to their agency, particularly among marginalized groups (Dutta-Bergman, 2004; Geist Martin, Ray, & Sharf, 2003). Understanding resistance comprises a key part of this development. Previous researchers sometimes equated "resistance" with a failure to comply with health directives (see, for example, Brashers, Haas, Klingle, & Neidig, 2000). Interpretive research sheds light on resistance as a means of facilitating autonomy and increased choice-making. For instance, Stivers' (2004) conversation analysis detailed parental resistance (both passive and active) to medical treatment recommendations for children as a normative, integral part of the clinical interaction. Thus, even pediatricians envision treatment conversations as negotiations. Though Stivers described this negotiation as problematic because parents often secure unnecessary antibiotics, interpretive/critical researchers are slowly overcoming the idea that resistance should be understood primarily as an irrational barrier to behavior change (see Sharf, 2005). For example, focus groups suggest that many audiences of direct-to-consumer marketing actively resist race-based pharmagenics, in contrast to popular fears about negative influences of genetic discourse on public opinion (Bates, Lynch, Bevan, & Condit, 2005). Zoller (2004) found that some manufacturing employees actively resisted the health promotion messages from their workplace recreation center by ignoring the advice, avoiding the center, and engaging in the proscribed behaviors. The critical lens conceptualizes these choices not as psychographic barriers but as reactions against authority and the disciplinary tone of health messages; thus, Zoller argued that employers should respond through more responsive, open, and participative promotion initiatives rather than alternate motivational messaging strategies.

Interpretive/critical research also highlights agency by promoting personal empowerment over the management of our health and illness. For instance, Sharf (1997) described how an online breast cancer discussion group empowered women by enhancing decision making and helping women to understand the experiences that they may face. Scholars increasingly examine community empowerment as a form of health promotion (see, for example, Ford & Yep, 2003; Harter, Scott, Novak, Leeman, & Morris, 2006).

Advocacy and Activism

Community empowerment is closely tied to health advocacy and activism. Interpretive/critical research brings particular attention to social change at the margins. Elwood, Dayton, and Richard (1996) observed HIV prevention outreach workers in Houston, Texas in the United States to understand the efficacy of street-level prevention work often focused on harm reduction. Using Burke's theory of identification, they conceptualized identity building as a communicative skill versus a demographic category, thereby facilitating a politically controversial but important health intervention among stigmatized groups.

Despite the key role that activists play in influencing the experience of health and illness, health communication research largely overlooked these often grassroots challenges to existing power relationships in health, focusing instead on the communication needs of established professionals. Interdisciplinary research in sociology and social movements describes how activists have established public health infrastructures, challenged social stigmas associated with illness, advocated for patient roles in scientific research, and agitated for health policies (Zoller, 2005a). In communication, rhetoric and social movement research has helped to redress the lack of attention to activism by investigating health-related social movements such as the HIV/AIDS activism of groups like Act Up! (Christiansen & Hanson, 1996). These studies highlighted the communicative strategies of AIDS activists to reduce stigma associated with the disease, spur research into treatments, and promote accessibility to those treatments (Fabj & Sobnosky, 1995; Sobnosky & Hauser, 1999).

Critical-cultural research has begun to address how activists both work with and resist the scientific community. Wood, Hall, and Hasian (2008) investigated grassroots resistance surrounding the Human Genome Diversity Project (HGDP). Their study highlights activism among subaltern groups aimed at shaping the course of genetic policy. Rhetorical analysis reveals how activists question and seek to revise the HDGP, which is a seemingly straightforward attempt to accrue diverse genetic samples to create a more complete genetic map. These groups embed the discussion of genetic diversity within larger contexts of participation and control in science, racism, colonialism, and Western exploitation. Additionally, environmental communication research investigates environmental health activism, and this area presents a significant opportunity for interdisciplinary collaboration. For instance, some radical counter-public groups resist the individualistic and medical model accompanying National Breast Cancer Awareness Month by highlighting the environmental risks of breast cancer including industrial toxins (Pezzullo, 2003). Local communities and grassroots groups, often organized by women, contest environmental damage out of concern for apparent cancer and birth defect clusters, such as groups in the Texas-Mexico border area concerned with outbreaks of anencephaly (T. R. Peterson, 1997).

Interpretive/critical health communication theories can contribute to interdisciplinary research by describing the political consequences of how activists define health, describe illness causality, attribute responsibility, and depict social identities for social change (Zoller, 2005a). Additional work should address linkages between health communication and the interdisciplinary research focused on globalization and resistance (discussed by Pal & Dutta, this volume), given the influence of these policies on global health status (Zoller & Dutta, 2008) and the field's concerns with global health disparities.

LESSONS LEARNED AND FUTURE DIRECTIONS

One of our primary purposes was to build the case for defining and conceptualizing the theoretical contributions that interpretive/critical research makes on its terms, rather than to compare it against the criteria of replication, generalizability, and prediction. While a number of ways exist to articulate the accomplishments of interpretive/critical research, our review suggests that interpretive/critical research addresses issues of health meanings; adds complexity to our understanding of health, health behaviors and identities; examines persuasion in health discourse from other points of view beside effectiveness; articulates linkages among communication and politics, policy, and social power; deconstructs taken-for-granted assumptions about health and illness and conceptualizing alternatives, and describes direct implications for practice. Given the highly interdisciplinary nature of the health communication research, the kinds of contributions identified in the chapter also apply to other areas of communication where interpretive/critical researchers also investigate meaning construction, build knowledge of communication and everyday experience, theorize the politics of identity construction and their relationship to social power, amplify marginalized voices, and develop systemic approaches to praxis.

Interpretive/critical researchers rely most often on qualitative inquiry but, more importantly, they embrace what can be learned uniquely through qualitative inquiry. For instance, the active participation of scholars in ethnographic inquiry gives us insight into what can be messy, embodied interaction in which body, mind, emotion and spirit interrelate in communicating about health. Rhetorical scholars delve into the latent meanings of public discourses, making sense of rhetorical style, artistry, hidden logics, and sociopolitical context. Critical cultural scholars attend to audience ability to negotiate meaning, positing more complex explanations than the linear or hypodermic models of the past.

We are encouraged by the growth of reflexivity in the reporting of interpretive/critical research. More work acknowledges the role of the authors in selecting what counts as data as well as how it is interpreted and written about. Scholars increasingly embrace the ethical commitments of humanistic research to address the broader political implications of our research.

Having articulated some of the positive contributions of interpretive/critical research, we turn now to some of the challenges that lie ahead. We identify areas for further development, focusing on the need for stronger articulation of the value of interpretive/critical work, greater theoretical range, and more direct engagement with praxis.

Validation

Communication scholarship would benefit from stronger and more consistent framing of the overall contributions of interpretive/critical studies, especially in the area of health communication. Some studies continue to describe interpretive methods as pre-scientific, suggesting that findings must be validated using quantitative measures (though we recognize that these choices could potentially reflect editorial requests). Nonetheless, when authors describe limitations such as smaller samples (thereby reducing generalization) (e.g.,

Clarke, 1999) or a lack of operationalization (thereby reducing replicability), they implicitly apply scientific criteria rather than the assessment criteria appropriate for interpretive/critical research. When Bull et al. (2002) reported their focus groups with women (in which the participants talked about the lived experience of condom use and negotiation to guide the development of condom promotion campaigns), they presented the idea that every campaign may need to do similar audience research as a limitation. The improvement of health campaigns through interpretive audience research could have been heralded as a central finding of the study, rather than a limitation. Dillard et al. (2004) limited the significance of their qualitative analysis of communication surrounding newborn cystic fibrosis screening by describing it as a "descriptive foundation for future research" (p. 195). Some doctor-patient researchers acknowledge the contributions of qualitative research to understanding how communication develops in a contextualized way in interactions and observe need for integration between quantitative and qualitative research (Roter & McNeilis, 2003). However, others continue to frame qualitative research as a hypothesis generator (J. B. Brown et al., 2003).

Theoretical Range

In addition to using validity criteria, interpretive/critical research could more incisively frame theoretical contributions by explicitly tracing the implications of local practices over time and across contexts. Doing so would facilitate broader explanations that account for individual and cultural differentiation and guide practice. As we mentioned in the introduction, this suggestion does not differ substantially from calls for more theory-driven work in post-positivistic research. However, potentially, the use of hypotheses may lead researchers to more closely align their studies with previous scholarship in the area than research with concepts grounded in local contexts. Interpretive researchers need to be vigilant about drawing linkages across individual interpretive/ critical analyses of various topics (e.g., breast cancer, tobacco use, diet, and exercise), contexts (e.g., interpersonal, social support, public discourse), and methodologies (e.g., ethnographic, rhetorical, critical cultural). We might ask, for example, what are the larger issues guiding the theory and application of audience research as a basis for developing campaigns? What do we learn across studies about audience interpretations and enactments of different types of health promotion campaigns? How can we bring research together theoretically to discuss the meaning of health and illness? How do individual studies inform our theories of power and resistance in health? Often, this sort of synthesis happens only in periodic review articles or books such as the *Handbook of Health Communication* (Thompson, Dorsey, Miller, & Parrott, 2003). Some of these results likely emerge in the forms of typologies, models, and schemas, too frequently discounted as theorizing. Yet, adopting contextual research means recognizing a broader array of theoretical advancements than just prediction, and forms of explanation may include arguments, comparisons, and conceptual development.

Interpretive/critical research that analyzes data in terms of emergent "themes" (usually described as grounded or thematic analysis), in particular, must articulate its theoretical import in stronger terms. Beck et al. (2004) detailed publication patterns in health communication—location of publication, topics, and methodologies. According to their assessment, 55% of the articles that reported their methods described using thematic analysis versus 27% using multivariate analysis. We should link individual thematic analyses to larger sociocultural processes of meaning and health communication theorizing. When we examine research into topics such as college drinking stories (Workman, 2001), defenses against anti-smoking messages (DeSantis, 2002), or condom-usage (Bull et al., 2002), we find useful insights into the contextual factors that influence how recipients interpret and respond to health promotion campaigns. They address the barriers to adopting health-promoting behavior, thereby promoting more appropriate and targeted campaigns. The field can investigate such themes for other audiences and contexts, thereby providing a fuller picture of the interpretive processes and contextual (and material) factors that should guide intervention. Grounded research can build theorizing as well as studies that adopt explicit theoretical lenses to the degree that individual studies speak to the larger research dialogue about the issues under discussion.

We also can promote more theory development by drawing from a greater range of existing perspectives and theories. In our review, we observed that narrative theory, the theory of Problematic Integration (Babrow, 1992, 2001), and the culture-centered approach have received a good deal of attention. Yet, for example, significant room remains for development of dialogic perspectives that help to focus on the role of language and the co-construction of meaning in health contexts. Likewise, though we occasionally found references to specific rhetorical theories (e.g., discussion of Burke's "representative anecdote" in Harter & Japp, 2001), the long tradition of rhetorical studies has generated numerous theories that could inform and/or be informed by interpretive/ critical research in health communication. Individual research projects need to articulate explicitly theoretical frameworks rather than merely allude to relevant perspectives and theory (as in the mass media research mentioned above that invoked the concept of preferred reading without overtly discussing the theory). Doing so would facilitate interpretive/critical health communication research contributions to the broader discipline.

The theoretical range of health communication research also would be enhanced by more explicitly critical research, especially in terms of cultural, subaltern, queer, and postmodern theories. This call is quite common across the discipline (German, 1995; Lannaman, 1992; Mumby, 1993). Despite recent research that explores issues of ideology and hegemony, health communication could benefit from continued work that elaborates how the social construction of health and illness relates to issues of power, politics, and resistance—and how those relate to individual and cultural identity. Future research should continue to connect the individual experience of health and illness with larger material and symbolic systems. Such investigations add complexity to our understanding of human agency among patients, clients, media audiences, research participants, and campaign targets. Critical perspectives can shed light on the potential paradoxes of resistance in health contexts given the gulf between personal/embodied and professional knowledge, where nonconformity can produce either better or worse health outcomes. Additionally, attention to other outcomes such as autonomy, voice, participation, and social change would add complexity to understanding of health and resistance.

Interpretive/critical scholars have made great strides in fostering inter-disciplinary connections, especially with sociology, medicine, public health, and nursing. A great deal of cross-pollination among interpretive/critical scholars in sub-disciplines of communication exists as well, including a significant amount of work in organizational and public communication. As this trend continues, we encourage greater collaboration between health communication and some areas with which we have had little dialogue, such as environmental communication and social movements. Working with these areas would broaden our conception of what constitutes health by better linking human health and the natural world and what constitutes health communication practice by investigating activism along with more traditional areas of communication. Moreover, areas of the discipline with strong contributions to health communication (such as technology and interpersonal studies) are rarely investigated using rhetorical analysis or ethnographic methods.

Theory and Praxis

We have described the evolution of interpretive/critical research concerned with the implications of relevant theorizing for the practice of health communication (i.e., praxis as theoretically informed social change). Deetz (2001) argued that the primary role of theorizing should be to enable useful responses. In this vein, as researchers uncover communication conceptions and problems as defined by everyday people (Craig, 2007), they should not only articulate what useful responses would look like (as many do) but investigate the actual processes through which alternative forms of practice can be put into place.

One of the most explicit linkages between interpretive research approaches and health communication practice pertains to the development of participatory models of health promotion and medical interaction. Interpretive/critical research, using multiple methodologies, investigates the potential of such models for practical intervention and for revising the guiding assumptions of some of the existing models of health communication (e.g., the Health Belief Model). Culture-centered research demands reflexivity, so that the voices of the marginalized are not merely co-opted to increase the effectiveness of professionals' existing goals but actually transform our understanding of what constitutes good health communication. The field requires additional investigation of participants' lived experience of participation, fostering a depth of insight into the challenges of including patients, audiences, and communities in substantive decision-making. These challenges are multiplied as we begin to address participatory systems that promote collaboration across economic, gender, ethnic, and national lines.

We also described growing interest in the role of communication in constituting, applying, and challenging health policy, though we noted that much more work remains to be done in this area. Moving forward, the connections between a broad array of research contexts and health policy can be made more explicit. We must give greater attention to changing health policy as an element of health communication practice, along with understanding the implications of these changes for health communication theorizing. Furthermore, reducing health inequities constitutes a key goal for many health communication researchers. Given the massive social change wrought by economic and cultural forms of globalization, investigating the relationships among international trade policy, health status, and social discourses about health is crucial for contemporary health communication.

In closing, we acknowledge that the "disciplinary" work of a chapter like this one comprises an act of construction and interpretation on the part of the authors. Reviews such as this chapter are disciplinary in the sense of drawing and defining disciplinary boundaries, and they may also "discipline" (in the Foucaultian sense, see Foucault, 1979) the field in terms of delimiting what counts as interpretive, cultural, and critical research and, indeed, a "contribution." Yet, we believe that continued dialogue across methodological and metatheoretical approaches about the mutual benefits of our research is necessary to the development of health communication research. Our analysis clearly shows that the flagship journals *Health Communication* and *Journal of Health Communication: International Perspectives* have become good places for such dialogue, given that both include work from across the spectrum of philosophies and methodologies. We hope, then, that readers take this chapter as an invitation for continued conversation about the growth and development of multiple theoretical perspectives in health communication, rather than as a definitive statement on the field.

ACKNOWLEDGMENTS

The authors acknowledge the invaluable assistance of the editor, Christina Beck, and the anonymous reviewers. We also appreciate insights from Shiv Ganesh, Mohan Dutta, and Austin Babrow.

NOTES

1. There has yet to be a broader description and assessment of the contributions of interpretive/critical research to theory and practice in health communication. A number of books (e.g., Elwood, 1999; Gwyn, 2002; Seale, 2004a, 2004b; Tulloch & Lupton, 1997), handbooks and edited volumes (Parrott & Condit, 1996; Thompson et al., 2003), and textbooks (Beck, 2001; duPre, 2000; Geist Martin et al., 2003; Jackson & Duffy, 1998; Kar & Alcalay, 2001) synthesize the studies in various domains of health communication; given their comprehensive examination of specific topics, these texts increasingly reference interpretive/critical analyses (and demonstrate for the attentive reader, the contributions of interpretive/critical research).
2. For instance, focus groups are one means of acquiring data. Many methods textbooks consider this a qualitative research method (e.g., Keyton, 2006), and one might erroneously assume that this positions focus group research within the interpretive/critical paradigm; yet, scholars who gather their data using focus groups can employ either quantitative or qualitative methods of analysis.
3. The methodological boundaries between interpretive/critical and quantitative content analyses often blur in the pursuit of descriptive and explanatory research (Kline, 2003).
4. The concept of "queer" allows us to go beyond simplified notions of homosexuality that, in effect, dichotomize sexuality along the lines of a heteronormative masculine/feminine dichotomy.

REFERENCES

Adelman, M., & Frey, L. (1997). *The fragile community: Living together with AIDS*. Mahwah, NJ: Erlbaum.

Airhihenbuwa, C. O. (1995). *Health and culture: Beyond the western paradigm*. Thousand Oaks, CA: Sage.

Airhihenbuwa, C. O., & Ludwig, M. J. (1997). Remembering Paolo Freire's legacy of hope and possibility as it relates to health education/promotion. *Journal of Health Education, 28*, 317-319.

Airhihenbuwa, C. O., & Obregon, R. (2000). A critical assessment of theories/ models used in health communication for HIV/AIDS. *Journal of Health Communication, 5*, 5-15.

Airhihenbuwa, C. O., & Webster, J. D. (2004). Culture and African contexts of HIV/AIDS prevention, care and support. *Journal of Social Aspects of HIV/AIDS Research Alliance, 1*, 4-13.

Andrews, J. R. (1990). *The practice of rhetorical criticism* (2nd ed.). New York: Longman.

Arrington, M. I. (2005). "She's right behind me all the way": An analysis of prostate cancer narratives and changes in family relationships. *Journal of Family Communication, 5*, 141-162.

Arrington, M. I., & Goodier, B. C. (2004). Prostration before the law: Representations of illness, interaction, and intimacy in the *NYPD Blue* prostate cancer narrative. *Popular Media, 2*, 67-84.

Ashing-Giwa, K. (1999). Health behavior change models and their socio-cultural relevance for breast cancer screening in African American women. *Women & Health, 28*(4), 53-71.

Aull, F., & Lewis, B. (2004). Medical intellectuals: Resisting medical orientalism. *Journal of Medical Humanities, 25*, 87-108.

Babrow, A. S. (1992). Communication and problematic integration: Understanding diverging probability and value, ambiguity, ambivalence, and improbability. *Communication Theory, 2*, 95-130.

Babrow, A. S. (2001). Uncertainty, value, communication, and problematic integration. *Journal of Communication, 51*, 553-573.

Babrow, A. S., Kasch, C. R., & Ford, L. A. (1998). The many meaning of 'uncertainty' in illness: Toward a systematic accounting. *Health Communication, 10*, 1-24.

Babrow, A. S., & Kline, K. (2000). From "reducing" to "coping with" uncertainty: Reconceptualizing the central challenge in breast self-exams. *Social Science and Medicine, 51*, 1805-1816.

Babrow, A. S., & Mattson, M. (2003). Theorizing about health communication. In T. L. Thompson, A. M. Dorsey, K. I. Miller & R. Parrott (Eds.), *Handbook of health communication* (pp. 35-61). Mahwah, NJ: Erlbaum.

Baglia, J. (2005). *The Viagra ad venture: Masculinity, media, and the performance of sexual health*. New York: Peter Lang.

Bakhtin, M. M. (1981). *The dialogic imagination*. Austin: University of Texas Press.

Bakhtin, M. M. (1993). *Toward a philosophy of the act* (V. Liapunov, Trans.). Austin: University of Texas Press.

Bartesaghi, M., & Castor, T. (2008). Social construction and communication: Re-constituting the conversation. In C. S. Beck (Ed.), *Communication yearbook 32* (pp. 3-39). New York: Routledge.

Bates, B. R., Lynch, J. A., Bevan, J. L., & Condit, C. M. (2005). Warranted concerns, warranted outlooks: A focus group study of public understandings of genetic research. *Social Science & Medicine, 60*, 331-344.

Beck, C. S. (2001). *Communicating for better health: A guide through the medical mazes*. Boston: Allyn & Bacon.

Beck, C. S. (2005). Becoming the story: Narratives as collaborative, social enactments of individual, relational, and public identities. In L. M. Harter, P. M. Japp, & C. S. Beck (Eds.), *Narratives, health, and healing: Communication theory, research, and practice* (pp. 61-81). Mahwah, NJ: Erlbaum.

Beck, C. S., Benitez, J. L., Edwards, A., Olson, A., Pai, A., & Torres, M. B. (2004). Enacting "health communication:" The field of health communication as constructed through publication in scholarly journals. *Health Communication, 16*, 475-492.

Bowers, J. W. (1972). The pre-scientific function of rhetorical criticism. In D. Ehninger (Ed.), *Contemporary rhetoric* (pp. 163-173). Glenview, IL: Scott Foresman.

Brashers, D. E., Haas, S. M., Klingle, R. S., & Neidig, J. L. (2000). Collective AIDS activism and individuals' perceived self-advocacy in physician-patient communication. *Human Communication Research, 26*, 372-402.

Braun, V. (2005). In search of (better) sexual pleasure: Female genital 'cosmetic' surgery. *Sexualities, 8*, 407-424.

Brown, G., & Maycock, B. (2005). Different spaces, same faces: Perth gay men's experiences of sexuality, risk and HIV. *Culture, Health & Sexuality, 7*, 59-72.

Brown, J. B., Stewart, M., & Ryan, B. L. (2003). Outcomes of patient-provider interaction. In T. L. Thompson, A. M. Dorsey, K. I. Miller, & R. Parrott (Eds.), *Handbook of health communication* (pp. 141-161). Mahwah, NJ: Erlbaum.

Buber, M. (1958). *I and thou*. New York: Macmillan.

Bull, S. S., Cohen, J., Ortiz, C., & Evans, T. (2002). The POWER campaign for promotion of female and male condoms: Audience research and campaign development. *Health Communication, 14*, 475-491.

Burgoon, M. (1995). *Navigating the treacherous waters of health communication: Dawning of the age of aquarius or the rule of Proteus?* Paper presented at the Speech Communication Association Summer Conference on Communication and Health, Washington, D. C.

Burrell, G., & Morgan, G. (1979). *Sociological paradigms and organisational analysis: Elements of the sociology of corporate life.* London: Heinemann.

Casas, J. M., Wagenheim, B. R., Banchero, R., & Menoza-Romero, J. (1994). Hispanic masculinity: Myth or psychological schema meriting clinical consideration. *Hispanic Journal of Behavioral Sciences, 16*, 315-331.

Chao, A. (2000). Global metaphors and local strategies in the construction of Taiwan's lesbian identities. *Culture, Health, & Sexuality, 2*, 377-390.

Charmaz, K. (2002). Qualitative interviewing and grounded theory analysis. In J. F. Gubrium & J. A. Holstein (Eds.), *Handbook of interview research* (pp. 675-694). London: Sage.

Christiansen, A., & Hanson, J. (1996). Comedy as cure for tragedy: ACT UP! and the rhetoric of AIDS. *Quarterly Journal of Speech, 82*, 157-170.

Cissna, K. N., & Anderson, R. (1994). Communication and the ground of dialogue. In R. Anderson, K. N. Cissna, & R. C. Arnett (Eds.), *The reach of dialogue: Confirmation, voice and community* (pp. 9-30). Creskill, NJ: Hampton.

Clarke, J. N. (1999). Prostate cancer's hegemonic masculinity in select print mass media depictions (1974-1995). *Health Communication, 11*, 59-74.

Cline, R. W. (2003). Everyday interpersonal communication and health. In T. L. Thompson, A. M. Dorsey, K. I. Miller, & R. Parrott (Eds.), *Handbook of health communication* (pp. 285-313). Mahwah, NJ: Erlbaum.

Conrad, C., & Jodlowski, D. (2008). Dealing drugs on the border: Power and policy in pharmaceutical reimportation debates. In H. Zoller & M. Dutta (Eds.), *Emerging perspectives in health communication: Meaning, culture, and power* (pp. 365-389). New York: Routledge.

Conrad, C., & McIntush, H. G. (2003). Organizational rhetoric and healthcare policymaking. In T. L. Thompson, A. M. Dorsey, K. I. Miller, & R. Parrott (Eds.), *Handbook of health communication* (pp. 403-422). Mahwah, NJ: Erlbaum.

Corea, G. (1985). *The hidden malpractice.* New York: Harper Colophon.

Courtenay, W. H. (2000). Engendering health: A social constructionist examination of men's health beliefs and behaviors. *Psychology of Men & Masculinity, 1*, 4-15.

Coyle, A., & Morgan-Sykes, C. (1998). Troubled men and threatening women: The construction of 'crisis' in male mental health. *Feminism & Psychology, 8*, 263-284.

Craig, R. T. (1999). Communication theory as a field. *Communication Theory, 9*, 119-161.

Craig, R. T. (2007). Issue forum introduction: Theorizing communication problems. *Communication Monographs, 74*, 103-105.

Crawford, R. (1977). You are dangerous to your health: The ideology and politics of victim blaming. *International Journal of Health Services, 7*, 663-680.

Crawford, R. (1980). Healthism and the medicalization of everyday life. *International Journal of Health Services, 10*, 365-388.

Crawford, R. (1984). A cultural account of "health": Control, release, and the social body. In J. B. McKinlay (Ed.), *Issues in the political economy of health care* (pp. 60-103). New York: Tavistock Publications.

Daly, M. (1990). *Gyn/ecology, the metaethics of radical feminism: With a new intergalactic introduction*. Boston: Beacon.

Daniels, M. J., & Parrott, R. L. (1996). Prenatal care from the woman's perspective: A thematic analysis of the newspaper media. In R. L. Parrott & C. M. Condit (Eds.), *Evaluating women's health messages: A resource book* (pp. 222-248). Thousand Oaks, CA: Sage.

Davis-Floyd, R. (1992). *Birth as an American rite of passage*. Berkeley: University of California Press.

de Certeau, M. (1984). *The practice of everyday life* (S. Rendall, Trans.). Berkeley: University of California Press.

De Moor, K. (2005). Diseased pariahs and difficult patients. *Cultural Studies, 19*, 737-754.

Deetz, S. A. (1992). *Democracy in an age of corporate colonization*. Albany: State University of New York Press.

Deetz, S. A. (2001). Conceptual foundations. In F. M. Jablin & L. L. Putnam (Eds.), *The new handbook of organizational communication* (pp. 3-47). Thousand Oaks, CA: Sage.

Dejong, W., & Wallack, L. (1999). A critical perspective on the drug czar's antidrug media campaign. *Journal of Health Communication, 4*, 155-160.

DeSantis, A. D. (2002). Smoke screen: An ethnographic study of a cigar shop's collective rationalization. *Health Communication, 14*, 167-198.

Dillard, J. P., Carson, C. L., Bernard, C. J., Laxova, A., & Farrell, P. M. (2004). An analysis of communication following newborn screening for cystic fibrosis. *Health Communication, 16*, 195-205.

Diop, W. (2000). From government policy to community-based communication strategies in Africa: Lessons from Senegal and Uganda. *Journal of Health Communication, 5*, 113-117.

Dow, B. J., & Condit, C. M. (2005). The state of the art in feminist scholarship in communication. *Journal of Communication, 55*, 448-478.

Dreifus, C. (Ed.). (1977). *Seizing our bodies: The politics of women's health*. New York: Vintage Books.

duPre, A. (2000). *Communicating about health: Current issues and perspectives*. London: Mayfield.

Dutta, M. J. (2007). Communicating about culture and health: Theorizing culture-centered and cultural sensitivity approaches. *Communication Theory, 17*, 304-328.

Dutta, M. J. (2008). *Communicating health: A culture-centered perspective*. London: Polity.

Dutta, M. J., & Basnyat, I. (in press). The Radio Communication Project in Nepal: A critical analysis. *Health Education and Behavior*.

Dutta, M. J., & Basu, A. (2007). Health among men in rural Bengal: Exploring meanings through a culture-centered approach. *Qualitative Health Research, 17*, 38-48.

Dutta-Bergman, M. (2004). Poverty, structural barriers, and health: A Santali narrative of health communication. *Qualitative Health Research, 14*, 1107-1123.

Dutta-Bergman, M. (2005). Theory and practice in health communication campaigns: A critical interrogation. *Health Communication, 18*, 103-122.

Eggly, S. (2002). Physician-patient co-construction of illness narratives in medical interview. *Health Communication, 14*, 339-360.

Ehrenreich, B., & English, D. (1978). *For her own good: 150 years of the experts' advice to women*. New York: Anchor Books.

Eisenberg, E., Murphy, A. G., Sutcliffe, K., Wears, R., Schenkel, S., Perry, S., et al. (2005). Communication in emergency medicine: Implications for patient safety. *Communication Monographs, 72*, 390-413.

Ellingson, L. L. (2003). Interdisciplinary health care teamwork in the clinic backstage. *Journal of Applied Communication Research, 31*, 93-117.

Ellingson, L. L. (2005). *Communicating in the clinic: Negotiating frontstage and backstage teamwork.* Cresskill, NJ: Hampton.

Ellingson, L. L., & Buzzanell, P. M. (1999). Listening to women's narratives of breast cancer treatment: A feminist approach to patient satisfaction with physician-patient communication. *Health Communication, 11*, 153-183.

Elwood, W. N. (Ed.). (1999). *Power in the blood: A handbook on AIDS, politics, and communication.* Mahwah, NJ: Erlbaum.

Elwood, W. N., Dayton, C., & Richard, A. (1996). Ethnography and illegal drug users: The efficacy of outreach as HIV prevention. *Communication Studies, 46*, 261-275.

Fabj, V., & Sobnosky, M. J. (1995). AIDS activism and the rejuvenation of the public sphere. *Argumentation & Advocacy, 31*, 163-184.

Farrell, K. P. (2006). HIV on TV: Conversations with young gay men. *Sexualities, 9*, 193-213.

Feinberg, L. (2001). Trans health crisis: For us it's life or death. *American Journal of Public Health, 91*, 897-900.

Finnegan, J. R. J., & Viswanath, K. (1990). Health and communication: Medical and public health influences on the research agenda. In E. B. Ray & L. Donohew (Eds.), *Communication and health: Systems and applications* (pp. 9-24). Hillsdale, NJ: Erlbaum.

Fisher, W. R. (1987). *Human communication as narration: Toward a philosophy of reason, value, and action.* Columbia: University of South Carolina Press.

Ford, L. A., & Yep, G. A. (2003). Working along the margins: Developing community-based strategies for communicating about health with marginalized groups. In T. L. Thompson, A. M. Dorsey, K. I. Miller, & R. Parrott (Eds.), *Handbook of health communication* (pp. 241-261). Mahwah, NJ: Erlbaum.

Foss, K. A., Foss, S. K., & Griffin, C. L. (1999). *Feminist rhetorical theories.* Thousand Oaks, CA: Sage.

Foucault, M. (1973). *The birth of the clinic: An archaeology of medical perception* (A. M. S. Smith, Trans.). New York: Vintage.

Foucault, M. (1979). *Discipline and punish: The birth of the prison* (A. Sheridan, Trans.). New York: Vintage.

Frank, A. W. (1995). *The wounded storyteller: Body, illness, and ethics.* Chicago: University of Chicago Press.

Gamble, V. N. (1997). Under the shadow of Tuskegee: African Americans and health care. *American Journal of Public Health, 87*, 1773-1778.

Gannon, L., & Stevens, J. (1998). Portraits of menopause in the mass media. *Women & Health, 27*(3), 1-15.

Geertz, C. (1973). *The interpretation of cultures.* New York: Basic Books.

Geertz, C. (1983). *Local knowledge: Further essays in interpretive anthropology.* New York: Basic Books.

Geist, P., & Dreyer, J. (1993). The demise of dialogue: A critique of medical encounter ideology. *Western Journal of Communication, 57*, 233-246.

Geist, P., & Hardesty, M. (1992). *Negotiating the crisis: DRGs and the transformation of hospitals.* Hillsdale, NJ: Erlbaum.

Geist Martin, P., Ray, E. B., & Sharf, B. F. (2003). *Communicating health: Personal, cultural, and political complexities.* Belmont, CA: Thomas Wadsorth.

German, K. M. (1995). Critical theory in public relations inquiry: Future directions for analysis in a public relations context. In W. N. Elwood (Ed.), *Public relations inquiry as rhetorical criticism* (pp. 279-294). Westport, CT: Praeger.

Gibbs, R. W., Jr., & Franks, H. (2002). Embodied metaphor in women's narratives about their experiences with cancer. *Health Communication, 14*, 139-165.

Giddens, A. (1984). *The constitution of society: Outline of the theory of structuration.* Berkeley: University of California Press.

Gillespie, S. R. (2001). The politics of breathing: Asthmatic Medicaid patients under managed care. *Journal of Applied Communication Research, 29*, 97-116.

Glaser, B., & Strauss, A. L. (1967). *The discovery of grounded theory.* Chicago: Aldine.

Greenhalgh, T., & Hurwitz, B. (Eds.). (1998). *Narrative based medicine: Dialogue and discourse in clinical practice.* London: BMJ books.

Gwyn, R. (2002). *Communicating health and illness.* Thousand Oaks, CA: Sage.

Hall, S. (Ed.). (1997). *Representation: Cultural representations and signifying practices.* Thousand Oaks, CA: Sage.

Hall, S., Hobson, D., Lowe, A., & Willis, P. (Eds.). (1980). *Culture, media, language.* London: Hutchinson.

Harcourt, J. (Ed.). (2006). *Current issues in lesbian, gay, bisexual, and transgender health.* New York: Harrington Park Press.

Harter, L. M., & Japp, P. M. (2001). Technology as the representative anecdote in popular discourses of health and medicine. *Health Communication, 13*, 409-425.

Harter, L. M., Japp, P. M., & Beck, C. S. (Eds.). (2005a). *Narratives, health, and healing: Communication theory, research, and practice.* Mahwah, NJ: Erlbaum.

Harter, L. M., Japp, P. M., & Beck, C. S. (2005b). Vital problematics of narrative theorizing about health and healing. In L. M. Harter, P. M. Japp & C. S. Beck (Eds.), *Narratives, health, and healing: Communication theory, research, and practice* (pp. 7-30). Mahwah, NJ: Erlbaum.

Harter, L. M., Scott, J., Novak, D., Leeman, M., & Morris, J. (2006). Freedom through flight: Performing a counter-narrative of disability. *Journal of Applied Communication Research, 34*, 3-29.

Harter, L. M., Sharma, D., Pant, S., Singhal, A., & Sharma, Y. (2007). Catalyzing social reform through participatory folk performances in rural India. In L. Frey & K. Carragee (Eds.), *Communication activism* (pp. 269-298). Cresskill, NJ: Hampton Press.

Harter, L. M., Stephens, R. J., & Japp, P. M. (2000). President Clinton's apology for the Tuskegee syphilis expiriment: A narrative of remembrance, redefinition, and reconciliation. *Howard Journal of Communications, 11*, 19-34.

Hazelton, M. (1997). Reporting mental health: A discourse analysis of mental health-related news in two Australian newspapers. *Australian & New Zealand Journal of Mental Health Nursing, 6*, 73-89.

Hines, S. C., Babrow, A. S., Badzek, L., & Moss, A. H. (1997). Communication and problematic integration in end-of-life decisions: Dialysis decisions among the elderly. *Health Communication, 9*, 199-217.

Hubbard, R. (1990). *The politics of women's biology.* Brunswick, NJ: Rutgers University.

Illich, I. (1976). *Medical nemesis.* New York: Pantheon Books.

Jackson, L. D., & Duffy, B. K. (1998). *Health communication research: A guide to developments and directions.* Westport, CT: Greenwood.

Jacobus, M., Keller, E. F., & Shuttleworth, S. (Eds.). (1990). *Body/politics: Women and the discourses of science.* New York: Routledge.

Johnson, D., Flora, J., & Rimal, R. N. (1997). HIV AIDS public service announcements around the world: A descriptive analysis. *Journal of Health Communication, 2,* 223-234.

Johnson, J. L., Bottorff, J. L., Browne, A. J., Grewal, S., Hilton, B. A., & Clarke, H. (2004). Othering and being othered in the context of health care services. *Health Communication, 16,* 253-271.

Kar, S. B., & Alcalay, R. (Eds.). (2001). *Health communication: A multicultural perspective.* Thousand Oaks, CA: Sage.

Keränen, L. (2007). "Cause someday we die": Rhetoric, agency and the case of the "patient" preferences worksheet. *Quarterly Journal of Speech, 93,* 179-210.

Keyton, J. (2006). *Communication research: Asking questions, finding answers* (2nd ed.). Boston: McGraw-Hill.

Kirkwood, W. G., & Brown, D. (1995). Public communication about the causes of disease: The rhetoric of responsibility. *Journal of Communication, 45,* 55-76.

Kleinman, A. (1988). *The illness narratives: Suffering, healing, and the human condition.* New York: Basicbooks.

Kline, K. N. (1999). Reading and re-forming breast self-examination discourse: Claiming missed opportunities for empowerment. *Journal of Health Communication, 4,* 119-141.

Kline, K. N. (2003). Popular media and health: Images, effects, and institutions. In T. L. Thompson, A. M. Dorsey, K. I. Miller, & R. Parrott (Eds.), *Handbook of health communication* (pp. 557-581). Mahwah, NJ: Erlbaum.

Kline, K. N. (2006). A decade of research on health content in the media: The focus on health challenges and sociocultural context and attendant informational and ideological problems. *Journal of Health Communication, 11,* 43-59.

Kline, K. N. (2007). Cultural sensitivity and health promotion: Assessing breast cancer education pamphlets designed for African American women. *Health Communication, 21,* 85-96.

Kline, K. N., & Mattson, M. (2000). Breast self-examination pamphlets: A content analysis grounded in fear appeal research. *Health Communication, 12,* 1-21.

Knuf, J., & Caughlin, J. (1993). Weighty issues: Semiotic notes on dieting as a secular ritual. *Health Communication, 5,* 161-179.

Lammers, J. C., & Geist, P. (1997). The transformation of caring in the light and shadow of "managed care." *Health Communication, 9,* 45-60.

Lannaman, J. W. (1992). Deconstructing the person and changing the subject of interpersonal studies. *Communication Theory, 2,* 139-148.

Lantz, P. M., & Booth, K. M. (1998). The social construction of the breast cancer epidemic. *Social Science & Medicine, 46,* 907-918.

Leeds-Hurwitz, W. (1995). Introducing social approaches. In W. Leeds-Hurwitz (Ed.), *Social approaches to communication* (pp. 3-20). New York: Guilford.

Lupton, D. (1992). Discourse analysis: A new methodology for understanding the ideologies of health and illness. *Australian Journal of Public Health, 16,* 145-150.

Lupton, D. (1994a). The condom in the age of AIDS: Newly respectable or still a dirty word? A discourse analysis. *Qualitative Health Research, 4,* 304-320.

Lupton, D. (1994b). 'The great debate about cholesterol': Medical controversy and the news media. *Australian & New Zealand Journal of Sociology, 30,* 334-339.

Lupton, D. (1994c). *Medicine as culture: Illness, disease, and the body in western societies.* Thousand Oaks, CA: Sage.

Lupton, D. (1994d). Toward the development of critical health communication praxis. *Health Communication, 6,* 55-67.

Lupton, D. (1995). *The imperative of health: Public health and the regulated body.* London: Sage.

Lupton, D. (1998). The end of AIDS?: AIDS Reporting in the Australian press in the mid-1990s. *Critical Public Health, 8*, 33-46.

Lupton, D. (1999). Archetypes of infection: People with HIV/AIDS in the Australian press in the mid-1990s. *Sociology of Health & Illness, 21*, 37-53.

Lupton, D. (2000). The social construction of medicine and the body. In G. L. Albrecht, R. Fitzpatrick, & S. C. Scrimshaw (Eds.), *The handbook of social studies in health and medicine* (pp. 50-63). Thousand Oaks, CA: Sage.

Lupton, D. (2008). 'You feel so responsible: Australian mothers' concepts and experiences related to promoting the health and development of their young children. In H. Zoller & M. Dutta (Eds.), *Emerging perspectives in health communication: Meaning, culture and power* (pp. 113-128). New York: Routledge.

Lynch, J., & Dubriwny, T. (2006). Drugs and double binds: Racial identification and pharmocogenomics in a system of binary race logic. *Health Communication, 19*, 61-73.

Lyons, A. C., & Willott, S. (1999). From suet pudding to superhero: Representations of men's health for women. *Health, 3*, 283-302.

Mann, M. (1986). *The sources of social power* (Vol. 1). New York: Cambridge Press.

Martin, J. N., & Nakayama, T. K. (1999). Thinking dialectically about culture and communication. *Communication Theory, 9*, 1-25.

McGrath, P. (2005). Developing a language for nonreligious spirituality in relation to serious illness through research: Preliminary findings. *Health Communication, 18*, 217-235.

McKnight, J. (1988). Where can health communication be found? *Journal of Applied Communication Research, 16*, 39-43.

McLean, S. (1997). A communication analysis of community mobilization on the Warm Springs Indian Reservation. *Journal of Health Communication, 2*, 113-125.

Melkote, S., Muppidi, S., & Goswami, D. (2000). Social and economic factors in an integrated behavioral and societal approach to communications and HIV/AIDS. *Journal of Health Communication, 5*, 17-27.

Mokros, H. B., & Deetz, S. (1996).What counts as real?: A constitutive view of communication and the disenfranchised in the context of health. In E. B. Ray (Ed.), *Communication and the disenfranchised: Social health issues and implications* (pp. 29-44). Mahwah, NJ: Erlbaum.

Mumby, D. K. (1988). *Communication and power in organizations: Discourse, ideology and domination.* Norwood, NJ: Ablex.

Mumby, D. K. (1993). Critical organizational communication studies: The next ten years. *Communication Monographs, 60*, 18-25.

Mumby, D. K. (1996). Feminism, postmodernism, and organizational communication studies: A critical reading. *Management Communication Quarterly, 9*, 259-295.

Mumby, D. K. (1997). Modernism, postmodernism, and communication studies: A rereading of an ongoing debate. *Communication Theory, 7*, 1-28.

Murphy, P. (2001). Framing the nicotine debate: A cultural approach to risk. *Health Communication, 13*, 119-140.

Nadesan, M. H. (2005). *Constructing autism: Unravelling the 'truth' and understanding the social.* London: Routledge.

Northridge, M. E. (Ed.). (2001). Advancing lesbian, gay, bisexual, and transgender health [Special Issue]. *American Journal of Public Health, 91*.

Oakley, A. (1984). *The captured womb: A history of medical care of pregnant women.* New York: Basil Blackwell.

Ott, B., & Walter, C. (2000). Intertextuality: Interpretive practice and textual strategy. *Critical Studies in Mass Communication, 17*, 429-446.

Ott Anderson, J., & Geist Martin, P. (2003). Narratives and healing: Exploring one family's stories of cancer survivorship. *Health Communication, 15*, 133-143.

Pal, M., & Dutta, M. J. (2008). Theorizing resistance in a global context: Processes, strategies, and tactics in communication scholarship. In C. S. Beck (Ed.), *Communication yearbook 32* (pp. 41-87). New York: Routledge.

Parrott, R., & Condit, C. (Eds.). (1996). *Evaluating women's health messages: A resource book*. Thousand Oaks, CA: Sage.

Patton, M. Q. (2002). *Qualitative research and evaluation methods* (3rd ed.). Thousand Oaks, CA: Sage.

Payer, L. (1992). *Disease-mongers: How doctors, drug companies, and insurers are making you feel sick*. New York: John Wiley & Sons.

Payer, L. (1996). *Medicine and culture: Varieties of treatment in the United States, England, West Germany, and France* (2nd ed.). New York: Henry Holt.

Perez, T. L., & Dionisopoulos, G. N. (1995). Presidential silence, C. Everett Koop, and the Surgeon General's Report on AIDS. *Communication Studies, 46*, 18-23.

Perloff, R. M., & Ray, G. B. (1991). An analysis of AIDS brochures directed at intravenous drug users. *Health Communication, 3*, 113-125.

Peterson, A. (2001). Biofantasies: Genetics and medicine in the print news media. *Social Science & Medicine, 52*, 1255-1268.

Peterson, A., & Lupton, D. (2000). *The new public health: Health and self in the age of risk*. London: Sage.

Peterson, T. R. (1997). *Sharing the earth: The rhetoric of sustainable development*. Columbia: University of South Carolina Press.

Petros, G., Airhihenbuwa, C., Simbayi, L., Ramlagan, S., & Brown, B. (2006). HIV/AIDS and "othering" in South Africa: The blame goes on. *Culture, Health & Sexuality, 8*, 67-77.

Pezzullo, P. C. (2003). Resisting "National Breast Cancer Awareness Month:" The rhetoric of counterpublics and their cultural performances. *Quarterly Journal of Speech, 89*, 345-365.

Pineau, E. (2000). Nursing mother and articulating absence. *Text and Performance Quarterly, 20*, 1-19.

Posner, T. (1991). What's in a smear? Cervical screening, medical signs and metaphors. *Science as Culture, 2*, 166-187.

Ragan, S. L., Mindt, T., & Wittenberg-Lyles, E. (2005). Narrative medicine and education in palliative care. In L. M. Harter, P. M. Japp, & C. S. Beck (Eds.), *Narratives, health, and healing: Communication theory, research, and practice* (pp. 259-275). Mahwah, NJ: Erlbaum.

Ratcliff, K. S. (2002). *Women and health: Power, technology, inequality, and conflict*. Boston: Allyn & Bacon.

Ratzan, S. C., Payne, J. G., & Bishop, C. (1996). The status and scope of health communication. *Journal of Health Communication, 1*, 25-41.

Rawlins, W. K. (1998). From ethnographic occupations to ethnographic stances. In J. S. Trent (Ed.), *Communication: Views from the helm for the 21st century* (pp. 359-362). Boston: Allyn and Bacon.

Rawlins, W. K. (2005). Our family's physician. In L. M. Harter, P. M. Japp, & C. S. Beck (Eds.), *Narratives, health, and healing: Communication theory, research, and practice* (pp. 197-216). Mahwah, NJ: Erlbaum.

Rice, P. L., & Ezzy, D. (1999). *Qualitative research methods: A health focus*. South Melbourne, Australia: Oxford University Press.

Rogers, E. M. (1996). The field of health communication today: An up-to-date report. *Journal of Health Communication, 1*, 15-23.

Roter, D., & McNeilis, K. S. (2003). The nature of the therapeutic relationship and the assessment of its discourse in routine medical visits. In T. L. Thompson, A. M. Dorsey, K. I. Miller, & R. Parrott (Eds.), *Handbook of health communication* (pp. 121-140). Mahwah, NJ: Erlbaum.

Rothman, B. K. (1989). *Recreating motherhood: Ideology and technology in a patriarchal society*. New York: W.W. Norton.

Salmon, C. T., & Atkin, C. (2003). Using media campaigns for health promotion. In T. L. Thompson, A. M. Dorsey, K. I. Miller, & R. Parrott (Eds.), *Handbook of health communication* (pp. 449-472). Mahwah, NJ: Erlbaum.

Scott, J. B. (2003). *Risky rhetoric: AIDS and the cultural practices of HIV testing*. Carbondale: Southern Illinois University Press.

Seale, C. F. (2004a). *Health and the media*. Oxford, England: Blackwell.

Seale, C. F. (2004b). *Media & health*. Thousand Oaks, CA: Sage.

Sharf, B. F. (1990). Physician-patient communication as interpersonal rhetoric: A narrative approach. *Health Communication, 2*, 217-231.

Sharf, B. F. (1997). Communicating breast cancer on-line: Support and empowerment on the Internet. *Women & Health, 26*(1), 65-84.

Sharf, B. F. (1999). The present and future of health communication scholarship: Overlooked opportunities. *Health Communication, 11*, 195-199.

Sharf, B. F. (2001). Out of the closet and into the legislature: Breast cancer stories. *Health Affairs, 20*(1), 213-218.

Sharf, B. F. (2005). How I fired my surgeon and embraced an alternative narrative. In L. M. Harter, P. M. Japp, & C. S. Beck (Eds.), *Narratives, health, and healing: Communication theory, research, and practice* (pp. 325-342). Mahwah, NJ: Erlbaum.

Sharf, B. F., & Freimuth, V. S. (1993). The construction of illness on entertainment television: Coping with cancer on *thirtysomething*. *Health Communication, 5*, 141-160.

Sharf, B. F., Freimuth, V. S., Greespon, P., & Plotnick, C. (1996). Confronting cancer on *thirtysomething*: Audience response to health content on entertainment television. *Journal of Health Communication, 1*, 157-172.

Sharf, B. F., & Vanderford, M. L. (2003). Illness narratives and the social construction of health. In T. L. Thompson, A. M. Dorsey, K. I. Miller, & R. Parrott (Eds.), *Handbook of health communication* (pp. 9-34). Mahwah, NJ: Erlbaum.

Signorielli, N. (1990). Television and health: Images and impact. In C. Atkin & L. Wallack (Eds.), *Mass communication and public health: Complexities and conflict* (pp. 96-113). Newbury Park: Sage.

Smith, D. H. (1988a). Communication as a reflection of and a source for, values in health. *Journal of Applied Communication Research, 16*, 29-38.

Smith, D. H. (Ed.). (1988b). Values in Health Communication [Special Issue]. *Journal of Applied Communication Research, 16*.

Smith, J. K., & Heshusius, L. (2004). Closing down the conversation: The end of the quantitative-qualitative debate among educational inquirers. In C. Seale (Ed.), *Social research methods: A reader* (pp. 499-504). New York: Routledge.

Sobnosky, M. J., & Hauser, E. (1999). Initiating or avoiding activism: Red ribbons, pink triangles, and public argument about AIDS. In W. N. Elwood (Ed.), *Power in the blood: A handbook on AIDS, politics, and communication* (pp. 25-38). Mahwah, NJ: Erlbaum.

Solomon, M. (1985). The rhetoric of dehumanization: An analysis of medical reports of the Tuskegee Syphilis Project. *Western Journal of Speech Communication, 49*, 233-247.

Sontag, S. (1978). *Illness as metaphor*. New York: Vintage.

Sontag, S. (1990). *Illness as metaphor and AIDS and its metaphors* (1st Anchor Books edition ed.). New York: Anchor Books.

Spivak, G. (1999). *A critique of postcolonial reason: Towards history of the vanishing present*. Cambridge, MA: Harvard University Press.

Stevens, P., & Hall, J. M. (2002). A critical historical analysis of the medical construction of lesbianism. In K. S. Radcliff (Ed.), *Women and health: Power, technology, inequality, and conflict* (pp. 21-30). Boston: Allyn & Bacon.

Stivers, T. (2004). Parent resistance to physician's treatment recommendations: One resource for initiating a negotiation of the treatment decision. *Health Communication, 18*, 41-74.

Stokes, A. Q. (2005). Healthology, health literacy, and the pharmaceutically empowered consumer. *Studies in Communication Sciences, 5*(2), 129-146.

Stone, K. (1999). Safer text: Reading biblical laments in the age of AIDS. *Theology & Sexuality: The Journal of the Institute for the Study of Christianity & Sexuality, 10*, 16-27.

Storey, D., Boulay, M., Karki, Y., Heckert, K., & Karmacha, D. (1999). Impact of the integrated radio communication project in Nepal, 1994-1997. *Journal of Health Communication, 4*, 271-294.

Tavris, C. (1992). *The mismeasure of woman*. New York: Touchstone.

Thompson, T. L. (1989). Editor's note. *Health Communication, 1*, 1-3.

Thompson, T. L. (2003). Introduction. In T. L. Thompson, A. M. Dorsey, K. I. Miller, & R. Parrott (Eds.), *Handbook of health communication* (pp. 1-8). Mahwah, NJ: Erlbaum.

Thompson, T. L., Dorsey, A. M., Miller, K. I., & Parrott, R. (Eds.). (2003). *Handbook of health communication*. Mahwah, NJ: Erlbaum.

Treichler, P. A. (1987). AIDS, homophobia and biomedical discourse. *Cultural Studies, 11*, 263-305.

Treichler, P. A. (1990). Feminism, medicine, and the meaning of childbirth. In M. Jacobus, E. F. Keller, & S. Shuttleworth (Eds.), *Body/politics: Women and the discourses of science* (pp. 113-138). New York: Routledge.

Treichler, P. A. (1999). *How to have theory in an epidemic: Cultural chronicles of AIDS*. Durham, NC: Duke University Press.

Tulloch, J., & Lupton, D. (1997). *Television, AIDS and risk: A cultural studies approach to health communication*. St. Leonards, Australia: Allen & Unwin.

Vanderford, M. L., Jenks, E. B., & Sharf, B. F. (1997). Exploring patients' experiences as a primary source of meaning. *Health Communication, 9*, 13-26.

Vanderford, M. L., & Smith, D. H. (1996). *The silicone breast implant story: Communication and uncertainty*. Mahwah, NJ: Erlbaum.

Vargas, L. (2000). Genderizing Latino news: An analysis of a local newspaper's coverage of Latino current affairs. *Critical Studies in Media Communication, 17*, 261-293.

Villagran, M., Collins, D., & Garcia, S. (2008). *Voces de las Colonias*: Dialectical tensions about control and cultural identification in Latinas' communication about cancer. In H. Zoller & M. Dutta (Eds.), *Emerging perspectives in health communication: Meaning, culture, and power* (pp. 203-223). New York: Routledge.

Waitzkin, H. (1991). *The politics of medical encounters: How patients and doctors deal with social problems*. New Haven, CT: Yale University Press.

Whaley, B. B. (Ed.). (1999). *Explaining illness: Research, theory, and strategies*. Mahwah, NJ: Erlbaum.

Witte, K. (1994). The manipulative nature of health communication research: Ethical issues and guidelines. *American Behavioral Scientist, 38*, 285-293.

Witte, K. (1998). A theoretically based evaluation of HIV/AIDS prevention campaigns along the Trans-Africa Highway in Kenya. *Journal of Health Communication, 3*, 343-363.

Witte, K., Meyer, G., Bidol, H., Case, M. K., Kopeman, J., Maduschke, K., et al. (1996). Bringing order to chaos: Communication and health. *Communication Studies, 47*, 229-242.

Wood, R., Hall, D. M., & Hasian, M. A., Jr. (2008). The human genome diversity debates: A case study in health activism. In H. Zoller & M. Dutta (Eds.), *Emerging perspectives in health communication: Meaning, culture, and power* (pp. 431-446). New York: Routledge.

Workman, T. A. (2001). Finding the meanings of college drinking: An analysis of fraternity drinking stories. *Health Communication, 13*, 427-447.

Yep, G. A., Lovaas, K., & Elia, J. P. (Eds.). (2003). *Queer theory and communication: From disciplining queers to queering the discipline*. Bingharton, NY: Harrington Park Press.

Yep, G. A., Reece, S., & Negron, E. (2003). Culture and stigma in a bona fide group: Boundaries and context in a "closed" support group for "Asian Americans" living with HIV infection. In L. Frey (Ed.), *Group communication in context: Studies of bona-fide groups* (pp. 157-180). Mahwah, NJ: Erlbaum.

Young, A. J., & Rodriguez, K. L. (2006). The role of narrative in discussing end-of-life care: Eliciting values and goals from text, context, and subtext. *Health Communication, 19*, 49-59.

Young, N. (2007). Identity trans/formations. In C. S. Beck (Ed.), *Communication yearbook 31* (pp. 224-273). Mahwah, NJ: Erlbaum.

Zola, I. K. (1972). Medicine as an institution of social control. *The Sociological Review, 20*, 487-504.

Zoller, H. M. (2000). "A place you haven't visited before:" Creating the conditions for community dialogue. *Southern Communication Journal, 2/3*, 191-207.

Zoller, H. M. (2003a). Health on the line: Identity and disciplinary control in employee occupational health and safety discourse. *Journal of Applied Communication Research, 31*, 118-139.

Zoller, H. M. (2003b). Working out: Managerialism in workplace health promotion *Management Communication Quarterly, 17*, 171-205.

Zoller, H. M. (2004). Manufacturing health: Employee perspectives on problematic outcomes in a workplace health promotion initiative. *Western Journal of Communication, 68*, 278-301.

Zoller, H. M. (2005a). Health activism: Communication theory and action for social change. *Communication Theory, 15*, 341-364.

Zoller, H. M. (2005b). Women caught in the multi-causal web: A gendered analysis of *Healthy People 2010. Communication Studies, 56*, 175-192.

Zoller, H. M., & Dutta, M. (Eds.). (2008). *Emerging perspectives in health communication: Meaning, culture, and power*. New York: Routledge.

CHAPTER CONTENTS

4 Meaningful Work and Personal/Social Well-Being

Organizational Communication Engages the Meanings of Work

George Cheney
University of Utah and
University of Waikato

Theodore E. Zorn, Jr.,
University of Waikato

Sally Planalp
University of Utah

Daniel J. Lair
University of Denver

This chapter argues for a broadening of organizational communication scholarship through the consideration of meanings of work including meaningful work. First, we define meaningful work especially within the frame of a broader examination of meanings of work. Along the way, we consider the concept of meaningful work within a constellation of terms that includes job enrichment, work-life balance, career path, leisure, life satisfaction, and so forth. Second, we consider the historical-cultural contexts for our understanding of meaningful work. Here we treat both synchronic and diachronic perspectives on the meaning of work and bring into view matters of difference, such as race, nationality, gender, and class, particularly to the extent that the extant literature treats these dimensions. Third, we consider contemporary discourses in and around workplaces concerning meaningful work—especially in advanced industrial societies. In particular, we interpret recent trends in work and workplace restructuring and how stakeholders discuss them in various parts of

Correspondence: George Cheney, University of Utah, E-mail: george.cheney@utah. edu; Theodore E. Zorn, Jr., University of Waikato, E-mail: tzorn@mngt.waikato.ac.nz; Sally Planalp, University of Utah, E-mail: sally.planalp@utah.edu; Daniel J. Lair, University of Denver, E-mail: dlair@du.edu the world. Though this review can in no way be comprehensive, we try to identify prevailing themes in the popular and quasi-popular literatures on the subject. Fourth, we argue for a communication-based perspective on meaningful work as distinct from more familiar sociological and psychological perspectives. Here we draw on extant and projected research in the areas of interpersonal/family communication, health communication, and religious/spiritual communication, in addition to the more usual emphasis on organizational communication. Fifth and finally, we point to three main avenues for communication research into this important area, including relationships between public discourses about work and work-related identities, re-conceptualizations of work beyond paid employment, and ways that organizational cultures can foster meaningful work.

INTRODUCTION: THE MEANINGS OF WORK AND MEANINGFUL WORK

Questions of Definition and Scope

Organizational communication scholars have long been concerned with the quantity and quality of communication at work, but they have given significantly less attention to the meanings associated with work itself and focused less on how those meanings contribute to overall life satisfaction. This slight is surprising, given the centrality of *meaning* to contemporary conceptualizations of communication since about 1980 (Cheney, 2000). When meaning has been the focus of investigation, it has usually been ascribed to particular organizational messages, workplace episodes, or narratives of events (see, e.g., Jablin & Putnam, 2001). Though "culture" has displaced "machine" as the prevailing root metaphor in organizational communication research, this shift has not uncovered our deepest assumptions about the experience of work itself, despite the potential to do so.

Investigations of the meaning of work, job, labor, and profession deserve wider attention within the empirical, interpretive, and critical epistemological frameworks of the field. For example, from an empirical standpoint, we must ask about the ways in which people actually structure and use their time vis-à-vis their stated life and professional goals (see Schor, 1992, 1997). From an interpretive perspective, we should probe individual and collective understandings of "career," "success," and "the good life" (Cheney, Ritz, & Lair, in progress). Finally, from a critical perspective drawing on the recent research on happiness and subjective well-being (e.g., Myers & Diener, 1995), we should inquire about whether our contemporary structures of work and productivity have delivered on their promise of fulfillment (see, e.g., Zorn, Page, & Cheney, 2000).

Until about 1990, the study of organizational communication remained "inside the box" in the sense that it focused almost entirely on the internal affairs of work-based and other organizations. Not only did organizational communication scholars neglect relations between work and home/family/community/public life, they also failed to pose penetrating questions about work itself and our orientations toward it, focusing instead on specific organizational patterns (Ashcraft, 2007; Carlone & B. C. Taylor, 1998; Lair, 2007). This myopia not only limited the horizons of organizational communication research vis-à-vis areas such as marketing, advertising, and public relations, but it restricted interchanges with specialties of the field such as interpersonal, family, group, health, environmental, intercultural, and spiritual/religious communication.

More recently, several trends have connected organizational communication scholarship with the "outside" and "inside" worlds. These research bridges include work-life balance (Edley, 2001, 2003; Gill, 2004; Golden, Kirby, & Jorgenson, 2006; Kirby, Golden, Medved, Jorgenson, & Buzzanell, 2003; Kirby & Krone, 2002; Medved & Kirby, 2005); the intersection between organizational life and cultural studies (Carlone & B. C. Taylor, 1998; Jackson, 2001; Lair, 2007; B. C. Taylor & Carlone, 2001); studies of friendship in and out of work contexts (Sias & Cahill, 1998; Zorn, 1995); understandings of career that connect individuals to larger cultural norms and assumptions (Buzzanell, 1997; Buzzanell & Goldzwig, 1991; Hylmö & Buzzanell, 2002); treatments of organizational identity on multiple societal levels (Cheney & Christensen, 2000); issues of gender, race, and class that span work and non-work domains (Allen, 1995, 1998; Ashcraft & Mumby, 2004; Cloud, 2001; Trethewey, 1999), and the broader processes of organizing that characterize not only formal organizations but also language and interaction (Cooren, 2000; J. R. Taylor & Van Every, 2000). For example, even an apparently innocuous expression such as "What do you do?" can, in certain contexts, carry racial, class-based, and gender-related implications (Williams, 2001).

We believe that communication studies stand to benefit from and contribute to the growing questioning about the roles of work in contemporary industrialized societies (see, e.g., V. Smith, 2001, 2006). As a first example, we offer the negotiation of terminology itself, considering words such as "standard of living," "professionalism," "success," and the like. As part of the present investigation, we consider both meanings of work and that which is accorded the status of "meaningful work" by individuals, groups, or society in general. Second, we find that both popular aphorisms and narratives, such as "Get a real job!" (Clair, 1996; Clair, Bell, Hackbarth, Mathes, & McConnell, 2008), as well as "local" ones (such as slogans for corporate training programs—which have been spoofed in Web sites such as www.despair.com) reveal a great deal about socially held and individually interpreted priorities. A third example comes from the relational impacts of work trends, such as the growing reliance on contingent or non-standard employment in many countries (e.g., Ballard & Gossett, 2007; Sennett, 1998; Spoonley, 2004). Fourth and finally, we recast the notion of communication networks in this context to consider how certain groups or communities of persons (in a single organization, locale, or profession) try to align their work with their understandings of the good life.

Meaningful Work: A Constellation of Concerns

Just as we may consider the individual-organizational relationship in terms of a constellation of words and concepts that includes commitment, identification, attachment, loyalty, and the like, we may also examine meaningful work in terms of a cluster that encompasses central life interest, job satisfaction, work-life balance, life satisfaction, perspectives on the career, spirituality, and the meaning of leisure (e.g., Dockery, 2003; Greenhaus & Powell, 2006; Haworth, 1997; Kendall, 2004). By introducing this array of concepts, we situate work personally and socially, suggesting points of view that call the very nature and goals of work into question—or at least bring them into sharp relief. For example, Pieper (2000) defended leisure against its usual attacks, which are based on what he sees as "an overvaluation of activity for its own sake" (p. 61), "an overvaluation of exertion and drudgery" (p. 61), and "an overvaluation of the social function of work" (p. 62). Such commentaries help to hone our understanding of work by highlighting its boundaries and reflecting deeply on what falls outside of work's accustomed domain.

Meaningful work clearly overlaps with but may also be distinguished from the traditional concept of job satisfaction. According to Terez (2002), scholars typically envision job satisfaction as a matter of specific needs and expectations met through the job as provided by an organization; whereas, meaningful work broadens the scope of analysis to include individuals' (or groups') dreams, hopes, and senses of fulfillment and contribution. The research on job satisfaction has one of the longest records of any concept or factor in organizational studies, dating back to the famous Hawthorne Studies of 1927-1932 (Roethlisberger & Dickson, 1939). However, if considered at all in job satisfaction studies, the meaningfulness of work is conceptualized by scholars as one of the multiple contributors to job satisfaction (Hackman & Oldham, 1976; van Saane, Sluiter, Verbeek, & Frings-Dresen, 2003), and most items in measures of job satisfaction (e.g., P. C. Smith, Kendall, & Hulin, 1969) emphasize immediate rather than transcendent concerns.

The same holds true for most of the organizational communication instruments used to assess information flow, organizational identification, and organizational culture (see, for example, Rubin, Palmgren, & Sypher, 1994). In fact, the popular notions of organizational identification, commitment, and loyalty all tend to privilege the specific organization or job as a point of reference, rather than asking broader, more fundamental questions about what work means to employees. Similarly, organizational socialization research, at least from an organizational communication perspective, has overwhelmingly focused on socialization as the assimilation of newcomers to specific organizations rather than on a broader process of developing orientations toward work itself (Bullis, 1993; Clair, 1996; Lair, 2007; R. C. Smith & Turner, 1995; Waldeck & Myers,

2007). Yet, as Medved, Brogan, McClanahan, Morris, and Shepherd (2006, p. 175) observed, "by examining discourses of work and family outside of any particular organizational context [we can further] our understandings of how people [relate to] work, family [and other spheres]."

In the context of work, well-being encompasses "objective" and "subjective" elements, with the largely objective parts including overall standard of living, workplace environment, and safety and hygiene factors. Subjective, psychological, or mental well-being focuses on satisfaction and happiness with work (Tuomi, Vanhala, Nykyri, & Janhonen, 2004). In fact, concerns about the physical well-being of workers have shifted significantly toward this more subjective domain in the wake of significant improvements to the material conditions of workplaces in many industrialized societies since the early 1970s (Price, 2006). Yet, we must emphasize the complex interrelations of material and non-material factors in the sense that one type of incentive or source of satisfaction often becomes a substitute for another in the eyes of the employee. Thus, so-called objective factors (such as pay increases) may take on symbolic significance far beyond their material value (Das, 2002). Also, employees may sometimes demand raises when, in fact, they really desire recognition and support (Quality of Worklife Committee, The University of Montana, 1996).

Research indicates that attainment of personally meaningful work goals contributes to subjective well-being (Harris, Daniels, & Briner, 2003) and that unemployment results in decreased well-being for most people (Haworth, 1997). Interestingly, however, a small minority of people report increased well-being resulting from unemployment, perhaps because they considered paid employment to be distinct from meaningful work (Fryer & Payne, 1984). As Hamilton (2003) argued, "Purposeful work, rather than paid employment, provides the rewards most people crave" (p. 157). Recent research on happiness, or subjective well-being, points to several overarching factors—a sense of personal control, optimism, and extraversion; solid, close relationships; satisfying work, and some kind of religious/spiritual faith or orientation (Myers & Diener, 1995).

According to Lips-Wiersma (2002, p. 500), "The many definitions of spirituality used in relation to work...have in common that spirituality is treated as a meaning-making construct." She contended that workplace spirituality entails finding meaning and purpose in one's work and living out deeply held beliefs. She elaborated three dimensions of meaning—purpose, sense making, and coherence—as the focus of her investigation on how spirituality influences career choices. Thus, she noted a close connection between workplace spirituality and meaningful work in that an important part of one's spirituality may be the choices made regarding work and career, and the meaningfulness of work may be closely tied to one's spiritual beliefs. In fact, a number of recent writings have attempted to re-infuse work and professional activities with spiritual concerns, including the Right Livelihood movement associated with Buddhist teachings (e.g., Whitmyer, 1994) and various Christian conceptions of work (e.g., Fox,

1995). Similarly, in their introduction to a special issue of *Communication Studies*, Buzzanell and Harter (2006, p. 1) called for organizational communication to overcome its "secular hegemony" by paying greater attention both to spirituality in secular organizations and to spiritually based organizations as well.

Consistent with this focus, organizational communication research has tended to stay within the bounds of the private and public sectors; only recently have organizational communication scholars taken a serious look at non-profits (e.g., Lewis, 2005), NGOs (e.g., Ganesh, 2004), and home-work relationships (e.g., Buzzanell, 1997). In fact, we consider this broadening of our scope critical to a consideration of meaningful work. Some recent social critics suggest that, in an era in which many societies experience relative abundance and in which technology enables more work to done by fewer people, societies must begin to value opportunities for meaningful work outside of paid employment (Gorz, 2000; Hamilton, 2003). As Wagner (2002, p. 16) asserted, "Such a narrow definition of work [as paid employment] puts the economic needs of society ahead of all the other purposes of our existence." Moreover, recent reconceptualizations of the gross domestic product (and of productivity more generally) insist that a much wider range of work activities should be incorporated in the assessment of a society's activity and "outputs" (Hamilton, 2003; Waring, 1988; see also http://www.adbusters.org). Volunteer activities, domestic work, study work, and hobbies or life interests should be included within this scope (see, e.g., Medved & Kirby, 2005). For many people, such secondary or even largely invisible activities may be far more meaningful than their paid employment.

From Individual Concerns to Social Issues

As a result of this conceptual expansion, the contemporary sub-discipline of organizational communication much more closely connects to the early works on modern organizations by Marx, Weber, and Durkheim than ever before. That is, organizational communication scholars are now just as likely to ask about the values of an organization or an entire institution as they are to consider the effectiveness of a job, decision, or supervisory relationship. In a sense, the full flowering of the organizational culture perspective is before us, and that perspective necessarily embraces intersections between organizational communication and other areas of the field, including studies of popular culture and health and well-being.

Looking beyond the discipline of communication, we find a convergence of several trends in current popular and academic considerations of work (see, e.g., Ackerman, Goodwin, Dougherty, & Gallagher, 1998; Ackerman, Kiron, Goodwin, Harris, & Gallagher, 1997; O'Toole & Lawler, 2006). Writings questioning the success of contemporary corporate capitalism, consumerist ideology, organizational well-being, and integrity at work all point to the role of happiness or subjective well-being (see, e.g., Hamilton, 2003; Lane, 2000; Schor,

1992, 2005). In fact, 30 or so years ago, many scholars and students would have found the study of happiness to be unnecessary or even trivial (for an exception, see Argyle, 1987); yet, few now wonder why we should tackle such topics.[1]

The themes of recent work on happiness are far less instrumental compared to the more traditional approaches to well-being and life satisfaction within the literature of work and organizations, where stakeholders perceive employee well-being largely as a step in the path between organizational policies and organizational productivity (Grawitch, Gottschalk, & Munz, 2006). That is, from the dawn of the Human Relations Movement around 1930 through its variants to the present, employee well-being has not generally been seen as a value in its own right. For various reasons, including the reinvigoration of economics with psychological and philosophical concerns, that view is beginning to be complemented by one that ascribes intrinsic and end-goal value to individual well-being. In this regard, we see a convergence of interests across the disciplines of economics, sociology, psychology, political science, management, philosophy, anthropology, and communication. In fact, the growing attention to the question of "work-life balance" attests to a broader humanistic impulse that guides much of the contemporary research on satisfaction at work (Bonney, 2005; Dex & Bond, 2005). Throughout the remainder of this chapter, we will draw freely on the literatures of those fields to support our analysis.

The renewed scholarly interest in happiness (e.g., Myers, 1992; Wilson & Gilbert, 2003) represents one example of how a deeper examination of the meaning of work—and, by implication, non-work—is called for within the context of (organizational) communication studies. A recent surge of interest in "positive organizational scholarship" parallels the rise of "positive psychology" (Diener & Seligman, 2004; Seligman, 2002), and it places happiness and human flourishing at the center of organizational studies (Cameron & Caza, 2004; Cameron, Dutton, & Quinn, 2003). "Positive" in this sense does not mean the absence of negativity, problems, or ethical breaches but rather satisfaction with life as a whole and human flourishing. Moreover, the research on overall life satisfaction obviously connects to the sub-disciplines of interpersonal, family, and health communication and relates to a growing interest in communication and spirituality.

Through this chapter, we join micro-level empirical and interpretive concerns about employees' relationships with work and one another to broad critical-reflective concerns about the fundamental purposes of work and organizations. We connect relevant pieces of extant research from organizational communication and other sub-disciplines of communication within a wider multidisciplinary examination of what makes work meaningful.

Outline of the Remainder of this Chapter

In the remainder of this chapter, we first consider the historical-cultural contexts for our understanding of meaningful work. Second, we examine contemporary discourses in and around workplaces concerning meaningful work—particularly in advanced industrial societies. Third, we argue for a communication-based perspective on meaningful work as distinct from more familiar sociological and psychological perspectives. Fourth, we point to three main avenues for communication research into this important area—relationships between public discourses about work and work-related identities, reconceptualizations of work beyond paid employment, and ways that organizational cultures can foster meaningful work.

HISTORICAL-CULTURAL VARIATIONS ON THE MEANING OF AND MEANINGFUL WORK

Work, Objectivity, and Subjectivity

Though what makes work meaningful for individuals varies, we suggest, building on Lips-Wiersma (2002), that meaningful work may be conceptualized as a job, a coherent set of tasks, or any endeavor requiring mental and/or physical exertion that an individual interprets as having a purpose (see also Pratt & Ashforth, 2003). By foregrounding the idea of purpose, meaningful work may be contrasted to other positively valenced constructions of work using Seligman's (2002) three general approaches to well-being—the pleasant life, the good life, and the meaningful life. He associated the pleasant life with hedonism—pursuing positive emotions and moods. The good life involves fulfilling our potential based on using and developing our talents. The meaningful life focuses on contributing to a greater good, a higher cause. Similarly, meaningful work, as work that contributes to a personally significant purpose, can be differentiated from work that simply makes us feel good or work that enables us to express and hone our talents.[2]

Clearly, any consideration of work's meaning within the context of "making a living" depends on having a job in the first place. When we speak about meaningful work as job or career, we want to recognize that it is a privilege to be able to have self-determination and to be able to reflect on such things. At the same time, we also acknowledge that a great deal of meaningful work occurs outside of paid work and that we must expand our vision to consider many types of work not ordinarily recognized as "productive" or as having official status in society, particularly in light of Wagner's (2002) observation that the work world of the future is likely to consist of episodic alternations between periods of frenetic, paid employment and relatively unstructured, unpaid activity. The bottom line is that we need to be inclusive in both our definitions and in our treatment of various segments of society.

What *does* it mean for work to be meaningful? In *whose* view? Further, what patterns as well as differences can we see across time, cultures, and categories of difference such as gender, race, nationality, culture, and class?

Obviously, questions of this scope suggest a much more expansive discussion than we have time or space for here. Nevertheless, we can identify some key positionings of work in culture and history, particularly with the assistance of in-depth treatments of the social history of work such as Beder (2000), Ciulla (2000), and Gini (2001).

As the song and film by the name of *Car Wash* (Linson & Schultz, 1976) illustrate, any type of work can be enriched, elevated, and seen as worthwhile or at least tolerable. Even work commonly identified as drudgery can be transformed through spiritual or secular reframing as duty, as meditation, or even as "flow" (Csikszentmihalyi, 1990). In fact, Isaksen (2000) concluded that people who do repetitive work often find meaning through attachment to the workplace and social relations at work, viewing work as a necessary part of a more meaningful purpose such as supporting the family. That said, here we advance some important preliminary observations about work, objectivity, and subjectivity.

Bowie (1998), for example, argued that we might take a subjective or objective stance on the question of what makes work meaningful for the worker/employee. Subjectively, meaningful work comprises whatever the individual says it is; thus, what is meaningful for one person may be insignificant for another. One housekeeper may consider his work to be "art," while another may assume a purely technical, instrumental approach to the task. Such differences are not surprising, given Pratt and Ashforth's (2003) insistence that meaningfulness is necessarily subjective. For example, Buss and Cheney (1983) determined that most of the well-paid assembly line workers that they interviewed defined their labor as "just a job," but a few took different perspectives—either getting into something of a meditative state (sometimes by singing to themselves) or finding pleasure in the image of the completed car (even though they usually didn't see it). Recent surveys of U.S. employees reveal the importance of this interpretive flexibility, where some highlight material benefits and others orient to recognition, autonomy, or trust in supervisors (Bullis, Planalp, Bell, & Brown, 2005; Freeman & Rogers, 1999).

Alternatively, one could posit a relatively objective set of criteria that would cross individual, cultural, and historical perspectives. A number of authors have chosen this path by identifying the constituent elements of meaningful work, either deductively (Bowie, 1998) or inductively (Gardner, Csikszentmihalyi, & Damon, 2001; Mitroff & Denton, 1999; Terez, 2002; Yankelovich, 1974). We review these studies later in the chapter.

We favor an approach that emphasizes *intersubjectivity*. That is, we argue for the need to acknowledge historical, economic, and cultural contexts but also to recognize shared conceptions of meaningful work within particular sites or networks at particular times. As such, even a commonly acknowledged component of meaningful work such as autonomy should be subject to some degree of interpretation, given individual and group variation in understanding of it and desire for it. Some people prefer to be told what to do at work. Thus, there must be an ongoing conversation between principles and situations: As such, no one size fits all persons or jobs.

A number of factors influence the meaningfulness of work, including expectations established by discourses prominent in a particular culture at a particular point in time (Fairclough, 1992; Foucault, 1984) and group-level norms (as was a major theme of the human relations movement, according to all accounts). Beder (2000) made the case that the celebrated (Protestant) work ethic has been exploited by corporations and political leaders in a number of Western industrialized nations to encourage individuals to work far more and harder than they would have otherwise. In contrast, Hasan (2004) found that Kuwaiti workers were more interested in extrinsic rewards (e.g., prestige, feeling important, or the chance to use skills) than in work as a life role (e.g., a source of self-respect, pride, or independence). Hasan argued that conservative societies tend to experience work as less central to life and that the educational system in Kuwait provides no clear vision of and orientation to the world of work. In a broader analysis, Schwartz (1999) assessed value orientations of different cultures and their implications for the centrality of work in people's lives, issues of entitlement versus work as obligation or duty, and variability in the purposes of work (personal growth, pay, sociality, and/or power).

A communication-based perspective requires an examination of the social construction of meaningful work by individuals and groups in addition to taking into account the broad socio-cultural discourses that contribute to that construction. The person who enters a work environment known for its use of the family metaphor to describe work relationships will also bring certain assumptions about the meaning of family and the appropriateness of the metaphor (R. Smith & Eisenberg, 1987). Looking through a rhetorical-communication lens at the meanings of work should not minimize the importance of the material conditions of work but should help us to understand how the symbols, messages, and narratives associated with work are both reflective of and contributory to material contexts for work (including class). Indeed, the meaning of work is constructed and negotiated on every societal level from interpersonal relationships to popular culture (Clair, 1996).

Key Historical-Cultural Themes in the Meanings Ascribed to Work

Perhaps the best single volume on the development of perspectives on work across time and cultures is Joanne Ciulla's (2000) *The Working Life* (but see also excellent books by Beder, 2000, and Gini, 2001). Ciulla's book masterfully interweaves practical trends and philosophical reflections, considering ideas about work within their socio-historical milieus. Ciulla's analysis, with an admittedly Western bias, details how work has been positioned by societies from those of ancient Athens to the 20th century United States. Ciulla helps us to see how individuals' interpretations of work partially stem from their context, age, and the sub-groups/cultures, illustrating the importance of critically examining presumptions about the nature of work from a standpoint that questions both universality and idiosyncrasy. For example, Ciulla described how the ancient Athenians sought to avoid work and relegated it to a status less than that of other public and private activities. Thus, they perceived democracy as irrelevant to work because work was not something done by those who made up the body politic—free, landed white males.

Given that the meaning of work radically varies across culture and history, we should consider a few broad, basic perspectives on work—perspectives that are often combined and whose distinctions are blurred in practice. In the most general sense, work may be perceived simply as labor: physical and/or mental exertion. From this point of view, nearly anything other than rest is work. A variation on this perspective is that work is intrinsically unpleasant labor (Thomas, 2000), as in the work-play, work-life, work-holiday, and work-rest dichotomies. Several people would exclude many types of mental and physical exertion from work; for example, some might not consider games, sports, and hobbies (such as "working out") to be work, even though those activities often require greater exertion than what some individuals consider work. Thus, even at this level, the very idea of what counts as work is contested.

Work may be understood as a direct source of personal expression and worth—that is, as a basis of achievement, personal growth, and self-efficacy. For example, Kant (1775/1963) argued that "[l]ife is the faculty of spontaneous activity, the awareness of all our human powers. Occupation gives us that awareness...Man feels more contented after heavy work than when he has done no work; for by work he has set his powers in motion" (pp. 160-161). This perspective depicts work as fundamentally human and as part of living a complete life. In this sense, not working means not experiencing life to the fullest, and everyone needs to do some form of work.

Work may also be perceived as an indirect source of personal worth via the income and other extrinsic rewards accrued. Income, like other external rewards such as grades and benefits, thus may support self-worth while also providing livelihood in the strict sense of that word (see Kohn, 1993). As Kant (1775/1963) explained, "If he earns his bread, he eats it with greater pleasure than if it is doled out to him.... By dependence on others, man loses in worth" (pp. 161, 175). Much of the political rhetoric behind welfare-to-work programs draws from this line of argument, emphasizing that people will feel better about themselves if they earn their income rather than receiving financial support from the state. Thus, it implies a sense of "ownership," and the current rhetoric of entrepreneurship stresses this same theme (du Gay, 1996).

Work as an intrinsic value (work as self-expression and self-worth) and work as an extrinsic value (work as instrumental means) may anchor the ends of a continuum. While it is tempting to read the former end as "meaningful" and the latter as meaningless, both Ciulla (2000) and Gini (2001) cautioned about the dangers of relying too heavily on work to be the primary source of self-esteem.

Such reliance is apt to make continually more intrusive claims on the worker, shattering work-life balance and eventually eroding, if not outright destroying, what the worker found so valuable in his or her work in the first place (Philipson, 2002). Anchoring self-esteem too firmly in work is particularly dangerous in an era marked by a conspicuously contingent employment environment, leaving workers at great psychological risk if work simply disappears. For example, Ehrenreich (2005) vividly described the despair of many former white-collar workers now in the ranks of the long-term un- and underemployed.

Work may also be treated as an indirect source of personal worth by conveying a sense of status and what we would call "hierarchical meaning." Thus, many people derive satisfaction from a belief that others respect their position or occupation, and this difference can be signaled by income. Mounting evidence suggests that an obsession with status as conveyed through position and income actually places undue stress on individuals (de Botton, 2004), with adverse effects on health as well as chilling effects on interpersonal relationships (Marmot, 2004). Accordingly, Pfeffer (1994) argued that organizations more likely create positive work experiences for people by reducing symbolic and material differences among staff, and the idea of the "flat" organization, as it has flourished especially in the high-tech and other creative sectors, aligns with this view.

Work may be conceived in terms of a web of interpersonal relationships. This perspective is still very much part of predominantly non-Western societies, such as we find with the emphasis on *palanca* in Latin American work politics. *Palanca* refers to the inherently social nature of work and of work-related decisions, including advancement and opportunity; it inscribes organizational relations with a sense of relations being more important than what might otherwise be called the substantive work activity (Archer & Fitch, 1994). This orientation toward work runs counter to the 20th century Western notions of career as something owned entirely by the individual and carried with her. In many industrialized nations, notably the United States and the United Kingdom, the trend has been away from the web concept of career and toward the portable, identity-based conception.[3]

Contrary to popular stereotypes, work may be seen as a *"flow"* or *optimal experience*. Csikszentmihalyi (1990, p. 4) described flow as "the state in which people are so involved in an activity that nothing else seems to matter; the experience itself is so enjoyable that people will do it even at great cost, for the sheer sake of doing it." In fact, he found that people reported flow four times as often when they were on the job than when they were watching television (1990, p. 83), and he noted that "what often passes unnoticed is that work is much more like a game than most other things we do during the day" (Csikszentmihalyi, 1997, p. 59). He also reported many examples of workers who do the job as its own reward and cannot distinguish between work and free time. For example, Serafina lived the traditional farming life in a high mountain village in Italy. When asked what she would do if she had all the time and money in the world, she laughed and said "she would milk the cows, take them to pasture, tend the orchard, card wool"—in other words, what she had been doing all along (Csikszentmihalyi, 1990, p. 146).

Work may be understood as the vehicle or means to a transcendent goal or as a celebration of the process of work itself. This conception of work most closely relates to the traditional religious and secular notion of "a calling," in that individuals do not fully own the work but rather that it connects them to higher purposes than their personal goals (Thomas, 2000; Wrzesniewski, 2003). Terkel (1972) described "a Chicago piano tuner, who seeks and finds the sound that delights; the bookbinder, who saves a piece of history; the Brooklyn fireman, who saves a piece of life..." (p. xi). Wrzesniewski, a management researcher, found that people more likely (re)interpret their work as a calling—than either "just a job" or as a linear career—after a catastrophic major event or personal loss.

These perspectives on work are neither ideal types (in the Weberian sense) nor necessarily stable representations for individuals or societies. Rather, they reflect a range of analytically distinct though in-practice overlapping understandings of work. Any person may adopt one or more stances toward work during the course of a lifetime. In fact, it is quite common to hear someone describe a job as temporary, or "just a job," and contrast it with a more fulfilling (and perhaps ongoing) position that links directly to a career and to a sense of self. Likewise, as Beder (2000) and Ciulla (2000) both observed, societies as a whole may well manifest changes in their dominant perspectives regarding work, just as Weber (1992) first noted in his controversial treatise, *The Protestant Ethic and the Spirit of Capitalism.*

Key Elements of Meaningful Work

A number of authors have attempted to identify the constituent elements of meaningful work. While we question whether any one set of criteria fits all situations, especially across time and cultures, the elements of meaningful work identified in previous research are important to consider with respect to both recurring themes and cases of exception.

Bowie (1998, p. 1083) identified six criteria for meaningful work deductively derived from Kant's (1775/1963, 1994) writings about personhood, ethical principles, and duty.

1. Meaningful work involves work that individuals freely agree to do.
2. Meaningful work allows workers to exercise their autonomy and independence.
3. Meaningful work enables workers to develop their rational capacities.
4. Meaningful work provides a wage sufficient for physical welfare.
5. Meaningful work supports the moral development of employees.
6. Meaningful work is not paternalistic in the sense of interfering with workers' conception of how they wish to obtain happiness.

Importantly, the theme of autonomy running through Bowie's (1998) criteria is supported empirically by the largest survey of U.S. workers ever conducted, which revealed that, above all else, workers wanted more meaningful influence on the constitution of their work environments (Freeman & Rogers, 1999).

As a complement to Bowie's (1998) deductive criteria, Mitroff and Denton (1999) identified a set of inductively derived characteristics through survey research. They discovered that the most common contributors to a sense of meaning and purpose in a job included: (1) interesting work, (2) realizing one's full potential as a person, (3) being associated with a good and ethical organization, (4) making money, (5) service to others, and (6) having good colleagues.

Similarly, Terez (2002) conducted focus groups and interviews and identified 22 characteristics of meaningful work. The most important characteristics included (1) purpose, or the sense that what one does as an individual, and what the organization does collectively, truly makes a difference; (2) a sense of ownership of the work and how it is done; (3) fit between the work and one's abilities, values, and interests; (4) a sense of oneness—or being united in a common mission—with colleagues, and (5) opportunities for relationship-building with colleagues, clients/customers, and others. Terez identified service, equality, validation, invention, and personal development as the next most important characteristics. Obviously, some overlap exists between Terez's list and Mitroff and Denton's (1999), in that each speaks to purposes and goals for work much broader than the self-oriented and instrumental, illustrating the importance of creating meaningful work through developing connections with a deeper sense of self, one's values, and colleagues.

Two other analyses of the constituents of meaningful work merit mention. Yankelovich (1974) concluded from his survey research that work is meaningful to the extent that it involves enabling participation in decision making and developing one's abilities. Gardner et al. (2001) argued that work becomes most meaningful when individuals consider it to be a calling with clear work values, practices, and societal contribution and when work reflects one's identity. These studies suggest that meaningful work needs to be understood in terms of both inward-focused characteristics influencing the experience of the worker and outward-focused qualities affecting the social consequences of the work.

While the findings in these studies differ in important ways, we also note recurring themes. Certainly, the importance of purpose comes through in several of the studies cited here. Beyond that criterion, the empirical studies reviewed indicate that meaningful work for many people (1) enables a sense of agency, (2) enhances belonging or relationships, (3) creates opportunities for influence, (4) permits one to use and develop one's talents, (5) offers a sense of making a contribution to a greater good, and (6) provides income adequate for a decent living.

However, Lips-Wiersma (2002) suggested that Mitroff and Denton's (1999) survey may be influenced by the highly individualistic U.S. culture in which it was conducted, and a similar charge could be leveled at the other studies cited here, which were all conducted in the United States. Diener, Suh, Lucas, and H. L. Smith (1999) likewise argued that the individualism-collectivism dimension of culture is particularly significant in differentiating cultural differences in subjective well-being and may be similarly important in conceptualizations of meaningful work. To note the most obvious examples, individuals in collectivist cultures value autonomy and individual purpose less and value connection to the group more. Research outside the United States is needed for cross-cultural comparisons.

Summary: "Difference" over Time and across Cultures

One must recognize that variations in the meaning of work can be broadly understood diachronically, over time, or synchronically, with respect to cultural difference. Such differences must be examined against any claims to consistent or universal patterns. Along both diachronic and synchronic dimensions, we acknowledge the power of subjectivity at play in terms of people's understandings of what work is, whether and how it relates to their identities, and what constitutes meaningful or valuable work for them. For example, notions of the individual career as possession now dominate thinking in many Western and Western-influenced countries (Inkson, 2006). Interestingly, this understanding of career may seem to be timeless and immutable for many who subscribe to it. Yet, even within the United States, older workers may find meaning in the transfer of knowledge and skills to younger generations in some lines of work (Mor-Barak, 1995). That is to say, the nature of the relationship between generations at work becomes as important as the categorization of workers by generation in understanding the meaning of work.

Throughout this chapter, we try to incorporate as many contexts and examples from around the world as available in recent published literature. While we cannot be comprehensive in this regard or in our treatment of history, we emphasize the situatedness of individuals' and groups' understandings of work—especially in an age that celebrates career, entrepreneurialism, and individual identity. Part of our consideration of culture—especially what is termed "popular culture"—must be matters and markers of "difference," such as gender, race/ethnicity, nationality, religion, age, and class. For example, workers in some countries and regions more likely identify the meaning of work as tied to religious conviction and, therefore, as part of an integrated perspective on the self (Harpaz, 1998). These categories or groupings expand the interpretive range of what culture *is*, and they remind us that multiple sub-cultures may exist simultaneously within a single organization, industry, region, or nation. In fact, individual or group differences in the conception of work can affect not only how people do work but how they interact with each other at work—especially concerning different concepts of duty (Mattson, 2003). Thus, differences and patterns need to be approached with an eye toward many diverse dimensions of work experience and subjectivity.

We should note here as well that much of our discussion of meaningful work to follow takes on the cast of a relatively white, middle-to-upper class, male-oriented and largely *corporate* perspective on the meaning of work and the issue of meaningful work. This bias largely reflects that of the larger interdisciplinary literature on meaningful work. Such a bias recalls Ciulla's (2000) discussion of what we really know about the ancient Greek view of work as limited to only the surviving opinions of well-to-do thinkers such as Aristotle; we simply do not know what the majority of individuals performing the labor necessary to sustain Athenian society had to say about their work. Accordingly, while we have already discussed the considerable social variability of definitions of "meaningful work," we observe that the relatively homogeneous tenor of the following discussion serves to underscore the importance of further investigation of such variability across cultural contexts.

CONTEMPORARY PUBLIC DISCOURSES ON MEANINGFUL WORK

A number of developments in contemporary society have converged to elevate the importance of considering the meaningfulness of work. In particular, we call attention to (1) the emphasis on and the questioning of the effects of productivity and economic growth; (2) changing organizational forms and their consequences, such as increased insecurity of employment; (3) the glorification of organizational change; (4) the effects of increased use of information and communication technologies (ICTs); (5) changes in work hours and work intensification, and (6) the simplicity movement. These trends are intricately interconnected, so we treat them separately only for the convenience of analysis.

The Discourse of Productivity and Economic Growth

Politicians, journalists, and business leaders commonly focus on productivity improvements and economic growth as important ends toward which policy should be directed. Until recently, people rarely questioned whether these goals were producing positive social outcomes (e.g., Heath, 2002). According to Heath, economists often assume that increases in productivity at the organizational level and economic growth at the national level (typically measured as gross national product or GNP) produce desirable social "goods," such as decreased poverty, relative economic equality, increased leisure, and availability of material goods. Within the discourse that embraces these assumptions, working smarter or harder contributes to achieving the organization or society's economic goals and, at the individual level, producing greater wealth, material rewards, and leisure (see Veblen, 1981).

In recent years, a backlash has ensued against the received wisdom of economic growth discourse, pointing out that the expected outcomes of productivity and growth efforts have either not materialized (as in the unfulfilled promises of increased affluence, equality, and leisure) or have not satisfied (in the case of more material goods). We have already pointed to a convergence of concerns among economists, sociologists, political scientists, some business writers, and others about a new evaluation of post-industrial capitalist democracies in terms of life satisfaction (Hamilton, 2003; Lane, 2000; Layard, 2005; Samuelson, 1997). Research on psychological well-being has recently been linked to the consequences of consumerism and of corporate-consumer capitalism (Diener & Seligman, 2004; Wachtel, 1989). Such a connection can help to move evaluation of the economy to the broadly utilitarian level, asking, "But, are most people happier for all this?" (e.g., Hamilton, 2003; Lane, 2000; Layard, 2005).

If working harder has not resulted in the hoped-for outcomes of economic growth—or, worse, has contributed collectively to increased ill-being, such as stress, anxiety, and loss of social connectedness (Diener & Seligman, 2004)—we must inquire about the value of work and the reasons why people continue to focus so much energy on work and careers. For many, work has meant and still means a path to the "good life" of wealth and material consumption—an upward spiral of production and consumption. Yet, recent research and experience have led many to question this association.

Changing Organizational Forms

In the quest for efficiencies and productivity gains and in the face of other forces such as globalized markets and new technologies, organizations have experimented in recent years with multiple organizational forms (e.g., V. Smith, 1997). From the industrial revolution until the 1980s, the traditional bureaucratic form was dominant, and organizations pursued a general strategy of increasing size and vertical integration as paths to greater growth and profits. Within this perspective, the meaning of work included loyalty toward and identification with one's employer, a career within the same organization, and again, a path to the good life through being a good "Organization Man" (Whyte, 1956).

In the last several decades, a new discourse of successful organizing has largely rejected the doctrine of large, bureaucratic, and vertically integrated organizations in favor of leaner, flatter, disaggregated, and networked organizations. In this new discourse, the successful organization identifies its core business and competencies, outsources non–core competencies to partners who can perform them more efficiently, and aggressively downsizes its permanent workers in favor of contingent workers, to become a lean and agile global competitor (e.g., Gee, Hull, & Lankshear, 1996; Parker, 1992; V. Smith, 1997). To be sure, large bureaucratic organizations remain alive and well; however, they have lost favor in the popular business press and among management gurus. Further, many organizations have, indeed, downsized, outsourced, and pursued alternative forms of organization.

Such organizational changes have developed in concert with a new discourse of careers that has had a significant influence on individuals' views of work. For example, comparatively flat organizations mean that fewer workers will have the opportunity for internal promotion; thus, many workers face the choice of finding satisfaction within their current job rather than looking at it as a means to a promotion into a meaningful position at a later date. In fact, some of the questioning of now-traditional notions of career and success result from individuals experiencing decreased job security and stability (see V. Smith, 2001), where stakeholders understand risk and opportunity in multiple senses. For some years, the popular business press has suggested that the nature of work, and particularly *career*, is changing. A common theme involves the argument that lifelong employment with a single organization is a thing of the past and that workers need to embrace the notion of a "portfolio career" (Edwards & Wajcman, 2005), considering themselves mobile, constantly upskilling and preparing themselves for the next opportunity (read, termination of employment). Business guru Tom Peters's (1999) book, *The Brand You 50*, perhaps captures this mentality best in the subtitle: "Fifty ways to transform yourself from an 'employee' into a brand that shouts distinction, commitment, and passion!" As du Gay (1996) asserted, the worker is cast (for better and for worse) within such discourse as an entrepreneur, "continuously engaged in a project to shape his or her life as an autonomous, choosing individual to optimize the worth of his or her existence" (p. 302).

Of course, the idea of "personal branding" raises other questions, besides challenging the notion of a constant, linear career path. An analysis of the personal branding literature (especially in books and Web sites) reveals an emphasis on projected image rather than introspection (Lair, Sullivan, & Cheney, 2005). Thus, this trend is hardly reminiscent of the idea of a "calling," featuring one's niche in and service to the world. Popular management discourses such as personal branding or Steven Covey's "effectiveness" movement (e.g., Carlone, 2001; Jackson, 2001) promote and even celebrate work success as the exclusive domain of the individual worker, whose "job" it becomes to improve her own self—whether viewed as externally projected "brand" or internally driven "habits." In this way, individuals displace organizational responsibility in considerations of work success and satisfaction. Moreover, these same discourses celebrate such an individualistic view of career by anchoring it in notions of the American Dream (Knights & McCabe, 2003) and tapping into what Jackson described as the "deep cultural proclivities of the American psyche" (p. 162). Such mythic characterizations are not limited to U.S. versions of entrepreneurialism. As Thrift (1997) observed, they fit centrally with global discourse of "soft capitalism," a celebratory narrative tying entrepreneurialism to human freedom that is just as much a part of economic globalization as the expansive movement of global capital.

The Glorification of Organizational Change

Closely related to the trends above is the elevation of valuing organizational change over organizational stability (Zorn, Christensen, & Cheney, 1999; Zorn, Page, & Cheney, 2000). While organizations have always faced a fundamental tension between stability and change, since about the 1980s, they have confronted not only an increasing proclivity toward change but also additional valuing of change in and of itself. As evidence, conceptualizations of organizational leadership have shifted away from influencing others toward goal attainment (e.g., Hersey & Blanchard, 1969; Rost, 1991) to a process of creating change (e.g., Kotter, 1990), and managers have come to be reconstituted as change masters (Kanter, 1983) and entrepreneurs (du Gay, Salaman, & Rees, 1996). A substantial scholarly literature has arisen around management fashions and the gurus that promulgate them (e.g., Abrahamson, 1996; Clark & Salaman, 1998; Jackson, 2001). This literature has documented managers' obsession with new management fads as they constantly attempt to position themselves as change agents and their organizations as innovative front-runners.

These shifts add force to the trends identified in the previous section in that workers are less prone to view their work as linear, stable, and tied to traditions built up over a long organizational history but increasingly as uneven, marked by upheaval, and dependent on the latest management movements. Managers and workers are encouraged by the dominant discourse of organizational change to see their work as romantic, heroic quests to achieve corporate "excellence" (Zorn et al., 1999). Managers, often cast as the heroes in these quests, may be particularly likely to see their work in this way. To the extent that workers buy into this discourse, work may also be meaningful via its links to cutting edge management movements such as total quality management (TQM) and business process reengineering (BPR) in the 1980s and 1990s, and e-business and knowledge management in the 2000s (Zorn & Taylor, 2004). On the other hand, workers who remain cynical about the faddishness of organizational change may experience work taking on quite a different set of meanings, finding themselves deprived of an important source of meaning as time-honored organizational traditions give way to new organizational practices. Further, employees may envision their work as both fragmented and temporary, subject to the waves of fashion and whims of managers, and, therefore, perceive themselves as pawns in the change game.

Increased Use of Information and Communication Technologies

Information and communication technologies, or ICTs, both enable the changes identified above and comprise a key feature of the contemporary organizational landscape. ICTs have made possible all four of the management fashions identified in the previous section (TQM, BPR, e-business, and knowledge management).

ICTs can affect workers' jobs in multiple ways. They may (1) *substitute* for worker skill, as is the case with expert systems used to enable unskilled (or low-skilled) computer operators to substitute for high skilled workers; (2) *complement* worker skills, such as when an expert system is used by skilled workers both to draw on and add to the information embedded in the system; (3) *debilitate* skills, such as when they are used to restrict the choices a skilled worker can make (e.g., a physician being forced to follow scripted procedures embedded in a software program), or (4) *elevate* skills, such as the increased demand for and value of skills, such as computer programming (Head, 2003). Obviously, each of these attributes can profoundly impact how workers perceive their jobs. Perhaps the component most common in studies of meaningful work involves work that uses and develops an individual's skills and abilities (Bowie, 1998; Mitroff & Denton 1999; Terez, 2002; Yankelovich, 1974). In very general terms, people will find work more meaningful to the extent that ICTs elevate or complement their skills and less so when they debilitate skills.

When ICT and other technologies substitute for workers, as they have increasingly over the last 150 years (Rifkin, 1995), workers often find themselves moved to new roles or without paid employment. Multiple studies have demonstrated that people associate unemployment with decreased well-being (Diener & Seligman, 2004). However, as explained earlier in this chapter, unemployment can, in some cases, lead people to reevaluate the kind of work that they find meaningful and to seek more satisfying options (Fryer & Payne, 1984). Some authors have argued that increasing substitution of technology for workers will soon result in a future with less paid work than people available, requiring us to re-think the types of work that we value (Gini, 2001; Gorz, 2000; Rifkin, 1995; for an opposing view, see Levy & Murnane, 2004).

ICT also enables increases in workplace surveillance (e.g., Sewell, 1998; Sewell & Barker, 2006)—especially real-time (versus after-the-fact) surveillance (Head, 2003). Surveillance initiatives may lead workers to re-think the meaning of their relationship with the employer in that a sense of mutual mistrust can extend beyond the break in the traditional social contract. Given the importance attributed to autonomy in conceptualizations of meaningful work (e.g., Bowie, 1998; Terez, 2002), increased surveillance poses a greater challenge for finding meaningful work in large organizations.

Changes in Work Hours and Work Intensification

Numerous authors have documented changes in the number of hours worked over the last several decades. Despite debates about the degree to which the work week has changed (Edwards & Wajcman, 2005; Green, 2001), evidence suggests that many countries where neo-liberal economic policies have predominated (e.g., the United Kingdom, Australia, and New Zealand) have experienced a leveling off in the average number of hours worked in the 1980s after a long historical decline. Since that time, according to this perspective, the mean has changed little, if at all, but working hours have separated the work force, with an increasing divide between those working very long hours and those working far less than the average (Callister, 2005; Cappelli et al., 1997; Green, 2001). A second perspective suggests that, in most European countries and Japan, the mean number of working hours declined over the last two decades, while in the United States, the work week actually increased (Gornick & Heron, 2006). According to this research, from 1973 to 2000, the average American added 199 hours—or five additional 40-hour work weeks—to his or her annual working schedule, over a time period in which worker productivity on a national level nearly doubled (Gornick & Heron, 2006; Schor, 2003).

A number of critics have decried the development of an "overwork culture" that has deleterious effects on personal and social well-being (e.g., Bunting, 2004; Galinsky et al., 2005; Schor, 1992). The relation between the number of hours worked and well-being is complex, and it depends on several moderating factors such as job complexity, voluntary nature of extra hours, and work-home conflict (Diener et al., 1999). Numerous studies document negative effects of overwork, such as increased stress, poor health, depression, and mistakes on the job (e.g., Galinsky et al., 2005), yet other studies suggest that culture and individual preferences can mitigate these effects substantially (McMillan & O'Driscoll, 2004; Spector et al., 2004).

Furthermore, research reveals that work has intensified in the last 25 years for many people (De Bruin & Dupuis, 2004; Green, 2001), resulting in a major cause of decreases in job satisfaction in some countries (Green & Tsitsianis, 2005). In pursuit of efficiency and productivity, managers have pursued "lean and mean" organizational forms in which the survivors of downsizing and reengineering work longer and harder and feel less satisfied (Gilson, Hurd, & Wagar, 2004; Kivimaki, Vahtera, Elovainio, Pentti, & Virtanen, 2003). Furthermore, technological changes have generally given managers greater control, and the decline in unions has afforded workers less power; both of these factors can significantly influence work intensification (Green, 2005).

Changes in both working hours and work intensification hold significant implications for the meaning of work. Certainly, some thrive on long hours and high pressure, at least for a contained period. Clinical psychologist Ilene Philipson (2002), who worked primarily with overworked Silicon Valley executives in the late 1990s, noted that such hours and pressures create a system wherein work replaces more traditional sources for self-esteem and social connection, such as families and communities. Additionally, Kuhn (2006) found that people working long hours draw on a variety of local and broader discourses to support work-related identities. In contrast with the manner in which families and communities (e.g., Putnam, 2000) have become less stable and more diverse in formulation, Philipson argued that "[t]he workplace offers embeddedness in social relationships, involvement in company gossip and intrigue, the opportunity for both individual and collective achievement, and recognition for that achievement" (p. 12). Increased work hours, then, often provide short-term benefits in a sort of positive feedback loop, until the system becomes radically unstable for the overworked, often resulting in psychological trauma.

The Simplicity Movement

Partly in response to the trends noted above, a significant number of people have chosen to engage in what Dominguez and Robin (1999) called a "widespread rethinking of the material interpretation of the American Dream" (p. xvi). This rethinking has occurred primarily through what Elgin (1998) termed "The Simplicity Movement" (or the Simple Living Movement), a loose collection of people developing ideas and initiatives devoted to the principles of simple, deliberate living. Drawing inspiration from Thoreau's *Walden* (1854), the simplicity movement encompasses a variety of alternative practices ranging from Dominguez and Robin's innovative approach to personal finance, to Andrews's (1998) call for voluntary simplicity "circles" of individuals to meet and share ways in which they can help each other achieve simplicity, to "Take Back Your Time Day," a nationwide initiative patterned after Earth Day, designed to spark a national dialogue on issues of work and time (e.g., de Graaf, 2003).

While the simplicity movement engages issues beyond work, it is precisely the question of the meaning of work that "may be the primary impediment to a simpler life" (Andrews, 2003, p. 142) According to Andrews, simplicity comprises not only a question of discovering meaningful, fulfilling work, but also of careful, deliberate decisions about what one *does* with the fruits of one's labor (see also Dominguez & Robin, 1999). In other words, the simplicity movement also involves redirecting consumerist impulses and discovering choices that allow individuals to use their money in more individually, socially, and environmentally responsible ways.

Conclusion: Implications for Communication

We acknowledge that some of the aspects of work noted thus far are not, at least on face value, communication-based. The physical environment of work, commuting distance, work hours, salary, and regular benefits all have a material standing that cannot be ignored or completely accounted for by blanket appeals to a "discursive perspective." However, even in these apparently solid domains, communication emerges as crucial in understanding how even seemingly objective issues, such as work time and technology, are symbolized, framed and discussed. For example, salaries and wages regularly take on great symbolic significance (Das, 2002); (tele)commuting directly impacts opportunities for interaction (Hylmö & Buzzanell, 2002), and policy makers integrate work hours within national-level persuasive discourses about "productivity" (e.g., in the public debate within the United States in the 1980s about "the Japanese miracle"). We may observe the complex interrelationships of the symbolic and the material with respect to many of these dimensions of work, just as we note with the matter of "class" (Cheney & Cloud, 2006). In short, work-related discourses are important not only for the ways in which they frame the changing material conditions of work but for the ways in which they influence workers' very conceptions of self. In the final sections of our paper, we highlight a number of areas where communication research can make worthwhile contributions to the understanding of meaning and work as well as acknowledge important influences from other disciplines.

COMMUNICATION-BASED STUDIES OF MEANINGFUL WORK

Much of the treatment of work in our field fits under the heading of organizational communication. However, as we have noted, the broadening concepts of work today necessarily implicate other areas of the discipline. After all, when we expand our ideas of work to consider their effects on other parts of an individual's life and their implications for society as a whole, these applications are natural and even necessary. In this section, we extend the application of meaningful work to areas beyond organizational communication, considering especially the relevance to interpersonal/family, health, and spiritual communication. Along the way, we highlight extant investigations that could be considered under the umbrella of meaningful work while also suggesting some new avenues for research. By way of other examples in this chapter, we mention intercultural communication and environmental communication, though we do not emphasize those two areas here.

Interpersonal/Family Communication

Though the area of interpersonal communication has been grounded largely, if not almost exclusively, in personal relationships rather than in work relationships, we find no inherent reason that this focus should be the case (for exceptions, see Sias, Krone, & Jablin, 2002; Zorn, 1995). As argued earlier in this chapter, people establish and maintain relationships at and through work, and those relationships play a very important part in making work and life meaningful. At the *Fortune* 500 company that Hochschild (1997) studied, when asked "Where do you have the most friends?" nearly half reported "at work." In another study (Lonkila, 1998), Helsinki teachers reported that work was nearly as prevalent a source of social connections (28%) as were kin (40%), and St. Petersburg teachers indicated more social ties through work (48%) than through kin (27%).

As we suggested earlier, meaningful work can be defined in terms of a web of interpersonal relationships, but that statement begs the question of why meaningful work includes other people. What is the active ingredient? Is it the camaraderie and sense of belonging (Baumeister & Leary, 1995)? Is it the satisfaction that comes with team efforts and accomplishments (Seashore, 1954)? Is it the gratification of seeing the impact of one's work on others (such as with work in the service sector)? Or is it simply that workers may have enjoyable interactions with others, making it fun to come to work?

One important question is how life priorities influence the meaning of both work and home relationships and vice versa. Put perhaps too simply: Do people work to live (including to support their personal relationships) or live to work? If they lean one way or another, what cultural, historical, developmental, and individual factors influence their orientations? What are the effects on families, especially children (Cummings, 2006), and the larger society when most people throw themselves (or are thrown) into one domain to the neglect of the other? If they reject the forced choice and try to achieve balance or integration, how do they manage? The topic of work-life/family balance/interaction has been engaged extensively by organizational scholars (see Kirby et al., 2003) and popular authors, but to a lesser degree by interpersonal and family communication scholars, even though, in principle, they share the research terrain (see Golden et al., 2006).

Researchers acknowledge satisfying relationships as one of the most stable and influential predictors of subjective well-being, with most studies focusing on marriage (Myers, 1999), but their effects may extend beyond the personal sphere. Ethnographic work by Hochschild (1997) challenged the assumption that interactions at home and relationships with family were inherently more satisfying than interactions and relationships at work. Workers found conflicts, demands, and screaming kids at home but laughing, joking, appreciation, and stimulation at work. Of course, many workers experience just the opposite, and one must be wary of generalizations based on ethnographic data. Hochschild's research invites more systematic inquiry into how interactions at home and at work function to pull or push in one direction or another, how individuals negotiate the two domains through talk, sources of social support for both work or family strains (Bansal, Monnier, Hobfoll, & Stone, 2000; Stackman & Pinder, 1999), the link between quality of time spent together and quantity, and other related issues, perhaps using diary methodologies with more representative samples.

Even the distinction between home and work domains is eroding with flexible hours, telecommuting, e-mail, cell phones, and other technological and policy changes in workplaces. However, home and work life have never been separate if one takes into account work at home (either for pay or not) and the fact that work has always been a site for friendships, romantic relationships, mentoring relations, and other types of personal connections established and perhaps largely sustained through work. Technological developments can free up workers to spend more time with their nearby families, friends, and neighbors, but they can also keep people at their desks "e-conversing" with long-distance associates as well (Wagner, 2002). The jury is still out on which pattern is better for well-being and, more importantly, why.

The relationship between home and work remains ripe for theorizing from the perspective of communication boundary management (see, e.g., Petronio, 2000). The realm of work adds a complication to the private/public dialectic which plays an important role in boundary management since work can be seen as both private and public. From a practical perspective, it would be useful to know more about what strategies people use to negotiate permeable boundaries between work and home.

Health Communication

Health care professions seem to be an obvious route to meaningful work via the goal of contributing to the health and well-being of others, as well as producing gratifying personal interactions. Rawlins (2005) reported that his physician father clearly thought of his work as a calling, in the sense of "a rich morally imbued identity" (p. 215) based on helping his community. To the senior Dr. Rawlins, "being a family physician...also meant being part of these families" (p. 206), and he was committed to understanding patients' health concerns in the contexts of their own lived stories. The themes of meaningful work as a web of relationships and as the pursuit of a transcendent goal (patients' well-being) shine through his narrative.

The same idealism and sense of calling does attract some people to the health care field, but they may later struggle on the job to maintain it. Numerous stressors (such as workload, role issues, scarce resources, physical strain, and lack of participation in decision making) can contribute to burnout, but support from co-workers (peers and supervisors) can also go a long way toward reducing it (Apker & Ray, 2003). It would be interesting to find out whether interactions with co-workers, supervisors, patients, and others can help to revitalize the idealism and sense of the work as meaningful, and if so, how. Having a strong sense of calling and contribution, on the other hand, could contribute to burnout if job pressures make it difficult to do the job adequately. Striving for work/life balance could fuel burnout as well if work stress leads to neglect of responsibilities for personal relationships (Ekstedt & Fagerberg, 2005).

Many health care jobs entail repetitive housekeeping, bookkeeping, and personal care tasks that can be described as drudgery. Nevertheless, as discussed earlier, some workers find meaning even in grim circumstances. Secrest, Iorio, and Martz (2005) discovered that nursing assistants in nursing homes, which they described as "an environment fraught with hostility, disrespect and lack of control" (p. 90), still found meaning by perceiving patients as like family to them, taking pride in doing what was right, and seeking control in attention to detail.

Meaningful work can also be of therapeutic value, especially to people with special challenges such as disabilities, trauma, or serious illness. For example, McReynolds (2001) reported that, for people with HIV/AIDS, work meant contributing as a member of society, and it served as a measure of health, in addition to providing affordable health care and a distraction from the disease. Kennedy-Jones, Cooper, and Fossey (2005) concluded that work gave meaning, purpose, structure, opportunities for social interactions, and a sense of belonging to people with mental illness. Kirsh (2000) noted the additional benefits of pride, feeling "normal," a sense of contribution, and personal challenges, though some respondents also acknowledged the risk of being overwhelmed by the challenges and the importance of co-worker and supervisor support.

In addition, the nature of the work may provide therapeutic benefit beyond that of work itself. Many injection drug users employed to provide risk reduction outreach to their peers attained a sense of meaning and purpose in their work, and they said that it motivated them to make other positive changes in their lives (Dickson-Goméz, Knowlton, & Latkin, 2004). One brain-injured person, however, observed that people are defined by their work. This individual expressed frustration that she could do better than her current job and wished that she had a job that said "who I am" (Oppermann, 2004, p. 946).

Spiritual Communication

The relatively new area of spiritual communication connects with meaningful work in several ways. First, work may be considered to be a time-consuming activity that interferes with more important spiritual pursuits. Miller and Joe (1993, p. 116) wrote that many Plains Indians believed that "dreaming *was* the proper work for young men, i.e., to dream, to search for their vision, for their identity, and for their purpose in life." Most of the highly traditional Navajos that Miller and Joe surveyed, however, did not seem to be torn between time to work and time to pray because of endemic unemployment and because a number of those employed full-time developed strategies to help blend traditional Navajo views with the demands of industrial work. Findings from another study (Harpaz, 1998) indicated that religiously oriented Jews in Israel did tend to view work as less important than their religion and as interfering with it to some extent. When asked why they would stop working if they won a lottery or inherited a large sum of money, "their overwhelmingly prevalent reply was 'to practice and study the Torah'" (p. 163).

Hoke (1968) argued that many workers are not pulled between time spent on work and on spiritual pursuits; rather they are pushed away from work in a technological society that itself may be dispiriting. According to Hoke, "The notion that each human life is a responsible pilgrimage seems absurd in a technological society where men are grouped, numbered, organized, stripped of differences, and treated as replaceable, manufactured, products" (p. 599).

Yet, some workers may escape dispiriting work and impersonal treatment if others experience and recognize their contributions as unique, creative, and significant.

At the other extreme, work may be perceived as a concrete and worldly enactment and pursuit of spiritual commitments or as a divine calling (as the etymology of the word "vocation" shows) (Byron, 1998; Dollarhide, 1997; Scott, 2007). According to Harpaz (1998), the Judeo-Christian ethic constitutes a prevalent philosophy of work as enacting spiritual commitments. Secular-oriented Israeli Jews influenced by a Zionist "religion of work" (p. 165) endorsed the spiritual value of work in contrast to highly religious Israeli Jews who were more likely to view work as detracting from spiritual pursuits. Christian workers in Germany and the Netherlands who had received a religious education also endorsed work as a spiritual value (Harpaz, 1998). Work as a spiritual calling can been found in artists who do creative and highly personalized work, often at some personal sacrifice. The artists studied by Mize Smith, Arendt, Bezek Lahman, Settle, and Duff (2006) did not use the term *calling* per se but spoke in ways that evoked a spiritual framework. They discussed what they "should" be doing, the work choosing them, or the work being a part of who they were.

The view that the work itself may not be inherently or even primarily spiritual falls between the previous two perspectives, but the potential ensues for imbuing the work with spirituality. A spiritual approach to distress and burnout in health care settings, for example, may involve reframing spiritual distress as necessary for seeking meaning and purpose in life and providing support such as quiet spaces for reflection, renewal days or staff retreats, classes on mediation or yoga (Bazan & Dwyer, 1998), and counselling oriented to finding meaning in work (Dollarhide, 1997).

Integrating work and spirituality, however, is not without its tensions. The faculty at the Jesuit university studied by Kirby et al. (2006) experienced three primary tensions: (1) between embracing and resisting Jesuit values and Catholicism as an integral part of their work and their students' education; (2) between inclusion and exclusion in campus events and prayer based on Catholic affiliation, and (3) between proclamation and silence about religion in a profession that is predominantly secular. Goodier and Eisenberg (2006) observed similar tensions in a large Catholic non-profit health care system whose leadership made a choice for a more "spiritual" approach to organizing through emphasizing loving one another, interconnectedness, purpose, and core values such as honesty, sacred communication, fairness, excellence, and celebration. The researchers concluded that "while spirituality may be inspiring to some it potentially oppresses and exploits others...this model of organizing was in the end more invitational and inspirational than oppressive" (p. 61).

FUTURE RESEARCH FOR COMMUNICATION STUDIES

We have explained how most of the extant research on the meaning of work has been conducted in sociology. However, as indicated by our citations throughout this chapter, important studies have emerged from the disciplines of psychology, organizational behavior, economics, leisure studies, and consumer and family studies as well. As we build on the body of interdisciplinary research and, especially, on the communication-based scholarship specified in the prior section, perhaps the most fundamental questions from a communication perspective relate to theorizing meaningful work. How can we best conceptualize what it means for work to be considered meaningful? With our discipline's historical emphasis on meaning creation/sharing/contestation, we should be able to offer theoretical insights into meaningful work that complement those of other disciplines. In addition, communication studies are well situated to theorize not only meaning construction but the enactment and co-production of meaningful work.

In fact, communication researchers are only beginning to consider issues of work meaning, the role(s) of work in our lives, and how they intersect with our larger social institutions. We have already suggested how individuals' own work meanings and understandings should be considered in relation to broader popular discourses about work, productivity, business, and professionalism. We would also emphasize the need to attend not only to the interpretations of material conditions of work but to those conditions themselves—even though such a treatment is beyond the scope of this chapter (see especially Cheney & Cloud, 2006; Cloud, 2001, 2005). In this final section of our chapter, we sketch ideas for further investigations into the meaning of work and meaningful work for our discipline, beginning with studies related to organizational communication and then moving beyond that arena.

Relationships Between Public Discourses about Work and the Expressions of Individual Professional or Work-oriented Identities

One of the ways in which we can develop understandings of what constitutes both the meaning of work and the nature of meaningful work involves exploring the ways in which such issues unfold in the public discourses that individuals rely on to draw such meanings. While such an avenue of inquiry is necessarily broad, we suggest several discourses which promise to be particular insightful.

Aphorisms and other Crystallizations of Cultural Meaning about Work

Folkways of understanding work are important not only as cultural repositories of knowledge but also as *topoi* or resources for persuasion. Thus, seemingly innocuous or even quaint maxims such as "Time is money" may not only reflect culturally shared knowledge but continue to persuade people in a variety of settings, work and otherwise. Clair (1996) demonstrated how the saying "Get a real job" holds important political implications on the levels at which it is uttered to sway individuals away from certain pursuits and toward others. In fact, the authors of this chapter have found that entire class sessions can be built around examinations of phrases including that one and others such as: "Act like a professional," "The market made me do it," and "It's just business" (see Cheney, Ritz, & Lair, in progress). Thus, the close examination of these crystallizations of meaning about work (and life) shows great promise for pedagogy as well as for research.

Popular Representations of Work

Popular movies, novels, songs, and other cultural artifacts also reflect widespread beliefs and values regarding the meanings of work. For example, Conrad (1988) analyzed the meanings conveyed in country-western work songs, demonstrating that such songs encourage the attribution of particular meanings to work experiences as well as certain hierarchical social and organizational power relationships. Ashcraft and Flores (2003) examined the ways in which several popular films employed a "masculinity-in-crisis" narrative in response to changing gender dynamics in the workplace. In perhaps the broadest treatment of popular cultural representations of work, Vande Berg and Trujillo (1989) examined the display of work on network television prime time dramas, revealing a relatively consistent pattern of work portrayals with "the potential to teach [viewers] many things about organizational life in America" (p. 242).

Such studies, however, have remained relatively sporadic, despite calls for a greater emphasis on exploring popular representations of work (Carlone & B. C. Taylor, 1998; B. C. Taylor & Carlone, 2001). In fact, the critical examination of such discourses has become even more important in the face of a proliferation of popular representations that explicitly engage work as a central topic (Turnquist, 2005). The last decade has witnessed a significant resurgence of such representations of work in both film (e.g., *Office Space*, *In the Company of Men*, and *In Good Company*) and television (e.g., the popular U.K. and U.S. sitcom *The Office* and a host of work-based reality television programs, most notably Donald Trump's *The Apprentice*; see, e.g., Lair, 2007). While popular entertainment featuring the workplace is certainly nothing new, this recent wave of representation explicitly engages work as a central theme, rather than relying on the workplace primarily as a context as in earlier eras. That is, many of these recent popular engagements place the content of work itself squarely in the foreground, rather than offering the workplace as a background against which ostensibly more important actions, such as the relationships between co-workers, take place. Such representations are important, Ashcraft and Mumby (2004) argued, because "presumably, 'real' people consume these representations, drawing on and/or resisting them in the performances of everyday organizational life" (pp. 18-19). As such, these popular representations serve as discursive resources playing a crucial role in the ongoing processes of work socialization, broadly conceived (Clair, 1996).

Current Manifestations of Work Myths Within and across Societies

To some extent, a society inherits the previous generations' stances toward work, even when the current wave runs counter to the old one. Many observers of contemporary U.S. society, for example, have argued that the seeds of individualism were sewn and sprouted by the time that Alexis de Tocqueville (1838/2001) toured the country in the 1830s. In particular, the stories of Horatio Alger, such as *Ragged Dick*, influenced several generations' ideas about success, wealth, and individual achievement. Kingwell (1998) drew on the work of Lasch (1978) to assert that, in the United States, even play has become work through a sort of pathological influence of the Protestant work ethic, in the form of competitive sports, "getting through" the list of leisure time activities, and even competitive drunkenness (see also Beder, 2000).

Similarly, in New Zealand, myths of rugged, independent settlers clearing and farming the land and making do with limited resources have no doubt influenced the widespread "number 8 wire" ethos, which refers to the idea that anything can be repaired or created with limited resources, such as a few pieces of number 8 wire. Many New Zealanders today proudly embrace the "can do," enterprising view of work embodied in such myths.

People's Narratives about Work and Life

While communication scholars have looked at narrative in terms of its roles in rhetorical discourse (notably, Fisher, 1985) and in terms of accounts of episodes at work (e.g., Brown, 1990; Trujillo & Dionisopoulos, 1987), little has been written about people's broader narratives of career, work, and life (for an exception, see J. Bowe, M. Bowe, & Streeter, 2000). We urge attention to both naturally occurring narratives of life's work as well as to prompted responses to researchers' questions such as, "If you had it to do all over again...?" In particular, we invite researchers to pay attention to the punctuation of such narratives, the varying emphasis of high and low points, and the overall framing of narratives (i.e., with root metaphors such as the ladder, the race, the journey, and the like). In his course on quality of work life, the first author asks students, in their first assignment, to "imagine your ideal job, work, or career, and describe the type of work, the scene, the relationships, and the uses of technology." This type of imaging process can produce interesting prospective narratives that the students can revisit later.

Hodson (2004) analyzed 124 book-length ethnographies about work to answer the "carrot or stick" question: Do people work because they are forced or are they drawn into it? His conclusion suggests a bifurcated work force. High-status employees find their work both materially and socially rewarding, and they feel a sense of fulfillment, pride and meaning. They are drawn to their work to the extent that it can sometimes compete with the satisfactions of home, as Hochschild (1997) warned, sometimes to the point of workaholism. Low-status employees, on the other hand, not only reap fewer material rewards but tend to have more limited social lives at work.

Organizational Rhetoric and Organizational Subjectivity

The promise of critical investigation of the influences of aphorisms, popular images of work, enduring work myths, and personal work narratives on the meaning of work and the development of meaningful work suggests a productive avenue from which to approach organizational rhetoric. The explicit study of organizational rhetoric traces its roots to the mid-1970s (e.g. P. K. Tompkins, Fisher, Infante, & E. L. Tompkins, 1975), and it has produced a sizeable body of scholarship exploring rhetoric as more or less intentional, persuasive communication by organizations to both internal and external audiences (see, for example, Cheney with Lair, 2005).

Organizational rhetoric, however, has focused less on the development of broader ideology-oriented theories of rhetoric that have emerged over the past two decades, particularly those emerging from the critical rhetoric project (McGee, 1990; McKerrow, 1989). While this research represents a growing body of scholarly literature, it has yet to be significantly engaged by scholars of organizational rhetoric—a point illustrated by the lack of citation of such work in Meisenbach and McMillan's (2006) state-of-the-art review of organizational rhetoric.

Broadening the purview of organizational rhetoric to include insights from the critical rhetoric project helps us to explore both the meaning of work and the perspective from which work becomes *meaningful* because, at its heart, critical rhetoric seeks to explore the relationship between rhetoric and subjectivity (Sloop, 1996). Here, the aphorisms, images, myths, and narratives framing the experience of work would be conceived of as the pool of available "discursive fragments" (McGee, 1990) from which subjects can create meanings of work. Consider, for example, inquiries into the various sources of meaning shaping the definition of "professional" (e.g., Cheney & Ashcraft, 2007) to the rhetorical construction of "white" and "blue-collar" work (e.g., Lair, 2004), to the various discourses surrounding the rise of 401k retirement plans over the last 20 years that have influenced a radical transformation of the relationship between work and retirement and between employee and organization (see, for example, the 2006 *Frontline* documentary, "Can You Afford to Retire?" [H. Smith, 2006]).

These examples illustrate a variety of work-related domains where stakeholders ultimately shape the meaning of work as they configure discursive fragments. These groups of fragments simultaneously constrain and enable because they limit the options available to individuals and provide resources that those individuals can use in shaping their own work-related meanings and identities (McKerrow, 1989). In short, expanding the domain of organizational rhetoric via the insights of contemporary rhetorical theory's encounter with poststructural and postmodern theory can help us to understand the construction of meaning about work and by workers.

The Reconceptualization of Work Beyond Paid Employment and the Implications for Culture and Relationships

Arguments about New Approaches to Work and Roles

Earlier in this chapter, we described growing academic and popular literatures since the mid-1990s (see Rifkin, 1995) that urge a reconsideration of work by individuals, organizations, and societies. Some of these writings have been in direct response to economic turbulence in North America, Europe, and Australasia (e.g., V. Smith, 2001). Others have taken an almost timeless philosophical position (Gorz, 2000). It is important to examine these works more closely, especially to see how they (re)frame issues of economic productivity (e.g., with alternative measures to the GDP), treat advertising and consumerism, and deal with the issue of long-term versus contingent employment. Certainly, one of the great contributions of these literatures has been a re-evaluation of housework, volunteer activities, and other forms of hidden labor (Bunting, 2004; Gini, 2001).

Similarly, trends such as the Simplicity Movement discussed earlier not only seek to limit or control work or to minimize abuse of workers but to pose more fundamental challenges to the dominant ways of understanding work in the Western industrialized world. Interestingly, many books and Web sites challenge neo-liberal market globalization and raise serious questions about the nature of work in the modern world. The best-known efforts include the Right Livelihood movement derived from Buddhist teachings (Whitmyer, 1994), which seeks to dignify work and to infuse work relations as well as the work itself with strong senses of purpose, mindfulness, and justice. The "Take Back Your Time" movement—a national initiative sponsored by the Simplicity Forum—encourages the re-thinking of work-time relationships through strategies such as comparisons of work weeks between nations and creative articulations of a wide range of disparate values and issues from family to health to the environment to the well-being of pets (http://www.timeday.org; see related arguments by Ballard & Gossett, 2007). We might also mention the Local Exchange and Trade Systems, which represent conscious attempts to localize control over labor as well as trade (http://www.lets-linkup.com/). All of these movements are ripe for investigation by communication scholars, in terms of their ethical positions as well as their political effectiveness.

Effects of Reassessment of Work and Productivity on Relationships

Social scientific and anecdotal evidence regarding Japan's economic downturn in the 1990s has yielded some unexpected social benefits. Reports show that some segments of the population have rejected their previously fast-paced lifestyle, re-embraced family, friendship, and community, and found higher levels of overall life satisfaction (see, e.g., Dourille-Feer, 2004). In fact, Fryer and Payne (1984) observed that a small number of individuals reported that unemployment had actually *increased* their well-being.

Organizational Cultures that Foster the Pursuit of Meaningful Work

The organizational (communication) culture perspective has been a dominant perspective on work life since the early 1980s across all fields that deal with the study of organizations. Moreover, this perspective has broadened research on organizations and communication to consider the full range of work situations and the understandings held by sub-cultures within organizations (e.g., Goodall, 1989; Trujillo, 1992). At the same time, this perspective has drawn careful attention to the relationships between the cultures of organizations, industries, and nations (e.g., Hofstede, 1980; Sackman, 1992), as well as inviting the exploration of how identities at work are aligned with and shaped by aspects of difference, such as gender, race/ethnicity and class (e.g., Allen, 1996; Ashcraft & Mumby, 2004; Cloud, 2005).

Remarkably, however, scholars in communication studies have attended less to the meaningful nature of work than their counterparts in, say, sociology. Organizational-industrial psychologists have long been concerned with the need for and paths to job enrichment (see, e.g., Firth, Mellor, Moore, & Loquet, 2004), inspired by findings from research on patterns of human motivation. Organizational and occupational sociologists have consistently examined the nature of the work itself and people's reactions to it (see, e.g., V. Smith, 2001), observing a strong connection, for example, between the conditions of many modern workplaces and individual alienation (Braverman, 1974; Hodson, 1996). Perhaps because of its fundamental concern for symbol, expression, and discourse, organizational communication—through research via the "cultural turn"—has been more interested in capturing that range of meanings about work and organizational life rather than attending to the conditions under which work is deemed especially meaningful. The latter is certainly concerned with the symbolic and the subjective, just as we have already indicated. However, it also suggests metaphysical concerns about values, on the one hand, and the physical conditions of work on the other. With a growing number of books, films, and websites centered on the re-evaluation of work itself (much of this under the heading of "work-life balance"), it is timely that organizational and other communication scholars consider how organizational culture relates to meaningful work. Certainly, it represents an important ethical and practical extension of the cultural perspective. We suggest two main areas for such investigations.

Investigations of Empirical Associations between Overall Life Satisfaction and Particular Dimensions of Work and Work(place) Culture

We envision research that connects broad indicators of perceived well-being, including alternatives to the most favored indices such as GDP, and specific aspects of work that are supported or not supported by the organization's culture. We include as key aspects of work the relationships with co-workers/ colleagues (in peer groups as well as between supervisors and subordinates), the intrinsic qualities of the work (e.g., its physicality or symbolicity), the level or status of the work (that is, how it is commonly "ranked" by others), the perceived contributions of the work to society (answering the question, "Am I making a difference?"), conditions for autonomy and voice (as featured in a number of national and international surveys), and the opportunity for self-development (as understood above all by the individual vis-à-vis her most cherished goals).

For communication scholars, the role of relationships at work is obvious— whether we examine them in terms of vertical hierarchy or with regard to comparatively power-neutral "horizontal" connections. However, we also highlight the ways in which individuals frame other aspects of work in conversation and how those framings relate to broader cultural influences. In this regard, it is important to consider how various groups talk about such mundane concepts as "creativity," "collaboration," and "opportunity" at work and how those understandings either relate to or are disconnected from organizational policies under the same rubrics. Indeed, we would expect to find differences across various demographic groups, communities of practice, cultures, and historical time periods. As of now, we know of no extant work in organizational communication or communication studies more generally that fills this niche.

Analyses of Specific Enlightened Work Cultures

We argue for additional treatments of cases and patterns of satisfying work environments. Around the world, magazines and organizations generate lists of "the best companies to work for," and some of these (as *Fortune* magazine's annual lists; e.g., Levering & Moskovitz, 2007) base their results in large part on employees' responses to surveys. Other cases can be found among the most highly touted ethical businesses (e.g., The Body Shop, Ben & Jerry's and Patagonia) and new arrivals in lists of *socially responsible* corporations. However, such research should be taken a step further, especially to consider how employee meanings of work are constructed and co-constructed in connection with specific organizational policies and work activities in exceptional organizations and work environments (compare Bullis et al., 2005). It is important to delve into self-identified cases of enlightened work practices, where organizations claim to be actively serving the interests of employees, to examine the consistency of responses to those policies and the policies' stated intentions, whether the organizations claim to be "employee friendly," "family friendly," or "socially responsible" (Caudron, 1997; Davis & Kalleberg, 2006; Gilla, 2001).

Researchers should pursue particular communication practices within organizations that may nurture a sense of meaningfulness (see Pratt & Ashforth, 2003) and well-being (Tuomi et al., 2004). Black's (2005, following Elster, 1983) notion of "by-products" is particularly appealing here. As Black argued, many contemporary organizational practices, such as self-managed teams, participation, and empowerment, are, at their core, attempts to enhance meaningfulness. Yet, employees often remain deeply cynical about direct or obvious attempts to infuse emotion or meaningfulness into their work. However, she found that employees experienced enhanced meaningfulness as by-products of training in dialogue skills. As participants tried out the skills, they sometimes discovered alternative ways of seeing and deepening connections to others. While it may be difficult to try to *make* work more meaningful, meaningfulness may be a by-product of efforts to develop valued communication skills or embrace new communication practices.

Studies beyond Organizational Communication

A penetrating, multi-dimensional, multi-methodological investigation of the meaning of work has the potential not only to enrich organizational communication research with a consideration of its most fundamental assumptions but to invite collaboration with scholars and projects representing interpersonal/family, health, religious/spiritual, environmental, and intercultural communication. For example, we can envision organizational and interpersonal/family communication scholars jointly investigating the ways that family and other personal relationships are affected by various constructions and material conditions of work, or alternatively, how relationships (e.g., marriage, parenthood) might influence individuals' meanings for work. In a related vein, scholars interested in parent-child interaction would do well to consider how telecommuting, job-sharing, and more conventional work arrangements impact children (Cummings, 2006). Similarly, we can imagine organizational and religious/spiritual communication scholars collaborating to explore how different metaphysical/transcendental belief systems encourage particular views of work and how individuals enact them. Further, the field would benefit from in-depth case studies of interaction, reported life satisfaction, and day-to-day decision making within the workforces and volunteer segments of avowedly spiritual organizations.

The possibilities for a broader view of health communication are apparent when we define well-being in large part by how, where, and when we work. Likewise, it is important to reconsider the role of "the environment" in organizational communication, which has been typically taken to refer to other organizations rather than the natural material world (Bullis, Cheney, & Kendall, in progress). This shift is crucial if we are to come to terms with consumption practices at the organizational as well as individual levels. We have already commented on the expansive opportunities for exploring the cultural situatedness of work. Studies in multiple national-ethnic settings should be undertaken not only with questionnaires, but also with observations, interviews, and textual analysis. This work can enlarge the horizons of intercultural communication by considering how stakeholders treat domains of interaction and life space differently. These recommendations encompass, of course, only a few of many possibilities for cross-specialization collaboration.

CLOSING

Research on the meaning of work and meaningful work can help to make visible what has so often been taken for granted in our studies of work and organizations—the actual work that people do, how they feel about it, how work can be more fully dignified, and how these issues relate to broader social, political, and economic trends. Communication scholars are uniquely positioned to contribute to the literature on meaningful work because of our historic emphasis on meaning and social interaction. Taking the meaning of work and its place in our lives as a starting point offers a way to re-examine and renew relationships, to assess the role of productivity in health and well-being, to re-evaluate the impact of our projects on the environment, and even to re-direct consumer capitalism toward more viable and worthy goals. Ultimately, we hope such research would contribute to increased awareness and understanding of why and how we work and to actions that would enhance the quality of our work experiences and our lives in general.

ACKNOWLEDGMENTS

Note: This chapter was initially prepared for the annual conference of the Australia–New Zealand Communication Association, Christchurch, July 2005.

The work is based on earlier research by the authors and their collaborators and was inspired by practical experiences in the classroom, through consulting, and in the community. We are grateful to Christie Beck and the three anonymous reviewers for helpful recommendations on previous drafts of this chapter. We welcome your comments on this emerging research agenda.

NOTES

1. For examples, see a recent cover story of *Time* magazine "The Science of Happiness" (1/17/2005), the 1998 best seller by the Dalai Lama and Howard Cutler, *The Art of Happiness*, and Ruut Veenhoven's World Database on Happiness (http://www2. eur.nl/fsw/research/happiness/index.htm).
2. Again, a more embracing understanding of work harks back to the early writings of Marx (see Fromm, 1961), who envisioned meaningful work as a defining characteristic of humanity and, thus, perceived structural alienation wherever people's labors were severed or separated from their purview and control.
3. The first author found the influence of the more individualistic version of career growing, even during the short span of the 1990s in the Basque Country, Spain (Cheney, 1999).

REFERENCES

Abrahamson, E. (1996). Management fashion. *Academy of Management Review, 21*, 254-285.

Ackerman, F., Goodwin, N. R., Dougherty, L., & Gallagher, K. (Eds.). (1998). *The changing nature of work*. Washington, DC: Island Press.

Ackerman, F., Kiron, D., Goodwin, N. R., Harris, J. M., & Gallagher, K. (1997). *Human well-being and economic goals*. Washington, DC: Island Press.

Allen, B. J. (1995). "Diversity" in organizations. *Journal of Applied Communication Research, 23*, 143-155.

Allen, B. J. (1996). Feminism and organizational communication: A Black woman's (re)view of organizational socialization, *Communication Studies, 47, 257-271.*

Allen, B. J. (1998). Black womanhood and feminist standpoints. *Management Communication Quarterly, 11*, 575-586.

Andrews, C. (1998). *The circle of simplicity: Return to the good life*. New York: Harper.

Andrews, C. (2003). The simple solution. In J. de Graaf (Ed.), *Take back your time: Fighting overwork and time poverty in America* (pp. 139-144). San Francisco: Berrett-Koehler.

Apker, J., & Ray, E. B. (2003). Stress and social support in health care organizations. In. T. L. Thompson, A. M. Dorsey, K. I. Miller, & R. Parrott (Eds.), *Handbook of health communication* (pp. 347-368). Mahwah, NJ: Erlbaum.

Archer, L., & Fitch, K. (1994). Communication in Latin American multinational organizations. In R. Wiseman & R. Shuter (Eds.), *Communicating in multinational organizations* (pp. 75-93). Thousand Oaks, CA: Sage.

Argyle, M. (1987). *The psychology of happiness*. London: Methuen.

Ashcraft, K. L. (2007). Appreciating the "work" of discourse: Occupational identity and difference as organizing mechanisms in the case of commercial airline pilots. *Discourse & Communication, 1*(1), 9-36.

Ashcraft, K. L., & Flores, L. (2003). "Slaves with white collars": Persistent performances of masculinity in crisis. *Text and Performance Quarterly, 23*, 1-29.

Ashcraft, K.L, & Mumby, D. K. (2004). *Reworking gender: A feminist communicology of organization*. Thousand Oaks, CA: Sage.

Ballard, D., & Gossett, L. (2007). Alternative times: Communicating the non-standard work relationship. In C. S. Beck (Ed.), *Communication yearbook 31* (pp. 274-321). Mahwah, NJ: Erlbaum.

Bansal, A., Monnier, J., Hobfoll, S. E., & Stone, B. (2000). Comparing men's and women's loss of perceived social and work resources following psychological distress. *Journal of Social and Personal Relationships, 17*, 265-281.

Baumeister, R. F., & Leary, M. R. (1995). The need to belong: Desire for interpersonal attachments as a fundamental human motivation. *Psychological Bulletin, 117*, 497-529.

Bazan, W. J., & Dwyer, D. (1998, March/April). Assessing spirituality: Healthcare organizations must address their employees' spiritual needs. *Health Progress, 79*(2), 20-24.

Beder, S. (2000). *Selling the work ethic: From Puritan pulpit to corporate PR*. London: Zed Books.

Black, L. (2005). Building connection while thinking together: By-products of employee training in dialogue. *Western Journal of Communication, 69*, 273-292.

Bonney, N. (2005). Overworked Britons? Part-time work and work-life balance. *Work, Employment and Society, 19*, 391-401.

Bowe, J., Bowe, M., & Streeter, S. (Eds.). (2000). *Gig: Americans talk about their jobs*. New York: Three Rivers Press.

Bowie, N. E. (1998). A Kantian theory of meaningful work. *Journal of Business Ethics, 17*(9/10), 1083-1092.

Braverman, H. (1974). *Labor and monopoly capital*. New York: Monthly Review Press.

Brown, M. H. (1990). Defining stories in organizations: Characteristics and functions. In J. A. Anderson (Ed.), *Communication yearbook 13* (pp. 162-190). Newbury Park, CA: Sage.

Bullis, C. (1993). Organizational socialization research: Enabling, constraining, and shifting perspectives. *Communication Monographs, 60*, 10-17.

Bullis, C., Cheney, G., & Kendall, B. E. (in progress). *Taking the "environment" seriously in organizational communication*. Unpublished manuscript, University of Utah.

Bullis, C., Planalp, S., Bell, S., & Brown, A. (2005). *The development of a multidimensional questionnaire to assess worklife quality*. Unpublished manuscript, University of Utah.

Bunting, M. (2004). *Willing slaves: How the overwork culture is ruling our lives*. London: Harper-Collins.

Buss, T. F., & Cheney, G. (1983). Personalizing the impact: Some case studies. In T. F. Buss, F. S. Redburn, & J. Waldron (Eds.), *Mass unemployment: Plant closings and community mental health* (pp. 91-132). Beverly Hills, CA: Sage.

Buzzanell, P. (1997). Toward an emotion-based feminist framework for research on dual career couples. *Women and Language, 20*(2), 40-48.

Buzzanell, P., & Goldzwig, S. R. (1991). Linear and nonlinear career models: Metaphors, paradigms, and ideologies. *Management Communication Quarterly, 4*, 466-505.

Buzzanell, P., & Harter, L. M. (2006). Introduction: (De)centering and (re)envisioning the secular hegemony of organizational communication theory and research. *Communication Studies, 57*, 1-3.

Byron, W. J. (1998). Spirituality for the workplace. *Spiritual Life, 44*, 67-75.

Callister, P. (2005). *The future of work within households: Understanding household-level changes in the distribution of hours of paid work.* Wellington, New Zealand: Department of Labour. Retrieved October 25, 2005, from http://www.dol.govt.nz/pdfs/fow-changes-in-working-hours.pdf

Cameron, K. S., & Caza, A. (Eds.). (2004). Special issue on positive organizational scholarship. *American Behavioral Scientist, 47, 731-866.*

Cameron, K. S., Dutton, J. E., & Quinn, R. E. (Eds.). (2003). *Positive organizational scholarship: Foundations of a new discipline.* San Francisco: Berrett-Koehler.

Cappelli, P., Bassi, L., Katz, H., Knoke, D., Osterman, P., & Useem, M. (1997). *Change at work: How American industry and workers are coping with corporate restructuring and what workers must do to take charge of their own careers.* New York: Oxford University Press.

Carlone, D. (2001). Enablement, constraint, and *The 7 Habits of Highly Effective People. Management Communication Quarterly, 14*, 491-497.

Carlone, D., & Taylor, B. C. (1998). Organizational communication and cultural studies: A review essay. *Communication Theory, 8*, 337-367.

Caudron, S. (1997). The search for meaning at work. *Training and Development, 51*, 24-27.

Cheney, G. (1999). *Values at work: Employee participation meets market pressure at Mondragón.* Ithaca, NY: Cornell University Press.

Cheney, G. (2000). On interpreting interpretive research: Toward perspectivism without relativism. In S. R. Corman & M. S. Poole (Eds.), *Perspectives on organizational communication: Finding common ground* (pp. 17-45). New York: Guilford.

Cheney, G., & Ashcraft, K. L. (2007). Considering "the professional" in communication studies: Implications for theory and research within and beyond the boundaries of organizational communication. *Communication Theory, 17*, 146–175.

Cheney, G., & Christensen, L. T. (2000). Identity at issue: Linkages between "internal" and "external" organizational communication. In F. M. Jablin & L. L. Putnam (Eds.), *The new handbook of organizational communication* (pp. 231-269). Thousand Oaks, CA: Sage.

Cheney, G., & Cloud, D. L. (2006). Doing democracy, engaging the material: Employee participation and labor activity in an age of market globalization. *Management Communication Quarterly, 19*, 501-540.

Cheney, G., with Lair, D. J. (2005). Theorizing about rhetoric and organizations. In S. May & D. K. Mumby (Eds.), *Engaging organizational communication theory and research* (pp. 55-84). Thousand Oaks, CA: Sage.

Cheney, G., Ritz, D., & Lair, D. J. (in progress). *Communication and professional ethics: How we talk about who we are at work and why it matters.* New York: Oxford University Press.

Ciulla, J. (2000). *The working life.* Pittsburgh, PA: Three Rivers Press.

Clair, R. P. (1996). The political nature of the colloquialism, "A real job": Implications for organizational socialization. *Communication Monographs, 63*, 249-267.

Clair, R. P., Bell, S. Hackbarth, K., Mathes, S., & McConnell, M. (2008). *Why work?: The perceptions of a 'real job' and the rhetoric of work through the ages.* West Lafayette, IN: Purdue University Press.

Clark, T., & Salaman, G. (1998). Telling tales: Management gurus' narratives and the construction of managerial identity. *Journal of Management Studies, 35*, 137-161.

Cloud, D. (2001). Laboring under the sign of the new: Cultural studies, organizational communication, and the fallacy of the new economy. *Management Communication Quarterly, 15*, 268-278.

Cloud, D. (2005). Fighting words: Labor and the limits of communication at Staley, 1993 to 1996. *Management Communication Quarterly, 18*, 509-542.

Conrad, C. (1988). Work songs, hegemony, and illusions of self. *Critical Studies in Mass Communication, 5*, 179-201.

Cooren, F. (2000). *The organizing property of communication.* Philadelphia: John Benjamins.

Csikszentmihalyi, M. (1990). *Flow: The psychology of optimal experience.* New York: Harper & Row.

Csikszentmihalyi, M. (1997). *Finding flow.* New York: HarperCollins.

Cummings, J. A. (2006, November). *Work-family balance in the lives of children: Giving voice to a silenced population.* Paper presented at the annual meeting of the National Communication Association, San Antonio, TX.

Dalai Lama, H. H., & Cutler, H. C. (1998). *The art of happiness.* New York: Penguin Putnam.

Das, H. (2002). The four faces of pay: An investigation into how Canadian managers view pay. *International Journal of Commerce & Management, 12*(1), 18-40.

Davis, A. E., & Kalleberg, A. L. (2006). Family-friendly organizations? Work and family programs in the 1990s. *Work and Occupations, 33*, 191-223.

de Botton, A. (2004). *Status anxiety.* New York: Pantheon.

De Bruin, A., & Dupuis, A. (2004). Work-life balance? Insights from non-standard work. *New Zealand Journal of Employment Relations, 29*(1), 21-37.

de Graaf, J. (Ed.). (2003). *Take back your time: Fighting overwork and time poverty in America.* San Francisco: Berrett-Koehler Publishers, Inc.

de Tocqueville, A. (2001). *Democracy in America.* New York: Penguin. (Original work published 1838)

Dex, S., & Bond, S. (2005). Measuring work-life balance and its covariates. *Work, Employment and Society, 19*, 627-637.

Dickson-Goméz, J. D., Knowlton, A., & Latkin, C. (2004). Values and identities: The meaning of work for injection drug users involved in a volunteer HIV prevention outreach. *Substance Use and Misuse, 39*, 1259-1286.

Diener, E., & Seligman, M. E. P. (2004). Beyond money: Toward an economy of well-being. *Psychological Science in the Public Interest, 5*, 1-31.

Diener, E., Suh, E. M., Lucas, R. E., & Smith, H. L. (1999). Subjective well-being: Three decades of progress. *Psychological Bulletin, 125*, 276-302.

Dockery, A. M. (2003, December). *Happiness, life satisfaction and the role of work: Evidence from two Australian surveys.* Paper presented at the 5th Path to Full Employment Conference and the 10th National Conference on Unemployment, Newcastle, Australia.

Dollarhide, C. T. (1997). Counseling for meaning in work and life: An integrated approach. *Journal of Humanistic Education & Development, 35*, 178-187.

Dominguez, J., & Robin, V. (1999). *Your money or your life* (2nd ed.). New York: Penguin Books.

Dourille-Feer, E. (2004, December). Future studies in Japan: From shaping change to adapting to change. *Futuribles, 303*, 73-83.

du Gay, P. (1996). *Consumption and identity at work.* London: Sage.

du Gay, P., Salaman, G., & Rees, B. (1996). The conduct of management and the management of conduct: Contemporary managerial discourse and the constitution of the 'competent' manager. *Journal of Management Studies, 33*, 263-282.

Edley, P. (2001). Technology, employed mothers, and corporate colonization of the lifeworld: A gendered paradox of work and family balance. *Women and Language, 24*, 28-35.

Edley, P. (2003). Entrepreneurial mothers' balance of work and family: Discursive constructions of time, mothering, and identity. In P. M. Buzzanell, H. Sterk, & L. H. Turner (Eds.), *Gender in applied communication contexts* (pp. 255-273). Thousand Oaks, CA: Sage.

Edwards, P., & Wajcman, J. (2005). *The politics of working life.* Oxford, England: Oxford University Press.

Ehrenreich, B. (2005). *Bait and switch.* New York: Henry Holt.

Ekstedt, M., & Fagerberg, I. (2005). Lived experiences of the time preceding burnout. *Journal of Advanced Nursing, 49*, 59-67.

Elgin, D. (1998). *Voluntary simplicity: Toward a way of life that is outwardly simple, inwardly rich* (Rev. ed.). New York: Harper Paperback.

Elster, J. (1983). *Sour grapes.* Cambridge, England: Cambridge University Press.

Fairclough, N. (1992). *Discourse and social change.* Cambridge, England: Polity Press.

Firth, L., Mellor, D. J., Moore, K. A., & Loquet, C. (2004). How can managers reduce employee intention to quit? *Journal of Managerial Psychology, 19*, 170-187.

Fisher, W. R. (1985). The narrative paradigm: In the beginning. *Journal of Communication, 35*, 74-89.

Foucault, M. (1984). *The Foucault reader.* New York: Pantheon.

Fox, M. (1995). *The reinvention of work.* San Francisco: HarperCollins.

Freeman, R. B., & Rogers, J. (1999). *What workers want.* Ithaca, NY: Cornell University Press.

Fromm, E. (1961). *Marx's concept of man.* New York: Frederick Ungar.

Fryer, D., & Payne, R. (1984). Proactive behavior in unemployment: Findings and implications. *Leisure Studies, 3*, 273-295.

Galinsky, E., Bond, J. T., Kim, S. S., Backon, L., Brownfield, E., & Sakai, K. (2005). *Overwork in America: When the way we work becomes too much.* Retrieved June 5, 2006, from http://familiesandwork.org/summary/overwork2005.pdf

Ganesh, S. (2004). *A multidisciplinary review of the research on NGOs and non-profits.* Unpublished manuscript, University of Montana-Missoula.

Gardner, H., Csikszentmihalyi, M., & Damon, W. (2001). *Good work: When excellence and ethics meet.* New York: Basic Books.

Gee, J. P., Hull, G., & Lankshear, C. (1996). *The new work order.* Boulder, CO: Westview Press.

Gill, R. (2004). *Alternative metaphors for work-life balance.* Unpublished manuscript, University of Utah.

Gilla, A. (2001). *A critical examination of the labor practices of socially responsible businesses.* Unpublished master's thesis, University of Montana.

Gilson, C., Hurd, F., & Wagar, T. (2004). Creating a concession climate: The case of the serial downsizers. *International Journal of Human Resource Management, 15*, 1056-1068.

Gini, A. (2001). *My job, my self: Work and the creation of the modern individual.* New York: Routledge.

Golden, A., Kirby, E. L., & Jorgenson, J. (2006). Work-life research from both sides now: An integrative perspective for organizational and family communication. In C. S. Beck (Ed.), *Communication yearbook 30* (pp. 143-196). Mahwah, NJ: Erlbaum.

Goodall, H. L., Jr. (1989). *Casing a promised land* (Expanded). Carbondale: Southern Illinois University Press.

Goodier, B. C., & Eisenberg, E. M. (2006). Seeking the spirit: Communication and the (re)development of a "spiritual" organization. *Communication Studies, 57*, 47-65.

Gornick, J. C., & Heron, A. (2006). The regulation of working time as work-family reconciliation policy: Comparing Europe, Japan, and the United States. *Journal of Comparative Policy Analysis, 8*, 149-166.

Gorz, A. (2000). *Reclaiming work: Beyond the wage-based society.* Cambridge, England: Polity Press.

Grawitch, M. J., Gottschalk, M., & Munz, D. C. (2006). The path to a healthy workplace: A critical review linking healthy workplace practices, employee well-being, and organizational improvements. *Consulting Psychology Journal: Practice and Research, 58*, 129-147.

Green, F. (2001). It's been a hard day's night: The concentration and intensification of work in late-twentieth century Britain. *British Journal of Industrial Relations, 39*, 53-80.

Green, F. (2005). Why has work effort become more intense? *Industrial Relations, 43*, 709-741.

Green, F., & Tsitsianis, N. (2005). An investigation of national trends in job satisfaction in Britain and Germany. *British Journal of Industrial Relations, 43*, 401-429.

Greenhaus, J. H., & Powell, G. N. (2006). When work and family are allies: A theory of work-family enrichment. *Academy of Management Review, 31*, 72-92.

Hackman, J. R., & Oldham, G. R. (1976). Motivation through the design of work: Test of a theory. *Organizational Behavior and Human Performance, 16*, 250-279.

Hamilton, C. (2003). *Growth fetish.* Sydney, Australia: Allen & Unwin.

Harpaz, I. (1998). Cross-national comparison of religious conviction and the meaning of work. *Cross-Cultural Research, 32*, 143-170.

Harris, C., Daniels, K., & Briner, R. B. (2003). A daily diary study of goals and affective well-being at work. *Journal of Occupational and Organizational Psychology, 76*, 401-410.

Hasan, I. (2004). Meaning of work among a sample of Kuwaiti workers. *Psychological Reports, 94*, 195-207.

Haworth, J. T. (1997). *Work, leisure, and well-being.* London: Routledge.

Head, S. (2003). *The new ruthless economy: Work and power in the digital age.* New York: Oxford University Press.

Heath, J. (2002). Should productivity growth be a social priority? *The Review of Economic Performance and Social Progress, 2*, 225-241.

Hersey, P., & Blanchard, K. H. (1969). Life-cycle theory of leadership. *Training and Development Journal, 23*, 26-34.

Hochschild, A.R. (1997). *The time bind.* New York: Metropolitan Books.

Hodson, R. (1996). Dignity in the workplace under participative management: Alienation and freedom revisited. *American Sociological Review, 61*, 719-738.

Hodson, R. (2004). Work life and social fulfillment: Does social affiliation at work reflect a carrot or a stick? *Social Science Quarterly, 85*, 221-239.

Hofstede, G. (1980). *Culture's consequences: International differences in work-related values.* Newbury Park, CA: Sage.

Hoke, B. (1968). The meaning of work: Contemporary views reviewed. *Archives of Environmental Health, 16*, 598-603.

Hylmö, A., & Buzzanell, P. M. (2002). Telecommuting as viewed through cultural lenses: An empirical investigation of the discourses of utopia, identity, and mystery. *Communication Monographs, 69*, 329-356.

Inkson, K. (2006). *Understanding careers: The metaphors of working lives.* London: Sage.

Isaksen, J. (2000). Constructing meaning despite the drudgery of repetitive work. *Journal of Humanistic Psychology, 40*(3), 84-107.

Jablin, F. M., & Putnam, L. L. (Eds.). (2001). *The new handbook of organizational communication.* Thousand Oaks, CA: Sage.

Jackson, B. (2001). *Management gurus and management fashions: A dramatistic inquiry.* London: Routledge.

Kant, I. (1963). *Lectures on ethics 1775.* New York: Harper Torchbooks. (Originally published in 1775)

Kant, I. (1994). *Ethical philosophy* (J. W. Ellington, Trans.). (Original work published 1775). Indianapolis, IN: Hackett. (Original work published 1775)

Kanter, R. M. (1983). *The change masters: Innovation for productivity in the American corporation.* New York: Simon & Schuster.

Kendall, B. E. (2004). *An exploratory investigation of leisure within the context of communication studies.* Unpublished manuscript, University of Utah.

Kennedy-Jones, M., Cooper, J., & Fossey, E. (2005). Developing a worker role: Stories of four people with mental illness. *Australian Occupational Journal, 52*, 116-126.

Kingwell, M. (1998). *In pursuit of happiness*. New York: Crown Publishers.

Kirby, E. L., Golden, A., Medved, C., Jorgenson, J., & Buzzanell, P. (2003). An organizational communication challenge to the discourse of work and family research: From problematics to empowerment. In P. Kalbfleisch (Ed.), *Communication yearbook 27* (pp. 1-44). Mahwah, NJ: Erlbaum.

Kirby, E. L., & Krone, K. J. (2002). "The policy exists but you can't really use it": Communication and the structuration of work-family policies. *Journal of Applied Communication Research, 30*, 50-77.

Kirby, E. L., McBride, M. C., Shuler, S., Birkholt, M. J., Danielson, M. A., & Pawlowski, D. R. (2006). The Jesuit difference (?): Narratives of negotiating spiritual values and secular practices. *Communication Studies, 57*, 87-105.

Kirsh, B. (2000). Work, workers, and workplaces: A qualitative analysis of narratives of mental health consumers. *Journal of Rehabilitation, 66*(4), 24-30.

Kivimaki, M., Vahtera, J., Elovainio, M., Pentti, J., & Virtanen, M. (2003). Human costs of organizational downsizing: Comparing health trends between leavers and stayers. *American Journal of Community Psychology, 32*, 57-67.

Knights, D., & McCabe, D. (2003). *Organization and innovation: Guru schemes and American dreams*. Berkshire, England: Open University Press.

Kohn, A. (1993). *Punished by rewards*. Boston: Houghton Mifflin.

Kotter, J. (1990). *A force for change: How leadership differs from management*. New York: Free Press.

Kuhn, T. (2006). A 'demented work ethic' and a 'lifestyle firm': Discourse, identity, and workplace time commitments. *Organization Studies, 27*, 1339-1358.

Lair, D. J. (2004, November). *"White collar" as cultural model: Discursive representations of "white collar" in the overtime regulation controversy*. Paper presented at the annual meeting of the National Communication Association, Chicago, Illinois.

Lair, D. J. (2007). *"Survivor for Business People": A critical-rhetorical engagement of* The Apprentice *as popular management discourse*. Unpublished doctoral dissertation, University of Utah.

Lair, D. J., Sullivan, K., & Cheney, G. (2005). Marketization and the recasting of the professional self: The rhetoric and ethics of personal branding. *Management Communication Quarterly, 18*, 307-343.

Lane, R. (2000). *The loss of happiness in market democracies*. New Haven, CT: Yale University Press.

Lasch, C. (1978). *The culture of narcissism*. New York: Norton.

Layard, R. (2005). *Happiness: Lessons from a new science*. New York: Penguin.

Levering, R., & Moskovitz, M. (2007, January 22). In good company. *Fortune, 155*(1), 94-116.

Levy, F., & Murnane, R.J. (2004). *The new division of labor: How computers are creating the next job market*. Princeton, NJ: Princeton University Press.

Lewis, L. (2005). The civil society sector: A review of critical issues and research agenda for organizational communication scholars. *Management Communication Quarterly, 19*, 238-267.

Lips-Wiersma, M. (2002). The influence of spiritual "meaning-making" on career behavior. *The Journal of Management Development, 21*, 497-520.

Linson, A. (Producer), & Schultz, M. (Director) (1976). *Car Wash* [motion picture]. United States: Universal Pictures.

Lonkila, M. (1998). The social meaning of work: Aspects of the teaching profession in post-Soviet Russia. *Europe-Asia Studies, 50*, 699-713.

Marmot, M. (2004). *The status syndrome: How social standing affects our health and longevity.* New York: Times Books.

Mattson, S. (2003, April-May). Cultural diversity in the workplace: How the meaning of work can affect the way we work. *AWHONN Lifestyles, 7*, 154-158.

McGee, M. C. (1990). Text, context, and the fragmentation of contemporary culture. *Western Journal of Speech Communication, 54*, 274-289.

McKerrow, R. E. (1989). Critical rhetoric: Theory and praxis. *Communication Monographs, 56*, 91-111.

McMillan, L. H. W., & O'Driscoll, M. P. (2004). Workaholism and health: Implications for organizations. *Journal of Organizational Change Management, 17*, 509-519.

McReynolds, C. J. (2001). The meaning of work in the lives of people living with HIV disease and AIDS. *Rehabilitation Counseling Bulletin, 44*, 104-115.

Medved, C. E., Brogan, S. M., McClanahan, A. M., Morris, J. F., & Shepherd, G. J. (2006). Family and work socializing communication: Messages, gender, and ideological implications. *Journal of Family Communication, 6*, 161-180.

Medved, C. E., & Kirby, E. L. (2005). Family CEOs: A feminist analysis of corporate mothering discourses. *Management Communication Quarterly, 18*, 435-478.

Meisenbach, R., & McMillan, J. J. (2006). Blurring the boundaries: Historical developments and future directions in organizational rhetoric. In C. S. Beck (Ed.), *Communication yearbook* 30 (pp. 99-142). Mahwah, NJ: Erlbaum.

Miller, D. L., & Joe, J. R. (1993). Employment barriers and work motivation for Navajo rehabilitation clients. *International Journal of Rehabilitation Research, 16*, 107-117.

Mitroff, I. I., & Denton, E. A. (1999). *A spiritual audit of corporate America.* San Francisco: Jossey-Bass.

Mize Smith, J., Arendt, C., Bezek Lahman, J., Settle, G. N., & Duff, A. (2006). Framing the work of art: Spirituality and career discourse in the nonprofit arts section. *Communication Studies, 57*, 25-46.

Mor-Barak, M. E. (1995). The meaning of work for older adults seeking employment: The generativity factor. *International Journal on Aging and Human Development, 41*, 325-344.

Myers, D. G. (1992). *The pursuit of happiness: Who is happy and why.* New York: William Morrow.

Myers, D. G. (1999). Close relationships and quality of life. In D. Kahneman, E. Diener, & N. Schwarz (Eds.), *Well-being: The foundations of hedonic psychology* (pp. 374-391). New York: Sage.

Myers, D. G., & Diener, E. (1995). Who is happy? *Psychological Science, 6*, 10-19.

Oppermann, J. D. (2004). Interpreting the meaning individuals ascribe to returning to work after traumatic brain injury: A qualitative approach. *Brain Injury, 18*, 941-955.

O'Toole, J., & Lawler, E.E. (2006). *The new American workplace.* New York: Palgrave.

Parker, M. (1992). Post-modern organizations or postmodern organization theory. *Organization Studies, 13*, 1-17.

Peters, T. J. (1999). *The brand you 50: Or: Fifty ways to transform yourself from an 'employee' into a brand that shouts distinction, commitment, and passion!* New York: Knopf.

Petronio, S. (2000). *Balancing the secrets of private disclosures.* Mahwah, NJ: Erlbaum.

Pfeffer, J. (1994). *Competitive advantage through people.* Boston: Harvard Business School Press.

Philipson, I. (2002). *Married to the job: Why we live to work and what we can do about it.* New York: The Free Press.

Pieper, J. (2000). Leisure and its threefold opposition. In G. C. Meilaender (Ed.), *Working: Its meaning and its limits* (pp. 61-63). Notre Dame, IN: University of Notre Dame Press.

Pratt, M. G., & Ashforth, B. E. (2003). Fostering meaningfulness in writing and at work. In K. S. Cameron, J. E. Dutton, & R. E. Quinn (Eds.), *Positive organizational scholarship: Foundations of a new discipline* (pp. 309-327). San Francisco: Berrett-Koehler.

Price, R. H. (2006). The transformation of work in America: New health vulnerabilities for Americn workers. In E. E. Lawler, & J. O'Toole (Eds.). *America at work: Choices and challenges* (pp. 23-35). New York: Palgrave.

Putnam, R. (2000). *Bowling alone: The collapse and revival of American community.* New York: Simon & Schuster.

Quality of Worklife Committee, The University of Montana (1996). *Report on campus-wide survey.* Missoula: University of Montana.

Rawlins, W. K. (2005). Our family's physician. In L. M. Harter, P. M. Japp, & C. S. Beck (Eds.), *Narratives, health, and healing* (pp.197-216). Mahwah, NJ: Erlbaum.

Rifkin, J. (1995). *The end of work.* New York: Putnam.

Roethlisberger, F. J., & Dickson, W. J. (1939). *Management and the worker.* Cambridge, MA: Harvard University Press.

Rost, J. C. (1991). *Leadership for the twenty-first century.* New York: Praeger.

Rubin, R., Palmgren, P., & Sypher, H. (1994). *Communication research measures: A sourcebook.* New York: Guilford.

Sackman, S. A. (1992). Culture and subcultures: An analysis of organizational knowledge. *Administrative Sciences Quarterly, 37*, 140-161.

Samuelson, R. J. (1997). *The good life and its discontents: The American Dream in the age of entitlement.* New York: Vintage.

Schor, J. B. (1992). *The overworked American.* New York: Basic Books.

Schor, J. B. (1997). *The overspent American.* New York: Basic Books.

Schor, J. B. (2003). The (even more) overworked American. In J. de Graaf (Ed.), *Take back your time: Fighting overwork and time poverty in America* (pp. 6-11). San Francisco: Berrett-Koehler.

Schor, J. B. (2005). *Born to buy: The commercialized child and the new consumer culture.* New York: Scribner.

Schwartz, S. H. (1999). A theory of cultural values and some implications for work. *Applied Psychology: An International Review, 48*, 23-47.

Scott, J. A. (2007). Our calling, our selves: Repositioning religious and entrepreneurial discourses in career theory and practice. *Communication Studies, 58*, 261-279.

Seashore, S. (1954). *Group cohesiveness in the industrial work group.* Ann Arbor: University of Michigan Press.

Secrest, J., Iorio, D. H., & Martz, W. (2005). The meaning of work for nursing assistants who stay in long-term care. *International Journal of Older People Nursing*, in association with *Journal of Clinical Nursing, 14*, 90-97.

Seligman, M. E. P. (2002). *Authentic happiness: Using the new positive psychology to realize your potential for lasting fulfillment.* New York: Free Press.

Sennett, R. (1998). *The corrosion of character: The personal consequences of work in the new capitalism.* New York: W.W. Norton & Co.

Sewell, G. (1998). The discipline of teams: The control of team-based industrial work through electronic and peer surveillance. *Administrative Science Quarterly, 43*, 397.

Sewell, G., & Barker, J. (2006). Coercion versus care: Using irony to make sense of organizational surveillance. *Academy of Management Review, 31*, 934-961.

Sias, P. M., & Cahill, D. J. (1998). From co-workers to friends: The development of peer friendships in the workplace. *Western Journal of Communication, 62*, 273-299.

Sias, P. M., Krone, K. J., & Jablin, F. M. (2002). An ecological systems perspective on workplace relationships. In M. L. Knapp & J. A. Daly (Eds.), *Handbook of interpersonal communication* (3rd ed., pp. 615-679). Thousand Oaks, CA: Sage.

Sloop, J. M. (1996). *The cultural prison: Discourse, prisoners, punishment.* Tuscaloosa: University of Alabama Press.

Smith, H. (Senior Producer). (2006, May 16). Can you afford to retire? *Frontline* [television documentary]. Arlington, VA: Public Broadcasting Service.

Smith, P. C., Kendall, L. M., & Hulin, C. L. (1969). *The measurement of satisfaction in work and retirement.* Chicago: Rand McNally.

Smith, R. C., & Eisenberg, E. (1987). Conflict at Disneyland: A root metaphor analysis. *Communication Monographs, 54*, 367-380.

Smith, R. C., & Turner, P. K. (1995). A social constructionist reconfiguration of metaphor analysis: An application of "SCMA" to organizational socialization theorizing. *Communication Monographs, 62*, 152-181.

Smith, V. (1997). New forms of work organization. *Annual Review of Sociology, 23*, 315-339.

Smith, V. (2001). *Crossing the great divide: Worker risk and opportunity in the new economy.* Ithaca, NY: Cornell University Press.

Smith, V. (Ed.). (2006). *Worker participation: Current research and future trends (Vol. 16; Research in the sociology of work).* Greenwich, CT: JAI Press.

Spector, P. E., Cooper, C. L., Poelmans, S., Allen, T. D., O'Driscoll, M., Sanchez, J. I., et al. (2004). A cross-national comparative study of work-family stressors, working hours, and well-being: China and Latin America versus the Anglo world. *Personnel Psychology, 57*, 119-142.

Spoonley, P. (2004). Is non-standard work becoming standard? Trends and issues. *New Zealand Journal of Employment Relations, 29*(3), 3-24.

Stackman, R. W., & Pinder, C. C. (1999). Context and sex effects on personal work networks. *Journal of Social and Personal Relationships, 16*, 39-64.

Taylor, B. C., & Carlone, D. (2001). Silicon communication: A reply and case study. *Management Communication Quarterly, 15*, 289-300.

Taylor, J. R., & Van Every, E. J. (2000). *The emergent organization: Communication as its site and surface.* Mahwah, NJ: Erlbaum.

Terez, T. (2002). *22 keys to creating a meaningful workplace.* Avon, MA: Adams Media Corporation.

Terkel, S. (1972). *Working: People talk about what they do all day and how they feel about what they do.* New York: Pantheon.

The Science of Happiness [Special Mind and Body Issue]. (2005, January 17), *Time,* pp. A1-A68.

Thomas, K. W. (2000). *Intrinsic motivation at work: Building energy and commitment.* San Francisco: Berrett-Koehler.

Thoreau, H. D. (1854). *Walden.* Boston: Ticknor and Fields.

Thrift, N. (1997). Soft capitalism. *Cultural Values, 1*, 29-58.

Tompkins, P. K., Fisher, J. Y., Infante, D. A., & Tompkins, E. L. (1975). Kenneth Burke and the inherent characteristics of formal organizations: A field study. *Speech Monographs, 42*, 135-142.

Trethewey, A. (1999). Disciplined bodies: Women's embodied identities at work. *Organization Studies, 20*, 423-450.

Trujillo, N. (1992). Interpreting (the work and talk of) baseball: Perspectives on ballpark culture. *Western Journal of Communication, 56*, 350-371.

Trujillo, N., & Dionisopoulos, G. (1987). Cop talk, police stories, and the social construction of organizational drama. *Central States Speech Journal, 38*, 196-209.

Tuomi, K., Vanhala, S., Nykyri, E., & Janhonen, M. (2004). Organizational practices, work demands and the well-being of employees: A follow-up study in the metal industry and retail trade. *Occupational Medicine, 54*, 115-121.

Turnquist, K. (2005, February 17). While you were at work today. *The Oregonian,* p. E-1.

van Saane, N., Sluiter, J. K., Verbeek, J. H. A. M., & Frings-Dresen, M. H. W. (2003). Reliability and validity of instruments measuring job satisfaction—a systematic review. *Occupational Medicine, 53*, 191-200.

Vande Berg, L., & Trujillo, N. (1989). *Organizational life on television.* Norwood, NJ: Ablex.

Veblen, T. (1981). *The theory of the leisure class.* Harmondsworth, England: Penguin. (Original work published 1899).

Wachtel, P. (1989). *The poverty of affluence.* Philadelphia: New Society Publishers.

Wagner, C. G. (2002). The new meaning of work. *The Futurist, 36*(5), 16-17.

Waldeck, J., & Myers, K. (2007). Organizational assimilation theory, research, and implications for multiple areas of the discipline: A state of the art review. In C. S. Beck (Ed.), *Communication yearbook 31* (pp. 322-369). Mahwah, NJ: Erlbaum.

Waring, M. (1988). *If women counted: A new feminist economics.* San Francisco: Harper & Row.

Weber, M. (1992). *The Protestant ethic and the spirit of capitalism.* London: Routledge.

Whitmyer, C. (1994). *Mindfulness and meaningful work: Explorations in right livelihood.* Berkeley, CA: Parallax Press.

Whyte, W. H. (1956). *The organization man.* New York: Simon & Schuster.

Williams, J. (2001). *Unbending gender: When work and family conflict and what to do about it.* New York: Oxford University Press.

Wilson, T. D. & Gilbert, D. T. (2003). Affective forecasting. In M. P. Zanna (Ed.), *Advances in experimental social psychology* (Vol. 35, pp. 345-411). San Diego, CA: Academic Press.

Wrzesniewski, A. (2003). Finding positive meaning in work. In K. S. Cameron, J. E. Dutton, & R. E. Quinn (Eds.), *Positive organizational scholarship: Foundations of a new discipline* (pp. 296-308). San Francisco: Berrett-Koehler

Yankelovich, D. (1974). The meaning of work. In J. M. Roson (Ed.), *The worker and the job: Coping with change* (pp. 19-47). Englewood Cliffs, NJ: Prentice-Hall.

Zorn, T. E. (1995). Bosses and buddies: A constructive/dramaturgical analysis of simultaneously close and hierarchical relationships in organizations. In J. T. Wood & S. Duck (Eds.), *Under-studied relationships: Off the beaten track* (pp. 122-147). Newbury Park, CA: Sage.

Zorn, T. E., Christensen, L. T., & Cheney, G. (1999). *Do we really want constant change?* San Francisco: Berrett-Koehler.

Zorn, T. E., Page, D., & Cheney, G. (2000). NUTS! about change: Multiple perspectives on change-oriented communication in a public-sector organization. *Management Communication Quarterly, 13*, 515-566.

Zorn, T. E., & Taylor, J. R. (2004). Knowledge management and/as organizational communication. In D. Tourish & O. Hargie (Eds.), *Key issues in organisational communication* (pp. 96-112). London: Routledge.

CHAPTER CONTENTS

5 Reconceptualizing Virtual Teaming from a Constitutive Perspective

Review, Redirection, and Research Agenda

Jennifer L. Gibbs
Rutgers University

Dina Nekrassova
Rutgers University

Svetlana V. Grushina
Rutgers University

Sally Abdul Wahab
Rutgers University

Despite the growing importance of virtual teams in modern organizations and the fundamental role played by discursive practices in enacting such teams across time, space, and cultural boundaries, the burgeoning literature on virtuality and virtual teams tends to be predominantly confined to management, computer science, and information systems journals; whereas, communication research has paid scant attention to virtual team interaction and processes. As a result, such research tends to take a functionalist approach, which regards communication as a variable, rather than examining how virtual teamwork is constituted through communicative practices. This chapter synthesizes the existing research on virtual teams and provides a critical reassessment of the literature from a constitutive perspective. We propose a conceptual framework that situates communication processes centrally as an alternative to the dominant inputs–processes–outcomes model and suggest a programmatic agenda of future

Correspondence: Jennifer L. Gibbs, Department of Communication, Rutgers University, 4 Huntington Street, New Brunswick, NJ 08901-1071; Phone: 732-932-7500 x8136; Fax: 732-932-6916; E-mail: jgibbs@scils.rutgers.edu research for communication scholars across a variety of areas—organizational, interpersonal, group, mediated, and intercultural communication.

New workplace trends toward distributed work, reliance on computer-mediated communication (CMC), and flexible work arrangements have led to the rise of virtual teams, which span boundaries of space, time, and culture. Virtual work arrangements—such as distributed product development or design teams, communities of practice, or telework—have become critical for organizational survival owing to intensified global competition and corporate restructuring, which often involve downsizing, outsourcing, and mergers and acquisitions (Martins, Gilson, & Maynard, 2004). As Lurey and Raisinghani (2001) contended, "globalization of the marketplace alone...makes...distributed work groups the primary operating units needed to achieve a competitive advantage in this ever-changing business environment" (p. 523). Virtual teams represent a particular type of new work arrangement that is characterized by varying degrees of geographic dispersion, dependence on communication technologies, cultural diversity, and dynamic structure (Gibson & Gibbs, 2006).

The landscape of communication research has been changing rapidly in light of the ubiquitous political, economic, and social changes worldwide, with increasing attention being directed to processes of global organizing (e.g., Stohl, 2005) and non-standard work arrangements (e.g., Ballard & Gossett, 2007). Virtual teams, in which individuals from diverse contexts and locations come in contact, often provide a critical coordination mechanism in integrating units across organizations. Understanding processes of organizing in virtual environments comprises an important issue that communication scholars are well equipped to address, but one that remains understudied in the communication discipline. This chapter reviews the virtual teams literature and recasts it from a constitutive perspective, inviting scholars from across the discipline to examine processes of virtual organizing and the centrality of communication in constituting such processes.

Virtual teamwork bridges a number of areas within the communication discipline—organizational, interpersonal, group, mediated, and intercultural communication. As interpersonal, group, and organizational interactions become increasingly mediated through technology, scholars in each of these areas may benefit from greater understanding of ways in which virtual relationships are constructed between individuals, in groups, and within and among organizations. This research can benefit a range of organizations, given virtual teaming's importance across many types of organizations—from multinational corporations to governmental and non-profit agencies to higher education. Further, exploring the ways in which stakeholders negotiate cultural differences in virtual contexts will enrich research in intercultural communication, which has largely been conducted in face-to-face settings. Finally, scholars in areas as diverse as information systems, instructional and developmental communication, health communication, and language and social interaction may also benefit from research on constitutive approaches to virtual teaming. Issues uncovered by studying virtual teams are relevant to an international community of scholars and practitioners.[1] Thus, we call for diverse communication scholars to devote greater attention to this important feature of the contemporary workplace.

Over the last decade, a burgeoning literature has emerged on virtual teams. Research provides critical understanding of various aspects of virtual work by illuminating unique characteristics of virtual teams, comparing them to traditional co-located teams, and identifying advantages and disadvantages of working across time and space by means of information and communication technologies (ICTs). Studies have focused on issues such as creating and maintaining trust (e.g., Coppola, Hiltz, & Rotter, 2004; Jarvenpaa, Shaw, & Staples, 2004; Krebs, Hobman, & Bordia, 2006; Piccoli & Ives, 2003; Walther & Bunz, 2005), conflict management (e.g., Hinds & Bailey, 2003; Hinds & Mortensen, 2005; Montoya-Weiss, Massey, & Song., 2001), leadership (e.g., Bell & Kozlowski, 2002; Connaughton & Daly, 2005; Kayworth & Leidner, 2001; Zaccaro & Bader, 2003), knowledge sharing (e.g., Cramton, 2001; Griffith, Sawyer, & Neale, 2003; Sole & Edmondson, 2002; Zakaria, Amelinckx, & Wilemon, 2004), and identification (e.g., Connaughton & Daly, 2004a; Fiol & O'Connor, 2005; Wiesenfeld, Raghuram, & Garud, 2001). Largely separate research streams have addressed challenges posed by geographic dispersion of team members, reliance on CMC, cultural diversity, and dynamic structural arrangements, though recent empirical studies are beginning to examine several or all of these factors together in a systematic fashion (c.f. Gibson & Gibbs, 2006).

Despite the growing importance of such teams in modern organizations and the fundamental role played by discursive practices in enacting such teams across time, space, and cultural boundaries, the burgeoning literature on virtuality and virtual teams tends to be predominantly confined to management, computer science, and information systems journals, while communication research has, until recently, paid scant attention to virtual team interaction and processes. As a result, most existing research on virtual teams takes a managerial or functionalist approach (also called post-positivist; see related arguments by Zoller & Kline, this volume). Indeed, most small group research has been conducted from a functionalist perspective (for a review, see Hollingshead et al., 2004), so, perhaps not surprisingly, virtual groups and teams research has continued in the same vein (e.g., Staples & Webster, 2007; Walther & Bazarova, 2007). The functionalist approach focuses on understanding and improving group performance effectiveness, which scholars in this tradition assume to be a causal outcome of internal and external input factors (Wittenbaum et al., 2004). Few studies examine how teaming (whether virtual or not) is constituted through communication among team members. As a review of research on virtual teams by Martins et al. (2004) suggests, the inputs–processes–outcomes model has become the dominant framework used to investigate virtual teams.

Input variables span group size, knowledge, skills and abilities of virtual team members, technology, task, and composition. Team processes include planning processes, action processes (team communication and participation), and interpersonal processes (conflict, uninhibited behavior, trust, or group cohesiveness). Finally, team outcomes encompass various affective states and performance indicators. According to the review by Martins et al., researchers discuss other factors that influence virtual working in terms of moderators of virtual performance such as task type, time, and social context. In other words, recent investigations of virtual teams are dominated by variable-analytic studies of factors that produce significant effects on work processes and may contribute to or interfere with virtual team effectiveness and productivity. In a similar vein, interpersonal processes—including communication itself—tend to be viewed as variables that may either improve overall team performance or disrupt completion of a task.

The functionalist perspective has its merits in precisely measuring and testing relationships among discrete variables and identifying best practices for team effectiveness. Communication scholars are, however, well positioned to extend this approach by conceptualizing and investigating organizational phenomena from alternative interpretive and critical perspectives that regard communication practices as central in virtual team processes, take a more discursive, constitutive view of communication, and examine how virtual teams are socially constructed through the communication practices of their members and larger organizational environment (for further explanations of social constructionist and interpretive/critical approaches, see Bartesaghi & Castor, this volume; Zoller & Kline, this volume). Such an approach calls attention to the diverse historical and cultural contexts of team members and their role(s) in shaping different meanings and interpretations of work processes, as well as power relations undergirding the negotiation of cultural practices and which interpretations and assumptions become privileged (for related arguments, see Lacy, this volume; Pal & Dutta, this volume).

This chapter synthesizes existing literature on virtuality and virtual teams and offers a critical reassessment of the literature from a constitutive perspective. We propose an alternative conceptual framework for studying virtual teams, which regards communication practices as constitutive of virtual teamwork and integrates key dimensions of virtuality (geographic dispersion, electronic dependence, cultural diversity, and dynamic structure) as well as key team processes (trust, conflict management, leadership, knowledge sharing, and identification). Rather than exclusively regarding these factors as variables to be operationalized and tested through quantitative research, we advocate the use of interpretive and critical approaches that examine teaming as a dynamic process that is socially constructed through intersubjective interactions among team members. In doing so, we identify gaps in the current literature and suggest a programmatic agenda for future research.

VIRTUALITY AND THE CENTRALITY OF COMMUNICATION

Defining Virtual Teams

Virtual teams have been defined as groups of geographically dispersed individuals who collaborate on mutual projects using ICTs to communicate (Townsend, DeMarie, & Hendrickson, 1998) and whose members are dispersed across geographic, temporal, organizational, and cultural boundaries (Jarvenpaa et al., 2004; Lurey & Raisinghani, 2001). Whereas early research relied heavily on laboratory studies contrasting purely "virtual" or 100% computer-mediated with non-virtual or 100% face-to-face groups (e.g., Burke & Chidambaram, 1995; Hollingshead, 1996; Kiesler, Siegel, & McGuire, 1984; Potter & Balthazard, 2002; Straus & McGrath, 1994; Walther, 1995; Warkentin, Sayeed, & Hightower, 1997), contemporary conceptualizations of virtuality have begun to treat it as a continuum (Gibson & Gibbs, 2006; Griffith, Sawyer, et al., 2003; Martins et al., 2004). As Martins et al. observed, in contemporary organizations, very few purely virtual or purely face-to-face teams exist. Rather than being a new and different breed of team, *all* teams can be characterized on a continuum of virtuality, ranging from low to high on each dimension.

Scholars commonly recognize virtuality as a multidimensional construct (Cohen & Gibson, 2003; Kirkman & Mathieu, 2005; Martins et al., 2004). Though the literature often imprecisely uses the term *virtual* to refer to many different types of teams, and specific dimensions of virtuality vary from study to study, the most common dimensions involve geographic dispersion, electronic dependence, cultural diversity, and dynamic structure (Gibson & Gibbs, 2006). *Geographic dispersion* refers to physical and temporal distance among team members as they are spread out across multiple locations and time zones.[2] *Electronic dependence* describes a substantial (though not necessarily exclusive) reliance of team members on electronic means of communication such as e-mail, instant messaging, videoconferencing, or groupware. *Cultural diversity* stems not only from the differences in nationality or ethnicity among team members but also from variations in professional, organizational, and project team cultures (Earley & Gibson, 2002; Goodman, Phillips, & Sackmann, 1999). Finally, as Gibson and Gibbs noted, *dynamic structure* refers to frequent change or turnover among members and their roles and relationships to one another.

The Centrality of Communication in Virtual Teams

Virtual work arrangements offer a number of competitive business advantages to organizations such as flexible jobbing (Stough, Eom, & Buckenmyer, 2000), spatial independence (Majchrzak, Malhotra, Stamps, & Lipnack, 2004), cost savings, quick information gathering and exchange, increased innovation through participation, and construction of mutual knowledge (for review, see

Gillam & Oppenheim, 2006). Interestingly, scholars also find that the same advantageous features lead to difficulties in establishing trust (Bradley & Vozikis, 2004; Jarvenpaa, Knoll, & Leidner, 1998; Kanawattanachai & Yoo, 2002; Murphy, 2004; Panteli, 2005), maintaining productive collaboration (Harvey, Novicevic, & Garrison, 2004; Jarvenpaa et al., 1998), executing effective leadership (Connaughton & Daly, 2005; Gillam & Oppenheim, 2006), dealing with disagreements and differences, negotiating task processes, group roles and work relationships, or resolving conflicts (Henderson, 1994) as well as breakdown of coordination, loss of communication "richness," and cultural misunderstandings (Gibbs, 2006). Hence, we emphasize that members enact virtual teams through communicative processes as they engage in various practices (e.g., information sharing, electronic message exchange, choice of a particular vocabulary, timeliness, and responsiveness), which may have positive or negative consequences, depending on the context and the particular communicative practices employed. Thus, we underscore the crucial role of communication in virtual teams. Though teaming, in general, may be conceptualized as constituted through communication, the constitutive role of communication may be even more pronounced in virtual teams because communication facilitates the team's existence (Ahuja, Galletta, & Carley, 2003).

In this chapter, we shift the view of virtual teams as predetermined by technological design (Lea, O'Shea, & Fung, 1995) or structural characteristics, and we set the stage for reconceptualizing virtual teaming as communicatively constituted through continuous mundane interactions among team members. In particular, the dynamism of virtual working is not necessarily revealed through unique technologies, performances of individual group members, or characteristics of media, but teaming evolves through reciprocal interactions between members through technology use. Thus, virtual teams must be considered relational and emergent (Boczkowski & Orlikowski, 2004). The following section reviews key areas of research on virtual teaming. We then critique several major assumptions running through the literature and offer a new conceptual framework and future research agenda that reconceptualizes each of these concepts as constituted through communication.

REVIEW OF THE VIRTUAL TEAMS LITERATURE

A comprehensive review of the virtual teams research published in communication, management, organizational behavior, small groups, computer science, and information systems journals revealed that the literature can be characterized by five key themes that are of particular interest to communication scholars: trust, conflict management, leadership, knowledge sharing, and identification. We elected to focus on these particular themes based on two criteria: the existence of a substantial body of research on each of them and their relevance to interpersonal and group communication processes. While input variables (such as demographic composition, team size, and task type) and outcome variables (such as satisfaction, time, decision quality, and creativity) have been commonly studied (Martins et al., 2004), communication scholars should also consider unpacking and articulating the ways in which interpretive and discursive practices work to construct these dynamic processes. We now discuss major findings in each of these areas.

Trust

Researchers have identified trust as a crucial ingredient in the productive and effective functioning of virtual teams (Goodbody, 2005; Govindarajan & Gupta, 2001; Jarvenpaa et al., 1998; Nandhakumar, 1999). Trust functions as an informal control mechanism that replaces traditional forms of control in post-bureaucratic organizations, and scholars regard it as more effective than formal control or authority status in getting members of decentralized virtual teams to work together (Handy, 1995; Murphy, 2004). Studies have determined that trust significantly impacts the efficiency, effectiveness, and quality of virtual team projects (Edwards & Sridhar, 2005). It is an important component for creating a safe environment (Gluesing & Gibson, 2004), increasing collaboration among members (Hossain & Wigand, 2004), and improving productivity (Govindarajan & Gupta, 2001). Furthermore, trust has been linked to power issues and shared goals (Panteli, 2005) because they serve as a foundation on which members build confidence in work partnerships and minimize the use of coercive power in pursuit of a collaborative partnership. In a similar vein, trust has been found essential for successful distanced leadership because it promotes effective communication and positive work relationships (Connaughton & Daly, 2004b, 2005).

Despite these benefits, research indicates that virtual work arrangements pose challenges to team members in terms of forming and maintaining trusting relationships (Millward & Kyriakidou, 2004). In particular, the lack of face-to-face communication characterizing virtual teams likely makes it more difficult to build trust among geographically dispersed team members who interact electronically. Some remain skeptical about the ability of virtual teams to perform well without face-to-face interaction—as Handy argued, "trust needs touch" (1995, p. 46). Trust can also be impeded by the inadequacy of CMC to provide access to the "backstage" of participants' activities (Nandhakumar, 1999). Further, virtual team members lack rich nonverbal and social context cues which help to convey tone, feelings, and nuances of meaning (Millward & Kyriakidou, 2004; Platt & Page, 2001; Stough et al., 2000). Because membership of virtual teams is often culturally diverse, cultural differences may present challenges for developing trusting relationships (Gibson & Manuel, 2003; Gillam & Oppenheim, 2006), given that people more likely trust members of their own cultural in-group and tend to distrust members of out-groups (Brewer, 1981). Finally, the dynamic structure and turnover characterizing many virtual teams can result in greater uncertainty and perceived risk owing to less stable and cohesive relationships, leading to lower trust among team members (Gibson & Gibbs, 2006).

Given the challenges of working virtually, experts commonly recommend establishing and cultivating trust to improve relationships among team members and raise productivity of virtual teams (Gluesing & Gibson, 2004; Grosse, 2002). The following practices can be employed to compensate for the lack of nonverbal cues in online interactions: rotating and diffusing team leadership, linking rewards to team performances, building social capital (e.g., building social networks among managers from different countries), scheduling face-to-face meetings (Govindarajan & Gupta, 2001), and cultivating face-to-face relationships among virtual team members (Nandhakumar, 1999). Another important strategy for overcoming difficulties in forming trust among virtual team members involves establishing and following a number of rules: (1) get started right away, (2) communicate frequently, (3) multitask getting organized and doing substantive work, (4) overtly acknowledge reading messages distributed by teammates, (5) be explicit about what one is thinking and doing, and (6) set deadlines and stick to them (Walther & Bunz, 2005). In their student sample, Walther and Bunz found strong support for the effectiveness of these rules to structure virtual team work, form trust in groups, and demonstrate better performance on tasks. However, behaviorial control mechanisms may also have a negative impact on trust development in temporary virtual teams because they increase the salience of incidents caused by reneging and incongruence (Piccoli & Ives, 2003).

Conflict Management

Conflict management comprises another major aspect of virtual teamwork that is fundamental to productive group functioning (Gillam & Oppenheim, 2006; Hinds & Bailey, 2003; Montoya-Weiss et al., 2001). Indeed, researchers suggest that conflict significantly affects group performance and satisfaction (DeChurch & Marks, 2001; Jehn, 1995, 1997). By definition, a team consists of a group of people who work interdependently. This interdependence entails processes of coordination, integration, and negotiation, thus making conflict an inherent feature of teamwork (Amason, 1996; DeChurch & Marks, 2001). Ting-Toomey (1994) defined *conflict* as "the perceived and/ or actual incompatibility of values, expectations, processes, or outcomes between two or more parties over substantive and/ or relational issues" (p. 360). According to conflict literature, teams experience three types of disagreement. *Relational conflict*, also known as affective conflict, refers to emotion-laden disputes about interpersonal issues (Amason, 1996; Griffith, Mannix, & Neale, 2003; Jehn, 1997). Amason labeled relational conflict as dysfunctional, and Jehn reported that it negatively impacts team performance. According to Jehn, *process conflict*, on the other hand, stems from disagreements about how to approach a particular task. Finally, *task conflict* refers to disagreements about the task itself (Amason, 1996; Griffith, Mannix, et al., 2003; Jehn, 1997). Dubbed as cognitive conflict by Amason, it can be advantageous or detrimental to team effectiveness depending on the situation (Jehn, 1995; Lovelace, Shapiro, & Weingart, 2001).

Virtual teams generally face greater conflict than traditional teams owing to their geographic dispersion, the reduction of social context cues in CMC, cultural differences, and dynamic structure. For example, the absence of important nonverbal cues may lead to misinterpretation of electronic messages and misunderstanding of other team members' intentions and expectations (DeSanctis & Monge, 1999), which increases the challenge of achieving a shared and unified understanding of the task among team members (Hinds & Bailey, 2003). Furthermore, geographically distributed teams do not benefit from *situated knowledge*, characterized by mutual engagement in activities, shared enterprise experience, and repertoire of resources (Sole & Edmondson, 2002), which may lead to communication difficulties and also result in misunderstanding among team members. Moreover, Montoya-Weiss et al. (2001) determined that virtual team members face temporal coordination challenges in resolving internal conflicts because groupware technologies do not have the capacity to convey the multiple nonverbal cues that characterize face-to-face interactions. The lack of such cues makes decision making and consensus building in teams more difficult, given that miscommunication and misunderstandings tend to occur, and, as a consequence, conflicts among team members are heightened and less easily dispelled (Zakaria et al., 2004).

Other sources of conflict include cultural differences, weak identity, and ambiguous tasks, group roles, and responsibilities (Maznevski, Davison, & Jonsen, 2006; Shin, 2005). For example, Mortensen and Hinds (2001) found that shared team identity was associated with less task conflict within distributed product development teams. They reported similar effects for affective conflict, suggesting that a shared identity may help distributed teams to better manage conflict. The results also suggest that teams relying heavily on CMC face more task conflict. Furthermore, despite the lack of socioemotional cues in CMC, affective conflict may be surprisingly more acute in computer-mediated groups because technology filters out much important social information which supports negotiation processes in face-to-face interactions. Moreover, Paul, Samarah, Seetharaman, and Mykytyn (2005) concluded that conflict management styles vary across cultures, with individualistic cultures preferring less collaborative styles and collectivistic cultures favoring more collaborative styles. Scholars have also used face-negotiation theory (Ting-Toomey, 1988; Ting-Toomey & Kurogi, 1998) to explain cultural differences in conflict management styles, given that those from individualistic cultures focus more on self-face concerns; whereas, those from collectivistic cultures tend to express more concern for the face of others and preserving mutual face (Cocroft & Ting-Toomey, 1994; Oetzel et al., 2001; Trubisky, Ting-Toomey, & Lin, 1991).

Leadership

Scholars have investigated issues of leadership according to the following themes. First, researchers generally define leadership in terms of functions that leaders should perform to build and to facilitate work processes within the team (e.g., performance management and team development; Bell & Kozlowski, 2002). Second, the managerial literature focuses primarily on developing prescriptive instructions to overcome challenges of leadership in virtual or distanced contexts to ensure leadership effectiveness. Challenges associated with leading from afar include "building trust, inspiring, managing conflict, preventing feelings of disconnectedness, monitoring and evaluating performance, communicating vision, establishing loyalty to the organization, and maintaining teamwork" (Connaughton & Daly, 2005, p. 188). Suggestions include establishing credibility at the executive level, selecting appropriate leadership style and strategies, building credibility, managing performance, and clearly defining tasks (Connaughton & Daly, 2004b; Kayworth & Leidner, 2001). Third, a number of research studies aim to distill similarities and differences between virtual and co-located teams, in which effective leadership practices in proximate teams serve as a benchmark to assess leadership in distanced ones (Bell & Kozlowski, 2002; Kerber & Buono, 2004). Fourth, researchers often conceptualize leadership as a set of observable and measurable variables (e.g., style, effectiveness, strategies, perception, character traits or personality, etc.) which produce impacts on team effectiveness (e.g., Kayworth & Leidner, 2001; Lurey & Raisinghani, 2001). Many studies seek to identify phenomena often conceptualized as input variables (e.g., task complexity, trust, identification, isolation, information equity) that produce significant impacts on leadership effectiveness. In other words, as Kayworth and Leidner explained, the main concern in studying leadership in the virtual environment has been unearthing factors that contribute to or contaminate leadership effectiveness and identifying a set of styles or behaviors suitable to improve leadership efficiently in a variety of situations.

Knowledge Sharing

Because researchers and practitioners agree that mutual or shared knowledge (Baba, Gluesing, Ratner, & Wagner, 2004; Cramton, 2001; Sarker, Sarker, Nicholson, & Joshi, 2005; Zakaria et al., 2004) comprises a critical asset for successful functioning of a social unit, transfer of knowledge appears to be especially important for virtual teams, in which knowledge is distributed and less likely to be shared (Baba et al., 2004; Sarker et al., 2005; Zakaria et al., 2004). The process of knowledge exchange may be conditioned by a number of factors. In particular, according to Sarker et al., the volume of communication, the credibility of the communicator, and cultural values held by the communicator impact the extent of knowledge transferred. Information access, storage, and retrieval also constitute key issues; successful collaboration in virtual teams requires having access to project-related information and sufficient channels to distribute information to all team members (Shin, 2005; Sivunen & Valo, 2006).

Researchers generally associate virtuality with challenges in terms of knowledge sharing. Virtual teams face difficulties in exchanging, disseminating, and sharing not only explicit knowledge (documents, reports, data, etc.) but also more subtle and less visible tacit knowledge which "is gained through social experience in a specific context and consists of cognitive knowledge (mental models or beliefs) and technical knowledge (skills or crafts)" (Flanagin, 2002, p. 243). Along these lines, research on distributed teams reveals that members in different locations often experience difficulty with sharing situated or tacit knowledge which is embedded in particular local contexts with members in other locations (Sole & Edmondson, 2002) and that they may not realize that certain knowledge is not shared, assuming that other members already know things that they take for granted (Cramton, 2001).

Another barrier to knowledge sharing in geographically distributed teams involves the tendency for subgroups or "faultlines" to form based on geographic location, particularly if they are aligned with demographic attributes (Cramton & Hinds, 2004). Subgroups also likely play a divisive role in moderately culturally diverse teams because conflict among strong cultural sub-factions can prevent such teams from transcending cultural differences and forming "hybrid cultures" or common understandings (Earley & Mosakowski, 2000). Gibson and Vermeulen (2003) determined that moderately diverse teams are, indeed, able to engage in learning behavior so long as subgroups do not become too strong and distinct. In addition to learning behavior, Cummings (2004) linked external knowledge sharing with the effectiveness of structurally diverse work groups, given that members benefit from knowledge gained from diverse geographic locations, organizational roles and affiliations.

Identification

Wiesenfeld, Raghuram, and Garud (1999, 2001) advocated identification as particularly critical in virtual contexts because it facilitates coordination and control of employees, which presents a key challenge owing to the lack of direct supervision or monitoring. Scholars argue that identification provides a type of "social glue" that holds virtual teams and organizations together and helps them cohere in the absence of face-to-face interaction (Fiol & O'Connor, 2005; Wiesenfeld et al., 1999). For instance, Mortensen and Hinds (2001) associated shared team identity with less task and affective conflict within distributed teams. These findings suggest that a shared identity may help distributed teams to manage different types of conflict in a more constructive way. In a similar vein, Connaughton and Daly (2004a) found significant relationships between trust and identification in dispersed settings.

Virtuality poses challenges to inducing identification, however. First, the temporary, project-based nature of many virtual work arrangements and the shifting nature of membership results in a more ephemeral environment (Kristof, Brown, Sims, & Smith, 1995), which leads to temporary rather than fixed identifications. Additionally, the existence of multiple identification targets tends to problematize identification among virtual team members (Scott, 1997). Given that virtual team members may perceive isolation from a team or an organization, identification with a team may be particularly important as well as problematic for virtual team members (Kirkman, Rosen, Gibson, Tesluk, & McPherson, 2002). Gossett (2002) determined that managers of temporary workers engage in strategic practices designed to limit, rather than promote, such identification to exclude such members from decision making and relieve the organization from feeling responsible for their general welfare. Overall, virtual work arrangements may be expected to pose challenges to identification owing to weakened identification across time and space and reduced loyalty owing to temporary relationships and the existence of multiple competing identity targets.

ASSUMPTIONS IN THE LITERATURE

The virtual teams literature can be characterized by several major assumptions. We argue for the need to reconceptualize the study of virtual teams from a constitutive perspective (e.g., Mokros, 2003; Putnam & Pacanowsky, 1983; Weick, 1979), and we call for rethinking these major premises. In this section, we critique several main assumptions underlying the dominant inputs–processes–outcomes model (e.g., Martins et al., 2004); in the following one, we outline how communication scholars may reconceptualize virtual teaming from a discursive, constitutive perspective. In the final section, we propose a new conceptual framework and outline a programmatic agenda for future research on virtual teams by communication scholars.

Communication as a Variable

As a review by Martins et al. (2004) suggests, the inputs–processes–outcomes model (e.g., Lurey & Raisinghani, 2001) has become the dominant framework for investigating virtual teams. As a result, according to Lurey and Raisinghani, virtual teams tend to be conceptualized as fixed and stable entities, and researchers treat team processes, communication patterns, and internal relations as internal or external variables that produce significant impacts on team performance and effectiveness. The literature has focused on identifying antecedents to conflict, leadership, trust, identification, and knowledge sharing and measuring the impact of these factors on outcomes such as satisfaction or productivity. Though identified as processes in the inputs-processes-outputs model, the dominant perspective taken in most managerial studies of virtual teams regards communication (and other constructs) as static variables rather than processes (e.g., Martins et al., 2004). Studies still tend to conceptualize communication among virtual team members as a physical process of transmitting instrumental and social information from one person to another, in line with the conduit metaphor (Axley, 1984). This process is constrained and conditioned by such factors as electronic dependence, geographic dispersion, cultural diversity, and dynamic structure. Such defining features of virtual teams serve as determinants that shape and constrict interactions among virtual workers. Even studies of virtual teams by communication scholars often take rather limited views of communication by measuring it in terms of variables, such as frequency or type of media use (e.g., Connaughton & Daly, 2004a; Timmerman & Scott, 2006). Such an approach adopts a mechanistic view of communication that overlooks its symbolic qualities and active role in creating and recreating social structures and processes of organizing (Putnam, 1983). As such, it fails to capture the dynamic nature of practices workers engage in to create and recreate the context of virtual teamwork. Furthermore, scholars and practitioners exploring various aspects of virtual work tend to treat the work context of virtual teams as a stable entity and, therefore, overlook the complex reciprocal interrelation between the context of virtual work, action, and human agency (Lea et al., 1995).

For example, studies of conflict in small groups tend to be conducted from a functionalist perspective (Wittenbaum et al., 2004), in which researchers generally conceptualize conflict as an output variable that is affected by the complex interrelationships of input variables (e.g., conflict resolution styles, trust variables, degree of identification with a team). Though research has shed light on diverse dimensions of virtual organizing, studies usually rest almost exclusively on an oversimplified view of the nature of conflict, negotiation, and conflict management processes. These studies typically consider relationships between parties in terms of competing interests and assess the outcomes of conflict in terms of winning or losing (Conrad & Poole, 2005).

Furthermore, scholars investigate communication as a variable that contributes to (or impedes) effective conflict resolution through various bargaining tactics. Such perspectives virtually ignore conflict framing, dynamic processes of socially developing interpretations of events, and socially constituted negotiating processes. For example, the few studies that examine cultural heterogeneity in virtual settings treated it as a variable that leads to increased conflict and has direct or indirect effects on performance (e.g., Mortensen & Hinds, 2001; Paul et al., 2005; Paul, Seetharaman, Samarah, & Mykytyn, 2004) and fail to consider processes through which it shapes conflict perceptions and dynamics among dispersed multicultural team members. However, cultural differences do not affect conflict levels or conflict management styles by virtue of their existence but, instead, because they shape the way that people perceive themselves, others, and the relationships between them (Singelis & Brown, 1995; Ting-Toomey & Oetzel, 2001). Thus, a better understanding of the effects of cultural differences on conflict in virtual teams may be attained by examining the ways in which these differences shape members' perceptions, behaviors, and interactions.

Deficiency Model of Virtuality

Another assumption prevalent in much of the emerging literature on global, virtual, and distributed teams relies on a "deficiency" model, which regards aspects of virtuality as detrimental to team performance. Definitions and operationalizations of virtuality vary, with geographic dispersion, electronic dependence, cultural diversity, and dynamic structure as the most common dimensions (Gibson & Gibbs, 2006). However, Gibson and Gibbs asserted that researchers tend to theorize that each of these features or *decoupling characteristics* (Gibbs, 2002) of virtual teams negatively affects teams.

For example, geographic dispersion presents potential challenges to effective team processes (Goodbody, 2005; Knoll & Jarvenpaa, 1998), leadership (Bell & Kozlowski, 2002; Connaughton & Daly, 2004a; Kerber & Buono, 2004; Maznevski et al., 2006), knowledge management (Cramton, 2001), and detection and management of conflict (Armstrong & Cole, 2002; Shin, 2005). Sole and Edmondson (2002) concluded that dispersed team members often have trouble with sharing situated knowledge of site-specific work practices, which is often taken for granted. Cramton determined that those team members also struggle to attain *mutual knowledge* owing to the lack of common ground.

Electronic dependence in virtual teams poses formidable problems owing to the lack of nonverbal cues that convey important social information in face-to-face interactions (Townsend et al., 1998) and, thus, may lead to misunderstanding, deterioration of trust, and escalation of conflict (Hinds & Weisband, 2003; Kirkman et al., 2002). This view is rooted in the cues-filtered-out perspective (Culnan & Markus, 1987), which suggests that the challenges of achieving mutual understanding and collaborating effectively in groups intensify as one moves from face-to-face to computer-mediated interaction. Early CMC theories, such as social presence theory (Short, Williams, & Christie, 1976) and media richness theory (Daft & Lengel, 1986), considered CMC to be deficient compared to face-to-face communication owing to the former's reduced social context cues (Sproull & Kiesler, 1986) and information richness. These perspectives frame CMC messages as impersonal and task-oriented in comparison to face-to-face interaction (Walther & Burgoon, 1992). In addition, Sproull and Kiesler concluded that the reduced social cues in CMC were prone to produce a *deregulating effect* in which people tended to exhibit self-focused and unrestrained behavior. More recent CMC theories, such as social information processing theory (Walther, 1992, 1997) and SIDE theory (Lea & Spears, 1992; Postmes, Spears, & Lea, 1998), depart from the traditional view of CMC as deficient and describe it instead as simply different and having unique characteristics (Walther & Parks, 2002). Much of the virtual teams literature, however, still relies on earlier cues-filtered-out perspectives which emphasize the limitations of CMC (e.g., Bell & Kozlowski, 2002; Hinds & Bailey, 2003; Kirkman et al., 2002).

Though empirical findings are mixed, researchers often cite cultural diversity in teams as detrimental to team performance, owing to the potential for differing values and norms to create conflict and misunderstanding (e.g., Elron, 1997; Jehn, Northcraft, & Neale, 1999; Kirchmeyer & Cohen, 1992; Kirkman & Shapiro, 1997, 2001; Maznevski, 1994). Elron noted that, though cultural heterogeneity may add to the group by enhancing creativity, homogeneous groups share greater similarities in attitudes, beliefs, and experiences. In a comprehensive literature review, Maznevski concluded that homogeneous teams performed better overall and engaged in less conflict than more diverse teams. Scholars have consistently found that demographic diversity, in particular, negatively affects group processes, owing to heightened emphasis by group members on social categories rather than project-related information (for a review, see Williams & O'Reilly, 1998). For example, though they reported a curvilinear effect such that highly diverse and homogeneous teams outperform moderately diverse teams over time, Earley and Mosakowski (2000) attributed team failures to individual members' cultural differences generating conflict and negatively affecting group dynamics. Conversely, for teams that functioned well, the authors ascribed the success to that team's particularly well-managed process, which included creating rules to follow throughout their meetings, being open with one another, showing respect for others' opinions, and so on. These two attributions for failure and success seem to indicate that, though success can be attributed to a successful process, group failure cannot be blamed for the failure of the process. The underlying premise, whether made explicit or not, seems to be that cultural difference begets communication breakdowns.

Finally, research has linked a dynamic structure with challenges related to sharing knowledge and developing strong relationship ties (Burt, 2004; Granovetter, 2005). The fluid structure and temporary nature of many virtual teams tends to create difficulties establishing identification, given the temporary (rather than ongoing) nature of relationships among members (Kristof et al., 1995). Further, virtual team members from different organizations less likely trust each other with confidential or proprietary information, which may also hinder knowledge sharing; indeed, greater diversity in organizational cultures (e.g., a greater number of cultures represented) has been associated with lower trust within virtual teams, owing to greater challenges connected to risk and interdependence (Gibson & Manuel, 2003).

Based on our review, deficiency models rely on the assumption that fostering shared understanding, cohesiveness, and frequent communication—features typically associated with traditional co-located teams—are prerequisites for virtual teams to be successful, rather than exploring the communicative practices through which virtuality features may become productive for team members. On the contrary, this review proposes that virtual teaming can be best understood by observing the way in which people structure their interactions and that failure to create such structures might be responsible for ultimate downfall of the group, not the innate cognitive or cultural characteristics of team members.

As an example, studies on leadership in virtual teams generally focus on identifying problematic areas in work processes, examining consequences (positive and negative) of these challenging aspects of virtual working, and developing specific recommendations to address the identified challenges and diminish the negative impact of reduced nonverbal cues in the context of virtual work. Similar to studies of trust and conflict, research on leadership is mainly conducted in the framework of the popular inputs-processes-outputs model of work processes, which defines successful team functioning in terms of measured effectiveness, productivity and efficiency, and reduction of problematic aspects (e.g., lack of commitment, difficulties developing trust, forming and maintaining group cohesiveness, etc.). Leadership, as well as other "human" or "social" aspects of teamwork, comprises important ingredients that need to be carefully performed to ensure productive team functioning (Connaughton & Daly, 2004b; Kerber & Buono, 2004).

Conceptualization and Measurement of Virtuality

Finally, conceptualizations and measures of virtuality have been limited in much of prior research. As mentioned earlier, many laboratory-based studies rely on dichotomous comparisons between virtual and non-virtual or co-located teams. Such measurement may explain the previous assumption that virtual teams are "deficient" compared to face-to-face teams. These studies compare purely "virtual" or computer-mediated to purely "face-to-face" teams and groups, and virtual/CMC teams generally come up short (e.g., Burke & Chidambaram, 1995; Kiesler et al., 1984; Potter & Balthazard, 2002; Straus & McGrath, 1994; Warkentin et al., 1997). Similarly, a largely separate body of research on team and group heterogeneity has followed the tradition of comparing heterogeneous to homogeneous teams, finding that culturally diverse teams face greater challenges than do homogeneous teams (e.g., Maznevski, 1994; Thomas, 1999; Williams & O'Reilly, 1998). Scholars in both of these areas have shifted away from dichotomous comparisons that inherently privilege traditional (face-to-face, homogeneous) over virtual or heterogeneous teams, reconceptualizing both virtuality (e.g., Gibson & Gibbs, 2006; Griffith, Sawyer, et al., 2003; Martins et al., 2004) and cultural diversity (e.g., Earley & Mosakowski, 2000; Gibson & Vermeulen, 2003) as continua on which all teams can be characterized rather than absolute conditions. We need more empirical work in this regard.

Methodologically, the findings of many studies on virtual teams may be limited because they are based on controlled laboratory studies using student samples. Many studies rely on samples of student teams performing class assignments (e.g., Burke & Chidambaram, 1995; Hollingshead, 1996;

Jarvenpaa & Leidner, 1999, Jarvenpaa et al., 2004; Walther & Bunz, 2005). As such, the virtual teams in many studies tend to be temporary and project-based, often purely virtual (e.g., Jarvenpaa & Leidner, 1999; Kristof et al., 1995) and composed of anonymous members with no history performing an artificial task (see, for example, much of the early GSS research as evident in the meta-analysis by McLeod, 1992). Such a focus limits generalizability of findings to the many ongoing virtual teams that perform real tasks, engage in at least some face-to-face contact, and function in the context of preexisting relationships. In addition, virtual teams are often nested in organizational or other social contexts, and lab research fails to account for the role of context in team functioning. Similarly, much of the research on culturally diverse groups has been conducted in highly controlled laboratory settings over short time periods and provides limited findings (Maznevski & Chudoba, 2000; Nkomo & Cox, 1996). As a result, findings on the impacts of cultural heterogeneity on team performance have been inconsistent and inconclusive (Gibson & Vermeulen, 2003; Hambrick, Davison, Snell, & Snow, 1998). More longitudinal field studies in naturalistic settings could clarify conflicting results, ensure ecological validity with continually evolving technological and organizational settings, and further articulate the communicative processes and practices through which members enact virtual teaming.

RECONCEPTUALIZING VIRTUAL TEAMING FROM A CONSTITUTIVE PERSPECTIVE

Though functionalist research has generated a great deal of knowledge about conditions leading to effective virtual team practices, additional conceptual tools may be applied to make sense of and understand emergent forms of virtual organizing. The so-called interpretive turn in organizational communication shifted scholars' focus away from viewing organizations as concrete, reified containers in which communication takes place through information exchange to more dynamic and constitutive views of organizing as socially constructed through communication (Taylor, Flanagin, Cheney, & Seibold, 2001; Weick, 1979). Rather than attempting to predict and control behavioral regularities, the goal of interpretive approaches is "...to explicate, and in some cases, to critique the subjective and consensual meanings that constitute social reality" (Putnam, 1983, p. 32). Interpretive or critical perspectives (Cheney, 2002; Deetz, 1994; Putnam & Pacanowsky, 1983; Zoller & Kline, this volume) would enable researchers to regard virtual team interactions as socially constructed (for related arguments, see Bartesaghi & Castor, this volume; Berger & Luckmann, 1966). Such alternative approaches envision communication not as a vehicle to transmit work-related information or a channel to deliver important social cues (see Axley, 1984) but as a process through which stakeholders accomplish teaming. We propose an alternative framework for conceptualizing and studying virtual teamwork that recognizes the dynamic nature of such team processes as trust, conflict management, leadership, knowledge sharing, and identification.

Rather than conceptualizing these processes as static variables that produce effects on various team outcomes, we suggest that virtual team members engage in various practices to form and maintain trusting relationships, navigate and resolve conflicts, enact leadership, share knowledge, and negotiate identities. Instead of assuming that fixed team characteristics determine communicative or other outcomes, we focus on those practices that constitute the very core of teaming as a communicative accomplishment. The meanings of events and processes emerge out of team members' engagement in communicative practices; in other words, members negotiate and actively (though often routinely and non-consciously) enact meaning through the use of verbal and nonverbal messages that create and sustain social reality (Polanyi, 1966; Polanyi & Prosch, 1975; Putnam, 1982). This approach is informed by the view of communication as constitutive (Mokros, 2003; Mokros & Deetz, 1996), which treats an instance of interaction as containing all the elements needed to understand socially constructed meanings: meanings co-created by participants in interaction. According to Mokros and Deetz, proponents of this perspective contend that people form their perceptions of reality by engaging in communication practices, as opposed to the view of communication as information exchange, where "communication is a phenomenon to be explained rather than a mode of explanation" (p. 31).

In shifting the focus of scrutiny away from team properties fixed in team input or outcome variables, we treat virtual teams as social collectives constituted and reconstituted continuously through goal-oriented communicative practices among their members (Mumby & Clair, 1997). The dynamism of virtual teaming is not necessarily revealed through unique properties of technologies in use but rather co-produced through a series of interaction incidents incorporating a set of decision processes configured by aspects of the team's structural elements (Maznevski & Chudoba, 2000). Our framework calls communication scholars to re-direct the focus of analysis from performances of individual group members or media characteristics to interactions among individuals through technology use by addressing social phenomena that are relational, emergent, and enacted (Boczkowski & Orlikowski, 2004). Following Weick (1979), virtual teaming involves "the inventions of people, inventions superimposed on flows of experience and momentarily imposing some order on these streams" (pp. 11-12).

The proposed framework presents a constitutive view of teaming as emerging through communication processes of virtual team members as they participate in everyday work practices. Just as Zoller and Kline (this volume) call for health communication scholars to employ more interpretive and critical approaches, we encourage communication scholars to embrace such alternative approaches in studying virtual teams, to further extend our knowledge of how teaming is discursively constructed. This framework opens up a new space to investigate virtual teams from different theoretical perspectives, broadens the spectrum of phenomena examined in virtual work contexts, and raises important new research questions to be addressed.

First, taking a constitutive approach allows and invites scholars to study virtual teaming from different theoretical perspectives such as the bona fide group perspective (Putnam & Stohl, 1996), sensemaking (Weick, 1995), structuration (Banks & Riley, 1993), or tensional perspectives (Tretheway & Ashcraft, 2004). Emerging research is beginning to adopt such perspectives. For example, Gibbs (2007) employed ethnographic methods to examine dialectical tensions of autonomy versus connectedness, inclusion versus exclusion, and cultural assimilation versus separation in a global software team and the ways in which such tensions were negotiated through communicative practices of team members. According to Gibbs, certain tensions were necessary and irresolvable given the complex nature of global organizing, and such tensions could be either productive or detrimental, depending on team members' communicative responses.. Another qualitative field study employed adaptive structuration theory to analyze the use of a collaborative technology in a virtual team, examining the types of structural adaptations that occurred within the team over time to resolve initial misalignments among organizational environment, group, and technology structures, and ways in which the team retained, modified, and reverted back to preexisting structures (Majchrzak, Rice, Malhotra, King, & Ba, 2000). As a third example, a recent case study investigated how a virtual team socially constructed and reinforced its boundaries and evolved a team identity over time, drawing on the bona fide group theory (Zhang, 2007). Such perspectives challenge notions of teams (and organizations) as stable, fixed sites of clarity and consensus as they recognize and capture the dynamic nature of teaming, the differences and disjunctures that often characterize virtual teams, and the permeability and flux of team boundaries. They also consider the organizational contexts in which virtual teams are embedded—an important (yet overlooked) influence on team interaction. We urge communication scholars to adopt such perspectives—still nascent in the virtual teams research—and to go beyond survey and experimental methods to study virtual teaming using more qualitative approaches such as ethnography, participant observation, and discourse analysis, as well as combining multiple methods (both qualitative and quantitative) in creative new ways.

Taking a constitutive approach also refocuses scholarship around new phenomena by examining virtual teaming as discursively constructed. Working in different parts of the world and being electronically dependent involves such mundane practices as checking one's e-mail, retrieving information from databases, and conducting virtual meetings, to name a few. Hence, team members continually reproduce the context of virtual working through recurrent discursive practices which bring into play a unique configuration of dimensions. A constitutive approach draws attention to understanding how team members reveal and enact virtual teaming during routine interactions. This perspective allows us to examine the specific practices, strategies, and messages that team members employ to sustain the ongoing process of organizing. As Boden (1994) observed, "It is through the telephone calls, meetings, planning sessions, sales talk, and corridor conversations that people inform, amuse, update, gossip, review, reassess, reason, instruct, revise, argue, debate, contest, and actually constitute the moments, myths and, through time, the very structuring of the organization" (p. 181).

Furthermore, because the proposed framework highlights the importance of understanding not only what aspects constitute the work of virtual teams but calls for investigation of specific processes through which members co-construct these unique work entities, the framework has implications for studying interpersonal and socialization processes in the context of virtual work (Jarvenpaa et al., 2004; Knoll & Jarvenpaa, 1998). In particular, certain technological choices help team members to establish interpersonal relationships, develop and maintain trust, facilitate and support knowledge exchange (Grosse, 2002). As Shin (2005) concluded, sources of conflict in virtual teams include difficulty in establishing trusting relationships with team members and confronting ambiguous tasks, roles, and responsibilities. Therefore, understanding the complexities of the interpersonal aspects of task-oriented activities may provide novel insights into the dynamics of team relationship building, conflict negotiation, and development of group cohesion. This research involves detailed analysis of message exchange, topic control and avoidance, and turn-taking in conversations and highlights issues of relationship building and maintenance in the virtual environment.

The final section outlines a conceptual framework for studying virtual team processes that integrates key structural features of virtuality with communicative processes characterizing such teams. Furthermore, we outline ways for researchers to reconceptualize each of these processes from a constitutive perspective and propose topics and questions for future research of virtual teams.

FUTURE RESEARCH AGENDA FOR VIRTUAL TEAMS

Advancing a New Conceptual Framework

The various dimensions of virtuality (geographic dispersion, electronic dependence, cultural diversity, and dynamic structure) tend to be studied largely independently. Because many teams rank high on multiple dimensions of virtuality (e.g., they are highly culturally diverse, geographically dispersed, and electronically dependent), we need more research that simultaneously examines the interrelationships among multiple dimensions. We propose a conceptual framework that integrates these four dimensions and the five key team processes described above (see Figure 5.1). The four dimensions of virtuality outside the box—geographic dispersion, electronic dependence, cultural diversity, and dynamic structure—comprise structural characteristics of teams. The five terms inside the box—trust, conflict management, leadership, knowledge sharing, and identification—represent key team processes that are shaped by communication.

Though incorporating all of these components in a single study may not be possible, we call on communication scholars from a variety of areas—organizational, interpersonal, group, mediated, and intercultural communication, among others—to engage in more programmatic research on virtual teams incorporating multiple components in examining the dynamic relationships and interdependencies among these processes and contexts. Our framework integrates the key pieces of a future research agenda for studying virtual teaming, which can also be unpacked and combined in various ways. A constitutive perspective is well suited for taking such a dynamic and integrative approach; rather than isolating variables and their interrelationships, it examines virtual team interaction as embedded in processes and contexts involving varying degrees of geographic dispersion, CMC use, cultural diversity, and dynamism of structural arrangements.

In particular, the suggested framework serves as a useful conceptual tool to explore social phenomena in new ways through research on virtual teams. Our review has illuminated scholarly interest in examining social aspects of virtual working such as identification (Fiol & O'Connor, 2005; Gossett, 2002; Wiesenfeld et al., 1999), knowledge networks (Monge & Contractor, 2003; Zakaria et al., 2004), leadership (Bell & Kozlowski, 2002; Connaughton & Daly, 2004b), trust (Jarvenpaa et al., 1998; Murphy, 2004), and conflict (Armstrong & Cole, 2002; Mannix, Griffith, & Neale, 2002; Mortensen & Hinds, 2001). Furthermore, the current project contributes to our understanding of virtual teaming by emphasizing the active role that members play in constructing the very context of virtual work. We not only focus on investigating structural and formative issues related to ICT use, but, by proposing a new framework, we recommend further exploration of critical constitutive processes, such as ways in which members deal with disagreements and differences, negotiate task processes, group roles, and work relationships, or resolve conflict situations (Henderson, 1994). The question is not *whether* geographically dispersed and culturally diverse team members are (or feel) connected through communication and information technologies but, rather, *how* (e.g., by what means and through which practices) they enact such connectivity in their mundane interactions. In this regard, adequate relational communication appears to be essential for developing and maintaining trust as this aspect of virtual working "pertains to the reciprocal process of how partners regard one another and how they express that regard" (Walther & Bunz, 2005, p. 830). Communication scholars, thus, need to investigate *how* members employ technology use in numerous practices

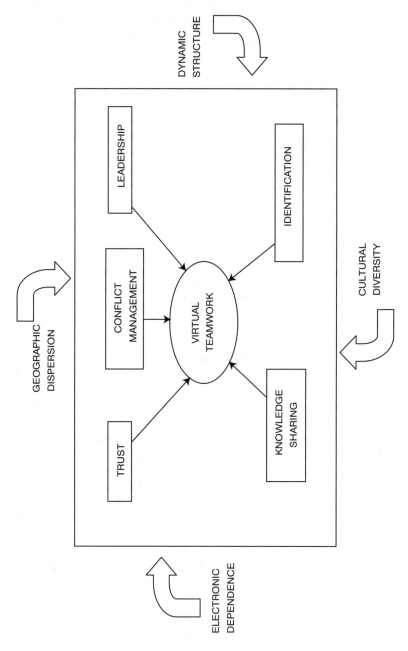

Figure 5.1 Conceptual framework for studying virtual team processes from a constitutive perspective

and *how* virtual team members negotiate assignments, build relationships, form impressions, or informally communicate with team members.

Reconceptualizing Trust

Researchers generally conceptualize trust in virtual teams research as an affective or cognitive construct (Kanawattanachai & Yoo, 2002; Millward & Kyriakidou, 2004); they treat it as a cognitive "belief" that determines the quality of team processes and outcomes (Jarvenpaa et al., 1998; Jarvenpaa & Leidner, 1999; Walther & Bunz, 2005). Therefore, the majority of research studies investigating this phenomenon in virtual environments have sought to unveil differences between low- and high-trust teams (e.g., Jarvenpaa et al., 1998; Jarvenpaa & Leidner, 1999). Prior studies have clearly demonstrated the importance of considering issues of trust when attempting to effectively manage virtual work processes. What remains virtually overlooked, however, involves *how* virtual workers develop, maintain, or break trust as they engage in various communicative practices. Communication scholars are well positioned to address this question by examining processes that constitute trusting relationships among virtual team members rather than explicating well-defined structures, roles and rules that purportedly ensure effective performance in the virtual context (Poole, 1999). This reconceptualization encourages scholars to reflect more on the relationships between trust and communication processes in virtual teams by conducting longitudinal observation- and interview-based studies in naturalistic organizational settings. In particular, the proposed framework sets the stage for examining trust as a communicative accomplishment achieved through a coordinated sequence of meaningful actions in routine interactions.

Reconceptualizing Conflict Management

Taking a more constitutive perspective offers unique conceptual tools to avoid the limitations of the inputs-processes-outputs model of conflict resolution in the context of virtual teams. Expressly, as a phenomenon of human communication, conflict comprises "a process in which a participant formulates interpretations that develop and change over time, contingent upon the prior and subsequent actions of the co-participant(s)" (Arundale, 1999, p. 126). From this perspective, researchers conceptualize framing as a dynamic process of collectively shaping, maintaining, and/or changing shared meanings (Gamson, Croteau, Hoynes, & Sasson, 1992). Furthermore, because all participants negotiate these issues, they serve as a framework for stakeholders' present and future actions in terms of sustaining or resolving a conflict and, thus, become collective action frames (Gamson, 2001). Several benefits exist in shifting the focus of analysis from examining properties of conflict situations to processes that constitute them.

First, this perspective conceptualizes participants in conflict as members of interpreting communities who continuously define and redefine their situations. Second, through their direct or indirect participation in framing a conflict, stakeholders co-construct collective knowledge about this conflict and, thus, shape and justify their actions (Shin, 2005). Therefore, a conflict is not a fixed and stable phenomenon but rather a complex continuous process in which each stakeholder actively participates in resolving a situation, aggravating polarization, and/or obscuring optimal conflict resolution. The aim of participants in the conflict situation entails not only reaching the settlement of immediate issues but "...transform[ing] the parties by giving them insights into themselves, insights into how they are contributing to the conflict and how they might change to improve the situation" (Conrad & Poole, 2005, p. 337). Future research on conflict should focus on the socially constituted communicative processes through which members frame conflicts and develop social interpretations of events.

Reconceptualizing Leadership

Research that challenges a functionalist approach to communication between leaders and subordinates in co-located settings calls for greater attention to processes or micro-practices through which stakeholders communicatively construct leadership. For instance, Fairhurst and Chandler (1989) described how a leader and employees utilized power and social distance as conversational resources to enact organizational structure. Moreover, these researchers suggested that "conversational resource use can create new structural forms, thereby altering the trajectory of the relationships" (p. 230). Fairhurst (2007) reviewed discourse approaches and applied a discourse approach to studying relationships between leaders and employees, which situates communicative interactions as central. Ford (2006) also explored leadership as a discursive accomplishment that shapes managerial workplace identities. Applied to the context of virtual teams, these approaches regard leadership as continually (re) negotiated through communicative interactions between team members.

Future research on leadership should investigate how leadership practices are constituted and negotiated through communicative practices. Communication scholars (for review, see Connaughton & Daly, 2005) have contributed to studies on distanced leadership by emphasizing the role of communication in dealing with paradoxes and challenges of leading from afar. For example, Connaughton and Daly (2004b) identified several communication processes that contribute to successful distanced leadership—building more personalized relationships through small talk and personalized textual message exchange, establishing expectations and ground rules about communication at the stage of initial team formation, and symbolically demonstrating leaders' commitment to team members through travel to distanced locations. These findings present fresh insights on the dynamics of virtual teaming and the role of team leaders in effective team functioning, and they also invite scholars and practitioners to set research agendas to further investigate the processes and implications of leadership and relationship building in the virtual work environment.

Reconceptualizing Knowledge Sharing

Knowledge and knowledge management tend to be defined in fairly narrow terms: (1) as cognitive structures of an individual that, once explicitly shared as information, become valuable resources for other individuals and (2) as technical information (explicit knowledge). Either way, researchers define knowledge in terms of information, and, as a consequence, "information is viewed as a kind of preliminary stage of knowledge" (Lueg, 2001, p. 151). Given the close relationship between knowledge and information, current research often reduces the complex processes of knowledge co-construction to simple information exchange among team members. However, recent studies of knowledge management in organizations (e.g., Heaton & Taylor, 2002) and online communication from an interpretive perspective (Ngwenyama & Lee, 1997) caution against such an approach because, as Lueg noted, it tends to overlook the representation problem, interpretation processes (Cramton, 2001; Lee, 1994), and organizational contextuality (Ngwenyama & Lee, 1997). We require further clarification of when/how information becomes knowledge and the underlying communication processes that transform information into knowledge.

Current perspectives (e.g., Griffith, Sawyer, et al., 2003) also tend to focus on knowledge as an individual property and, thus, virtually ignore social aspects of constructing mutual knowledge. Information becomes transformed into social knowledge when the same information becomes internalized by several persons in a similar way and converges individual cognitive structures into collective ones (Baba et al., 2004). Though this approach to establishing common ground in teamwork alludes to communal aspects of knowledge creation, this perspective still promotes the idea that "knowledge originates in the individual and that, once made explicit, subsequent interpretation of the representations of knowledge in symbolic form is unproblematic" (Heaton & Taylor, 2002, p. 232). Furthermore, though researchers generally acknowledge the importance of communicating and retaining contextual information (Cramton, 2001), they seem to characterize knowledge by specific properties that are drawn from disparate sources (Baba et al., 2004). Finally, the most efficient use of knowledge may be based on the ability of individual team members to separate knowledge from actions (Sarker et al., 2005).

We argue that communication as a mode of explanation (Deetz, 1994) offers fresh insights into how virtual team members constitute knowledge in interactions without separating knowledge from actions yet conceptually distinguishing between knowledge and information. First, Zorn and Taylor (2004) suggested that knowledge management constitutes "a process of organizational communication…because knowledge management is fundamentally concerned with sensemaking: the construction of meaning by people who are caught in a practical world of work, with multiple and frequently immediate concerns" (p. 104). In contrast to functionalist approaches, such scholars do not consider meaning to be an outcome of cognitive processes that reside within individuals, nor do meanings have stable properties that prompt similar interpretations by different individuals and, thus, result in predicted behavioral outcomes. Conversely, from a constitutive perspective, meanings are public (Geertz, 1973, 1983) and emerge in the process of people's engagement with each other. Communicative practices involve information sharing but are not limited to mere exchange of social or technical information. To become knowledge, information must be interpreted with reference to cultural meanings, acted on in specific situations, and situated in a particular social and historical context.

In this regard, Sole and Edmondson's (2002) conceptualization of situated knowledge is particularly useful in overcoming some of the limitations above. Indeed, the researchers appropriated a communicative view of knowledge sharing in the context of virtual teams and introduced the concept of situated knowledge, which refers to site-specific work practices. This perspective emphasizes both knowledge creation and its enactment in organizational practices. Such an approach allows researchers to uncover processes through which contextual elements both shape and are shaped by social practices performed by individual virtual team members. Thus, participants actively take part in constituting every aspect of virtual teamwork. Through collaboration on projects, team members and leaders learn to adjust their styles, incorporate professional expertise, negotiate work roles, appropriate relevant knowledge, and overcome challenges associated with geographic dispersion, electronic dependence, cultural diversity, and dynamic structure.

Future research should further explore conceptual distinctions and the relationship between information and knowledge, terms that researchers often use interchangeably. We invite scholars to critically appraise the communicative aspects of information sharing and exchange by exploring conceptual links between these two phenomena as well as differences in meaning. Research should examine knowledge sharing as a sense-making process (Weick, 1995). The following question deserves particular attention: How do team members use bodies of knowledge to make sense of information? If they create knowledge through sense making or interpretation of different kinds of information and communicative enactment of these knowledge claims, then mutual knowledge is situated in a specific interactional context and should be viewed a communicative accomplishment.

Reconceptualizing Identification

Though scholars call for investigation of identification processes in virtual teams (e.g., Fiol & O'Connor, 2005), they seem to be focused on unearthing stable antecedents that produce certain effects on the processes of identification and, therefore, would allow for reliable predictions about psychological and behavioral outcomes. Dominant conceptualizations of identification have been rooted in social identity and self-categorization theories (Tajfel, 1982; Tajfel & Turner, 1986), which argue that individuals locate or define themselves in terms of their social categories or groups and that they classify themselves and others as members of social in-groups and out-groups, based on differentiation of themselves from others (Ashforth & Mael, 1989). Furthermore, scholars conceptualize and measure the "processes" of identification in terms of individual perceptions, psychological attachment, feelings of trust, and commitment. Though the findings of such studies suggest important clear-cut managerial implications of the most efficient strategies to facilitate collaboration in virtual teams, these findings provide limited insights into what virtual team members actually do to identify with a group and how they communicatively enact identifications with (possibly) multiple targets. In addition, the dominant managerial approach takes a limited view of identification as a control mechanism, which arguably removes agency from employees. Taking a more interpretive approach allows for exploration of communicative strategies through which identified employees seek coordination and connections within virtual teams, rather than focusing exclusively on management efforts.

Communication scholars as far back as Burke (1950/1969) have viewed identification as symbolically and socially constructed, and more recent scholars in the field have adopted conceptualizations with an emphasis on communicative practices rather than cognition (see Cheney, 1983, 1991; Kuhn & Nelson, 2002; Larson & Pepper, 2003; Scott, Corman, & Cheney, 1998). Scott et al. developed a structurational view of identification, which regards it as inherently communicative—situated in everyday social interaction—and shows how organizational identities become meaningful in action by structuring employees' experiences. Scott et al. conceptualized identity as a structure that constitutes a set of rules and resources that may be drawn on by an organizational member. Thus, members constantly produce and reproduce identity through processes of identification, which represent "the forging, maintenance, and alteration of linkages between persons and groups" (p. 304). Hence, communicative manifestations of identification can be observed as they occur in social interactions with other organizational members. Organizational communication studies are starting to adopt this view of identification (e.g., Kuhn & Nelson, 2002; Larson & Pepper, 2003), but it has yet to be extended to virtual work contexts.

The desirability of identification in the virtual context has been both asserted and questioned by extant research. In our review, we tracked salient developments in conceptualizing the relationship between identification and team processes. Yet, future research should further explore the relation between teaming and processes of identification. For instance, the proposed framework calls scholarly attention to the following issues of central concern. Are processes of teaming and identification (construction of group identity) in reciprocal relationship? How does teaming become a resource for group identity and identification? How do expressions of identification become relevant in a particular context? How are particular identities enacted and negotiated in interactions between group members? What communication practices constitute processes of identification? Do processes of identification vary situationally in the virtual context (as argued by Scott et al., 1998)? What rhetorical strategies (Cheney, 1983) facilitate construction of team and individual team members' identity(ies) in the process of identification? What discourses of identity construction exist in the virtual context?

New Areas of Study

In addition to reconceptualizing the areas specified by our framework, embracing a constitutive approach also draws our attention to new areas that have not previously been studied in virtual teams research. One important area is the role of emotions and emotionality in virtual teaming. First, examining how emotive displays contribute to or impede the development of productive working relationships might enable us to challenge the widely accepted but overly simplistic view of virtual working as essentially the mechanistic exchange and transmission of work-related information. Second, such an approach allows us to gain a better sense of the communicative aspects of emotional enactment in group processes. Despite a wide range of approaches to defining emotions (Denzin, 1984; Harré, 1986; Lazarus, 1991; Lupton, 1998; Zajonc, 1980), researchers generally agree that emotions carry their communication function through their expressions—facial expressions, vocal cues, physiological cues, gestures or body movements, and action cues (Burleson & Planalp, 2000; Planalp, 1999; Planalp & Knie, 2002). The proposed framework serves as a point of departure for studies that seek to investigate expressive aspects of emotions in the virtual environment as well as the role of emotion work in communicative processes through which the context of virtual group work is constructed, maintained, and altered. In this sense, it continues the line of research (Ellison, Heino, & Gibbs, 2006; Orlikowski, Yates, Okamura, & Fujimoto, 1995; Tanis & Postmes, 2003; Walther & Parks, 2002) questioning the cues-filtered-out model (Culnan & Markus, 1987), which suggests that, with cues filtered out, communicators are less able to "alter the mood of a message, communicate a sense of individuality, or exercise dominance or charisma" (Kiesler, 1986, p. 48). Third, revealing how and why employees choose to enact certain feelings while hiding others in mundane organizational practices might shed light on why some teams (including virtual teams) that consist of workers who are highly knowledgeable and experienced in the field of their specialization turn out to be unproductive, inefficient, and unsuccessful compared to others. Member performance of emotions through communication in the virtual environment also warrants further investigation, for the very notions of emotional labor, emotion management, and emotion work within organizational settings have been ongoing topics of interest for organizational scholars and practitioners (Fineman, 2000; Hochschild, 1983; Rafaeli & Sutton, 1989; Tracy, 2005; Van Maanen & Kunda, 1989).

Next, an interpretive approach provides a useful means of studying issues related to different meanings of work. Cheney, Zorn, Planalp, and Lair (this volume) instructed scholars to "consider how employee meanings of work are constructed and co-constructed in connection with specific organizational policies and work activities" (p. 171). Such an approach emphasizes understanding different perspectives, a particularly important matter in virtual teams that cut across diverse geographic, temporal, and cultural contexts. For example, notions of work-life balance, work ethic, and the meaning of work likely vary across cultures and geographic locations and, thus, offer fruitful topics for future research on virtual teams.

Finally, the proposed framework opens up new directions for investigating power dynamics in the context of global working. On the one hand, scholars argue that geographic dispersion and electronic dependence flatten the hierarchical structure of virtual organizations (Majchrzak et al., 2000; Saunders, Van Slyke, & Vogel, 2004; Workman, 2004) and, thus, "filter out" social and structural differences and inequalities. On the other hand, virtuality seems to transform the nature of authority and control structures, raising questions of power relations, power differences, and emergent practices of power construction in the virtual context to the forefront. Interestingly, researchers of virtual teams have commonly focused on assessing those aspects/variables (e.g., trust, identification, commitment, group cohesion) which supposedly "glue" individual members together into an efficient entity transcending geographic dispersion and time differences. The issues pertaining to the politics of everyday life and power struggles in virtual teams—including access to and control of information, negotiation of team norms and member status, allocation of resources and decision-making processes—often remain unnoticed and ignored. In contrast, the proposed framework advocates a more detailed emphasis on the process through which team members communicatively construct teaming during interactions (e.g., telephone conversations, e-mail exchanges, and the like).

A possible approach to investigate power dynamics entails examining how team members negotiate different issues, the strategies that members use to exert social influence during collaboration on projects, and how competing interests get resolved through the control and manipulation of symbolic and discursive recourses. Though research has successfully demonstrated far-reaching implications for managerial practices (Gillam & Oppenheim, 2006; Gluesing & Gibson, 2004; Grosse, 2002; Harvey, Novicevic, & Garrison, 2004; Stough et al., 2000), virtual teams are generally overlooked as unique sites of decision making characterized not only by cultural, ethnic, or territorial differences but by power struggles emanating from diverse individual perceptions, attitudes, expectations, goals, and agendas. We may believe that the virtual team context reduces, filters out, or even eliminates those cues that point to differences and, therefore, creates an illusion of virtual teams as devoid of power relations. However, the persistent focus on consensus, best practices, and commonalities may "preclude debate and conflict, that substitute images and imaginary relations for self-presentation and truth claims, that arbitrarily limit access to communication channels and forums, and that then lead to decisions based on arbitrary authority relations" (Deetz, 2001, p. 29). Based on our proposed framework, we recommend a critical investigation of decision making in virtual teams and consent as a hidden side of power relations. Researchers should pursue questions such as who controls or monitors the flow of information? Under what conditions or structural circumstances is such control exerted? How do members achieve consensus or agreement? What are consequences/ implications of control/monitoring practices for decision making in virtual teams? How is control and resistance enacted in virtual contexts?

As suggested by Pal and Dutta in this volume, scholars should place studies of global teams, in particular, in the context of globalization and resistance and pursue ways in which processes of transnational hegemony and resistance play out in the micro-practices of team members. For example, global software teams involve power relations and inequalities, owing to the different national economic and political contexts in which teams are embedded, especially in the arena of off-shore outsourcing (Gibbs, 2007). Rhetorical studies of global teams may illuminate ways in which team culture inadvertently or unconsciously privilege "white" or dominant cultural assumptions, thus excluding or undermining racial or cultural positions of other team members (see Lacy, this volume). Future research should also examine the tensions between control and resistance, disjunctures, disruptions, and reconfigurations of traditional identity and culture owing to globalization and time-space distantiation as well as implications for the experience and identities of global team members, who remain deeply impacted by processes of global organizing.

In summary, virtual teamwork constitutes a timely topic that bridges a number of areas of the communication discipline—namely, organizational, interpersonal, group, mediated, and intercultural communication, among others—and in which processes of communication are central. We have proposed an alternative conceptual framework and constitutive perspective that broaden the role of communication in processes of virtual organizing by regarding them as communicatively or discursively constructed. While we advance this framework primarily to help direct and advance theory and research on virtual teaming, it offers practical benefits as well. Though we hope to expand attention beyond an exclusive focus on effectiveness, the knowledge generated from taking a constitutive perspective may be used to improve virtual team performance and enhance employee well-being within such teams. For example, it is useful in identifying and understanding differing perspectives and concerns which may not be compatible with management views. Managers and practitioners can also draw on the context-specific knowledge gained to generate customized solutions and best practices that would work in their particular organizations. This research area is also important in appealing to a global audience of scholars within the discipline, helping to foster international research collaborations, and generating insights from research conducted in diverse international settings. As such, we encourage communication scholars from a variety of epistemological perspectives, subdisciplines, and nations to devote greater attention to this important arena of the contemporary workplace.

ACKNOWLEDGMENTS

We acknowledge the helpful comments of Stacey Connaughton and three anonymous reviewers.

NOTES

1. First, research on virtual teams is conducted by scholars in different parts of the world: the United Kingdom (Crossman & Lee-Kelley, 2004; Matlay & Westhead, 2005), the Netherlands (Rasters, Vissers, & Dankbaar, 2002), Australia (Anawati & Craig, 2006), Canada (Aubert & Kelsey, 2003), New Zealand (Pauleen & Yoong, 2001), Finland (Leinonen, Järvelä, & Häkkinen, 2005), and the United States (Baba et al., 2004; Fiol & O'Connor, 2005; Lurey & Raisinghani, 2001; Maznevski & Chudoba, 2000). Other studies are the product of international collaboration among scholars from multiple countries: the United Kingdom and Hong Kong (Panteli & Davidson, 2005); the United States and China (Qureshi, Liu, & Vogel, 2006; Saunders et al., 2004); Australia and the United States (Hossain & Wigand, 2004); the Netherlands, China, and France (Rutkowski, Vogel, van Genuchten, Bemelmans, & Favier, 2002); the United States and India (Edwards & Sridhar, 2005); the United States and the Netherlands (Huysman et al., 2003); and the United States and France (Jarvenpaa et al., 1998). Finally, empirical research often examines global virtual teams that span multiple countries: the United States and the Netherlands (Huysman et al., 2003); the United States, Canada, Australia, and Portugal (Cramton, 2001); Canada and India (Edwards & Sridhar, 2005); Europe, Mexico, and the United States (Kayworth & Leidner, 2001); Thailand and the United States (Kanawattanachai & Yoo, 2002); the United Kingdom and Western Europe (Crossman & Lee-Kelley, 2004), and North America, Europe, Asia, and South America (Baba et al., 2004; Gibbs, 2007), to name just a few. Thus, extant research projects investigating various aspects of virtual work in the global environment present not only a scholarly interest as they uncover processes of teaming under novel but increasingly common circumstances. These studies and research collaborations also exemplify the very global trends that they set out to examine.

2. It should be noted that research increasingly differentiates between spatial and temporal dispersion, which are both captured within our notion of geographical dispersion. For example, a team that is geographically dispersed over multiple locations across several time zones likely faces a different set of challenges in coordinating work than a team that is dispersed between multiple locations within the same time zone, in which case it may be easier to meet and interact synchronously. Research increasingly focuses on the temporal dimension (e.g., Ballard & Gossett, 2007; Rutkowski, Saunders, Vogel, & van Genuchten, 2007; Saunders et al., 2004); whereas, other research further explores the multiple dimensions of geographical dispersion (see O'Leary & Cummings, 2001). We acknowledge these differences and encourage scholars to further explore their nuances.

REFERENCES

Ahuja, M., Galletta, D., & Carley, K. (2003). Individual centrality and performance in virtual R&D groups: An empirical study. *Management Science, 49*, 21-38.

Amason, A. C. (1996). Distinguishing the effects of functional and dysfunctional conflict on strategic decision making: Resolving a paradox for top management teams. *Academy of Management Journal, 39*, 123-148.

Anawati, D., & Craig, A. (2006). Behavioral adaptation within cross-cultural virtual teams. *IEEE Transactions on Professional Communication, 49*, 44-56.

Armstrong, D. J., & Cole, P. (2002). Managing distances and differences in geographically distributed work groups. In P. M. Hinds & S. Kiesler (Eds.), *Distributed work* (pp. 167-186). Cambridge, MA: MIT Press.

Arundale, R. B. (1999). An alternative model and ideology of communication for an alternative to politeness theory. *Pragmatics, 9*, 119-153.

Ashforth, B. E., & Mael, F. (1989). Social identity theory and the organization. *Academy of Management Review, 14*, 20-39.

Aubert, B. A., & Kelsey, B. L. (2003). Further understanding of trust and performance in virtual teams. *Small Group Research, 34*, 575-618.

Axley, S. (1984). Managerial and organizational communication in terms of the conduit metaphor. *Academy of Management Review, 9*, 428–437.

Baba, M. L., Gluesing, J., Ratner, H., & Wagner, K. H. (2004). The contexts of knowing: Natural history of a globally distributed team. *Journal of Organizational Behavior, 25*, 547-587.

Ballard, D. I., & Gossett, L. M. (2007). Alternative times: Communicating the non-standard work arrangement. In C. S. Beck (Ed.), *Communication yearbook 31* (pp. 274-321). Mahwah, NJ: Erlbaum.

Banks, S. P., & Riley, P. (1993). Structuration theory as an ontology for communication research. In S. Deetz (Ed.), *Communication yearbook 16* (pp. 167-196). Newbury Park, CA: Sage.

Bartesaghi, M., & Castor, T. (2008). Social construction in communication: Reconstituting the conversation. In C. S. Beck (Ed.), *Communication yearbook 32* (pp. 3-39). New York: Routledge.

Bell, B. S., & Kozlowski, S. W. J. (2002). A typology of virtual teams: Implications for effective leadership. *Group & Organization Management, 27*, 14-49.

Berger, P. L., & Luckmann, T. (1966). *The social construction of reality: A treatise in the sociology of knowledge.* Garden City, NY: Doubleday & Company.

Boczkowski, P. J., & Orlikowski, W. J. (2004). Organizational discourse and new media: A practice perspective. In D. Grant, C. Hardy, C. Oswick, & L. Putnam (Eds.), *The Sage handbook of organizational discourse* (pp. 359-377). London: Sage.

Boden, D. (1994). *The business of talk: Organizations in action.* Cambridge, England: Polity Press.

Bradley, W. E., & Vozikis, G. S. (2004). Trust in virtual teams. In S. H. Godar & S. P. Ferris (Eds.), *Virtual and collaborative teams: Process, technologies, and practice* (pp. 99-113). Hershey, PA: Idea Group Publishing.

Brewer, M. B. (1981). Ethnocentrism and its role in interpersonal trust. In M. B. Brewer & B. E. Collins (Eds.), *Scientific inquiry and the social sciences* (pp. 345-360). New York: Jossey-Bass.

Burke, K. (1969). *A rhetoric of motives.* Berkeley: University of California Press. (Original work published 1950)

Burke, K., & Chidambaram, L. (1995). Developmental differences between distributed and face-to-face groups in electronically supported meeting environments: An exploratory investigation. *Group Decision and Negotiation, 4,* 213-233.

Burleson, B. R., & Planalp, S. (2000). Producing emotion(al) messages. *Communication Theory, 10,* 221-250.

Burt, R. S. (2004). Structural holes and good ideas. *American Journal of Sociology, 110,* 349-399.

Cheney, G. (1983). The rhetoric of identification and the study of organizational communication. *Quarterly Journal of Speech, 69,* 143-158.

Cheney, G. (1991). *Rhetoric in an organizational society: Managing multiple identities.* Columbia: University of South Carolina Press.

Cheney, G. (2002). *Values at work.* Ithaca, NY: Cornell University Press.

Cheney, G., Zorn, T., Planalp, S., & Lair, D. (2008). Meaningful work and personal/social well-being: Organizational communication engages the meanings of work. In C. S. Beck (Ed.), *Communication yearbook 32* (pp. 137-185). New York: Routledge.

Cocroft, B., & Ting-Toomey, S. (1994). Facework in Japan and the United States. *International Journal of Intercultural Relations, 18,* 469-506.

Cohen, S. G., & Gibson, C. B. (2003). In the beginning: Introduction and framework. In C. B. Gibson & S. G. Cohen (Eds.), *Virtual teams that work: Creating conditions for virtual team effectiveness* (pp. 1-13). San Francisco: Jossey-Bass.

Connaughton, S. L., & Daly, J. A. (2004a). Identification with leader: A comparison of perceptions of identification among geographically dispersed and co-located teams. *Corporate Communication, 9,* 89-103.

Connaughton, S. L., & Daly, J. A. (2004b). Leading from afar: Strategies for effectively leading virtual teams. In S. H. Godar & S. P. Ferris (Eds.), *Virtual and collaborative teams: Process, technologies, and practice* (pp. 49-75). Hershey, PA: Idea Group Publishing.

Connaughton, S. L., & Daly, J. A. (2005). Leadership in the new millennium: Communicating beyond temporal, spatial, and geographical boundaries. In P. Kalbfleisch (Ed.), *Communication yearbook 29* (pp. 187-213). Mahwah, NJ: Erlbaum.

Conrad, C., & Poole, M. S. (2005). *Strategic organizational communication in global economy.* Belmont, CA: Thomson.

Coppola, N. W., Hiltz, S. R., & Rotter, N. G. (2004). Building trust in virtual teams. *IEEE Transactions on Professional Communication, 47*, 95-104.

Cramton, C. D. (2001). The mutual knowledge problem and its consequences for dispersed collaboration. *Organization Science, 12*, 346-371.

Cramton, C. D., & Hinds, P. J. (2004). Subgroup dynamics in internationally distributed teams: Ethnocentrism or cross-national learning? *Research in Organizational Behavior, 26*, 231-263.

Crossman, A., & Lee-Kelley, L. (2004). Trust, commitment and team working: The paradox of virtual organizations. *Global Networks, 4*, 375-390.

Culnan, M. J., & Markus, M. L. (1987). Information technologies. In F. M. Jablin, L. L. Putnam, K. H. Roberts, & L. W. Porter (Eds.), *Handbook of organizational communication: An interdisciplinary perspective* (pp. 420-443). Thousand Oaks, CA: Sage.

Cummings, J. N. (2004). Work groups, structural diversity, and knowledge sharing in a global organization. *Management Science, 50*, 352-364.

Daft, R. L., & Lengel, R. H. (1986). Organizational information requirements, media richness and structural design. *Management Science, 32*, 554-571.

DeChurch, L. A., & Marks, M. A. (2001). Maximizing the benefits of task conflict: The role of conflict management. *International Journal of Conflict Management, 12*, 4-22.

Deetz, S. (1994). Representational practices and the political analysis of corporations: Building a communication perspective in organizational studies. In B. Kovačić (Ed.), *New approaches to organizational communication* (pp. 211-243). Albany: State University New York Press.

Deetz, S. (2001). Conceptual foundations. In F. M. Jablin & L. Putnam (Eds.), *The new handbook of organizational communication: Advances in theory, research, and methods* (pp. 3-46). Thousand Oaks, CA: Sage.

Denzin, N. K. (1984). *On understanding emotion* (1st ed.). San Francisco: Jossey-Bass.

DeSanctis, G., & Monge, P. (1999). Introduction to the special issue: Communication processes for virtual organizations. *Organization Science, 10*, 693-703.

Earley, P. C., & Gibson, C. B. (2002). *Multinational work teams: A new perspective.* Mahwah, NJ: Erlbaum.

Earley, P. C., & Mosakowski, E. (2000). Creating hybrid team cultures: An empirical test of transnational team functioning. *The Academy of Management Journal, 43*, 26-29.

Edwards, H. K., & Sridhar, V. (2005). Analysis of software requirements for engineering exercises in a global virtual team setup. *Journal of Global Information Management, 13*(2), 21-41.

Ellison, N., Heino, R., & Gibbs, J. (2006). Managing impressions online: Self-presentation processes in the online dating environment. *Journal of Computer-Mediated Communication, 11*(2). Retrieved June 11, 2006, from http://jcmc.indiana.edu/vol11/issue2/ellison.html

Elron, E. (1997). Top management teams within multinational corporations: Effects of cultural heterogeneity. *Leadership Quarterly, 8*, 393-412.

Fairhurst, G. T. (2007). *Discursive leadership: In conversation with leadership psychology.* Thousand Oaks, CA: Sage.

Fairhurst, G. T., & Chandler, T. A. (1989). Social structure in leader-member interaction. *Communication Monographs, 56*, 215-239.

Fineman, S. (Ed.). (2000). *Emotion in organizations* (2nd ed.). London: Sage.

Fiol, C. M., & O'Connor, E. J. (2005). Identification in face-to-face, hybrid, and pure virtual teams: Untangling the contradictions. *Organization Science, 16*, 19-32.

Flanagin, A. J. (2002). The elusive benefits of the technological support of knowledge management. *Management Communication Quarterly, 16*, 242-248.

Ford, J. (2006). Discourses of leadership: Gender, identity and contradiction in a UK public sector organization. *Leadership, 2*(1), 77-99.

Gamson, W. A. (2001). Promoting political engagement. In W. L. Bennett & R. M. Entman (Eds.), *Mediated politics: Communication in the future democracy* (pp. 56-74). New York: Cambridge University Press.

Gamson, W. A., Croteau, D., Hoynes, W., & Sasson, T. (1992). Media images and the social construction of reality. *Annual Review of Sociology, 18*, 373-394.

Geertz, C. (1973). *The interpretation of cultures*. New York: Basic Books.

Geertz, C. (1983). *Local knowledge: Further essays in interpretive anthropology*. New York: Basic Books.

Gibbs, J. L. (2002). *Loose coupling in global teams: Tracing the contours of cultural complexity*. Unpublished doctoral dissertation, University of Southern California, Los Angeles.

Gibbs, J. L. (2006). Decoupling and coupling in global teams: Implications for human resource management. In G. K. Stahl & I. Björkman (Eds.), *Handbook of research in international human resource management* (pp. 347-363). Northampton, MA: Edward Elgar.

Gibbs, J. L. (2007). *Loose coupling in global teams: Negotiating tensions across time, space, and culture*. Manuscript submitted for publication.

Gibson, C. B., & Gibbs, J. L. (2006). Unpacking the concept of virtuality: The effects of geographic dispersion, electronic dependence, dynamic structure, and national diversity on team innovation. *Administrative Science Quarterly, 51*, 451-495.

Gibson, C. B., & Manuel, J. (2003). Building trust: Effective multicultural communication processes in virtual teams. In C. B. Gibson & S. G. Cohen (Eds.), *Virtual teams that work: Creating conditions for virtual team effectiveness* (pp. 59-86). San Francisco: Jossey-Bass.

Gibson, C. B., & Vermeulen, F. (2003). A healthy divide: Subgroups as a stimulus for team learning behavior. *Administrative Science Quarterly, 48*, 202-239.

Gillam, C., & Oppenheim, C. (2006). Review article: Reviewing the impact of virtual teams in the information age. *Journal of Information Science, 32*, 160-175.

Gluesing, J. C., & Gibson, C. B. (2004). Designing and forming global teams. In H. W. Lane, M. L. Maznevski, M. E. Mendenhall, & J. McNett (Eds.), *Handbook of global management* (pp. 199-226). Malden, MA: Blackwell.

Goodbody, J. (2005). Critical success factors for global virtual teams. *Strategic Communication Management, 9*(2), 18-21.

Goodman, R. A., Phillips, M. E., & Sackmann, S. A. (1999). The complex culture of international project teams. In R. A. Goodman (Ed.), *Modern organizations and emerging conundrums: Exploring the post industrial subculture of the third millennium* (pp. 23-33). Lanham, MD: Lexington Books.

Gossett, L. M. (2002). Kept at arm's length: Questioning the organizational desirability of member identification. *Communication Monographs, 69*, 385-404.

Govindarajan, V., & Gupta, A. K. (2001). Building an effective global business team. *MIT Sloan Management Review, 42*(4), 63-71.

Granovetter, M. S. (2005). The impact of social structure on economic outcomes. *Journal of Economic Perspectives, 19*, 33-50.

Griffith, T. L., Mannix, E. A., & Neale, M. A. (2003). Conflict and virtual teams. In C. B. Gibson, & S. G. Cohen (Eds.), *Virtual teams that work: Creating conditions for virtual team effectiveness* (pp. 335-352). San Francisco: Jossey-Bass.

Griffith, T. L., Sawyer, J. E., & Neale, M. A. (2003). Virtualness and knowledge in teams: Managing the love triangle of organizations, individuals, and information technology. *MIS Quarterly, 27*, 265-287.

Grosse, C. U. (2002). Managing communication within virtual intercultural teams. *Business Communication Quarterly, 65*(4), 22-38.

Hambrick, D. C., Davison, S. C., Snell, S., & Snow, C. C. (1998). When groups consist of multiple nationalities: Towards a new understanding of the implications. *Organization Studies, 19*, 181-205.

Handy, C. (1995). Trust and the virtual organization. *Harvard Business Review, 73*(3), 40-50.

Harré, R. (Ed.). (1986). *The social construction of emotions*. Oxford, England: Basil Blackwell.

Harvey, M., Novicevic, M. M., & Garrison, G. (2004). Challenges to staffing global virtual teams. *Human Resource Management Review, 14*, 275-294.

Heaton, L., & Taylor, J. R. (2002). Knowledge management and professional work: A communication perspective on the knowledge-based organization. *Management Communication Quarterly, 16*, 210-236.

Henderson, G. (1994). *Cultural diversity in the workplace: Issues and strategies*. Westport, CT: Quorum Books.

Hinds, P. J., & Bailey, D. E. (2003). Out of sight, out of sync: Understanding conflict in distributed teams. *Organization Science, 14*, 615-632.

Hinds, P. J., & Mortensen, M. (2005). Understanding conflict in geographically distributed teams: The moderating effects of shared identity, shared context, and spontaneous communication. *Organization Science, 16*, 290-307.

Hinds, P. J., & Weisband, S. P. (2003). Knowledge sharing and shared understanding in virtual teams. In C. B. Gibson & S. G. Cohen (Eds.), *Virtual teams that work: Creating conditions for virtual team effectiveness* (pp. 21-36). San Francisco: Jossey-Bass.

Hochschild, A. R. (1983). *The managed heart: Commercialization of human feeling*. Berkeley: University of California Press.

Hollingshead, A. B. (1996). Information suppression and status persistence in group decision making: The effects of communication media. *Human Communication Research, 23*, 193-219.

Hollingshead, A. B., Wittenbaum, G. M., Paulus, P. B., Hirokawa, R. Y., Ancona, D. G., Peterson, R. S., et al. (2004). A look at groups from the functional perspective. In M. S. Poole & A. B. Hollingshead (Eds.), *Theories of small groups: Interdisciplinary perspectives* (pp. 21-62). Thousand Oaks, CA: Sage.

Hossain, L. W., & Wigand, R. T. (2004). ICT enabled virtual collaboration through trust. *Journal of Computer Mediated Communication, 10*(1). Retrieved June 5, 2006, from http://jcmc.indiana.edu/vol10/issue1/hossain_wigand.html

Huysman, M., Steinfield, C., Jang, C. Y., David, K., in't Veld, M. H., Poot, J., et al. (2003). Virtual teams and the appropriation of communication technology: Exploring the concept of media stickiness. *Computer Supported Cooperative Work, 12*, 411-436.

Jarvenpaa, S. L., Knoll, K., & Leidner, D. E. (1998). Is anybody out there? Antecedent of trust in global virtual teams. *Journal of Management Information Systems, 14*(4), 29-64.

Jarvenpaa, S. L., & Leidner, D. E. (1999). Communication and trust in global virtual teams. *Organization Science, 10*, 791-815.

Jarvenpaa, S. L., Shaw, T. R., & Staples, D. S. (2004). Toward contextualized theories of trust: The role of trust in global virtual teams. *Information Systems Research, 15*, 250-264.

Jehn, K. A. (1995). A multimethod examination of the benefits and detriments of intragroup conflict. *Administrative Science Quarterly, 40*, 256-282.

Jehn, K. A. (1997). A qualitative analysis of conflict types and dimensions in organizational groups. *Administrative Science Quarterly, 42*, 530-557.

Jehn, K. A., Northcraft, G. B., & Neale, M. A. (1999). Why differences make a difference: A field study of diversity, conflict, and performance in workgroups. *Administrative Science Quarterly, 44*, 741-763.

Kanawattanachai, P., & Yoo, Y. (2002). Dynamic nature of trust in virtual teams. *The Journal of Strategic Information Systems, 11*, 187-213.

Kayworth, T. R., & Leidner, D. E. (2001). Leadership effectiveness in global virtual teams. *Journal of Management Information Systems, 18*(3), 7-40.

Kerber, K. W., & Buono, A. F. (2004). Leadership challenges in global virtual teams: Lessons from the field. *SAM Advanced Management Journal, 69*(4), 4-10.

Kiesler, S. (1986). Thinking ahead: The hidden messages in computer networks. *Harvard Business Review, 64*(1), 46-60.

Kiesler, S., Siegel, J., & McGuire, T. W. (1984). Social psychological aspects of computer-mediated communication. *American Psychologist, 39*, 1123-1134.

Kirchmeyer, C., & Cohen, A. (1992). Multicultural groups: Their performance and reactions with constructive conflict. *Group & Organization Management, 17*, 153-170.

Kirkman, B. L., & Mathieu, J. E. (2005). The dimensions and antecedents of team virtuality. *Journal of Management, 31*, 700-718.

Kirkman, B. L., Rosen, B., Gibson, C. B., Tesluk, P. E., & McPherson, S. O. (2002). Five challenges to virtual team success: Lessons from Sabre, Inc. *Academy of Management Executive, 16*(3), 67-79.

Kirkman, B. L., & Shapiro, D. L. (1997). The impact of cultural values on employee resistance to teams: Toward a model of globalized self-managing work team effectiveness. *Academy of Management Review, 22*, 730-757.

Kirkman, B. L., & Shapiro, D. L. (2001). The impact of cultural values on job satisfaction and organizational commitment in self-managing work teams: The mediating role of employee resistance. *Academy of Management Journal, 44*, 557-569.

Knoll, K., & Jarvenpaa, S. L. (1998). Working together in global virtual teams. In M. Igbaria & M. Tan (Eds.), *The virtual workplace* (pp. 2-23). Hershey, PA: Idea Group Publishing.

Krebs, S. A., Hobman, E. V., & Bordia, P. (2006). Virtual teams and group member dissimilarity: Consequences for the development of trust. *Small Group Research, 37*, 721-741.

Kristof, A. L., Brown, K. G., Sims, H. P., & Smith, K. A. (1995). The virtual team: A case study and inductive model. In M. M. Beyerlein, D. A. Johnson & S. T. Beyerlein (Eds.), *Advances in interdisciplinary studies of work teams* (Vol. 2, pp. 229-253). Greenwich, CT: JAI Press.

Kuhn, T., & Nelson, N. (2002). Reengineering identity: A case study of multiplicity and duality in organizational identification. *Management Communication Quarterly, 16,* 5-38.

Lacy, M. (2008). Exposing the spectrum of whiteness: Rhetorical conceptions of white absolutism. In C. S. Beck (Ed.), *Communication yearbook 32* (pp. 227-311). New York: Routledge.

Larson, G. S., & Pepper, G. L. (2003). Strategies for managing multiple organizational identifications: A case of competing identities. *Management Communication Quarterly, 16,* 528-557.

Lazarus, R. S. (1991). *Emotion and adaptation.* New York: Oxford University Press.

Lea, M., O'Shea, T., & Fung, P. (1995). Constructing the networked organization: Content and context in the development of electronic communications. *Organization Science, 6,* 462-478.

Lea, M., & Spears, R. (1992). Paralanguage and social perception in computer-mediated communication. *Journal of Organizational Computing & Electronic Commerce, 2,* 321-341.

Lee, A. S. (1994). Electronic mail as a medium for rich communication: An empirical investigation using hermeneutic interpretation. *MIS Quarterly, 18,* 143-157.

Leinonen, P., Järvelä, S., & Häkkinen, P. (2005). Conceptualizing the awareness of collaboration: A qualitative study of a global virtual team. *Computer Supported Cooperative Work: The Journal of Collaborative Computing, 14,* 301-322.

Lovelace, K., Shapiro, D. L., & Weingart, L. R. (2001). Maximizing cross-functional new product teams' innovativeness and constraint adherence: A conflict communications perspective. *Academy of Management Journal, 44,* 779–793.

Lueg, C. (2001). Information, knowledge, and networked minds. *Journal of Knowledge Management, 5,* 151-159.

Lupton, D. (1998). *The emotional self: A sociocultural exploration.* London: Sage.

Lurey, J. S., & Raisinghani, M. S. (2001). An empirical study of best practices in virtual teams. *Information and Management, 38,* 523-544.

Majchrzak, A., Malhotra, A., Stamps, J., & Lipnack, J. (2004). Can absence make a team grow stronger? *Harvard Business Review, 82*(5), 131-137.

Majchrzak, A., Rice, R. E., Malhotra, A., King, N., & Ba, S. (2000). Technology adaptation: The case of a computer-supported inter-organizational virtual team. *MIS Quarterly, 24,* 569-600.

Mannix, E. A., Griffith, T., & Neale, M. A. (2002). The phenomenology of conflict in distributed work teams. In P. M. Hinds & S. Kiesler (Eds.), *Distributed work* (pp. 213-233). Cambridge, MA: MIT Press.

Martin, J. (1992). *Cultures in organizations.* New York: Oxford University Press.

Martins, L. L., Gilson, L. L., & Maynard, M. T. (2004). Virtual teams: What do we know and where do we go from here? *Journal of Management, 30,* 805-835.

Matlay, H., & Westhead, P. (2005). Virtual teams and the rise of e-entrepreneurship in Europe. *International Small Business Journal, 23,* 279-302.

Maznevski, M. L. (1994). Understanding our differences: Performance in decision-making groups with diverse members. *Human Relations, 47,* 531-552.

Maznevski, M. L., & Chudoba, K. M. (2000). Bridging space over time: Global virtual team dynamics and effectiveness. *Organization Science, 11,* 473-492.

Maznevski, M. L., Davison, S. C., & Jonsen, K. (2006). Global virtual team dynamics and effectiveness. In G. K. Stahl & I. Björkman (Eds.), *Handbook of research in international human resource management* (pp. 364-384). Northampton, MA: Edward Elgar.

McLeod, P. L. (1992). An assessment of the experimental literature on electronic support of group work: Results of a meta-analysis. *Human-Computer Interaction, 7*, 257–280.

Millward, L. J., & Kyriakidou, O. (2004). Effective virtual teamwork: A socio-cognitive and motivational model. In S. H. Godar & S. P. Ferris (Eds.), *Virtual and collaborative teams: Process, technologies, and practice* (pp. 20-34). Hershey, PA: Idea Group Publishing.

Mokros, H. B. (Ed.). (2003). *Identity matters: Communication-based explorations and explanations*. Cresskill, NJ: Hampton Press.

Mokros, H. B., & Deetz, S. (1996). What counts as real? A constitutive view of communication and the disenfranchised in the context of health. In E. B. Ray (Ed.), *Communication and the disenfranchised: Social health issues and implications* (pp. 29-44). Hillsdale, NJ: Erlbaum.

Monge, P. R., & Contractor, N. S. (2003). *Theories of communication networks*. New York: Oxford University Press.

Montoya-Weiss, M. M., Massey, A. P., & Song, M. (2001). Getting it together: Temporal coordination and conflict management in global virtual teams. *Academy of Management Journal, 44*, 1251-1262.

Mortensen, M., & Hinds, P. J. (2001). Conflict and shared identity in geographically distributed teams. *International Journal of Conflict Management, 12*, 212-238.

Mumby, D. K., & Clair, R. (1997). Organizational discourse. In T. A. V. Dijk (Ed.), *Discourse as social interaction* (Vol. 2, pp. 181-205). London: Sage.

Murphy, P. (2004). Trust, rationality and the virtual team. In D. Pauleen (Ed.), *Virtual teams: Projects, protocols and processes* (pp. 317-343). Hershey, PA: Idea Group Publishing.

Nandhakumar, J. (1999). Virtual teams and lost proximity: Consequences on trust relationships. In P. J. Jackson (Ed.), *Virtual working: Social and organizational dynamics* (pp. 46-56). London: Routledge.

Ngwenyama, O. K., & Lee, A. S. (1997). Communication richness in electronic mail: Critical social theory and the contextuality of meaning. *MIS Quarterly, 21*, 145-167.

Nkomo, S. M., & Cox, T., Jr. (1996). Diverse identities in organizations. In S. R. Clegg, C. Hardy, & W. R. Nord (Eds.), *Handbook of organization studies* (pp. 338-356). London: Sage.

Oetzel, J. G., Ting-Toomey, S., Masumoto, T., Yokochi, Y., Pan, X., Takai, J., et al. (2001). Face and facework in conflict: A cross-cultural comparison of China, Germany, Japan, and the United States. *Communication Monographs, 68*, 235-258.

O'Leary, M., & Cummings, J. (2001). *The spatial, temporal, and configurational characteristics of geographic dispersion in work teams*. Working Paper, 148, Cambridge, MA: MIT Press.

Orlikowski, W. J., Yates, J., Okamura, K., & Fujimoto, M. (1995). Shaping electronic communication: The metastructuring of technology in the context of use. *Organization Science, 6*, 423-444.

Pal, M., & Dutta, M. J. (2008). Theorizing resistance in a global context: Processes, strategies, and tactics in communication scholarship. In C. S. Beck (Ed.), *Communication yearbook 32* (pp. 41-87). New York: Routledge.

Panteli, N. (2005). Trust in global virtual teams. *Ariadne, 43*. Retrieved May 29, 2006, from http://www.ariadne.ac.uk/issue43/

Panteli, N., & Davidson, R. M. (2005). The role of subgroups in the communication patterns of global virtual teams. *IEEE Transactions on Professional Communication, 48*, 191-200.

Paul, S., Samarah, I. M., Seetharaman, P., & Mykytyn Jr., P. P. (2005). An empirical investigation of collaborative conflict management style in group support system-based global virtual teams. *Journal of Management Information Systems, 21*(3), 185-222.

Paul, S., Seetharaman, P., Samarah, I. M., & Mykytyn Jr., P. P. (2004). Impact of heterogeneity and collaborative conflict management style on the performance of synchronous global virtual teams. *Information & Management, 41*, 303-321.

Pauleen, D. J., & Yoong, P. (2001). Relationship building and the use of ICT in boundary-crossing virtual teams: A facilitator's perspective. *Journal of Information Technology, 16*, 205-220.

Piccoli, G., & Ives, B. (2003). Trust and the unintended effects of behavior control in virtual teams. *MIS Quarterly, 27*, 365-395.

Planalp, S. (1999). *Communicating emotion: Social, moral, and cultural processes.* New York: Cambridge University Press.

Planalp, S., & Knie, K. (2002). Integrating verbal and nonverbal emotion(al) messages. In S. R. Fussell (Ed.), *The verbal communication of emotions: Interdisciplinary perspectives* (pp. 55-78). Mahwah, NJ: Erlbaum.

Platt, R., & Page, D. (2001). Managing the virtual team: Critical skills and knowledge for successful performance. In N. J. Johnson (Ed.), *Telecommuting and virtual offices: Issues and opportunities* (pp. 130-147). Hershey, PA: Idea Group.

Polanyi, M. (1966). *The tacit dimension.* New York: Doubleday.

Polanyi, M., & Prosch, H. (1975). *Meaning.* Chicago: University of Chicago Press.

Poole, M. S. (1999). Organizational challenges for the new forms. In G. DeSanctis & J. Fulk (Eds.), *Shaping organization form: Communication, connection, and community* (pp. 453-495). Thousand Oaks, CA: Sage.

Postmes, T., Spears, R., & Lea, M. (1998). Breaching or building social boundaries? Side-effects of computer-mediated communication. *Communication Research, 25*, 689-715.

Potter, R. E., & Balthazard, P. S. (2002). Understanding human interaction and performance in the virtual team. *Journal of Information and Technology Theory and Applications, 4*, 1-23.

Putnam, L. L. (1982). Paradigms for organizational communication research: An overview and synthesis. *Western Journal of Speech Communication, 46*, 192-206.

Putnam, L. L. (1983). The interpretive perspective: An alternative to functionalism. In L. L. Putnam & M. E. Pacanowsky (Eds.), *Communication and organization: An interpretive approach* (pp. 31-54). Beverly Hills, CA: Sage.

Putnam, L. L., & Pacanowsky, M. E. (Eds.). (1983). *Communication and organizations: An interpretive approach.* Beverly Hills, CA: Sage.

Putnam, L. L., & Stohl, C. (1996). Bona fide groups: An alternative perspective for communication and small group decision making. In R. Y. Hirokawa & M. S. Poole (Eds.), *Communication and group decision making* (2nd ed., pp. 147-178). Thousand Oaks, CA: Sage.

Qureshi, S., Liu, M., & Vogel, D. (2006). The effects of electronic collaboration in distributed project management. *Group Decision and Negotiation, 15*(1), 55-75.

Rafaeli, A., & Sutton, R. I. (1989). The expression of emotion in organizational life. *Research in Organizational Behavior, 11*, 1-42.

Rasters, G., Vissers, G., & Dankbaar, B. (2002). An inside look: Rich communication through lean media in a virtual research team. *Small Group Research, 33*, 718-754.

Rutkowski, A., Saunders, C., Vogel, D., & van Genuchten, M. (2007). "Is it already 4 a.m. in your time zone?": Focus immersion and temporal dissociation in virtual teams. *Small Group Research, 38*(1), 98-129.

Rutkowski, A. F., Vogel, D. R., van Genuchten, M., Bemelmans, T. M. A., & Favier, M. (2002). E-collaboration: The reality of virtuality. *IEEE Transactions on Professional Communication, 45*, 219-230.

Sarker, S., Sarker, S., Nicholson, D. B., & Joshi, K. D. (2005). Knowledge transfer in virtual systems development teams: An exploratory study of four key enablers. *IEEE Transactions on Professional Communication, 48*, 201-218.

Saunders, C., Van Slyke, C., & Vogel, D. R. (2004). My time or yours? Managing time visions in global virtual teams. *Academy of Management Executive, 18*(1), 19-31.

Scott, C. R. (1997). Identification with multiple targets in a geographically dispersed organization. *Management Communication Quarterly, 10*, 491-522.

Scott, C. R., Corman, S. R., & Cheney, G. (1998). Development of a structurational model of identification in the organization. *Communication Theory, 8*, 298-336.

Shin, Y. (2005). Conflict resolution in virtual teams. *Organizational Dynamics, 34*, 331-345.

Short, J., Williams, E., & Christie, B. (1976). *The social psychology of telecommunications*. London: John Wiley.

Singelis, T. M., & Brown, W. J. (1995). Culture, self, and collectivist communication: Linking culture to individual behavior. *Human Communication Research, 21*, 354-389.

Sivunen, A., & Valo, M. (2006). Team leaders' technology choice in virtual teams. *IEEE Transactions on Professional Communication, 49*, 57-68.

Sole, D., & Edmondson, A. (2002). Situated knowledge sharing in dispersed teams. *British Journal of Management, 13*, S17-S34.

Sproull, L. S., & Kiesler, S. (1986). Reducing social context cues: Electronic mail in organizational communication. *Management Science, 32*, 1492-1512.

Staples, D. S., & Webster, J. (2007). Exploring traditional and virtual team members' "best practices": A social cognitive theory perspective. *Small Group Research, 38*, 60-97.

Stohl, C. (2005). Globalization theory. In S. May & D. K. Mumby (Eds.), *Engaging organizational communication theory and research* (pp. 223-261). Thousand Oaks, CA: Sage.

Stough, S., Eom, S., & Buckenmyer, J. (2000). Virtual teaming: A strategy for moving your organization into the new millennium. *Industrial Management & Data Systems, 100*, 370-378.

Straus, S., & McGrath, J. E. (1994). Does the medium matter? The interaction of task type and technology on group performance and member reactions. *Journal of Applied Psychology, 79*, 87-97.

Tajfel, H. (1982). Social psychology of intergroup relations. *Annual Review of Psychology, 33*, 1-39.

Tajfel, H., & Turner, J. C. (1986). The social identity theory of intergroup behavior. In W. G. Austin & S. Worchel (Eds.), *The psychology of intergroup relations* (pp. 7-24). Chicago: Nelson-Hall.

Tanis, M., & Postmes, T. (2003). Social cues and impression formation in CMC. *Journal of Communication, 53*, 676-693.

Taylor, J. R., Flanagin, A. J., Cheney, G., & Seibold, D. R. (2001). Organizational communication research: Key moments, central concerns, and future challenges. In W. Gudykunst (Ed.), *Communication yearbook 24* (pp. 99-137). Thousand Oaks, CA: Sage.

Thomas, D. C. (1999). Cultural diversity and work group effectiveness. *Journal of Cross-Cultural Psychology, 30*, 242-263.

Timmerman, C. E., & Scott, C. R. (2006). Virtually working: Communicative and structural predictors of media use and key outcomes in virtual work teams. *Communication Monographs, 73*, 108-136.

Ting-Toomey, S. (1988). Intercultural conflict style. In Y. Kim & W. Gudykunst (Eds.), *Theories in intercultural communication* (pp. 213-235). Newbury Park, CA: Sage.

Ting-Toomey, S. (1994). *The challenge of facework: Cross-cultural and interpersonal issues*. Albany: State University of New York Press.

Ting-Toomey, S., & Kurogi, A. (1998). Facework competence in intercultural conflict: An updated face-negotiation theory. *International Journal of Intercultural Relations, 22*, 187-225.

Ting-Toomey, S., & Oetzel, J. G. (2001). *Managing intercultural conflict effectively.* Thousand Oaks, CA: Sage.

Townsend, A. M., DeMarie, S. M., & Hendrickson, A. R. (1998). Virtual teams: Technology and the workplace of the future. *Academy of Management Executive, 12*(3), 17-29.

Tracy, S. J. (2005). Locking up emotion: Moving beyond dissonance for understanding emotion labor discomfort. *Communication Monographs, 72*, 261-283.

Tretheway, A., & Ashcraft, K. L. (2004). Special issue introduction. Practicing disorganization: The development of applied perspectives on living with tension. *Journal of Applied Communication Research, 32*, 81-88.

Trubisky, P., Ting-Toomey, S., & Lin, S.-L. (1991). The influence of individualism-collectivism and self-monitoring on conflict styles. *International Journal of Intercultural Relations, 12*, 269-289.

Van Maanen, J., & Kunda, G. (1989). "Real feelings": Emotional expression and organizational culture. *Research in Organization Behavior, 11*, 43-103.

Walther, J. B. (1992). Interpersonal effects in computer-mediated interaction: A relational perspective. *Communication Research, 19*, 52-91.

Walther, J. B. (1995). Relational aspects of computer-mediated communication: Experimental observations over time. *Organization Science, 6*, 186-203.

Walther, J. B. (1997). Group and interpersonal effects in international computer-mediated collaboration. *Human Communication Research, 23*, 342-369.

Walther, J. B., & Bazarova, N. N. (2007). Misattribution in virtual groups: The effects of member distribution on self-serving bias and partner blame. *Human Communication Research, 33*, 1-26.

Walther, J. B., & Bunz, U. (2005). The rules of virtual groups: Trust, liking, and performance in computer-mediated communication. *Journal of Communication, 55*, 828-846.

Walther, J. B., & Burgoon, J. K. (1992). Relational communication in computer-mediated interaction. *Human Communication Research, 19*, 50-88.

Walther, J. B., & Parks, M. R. (2002). Cues filtered out, cues filtered in: Computer-mediated communication and relationships. In M. L. Knapp & J. A. Daly (Eds.), *Handbook of interpersonal communication* (3rd ed., pp. 529-563). Thousand Oaks, CA: Sage.

Warkentin, M. E., Sayeed, L., & Hightower, R. (1997). Virtual teams versus face-to-face teams: An exploratory study of a web-based conference system. *Decision Sciences, 28*, 975-996.

Weick, K. E. (1979). *The social psychology of organizing* (2nd ed.). Reading, MA: Addison-Wesley.

Weick, K. E. (1995). *Sensemaking in organizations.* Thousand Oaks, CA: Sage.

Wiesenfeld, B. M., Raghuram, S., & Garud, R. (1999). Communication patterns as determinants of organizational identification in a virtual organization. *Organization Science, 10*, 777-790.

Wiesenfeld, B. M., Raghuram, S., & Garud, R. (2001). Organizational identification among virtual workers: The role of need for affiliation and perceived work-based social support. *Journal of Management, 27*, 213-229.

Williams, K., & O'Reilly, C. (1998). Demography and diversity in organizations: A review of 40 years of research. *Research in Organizational Behavior, 20*, 77-140.

Wittenbaum, G. M., Hollingshead, A. B., Paulus, P. B., Hirokawa, R. Y., Ancona, D. G., Peterson, R. S., et al. (2004). The functional perspective as a lens for understanding groups. *Small Group Research, 35*, 17-43.

Workman, M. (2004). Goals, relationships, information and processes in global virtual team performance. *International Journal of Management and Decision Making, 5*, 348-372.

Zaccaro, S. J., & Bader, P. (2003). E-leadership and the challenges of leading e-teams. *Organizational Dynamics, 31*, 377-387.

Zajonc, R. B. (1980). Feeling and thinking: Preferences need no inferences. *American Psychologist, 35*, 151-175.

Zakaria, N., Amelinckx, A., & Wilemon, D. (2004). Working together apart? Building a knowledge-sharing culture for global virtual teams. *Creativity and Innovation Management, 13*, 15-29.

Zhang, H. (May, 2007). *A case study of boundary and identity management in a virtual team.* Paper presented at the annual meeting of the International Communication Association, San Francisco.

Zoller, H., & Kline, K. (2008). Theoretical contributions of interpretive and critical research in health communication. In C. S. Beck (Ed.), *Communication yearbook 32* (pp. 89-135). New York: Routledge.

Zorn, T. E., & Taylor, J. R. (2004). Knowledge management and/as organizational communication. In D. Tourish & O. Hargie (Eds.), *Key issues in organizational communication* (pp. 96-112). London: Routledge.

CHAPTER CONTENTS

6 "Oxygen of Publicity" and "Lifeblood of Liberty"

Communication Scholarship on Mass Media Coverage of Terrorism for the Twenty-first Century

Lisa Keränen
University of Colorado at Boulder

Virginia Sanprie
University of Colorado at Boulder

Scholarly literature concerning terrorism and the media spans decades and disciplines with a dramatic increase after 9/11. This state-of-the-art review assesses strengths, limitations, and gaps in recent scholarship on mainstream mass-mediated news coverage of terrorism and outlines an agenda for research that cuts across traditional context-based divisions of communication research. It begins by synthesizing various conceptions of terrorism as communication and discussing models of terrorism's relationship to the media. It then considers empirical studies of media content in television, print, Internet, and multimodal contexts. Finally, it identifies the need for expanded studies of multi-modal international news coverage of terrorism that cut across interpersonal, organizational, religious, and new media subfields of the communication discipline.

INTRODUCTION: INVESTIGATING MEDIA COVERAGE OF TERRORISM

In the weeks immediately following 9/11, the world watched as two towering symbols of U.S. economic and political might turned to rubble. Global citizens tuned in to sights and sounds of despair as survivors, emergency

Correspondence: Lisa Keränen, Department of Communication, 270 UCB, Boulder, CO 80309-0270; Phone: 303-735-5119; E-mail: keranen@colorado.edu workers, and those who lost loved ones in the attacks shared their grief and horror. Shots of the second plane hitting the high rise melded into scenes of Manhattan street chaos that shifted again to President Bush's steely resolve. These endlessly repeated and highly ritualized scenes of disaster achieved iconic status, reaching inhabitants of nations far removed from the geographical sites of devastation. As Debatin (2002) noted, "In the case of the 9/11 media events, the global media system—the infosphere—created a worldwide synchronization of attention, thus establishing an extraordinary order of time and life" (p. 165). Debatin observed that "the whole world was watching the events in real time or very shortly after the events occurred" (p. 165).

Incessant replay of 9/11's human and physical wreckage triggered international debate about the role of the media in times of terror. While some praised the media's "importance and excellence" in information sharing (Greenberg & Hofschire, 2002, p. 317), others signaled clarion calls for restraint.[1] As early as September 14, 2001, *Washington Post* political commentator Howard Kurtz (2001b) pled with television producers to stop rehashing the carnage. Three days later, he asked, "Why did the networks keep showing the planes crashing into the World Trade Center as scene-setters for their opening credits? As 'bumpers' before breaks? As video wallpaper while talking heads are opining?" (Kurtz, 2001a, p. C1). Kurtz maintained that, by turning catastrophe into a show-business spectacular, the networks trivialized shattered lives.

Kurtz's (2001a, 2001b) disquiet that the endless disaster of marathon media coverage dehumanized tragedy was not the first time that a prominent public figure had expressed alarm about terrorism's media prominence. Sixteen years earlier, former British Prime Minister Margaret Thatcher famously decried mass media coverage of terrorism in the wake of the 1985 hijackings of TransWorld Airlines. The press, Thatcher explained, "must try to find ways to starve the terrorist and the hijacker of the oxygen of publicity on which they depend" (Apple, 1985, p. A3). Although Thatcher's comment emphasized the potential harms of media dissemination of terrorist messages over Kurtz's later lament about dehumanization, both comments reflected deep ambivalence about the respective roles of—and relationships between—media, terrorism, and society; both signaled a desire for more reflection about how the press can best serve democratic ends in times of terror and disaster.

Years later, Thatcher and Kurtz's hope for a more reticent press remains unrealized. To the contrary, heightened awareness of globalization, a 24-hour news cycle, and evolving media technologies carry escalating and increasingly violent terrorism (Glasser, 2005) to strangers in far-flung corners of the globe. The role of the media in cultivating perceptions of terrorist and counterterrorist action is paramount. As Dobkin (1992) explained, "since terrorism is not privately experienced by most Americans, public understanding must come from mass-mediated representations of terrorism and institutional reactions to it" (p. 2). In fact, the vast majority of Americans turned to media for information, sense-making, and therapeutic consolation about 9/11 (Greenberg, Hofschire, & Lachlan, 2002). The media, in general, and the news media, in particular, thus encompass a primary point of contact between terrorists, states, and the citizenry.

Mediated reporting of terrorism has long been a noticeable part of our geopolitical landscape and, hence, the subject of academic research. Extant reviews surveying the state of this scholarship pre-date 9/11 (Alali & Byrd, 1994; Dobkin, 1992; Lakos, 1986; Paletz & Boiney, 1992; Schmid & de Graaf, 1982; Signorielli & Gerbner, 1988) and reveal a robust but fragmented series of case studies as well as critical indictments of media coverage that lack empirical data (Paletz & Boiney, 1992).[2] During the last several years, the events of 9/11 have triggered renewed scholarly attention to the relationships and broader antagonisms among terrorism, the media, citizens, and states. Though 9/11 may not have been the radical break with the past that some have argued, it did usher in a new era of heightened research on media and terror. A July, 2007, search of the multi-disciplinary online database *Academic Search Premier* revealed 1,368 scholarly articles concerning media and terrorism published since 2001, of which 491 are peer-reviewed, while *Communication & Mass Media Complete* gleaned 211 peer-reviewed articles of 425 total hits. The sheer quantity and breadth of this work require a state-of-the-art review that synthesizes existing lines of scholarship with an eye toward contributions that communication scholars can make to this topic of global political significance.

In this chapter, we strive to summarize, synthesize, and assess the surge in scholarship concerning mainstream mass media news coverage of terrorism following 9/11.[3] While we acknowledge and critique pivotal contributions of research published before 9/11, particularly when it remains heavily cited, we aim to provide an evaluation of contemporary themes and *foci* within this rapidly growing body of work to address how communication scholars can enrich, expand, and further develop this consequential line of inquiry. In what follows, we close our introductory section by discussing the global significance of this scholarship. We then outline the definitions, scope, and parameters of this review before turning to our two main content areas—reviewing conceptual scholarship theorizing media and terrorism and content analyses of news media coverage of terrorism. We conclude by assessing the strengths and limitations of this research and advancing an agenda for communication scholarship that cuts across traditional context-based divisions of communication scholarship.

SIGNIFICANCE OF RESEARCH ON MEDIA COVERAGE OF TERRORISM

Research on media coverage of terrorism has significant international import. Many scholars argue that globalization itself has supplied conditions that accommodate terrorist action and that, in the global village, even local or regional terrorism can achieve world-wide mediated and political focus (see G. Martin, 2006). The compression of time and space that comprises the hallmark of globalization leads to greater interaction between members of different nations, corporations, and organizations, thereby fueling increased levels of interdependence and interconnectedness (Ietto-Gillies, 2003; see related arguments by Pal & Dutta, this volume). This interconnection allows terrorists to strategically engage the media to reach broader audiences. G. Martin observed that "globalized political and economic arrangements offer terrorists the capability to affect the global community much faster, and much more intensely, than could previous generations of terrorists" (p. 269). Accordingly, Kavoori (2006) advanced the notion of a global "terrorscape"—simultaneously "an objective presence" and a "discursive one" that involves the international news media "from neonationalist American media, through al-Hura and al-Jazeera, to the very niched manifestations of Webcasting and rejuvenated traditional media" (p. 191). In such a terrorscape, local and regional incidents can quickly attain worldwide scrutiny. According to G. Martin, a "spillover effect" occurs when media catapult violent local or domestic skirmishes onto the global stage (p. 274). Hence, globalization and terrorism powerfully interlace in ways ever more prominent after 9/11. For instance, Rojecki (2005) noted that, whereas 2% of *New York Times* stories concerning terrorism in the months leading up to 9/11 mentioned globalization, one-third of the stories in the three months following 9/11 addressed the topic, making terrorism "a significant part of the issue culture of globalization" (p. 68).

Given that English-language news dominates global television journalism (Thussu, 2006), U.S. and Western perspectives and studies unsurprisingly preponderate. Yet, a growing number of studies investigate media coverage of terrorism from non-U.S. and non-Western perspectives (e.g., Abdulla, 2005; Achugar, 2004; Baiocchi, 2002; Banaji & Al-Ghabban, 2006; Ben-Shaul, 2006; Chakravartty, 2002; Eickelman, 2004; Erjavec & Volčič, 2006; Ilter, 2003; Lankala, 2006; Mohamad, 2004; Sádaba, 2002; Sádaba & La Porte, 2006; Sakai, 2003; van der Veer, 2004; Yinbo, 2002). van der Veer stated that "the media coverage of the events of 9/11 in the United States and their aftermath has shown us more than ever before some of the differences in perspectives between the United States, Europe, the Middle East, and Asia" (p. 5). In the global village, few among us are immune to the long arm of terrorism, even if exposure occurs in mediated ways filtered through divergent worldviews and perspectives.

Undoubtedly, communication researchers are well poised to play a pivotal role in investigating, explaining, and critiquing how these processes occur. Indeed, as we detail at the conclusion of this chapter, while scholarship on media coverage of terrorism obviously pertains to scholars of mediated and political communication, it also holds implications for scholars working across several disciplinary subfields in communication, encompassing but not limited to interpersonal and family communication, organizational communication, religious communication, and new media technology studies. In the next section of our chapter, we outline the definitions and parameters of our review.

TERRORISM AND MEDIA: DEFINITIONS AND SCOPE

Defining Terrorism

During its several hundred year history, the term *terrorism* has undergone a dramatic reversal in meaning. British statesman Edmund Burke coined the term during Revolutionary France when he described the *régime de la terreur*, during which 17,000 to 40,000 putative enemies of the radical Jacobian government met their end at the guillotine while tens of thousands of political prisoners died in jail (G. Martin, 2006). Whereas terrorism originally referred to acts of brutal state repression (*violence from above*), the term today carries a pointedly pejorative connotation of non-state violence (*violence from below*). Far from being monolithic, *terrorism* has been used to refer to a vast array of heterogeneous practices that generally involve "violence or the threat of violence against ordinary civilians, against their life, their property, their well-being" (Gasser, 2002, p. 553).[4]

Given the many guises of terrorism, definitions of the term are multiple and highly contested within both academic and political circles (see, e.g., Center for Defense Information, 2003; Horsman, 2005). Because states can and do sponsor terrorism, arriving at a widely shared definition has proven elusive. Nevertheless, scholars have devoted significant labor to the task of arriving at a widely agreeable definition (for discussions and assessment of various definitions, see Gasser, 2002; Schmid & Jongman, 1988). Laqueur (1999) found more than 100 definitions of terrorism with the "only general characteristic generally agreed upon is that terrorism involves violence and the threat of violence" (p. 6).[5] Numerous scholars documented indiscriminate, amorphous, and contradictory uses of definitions of terrorism by states and others, often to achieve political ends (Bhatia, 2005; Kapitan & Schulte, 2002; Laqueur, 1999; J. L. Martin, 1985). Bhatia maintained that the lack of an international definition of either "terrorism" or "terrorist"—under debate since the 1972 Munich Olympics—was "complicated by tense differences over issues of occupation, liberation movements and state-terrorism" (p. 15). Despite lingering disagreements, G. Martin (2006) noted "some consensus... but no unanimity" (p. 31) among scholarly and government definitions and identified six features common to most definitions: illegal force, subnational agents, unconventional methods, political motives, attacks on soft or civilian targets, and acts designed to affect audiences.

While recognizing the "problem of definition" (Cooper, 2001, p. 881) and the politics inherent in the act of defining (Schiappa, 2003), we nevertheless adopt the U.S. Department of State's definition as it appears in the Foreign Relations Authorization Act, Fiscal Years 1988, 1989. In that definition, terrorism constitutes "premeditated, politically motivated violence perpetrated against noncombatant targets by subnational groups or clandestine agents." According to this legislation, *international*, when compared to *domestic* terrorism, involves "citizens or the territory of more than one country." While these definitions delimit a more narrow view of terrorism than some critical scholars would advocate, they generally resonate with those accepted in the scholarly literature and capture G. Martin's (2006) consensus features.[6] Moreover, we note that many communication scholars conducting empirical media analyses of terrorism coverage accept the label of terrorism as applied by the media, though exceptions exist (see, e.g., Delli Carpini & Williams, 1987; Norris, Kern, & Just, 2002; Wittebols, 1992).

Focusing on post 9/11 Media Coverage of Terrorism with Reference to the Past

Just as terrorism is multifaceted and complex, the media too are not monolithic. Our review includes studies of mainstream print, television, and new media focusing on terrorism news. We are particularly interested in studies of new media coverage of terrorism. By "new media," we refer to Internet-based electronic media such as the World Wide Web, Weblogs (known as blogs), chat rooms, bulletin boards, and discussion lists. While our chapter focuses on mainstream mass media scholarship of terrorism news after 9/11, we incorporate pivotal, groundbreaking, or enduring work from pre-9/11 scholarship, particularly when addressing the conceptual foundations of this work. Books, edited collections, and journal articles culled using the electronic databases *Communication and Mass Media Complete*, *Web of Science*, and *ComAbstracts* form the basis of our review. In addition, we concentrate on English-language sources available in these Western-based databases. While we will not posture to have achieved a comprehensive review of such a large body of literature, we do believe that the articles that we cover in this chapter capture the thrust of academic literature on news media coverage of terrorism.[7]

In the next section of our chapter, we take our cue from scholarship predating 9/11 to consider major themes that have provoked debate or structured subsequent lines of inquiry. We also chronicle new developments within the scholarship, which we believe suggest promising avenues of inquiry. More specifically, we examine theoretical approaches to terrorism and the mass media along the following two subcategories: terrorism as communication and the relationship between terrorism and the mass media.

CONCEPTUAL ORIENTATIONS: THE ONTOLOGY OF MEDIA AND TERROR

Terrorism as Communication

The conception of terrorism as a fundamentally communicative act is a premise held by many scholars working across disciplinary divides (see, e.g., Leeman, 1991; Schmid & de Graaf, 1982; Tuman, 2003; Weimann, 2004). According to Weimann, if terrorism is symbolic, then it can be analyzed much as any other form of communication. Indeed, the act of terrorism itself, amplified through the mass media, arguably marks one stage of a much larger communicative process involving intrapersonal conviction, interpersonal suasion, group organizing, public ventilation, mediated magnification, and counter-terrorist response. Our survey of scholarship concerning mediated communication about terrorism features the stage in which most of us can expect to encounter terrorism. As Chermak and Gruenewald (2006), drawing from Slone (2000), asserted, "most people base their assessment of national security threats on indirect exposure through the media" (p. 431).

While many scholars begin with the premise that terrorism is communication, they have applied various communicative lenses in conceptualizing it. Historically, scholars have examined terrorism as a particular genre or type of communication ranging from rhetoric (e.g., Leeman, 1991; Tuman, 2003) to international media-oriented event (Weimann, 1987a, 1990) and spectacle (e.g., Chaliand, 1987; Der Derian, 2005). With regard to media coverage, Dowling (1986) argued that mediated coverage of terrorism constituted a distinct genre, while Leeman insisted scholars should study terrorist rhetoric as a dialectical counterpart to counter-terrorist messages. Other scholars have offered typologies of news stories on terrorism (Wittebols, 1992) or considered it from the generic perspective of ceremonial media events (Dayan & Katz, 1992) and disaster marathons (Blondheim & Liebes, 2002), the latter assuming greater prominence in recent years. Schirato and Webb (2004) identified a large number of genres involved in news reports of 9/11, including reality television, drama, action adventure, rescue shows, current affairs, the Western, and sports. Despite such generic diversity, Schirato and Webb argued that televised news reports of 9/11 best fit the genre of soap opera and its accompanying hysteria. Conceiving of terrorism news coverage through particular generic lenses helps scholars to identify, classify, and critique relevant substantive, stylistic, and structural tendencies of that coverage as compared to existing conventions of a genre. In this section of our chapter, we thus consider terrorism as communication from the perspectives of rhetoric and persuasion, narrative and myth, media-oriented events, and spectacle.

Rhetoric and Persuasion

Scholars who view terrorism and its news coverage through the lens of persuasion or rhetoric (e.g., Brock & Howell, 1988; W. J. Brown, 1990; Dowling, 1986, 1989; Leeman, 1991; Palmerton, 1988; Parry-Giles, 1995; Patkin, 2004; Tuman, 2003) emphasize the persuasive dimensions of strategic messages adapted to audience and occasion. Recently, Rowland and Theye (2006) asserted that "terrorism by its very nature is a rhetorical act," noting that Al Qaeda sent several messages to the United States in attacking its institutions of power (p. 1). Prior to 9/11, the subfield of rhetoric tended to produce isolated case studies of media coverage of particular incidents of terrorism (e.g., Brock & Howell, 1988; W. J. Brown, 1990; Dowling, 1989; Palmerton, 1988). Subsequent to it, the "War on Terror" comprises a significant focus of rhetorical criticism (e.g., Biesecker, 2007; Hartnett & Stengrim, 2006; Ivie, 2005, Noon, 2004; Simons, 2007) with analyses of presidential rhetoric and government strategies achieving increasing study (e.g., Bostdorff, 2003; Gunn, 2004; Murphy, 2003).[8] When considered as a whole, rhetorical studies of media coverage of terrorism produce qualitative textual explorations of the suasive dimensions of specific cases. Like their counterparts in critical and cultural studies, they tend to foreground ideological dimensions. These studies honor the richly nuanced, humanistic rhetorical tradition, which views rhetoric as emergent from sociohistorical particulars and, thereby, as warranting a case-study approach; rhetoricians are thus well poised to extend their contributions through projects that identify and critique recurrent patterns of terrorism news reportage across multiple and international sites and connect those patterns to broader cultural practices and rhetorical forms.

Narrative and Myth

Approaches that feature narrative (e.g., Dobkin, 1992, 1994; Goodall, 2006; Kitch, 2003; Nacos, 2003; Nossek & Berkowitz, 2006; Picard & Adams, 1987) and myth (e.g., Lule, 1993, 2002; Nossek & Berkowitz, 2006; Rowland & Theye, 2006; Thussu, 2006) feature the storied dimensions of terrorism reportage. Narrative approaches to terrorism in the media focus on characters, plots, and moral lessons (see Kitch, 2003; Nacos, 2003; Picard, 1993). Dobkin (1992) examined the ideological work of terrorism news. She found that stories about terrorism in U.S. television network newscasts from 1981 to 1986 reproduced "basic fears about the unknown and dying" and suggested "a deeper, uglier level of evil due to the sacrificial nature of the victim and the nefarious intent of the terrorist to terrorize" (p. 41). These stories tended to cast terrorists as "archetypal enemies" and characterized the United States as "champions of the 'free world'" (p. 52). Such polarity of characterization (us versus them, good versus evil) in elite discourse and subsequent news reports of terrorism is a phenomenon that scholars have continued to identify and critique in post-9/11 coverage (see, e.g., Hartnett & Stengrim, 2006; Kellner, 2002; Thussu, 2006).

A growing portion of empirical and critical work both before and after 9/11 treats the news media as mythmaker about terrorism. Nossek and Berkowitz (2006) dubbed this phenomenon "mythical newswork" to emphasize the dominance of media in propagating myths of heroism and victimage, innocence and guilt (p. 691). Der Derian (2005) wrote of "mytho-terrorism" in reference to the broader cultural tales that get retold through the media (p. 31). According to Der Derian, the media reports terrorist incidents in ways that recirculate dominant or, as Lule (2002) observed, even archetypal cultural myths. Lule, for example, identified four central myths present in *New York Times* editorials concerning 9/11—the end of innocence, the victims, the heroes, and the foreboding future. By contrast, Nossek and Berkowitz focused on the social functions of media-circulated myths about terrorism. These authors analyzed U.S. and Israeli coverage of two terrorist incidents in Israel to argue that news of terrorism retells societal master narratives in conservative ways. When core national values are threatened, journalists switch from everyday news practices of *professional narratives* to *cultural narratives*, which hasten return to dominant cultural values and social order.

A related conceptual approach employs the lens of drama. As early as 1975, Jenkins (1975) noted the choreography inherent in modern terrorism and called it "theater" (p. 4). Weimann and Winn's (1994) metaphor of the "theater of terror" stressed how "modern terrorism can be understood in terms of the production requirements of theatrical engagements. Terrorists pay attention to script preparation, cast selection, sets, props, role playing, and minute-by-minute stage management" (p. 52). Much like Kenneth Burke's (1969) dramatistic pentad of act, scene, agent, agency, and purpose, the metaphor of theater supplies an analytic vocabulary for dissecting the components of terrorism and shows its relationship to larger cultural patterns and scripts. When Debatin (2002) wrote that endless media attention "allowed the terrorist attacks to turn into a globally disseminated *plane wreck with spectators*" that "glued millions of people to their TV sets, even though they would not learn anything new and would only see the same horrible sequence again and again," he implicitly indexed the staged, theatrical dimensions of mediated representations of terrorism (p. 169; emphasis in original).

Media-oriented Events

The lenses of narrative, myth, and theater each call attention to characterization, emplotment, ritual dimensions, and temporality in media coverage of terrorism. Yet, our "stories" about terrorism evolve to fit the demands of the communication technologies du jour. Starting in the latter half of the 20th century, following the rise of electronic media, terrorists increasingly relied on media-sensitive strategies. Several conceptions of terrorism media coverage reflect sensitivity to this fact, including international media events, media-oriented terrorism, and mass mediated terrorism. Weimann (1987a) advanced the enduring and much referenced concept of terrorism as "international media event," noting that "terrorist attacks are increasingly being planned with care to attract the attention of the media" (p. 23). Terrorist attacks as international media events encompass live broadcasting, preplanning, elements of high drama, obligatory viewing, personification of events (heroes and villains), and the priestly role of media as "go betweens in the effort to resolve the conflict" (p. 29). Whatever the intention of terrorists with regard to the media, the media's coverage of these events, for Weimann (1987a), includes an ideological confrontation in which viewers are called on to maintain social order and prevailing societal norms. The monikers "media-oriented terrorism" (Weimann, 1990) and "mass-mediated terrorism" (Nacos, 2002, 2003) highlight "the centrality of media considerations in the calculus of political violence that is committed by nonstate actors against civilians" (Nacos, 2003, p. 23).

Spectacle

In an era dominated by the image, studies of media-oriented terrorism require appreciation of the visual components of terrorism news. Not surprisingly, then, scholars increasingly attend to the imagistic dimensions of terrorism, replicated and broadcast through visual media across the globe. Der Derian (2005, p. 23) explained that "thanks to the immediacy of television, the Internet and other networked information technology, we see terrorism everywhere in real time, all the time." As a result, Der Derian asserted that "terrorism has taken on an iconic, fetishised and, most significantly, highly optical character" (p. 23). *Spectacle* (Kellner, 2003; Livingston, 1994), therefore, comprises one of the most significant—and, we believe, heuristically valuable—contemporary lenses applied to media and terrorism. Indebted to Debord's *Society of the Spectacle* (1967/1994), this work often adopts a critical theory or Marxian approach that emphasizes the cultural alienation entailed in spectatorship. Debord, in particular, linked the mass media and spectacle, noting that the former is the most obvious manifestation of the latter. Spectacle relies on separation, in which passive viewers are distanced from those in power, the elites who control the media and the powerful celebrities whose foibles we watch. Crary (1999) extended Debord's conception of spectacle by observing that it "is not primarily concerned with a looking at images but rather with the construction of conditions that individuate, immobilize, and separate subjects" (p. 73). Thus, whereas narrative and mythical approaches to terrorism emphasize shared commonalities, spectacle entails a sense of distance and hidden promotion of capitalist values. Rather than reach out to one another, we engage the media. Postmodern thinkers such as Baudrillard (2002), Virilio (2002), and Žižek (2002) have further theorized 9/11 as media spectacle *par excellence*. "We can perceive the collapse of the WTC towers,"

Žižek wrote, "as the climactic conclusion of 20th century art's 'passion for the real'—the 'terrorists' themselves did not do it primarily to provoke real material damage, *but for the spectacular effect of it*" (p. 11).

A number of scholars conceptualize the media spectacle of terrorism in terms of witnessing, trauma, and suffering (see Chouliaraki, 2004; Rentschler, 2004; Zelizer, 2002). Rentschler, for instance, connected the act of witnessing terrorism to vicarious suffering. In watching disaster unfold across a mediated screen, we experience a "'modern' mass mediated form of suffering" (p. 296). This act entails identification with those whose suffering matters and a separation from those whose suffering does not. Chouliaraki similarly conceived the mediation of 9/11 in terms of "distant suffering" in which the "politics of pity" established proximity between spectators and events (p. 185). More specifically, Chouliaraki posited that the "television spectacle [of 9/11] engages the affective potential of the spectator and evokes a specific disposition to act upon the suffering–thus, its *moralizing effects* on the spectator" (p. 185). These authors offer conceptual schema with strong heuristic potential that can only be enhanced by additional empirical studies. While witnessing for Rentschler and Chouliaraki thus bears inherently political entailments, it does not necessarily carry connotations associated with othering and moralizing in all of its treatments. Zelizer, for example, linked witnessing with acts of commemoration honoring the dead. Here, witnessing transcends the passive spectator role and becomes an act of critical invention.

Considered together, these diverse conceptions share a focus on the symbolic and suasive dimensions of terrorism as covered in the media. While each of these lenses accentuates different features of terrorism and its reportage as communicative events, they nonetheless share the idea that terrorism as presented in the mass media draws from powerful cultural scripts in ritualized ways that often evoke a desire for a return to social order or promote a sense of distance and alienation. The relationship between the media and terrorism, itself, however, also needs to be explored.

The Relationship between Terrorism and the Mass Media in a Globalized World

A major plank of scholarship that pre-dated 9/11 concerned the relationship between terrorism and the mass media (see, e.g., Wilkinson, 1997). This section traces differing models of this relationship as depicted in contagion theory, framing and agenda-setting theories, and those entailed by globalization theory.

Contagion Theory

Many scholars noted a "symbiotic" relationship between terrorists and the media (Long, 1990). As Jablonski and Sullivan (1996) explained, "terrorists supply the media with interesting material for stories, while the media provide coverage to the terrorists" (p. 191). Though the model of symbiosis has lost some salience, one of the most debated propositions regarding a relationship between the media and terrorism involved the so-called contagion theory—the idea that coverage of terrorism emboldens terrorists and encourages more terrorism (see Brosius & Weimann, 1991; Weimann & Winn, 1994). Margaret Thatcher's "oxygen of publicity" metaphor expressed precisely this sentiment. Dobkin (1992) and Picard (1993) criticized contagion theory, citing a lack of empirical evidence, and an early analysis of terrorism content in the *New York Times* and the *London Times* concluded that, "while transnational terrorism does generate a considerable amount of press attention, the particular type of coverage it receives would appear to undermine the effectiveness of terrorism as a communications strategy" (Kelly & Mitchell, 1981, p. 269). In lieu of contagion, Wieviorka (1988/1993) posited four relationships between the media and terrorism, which range from total indifference to making the media the target of attack. Recent work stresses the complexity of relations between media and terrorism, suggesting that "routinization" rather than contagion might be occurring (Liebes & Kampf, 2007). In other words, the more the media covers terrorist incidents, the more restrained, distanced, and predictable the coverage becomes.

Framing and Agenda Setting

The concepts of framing and agenda setting, which reference two related processes, capture some of the intricacies of the relationships between terrorism and the mass media. News frames constitute "persistent patterns of selection, emphasis, and exclusion that furnish a coherent interpretation and evaluation of events" (Norris, Just, & Kern, 2002, p. 4). Researchers have studied them widely with regard to terrorism (e.g., Eisman, 2003; Entman, 1991; Jasperson & El-Kikhia, 2002; Reynolds & Barnett, 2003b; Ruigrok & van Atteveltd, 2007; Schaefer, 2002). Framing theory originated with Goffman's (1974) *Frame Analysis*, which argued that "schemata of interpretation," or frames, enable individuals to "locate, perceive, identify, and label" experiences and events in ways that shape interpretation and response (p. 21). As such, frames often supply the issues and terms of public attention.

Agenda-setting theory, advanced by McCombs and Shaw (1972), posits that the mass media play a large role in determining the issues to which publics attend. In this view, media prime public interest in certain topics over others. They determine the topics that users take up for consideration. Conventional news frames give order and meaning to unfolding stories in consistent and familiar terms. They alert publics to the problem of terrorism and other international affairs (see Wanta & Hu, 1993) and, thereby, shape the issues publics deem to be pressing. However, they also limit the horizon of acceptable action and "alter interpretations of topics treated" (Cappella & Jamieson, 1997,

p. 40). Studies of agenda setting in news media on terrorism find support for its role in establishing international terrorism as a significant issue (Christie, 2006; Craft & Wanta, 2004) and even in establishing the salience of bioterrorism (Aldoory & Van Dyke, 2006).

Global, Local, and Glocal Perspectives

Media coverage often characterizes terrorism as global or local, depending on physical proximity to and "local angle" of the attack. Schaefer (2002), for instance, found that proximity and local/national frames influenced the amount of coverage of the 1988 Kenya and Tanzania Embassy bombings in prominent African and U.S. newspapers. Ruigrok and van Atteveldt (2007), by contrast, concluded that framing of the 9/11, Madrid, and London attacks in American, Dutch, and British papers was more affected by 9/11 as a global event than by proximity and local-angle considerations. A majority of studies both before and after 9/11 found, however, a marked tendency for national news outlets to frame international terrorist incidents in terms of domestic agendas (e.g., Achugar, 2004; Fawcett, 2002; Parry-Giles, 1995; Sádaba & La Porte, 2006). Ben-Shaul's (2006) qualitative research, for example, compared televised audiovisuals of CNN, Israel's Channels 1 and 2, and Palestinian Authority Television news coverage of 9/11, the U.S.–Al Qaeda conflict, and the al Aksa Intifada. According to Ben-Shaul, when the Palestinian Authority Television— which featured 9/11 far less than the other sources—did mention 9/11, they "constantly related" it "to reports on Israeli military deployments and movements in the West Bank and Gaza Strip" (p. 77). He wrote that comparing coverage of these events showed "the high degree of divergence between the different points of view" and noted that they reflected the ideologies of their respective elites (p. 77). This finding has implications for international communication in that it suggests how past domestic experience with terrorism, combined with ongoing elite agendas, can color domestic media frames, thereby encouraging conflicting understandings of events.

More recent conceptualizations of the relationship between the media and terrorism represent a complex and multivalent association between the two and account for the interplay of state and elite discourse as well. A number of studies note the tendency of media to parrot elite discourse and to adopt state frames uncritically (e.g., Billeaudeux, Domke, Hutcheson, & Garland, 2003; Domke, Graham, Coe, John, & Coopman, 2006; Hutcheson, Domke, Billedeaux, & Garland, 2004; Snow & Taylor, 2006). Clearly, models of mediated terrorism as communication that stress interpenetration of local, regional, international, and elite players on a global stage are warranted. Such *glocalization*, or "the interpenetration of the global and local resulting in unique outcomes in different geographic areas," presents a promising avenue of consideration (Ritzer, 2004, p. 77).

CONTENT ANALYSES

Content analyses of mass-mediated terrorism coverage are legion. They also exhibit variation in scope, method, and findings. Scholars have devoted much attention to analyzing media coverage of terrorism on and after September 11, 2001, across a range of media. Though a share of literature focuses on fictional or popular culture references to 9/11 and terrorism (Boggs & Pollard, 2006; Chermak, Bailey, & Brown, 2003; Gans-Boriskin & Tisinger, 2005; R. Jones & Dionisopoulos, 2004; Wilkins & Downing, 2002), a substantial expanse of work addresses news coverage of terrorism, in general, and September 11, specifically. We discuss this larger body of news work next through a synthesis of empirical studies of media coverage of terrorism. In large part, this research revolves around news coverage in three primary forms—television, print, and the Internet, though we make reference to multi-modal content as well.

Media Coverage

Media representations of terrorism are largely the source for our information about terrorism, and, as Dobkin (1992) emphasized, scholars must extrapolate what this coverage entails. A 1987 content analysis of the three major U.S. network news broadcasts from 1969 to 1980 compared coverage of terrorism to actual international terrorist events and revealed that network reports did not match real events. The coverage tended to be erratic and "quite inaccurate," over-emphasizing, for example, both acts of terrorism in the Middle East and terrorist incidents directed at private U.S. citizens (Delli Carpini & Williams, 1987, p. 60). Chermak and Gruenewald's (2006) longitudinal overview of the media's coverage of domestic terrorism exposed similar tendencies. When comparing a list of actual terrorist incidents in the United States from 1980 to September 10, 2001, to the *New York Times'* coverage of terrorism for the same period, the authors determined multiple discrepancies. Of the 412 actual incidents of terrorism, only 228 received coverage in the *Times*. Further, a majority of the articles discussed a minority of the incidents. Fifteen terrorism incidents received coverage in 79% of the total amount of articles regarding all incidents. Chermak and Gruenewald concluded their article by calling for more systematic evaluations of media representations of terrorism, especially considering the impact of September 11.

Indeed, much of the work analyzing media content of terrorism revolves around the news coverage of 9/11 and presents a rather vexing picture of what such coverage entailed. In his article for the Joan Shorenstein Center on the Press, Politics and Public Policy titled, "While America Slept: Coverage of Terrorism from 1993 to September 11, 2001," Storin (2002), a Shorenstein Fellow and former editor of the *Boston Globe*, evaluated content from the *New York Times* and the *Washington Post* over an eight and a half year period to determine the extent to which these papers covered issues relating to the possibility of a terrorist attack in the United States. Although he gave credit to a few in-depth and highly informative news pieces and cautioned against concluding that the media wholly "missed" the story of a terrorism threat against the United States, Storin also noted a lack of urgency and inconsistency and inattention in both papers. According to Storin, "For the 11 months between October 12, 2000, and September 11, 2001, a Nexis search indicates that the *Times* published only six stories on page A1 that prominently mentioned a threat of terrorists or terrorism" (p. 28).

In many ways, as scholarship delves more deeply into the specifics of this content, including coverage in the hours, weeks, and months following 9/11, the picture does not greatly improve. Analyses of news coverage of 9/11 reveal it to be largely characterized by limited perspectives, moral positioning fueled by nationalism, and scant analysis and questioning. A few bright spots exist, including from sources such as Germany's popular newsmagazine, *Der Spiegel* (Haes, 2002) but, by and large, an examination of the content devoted to news coverage of 9/11 and terrorism raises questions about the content covered and slighted by international news media.

Television Content

September 11 has been called an event "made to order for television news" (Stempel & Hargrove, 2003, p. 55; see also Debatin, 2002). The intense, blockbuster movie–like graphics, raw emotional content, and real-time coverage contributed to the feeling of a "made-for-TV" moment, and American viewers tuned in. According to surveys conducted by The Pew Internet and American Life Project as well as Ohio University and Scripps Howard News Service, television emerged as the medium of choice on 9/11 and the days following. Notably, 81% of Americans reported getting information from television in the days after the attack, although use of all news-gathering media reportedly rose during this time (Pew Internet & American Life Project, 2001; Stempel & Hargrove, 2003).

Although analyses of television content range from the short-term to the more extended, results remain consistent. Scholars describe the immediate coverage of 9/11 as narrow and unidirectional. Mogensen, Lindsay, Li, Perkins, and Beardsley (2002) found that fact presentation served as a staple of coverage run on Fox News, CNN, ABC, NBC, and CBS. It dominated broadcasts to the detriment of other media functions such as guiding the audience, consoling trauma, or alleviating stress or anxiety. Further, according to Mogensen et al., half of news stories appearing on the networks in the first eight hours of the event were framed as a disaster.

The challenges and demands of a breaking news story factored strongly into the nature of 9/11 news coverage. In an analysis of the first five hours of coverage after the attack aired by ABC, CBS, CNN, and NBC, Reynolds and Barnett (2003b) explored how journalists operate in a breaking-news situation as well as how breaking news impacts content and journalists' roles. In part, they asked whether journalists performed the role of traditional disseminator, for example, or operated as social commentator. They also considered the extent to which reporters relayed unconfirmed reports and rumors in the broadcasts, used anonymous sources, and varied from journalistic conventions. Reynolds and Barnett acknowledged that journalists retracted earlier statements, admitted violating journalistic conventions, and served roles such as eyewitness, expert, and social commentator; yet, most of the time they functioned as traditional journalists and spent a small segment of time referring to anonymous sources and reporting rumors. However, the authors cautioned readers not to dismiss the significance of the occasions when journalists violated conventions because they may have had tremendous social impact. Reynolds and Barnett included an excerpt from then ABC anchorman Peter Jennings's live broadcast to illustrate this point. Jennings commented that, "[a]s you look at these scenes, you can feel absolutely clear that you are looking at the results of the United States at war with angry and vicious people who will do in the future as they have done in the past, whatever they can to get at the United States, this huge presence in the world" (Reynolds & Barnett, p. 698).

Silence comprises a revealing element of live, breaking-news coverage as well. According to Jaworski, Fitzgerald, and Constantinou (2005), the BBC News 24's coverage of 9/11 on that day can partly be characterized by silence, both concrete silence—the lack of sound or talk—and metaphorical silence— absence of new information and reliance on the repetition of old information or irrelevant talk. In a divergence from the indicting conclusions offered by the scholars assessing the content of 9/11 coverage (e.g., Anker, 2005; Eisman, 2003; Kellner, 2002; Mogensen et al., 2002), Jaworski et al. interpreted the BBC's coverage—including the silences—as an aid to shocked viewers in need of help with coming to terms with the situation.

For the most part, analyses of news coverage consistently reveal that media sources framed and presented stories in ways that narrowed the discourse surrounding 9/11 and discouraged alternative responses to military retaliation (Reynolds & Barnett, 2003a). In fact, Eisman's (2003) study of the three major U.S. television networks broadcasts in the two weeks after the attacks found that U.S. news media avoided difficult questions, alternative perspectives, and dissenting opinions and thereby "degenerated almost completely into blatant propaganda" (p. 65). Kellner (2002) similarly proffered a strong indictment of television news programs' reporting after 9/11. Far from critically debating the issues and questions surrounding the terrorist attack on 9/11, Kellner argued that the U.S. media whipped up war hysteria after 9/11, promoting military action as the solution to global terrorism. In a qualitative analysis of 9/11 coverage aired on Fox News, Anker (2005) explored how news coverage of 9/11 incorporated melodrama and, in so doing, fostered a particular American collective identity—one in which the United States became a moral victim called on to defend itself. The presence of melodrama and the implications of its moral casting served to direct public sentiment and cloak state power in an aura of righteousness. According to Anker, "The most dangerous implication of the melodramatic national identity during September 11 was that it took power away from citizens by encouraging them to assume that state power was an unquestionable moral imperative in fighting the eternal battle between good and evil" (p. 36).

Two studies conducted in part by the Project for Excellence in Journalism (2001, 2006) identified a shift in news content, including a larger percentage of newscasts devoted to hard news, foreign policy, and terrorism. The 2001 study examined ABC's, CBS's, and NBC's evening and morning newscasts over two week-long periods in June of 2001 and two week-long periods in October of 2001. A comparison of the data collected in June versus those from October revealed striking differences. Whereas lifestyle and feature stories comprised nearly 20% of evening newscasts in June of 2001, that figure dropped to 1% in October. Additionally, the percentage of the newscast devoted to hard news nearly doubled from June (45.5%) to October (82%). The numbers related to the morning news tell an even more dramatic story. Hard news jumped from less than 7% of the newscast in June to more than 58% in October. The study includes a caveat, however. Though the figures suggest that newscasts have become more serious after 9/11, a vast majority of the coverage is devoted to the war, "which suggests that the networks may have simply changed *subjects* rather than changed their *approach* to the news" (p. 1; emphasis in original).

The 2006 study by the Project for Excellence in Journalism assessed how 9/11 changed the evening news over a five year period. An examination and comparison of network evening newscasts in the four years prior to 9/11 and the four years after demonstrates a sharp increase in the amount of time devoted to foreign policy (up 102%), armed conflict (69%), and terrorism (135%). These numbers come with a price, namely the amount of coverage allotted to domestic issues. The study also reported a serious decline in the coverage of domestic stories relating to crime and law enforcement (down 47%), science and technology (down 50%), and drugs, alcohol, and tobacco (down 66%). While foreign policy, conflict, and terrorism remained strong elements of evening newscasts five years after 9/11, it appears that the sizable growth in hard news coverage did not continue. The study reported a 2% increase in the minutes devoted to hard news after the attacks and a 5% decrease in softer new coverage.

While the amount of airtime devoted to covering terrorism, foreign policy, and armed conflict may appear to be a positive change for a news industry accused of dropping the ball regarding terrorism coverage in the years proceeding 9/11, research by Chermak and Gruenewald (2006), Delli Carpini and Williams (1987), and Storin (2002) tempers any impulses to equate an increase in coverage with an increase in the quality and accuracy of coverage. Future work must, therefore, heed Chermak and Gruenewald's call for additional longitudinal studies that track media coverage of worldwide terrorist incidents and continue to assess the quality of this vast increase in terrorism coverage.

Further, the analysis of the BBC's content stands out as a positive assessment of 9/11 news coverage (Jaworski et al., 2005), which raises questions and additional research possibilities, including the need for extended comparative analyses between U.S. and international coverage. One can imagine differences in the coverage between U.S. and international sources, but how do those differences manifest themselves and to what extent? How was 9/11 covered across the globe? The May 2002 issue of *Television & New Media* focused on answering these questions, and many of the authors shared their assessment of content that tried to make sense of the event and its impact on their nation as well as contextualized the incident in accordance with various local experiences with terrorism and relations with the United States. Baiocchi (2002) argued that Brazil's print and television coverage of 9/11 and the subsequent war in Afghanistan can be characterized as ambiguous, demonstrating both solidarity with and criticism of the United States. Chakravartty (2002) explored how India's English-language media made sense out of 9/11 and the days following through "locally resonant narratives about terror, Islam, U.S. foreign policy, and the looming military response" (p. 205). Basque media coverage of 9/11 mirrored analogies to the problems experienced in the Basque provinces (Sádaba, 2002), and Buonanno (2002) referred to feelings of déjà vu conjured by coverage of 9/11 as it related to Italy's own experiences of domestic terrorism. These essays, and the May 2002 issue of *Television & New Media* as a whole, provide an informative glimpse of international coverage of 9/11 and the various ways in which the media framed the incident in accordance with local concerns, experiences, and politics.

In large part, scholarship regarding television news representations of 9/11 presents a rather severe assessment of news content and style. Although television comprised the medium of choice for American viewers on and after 9/11, research reveals television coverage of the incident to be largely narrow, sensational, and of a single, un-reflexive voice (Anker, 2005; Eisman, 2003; Kellner, 2002; Mogensen et al., 2002; Reynolds & Barnett, 2003a). September 11 did spur changes in news coverage—notably, a rise in the time and attention devoted to hard news issues including foreign policy, armed conflict, and terrorism (Project for Excellence in Journalism, 2001, 2006). While such a trend may, at first glance, appear to be wholly positive, an increase in coverage does not necessarily equate to an increase in quality coverage—and may not have held over time. Additional longitudinal work is needed to assess shifts in news coverage since 9/11. Further, we should consider differences in international coverage of 9/11. Such efforts must attend not only to non-English news sources but also move beyond the scope of this project to collect and review the scholarship published in non-English outlets around the globe.

Print Content

Despite recognition of 9/11's suitability for television coverage (Debatin, 2002), newspapers and newsmagazines also played an integral role in reporting the event and terrorism in general, and a large body of work addresses the content of such reporting. In fact, one may call the work devoted to analyses of print content disproportionately large in lieu of news media consumption patterns in the days and weeks following 9/11, since most Americans turned to television for news and information after the attack (Pew Internet and American Life Project, 2001; Stempel & Hargrove, 2003). Nonetheless, the scholarship involving analyses of content do not reflect these consumption figures; instead, it heavily favors print and newsmagazine content, as the scope of the following section indicates. The work concerning print content bestows several of the same criticisms on newspapers and newsmagazines that the previous section detailed regarding television content, but, in many ways, it provides a less indicting picture. Further, analyses of print content also encompass a variety of additional perspectives and approaches, including portrayals of "the Other" as well as consideration of international coverage of 9/11 and terrorism.

A synthesis of the work involving print content reveals a complex assessment. Some researchers characterized print news coverage following 9/11 as limited, inaccurate, and couched in fear and nationalism. Kitch (2003) revealed the 9/11 coverage in *Time, Newsweek*, and *U.S. News and World Report* in the month after the attack to be largely uniform, a point echoed by Ryan (2004). Ryan's analysis of the nation's ten largest newspapers immediately following 9/11 and leading up to the bombing of Afghanistan focused on each paper's official position on the War on Terror and the invasion of Afghanistan as communicated through the papers' editorials. He concluded that the newspapers explained the issues involved narrowly and through a singular narrative and frame that supported a military response and predicted a positive outcome. According to Ryan, "The ultimate question, of course, is: did the US news media serve Americans well during the critical period 12 September–8 October 2001? This study suggests the answer is no for those who think the media should explore, analyze, evaluate and publicize alternative strategies and ideas" (p. 380).

As Chermak and Gruenewald (2006) conveyed, discrepancies between unfolding geopolitical events and their appearance in mainstream media are rife in news coverage of terrorism. Their 20 year overview of the print media's coverage of domestic terrorism from 1980 to just prior to 9/11 reveals inconsistencies in reporting terrorism incidents, including an overemphasis of those incidents involving death and of events occurring in the Northeast region of the United States compared to events occurring in the South. In his exploration of five national newspapers in the 18 months proceeding and the 18 months following 9/11, Altheide (2006) discovered that, after 9/11, the print news media played a central part in promoting the politics of fear, conveying a sense of terrorism as "a monstrous black hand that was invisible, omnipresent, all powerful" (p. 433). Beyond inducing fear, newspapers and newsmagazines also sought to elicit and allow for expression of feelings of grief and nationalism. The text, photographs, letters, and images of U.S. newsmagazines "not only covered, but conducted a public funeral ceremony" in the month after 9/11 (Kitch, 2003, p. 215). National identity emerged as a strong element of discourse post 9/11, and government officials and military officials appeared to use extensive strategic communication relating to national identity. That language was, in turn, echoed by journalists (Hutcheson et al., 2004). Analyses of print content disclosed a dearth in distinctions between information relating to 9/11 and the War on Terror; an examination of 34 issues of *Time* and *Newsweek* from September of 2002 and the first few months of 2003 revealed a convergence in coverage of 9/11 and the Iraq war (Fried, 2005).

Much of the work involving analyses of print content offers a critical read of print news' coverage of 9/11 and terrorism, but, far from wholly indicting, this work provides a complicated picture of the terrain. By contrast to television, print media contained less emotional content, and it was not related to audiences' negative emotional response to the 9/11 terrorist attack (Cho et al., 2003). However, a portion of the print research recognizes the role of this medium in generating support and solidarity among a shocked citizenship. Kitch's (2003) study regarding the ritual of public funeral indicated how the news media allowed people across the nation to take part in the ceremony post 9/11 and experience a connection to the event. Though they critiqued the "inexorable intertwining of political leaders and mass media… in the construction, articulation, and dissemination of national identity" (p. 47), Hutcheson et al. (2004) found that all of the investigated groups—U.S. government and military officials, non-government elites, citizens, and journalists—employed a large amount of national identity discourse after 9/11.

Moreover, newspapers can serve as unifying sources when local citizen involvement in terrorism events occurs. Gartner (2004) explored whether local casualties influenced U.S. regional media coverage of international events by charting the presence of stories about the USS Cole attacks on online newspaper homepages. Gartner found support for the hypothesis that newspapers from areas that sustained a casualty would give the incident more attention, though coverage predictably fades over time. Thus, local relationship to an international event influences global news coverage and consequently, serves as a potent site for representations of international affairs.

Depictions of Arabs, Arab Americans, and Middle-Eastern Populations

Scholarship concerning media coverage of terrorism includes a consideration of the depictions and reference to Arabs, Arab Americans, and Middle Eastern populations. September 11 ushered in a period of uncertainty and potential danger for many Arab Americans, who frequently suffered—and continue to endure—social, economic, and political injustices after the attack (Prashad, 2005; Salaita, 2005; see also Domke, Garland, Billeaudeaux, & Hutcheson, 2003). Salaita argued that hostile attitudes toward Arab communities and populations in the United States after 9/11 were not new; such views have been harbored for decades and reignited during the response to 9/11. A strong vein of the work concerned with print content explores the news media's role in that response and examines how news media portrayed Arabs, Arab Americans, and those from the Middle East in general. This body of literature reveals that many of the newspaper and newsmagazine stories and messages concerning 9/11 and terrorism reinforced stereotypes and the sense of a dualistic battle between the U.S. and the terrorists—a dichotomy frequently conflated to "us" and "them."

In an analysis of 9/11 coverage within the *Gazette*, Quebec's English-language newspaper, Jiwani (2004) asserted that representations of Muslim women within the stories did not deviate from traditional stereotypes. The veiled woman, in particular, receives much media coverage; she is "depicted as being both oppressed by and subjugated under Islam, as well as unable to liberate herself without the help of Western powers" (p. 287). Jiwani argued such representations serve to reinforce binary thinking and an "us" versus "them" mentality. Representations and language use direct audience interpretations regarding notions of terrorism and terrorists. Dunn, Moore, and Nosek (2005) studied linguistic differences in newspaper content and the extent to which those differences shaped perceptions and audiences' attitudes concerning terrorism and their memory of violent events. Their content analysis of regional newspapers from July 2003 to January 2004 exposed that journalists more likely employed "benign" words in reference to violent action connected to the United States and its allies, and they used "devious" words more often in conjunction with violent action associated with Iraq and non-U.S. allies. The authors observed that "even minor linguistic variations can influence whether an act of violence is perceived as terrorism versus patriotism" (p. 83).

Vultee (2006) traced the transformation of the term *fatwa* "from a simple term of Islamic law into a compact signal of Western stereotypes of the Middle East" (p. 319). An Arabic word, fatwa refers to an authority's ruling regarding religious law but, as it has been employed in Western media, it has shifted in meaning to "'death sentence' and 'religious execution decree'" (p. 320). According to Vultee, the shift of the term fatwa exemplifies "linguistic demonization" and "reinforces an image of Islam as uniquely prone to political violence" (p. 319).[9]

Evidence suggests that anti-Arab sentiment after 9/11 met at least a modicum of resistance, however. In a comparison of the rhetorical strategies employed in *New York Times* articles, editorials, columns, and advertisements in describing Japanese Americans following the attack on Pearl Harbor to representations and references to Arab Americans after 9/11, Brennen and Duffy (2003) asserted that, while, "ultimately, the coverage of Japanese Americans as well as Muslim and Arab Americans is framed to evoke a pervading sense of fear about the Other" (p. 13), a primary difference between the two content areas involved the condemnation of anti-Arab racism after 9/11.

Several additional studies unpack the linguistic functions of naming (Bhatia, 2005; Kapitan & Schulte, 2002). Kapitan and Schulte, for example, explained that the label "terrorist" functions in international communication to discredit those to whom it is attached, dehumanizing them, and suggesting that they lack reason. The resultant rhetoric "erases any incentive an audience might have to understand the point of view of those individuals and groups so it can ignore the history behind their grievances" and "deflects attention away from one's own policies that might have contributed to those grievances" (p. 178).

International Perspectives

Similar to conducting television analyses, scholars studying print have also conducted analyses of content from a number of international perspectives as well, exploring the interplay between terrorism, domestic issues, and the media. Achugar's (2004) examination of Uruguayan newspapers highlights how the discourse of 9/11 was re-appropriated into explanations for Uruguay's dictatorship period and its causes. Others considered the events of 9/11 and their meaning for Japanese domestic and international relations through explorations of newspaper content (Nanri, 2005; Sakai, 2003). An analysis of how an annual local Irish parade was framed in local newspapers allowed Fawcett (2002) to study the appeal of conflict frames and the constraints involved in studying such conflict. He concluded that the frames employed by a newspaper resulted, at least partly, from the role that the paper plays as a storyteller and politician. A sample of four newspapers from different countries and their coverage of 9/11 in the four days after the attack revealed not only that journalists fall back on the daily routines that govern newsrooms but that a nation's geographic and cultural distance from an event functions as a buffer between the propaganda of the nation directly involved and the distant nation's policy (Josephi, 2004). Haes (2002) provided insight into how European journalism addressed 9/11 through his analysis of Germany's *Der Spiegel*, its most influential newsmagazine. He noted that the quality, depth, and difference in coverage compared to what many audiences had received in Germany and abroad in the previous days; specifically, the newsmagazine provided extensive background information, questioned calls for war, and asked the question lacking in a vast majority of other coverage: why?

In short, the work regarding coverage of terrorism in print content in many ways addresses some of the thin areas in television analyses. Research devoted to print includes a more complex picture of what the media provided in the days and weeks following 9/11. Though print coverage of the incident also elicits strong criticism, it offers some of the more mundane and sometimes helpful aspects of the coverage (e.g., Cho et al., 2003; Hutcheson et al., 2004; Kitch, 2003).

Further, the vein of investigations addressing portrayals of Arabs, Arab Americans, and Middle-Eastern populations provides much-needed critical reflection. Though it appears that the United States has learned something through its past mistakes of mistreating minority populations in times of war (Brennen & Duffy, 2003), much work remains in revealing and adjusting representations of populations that are reduced to the "Other." Brennen and Duffy's work must also be extended: What has the U.S. media learned since the attack on Pearl Harbor and the internment of Japanese Americans? Specifically, how have resistance to racism and stereotypes manifested in print content? What strategies are used to counter demonizing discourse and the rhetoric of blame? Who employs these strategies—officials, ordinary citizens, editors?

Finally, the international element of print content analyses is rich and multi-faceted. The variety of perspectives discloses the myriad ways in which the print media addresses terrorism and 9/11 and covers the topic from the position of nations. A domestic lens comprises a consistent element within this coverage, which affords extensive insight into the sentiment of the international community and the international response to the War on Terror. Future research may consider how this coverage paralleled or deviated from the events that played out in nations' political behavior and response to 9/11. While analyses of print coverage help to craft a more nuanced picture of media's representations of 9/11 and terrorism, the picture remains incomplete. Americans did not rely on the Internet for information about the attacks in large numbers in the days following 9/11, but Internet audiences have grown exponentially since 2001, and many now turn to it for news. As Roessler (2007) explained, "the Internet provides an endless variety of alternative sources, opening up a new area of research that explores the interplay between traditional media and the new digital environment" (p. 495). Today, scholars must consider the diversity of such content, including the information and services that audiences find through such sources.

Internet Content

Although the theoretical contextualizing of the Internet and new media (including Weblogs, or blogs, and list-serves, for example) constitutes a prominent component of the scholarship regarding media representations of terrorism, empirical research analyzing the content of Internet coverage and alternative news practices remains less robust but growing (see, e.g., Dooley & Corman, 2002). The attacks of 9/11 and the subsequent War on Terror have been called the first war of the Internet age, but news consumption figures depict that audiences did not largely turn to the Internet for their news in the days following 9/11 (Glass, 2002). Galvin (2004) noted that 9/11 brought into high relief "a new and unprecedented, technologically mediated, communications environment" (p. 14). Although most Americans still gathered their 9/11 information primarily from television, more than 30 million people went online in search of news in the wake of that tragic day (Pew Internet and American Life Project, 2001). Moreover, numerous less-formal news Web sites picked up slack in reporting, "making publicly available eyewitness accounts, personal photographs, and in some cases video footage of the unfolding disasters," which signified "something of a first-person news network" (Allan, 2002, p. 127). A small number of Americans—only 3%—reported getting most of their information from the Internet. According to the Pew Internet and American Life Project, although traffic on news sites increased in the days following the attack, overall reliance on the Internet remained smaller than normal. In fact, a subsequent study determined that the number of people using the Internet on a "typical day" did not assume usual levels until early October (Pew Internet & American Life Project, 2002).

Scholarly investigations concerning Internet content related to terrorism and 9/11 come from individual and groups of scholars, as well as research foundations such as the Pew Internet and American Life Project, with varying findings. While some studies found the Internet as a news source somewhat deficient (M. Brown, Fuzesi, Kitch, & Spivey, 2003; Randle, Davenport, & Bossen, 2003), analyses of sites over a longer period reveal that the Internet provided a variety of helpful content following 9/11 (Pew Internet & American Life Project, 2002). Based on research by M. Brown et al. and Randle et al., in spite of the Internet rapidly becoming more integrated into news gathering, many online news sources did not fully utilize available Internet tools in times of crisis. Randle et al.'s study of local newspaper Web sites in the hours following 9/11 determined that a majority of sites did not cover the attacks. According to M. Brown et al., sites that did cover 9/11 in the subsequent weeks largely mimicked more traditional news media and failed to realize the Internet's potential as a space for new, original, and alternative representations. Like more traditional forms of news, Web sites, perhaps understandably, lacked explanations for the event, and they neglected meaning, context, and perspective in their coverage of 9/11. Content analyses of news organizations' Web sites indicated consistent elements among the sites, including timelines and summaries, continuing war coverage, threats and risks, Bin Laden, chat rooms, emergency information and victim links, audio/video coverage, interactives, and advertisements. Regardless of their immediate utility, M. Brown et al. asserted that these sites do function as context for generating public memory and vary from other media in their "incorporation of a wide array of technologies and media forms dedicated to the preservation and reproduction of September 11 in a manner that is perpetually and immediately available" (p. 109).

A comprehensive report compiled by the Pew Internet and American Life Project (2002), an analysis of 247 various Web sites and the results of daily telephone surveys over the course of three to four months revealed that the

Internet provided a variety of content and services in the months following 9/11 and that many people took advantage of what appeared on the Internet. Of the sites analyzed, 63% provided direct information about the events of 9/11; 55% allowed users to view and experience the personal expressions of others; 44% enabled users to present their own personal expressions online; 36% of sites provided assistance; 26% helped users locate assistance; 11% permitted users to supply information themselves, and 6% of sites enabled users to participate in some sort of political advocacy. An additional component to the Pew's report concerned the emergence of "do-it-yourself" journalism after 9/11. According to the study, personal stories, eye-witness accounts, pictures, commentary, and first-hand knowledge of the events surrounding 9/11 flourished on the Internet in the days after the attack, granting new weight and standing to the phenomenon of do-it-yourself online journalism. In many ways, these non-traditional news sources helped to fuel the stamina of continuing online journalism trends.

The Internet not only provided alternatives to traditional news sources in the period after September 11, but it afforded the space for alternative means of expression as well. Frank (2004) explained electronic folklore related to the news and events of 9/11 that circulated electronically via e-mail or Web sites. Specifically, Frank examined the "newslore" form of photo shops: photographs digitally altered for humorous effect. According to Frank, newslore, and particularly photo shops, became an outlet for the hurt and anger experienced by the public but not seen or heard in mainstream media's telling of the story. Attention to the feelings and mindsets depicted through these counter-images and feelings demonstrates the need to consider information and expression found in places other than the mainstream news media. As Frank asserted, "[a] ny future attempt to research the national mood after September 11 through the mainstream news media alone, without recourse to the netlore, would be woefully incomplete" (p. 654).

To review, scholarship concerning the Internet's coverage of 9/11 and terrorism constitutes a growing body of work, reflecting a variety of assessments. While a few of the researchers found Internet coverage uneven (M. Brown et al., 2003; Randle et al., 2003), others revealed that the Internet provided an assortment of content, services, and possibilities for expression (Frank, 2004; Pew Internet & American Life Project, 2002). Although 9/11 may not have been the Internet's finest hour, the World Wide Web and its uses—both by new organizations and audiences—continue to evolve and must likewise continue to be tracked and analyzed with regard to terrorism. According to Seib (2004), "the Internet's traffic is estimated to double every hundred days. This underscores its expanding importance and the need for it to be reevaluated as a topic for news coverage" (p. 103). Will Internet content and coverage simply mimic the content of television broadcasts and newspapers as some studies indicate (e.g., M. Brown et al., 2003; Randle et al., 2003), or will it grow into a more nuanced resource beyond that of traditional news reporting as the data uncovered by the

Pew Internet and American Life Project (2001, 2002) suggests? Determining the answers to such relevant questions is not without difficulty. The Internet poses new challenges to researchers seeking to analyze content, including how to address the often fleeting nature of online information and the never-ending possibilities posed by hyperlinks (see Weare & Lin, 2000). However, as user populations continue to grow, researchers must address these challenges and the possibilities of Internet content. In particular, its use in non-Western populations deserves special scrutiny (see Abdulla, 2005).

Multi-modal Content

A majority of Americans reported using more than one medium in collecting news about terrorism during and after September 11, a statistic that reflects contemporary news-gathering trends (Stempel & Hargrove, 2003). More than ever, source variety comprises a staple of our media landscape. Wakshlag (2002) asserted:

> If anything distinguishes today's media environment from that of the past it is the abundance of choice, and not only in the United States. Newspapers, magazines, radio, television, and the latest communication innovation, the Internet, combine with interpersonal sources to create a huge matrix of communication options. (p. xiii)

Although a portion of the work regarding the content of media representations of terrorism reflects this trend, a majority of such research considers television in accordance with print (Cho et al., 2003; Eisman, 2003; Nord & Strömbäck, 2003; Ryan, 2006). Future investigations must account for the reality and diversity of news consumption patterns in analyzing content. P. Martin and Phelan (2002) addressed this need in their analysis of television broadcasts and message boards. The authors examined the transcripts of CNN, ABC, CBS, NBC, and Fox and the transcripts from the CNN message board in the week following 9/11, to explore the cognitive map that emerged around the word *Islamic*. They found "Islamic" in both contexts to be paired with a number of what the authors called unfavorable words such as terrorist(s), militant(s), fundamentalist(s), radical(s), jihad, struggle, extremist(s), or militant(s). They observed the similarities in the television broadcasts and the messageboards and noted with interest "the dominance of a particular cultural stereotype in both media fora, and their even greater usage and virulence on the messageboard, less bound, as it is, by television's obligation to frame events in official, and perhaps somewhat euphemized terms" (p. 267).[10]

As this section has demonstrated, television, print, and the Internet each allow for subtle and sometimes not-so-subtle differences in reporting and covering terrorism. As measures of news consumption patterns continue to depict a confluence of sources, researchers must address how these media vehicles interact as well as note similarities and differences in content. Considered as a whole, the picture painted here of media content regarding terrorism, in general, and 9/11, in particular, outlines how the media sometimes failed to best serve audiences in a time of crisis.

However, the media did not fail completely. In the days and weeks following 9/11, the media received high marks from audiences for a few reasons, including the steady flow of information, the media's help in getting information to the public from crisis managers, the media's participation in an outpouring of patriotism and unity instead of attack journalism and negativity, and the provision of forums for discussion and connection (Nacos, 2003). In many ways, the media served audiences to the best of its ability, given the confines and demands of the situation. However, a critical examination of the news media offers provocative insight and, in part, serves as a stern reprimand to an often recalcitrant and profit-driven institution. Future work must continue to reflect critically on the role of the media in its terrorism coverage and to assess its potential for sharing information, sparking conversation, and nurturing understanding about geopolitical events. The social constructivist leanings of communication scholarship mean that communication "researchers are well-poised to interrogate how these situations are discursively constructed and to explore alternatives" (Bartesaghi & Castor, 2008, p. 24). Both the critical impulse toward deconstructing media content and exposing its operations and the productive aspects of communication scholarship that outline future possibilities and discourses are invaluable in this process.

FUTURE DIRECTIONS: EXTENDING COMMUNICATION CONTRIBUTIONS TO MEDIA COVERAGE OF TERRORISM SCHOLARSHIP

Scholarship on mainstream media coverage of terrorism continues to multiply, reflecting the prominence of terrorism in our contemporary globalized world. While existing research varies in scope and methodology, it evidences a lively and socially important body of work with international implications. The diversity and complexity of media coverage of terrorism—even if at times stereotyped and predictable—and the myriad communicative functions that it plays in an ever-shrinking world are staggering. J. N. Henderson, J. C. Henderson, Raskob, and Boatright (2004) observed:

> The post-9/11 era is characterized by the experience of large-scale, coordinated terrorism with massive loss of life, continuous media discussion of potential threats, frequent alerts…more or less constant news about Al-Qaeda activities, and regular discussion of chemical, biological, radiological, and nuclear agents…In such a context, communication about

threats, about safety and health, and about protective actions becomes a life-or-death matter. (p. 225)

The findings of this review suggest the significance of—and the considerable need for—communication research that synthesizes the enormous number of case studies and theoretical essays that attempt to probe the role of the mass media in covering terrorism. While much of the content synthesized here revolves around media coverage of 9/11, scholars must heed the call of Chermak and Gruenewald (2006) and conduct longer-term, systematic studies of media coverage of terrorism on international levels. Because coverage is dynamic and fluid over time, scholars should continually gauge and evaluate the media content devoted to terrorism; perhaps such research can help to provide needed critical distance concerning the integrity, nuance, and ideological underpinnings of global terrorism news.

We also note a need for theories and accompanying studies of terrorism and the mass media that better account for the relationship between media coverage of terrorism, state response to terrorism, and terrorist action. While many have critiqued the so-called contagion theory of mass mediated coverage of terrorism (see, e.g., Dobkin, 1992; Picard, 1993), further studies should determine the contours of the complex interplay between (counter) terrorism and the media and between terrorists, governments and citizens. LaFree, Korte, and Dugan (2006) anticipated a promising line of research in this area. Their preliminary work with the Global Terrorism Database shows how state military response to terrorism can exacerbate terrorist actions. Exposing the media's role in making terrorist organizations aware of state responses would significantly extend communication contributions to this area.

While this body of scholarship reveals much about the role of media in disseminating information and cultivating interpretation and understanding about terrorism on its own terms, this research can only be enriched by collaborations involving scholars across the communication discipline and cognate fields. In the opening section of this chapter, we previewed four potential areas that relate to our understanding of media coverage of terrorism—interpersonal and family communication, organizational communication, religious communication, and new media technology. In reflecting on the literature reviewed in this chapter, we revisit potential areas of inquiry across these four avenues.

First, citizens form, extend, and modify their opinions of world events through interpersonal communication, routinely discussing these affairs at home and work (Yang & Stone, 2003). Because media coverage and interpersonal and/or family communication about terrorism coincide (see S. Jones & Rainie, 2002; see related review by Southwell & Yzer, 2007), interpersonal and family scholars are well poised to explore how dyads and small groups influence the media's terrorism agenda-setting function. Dutta-Bergman's (2004) analysis of post-9/11 Pew Research Center survey data, for example, found that people who used telephone-based interpersonal communication to contact friends after 9/11 were more likely to use the Internet and to e-mail family than those who did not use the telephone. Though Dutta-Bergman's study focused on supportive communication, it raises questions about the interaction of electronic media and interpersonal/family communication in setting the public agenda about terrorism. Does interpersonal communication surrounding television coverage of terrorism differ from that of newspapers or online content? How are media frames interpreted and refined during interpersonal encounters? Does the type of terrorism and the age and/or socio-economic status of interlocutors matter?

Second, the institutional and organizational aspects of media news production and circulation cannot be ignored (see Sparrow, 2006; see related review by Roessler, 2007). Because the organizational facets of news production shape news content, studying media content can shed insight into the organizational culture of news production (Reynolds & Barnett, 2003a, p. 87). Lepre and Luther (2007) noted that, since 9/11, news organizations "have actively engaged in preparing journalists as 'first responders' to acts of terrorism" and speculated that this move would require special training and skills, arguably influencing news reports and practices (p. 363). Accordingly, rising interest about and possible shifts in journalist's roles during times of terror and crises (Sylvester & Hoffman, 2002; Zandberg & Neiger, 2005; Zelizer & Allan, 2002), and the way in which institutional imperatives and norms shape these roles presents opportunities for research that crosses media and organizational communication subfields. This line of inquiry would benefit from ethnographic and qualitative studies of newsroom practices with particular focus on the institutional constraints affecting media content production and circulation. Additionally, organizational scholars could unpack how journalists maintain, challenge, or thwart group norms and institutional frames in covering terrorism news. Pal and Dutta's review of resistance literature in this volume proves pertinent here to the extent that resistance theories can help scholars understand how journalists "seek to transform the ideologies, practices, and institutions that serve as sites of dominant hegemony in the realm of transnationalism" (p. 43).

Third, religious terrorism "has become the predominant model for political violence in the modern world," and it has "increased in frequency, scale of violence, and global reach" (G. Martin, 2006, p. 183). This fact has important implications for communication scholars who can investigate how religious discourse is both implicated in and resistant to terrorism. Moreover, the rise of religiously motivated terrorism among factions of larger believers raises ethical considerations about symbolic conflation of religious devotion and terrorism. Numerous scholars have called attention to "media projection of Islam as violence," screened in Western and dominant global media (Baker, 2003, p. 35; see also Akram, 2002; Jackson, 2005; Nacos & Torres-Reyna, 2002, 2007), although Nacos and Torres-Reyna (2002) noted debate about whether post-9/11 constructions of Muslims, Arabs, and Muslim- and Arab Americans portrayed these groups as villains or were more "comprehensive, inclusive, and less stereotypical" than previous constructions (p. 151). That news coverage of terrorism implicates identities produced, interpreted, negotiated, and challenged (inter)culturally demonstrates the importance of examining the role of media coverage in promoting or quashing international dialogue about religion and terrorism, cultural identity, and othering.

Fourth, new media dimensions of terrorism coverage provide occasions for promising research intersections involving scholars of new media technology. The growth of international electronic communication and its use during recent disasters such as Hurricane Katrina suggests that this medium will achieve even greater prominence during future times of crisis (Garrison, 2005; Li, 2006). While scholars are beginning to make inroads in understanding the Internet's role following terrorism, innovations in existing technologies (blogs, instant messaging, and so on) require additional and ongoing attention. Are online newspapers potent agenda-setters with regard to terrorism? Does their content differ from more traditional media outlets? Do hyperlinks and discussion boards foster civic involvement or reproduce dominant, polarized discourse? Does citizen blogging change media reportage of terrorism content in the aftermath of a disaster? More specifically, drawing from Pal and Dutta's review in this volume, we might ask, in a globalized world, does the Internet allow "alternative entry points for the articulation of hitherto-silenced voices on key issues that have typically been played out by powerful social actors in traditional domains" (p. 44)? And finally, what are the cross-cultural differences in online news production and consumption in the aftermath of terrorism and disaster?

In addition, the international dimensions of online terrorism news coverage and Internet use deserve special scrutiny. As Anderson (2003) explained, "electronic media transcend spatial and temporal boundaries, creating new forms of interaction on a global scale" (p. 24). Access to the Internet in the Arab world, for example, grows steadily, approaching 8 million of 280 million citizens (Abdulla, 2005). According to Abdulla, although overall Internet penetration remains small in the Arab world where multiple users share scarce Internet service provider accounts, Muslims and Arabs turn to the Web following terrorist events in noticeable numbers. In the face of censorship and state-controlled media, Internet portals and online media outlets/discussion boards afford rare opportunities for voicing citizen concerns and expressing non-dominant viewpoints. Comparative content studies of electronic media and discussion boards in the non-Western world can expose the similarities and differences between how state-owned media outlets and citizens respond to terrorism, assess blame and responsibility, and frame related geopolitical events.

Finally, great geographical imbalance regrettably exists regarding the subject of terrorism research. Regions high in overall terrorism incidents receive a disproportionately small number of scholarly inquiries, and studies of 9/11 vastly outnumber those of all other terrorist incidents combined. According to

Dugan, LaFree, and Fogg's (2006) analysis of the Global Terrorism Database, Latin America suffers 40 times more terrorist attacks than North America, leads the world in terrorism-related fatalities, and comes under attack twice as often as other regions of the world. Yet, 9/11 and Middle-East terrorism receive the lion's share of published scholarship in major English-language academic journals, and international terrorism commands more media attention, and scholarly analysis, than domestic terrorism incidents. These disparities require redress.

In sum, interdisciplinary research concerning mass mediated coverage of terrorism is vibrant and varied. Nevertheless, communication scholars would benefit from continuing to probe the complexity of interactions among the media, terrorists, governments and citizens and from conducting empirical studies that cut across contexts of communication and media formats. Responding to Margaret Thatcher's news as "oxygen of publicity" characterization, former *Washington Post* chief executive officer Katharine Graham (1986) wrote that "publicity may be the oxygen of terrorists. But I say this: News is the lifeblood of liberty" (p. C1). This review suggests that the relationships between media and terrorism are far more complicated and multivalent than the simplistic "oxygen" versus "liberty" dichotomy. Media coverage of terrorism is rich and textured, multifaceted and dynamic, even when it is ritualized, inaccurate, and stereotypical; yet, it ultimately both reproduces and responds to underlying social conditions. Communication scholars are well-poised to show how and why such patterns hold and to produce richly practical, socially salient, international studies that demonstrate the subtle workings and impacts of mediated terrorism coverage and its role in shaping geopolitical events.

AUTHORS' NOTE

This research was sponsored by the United States Department of Homeland Security (DHS) through the National Consortium for the Study of Terrorism and Responses to Terrorism (START), grant number N00140510629. However, any opinions, findings, and conclusions or recommendations in this document are those of the authors and do not necessarily reflect the views of the U.S. Department of Homeland Security. The authors appreciate Katherine Cruger's impeccable research assistance, Christina Beck's judicious editing, anonymous reviewers' perspicacious feedback, and Hamilton Bean's intellectual energy— especially for START research.

NOTES

1. Greenberg and Hofschire (2002) characterized the sentiment of others' content analyses of post-9/11 media coverage, included in Greenberg's (2002) edited volume.

2. Picard (1994) noted that, despite some exceptions, the 1980s marked the beginning of substantive scholarly inquiry on mass communication and terrorism. For a recent examination of how journalism and mass communication programs have incorporated terrorism into their curricula, see Lepre and Luther (2007).

3. Interestingly, the Global Terrorism Database recorded 69,088 domestic and international terrorism incidents between 1970 and 1997 with pre-9/11 peak years occurring in 1992 with 5324 incidents, a number that declined to 3,500 incidents by 1997 (see Dugan et al., 2006). No corresponding spike in terrorism research occurred in the early 1990s. Notably, 61,000 or so of these total incidents occurred domestically—by terrorists attacking on their own soil, a finding not reflected in corresponding (disproportionately small) rates of scholarship examining domestic terrorism. According to U.S. State Department figures, terrorism is again increasing globally (Glasser, 2005). Glasser noted that the number of significant attacks more than tripled from 175 to 633 between 2003 and 2004, while terrorist incidents in Iraq increased nine times during this same time period.

4. These practices can emerge from state, sub-state, non-state, religious, revolutionary, sectarian, criminal, psychopathic, ideological, or dissident origins and include tactics such as hijackings, bombings, abductions, assassinations, biochemical weapons release, threats, torture, and extortion, to name a few. For reviews of definitions of terrorism and their common components, see Center for Defense Information (2003), Gasser (2002), and Schmid & Jongman (1988). Gasser, in particular, discussed the lack of a comprehensive and widely acceptable definition in either international treaties or government documents.

5. Schmid spent more than 100 pages reviewing 109 definitions of terrorism, finding 83.5% included violence and force, 65% emphasized political motives, and 50% mentioned threat (see Schmid & Jongman, 1988). Other components such as victim-target differentiation, intimidation, and method of combat appeared in fewer than 50% of definitions.

6. These definitions mask that state terrorism has been responsible for many more deaths than non-state terrorism (G. Martin, 2006, p. 47).

7. Because literature in the sprawling interdisciplinary subfield of terrorism studies is expanding exponentially (Ross, 2006), a full review of all relevant topics concerning terrorism and media would require at least book-length treatment. Therefore, in concentrating our review on conceptual and empirical essays concerning mainstream news media coverage of terrorism, we necessarily, but with some regret, exclude six significant related areas of scholarship. These areas include (1) studies of terrorist use of media (see, e.g., Conway, 2006; Qin, Zhou, Reid, Lai, & Chen, 2007; Reid et al., 2005; Weimann, 2004); (2) prescriptive media "best practices" literature (see, e.g., Cohen-Almagor, 2005; Covello, 2003; Edwards-Winslow, 2003; O'Hair, Heath, & Ledlow, 2005; Sandman, 2006); (3) conceptual and empirical essays analyzing discourses of the broader War on Terror (see, e.g., Biesecker, 2007; Cloud, 2004; Hartnett & Stengrim, 2006; Ivie, 2005; Noon, 2004; Ryan, 2004; Simons, 2007; Spielvogel, 2005); (4) media effects of terrorism reportage (see, e.g., Blanchard et al., 2004; Cardeña, Dennis, Winkel & Skitka, 2005; Cohen et al., 2006; Fremont, 2004; Haridakis & Rubin, 2005; Hindman, 2004; Keinan, Sadeh, & Rosen, 2003; Saylor, Cowart, Lipovsky, Jackson, & Finch, 2003; Scheufele, Nisbet, & Ostman, 2005; Smith, Moyer, Boyson, & Pieper, 2002; Weimann, 1987b); (5) studies of terrorism and entertainment media (see e.g., Boggs & Pollard, 2006; Chermak et al., 2003; Gans-Boriskin & Tisinger, 2005; Jones & Dionisopoulos, 2004; McNee, 2002; Wilkins & Downing, 2002, and (6) media functions and uses literature (see e.g., Althaus, 2002; Perse et al., 2002; Roeser & Schaefer, 2002; Ruggiero & Glascock, 2002; Seeger, Vennette, Ulmer, & Sellnow, 2002).

8. Thematizing the ever-growing body of research on the War on Terrorism unfortunately exceeds the bounds of our review (see Simons, 2007). However, we

note the significant need for future review and synthesis of scholarship in this area. A related conceptual approach to the rhetorical one employs the lens of propaganda (e.g., Cottle, 1997; Eisman, 2003; Graber, 2003; Kellner, 2003; Plaisance, 2005; Snow, 2006; Snow & Taylor, 2006). Plaisance, for instance, analyzed the U.S. media campaign "Shared Values," developed by Charlotte Beers for then Secretary of State Colin Powell and broadcast in Muslim countries in 2003. For Plaisance, this media campaign exhibited the hallmarks of propaganda and had serious ethical shortcomings in treating Muslims as means to an end instead of a people deserving to be engaged in their own terms. Snow examined the potentially harmful consequences of strategic state communication on democracy when she delineated public diplomacy, public relations, and propaganda in the "Cold War–centric paradigm currently being used in the war on terrorism" (p. 145). Kellner similarly interrogated the propaganda functions of media coverage of elite discourse in the War on Terror.

9. Vultee (2006) noted the evolution of the term was not a conspiracy but a failure on the part of gatekeepers to provide greater context, processing, and layering of information in favor of an easy-to-fall-back on cultural construct.

10. We further note that a growing body of literature examines the content of anthrax and bioterrorism reportage, as well as public and institutional responses to this media exposure (Bar-Ilan & Escherman, 2005; Covello, Peters, Wojtecki, & Hyde, 2001; Dougall, Hayward, & Baum, 2005; Meredith, Eisenman, Rhodes, Ryan, & Long, 2007; Pollard, 2003; Robinson & Newstetter, 2003; Sandman, 2003). Because naturally occurring pandemics are hard to distinguish from intentional attacks, the literature in this area increasingly intersects with public health risk communication (e.g., Freimuth, Linnan, & Potter, 2000). This scholarship raises important considerations for science communication and the rhetoric of science. In terms of gaps in existing knowledge, we believe the place of science and technology in mediated reportage of terrorism has yet to be fully examined. The so-called new face of terrorism increasingly relies on scientific and technological advances to threaten cyber and WMD attacks (Gurr & Cole, 2000). Scholars in science communication and the rhetoric of science should explore how and with what effect new technological developments and counter-measures are being thematized, framed, and understood by both terrorists and the mass media. In particular, are mediated reports of technological solutions to terrorism encouraging heightened technological sophistication in terrorist plans or encouraging conventional or asymmetrical attacks? Are they prompting new assessments of risk? How are differences between new technologies of weaponry (biological, chemical, and improvised explosive devices) being reported in preparation for potential attacks (see Vanderford, 2004)? In the case of the anthrax mailings of October 2001, a lack of technical consensus about features of a bioterrorism attack conveyed in mass mediated reports may have hampered public risk assessment (Anderson, 2003). Future studies are needed to understand how reportage of technically sophisticated terrorist threats functions for different audiences across a variety of contexts and how technical information regarding terrorist attacks interacts with media literacy (Rosenbaum, Beentjes, & Konig, this volume).

REFERENCES

Abdulla, R. A. (2005). Why they post: Arabic-language message boards after the September 11 attacks. In M. B. Salwen, B. Garrison, & P. D. Driscoll (Eds.), *Online news and the public* (pp. 279-302). Mahwah, NJ: Erlbaum.

Achugar, M. (2004). The events and actors of 11 September 2001 as seen from Uruguay: Analysis of daily newspaper editorials. *Discourse & Society, 15*, 291-320.

Akram, S. M. (2002). The aftermath of September 11, 2001: The targeting of Arabs and Muslims in America. *Arab Studies Quarterly, 24*, 61-118.

Alali, O., & Byrd, G. (1994). (Eds.). *Terrorism and the news media: A selected and annotated bibliography*. Jefferson, NC: McFarland.

Aldoory, L., & Van Dyke, M. A. (2006). The roles of perceived "shared" involvement and information overload in understanding how audiences make meaning of news about bioterrorism. *Journalism & Mass Communication Quarterly, 83*, 346-361.

Allan, S. (2002). Reweaving the internet: Online news of September 11. In B. Zelizer & S. Allan (Eds.), *Journalism after September 11* (pp. 119-140). London: Routledge.

Althaus, S. (2002). American news consumption during times of national crisis. *Political Science & Politics, 35*, 517-521.

Altheide, D. L. (2006). Terrorism and the politics of fear. *Cultural Studies ↔ Critical Methodologies, 6*, 413-439.

Anderson, A. (2003). Risk, terrorism, and the internet. *Knowledge, Technology, & Society, 16*, 24-33.

Anker, E. (2005). Villains, victims and heroes: Melodrama, media, and September 11. *Journal of Communication, 55*, 22-37.

Apple, R. W., Jr. (1985, July 16). Thatcher urges press to help 'starve' terrorists. *The New York Times*, p. A3.

Baiocchi, G. (2002). Media coverage of 9-11 in Brazil. *Television & New Media, 3*, 183-189.

Baker, R. W. (2003). Screening Islam: Terrorism, American Jihad, and the new Islamists. *Arab Studies Quarterly, 25*, 33-56.

Banaji, S., & Al-Ghabban, A. (2006). 'Neutrality comes from inside us': British-Asian and Indian perspectives on television news after 11 September. *Journal of Ethnic and Migration Studies, 32*, 1005-1026.

Bar-Ilan, J., & Escherman, A. (2005). The anthrax scare and the web: A content analysis of web page linking to resources on anthrax. *Scientometrics, 63*, 443-462.

Bartesaghi, M., & Castor, T. (2008). Social construction in communication: Revisiting the conversation. In C. S. Beck (Ed.), *Communication yearbook 32* (pp. 3-39). New York: Routledge.

Baudrillard, J. (2002). *The spirit of terrorism: And requiem for the Twin Towers* (C. Turner, Trans.). London: Verso.

Ben-Shaul, N. (2006). *A violent world: TV news images of Middle Eastern terror and war*. New York: Rowman & Littlefield.

Bhatia, M. V. (2005). Fighting words: Naming terrorists, bandits, rebels and other violent actors. *Third World Quarterly, 26*, 5-22.

Biesecker, B. (2007). No time for mourning: The rhetorical production of the melancholic citizen-subject in the War on Terror. *Philosophy & Rhetoric, 40*, 147-169.

Billeaudeux, A., Domke, D., Hutcheson, J. S., & Garland, P. (2003). Newspaper editorials follow lead of Bush Administration. *Newspaper Research Journal, 24*, 166-184.

Blanchard, E. B., Kuhn, E., Rowell, D. L., Hickling, E. J., Wittrock, D., Rogers, R. L., et al. (2004). Studies of the vicarious traumatization of college students by the September 11th attacks: Effects of proximity, exposure and connectedness. *Behavior Research & Therapy, 42*, 191-205.

Blondheim, M., & Liebes, T. (2002). Live television's disaster marathon of September 11 and its subversive potential. *Prometheus, 20*, 271-276.

Boggs, C., & Pollard, T. (2006). Hollywood and the spectacle of terrorism. *New Political Science, 28*, 335-351.

Bostdorff, D. (2003). George W. Bush's post-September 11 rhetoric of covenant renewal: Upholding the faith of the greatest generation. *Quarterly Journal of Speech, 89*, 293-319.

Brennen, B., & Duffy, M. (2003). "If a problem cannot be solved, enlarge it": An ideological critique of the "Other" in Pearl Harbor and September 11 *New York Times* coverage. *Journalism Studies, 4*(1), 3-14.

Brock, B. L., & Howell, S. (1988). The evolution of the PLO: Rhetoric of terrorism. *Central States Speech Journal, 39*, 281-292.

Brosius, H., & Weimann, G. (1991). The contagiousness of mass-mediated terrorism. *European Journal of Communication, 6*, 63-75.

Brown, M., Fuzesi, L., Kitch, K., & Spivey, C. (2003). Internet news representation of September 11: Archival impulse in the age of information. In S. Chermak, F. Y. Bailey, & M. Brown (Eds.), *Media representations of September 11* (pp. 103-116). Westport, CT: Praeger.

Brown, W. J. (1990). The persuasive appeal of mediated terrorism: The Case of the TWA Flight 847 hijacking. *Western Journal of Communication, 54*, 219-236.

Buonanno, M. (2002). Italian ambivalence. *Television & New Media, 3*, 177-181.

Burke, K. (1969). *A grammar of motives*. Berkeley: University of California Press.

Cappella, J., & Jamieson, K. (1997). *The spiral of cynicism: The press and the public good*. New York: Oxford University Press.

Cardeña, E., Dennis, J. M., Winkel, M., & Skitka, L. J. (2005). A snapshot of terror: Acute posttraumatic responses to the September 11 attack. *Journal of Trauma and Dissociation, 6*, 69-84.

Center for Defense Information. (2003). *Terrorism: The problems of definition*. Retrieved February 26, 2007, from http://www.cdi.org/friendlyversion/printversion. cfm? documentID=1564

Chaliand, G. (1987). *Terrorism: From popular struggle to media spectacle*. London: Saqi Books.

Chakravartty, P. (2002). Translating terror in India. *Television & New Media, 3*, 205-212.

Chermak, S. M., Bailey, F. Y., & Brown, M. (Eds.). (2003). *Media representations of September 11*. Westport, CT: Praeger.

Chermak, S. M., & Gruenewald, J. (2006). The media's coverage of domestic terrorism. *Justice Quarterly, 23*, 428-463.

Cho, J., Boyle, M. P., Keum, H., Schevy, M. D., McLeod, D. M., Shah, D. V., et al. (2003). Media, terrorism, and emotionality: Emotional difference in media content and public reactions to the September 11th terrorist attacks. *Journal of Broadcasting & Electronic Media, 47*, 309-327.

Chouliaraki, L. (2004). Watching 11 September: The politics of pity. *Discourse & Society, 15*, 185-198.

Christie, T. B. (2006). Framing rationale for the Iraq War: The interaction of public support with mass media and public policy agendas. *International Communication Gazette, 68*, 519-532.

Cloud, D. (2004). "To veil the threat of terror": Afghan women and the <clash of civilizations> in the imagery of the U.S. war on terrorism. *Quarterly Journal of Speech, 90*, 285-306.

Cohen, P., Kasen, S., Chen, H., Gordon, K., Berenson, K., Brook, J., et al., (2006). Current affairs and the public psyche: American anxiety in the post 9/11 world. *Social Psychiatry & Psychiatric Epidemiology, 41*, 251-260.

Cohen-Almagor, R. (2005). Media coverage of acts of terrorism: Troubling episodes and suggested guidelines. *Canadian Journal of Communication, 30*, 383-409.

Conway, M. (2006). Terrorism and the internet: New media - new threat? *Parliamentary Affairs, 59*, 283-298.

Cooper, H. H. A. (2001). Terrorism: The problem of definition revisited. *American Behavioral Scientist, 44*, 881-893.

Cottle, S. (1997). Reporting the troubles in Northern Ireland: Paradigms and media propaganda (Review Essay). *Critical Studies in Mass Communication, 14*, 282-296.

Covello, V. T. (2003). Best practice in public health and risk communication. *Journal of Health Communication, 8*, 5-8.

Covello, V. T., Peters, R. G., Wojtecki, J. G., & Hyde, R. C. (2001). Risk communication, the West Nile virus epidemic, and bioterrorism: Responding to the communication challenges posed by the intentional or unintentional release of a pathogen in an urban setting. *Journal of Urban Health, 78*, 382-391.

Craft, S., & Wanta, W. (2004). U.S. public concerns in the aftermath of 9-11: A test of second level agenda-setting. *International Journal of Public Opinion Research, 16*, 456-463.

Crary, J. (1999). *Suspensions of perception: Attention, spectacle, and modern culture.* Cambridge, MA: MIT Press.

Dayan, D., & Katz, E. (1992). *Media events: The live broadcasting of history.* Cambridge, MA: Harvard University Press.

Debatin, B. (2002). "Plane wreck with spectators": The semiotics of terror. In B. S. Greenberg (Ed.), *Communication and terrorism: Public and media responses to 9/11* (pp. 163-174). Cresskill, NJ: Hampton Press.

Debord, G. (1967/1994). *The society of the spectacle.* New York: Zone Books.

Delli Carpini, M. X., & Williams, B. A. (1987). Television and terrorism: Patterns of presentation and occurrence, 1969 to 1980. *The Western Political Quarterly, 40*, 45-64.

Der Derian, J. (2005). Imaging terror: Logos, pathos and ethos. *Third World Quarterly, 26*, 23-47.

Dobkin, B. A. (1992). *Tales of terror: Television news and the construction of the terrorist threat.* New York: Praeger.

Dobkin, B. A. (1994). Paper tigers and video postcards: The rhetorical dimensions of narrative form in ABC News coverage of terrorism. *Western Journal of Communication, 56*, 143-160.

Dooley, K. J., & Corman, S. R. (2002). The dynamics of electronic media coverage. In B. S. Greenberg (Ed.), *Communication and terrorism: Public and media responses to 9/11* (pp. 121-136). Cresskill, NJ: Hampton Press.

Domke, D., Garland, P., Billeaudeaux, A., & Hutcheson, J. (2003). Insights into U.S. racial hierarchy: Racial profiling, news sources, and September 11. *Journal of Communication, 53*, 606-623.

Domke, D., Graham, E. S., Coe, K., John, S. L., & Coopman, T. (2006). Going public as political strategy: The Bush Administration, the echoing press, and the passage of the Patriot Act. *Political Communication, 23*, 291-312.

Dougall, A. L., Hayward, M. C., & Baum, A. (2005). Media exposure to bioterrorism: Stress and the anthrax attacks. *Psychiatry, 68*, 28-42.

Dowling, R. E. (1986). Terrorism and the media: A rhetorical genre. *Journal of Communication, 36*, 12-24.

Dowling, R. E. (1989). Print journalism as political communication: The Iran Hostage Crisis. *Political Communication & Persuasion, 6*, 129-150.

Dugan, L., LaFree, G., & Fogg, H. V. (2006). *A first look at domestic and international global terrorism events, 1970-1997.* Paper presented at the Institute of Electrical and Electronics Engineers International Conference on Intelligence and Security Informatics, San Diego. Retrieved July 12, 2007, from http://www.start.umd.edu/publications/IEEE_terrorism_overview.pdf

Dunn, E. W., Moore, M., & Nosek, B. A. (2005). The war of the words: How linguistic differences in reporting shape perceptions of terrorism. *Analyses of Social Issues and Public Policy, 5*, 67-86.

Dutta-Bergman, M. (2004). Interpersonal communication after 9/11 via telephone and internet: A theory of channel complementarity. *New Media & Society, 6*, 659-673.

Edwards-Winslow, F. (2003). Telling it like it is: The role of the media in terrorism response and recovery. In J. N. Kayyem & R. L. Pangi (Eds.), *First to arrive: State and local responses to terrorism* (pp. 59-75). Cambridge, MA: MIT Press.

Eickelman, D. F. (2004). The Middle East's democracy deficit and the expanding public sphere. In P. van der Veer (Ed.), *Media, war, and terrorism: Responses from the Middle East and Asia* (pp. 61-73). London: RoutledgeCurzon.

Eisman, A. (2003). The media of manipulation: Patriotism and propaganda—mainstream news in the United States in the weeks following September 11. *Critical Quarterly, 45*, 55-72.

Entman, R.M. (1991). Framing U.S. coverage of international news: Contrasts in narratives of the KAL and Iran Air Incidents. *Journal of Communication, 41*, 6-25.

Erjavec, K., & Volčič, Z. (2006). Mapping the notion of "terrorism" in Serbian and Croatian newspapers. *Journal of Communication Inquiry, 30*, 298-318.

Fawcett, L. (2002). Why peace journalism isn't news. *Journalism Studies, 3*, 213-223.

Foreign Relations Authorization Act, Fiscal Years 1988 and 1989, 22 U.S.C. § 2656f(d)(1)-(2) (1987).

Frank, R. (2004). When the going gets tough, the tough go photoshopping: September 11 and the newslore of vengeance and victimization. *New Media and Society, 6*, 633-658.

Freimuth, V., Linnan, H. W., & Potter, P. (2000). Communicating the threat of emerging infections to the public. *Emerging Infectious Diseases, 6*, 337-347.

Fremont, W. P. (2004). Childhood reactions to terrorism-induced trauma: A review of the past 10 years. *Journal of the American Academy of Child and Adolescent Psychiatry, 43*, 381-392.

Fried, A. (2005). Terrorism as a context of coverage before the Iraq war. *Press/Politics, 10*, 125-132.

Galvin, M. (2004). Converging and hybrid communications systems and September 11: A case study. In S. Venkatraman (Ed.), *Media in a terrorized world: Reflections in the wake of 9/11* (pp. 14-33). London: Eastern Universities Press.

Gans-Boriskin, R., & Tisinger, R. (2005). The Bushlet administration: Terrorism and war on *The West Wing. The Journal of American Culture, 28*, 100-115.

Garrison, B. (2005). Online newspapers. In M. B. Salwen, B. Garrison, & P. D. Driscoll (Eds.), *Online news and the public* (pp. 3-46). Mahwah, NJ: Erlbaum.

Gartner, S. S. (2004). Making the international local: The terrorist attack on the USS Cole, local casualties, and media coverage. *Political Communication, 21*, 139-159.

Gasser, H.-P. (2002). Acts of terror, 'terrorism,' and international humanitarian law. *International Review of the Red Cross, 84*, 547-570.

Glass, A. J. (2002). *The war on terrorism goes online: Media and government response to first post-internet crisis.* Cambridge, MA: Harvard University, The Joan Shorenstein Center on the Press, Politics and Public Policy

Glasser, S. B. (2005, April 27). U.S. figures show sharp global rise in terrorism: State dept. will not put data in report. *Washington Post*, p. A1.

Goffman, E. (1974). *Frame analysis: An essay on the organization of experience.* London: Harper and Row.

Goodall, H. L. (2006). Why we must win the War on Terror: Communication, narrative, and the future of national security. *Qualitative Inquiry, 12*, 30-59.

Graber, D. (2003). Styles of image management during crises: Justifying press censorship. *Discourse and Society, 14*, 539-557.

Graham, K. (1986, April 20). Safeguarding our freedoms as we cover terrorist acts. *The Washington Post*, p. C1.

Greenberg, B. S. (2002). (Ed.). *Communication and terrorism: Public and media responses to 9/11.* Cresskill, NJ: Hampton Press.

Greenberg, B. S., & Hofschire, L. (2002). Summary and discussion. In B. S. Greenberg (Ed.), *Communication and terrorism: Public and media responses to 9/11* (pp. 317-332). Cresskill, NJ: Hampton Press.

Greenberg, B. S., Hofschire, L., & Lachlan, K. (2002). Diffusion, media use, and interpersonal communication behaviors. In B. S. Greenberg (Ed.), *Communication and terrorism: Public and media responses to 9/11* (pp. 3-16). Cresskill, NJ: Hampton Press.

Gunn, J. (2004). The rhetoric of exorcism: George W. Bush and the return of political demonology. *Western Journal of Communication, 68*, 1-23.

Gurr, N., & Cole, B. (2000). *The new face of terrorism: Threats from weapons of mass destruction.* New York: I. B. Tauris.

Haes, J. W. H. (2002). Catching the wave: German media on September 11. *Prometheus, 20*, 277-282.

Haridakis, P. M., & Rubin, A. M. (2005). Third-person effects in the aftermath of terrorism. *Mass Communication, 8*, 39-59.

Hartnett, S. J., & Stengrim, L. A. (2006). *Globalization and empire: The U.S. invasion of Iraq, free markets, and the twilight of democracy.* Tuscaloosa: University of Alabama Press.

Henderson, J. N., Henderson, J. C., Raskob, G. E., & Boatright, D. T. (2004). Chemical (VX) terrorist threat: Public knowledge, attitudes, and responses. *Biosecurity & Bioterrorism: Biodefense Strategy, Practice and Science, 2*, 225-228.

Hindman, D. B. (2004). Media system dependency and public support for the press and president. *Mass Communication & Society, 7*, 29-42.

Horsman, S. (2005). Themes in official discourses on terrorism in Central Asia. *Third World Quarterly, 26*, 191-213.

Hutcheson, J., Domke, D., Billeaudeaux, A., & Garland, P. (2004). U.S. national identity, political elites, and a patriotic press following September 11. *Political Communication, 21*, 27-50.

Ietto-Gillies, G. (2003). The role of transnational corporations in the globalization process. In J. Michie (Ed.), *The handbook of globalization* (pp. 139-149). Northhampton, MA: Edward Elgar.

Ilter, T. (2003). The framing of 11 September in the Turkish media: Moder(n)ating Turkey's oriental identity. *Arab Studies Quarterly, 25*, 179-196.

Ivie, R. L. (2005). *Democracy and America's war on terror*. Tuscaloosa: University of Alabama Press.

Jablonski, P. M., & Sullivan, C. (1996). Building the terrorism agenda, 1981-1994: The media, the president, and real world cues. *World Communication, 25*, 191-201.

Jackson, R. (2005). *Writing the war on terrorism: Language, politics and counterterrorism*. Manchester, England: Manchester University Press.

Jasperson, A. E., & El-Kikhia, O. E. (2002). CNN and al Jazeera's media coverage of America's war in Afghanistan. In P. Norris, M. R. Just, & M. Kern (Eds.), *Framing terrorism: The news media, the government, and the public* (pp. 93-112). New York: Routledge.

Jaworski, A., Fitzgerald, R., & Constantinou, O. (2005). Busy saying nothing new: Live silence in TV reporting of 9/11. *Multilingua, 24*, 121-144.

Jenkins, B. M. (1975). *International terrorism: A new mode of conflict*. Los Angeles: Crescent.

Jiwani, Y. (2004). Gendering terror: Representations of the Orientalized body in Quebec's post-September 11 English-language press. *Critique: Critical Middle Eastern Studies, 13*, 265-291.

Jones, R., & Dionisopoulos, G. N. (2004). Scripting a tragedy: The "Isaac and Ishmael" episode of *The West Wing* as parable. *Popular Communication, 2*, 21-40.

Jones, S., & Rainie, L. (2002). Internet use and the terror attacks. In B. S. Greenberg (Ed.), *Communication and terrorism: Public and media responses to 9/11* (pp. 27-38). Cresskill, NJ: Hampton Press.

Josephi, B. (2004). Media terrorism or culture of peace: Reporting September 11. In S. Venkatraman (Ed.), *Media in a terrorized world: Reflections in the wake of 9/11* (pp. 34-53). London: Eastern Universities Press.

Kapitan, T., & Schulte, E. (2002). The rhetoric of 'terrorism' and its consequences. *Journal of Political & Military Sociology, 30*, 172-196.

Kavoori, A. P. (2006). International communication after terrorism: Toward a postcolonial dialectic. In A. P. Kavoori & T. Fraley (Eds.), *Media, terrorism, and theory: A reader* (pp. 179-197). New York: Rowman & Littlefield.

Keinan, G., Sadeh, A., & Rosen, S. (2003). Attitudes and reactions to media coverage of terrorist acts. *Journal of Community Psychology, 31*, 149-165.

Kellner, D. (2002). September 11th, terrorism, and blowback. *Cultural Studies ↔ Critical Methodologies, 2*, 27-39.

Kellner, D. (2003). *Media spectacle*. New York: Routledge.

Kelly, M. J., & Mitchell, T. H. (1981). Transnational terrorism and the Western elite press. *Political Communication and Persuasion, 1*, 269-296.

Kitch, C. (2003). "Mourning in America": Ritual, redemption, and recovery in news narrative after September 11. *Journalism Studies, 4*, 213-224.

Kurtz, H. (2001a, September 17). Journalism's surreal reality check. *The Washington Post*, p. C1.

Kurtz, H. (2001b, September 26). The line between journalism and sensationalism. *CNN.com/COMMUNITY*. Retrieved July 15, 2007, from http://archives.cnn.com/2001/COMMUNITY/09/kurtz/index.html

LaFree, G., Korte, R., & Dugan, L. (2006, June 28). *Deterrence and defiance in models of terrorist violence in Northern Ireland, 1969-1992*. Research symposium presented at the annual meeting of the National Consortium for Terrorism and the Study of Terrorism (START), College Park, Maryland.

Lakos, A. (1986). *International terrorism: A bibliography*. Boulder, CO: Westview Press.

Lankala, S. (2006). Mediated nationalisms and 'Islamic terror': The articulation of religious and postcolonial secular nationalisms in India. *Westminster Papers in Communication & Culture, 3*, 86-102.

Laqueur, W. (1999). *The new terrorism: Fanaticism and the arms of mass destruction*. New York: Oxford University Press.

Leeman, R. W. (1991). *The rhetoric of terrorism and counterterrorism*. New York: Greenwood Press.

Lepre, C. R., & Luther, C. A. (2007). The incorporation of terrorism coverage in academic journalism programs. *Journalism & Mass Communication Educator, 61*, 362-377.

Li, X. (2006). Introduction. In X. Li (Ed.), *Internet newspapers: The making of a mainstream media* (pp. 1-9). Mahwah, NJ: Erlbaum.

Liebes, T., & Kampf, Z. (2007). Routinizing terror: Media coverage and public practices in Israel, 2000-2005. *Harvard International Journal of Press/Politics, 12*, 108-116.

Livingston, S. (1994). *The terrorism spectacle*. Boulder, CO: Westview Press.

Long, D. E. (1990). *The anatomy of terror*. New York: The Free Press.

Lule, J. (1993). Murder and myth: *New York Times* coverage of the TWA 847 hijacking victim. *Journalism Quarterly, 70*, 26-39.

Lule, J. (2002). Myth and terror on the editorial page: The *New York Times* responds to September 11, 2001. *Journalism & Mass Communication Quarterly, 79*, 275-293.

Martin, G. (2006). *Understanding terrorism* (2nd ed.). New York: Sage.

Martin, J. L. (1985). The media's role in international terrorism. *Terrorism: An International Journal, 8*, 127–146.

Martin, P., & Phelan, S. (2002). Representing Islam in the Wake of September 11: A comparison of U.S. television and CNN online messageboard discourses. *Prometheus, 20*, 263-269.

McCombs, M., & Shaw, D. (1972). The agenda-setting function of mass media. *The Public Opinion Quarterly, 36*, 176-187.

McNee, F. (2002). Something's happened: Fictional media as a coping mechanism. *Prometheus, 20*, 281-287.

Meredith, L. S., Eisenman, D. P., Rhodes, H., Ryan, G., & Long, A. (2007). Trust influences response to public health messages during a bioterrorist event. *Journal of Health Communication, 12*, 217-232.

Mogensen, K., Lindsay, L., Li, X., Perkins, J., & Beardsley, M. (2002). How TV news covered the crisis: The content of CNN, CBS, ABC, NBC, and Fox. In B. S. Greenberg (Ed.), *Communication and terrorism: Public and media responses to 9/11* (pp. 101-120). Cresskill, NJ: Hampton Press.

Mohamad, G. (2004). War, words, and images. In P. van der Veer (Ed.), *Media, war, and terrorism: Responses from the Middle East and Asia* (pp. 187-196). London: RoutledgeCurzon.

Murphy, J. M. (2003). "Our mission and our moment": George W. Bush and September 11th. *Rhetoric & Public Affairs, 6*, 607-632.

Nacos, B. L. (2002). *Mass-mediated terrorism.* Lanham, NJ: Rowman & Littlefield.

Nacos, B. L. (2003). Terrorism as breaking news: Attack on America. *Political Science Quarterly, 118*, 23-53.

Nacos, B. L., & Torres-Reyna, O. (2002). Framing Muslim Americans before and after 9/11. In P. Norris, M. R. Just, & M. Kern (Eds.), *Framing terrorism: The news media, the government, and the public* (pp. 133-158). New York: Routledge.

Nacos, B. L., & Torres-Reyna, O. (2007). *Fueling our fears: Media coverage, and public opinion of Muslim Americans.* Lanham, MD: Rowman & Littlefield.

Nanri, K. (2005). The conundrum of Japanese editorials: Polarized, diversified and homogeneous. *Japanese Studies, 25*, 169-186.

Noon, D. H. (2004). Operation enduring analogy: World War II, the War on Terror, and the uses of historical memory. *Rhetoric & Public Affairs, 7*, 339-365.

Nord, L. W., & Strömbäck, J. (2003). Making sense of different types of crises: A study of the Swedish media coverage of the terrorist attacks against the United States and the U.S. attacks in Afghanistan. *Harvard International Journal of Press/Politics, 8*, 54-75.

Norris, P., Just, M. R., & Kern, M. (2002). (Eds.). *Framing terrorism: The news media, the government, and the public.* New York: Routledge.

Norris, P., Kern, M., & Just, M. R. (2002). Framing terrorism. In P. Norris, M. R. Just, and M. Kern (Eds.), *Framing terrorism: The news media, the government, and the public* (pp. 3-25). New York: Routledge.

Nossek, H., & Berkowitz, D. (2006). Telling "our" story through news of terrorism. *Journalism Studies, 7*, 691-707.

O'Hair, D., Heath, R., & Ledlow, G. (Eds). (2005). *Community preparedness and response to terrorism.* Westport, CT: Praeger.

Pal, M., & Dutta, M. (2008). Theorizing resistance in a global context: Processes, strategies, and tactics in communication scholarship. In C. S. Beck (Ed.), *Communication yearbook 32* (pp. 41-87). New York: Routledge.

Paletz, D. L., & Boiney, J. (1992). Researchers' perspectives. In D. L. Paletz & A. P. Schmid (Eds.), *Terrorism and the media* (pp. 6-28). Newbury Park, CA: Sage.

Palmerton, P. R. (1988). The rhetoric of terrorism and media response to the 'Crisis in Iran.' *Western Journal of Speech Communication, 52*, 105-121.

Parry-Giles, T. (1995). Ideology and poetics in public issue construction: Thatcherism, civil liberties and 'terrorism' in Northern Ireland. *Communication Quarterly, 43*, 182-196.

Patkin, T. T. (2004). Explosive baggage: Female Palestinian suicide bombers and the rhetoric of emotion. *Women and Language, 27*, 79-88.

Perse, E., Signorielli, N., Courtright, J., Samter, W., Caplan, S., Lambe, J., et al. (2002). Public perceptions of media functions at the beginning of the War on Terrorism. In B. S. Greenberg (Ed.), *Communication and terrorism: Public and media responses to 9/11* (pp. 39-52). Cresskill, NJ: Hampton Press.

Pew Internet and American Life Project. (2001, September 15). *How Americans used the Internet after the terror attack.* Washington, DC: Pew. Retrieved November 15, 2006, from http://www.pewinternet.org/

Pew Internet and American Life Project. (2002, September 5). *One year later: September 11 and the internet.* Washington, DC: Pew. Retrieved November 15, 2006, from http://www.pewinternet.org/

Picard, R. G. (1993). *Media portrayals of terrorism: Functions and meaning of news coverage.* Ames: Iowa State University Press.

Picard, R. G. (1994). The maturation of communication and terrorism studies. *Journal of Communication, 44,* 122-127.

Picard, R. G., & Adams, P. D. (1987). Characterizations of acts and perpetrators of political violence in three elite U.S. daily newspapers. *Political Communication and Persuasion, 4,* 1-9.

Plaisance, P. L. (2005). The propaganda War on Terrorism: An analysis of the United States' "Shared Values" public-diplomacy campaign after September 11, 2001. *Journal of Mass Media Ethics, 20,* 250–268.

Pollard, W. E. (2003). Public perceptions of information sources concerning bioterrorism before and after the anthrax attacks. *Journal of Health Communication, 8,* 148-151.

Prashad, V. (2005). How the Hindus became Jews: American racism after 9/11. *South Atlantic Quarterly, 104,* 583-606.

Project for Excellence in Journalism. (2001, November 19). *Before and after: How the War on Terrorism has changed the news agenda, network television, June to October 2001.* Washington, DC: PEJ. Retrieved March 29, 2007, from http://journalism.org

Project for Excellence in Journalism. (2006, September 11). *How 9-11 changed the evening news: PEJ analysis.* Retrieved March 29, 2007, from http://journalism.org/node/1839/

Qin, J. L., Zhou, Y. L., Reid, E., Lai, G. P., & Chen, H. C. (2007). Analyzing terror campaigns on the internet: Technical sophistication, content richness, and Web interactivity. *International Journal of Human-Computer Studies, 65,* 71-84.

Randle, Q., Davenport, L. D., & Bossen, H. (2003). Newspapers slow to use websites for 9/11 coverage. *Newspaper Research Journal, 24,* 58-71.

Reid, E., Qin, J. L., Zhou, Y. L., Lai, G. P., Sageman, M., Weimann, G., et al. (2005). Collecting and analyzing the presence of terrorists on the web: A case study of Jihad Websites. In *IEEE Intelligence and Security Informatics, Proceedings* (Vol. 3495, pp. 402-411). Atlanta, GA: ISI.

Rentschler, C. A. (2004). Witnessing: U.S. citizenship and the vicarious experience of suffering. *Media, Culture & Society, 26,* 296-304.

Reynolds, A., & Barnett, B. (2003a). "America's under attack": CNN's verbal and visual framing of September 11. In S. Chermak, F. Y. Bailey, & M. Brown (Eds.), *Media representations of September 11* (pp. 85-101). Westport, CT: Praeger.

Reynolds, A., & Barnett, B. (2003b). This just in . . . How national TV news handled the breaking "live" coverage of September 11. *Journalism & Mass Communication Quarterly, 80,* 689-703.

Ritzer, G. (2004). *The globalization of nothing.* Thousand Oaks, CA: Sage.

Robinson, S. J., & Newstetter, W. C. (2003). Uncertain science and certain deadlines: CDC responses to the media during the Anthrax attacks of 2001. *Journal of Health Communication, 8,* 17-34.

Roeser, J., & Schaefer, G. (2002). Media use in Germany around the attacks in the United States. In B. S. Greenberg (Ed.), *Communication and terrorism: Public and media responses to 9/11* (pp. 85-97). Cresskill, NJ: Hampton Press.

Roessler, P. (2007). Media content diversity: Conceptual issues and future directions for communication research. In C. S. Beck (Ed.), *Communication yearbook 31* (pp. 457-513). Mahwah, NJ: Erlbaum.

Rojecki, A. (2005). Media discourse on globalization and terror. *Political Communication, 22*, 63-81.

Rosenbaum, J. E., Beentjes, J. W. J., & Konig, R. P. (2008). How media literacy is defined: A review. In C. S. Beck (Ed.), *Communication yearbook 32* (pp. 313-352). New York: Routledge.

Ross, J. (2006). *Political terrorism: An interdisciplinary approach.* New York: Peter Lang.

Rowland, R. C., & Theye, K. (2006, November). *Terrorism, rhetoric, and myth.* Paper presented at the annual meeting of the National Communication Association, San Antonio, TX.

Ruggerio, T., & Glascock, J. (2002). Tracking media use and gratifications. In B. S. Greenberg (Ed.), *Communication and terrorism: Public and media responses to 9/11* (pp. 65-74). Cresskill, NJ: Hampton Press.

Ruigrok, N., & van Atteveldt, W. (2007). Global angling with a local angle: How U.S., British, and Dutch newspapers frame global and local terrorist attacks. *Harvard International Journal of Press-Politics, 12*, 68-90.

Ryan, M. (2004). Framing the war against terrorism: U.S. newspaper editorials and military action in Afghanistan. *Gazette: International Journal for Communication Studies, 66*, 363-382.

Ryan, M. (2006). Mainstream news media, an objective approach, and the march to war in Iraq. *Journal of Mass Media Ethics, 21*, 4–29.

Sádaba, T. (2002). "Each to his own . . ." September 11 in Basque media. *Television & New Media, 3*, 219-222.

Sádaba, T., & La Porte, T. (2006). Mediated terrorism in comparative perspective: Spanish press coverage of 9/11 vs. coverage of Basque terrorism. In A. P. Kavoori & T. Fraley (Eds.), *Media, terrorism, and theory: A reader* (pp. 69-89). New York: Rowman & Littlefield.

Sakai, K. (2003). 11 September and the clash of civilizations: The role of the Japanese media and public discourse. *Arab Studies Quarterly, 25*, 159-178.

Salaita, S. (2005). Ethnic identity and imperative patriotism: Arab Americans before and after 9/11. *College Literature, 32*, 146-168.

Sandman, P. M. (2003). Bioterrorism risk communication policy. *Journal of Health Communication, 8*, 146-147.

Sandman, P. M. (2006). Crisis communication best practices: Some quibbles and additions. *Journal of Applied Communication Research, 34*, 257-262.

Saylor C. F., Cowart, B. L., Lipovsky, J. A., Jackson, C., & Finch, A. J., Jr. (2003). Media exposure to September 11. *American Behavioral Scientist, 46*, 1622-1642.

Schaefer, T. M. (2002). Framing the U.S. Embassy bombings and September 11 attacks in African and U.S. Newspapers. In P. Norris, M. R. Just, & M. Kern (Eds.). *Framing terrorism: The news media, the government, and the public* (pp. 93-112). New York: Routledge.

Scheufele, D. A., Nisbet, M. C., & Ostman, R. E. (2005). September 11 news coverage, public opinion, and support for civil liberties. *Mass Communication & Society, 8*, 197-218.

Schiappa, E. (2003). *Defining reality: Definitions and the politics of meaning.* Carbondale: Southern Illinois University Press.

Schirato, T., & Webb, J. (2004). The media as spectacle: September 11 as soap opera. *Journal for Cultural Research, 8*, 411-423.

Schmid, A. P. & de Graaf, J. (1982). *Violence as communication: Insurgent terrorism and the Western news media*. London: Sage.

Schmid, A. P., & Jongman, A. J. (Eds.). (1988). *Political terrorism: A new guide to actors, authors, concepts, data bases, theories, and literature*. New Brunswick, NJ: Transaction Books.

Seeger, M. W., Vennette, S., Ulmer, R. R., & Sellnow, T. (2002). Media use, information seeking, and reported needs in post-crisis contexts. In B. S. Greenberg (Ed.), *Communication and terrorism: Public and media responses to 9/11* (pp. 317-332). Cresskill, NJ: Hampton Press.

Seib, P. (2004). *Beyond the front lines: How the news media cover a world shaped by war*. New York: Palgrave Macmillan.

Signorielli, N., & Gerbner, G. (1988). *Violence and terror in the mass media*. Westport, CT: Greenwood.

Simons, H. W. (2007). Introduction to special issue on rhetoric and the war in Iraq. *Rhetoric & Public Affairs, 10*, 177-182.

Slone, M. (2000). Responses to media coverage of terrorism. *Journal of Conflict Resolution, 44*, 508-22.

Smith, S. L., Moyer, E., Boyson, A. R., & Pieper, K. M. (2002). Parent's perceptions of children's fear responses. In B. S. Greenberg (Ed.), *Communication and terrorism: Public and media responses to 9/11* (pp. 193-208). Cresskill, NJ: Hampton Press.

Snow, N. (2006). Terrorism, public relations, and propaganda. In A. P. Kavoori & T. Fraley (Eds.), *Media, terrorism, and theory: A reader* (pp. 145-160). New York: Rowman & Littlefield.

Snow, N., & Taylor, P. (2006). The revival of the propaganda state: U.S. propaganda at home and abroad since 9/11. *The International Communication Gazette, 68*, 389-407.

Southwell, B., & Yzer, M. (2007). The roles of interpersonal communication in mass media campaigns. In C. S. Beck (Ed.), *Communication yearbook 31* (pp. 420-463). Mahwah, NJ: Erlbaum.

Sparrow, B. (2006). A research agenda for institutional media. *Political Communication, 23*, 145-157.

Spielvogel, C. (2005). "You know where I stand": Moral framing of the War on Terrorism and the Iraq War in the 2004 presidential campaign. *Rhetoric & Public Affairs, 8*, 549-570.

Stempel, G. H., III, & Hargrove, T. (2003). Newspapers played major role in terrorism coverage. *Newspaper Research Journal, 24*, 55-58.

Storin, M. V. (2002). *While America slept: Coverage of terrorism from 1993 to September 11, 2001* (#2002-7). Cambridge, MA: Harvard University, The Joan Shorenstein Center on the Press, Politics and Public Policy.

Sylvester, J., & Hoffman, S. (2002). *Women journalists at ground zero*. Lanham, MD: Rowman & Littlefield.

Thussu, D. K. (2006). Televising the 'War on Terrorism': The myths of morality. In A. P. Kavoori & T. Fraley (Eds.), *Media, terrorism, and theory: A reader* (pp. 3-17). New York: Rowman & Littlefield.

Tuman, J.S. (2003). *Communicating terror: The rhetorical dimensions of terrorism*. Thousand Oaks, CA: Sage.

van der Veer, P. (2004). Introduction. In P. van der Veer (Ed.), *Media, war, and terrorism: Responses from the Middle East and Asia* (pp. 1-8). London: RoutledgeCurzon.

Vanderford, M. (2004). Breaking new ground in WMD risk communication: The pre-event message development project. *Biosecurity & Bioterrorism: Biodefense Strategy, Practice and Science, 2*, 193-194.

Virilio, P. (2002). *Ground zero* (C. Turner, Trans.). New York: Verso.

Vultee, F. (2006). Fatwa on the bunny: News language and the creation of meaning about the Middle East. *Journal of Communication Inquiry, 30*, 319-336.

Wakshlag, J. (2002). Introduction: Reflection on media in times of crisis. In B. S. Greenberg (Ed.), *Communication and terrorism: Public and media responses to 9/11* (pp. xiii-xv). Cresskill, NJ: Hampton Press.

Wanta, W., & Hu, Y.W. (1993). The agenda-setting effects of international news coverage: An examination of differing news frames. *International Journal of Public Opinion Research, 5*, 250-264.

Weare, C., & Lin, W. (2002). Content analysis of the World Wide Web: Opportunities and challenges. *Social Science Computer Review, 18*, 272-292.

Weimann, G. (1987a). Media events: The case of international terrorism. *Journal of Broadcasting and Electronic Media, 31*, 21-39.

Weimann, G. (1987b). Conceptualizing the effects of mass mediated terrorism. *Political Communication and Persuasion, 4*, 213-216.

Weimann, G. (1990). 'Redefinition of image': The impact of mass-mediated terrorism. *International Journal of Public Opinion Research, 2*, 16-29.

Weimann, G. (2004, March). *www.terror.net: How modern terrorism uses the internet (Special Report 116)*. Washington, D.C.: United States Institute of Peace.

Weimann, G., & Winn, C. (1994). *The theater of terror: Mass media and international terrorism*. New York: Longman.

Wieviorka, M. (1988/1993). *The making of terrorism* (D. Gordon, Trans.). Chicago: University of Chicago Press.

Wilkins, K., & Downing, J. (2002). Mediating terrorism: Text and protest in interpretations of *The Siege*. *Critical Studies in Media Communication, 19*, 419-437.

Wilkinson, P. (1997). The media and terrorism: A reassessment. *Terrorism and Political Violence, 9*, 53-64.

Wittebols, J. H. (1992). Media and the institutional perspective: U.S. and Canadian coverage of terrorism. *Political Communication, 9*, 267-278.

Yang, J., & Stone, G. (2003). The powerful role of interpersonal communication in agenda setting. *Mass Communication & Society, 6*, 57-74.

Yinbo, L. (2002). How Chinese television and new media presented the U.S. 9-11 tragedy: A comparative study of SINA, CCTV, and Phoenix TV. *Television and New Media, 3*, 223-230.

Zandberg, E., & Neiger, M. (2005). Between the nation and the profession: Journalists as members of contradicting communities. *Media, Culture & Society, 27*, 131-141.

Zelizer, B. (2002). Photography, journalism, and trauma. In B. Zelizer & S. Allan (Eds.), *Journalism after September 11* (pp. 48-68). London: Routledge.

Zelizer, B., & Allan, S. (Eds.). (2002). *Journalism after September 11*. London: Routledge.

Žižek, S. (2002). *Welcome to the desert of the real*. New York: Verso.

CHAPTER CONTENTS

7 Exposing the Spectrum of Whiteness

Rhetorical Conceptions of White Absolutism

Michael G. Lacy
DePaul University

This chapter continues a practice introduced by critical communication scholars to produce insightful analyses of whiteness. Specifically, this chapter synthesizes a body of rhetorical studies in which rhetors explicitly offered ideal white racial identities and cultural norms to establish and justify white supremacy in Western societies. I call this discourse "white absolutism," which consists of absolutist religious and scientific appeals, tribalism, and scapegoating. White absolutism centers white masculinity and justifies restoring white patriarchal heterosexual control by negating black, nonwhite, and feminine archetypes that offer motives to conquer, control, and kill nonwhites. White absolutism still exists in coded and postmodern forms, and its scholarly analyses have generated four important areas of communication research: (1) cyberspace hate rhetoric, (2) cultural (re)productions of white superiority, (3) historical studies of whiteness, and (4) new, redemptive, and innocent white identity studies.

INTRODUCTION

Communication scholars across the discipline apply a variety of approaches, methods, analytical tools, and critical vocabularies and frameworks to cultural practices that construct, constitute, and discursively form whiteness—white racial identities[1] that reproduce white supremacist ideologies and white privilege every day, situated in interaction, conversations, interviews, diaries, ethnographies, literature, performance, public speeches, political debates, media discourse, and cultural artifacts and representations. These scholars show how whiteness shapes and affects our (1) identity (e.g., authentic, imagined, subaltern, transnational, hybrid and non-white) and interpersonal relationships; (2) cultural norms, values, and practices; (3) civic and public policies (e.g., immigration, nationhood, citizenship,

Correspondence: Michael G. Lacy, DePaul University, 2320 North Kenmore Avenue, Suite 589, Chicago, IL 60604; Phone: 773-325-4352; E-mail: mlacy2@depaul.edu affirmative action, multiculturalism, reconciliation, and reparations), and (4) intercultural and global alliances to reduce conflict. Whether we are conscious of it or not, constructions of whiteness affect who we are, why we are here, where we and our ancestors came from, and what we will become antiracist and postcolonial people.

Since Nakayama and Krizek (1995) introduced *whiteness studies* to the field of communication, communication scholars have imported theories of whiteness from various disciplines (e.g., history, sociology, literary studies, cultural studies, critical race theory, film studies, African American studies, black feminist thought, feminist theory, women's studies, and education) to examine bodies of scholarly literature for constructions of white racial identities that have escaped critical scrutiny (Dyer, 1988; Moon, 1999; Morrison, 1989; Shome, 2000; Supriya, 1999). Such scholarship exposes the dominance, complexities, and ubiquitousness of whiteness in communication practices that shape and control people's lives and reproduce white racial power and privilege, often without their knowledge or consent (Wander, Nakayama, & Martin, 1999).

Communication scholars have primarily used critical and interpretative methods and frameworks to expose whiteness in discursive practices because of the overgeneralizations, reductions, and stereotypes of racial Others reified by traditional or positivistic social scientific research (Essed, 1991; Essed & Goldberg, 2002; Goldberg, 1995; McPhail, 2002) and the absence of analyses of discursive practices that constitute whiteness and cultural norms (Hall, 2003; Nakayama & Krizek,1995; Shome, 2000; West, 1982). Communication scholars have employed poststructural theories and frameworks to reveal whiteness as "strategic rhetoric" (Nakayama & Krizek, 1995) in hate crimes (Moon & Nakayama 2005), "strategic whiteness" in popular films (Dyer, 1988; Projansky & Ono, 1999; Shome, 1996, 2000), and "strategic silence" in politics (Crenshaw, 1997). Critical communication scholars have utilized poststructuralism to describe whiteness as a distinctive culturally produced identity (Jackson, 1999b; Steyn, 2004), a historical, dominant, colonial, and globally imposed identity experienced by nonwhite women (Frankenberg, 1993; Shome, 1996, 1999; Toyosaki, 2007; see also related works by Gresson, 2004; Jensen, 2005), or a legal category used by judges, policymakers, and journalists to determine the national identity of nonwhite immigrants (Flores, 2003; Shah, 1999). Further, Delgado and Stefancic (1997) employed critical race theory and historical studies as a framework to expose whiteness.

Postructuralism has informed investigations of whiteness in popular culture productions (Calhoun, 2005; Lipari, 2004; Madison, 1999; Rockler, 2002; Shome, 2000; Watts, 2005), performances (Cooks, 2003; Warren, 2001), as a pedagogical tool or "invention" (Cooks & Simpson, 2007; Middleton, 2004; Morrison, 1989), or discursive practice, Moon (1999) argued, used by "good (white) girls" to maintain solidarity with white heterosexual men and reproduce white privilege (p. 254; see also Houston, 2002; Lee, 1999; McIntosh, 2001).

Moon synthesized bell hooks' (1992) and Collins' (1990) conceptions of black feminist thought with womanist and feminist theory to develop conceptions and descriptions of whiteness.

In addition, rhetorical frameworks have guided analyses of whiteness (Cloud, 2004; Crenshaw, 1997; Dickinson, Ott, & Aoki, 2005; Flores, 2003; Gordon & Crenshaw, 2004; Gresson, 1995; Marty, 1999; Tierney & Jackson, 2003; Watts, 2005), but few communication scholars have used rhetorical studies to examine, expose, and describe explicit forms of whiteness. This latter approach underscores the rhetorical roots and relatively stable structures of white supremacy in contemporary hate rhetoric, popular culture productions, historical treatments, and civic discourse.

In this chapter, I synthesize rhetorical studies that describe rhetors who offer ideal white identities to establish and defend white supremacy in Western societies as African slavery debates peaked (Montagu, 1997) and modernism emerged in the late 17th, 18th, and 19th centuries (West, 1982). Specifically, I analyze and describe seminal rhetorical case studies of mythic rhetoric (particularly the works of Kenneth Burke, 1973; see also McGuire, 1977; Roy & Rowland, 2003), oppression (Bosmajian, 1983), coercion (Burgess, 1973), social movements, demagoguery, hate rhetoric (D. E. Whillock, 1995; R. K. Whillock, 1995), xenophobia and nationalism (Shah, 1999). In these studies, communication scholars examined instances in which rhetors (e.g., presidents, politicians, clergy, judges, lawyers, scientists, and cultural artists) justified and defended slavery (Grade, 1984; Wander, 1972), Reconstruction (Kinney, 1982; Logue, 1976; B. R. McGee, 2000; Wilson, 2002), desegregation (Braden, 1980; Clark, 1993; Hillbruner, 1960), colonialism and dislocation (Lake, 1991; Wander, 1972), and fascism (Burke, 1973; Bytwerk, 2004; McGee, 1975; Murray, 1998; Perry, 1983). Jamieson (1992) also provided a review of racial (and especially anti-black) and ethnic appeals in U. S. political discourse. I also cull and present rhetorical examples and representative anecdotes from anthologies of critical race and whiteness theories (Delgado & Stefancic, 1997; Essed & Goldberg, 2002; Montagu, 1997; Myrdal, 1962) that scholars engage to illustrate their seminal racial theories and constructs (e.g., *whiteness, Orientialism, modern racism,* and *everyday racism*).

I argue that this diffuse discourse (consisting of multiple white identities) centers white masculinity by negating black, nonwhite, and feminine archetypes and providing people with motives to control and kill nonwhites to establish and restore white heterosexual patriarchal power and control. I call this discourse *white absolutism.* This term highlights the rhetorical character (based on established rhetorical conceptions) of discourse that forms, affirms, and produces white supremacist ideology. Previously, historians, sociologists, and social scientists have described this discourse in historical or deterministic terms as *old racism* or *traditional racism* (see McPhail, 2002). Second, white absolutism emphasizes the absolutist character of this racialized discourse, distinguishing it from the ambivalent, contradictory, and implicit constructions of modern racism (West, 1982), which reproduce white racial advantages and privileges in post-colonial and post–civil rights contexts (see Shome, 2000; Wander et al., 1999).

The features of white absolutism include (1) absolutism, or using religion and science to explain the origins of white supremacy and justify its necessity and persistence; (2) tribalism, or exploiting blood and sexual metaphors to arouse deep fears of racial invasion, annihilation, or death, and (3) scapegoating, or blaming an external (nonwhite) racial devil for loss and polarizing essential differences to unify whites. In the final section, I contend that white absolutism still exists in coded and postmodern (i.e., mediated, diffuse, fragmented, asymmetrical, and contrastive) form, and its analyses by communication scholars have produced four important areas of research: (1) cyberspace and postmodern hate rhetoric, (2) cultural (re)productions of white superiority and supremacy, (3) historical studies of whiteness, and (4) new, redemptive and innocent white identity studies.

ABSOLUTISM

Rhetors who offer explicit appeals for white supremacy constitute "absolutists" who operate from a "positivistic or classic world view," which is "populated with essences, realities, intrinsic good and evils, and absolutes that exist and can clearly be known so the moral rules can be declared with objective validity" (Jamieson, 1976, p. 8; see also Hart, 1976). White absolutists exploit religion and science to explain and justify white supremacy over nonwhites as a divine and natural order, or a *Great Chain of Being* (Hillbruner, 1960; see also Lovejoy, 1957).

Religious Authority

Since the 16th century, prominent clergymen and politicians have cited Judeo-Christian scripture as authority to explain the origins of negative racial differences and white supremacy. Doctrinaire Catholic officials or monotheists, for example, held that blacks and Indians "fell" from God's grace beginning with Adam and Eve (Gould, 1981). Secularists argued that blacks, Indians, and nonwhites descended from more separate and inferior origins than whites (e.g., philosopher David Hume, see Gould, 1981; West, 1982).

By the 17th century, divine intervention comprised the dominant way that people in Western societies accounted for dark skin and racialized differences (Banton, 1988; Gould, 1981; Miles, 1989; Pieterse, 1992; West, 1982). Slavery advocates before and after the U.S. Civil War (Banton, 1988; Hillbruner, 1960; Montagu, 1997), segrationists in the late 1950s (Toch, Deutsch, & Wilkens, 1960), and Mormon church officials until the 1970s cited Genesis as proof that blacks descended from Cain, Canaan, Ham, and other ignoble biblical characters whom God "marked" owing to transgression and sin (Trank, 1970, p. 220; see also Banton, 1988). The Africans' dark skin served as a permanent and perpetual sign of moral turpitude and inferiority (Montagu, 1997; Myrdal, 1962; Trank, 1970; Wander, 1972).

Since modernity emerged in the late 17th and 18th centuries (West, 1982), white absolutists (e.g., white supremacists, Ku Klux Klansmen, Nazis, fascists, and hate groups) appropriated the mythic structures and archetypes found in Christian scriptures. These narrative structures equip deeply dissatisfied, lost, and fragmented publics with a coherent framework or worldview that explains who they are as a "chosen people" or "master race" and what they must do to return to greatness (see Burke, 1973). Such greatness never really existed, explained Burke, but the discourse provides a heroic identity for those lacking one, often prompting scapegoating, violence, and holocaust to reclaim their illusory mythic identity (Burke, 1973; Carter, 1999; McGuire, 1977; Roy & Rowland, 2003; Rueckert, 1982). Burke observed that, since the Civil War ended in 1865, Aryans in the United States and later in Hitler's Nazi Germany inverted, twisted, and perverted Christian theology to convert their material poverty into a spiritual quest to reclaim their white heterosexual masculine Aryan identity and, with it, the material control of the state. Before and after the Civil War, white absolutists offered utopian religious images (B. R. McGee, 2000) of white patriarchs acting with "civility" and "benevolence" toward their "faithful souls," "happy darkies," or "savage children" (Wander, 1972, p. 357), working on their plantations. Such romanticism helped justify and resolve the United States's moral dilemma over slavery (Fredrickson, 1988; Riggs & Salmon, 1987) and conceal the Confederacy's oppression of blacks (Crenshaw, 1997).

In response to losing the Civil War and Southern autonomy, *The Lost Cause* emerged. The Lost Cause constitutes a rhetorical fantasy theme, or group-specific myth, and populist narrative (M. J. Lee, 2006) that describes the Southerners' exceptional virtues (e.g., see Grade, 1984, for discussion of love for home, region, and God). Those virtues especially included, according to M. J. Lee, their spiritual closeness to God and one another (e.g., "Southern by the grace of God," p. 370). The Lost Cause continues to offer white Southerners a shared vision that the South will rise again and restore white Anglo-Saxon supremacy (Clark, 1993). Romantic visions of the Confederacy, the Old South, and The Lost Cause collide with collective memories of the antiblack violence and lynchings that triggered the iconic civil rights movement (Williamson, 2002), thereby fueling intense debates about the meaning and national status of the Confederate flag, museums, and memorabilia (Crenshaw, 1997; Gabriel, 1998; Lacy, 2007b).

White absolutists also use religious doctrines to prescribe restrictive roles for their leaders, who must be charismatic, patriarchal, and prophetic, as well as for followers, who must abandon their individuality and rationality and adopt an anonymous group mask that makes violence more likely (Bytwerk, 2004; M. McGee, 1975). Such commitments are reinforced by melodrama, make-believe, and hyper-rhetorical activities (such as uniforms, hoods, masks, loyalty oaths, emblems—crosses and swastikas—and flags) seemingly everywhere, asserted Braden (1980), intensifying the individual's adherence to a white supremacist ideology. Murray (1998) discovered that Nazis strategically deployed propaganda, legislative action, and performances constituting a mythic or ideal Nazi citizen at critical times over decades, producing an ideology in which ordinary citizens became complicit or willing participants of atrocities.

Film and propaganda historians believe that Leni Riefenstahl's 1935 documentary film, *Triumph of the Will*, in particular, generated widespread support among Germans and universal and absolute loyalty to the Nazis by 1939. The film did so, D. E. Whillock (1995) contended, by offering iconic images that vividly described the devastation, suffering, and mental anguish of German people (at the hands of Jews and Bolsheviks) after World War I, while glorifying Teutonic gods of the past and the true belief, passion, and conformity of Hitler's youth brigades, affirming a new generation of Aryan rulers. Braden (1980) maintained that the barrage of symbolism used in "closed rhetorical societies" (p. 334; e.g., Hitler's Nazi Germany, Fascist Italy, or Mississippi from 1954 to 1964) is reinforced by ritual, coercive rhetoric, threats, terrorism, and violence sanctioned by the state to intimidate onlookers, dissenters, and backsliders (see also Bosmajian, 1983; Burke, 1973; Ellul, 1964; Montagu, 1997; D. E. Whillock, 1995).

By referring to religious doctrines, absolutists refute relativistic, secular, and egalitarian arguments by those who accept common articles of faith and biblical scriptures (Hart, 1984; see also Hillbruner, 1960). Racist hardliners in the 19th century believed that God divined black inferiority and, therefore, abolitionists need not waste their time educating blacks; slavery was good for the slave's "savage soul," they argued (Montagu, 1997, p. 58; see also Gould, 1981; Hillbruner, 1960; Wander, 1972; West, 1982). Absolutism also produces a linguistic firmness, rigidity, and defensiveness (Hart, 1984). After the death of white supremacist and journalist Robert Edward Edmunds in 1959, hate groups in a letter-writing campaign used slogans like integration or "race mixing" in a plot to destroy "White America and Christianity" (Toch et al., 1960, p. 179). Arguing like fundamentalist preachers, white segregationists in the 1950s and early 1960s resisted federal desegregation orders by adopting a defensive posture, confrontational tone, categorical absolutes (e.g., "total mobilization," "fight to the death" and "all or nothing") and an "us versus them" orientation (Braden, 1980, p. 346). "Segregation Now, Segregation Tomorrow, Segregation Forever!," proclaimed Alabama Governor George Wallace during his 1963 inaugural address, two months before standing in front of the school house door at the University of Alabama in defiance of federal authority and the Kennedy Administration (Clark, 1993, p. 168; see also Jamieson, 1992, p. 80). Wallace's resistance and carefully orchestrated surrender mediated the loss of public support for segregation, Clark asserted, while reaffirming the "inevitability" and "self-fulfilling logic" of white supremacy (p. 195), especially for angry and perplexed whites who believed in the state's right to subordinate its black citizens.

White absolutists also cite Christian doctrine to suggest that the end-state is known, certain, and forthcoming for true believers (Hoffer, 1951). Anglican and Puritan preachers and U.S. politicians argued that white souls would be saved, but the vast majority of Indian souls would be damned forever. Preachers and leading politicians invoked "God's will" to justify the extreme dominance, brutality, cruelty, and destruction of Native American and Mexican cultures in North America after the emergence of capitalism (Smedley, 1993, pp. 81-82), culminating in *Manifest Destiny*, a term coined by John L. O'Sullivan in 1845. According to Smedley, Manifest Destiny not only became a doctrinaire movement that expanded white Anglo-Saxon rule over North American lands, its peoples, and its resources, it unified white Anglo Americans (Stratton, 2005) by encouraging them to see themselves as God's "chosen people" (Smedley, p. 191). Indeed, B. R. McGee claimed that Armageddon, dystopian, and utopian fantasies were dramatically played out in 1915 by D. W. Griffith's infamous and groundbreaking film, *Birth of a Nation*. At the end of the film, a transcendent figure of Jesus Christ appears to sanctify the unification of white Northerners and Southerners and the birth of a new, white Aryan nation.

Natural Law

During and after the European and American Enlightenments in the late 18th and early 19th centuries, important scholars, writers, politicians, and artists fused racial discourse with modernism, influencing elite visual arts, popular novels, and images (Goldberg, 1993; McGary, 2002; Stoler, 1995; West, 1982), shifting the grounds of authority for white absolutism from religion to science. In doing so, white absolutists reinforced, complemented, and reified religious appeals for white supremacy with natural law, thereby making white supremacy seem objective, essential, and natural (Hall, 2003). Rhetorical scholars have observed that white politicians and public figures in the United States, especially in the South, combine religious and scientific justifications for white supremacy and antiblack racism (see Braden, 1980; Jamieson, 1992; Wilson, 2002). However, West (1982) and Gould (1981) reported that influential rhetorical documents, scientific treatises, cultural (aesthetic) artifacts, and productions reflect a paradigm shift from religious justifications of race and racism toward scientific modernism.

In the 19th century, influential anthropologists, naturalists, and pseudo-scientists (such as Linnaeus, Buffon, Blumenbach, and Gobineau) appropriated Aristotelian classifications. Campbell (1974) argued that European clerics and philosophers, as well as slave masters and educators in the Old South, cited Aristotle as an authority to justify black slavery. Aristotle is cited second only to the Bible as the primary authoritative source to justify slavery (p. 283). Montagu (1997) also found references to Aristotle in scientific racial discourse in the 19th and 20th centuries. Gould (1981) demonstrated that Plato's Socrates expressed a belief in biological determinism, essential differences, and innate social rank.

Leading scientists appropriated Darwinian taxonomies and natural history schemes to provide "proof" that blacks and Indians were separate, distinct, and *naturally* inferior species in a *Great Chain of Being* (Hillbruner, 1960; see also Crable, 2003; Lovejoy, 1936/1957) in which whites were on top followed by (native) Indians, blacks, and other nonwhites (Gould, 1981; Montagu, 1997; West, 1982). Crable observed that, as early as 1684, Bernier and other theorists (e.g., Kant, Blumebach, and Gobineau) divided humankind into finite groups and racial ranks based on *naturally* occurring features. In doing so, prominent naturalists and theorists produced distorted rhetorical bodies that specify, describe, and rank nonsymbolic or motionless "natural" subjects (e.g., "races") while concealing the symbolic processes (e.g., meanings, values, and hierarchies) that *naturalize* kinds of people, devoid of human action (p. 133). According to Crable, similar rhetorical distortions can be found in contemporary discourse on race and racial identity (e.g., U.S. Census questionnaires).

Banton (1988) claimed that scholars first advanced theories of "scientific racism" in the 1850s. Gould (1981) traced the studies of leading scientists in the 19th century (e.g., Linnaeus, Cuvier, Agazziz, and Morton) who argued that obvious visible, physical, empirical, or phenotypical traits (e.g., cranium size, hair texture, skin color, sexual organs, and various body parts) determined a race's intelligence, predispositions, cultural achievements, and destiny. These studies reified African or black inferiority and white supremacy, fostering the belief that whites were permanently superior to blacks. White absolutism produced a normative, white heterosexual male "gaze," idealizing European and Greek forms (West, 1982), while contrasting caricatures of black or nonwhite women's bodies, buttocks, and sexual organs (e.g., *Hottentot Venus*) as signs of innate black inferiority (Gilman, 1986). Southern demagogues in the 1950s and 60s resisted integration and federal desegregation orders by citing numerous pseudo-scientific books and treatises as evidence of black inferiority (Braden, 1980). One of the most influential, Shufeldt's (1907) *The Negro a menace to American civilization*, depicted blacks as subhuman monkeys, purportedly based on biology and ethnography (see also Jamieson, 1992; Myrdal, 1962). According to Braden, from 1954 to 1964, white Mississippians craved hearing self-proclaimed anthropologist Carleton Putnam's speeches that attacked Franz Boaz for his egalitarianism, or Judge Thomas P. Brady's conclusions that black or Negro inferiority was a "fact" of "nature," based on their low I.Q. test scores, indifference, and indolence (p. 341).

After World War I, scientists and U.S. government officials opposed using biological measurements because they were too absolutist and erroneous. In their place, psychological measurements and I.Q. tests were deployed against waves of "not-yet-white" European immigrants (e.g., Irish, Jews, Sicilian Italians, and Poles; see Jacobson, 1998; Roediger, 1994), competing for domestic resources against African Americans and other immigrants (Gould, 1981; Pieterse, 1992; Roediger, 1991, 1994). As Gould (1995) observed, after World War II, U.S. officials rejected old biological racism, or eugenics, owing to the public's abhorrence of the Nazi's racial sterilization and purification programs (not because racial notions were refuted by new evidence or scientific advances). Gould and other prominent scholars believe that Hernstein and Murray's (1994) *The Bell Curve* merely rehashes scientific racism to mobilize public opinion against affirmative action policies (see also Grey, 1999; Jacoby & Glauberman, 1995; Stoler, 1995).

In their study of audience reception, Ramsey, Achter, and Condit (2001) found that the book and its reviews did not increase antiblack racism by recirculating racist views (e.g., whites who held strong negative perceptions of other races appropriated genetic and environmental reasons to justify their beliefs, while egalitarian whites and blacks incorporated genetic accounts to their schemas). Unfortunately, Ramsey et al. concluded that the book and its reviews encouraged a less-than-ideal starting point for the debate, focusing on nature (genetics) versus nurture (environment), instead of individual versus social responsibility.

European imperialists produced "knowledge" about racial Others that inscribed and disseminated ethnic notions and stereotypes of Africans, Arabs, Asians, and nonwhites throughout the West (Hall, 2003; Said, 1978; see related argument by Keränen & Sanprie, this volume, regarding the negative stereotypes and media representations of Arabs and Muslims since September 11, 2001). Said (1978, 1993) argued that, beginning in 1787, Napoleon and other European colonial powers employed engineers, cartographers, and pseudo-scientists to produce static representations and stereotypes of diverse peoples, religions, and cultures over vast geographic spaces in the Middle East and East as mysterious, strange, exotic, and different, or what Said calls *Orientalism*, a "colonial form of racism." Nakanishi (1988) described a similar process that he called "lumping," in which whites and nonwhites claim that all Asians or pan-Asians (e.g., Chinese, Japanese, and Japanese Americans) share the same, homogeneous, monolithic, and stereotypical traits.

Similarly, Lake (1991) and Morris and Wander (1990) found that cultural histories of Anglo Americans typically erase and exclude Native Americans from the mythic Western Frontier, thereby justifying their violent removal and extermination from the land and the appropriation of their vital and sacred resources. Trimble (1988) reported that documentaries, textbooks, novels, and infamous Hollywood *Western* films and cartoons present American Indians as "frozen in time" (as savage, stoic, silent, or drunken). According to Trimble, these notions still shape contemporary beliefs, cultural memories, and histories about American Indians (see also Dickinson et al., 2005). White absolutists combine science, cultural aesthetics, and popular culture productions to produce "knowledge" of racial Others (Hall, 2003; West, 1982).

TRIBALISM

White absolutism is tribal. It exploits inherited familial characteristics to suggest that the body politic has been invaded by an insidious parasite, vampire, savage, or monstrous black brute (e.g., Shakespeare's Calaban), capable of destroying civilization. Therefore, blacks, natives, nonwhites, and Jews (who were considered "black" from the 16th to the 19th centuries; see Gilman, 1991) need to be controlled, segregated, removed, or killed. Thus, white absolutists equip whites with redemption dramas that justify the violence of white heterosexual masculine heroes in their quest to restore absolute, white patriarchal control and civilization. They do so by exploiting blood metaphors and dystopian heterosexual fantasy themes that heighten whites' senses of fear, loss, and death.

Blood Metaphors

Montagu (1997) contended that modern science disproved folk and classical ideas that "blood" determined or passed hereditary and character traits (biological traits are passed through the genes). Yet, Campbell (1974) noted that, in ancient Greece, Aristotle and other philosophers believed that one's blood determined inherited character traits. Christian scripture (Burke, 1973), legal and government institutions (e.g., blood segregation laws), as well as popular culture vehicles all reify "blood" as a stable signifier of "race" (see Montagu, 1997). As Montagu explained, according to white absolutists, God divined whites with "pure" or "full" blood, which made them an exclusive, superior, and elevated or civilized racial tribe. They defined "pure blood" in terms of their own ethnocentric whiteness, over time, reifying and elevating northern European or Aryan Nordic blood as the most precious and superior blood (Montagu, p. 362; see also Myrdal, 1962; Pieterse, 1992), relegating the "blood" of southern and eastern Europeans to second class status because they did not maintain their blood purity and risked genetic annihilation (Jackson, 1999a, p. 26). According to Montagu, Nazi propagandist Alfred Rosenburg, for example, argued that Aryan blood comprised the primary source of their eternal values, superior character, and political destiny, which justified their moral, cultural, and political authority.

White absolutism exploits dystopian fears of the body to arouse deep public fears of death by racial invasion (see Burke, 1973; Montagu, 1997; Myrdal, 1962). Aryans, for example, asserted that their pure blood and racial superiority were being "mixed," diluted, contaminated, or polluted with an inferior stock (through immoral sexual intercourse, producing inferior offspring), which had weakened their "God-given" and "natural" supremacy. Like the conservative rightists in the United States during the *Cold War*, who used the cancer metaphor as a symbolic token to signify danger and threat from an invisible and internal enemy (e.g., "communists;" Black, 1970; Fisher, 1970), white European fascists argued that a Jewish parasite infested their precious Aryan blood and, therefore, sterilization, ethnic cleansing, or *The Final Solution* (i.e., the extermination of European Jewry) was necessary to save the body politic (Bosmajian, 1983; Burke, 1973; Perry, 1983). The fear of contamination helped "white Anglo Americans" mobilize broad public resistance against the citizenship of Chinese laborers working on U.S. railroads in the 19th century, culminating in the Exclusion Act of 1882 and laws banning new Chinese immigration, interracial marriage, and miscegenation until the mid-20th century (G. Lee, 1996; Takaki, 1993). Flores (2003) documented that major U.S. newspaper reports in the 1930s depicted Mexicans as "imported vermin" and "foreign criminals" to resist Mexican immigration to the United States and assuage Americans' fears over competition for jobs (p. 376).

While eugenicists attributed the eloquence and accomplishments of Phillis Wheately, Booker T. Washington, Frederick Douglass, and George Washington Carver to their "white European bloodlines" (Gates, 1986; Spickard, 1992), white absolutists primarily use blood metaphors to expose the inferiority of racial others and justify their subordination. In his seminal treatise of antiblack racism in the United States during the 1930s, Myrdal (1962) observed that, if a race that possesses the blood of high status mixes with the lower stock, the result was an inferior race; the "cross between a white and a Hindu produces a Hindu, and a cross between any European race and a Jew is a Jew" (p. 14). Such inclusiveness made "inferior" races the "natural" subjects for subordinate roles. One drop of black blood, for example, made one black and subhuman during slavery in the United States, increasing the number of slaves and domestic workers (Fredrickson, 1988; Montagu, 1997; Myrdal, 1962). When minorities are no longer useful as slaves, domestics, subordinate workers, laborers, or political antagonists, Wilhelm (1980) warned that dominant racial groups (whites) exterminate them (e.g., Jews in Nazi Germany and Native Americans in the United States.

Infamous white supremacists (e.g., Thomas Dixon) and Klansmen in their popular literature, films, and public speeches (particularly after Reconstruction and "Negro disenfranchisement" in 1901) claimed that "blood mixing" created a "mulatto" race that was capable of destroying both races because they possessed the negative characteristics of "power-hungry and guilty" whites and "immoral and sexually aggressive" blacks (Kinney, 1982). Popular plays, novels, films, and contemporary television productions in the 20th century depicted the "tragic female mulatto" as hypersexual, devious, tormented, despised, and insane, due to her mixed breeding and blood (Bogle, 1996; Orbe & Strother, 1996; Spickard, 1992).

White absolutists use racialized blood to deny national status and legitimacy to ethnic others, thereby expanding ideas of racial subordination to include ethnic groups in the United Kingdom and United States (Gilroy, 1987; Jacobson, 1998; Pieterse, 1992). Once established, antiblack racism served as the prototype to oppress new, "not yet white" immigrants (e.g., Irish, Jews, Chinese, Italians, and others) arriving in the United States (Roediger, 1994), who were morphed into "white negroes" (Pieterse, 1992) or "niggers turned inside out" in the case of the Irish (Gabriel, 1998, p. 50; see also Ignatiev, 1995; Stratton, 2005), with purportedly the same stereotypical features and traits of blacks, owing to their inferior bloodlines (Pieterse, 1992).

In response, Irish and other ethnic groups demonstrated their commitment to white supremacy and nationalism by vilifying blacks in extreme ways (Stratton, 2005) and identifying themselves as "white" (Sullivan & Goldzwig, 2004, p. 273). Racialized blood arguments justified denying immigrants entry to the United States, United Kingdom, and North America during the 18th and 19th centuries (Gilroy, 1987; Smedley, 1993). Shah (1999) found that "high caste" Asian Indians justified their U.S. naturalization and citizenship by distinguishing their "white" bloodlines from "dark" "low caste" Asian Indians, as did Akhay Kumar Mazumar, who stated "I am a high-caste Hindu of pure blood belonging to a Warrior ruling caste. High-caste Hindus always consider themselves to be members of the Aryan race" (as cited in Shah, p. 256). After the "Hindu Conspiracy" trial of San Francisco in 1917, in which 32 prominent Asian Indian leaders were accused of conspiring to overthrow British rule, Shah noted that white absolutists roundly characterized Asian Indians as nonwhite, subversive, and dangerous. According to Shah, news reports and editorials in the *San Francisco Chronicle* and the *New York Times*, as well as the rhetoric offered by public officials and the courts at the time, reflected the widespread belief that "only Whites could be true Americans," culminating in a unanimous Supreme Court decision *(United States* v. *Bhagat Singh Thind,* 1922)* in February, 1923, defining whiteness as the criterion for citizenship (p. 259).

Heterosexual Symbolism

White absolutists also exploit masculine heterosexual fears and dystopian fantasies and metaphors to expose how dangerous black brutes or seductive male vampires sought to rape or seduce white women and to weaken or destroy their white nationalistic identity. These narratives prompt extreme, heterosexual masculine violence (as warriors, knights, frontiersmen, etc.) to separate, segregate, castrate, and kill black beasts and to preserve white, Aryan nations and civilization.

Rape

Before and after the Civil War, whites circulated blatant jokes and stories about erotic black and mulatto temptresses and Jezebels who enjoyed the sexual advances of white males (Edelman, 1988; hooks, 1981). More pervasively, however, they produced lurid stories in which their *own* white women were chased and raped by "black brute niggers," as in popular southern literature, or what Cash (1941, p. 118) called "the Southern rape complex." Although "myths of the black male rapist" were present in early American newspaper reports (Block, 2001), a black male's rape (or implied rape) of a Southern white woman only appeared once in popular literature before Thomas Dixon's ghastly innovation of bloody victimage in *The Leopard's Spots* in 1902, which became a runaway best seller throughout the South. The novel featured black freedmen as the enemy but indirectly blamed the Northern politicians, carpetbaggers, and scalawags for unleashing black males to roam, plunder, and rape the South (Bloomfield, 1964; Gilmore, 1994; Kinney, 1982). The lurid attacks on Southern belles, the symbols of the Southern aristocracy, romantically suggested that violent white heterosexual masculine gallantry or chivalry (*Knights* of the White Camellias or Ku Klux Klan) was necessary to save and protect white women from dangerous black brutes. This calling served to restore the southern white male ego after losing the Civil War. As lynching rose and calls for anti-lynching legislation increased in 1892, popular writers, politicians, and orators used the black male murderer and rapist formula to justify an epidemic of lynching blacks (a barbaric phenomenon meant to terrorize blacks and voyeuristically entertain whites, which popular singer Billie Holliday called "Strange Fruit;" see Jackson, 2006, p. 17) that continued in the late 19th and early 20th centuries. White supremacists argued that the lynchings were caused by the murder and rape committed by black male brutes who violated white purity. In *The Negro: The Southerner's Problem*, Thomas Nelson Page argued that lynching "put an end to the ravishing of their women by an inferior race" (as cited in Jamieson, 1992, p. 77). Thomas Dixon (1902, p. 371) argued in his polemic:

> The black man is a damned black beast who will rape and destroy Anglo-Saxon racial purity. Once the human control provided by whites is taken away, the result is inevitable: Such crimes…were unknown to slavery… Now, scarcely a day passes without an atrocity, swiftly followed by a lynching.

Kinney (1982) reported that more than 2,500 African Americans were lynched by whites during 1880 through 1900; whereas, Pinar (2001) estimated that nearly 4,500 blacks were lynched in the United States between 1882 and 1927 (see also Jackson, 2006). During this period, virulent antiblack stereotypes (as unintelligent, dangerous, and sexually immoral) were commonplace in elite political discourse (Jamieson, 1992, p.77), major southern newspapers (Logue, 1976), and popular literature. According to Kinney, during this "progressive era" (1880–1910), Dixon's novels "struck a chord with the white populous," making him the most popular novelist of his era (p. 146). Dixon's antiblack themes and storylines were incorporated into D. W. Griffith's 1915 *The Birth of a Nation*, which President Wilson referred to as "history writ in lighting." The film served as everyday realities for whites who had never seen blacks before (Bogle, 1996; Riggs & Salmon, 1987).

Popular films, literature, narratives, and public speeches that featured black brutes raping and trying to possess white virgins diverted attention from white patriarchs, who had sexual relationships with young, subservient black women, including infamous public figures and respected politicians, who expressed white supremacist views about blacks (e.g., Thomas Jefferson, Thomas Dixon, Sr., and Strom Thurmond, all of whom apparently had sex and children with young, subordinate black women; see Gilmore, 1994; Mattingly, 2003; Turner, 2001). Though rape, sexual assault, and torture were used to terrorize, control and dehumanize black girls and women during legalized slavery, hooks (1981, pp. 35-37) contended that white male rapes of black girls and women are noticeably absent from popular southern literature and political discourse because, as Myrdal (1962) argued, such practices would have outraged puritanical white Northerners. Instead, according to hooks, whites and prominent black male politicians labeled black women prostitutes, temptresses, and Jezebels for having sexual relationships and "illegitimate offspring" with their white male patriarchs (p. 33).

Seduction and Emasculation

White imperialists and colonizers frequently described their adventures as patriarchal conquests, penetrations, or invasions into "feminine" foreign lands, continents, or nations (e.g. Africa; see Young, 1996). However, white absolutists generally use heterosexual metaphors to restore their masculine national identity, which they maintain has been emasculated, feminized, and weakened by a seductive rival male, or vampire, causing social, economic and moral decline. Hitler, for example, argued that a rival Jewish male seduced and "intermingled" with Germans, producing prostitution, incest, and syphilis in Germany (Burke, 1973, p. 195). The high amount of heterosexual imagery in Hitler's rhetoric comprises a form of "symbolic incest" or "narcissism," Burke suggested, or an intense focus on the self or ego, universal loss, and a desire for personal and cultural purification of essentialized demons. Hitler obliterated the Nazis' ancestral past (from Hebrew patriarchs found in Judeo-Christianity) to induce a complete symbolic rebirth or change of identity. Burke asserted that such rhetoric also implies an absolute desire for Germans to be led by one dominating male. In response to the historical and ideological inscriptions of hypersexual black males (Jackson, 2006), black nationalism, realism, and resistance rhetoric shared the same heterosexist and patriarchal ideology and values as white supremacists (hooks, 1981; Hope, 1975; see also McPhail, 2002). They did so, Hope argued, by treating "women as property" and featuring black male seduction and the rape of white women as symbolic revenge for the emasculation of black males by whites (p. 19-20; see also hooks, 1981). Rather than black males being emasculated, hooks argued that black women were "masculinized" and forced to work in fields along side men, or transformed into mammies and matriarchs (pp. 47-49; see also Collins, 1990).

African and Irish novelists and playwrights offered patriarchal narratives featuring anti-colonial warriors reclaiming their mothers and mistresses from imperial aggressors (Innis, 1994). African and black heterosexism seems to be a post-colonial and European adaptation, Asante (1987) contended, since in Afrocentric cultures, women play a central role and property rights are virtually unknown. Whether united by heterosexism and patriarchal control— that produces multiple and interlocking forms of oppression for black women (Collins, 1990; hooks, 1981; McIntosh, 2001)—or a black masculine response to white oppression, absolutism and patriarchy go hand in hand.

In sum, white absolutists use blood metaphors and dystopian heterosexual fantasies to arouse fear of monstrous black brutes or deadly parasites and vampires to purge blacks, Jews, and nonwhites from the nation or region and to restore their absolute white heterosexual masculine identity, offering in Burkean vernacular and imagery "equipment for killing."

SCAPEGOATING

White absolutists engage in scapegoating, a primitive ritual in which they project human guilt, sins, and weaknesses onto a beast that they violently beat and slay, completely purging and eliminating sin and generating a sense of catharsis, rebirth, redemption, or renewal (Burke, 1973, 1984). According to Burke, to exorcise the anxieties and feelings of loss arising from modern plagues and capitalism, white absolutists "magically" substitute people for goats (i.e., clear, personal targets), thereby offering a simplistic, perverse and poisonous cure for complex social and economic problems. Left unchecked, Burke (1973) argued that scapegoating becomes sanctioned by the state and produces genocide, holocausts and atrocities (see also Carter, 1999; Rueckert, 1982), as it has for blacks in Africa, Jews in Nazi Germany, and blacks and Native Americans or Indians in the United States (Pieterse, 1992). On a smaller scale, Roy and Rowland (2003) found that Hindu Nationalists (Shiv Sena rhetoric) target "bad" Muslims as scapegoats for subverting Hindu heroism (as great warriors) and a mythic return of their past, resulting in violence against Muslims in 2002. This research suggests various forms of racial/religious forms of absolutism (and scapegoating) that deserve scholarly attention. In sum, scapegoating externalizes blame for loss, polarizes essential differences, and unifies people against a common enemy.

Externalizing Blame

Absolutists blame an external racial scapegoat for real or perceived loss, competition, economic catastrophe, or social upheaval. In doing so, they resist blaming themselves, challenging their absolutist worldview, or subverting their regressive tribal customs. For example, Burke (1984) noted that poor and middle-class whites in the South during the 1930s became convinced that they would prosper by eliminating their black competitors through lynching. Pease (2003) observed that Ralph Ellison's innovations and descriptions of white American racists who lynched Negroes as a sacrificial ritual to demonstrate and reaffirm white supremacy (found in his short stories and his classic novel, *Invisible Man*) were inspired by Kenneth Burke's "scapegoat mechanism" (merger, division, and reunification), in which Hitler targeted "the Jew" in Nazi Germany.

Takaki (1993) found that working-class whites and poor disenfranchised blacks living in major industrial inner cities perceived Asian Americans as foreign (Japanese and Korean) competitors, scapegoating and blaming them for the economic depression in major cities during the 1980s and 1990s. To externalize blame, white absolutists produce apocalyptic discourse (primordial objects, images, and visions) that reveals and enlarges the sense of catastrophe or crisis, providing ready-made symptoms of loss and ample opportunities to blame racial Others. Apocalyptic discourse becomes popular in times of great social upheaval, says Edinger (1999), fueling popular racist uprisings during Reconstruction in the Old South after the Civil War, the economic depression in post World War I Germany, and the post-industrial decline of the British Empire. White absolutists operate like "medicine men" (Burke, 1973, p. 201) who quickly diagnose the symptoms of a larger national or regional illness by employing a causal design and cataloging a series of unpleasant conditions or signs of anarchy and social unrest. Once diagnosed, they heap social ills on an enemy. According to Burke, Hitler cited the Vienna Parliament's "babble of voices" and business conflicts as symptoms of a larger disorder, all of which was said to be caused by a rapacious Jewish plot (p. 201). R. K. Whillock (1995) determined that hatemongers use *synecdoche*, or isolate small events that stand for the larger whole, to imply a larger scheme, plot, or great conspiracy is at work.

Polarizing and Exacerbating Difference

White absolutists who scapegoat exploit archetypal discourse to define racial others in concrete or material ways (e.g., dirt, sin, and the devil), with animalistic and fecal motives (urine, feces, and semen), preparing them for expulsion and slaughter. By antithesis, white absolutists define themselves in abstract and spiritual ways (angels, grace, virtue, purity, and intelligence) to reify their purification (Burke, 1973; Myrdal, 1962; Rueckert, 1982). The sharp dualities of opposites (e.g., biology and spirituality) is a recurring dialectic found in Enlightenment ideologies, reflecting a Manichean duality, binary and allegory (Self versus Others), that signifies imperial and colonial economic domination (Billig et al., 1988; Goldberg, 1993; Jackson, 1999b; Shome, 1996; West, 1982). According to Rueckert, the sharp dialectic is also based on archetypes of purification and redemption that, Myrdal contended, transform light and dark metaphors into racial masks and uniforms that represent good and evil to overshadow human similarities and intensify feelings of danger and fear. For white absolutists, light skin had angelic associations, and dark skin and wooly hair signifies the devil (Bosmajian, 1983; Fanon, 1967; Myrdal, 1962), erecting a light-dark hierarchy (or "antiblackness") that has been inscribed, internalized, and reproduced among subaltern (including subaltern whites) and ethnic minority groups within Western societies. This light–dark hierarchy still prompts racial chauvinism, confusion, shame, and pain (Gresson, 2004). Racial pain is acute for young children and adults (and their parents), growing up in the United States and South Africa, Gresson observed, as they experience the political and psychological ramifications of labeling or being labeled as "white," "nonwhite," or "black."

To further polarize essential differences, white absolutists vilify and name their racial enemy in extreme ways, by using crude references, racial slurs, epithets, ridicule, jokes, and obscenities to generate hate and alert complacent publics that a racial devil violated their sacred, moral, civil and social values. Based on Sartre's and Freud's theories of humor, Billig (2001) argued that bigots, fascists, and the KKK take pleasure and joy in racist and anti-Semitic jokes because, by dehumanizing and mocking their racial target, they suspend human empathy and violate social taboos (about sex, violence, and aggression) without conscience, backed by the righteousness of white supremacist ideology.

White racists exploit visual rhetoric and imagery (in fiction, pamphlets, newspaper sketches, cartoons, film) to enlarge, exaggerate, and distort physical and cultural differences of the racial enemy, generating motives to restore white supremacy. Logue (1976) found that Southern newspapers in the United States (e.g., the *Atlanta Constitution*) commonly printed caricatures and satirical sketches mocking the language and intelligence of black legislators, reviving antiblack hostility, and reinscribing white supremacy back into dominance after the Civil War. Popular cartoons in the early and mid-20th century featured extreme and sadistic violence against black children, called "pickanninies," to suggest that black children were expendable little creatures, reflecting a desire to be rid of blacks (Riggs, 1987). D. E. Whillock (1995) observed that hate mongers use visual rhetoric (icons, imagery, and symbols) to reinforce the dominant white supremacist ideology. They do so by providing recurrent storylines (of tragic loss, past heroes, subhuman racial enemies, and the eventual return of greatness) from public speeches, musical hymns, performances, and cultural events, thereby generating a sense of conformity and overwhelming support. According to D. E. Whillock, historical and cultural memories continue through visual images (e.g., swastikas, the Rising Sun, and combat uniforms) that still resonate over time.

Visual hate rhetoric circulated by popular culture productions makes it easy for isolated and unsophisticated publics (including children) to identify with white supremacist ideologies, primarily because visual rhetoric merely requires a heuristic in which people make simple, reductive, clear-cut generalizations of others based on empirical (visual) or obvious differences. Because racists typically make broad generalizations and ignore individual differences, Allport (1954) observed that racist bigots are likely to be religious, ideological, political, or out-group bigots too. Nazis had an "extended family of enemies," in addition to Jews and blacks, including Communists, Freemasons, gypsies, and homosexuals (Pieterse, 1992, p. 218). U.S. politicians (particularly in the South) have historically linked their political opponents to blacks, Catholics, Irish, and other despised ethnic and political groups (e.g., communists) to generate hate and fear of their enemies (Jamieson, 1992). Racist bigots in the United States connected Jews and blacks with communism, Catholics, and Semites in a plot to destroy America (Toch et al., 1960; see also Hart, 1997). Such negativity allows hate mongers to stand in mortal combat against their mythic enemies, reviving their cause and making it seem sacred.

Unification by Perfecting Evil

White absolutists demonize racial Others by conjuring up a "perfect" racial devil to unify disparate, lost, and dissatisfied people "who share no allegiance, but for a common foe" (Burke, 1973, p. 193). Jews and blacks have historically served as perfect devils, or sources of anti-Christian immorality, national perversion, and cultural decay (Gabriel, 1998; Pieterse, 1992). Essentially, white racists *dehumanize* their racial scapegoats, preparing them for possession, servitude, and slaughter. Racial and ethnic minorities have been dehumanized in at least three ways. First, they have been characterized as nonhuman (as vermin, parasites, infestations), coming from exogenous origins with extraordinary destructive powers, which justifies extreme (necessary and moral) measures to totally exterminate them (Bosmajian, 1983; Flores, 2003; Perry, 1983). For instance, U.S. newspapers used infestation metaphors that served to generate xenophobia and mobilize white resistance against "low caste" black Asian Indians, Chinese, and Mexican immigrants in the 19th and early 20th centuries, who were depicted as the carriers of filth, dirt, pestilence, and hookworm (Flores, 2003; W. Lee, 1999; Shah, 1999; Takaki, 1993). Second, white absolutists have depicted racial scapegoats (e.g., blacks, Latinos, and Native Americans) as subhuman, animalistic, and bestial (as "apes," "savages" and "brutes") to justify enslaving, controlling, moving, dislocating, segregating, and killing the "beasts" (Jackson, 2006; Logue, 1976; Riggs, 1987; Trimble, 1988). Third, white absolutists have described blacks, browns, reds, and nonwhites as primitive, barbaric, and immature (feminine and childlike) or incapable of governing themselves, making white paternalism and colonialism seem necessary, benevolent, comfortable, and moral (Flores, 2003; Jackson, 2006; Logue, 1976; Shome, 1996; Takaki, 1993).

Rhetors who deploy white absolutism engage in scapegoating to externalize blame for material loss, complex problems, capitalism, and modernity and to unify lost and dissatisfied publics by polarizing others and creating racial devils. Scapegoating "magically" relieves human suffering while prompting sacrifices and killing.

STUDYING WHITE ABSOLUTISM AND WHITENESS

White absolutism affirmed, established, and reified white supremacy as a dominant ideology in Western societies since the 18th century. These societies did so by exploiting Christianity, natural law, tribal fear, and scapegoats to justify negating, segregating, enslaving, colonizing, expelling, and killing nonwhites while securing white masculine heterosexual control. Communication scholars suggest that white absolutism still exists in coded and postmodern form, and their analyses of it have produced four areas of communication research: (1) cyberspace and postmodern hate rhetoric, (2) cultural (re)productions of white superiority and supremacy, (3) historical studies of whiteness, and (4) new, redemptive, and innocent white identity studies.

Cyberspace and Postmodern Hate Rhetoric

Communication researchers have found mythic forms of white absolutism in contemporary hate rhetoric. Waltman and Davis (2005) reported that *The Turner Diaries* is considered essential reading for "proper" hate mongers on racist Web sites (p. 38), allegedly inspiring Timothy McVeigh's bombing of the Oklahoma City federal building and the dragging and killing of a black man, James Byrd, behind a pick-up truck by white supremacists in Texas. The book offers mythic Aryan structures and fantasy-themes of a morally superior worldview, Aryan heroes and martyrs, Jewish vampires and black predators, and an inevitable apocalyptic racial holy war (RAHOWA) with the Zion Occupied Government, which controls African Americans bent on destroying white Christian Americans. D. E. Whillock (1995) argued that young neo-Nazis and Skinheads wore Doc Marten shoes, laced with red and white shoe laces, to signify the spilt blood of their enemies and Aryan racial purity respectively, to link their modern day hate of blacks, Asians, and Jews with the past. Such rhetoric provides would-be haters with a collective memory of

Aryan ideology to unify them into a new hate group and justify their individual acts of ethnoviolence against their enemies.

One of the most compelling and vital areas of communication research examines hate rhetoric generated by hate groups (e.g., KKK, Neo-Nazi, Christian Identity, and Neo-Confederates) and disseminated in cyberspace through Internet Web sites to increase their membership, especially among children and young white males. In 2002, the Southern Poverty Law Center documented 708 organized hate groups in the United States using Internet Web sites (excluding sites without individual Web publishers (Yousman, 2003). Hate groups increased 20% from 1999 to 2000 (Williamson & Pierson, 2003) and, according to Yousman, climbed another 9% between 2002 and 2003. Waltman (2003) and Williamson and Pierson found that modern white supremacists' Web sites (e.g., KKK Youth Corp 's "Just for Kids") offers a "hate stratagem" (i.e., artifice or trickery; see R. K. Whillock, 1995) and persuasive heuristic framework that encourages children to uncritically engage, consume, and participate in the Web sites, recruiting them into a virtual hate community (see related arguments by Keränen & Sanprie, this volume, regarding the global recruitment of terrorists via the Internet as well as Gibbs, Nekrassova, Grushina, & Wahab, this volume, for a review of virtual communities).

Hate mongers use visual cues and diffuse textuality (icons, interactive videogames, chat rooms, music videos, and "informational educational sites" (Williamson & Pierson, 2003, p. 252), which deceptively cast the hate group's identity and motives into a positive light (as "pride" or "traditions") while deflecting their most vile claims and activities (e.g., cross burnings as "illuminations;" Waltman & Davis, 2005, p. 32, 35). Williamson and Pierson observed that the cyber-rhetors and users create and play interactive games with complete anonymity, situating children in "a diffuse hypertextual universe where stereotyping others is as natural as zapping 'niggers,' 'spics,' and 'Jews' who inhabit familiar video game formats" (see also Ryan, 2005). Furthermore, Waltman and Davis asserted that the humor and racist cartoons posted on Internet Web sites by white supremacists (Vanguard News Network, White Aryan Resistance Webpage and the Jim Crow Museum of Racist Memorabilia) justify symbolic ethnoviolence against racial and ethnic groups as a perverse form of superiority (see also Billig, 2001). Billig determined that the KKK's Web sites use the "just a joke" disclaimer to avoid social and cultural (i.e., egalitarian) sanctions against racist expressions as well as legal liability for hate crimes by consumers of their sites (to whom the Klan refers as the *real* racists). They do so by presenting black inferiority as a scientific "fact," dehumanizing blacks, using abusive and extreme racist slurs ("nigger jokes"), and caricatures and engaging in violent fantasies of lynching blacks, with laughter. Billig concluded that these jokes are "not just jokes," but meta-discourse designed to subvert restraints against racist violence (p. 286).

"Hateporn" (a cousin of cyberporn) promotes intolerance, bigotry, violence, and vengeance, argued Williamson and Pierson (2003), but it defies legal sanction given First Amendment freedom of speech laws, which coincide with the public's views of "symbolic hate" (Leets, 2001, p. 309; see also Goldberg, 1995) and, as Williamson and Pierson noted, postmodern ethics of tolerance. Williamson and Pierson contended that these circumstances make the researchers' task of disclosing hate and proposing a moral ethic to cope with postmodern racism difficult and imperative. Waltman (2003) maintained that few communication scholars examine hate rhetoric, but he implored them to decode hate messages, and begin fulfilling their antiracist mission called for by whiteness scholars (Moon & Flores, 2000; see Ignatiev & Garvey, 1996). After all, Waltman warned, the Klan's Web site states, "Youth today, leaders tomorrow" (p. 35).

Cultural (Re)Productions of White Superiority and Supremacy

Cultural studies communication scholars have exposed radical white absolutist narratives in contemporary popular music (Jackson, 2006; Yousman, 2003), films, and television shows (Gresson, 1995; Stratton, 2005; Tierney, 2006) that culturally reproduce white superiority in response to losing white supremacy. Yousman suggested that white suburban male and female youth culture's identification with and adoration of black brute representations is a form of white supremacy, albeit contradicted and coded. White youth culture's intense fascination and consumption of violent, hypermasculine (misogynistic, homophobic) representations of blacks in hip hop and gangsta rap music (or "blackophilia") is coupled with fear and dread of African Americans ("blackophobia"), which justifies white violence by white hate groups on their Web sites and music (p. 370, 379). However, most commonly, according to Yousman, consumers combine blackophilia and blackophobia, revealing a liminal white identity, caught between absolute white supremacy and the loss of "inherent" white power and privileges in the 21st century (p. 381).

To manage this crisis, according to Yousman (2003), white youth obsessively identify with cultural Others and consume "authentic" black cultural artifacts to assert their white superiority over nonwhites by economically controlling blackness (p. 375), producing "domestic Orientialism" (p. 378); that is, the gaze and possession of nonwhites' cultural artifacts; see Watts, 1997 as well as related discussion by Pal & Dutta, this volume). Such consumption produces an apolitical, privatized, individualistic consumerism ethos that resists collective challenges to institutional racism and affirmative action.

Tierney (2006) reported that three major films in 2003 (*Bulletproof Monk, Kill Bill,* and *The Last Samurai*) featured white protagonists who mastered Asian martial arts and demonstrated white superiority over Asians (i.e., pan-Asian ethnic ethnicities lumped together) by killing them. These films reproduced white absolutist Orientialism by showing whites (1) easily crossing boundaries to master martial arts skills at breakneck speed, (2) defeating multitudes of Asians as an Asian practitioner, (3) encountering Asian hostility, which is violently disavowed by an Asian cohort, and (4) developing and demonstrating their exemplary skills in the presence of a helpful Asian master who bestows weapons capable of great power on them (e.g., Samurai sword).

These film narratives mirror the white patriarchal colonial adventures found in mythic stories and museums of Western frontiersmen and cowboys who killed scores of Indians and become keepers of their vanishing (appropriated) sacred Native American artifacts and traditions, rendering the Indians worthless. The carnival-like violence in Western films and museums (e.g., Buffalo Bill's Wild West museum) works to justify the violence against Native Americans and the slaughter and exploitation of natural resources (e.g., bison) in terms of progress and implicitly privileges white masculinity (Dickinson et al., 2005). Do cultural artifacts that invoke white superiority over Asians reflect the West's self-image as a superior civilization or global anxieties about white/national economic supremacy? Do these conquering narratives portend conflict and war, and are Americans being enlisted as God's "chosen people" in a global version of Manifest Destiny to conquer foreign lands to restore our white/national global economic dominance and influence? What effects do they have on nonwhite global viewers? I raise these serious and important questions, but only more research and insightful interpretation will tell us what such popular culture artifacts mean, especially while the United States remains at war.

Stratton (2005) revealed that the "camp," or cult classic television show, *Buffy the Vampire Slayer*, inverts tribal storylines that still signify threat from nonwhites and the loss of white supremacy. Buffy, a tough Anglo American Jew (and her weak Jewish sidekick, Willow) confront and slay evil vampires and Nazis to save an all-white United States from a demonic Holocaust and racial apocalypse. The narrative structure justifies the fear of young white women and men who feel threatened by losing white supremacy due to Mexicans, Latinos, nonwhites, and transnational people migrating to California, legitimizing white people's aggression. Stratton argued that Buffy's apocalyptic story implicates anti-immigration and affirmative action Propositions in California during the 1990s, reflecting Anglo American backlash. Proposition initiatives or immigration politics have been an insightful and productive area of research for communication scholars that has exposed explicit forms of scapegoating, of Mexicans and Latinos in media discourse (Flores, 1996, 2003; Hasian & Delgado, 1998; Ono & Sloop, 2002; see also related arguments by del Rio, 2006), conflating whiteness with nationality through thinly veiled themes (e.g., taxes, affirmative action, less dependency, moral accountability; see Gabriel, 2000). According to Gabriel, these studies hold global implications because other countries (e.g., United Kingdom) look to the United States for models and patterns of immigration, affirmative action, community policing, and indicators of "race riots," but sadly, Gabriel found Old European fears and anxieties being played out in new ways in the United States.

Historical Studies of Whiteness

Rhetorical, feminist, and cultural studies scholars open new vistas of communication research and whiteness studies by examining historical documents and rhetorical materials (Murray, 1998), women's publications (Cramer, 2003), archival materials (Lipari, 2004), historical museums (Dickinson et al., 2005), journalistic discourse and media representations (del Rio, 2006; Flores, 2003; Shah, 1999), citizen discourse (e.g., letters to the editor; Lacy, 2007b; Steyn, 2004), popular films (B.R. McGee, 2000; see also Gresson, 2004; Projansky & Ono, 1999; Supriya, 1999), and performances (Murray, 1998). These scholars examine communication in contexts in which white absolutism or defenses for white supremacy were dominant or explicit, thereby contesting, reworking, and clarifying scholarly assumptions and conceptual issues such as (1) the role that everyday discourse and diffuse rhetorical texts play in forming oppressive ideologies and the complicity of ordinary citizens in committing atrocities and hate crimes; (2) the dualism between whites and nonwhites, revealing complex intersections and *intraracial* (white) competition that promotes white supremacy, and (3) the roots and origins of contemporary whiteness discourse, including implicit forms of whiteness, which are supposed to be now dominant.

Whiteness studies researchers do not examine "overt, identifiable and socially acknowledged forms of whiteness," asserted Shome (2000, p. 366), but instead, they attempt to capture the "invisible," "everyday," and systemic discursive practices (especially popular culture representations) that reproduce white privilege, primarily in postcolonial and post–Civil Rights contexts (p. 366; see also Nakayama & Krizek, 1995, as well as related arguments by Pal & Dutta, this volume). However, a new trend is developing. Communication scholars also examine historical and archival communication materials in contexts in which white supremacy was presumably explicit and dominant; by doing so, these scholars make new discoveries. For instance, after examining a variety of rhetorical texts from 1918 to 1941, Murray (1998, p. 43) concluded that "ordinary Germans" were neither all "coerced" victims or "willing executioners" of Europeans Jews, as leading historians have argued. "Ordinary Germans" became subjects constantly and continually constituted as ideal Nazis through rhetorical acts (propaganda, legislation, performances) that were invoked and occupied by citizens at critical moments over two decades to form a Nazi ideology, leading to atrocities and Holocaust. Such research challenges conventional historical knowledge about ordinary people and everyday discourse by examining diffuse rhetorical materials over time.

Critical race and whiteness scholars have found stable, dualistic representations of white and nonwhite representations that affirm white superiority by negating blackness (e.g., "black beasts," "white negroes" and "the black underclass"). However, Cramer (2003) suggested that 19th century white women missionary publications reflected ambivalence toward "native" women unseen in white patriarchal colonial discourse. They did so by constructing a morally superior Christian mission by saving African, Indian, Chinese, Japanese, Cuban, and Filipino women from "impurity" and "heathenism" (p. 215) while affirming "sisterhood" with indigenous women's shared destiny (for education, respect, honor, desegregation) against brute violence from their "ungodly husbands" (p. 219). Supriya (1999, p. 160) exposed a "synchronous white identity" (see also McCarthy, 1988) or a distinctive white identity and consciousness that operates on the periphery of Indian identity through expressions of sympathy, appreciation, and mystery of Indian gods and a young Indian doctor in *Passage to India*. I argue that these representations are more asymmetrical than ambivalent, but these researchers importantly invite us to interrogate strict dichotomous binaries of race and to explore the complex intersections of whiteness that are interwoven in representations.

In addition, communication researchers have found competing and antagonistic *intraracial* white identities that reinforce the dominance of white absolutism and white supremacy. For example, Gabriel (1998) asserted that Afrikaners have expressed a "subaltern whiteness" (p.184), in which they affirmed their white supremacy over blacks, coloureds, whites and Indians in South Africa based on their "mythic" national bloodlines and status as chosen people, while historically contending with a "white on white overlordship" by the British Empire (pp. 147-148). Furthermore, whiteness can be extinguished. Flores (2003) and Shah (1999) documented separately and respectively that Mexicans and Asian Indian immigrants in the early 20th century were legally considered "white," until they were perceived as a social, political, and economic threats culminating in legislation banning their immigration.

Historical studies of whiteness not only challenge our knowledge and conceptions about particular people, places, events, and cultural practices that constitute and reify whiteness everyday, but, as Wander et al. (1999) contended, they may expose the horrors of genocide that remain hidden (in Australia, New Zealand, the United States Midwest, for example) because of the ideological blinders formed by our words and thoughts.

New, Redemptive (Purified), and Innocent White Identity Studies

Communication scholars have described caricatures of white absolutism in popular films (Brinson, 1995; Gresson, 2004; Madison, 1999) and screen plays (Lipari, 2004), public trials (Williamson, 2002), media spectacles (Giroux, 2003), antiracist apologias (Gordon & Crenshaw, 2004; Marty, 1999), denials of racism by politicians (Crenshaw, 1997; Lacy, 2007a), citizen discourse (Lacy, 2007b), and everyday discourse (Moon, 1999). In these sites, whites offered radically new and innocent white identities from white racists through killing, trial, denial, and silence. "Antiracist white heroes" in popular films (e.g., *Mississippi Burning*) subverted, hunted, and killed white supremacists in the southern United States or South Africa to save blacks, nonwhites, and women in antiracist white hero films, thereby situating racism in the past while securing white privilege (Madison, 1999). Neoliberals used media spectacle to disavow Southern Dixie-style white racists while reinforcing rapacious forms of individualism, privatizations, and universal standards of colorblindness (Crenshaw, 1998; Giroux, 2003; Gresson, 2004).

White politicians, elites, and citizen critics have denied racism (by negating old white racists; Billig, 2001; Lacy, 2007b; van Dijk, 1992) and quibbled about the meaning of racism to deflect racist accusations and sanitize their personal and cultural histories of racism, while offering motives to maintain white racial privilege (Lacy, 2007a). Crenshaw (1997) argued that Senator Jesse Helms attempted to legally reinscribe the white patriarchal Confederacy and insignia into national heroic consciousness by remaining "strategically silent" about the institutional oppression of poor black female and male slaves at the hands of the Confederacy while offering patriotic images of white Southern "gentle elderly ladies" too benign to be racists (p. 258). Lipari (2004) found that Columbia Pictures executives omitted one-third of Lorraine Hansberry's award-winning screen play, *A Raisin in the Sun*, that dramatized the intersections of white privilege on black life in Southside Chicago, while featuring a *sole*, extreme white racist to reinforce white goodness, universal norms, and innocence, fulfilling the economic demands of white audiences at the box office. Williamson (2002) contended that a public trial that sentenced a perfect racist villain, William King, to death (and imprisoning two other white supremacists) for the dragging and killing of James Byrd offered whites in Jasper, Texas "perfect redemption," purging their ancestral ghosts of white lynching and terrorism of blacks throughout the South. According to Williamson, the "Dragging Trial" created a ritualistic space for whites and blacks to openly express prejudices and tolerance, but it also oversimplified racial progress and concealed the everyday racism experienced by blacks and produced images that white supremacists canonized as martyrdom on their Web sites.

Communication scholars argue that contemporary popular discourse offers metonymies or caricatures of old, white racists (typically Southern white racists using extreme racial epithets or violence, or "essentialist racism;" see Frankenberg, 1993, p. 193; see also Guillaumin, 1995), which oversimplify, reduce, and conceal the hegemonic force, intersections, and persistence of white supremacy. It does so by offering deterministic histories and cultural memories of racial progress. These narratives also conceal how white elites (many of whom are considered national cultural heroes produced modern racist arguments (West, 1982) with "civility," "hyperpoliteness" and decorum (Gould, 1981; Lacy, 1992; Moon, 1999; West, 1982). Indeed, Gould argued that Presidents Jefferson and Lincoln (before the success of the black troops in the Civil War) and Benjamin Franklin expressed soft-line racist attitudes about blacks. Gould concluded that the American Founding Fathers as well as other cultural heroes in the United States often showed a commitment to white supremacy, which is frequently ignored by scholars.

The narratives also undermine and appropriate the role that blacks and nonwhites play in their own emancipation and liberation. White media elites, neoconservatives, and black conservatives invoked cultural memories of white paternalism as a potent defense against affirmative action, reparations (Bacon, 2003) and atonement (Gresson, 2004).

CONCLUSION

This examination of a rhetorical body of scholarship exposed white absolutist discourse that glorifies and reifies white superiority, preys on heterosexual bodily fears, and blames nonwhites for societal problems. Such rhetoric goads white people to restore white masculine heterosexual power and usurp material possessions by committing horrifying acts of violence against nonwhite people. Such actions become the voice and practice of the oppressor. Communication scholars now believe that claims of white supremacy are more complex, feminine, ambivalent, implicit, presumptive, and antagonistic toward other white identities than initially conceived and, therefore, deserve more scholarly attention. Other scholars note a resurgence of white absolutism in new technologies, popular culture, and caricatures presented like curios from a time gone by. These instances merit more scholarly attention as well. Scholars from a variety of disciplines worry that, by centering and focusing on constructions of white racial identities, whiteness studies research produces narcissistic displays of white pain (Gresson, 2004; hooks, 1992; McIntosh, 2001; Moon & Flores, 2000; Shome, 2000), without showing how whiteness oppresses and affects nonwhite people (Projansky & Ono, 1999). Finally, this synthesis encourages communication scholars to examine other bodies of communication literature to expose constructions of white racial identities that are taken for granted and reproduce white power and privilege. Such an enterprise might show what whiteness is doing to us, so that we might eradicate it and set us free.

NOTE

1. Because racial names are socially constructed and ideologically formed and, therefore, a non-essential human category, I did not capitalize racial terms for people (e.g., "whites," or "blacks") throughout this chapter. Some critical race

scholars place quotation marks around the racial and ethnic terms, such as "whites" or "blacks," to make this point (see Essed & Goldberg, 2002; Jacobson, 1998).

REFERENCES

Allport, G. W. (1954). *The nature of prejudice.* Reading, MA: Addison-Wesley.

Asante, M. K. (1987). The *Afrocentric idea.* Philadelphia: Temple University Press.

Bacon, J. (2003). Reading the reparations debate. *Quarterly Journal of Speech, 89,* 171-195.

Banton, M. (1988). *Racial consciousness.* New York: Longman.

Billig, M. (2001). Humor and hatred: The racist jokes of the Ku Klux Klan. *Discourse and Society, 12,* 267-289.

Billig, M., Condor, S., Edwards, D., Gane, M., Middleton, D., & Radley, A. (1988). Prejudice and tolerance. In M. Billig (Ed.), *Ideological dilemmas: A social psychology of everyday thinking* (pp. 100-123). London: Sage.

Black, E. (1970). The second persona. *Quarterly Journal of Speech, 56,* 109-119.

Block, S. (2001). Rape and race in colonial newspapers, 1728-1776. *Journalism History, 27,* 147-155.

Bloomfield, M. (1964). Dixon's *The Leopard's Spots*: A study in popular racism. *American Quarterly, 16,* 387-401.

Bogle, D. (1996). *Toms, coons, mulattoes, mammies and bucks: An interpretive history of blacks in American film* (4th ed.). New York: Continuum.

Bosmajian, H. (1983). *Language of oppression.* Lanham, MD: University of American Press.

Braden, W. W. (1980). The rhetoric of a closed society. *Southern Speech Communication Journal, 45,* 332-351.

Brinson, S. L. (1995). The myth of white superiority in *Mississippi Burning. Southern Communication Journal, 60,* 211-221.

Burke, K. (1973). *Philosophy of literary form: Studies in symbolic action* (3rd ed.). Berkeley: University of California Press.

Burke, K. (1984). *Permanence and change: An anatomy of purpose* (3rd ed.). Berkeley: University of California Press.

Burgess, P. G. (1973). Crisis rhetoric: Coercion vs. force. *Quarterly Journal of Speech, 59,* 61-73.

Bytwerk, R. L. (2004). *Bending spines: The propagandas of Nazi Germany and the German Democratic Republic.* East Lansing: Michigan State University Press.

Calhoun, L. R. (2005). "Will the real Slim Shady please stand up?": Masking whiteness, encoding and hegemonic masculinity in Eminem's *Marshall Mathers LP. Howard Journal Communication, 16,* 267-294.

Campbell, M. (1974). Aristotle and black slavery: A study in race prejudice. *Race, Journal of Race and Group Relations, 15,* 283-298.

Carter, C. A. (1999). *Kenneth Burke and the scapegoat process.* Norman: University of Oklahoma Press.

Cash, W. J. (1941). *The mind of the South.* New York: Vintage-Knopf.

Clark, E. C. (1993). *The schoolhouse door: Segregation's last stand at the University of Alabama.* New York: Oxford University Press.

Cloud, D. (2004). "To the veil and threat of terror": Afghan women and the <clash of civilizations> in the imagery of the U.S. War on Terrorism. *Quarterly Journal of Speech, 90*, 285-306.

Collins, P. H. (1990). *Black feminist thought: Knowledge, consciousness and the politics of empowerment.* London: Unwin Hyman.

Cooks, L. (2003). Pedagogy, performance and positionality: Teaching whiteness in interracial communication. *Communication Education, 52*, 245-257.

Cooks, L. M., & Simpson, J. S. (2007). *Whiteness, pedagogy, and performance: Dis/placing race.* Lanham, MD: Rowman & Littlefield.

Crable, B. (2003). Symbolizing motion: Burke's dialectic and rhetoric of the body. *Rhetoric Review, 22*, 121-137.

Cramer, J. M. (2003). White womanhood and religion: Colonial discourse in the U.S. women's missionary press, 1869-1904. *The Howard Journal of Communication, 14*, 209-224.

Crenshaw, C. (1997). Resisting whiteness' rhetorical silence. *Western Journal of Communication, 61*, 253-278.

Crenshaw, C. (1998). Colorblind rhetoric. *The Southern Communication Journal, 63*, 244-256.

Delgado, R., & Stefancic, J. (1997). *Critical white studies: Looking behind the mirror.* Philadelphia: Temple University Press.

del Rio, E. (2006). The Latina/o problematic: Categories and questions in media communication research. In C. S. Beck (Ed.), *Communication yearbook 30* (pp. 387-430. Mahwah, NJ: Erlbaum.

Dickinson, G., Ott, B. L., & Aoki, E. (2005). Memory and myth at the Buffalo Bill museum. *Western Journal of Communication, 69*, 85-108.

Dixon, T. (1902). *The leopard's spots.* New York, Doubleday, Page, & Company.

Dyer, R. (1988). White. *Screen, 29*, 44-65.

Edelman, M. (1988). *Constructing the political spectacle.* Chicago: University of Chicago Press.

Edinger, E. F. (1999). *Archetypes of the apocalypse: Divine vengeance, terrorism and the end of the world.* Peru, IL: Open Court Publishing Co.

Ellul, J. (1964). *Propaganda: The formation of men's attitudes.* New York: A. A. Knopf.

Essed, P (1991). *Understanding everyday racism: An interdisciplinary theory.* London: Sage.

Essed, P., & Goldberg, D. T. (Eds.). (2002). *Race critical theories.* Malden, MA: Blackwell.

Fanon, F. (1967). *Black skins, white masks.* New York: Grove Press.

Fisher, W. (1970). A motive view of communication. *Quarterly Journal of Speech, 56*, 131-139.

Flores, L. A. (1996). Creating discursive space through a rhetoric of difference. *Quarterly Journal of Speech, 82*, 142-156.

Flores, L. A. (2003). Constructing rhetorical borders: Peons, illegal aliens, and competing narratives of illegal immigration. *Critical Studies in Media Communication, 20*, 362-387.

Frankenberg, R. (1993). *White women, race matters: The sociological construction of whiteness.* Minneapolis: University of Minnesota Press.

Frederickson, G. M. (1988). *The arrogance of race: Historical perspectives on slavery, racism and social inequality.* Middletown, CT: Wesleyan University Press.

Gabriel, J. (1998). *Whitewash: Racialized politics and the media.* London: Routledge.

Gabriel, J. (2000). On propositions, racism & democracy. *Discourse & Society, 11,* 570-572.

Gates, Jr., H. L. (Ed.). (1986). *"Race," writing and difference.* Chicago: University of Chicago Press.

Gibbs, J., Nekrassova, D., Grushina, S. & Wahab, S. (2008). Reconceptualizing virtual teaming from a constitutive perspective. In C. S. Beck (Ed.), *Communication yearbook 32* (pp. 187-229). New York: Routledge.

Gilman, S. L. (1986). Black bodies, white bodies: Toward an iconography of female sexuality in the late 19th-century art, medicine and literature. In H. L. Gates, Jr. (Ed.), *"Race," writing and difference* (pp. 223-261). Chicago: University of Chicago Press.

Gilman, S. L. (1991). *The Jew's body.* London: Routledge.

Gilmore, G. E. (1994). "One of the meanest books": Thomas Dixon, Jr. and the Leopard's Spots. *North Carolina Literary Review, 2,* 87-101

Gilroy, P. (1987). *There ain't no black in the Union Jack.* London: Hutchinson.

Giroux, H. A. (2003). Spectacles of race and pedagogies of denial: Anti-black racist pedagogy under the reign of neoliberalism. *Communication Education, 52,* 191-211.

Goldberg, D. T. (1993). *Racist culture: Philosophy and the politics of meaning.* Cambridge, MA: Blackwell.

Goldberg, D. T. (1995). Afterword: Hate, or power? In R. K. Whillock & D. Slayden (Eds.), *Hate speech* (pp. 122-141). Thousand Oaks, CA: Sage.

Gordon, D. B., & Crenshaw, C. (2004). Racial apologies. In P.A. Sullivan & S. R. Goldzwig (Eds.), *New approaches to rhetoric* (pp. 245-266). Thousand Oaks, CA: Sage.

Gould, S. J. (1981). *The mismeasure of man.* New York: W. W. Norton.

Gould, S. J. (1995). Mismeasure by any measure. In R. Jacoby & N. Glauberman (Eds.), *The bell curve debate: History, documents, opinions* (pp. 3-13). New York: Random House.

Grade, R. D. (1984). Origin of the 'Lost Cause' argument: Analysis of civil war letters. *Southern Speech Communication Journal, 49,* 420-430.

Gresson III, A. D. (1995). *The recovery of race in America.* Minneapolis: University of Minneapolis Press.

Gresson III, A. D. (2004). *America's racial atonement: Racial pain, recovery rhetoric, and the pedagogy of healing.* New York: Peter Lang.

Grey, S. H. (1999). The statistical war on equality: Visions of American virtuosity in *The Bell Curve. Quarterly Journal of Speech, 85,* 303-329.

Guillaumin, C. (1995). *Racism, sexism, power and ideology.* New York: Routledge.

Hall, S. (2003). The whites of their eyes: Racist ideologies and the mass media. In G. Dines & J. M. Humez (Eds.), *Gender, race & class in media* (2nd ed., pp. 89-93). London: Sage.

Hart, R. P. (1976). Absolutism and situation: *Prolegomena* to a rhetorical biography of Richard M. Nixon. *Communication Monographs, 43,* 204-228.

Hart, R. P. (1984). The function of human communication in the maintenance of public values. In C. A. Arnold & J. W. Bowers (Eds.), *Handbook of rhetorical and communication theory* (pp. 249-261). Boston: Allyn & Bacon.

Hart, R. P. (1997). *Modern rhetorical criticism.* Needham, Heights, MA: Allyn & Bacon.

Hasian Jr., M., & Delgado, F. (1998). The trials and tribulations of racialized critical rhetorical theory: Understanding the rhetorical ambiguities of Proposition 187. *Communication Theory, 83,* 245-270.

Hernstein, R. J., & Murray, C. (1994). *The bell curve: Intelligence and class structure in American life.* New York: The Free Press.

Hillbruner, A. (1960). Inequality, the great chain of being, and ante-bellum Southern oratory. *Southern Speech Communication Journal, 25,* 172-189.

Hoffer, E. (1951). *The true believer: Thoughts on the nature of mass movements.* New York: Harper & Row.

hooks, b. (1981). *Ain't I a woman: Black women and feminism.* Boston: South End Press.

hooks, b. (1992). *Black looks: Race and representation.* Boston: South End Press.

Hope, D. S. (1975). Redefinition of self: A comparison of the rhetoric of the women's liberation and black liberation movements. *Today's Speech, 23,* 17-25.

Houston, M. (2002). Seeking difference: African Americans in interpersonal communication research, 1975-2000. *Howard Journal of Communications, 13,* 25-41.

Ignatiev, N. (1995). *How the Irish became white.* New York: Routledge.

Ignatiev, N. & Garvey, J. (1996). *Race traitor.* New York: Routledge.

Innis, C. (1994). Virgin territories and motherlands: Colonial and nationalist representations of Africa and Ireland. *Feminist Review, 47,* 1-14.

Jackson, R. L. (1999a). *The negotiation of cultural identity: Perceptions of European and African Americans.* Westport, CT: Praeger.

Jackson, R. L. (1999b). White space, white privilege: Mapping discursive inquires into self. *Quarterly Journal of Speech, 85,* 38-54.

Jackson, R. L. (2006). *Scripting the black masculine body: Identity, discourse and racial politics in popular media.* Albany: State University of New York Press.

Jacobson, M. F. (1998). *Whiteness of a different color: European immigrants and the alchemy of race.* Cambridge, MA: Harvard University Press.

Jacoby, R., & Glauberman, N. (1995). *The bell curve debate: History, documents, and opinions.* New York: Time Book.

Jamieson, K. (1976). The rhetorical manifestation of *Weltanschauung. Central States Speech Journal, 27,* 4-14.

Jamieson, K. H. (1992). *Dirty politics: Deception, distraction and democracy.* New York: Oxford University Press.

Jensen, R. (2005). *The heart of whiteness: Confronting race, racism and white privilege.* San Francisco: City Lights Publishers.

Keränen, L., & Sanprie, V. (2008). "Oxygen of publicity" and "lifeblood of liberty:" Communication scholarship on mass media coverage of terrorism for the twenty-first century. In C. S. Beck (Ed.), *Communication yearbook 32* (pp. 231-275). New York: Routledge.

Kinney, J. (1982). The rhetoric of racism: Thomas Dixon and the "damned black beast." *American Literary Realism, 1870-1910, 15,* 145-154.

Lacy, M. G. (1992). *Toward a conception of civil racism.* Unpublished doctoral dissertation, University of Texas, Austin.

Lacy, M. G. (2007a). *Clown hero: A mythic analysis of David Duke's battle.* Manuscript submitted for publication.

Lacy, M. G. (2007b). *Modern antiblack myths in post Civil Rights citizen discourse, the progressive era (1974-1988).* Manuscript submitted for publication.

Lake, R. (1991). Between myth and history: Enacting time in Native American protest rhetoric. *Quarterly Journal of Speech, 77,* 123-132.

Lee, G. (1996). *Troubadours, trumpeters, trouble makers: Lyricism, nationalism and hybridity in China and its others.* Durham, NC: Duke University Press.

Lee, M. J. (2006). The populist chameleon: The people's party, Huey Long, George Wallace, and the populist argumentative frame. *Quarterly Journal of Speech, 92,* 355-378.

Lee, W. (1999). One whiteness veils three uglinesses: From border crossing to a womanist interrogation of gendered colorism. In T. K. Nakayama & J. N. Martin (Eds.), *Whiteness: The communication of social identity* (pp. 279-298). Thousand Oaks, CA: Sage.

Leets, L. (2001). Response to internet hate sites: Is free speech too free in cyberspace. *Communication Law & Public Policy, 6,* 287-316.

Lipari, L. (2004). "Fearful of the written word": White fear, black writing, and Lorraine Hansberry's *A Raisin in the Sun* screenplay. *Quarterly Journal of Speech, 90,* 81-102.

Logue, C. (1976). Rhetorical ridicule of reconstruction blacks. *Quarterly Journal of Speech, 62,* 400-409.

Lovejoy, A. (1957). *The great chain of being: A study of the history of ideas.* Cambridge, MA: Harvard University Press. (Original work published 1936)

Madison, K. J. (1999). Legitimation crisis and containment: The "anti-racist-white-hero" film. *Critical Studies in Mass Communication, 16,* 399-416.

Marty, D. (1999). White antiracist rhetoric as apologia: Wendell Berry's *The Hidden Wound.* In T. K. Nakayama & J. N. Martin (Eds.), *Whiteness: The communication of social identity* (pp. 51-68). Thousand Oaks, CA: Sage.

Mattingly, D. (2003, December 16). Strom Thurmond's family confirms paternity claim. CNN Washington Bureau. CNN.com, December 16, 20. Retrieved on November 10, 2007, from http://www.cnn.com/2003/US/12/15/thurmond.paternity

McCarthy, C. (1988). Rethinking liberal and radical perspectives on racial inequality in schooling: Making the case for nonsynchrony. *Harvard Education Review, 58,* 265-279.

McGary, H. (2002). Reflections on a genealogy of modern racism. In P. Essed & D. T. Goldberg (Eds.), *Race critical theories* (pp. 433-436). Malden, MA: Blackwell.

McGee, B. R. (2000). Thomas Dixon's *The Clansman*: Radical, reactionaries, and the anticipated utopia. *Southern Communication Journal, 65,* 300-317.

McGee, M. (1975). In search of "the people": A rhetorical alternative. *Quarterly Journal of Speech, 61,* 235-49.

McGuire, M. (1977). Mythic rhetoric in *Mein Kampf*: A structuralist critique. *Quarterly Journal of Speech, 63,* 1-13.

McIntosh, P. (2001). White privilege: Unpacking the invisible knapsack. In P. S. Rothenberg (Ed.), *Race, class, and gender in the United States: An integrated study* (5th ed., pp. 163-167). New York: Worth Publishers.

McPhail, M. (1996). Race and sex in black and white: Essence and ideology in the Spike Lee discourse. *Howard Journal of Communications, 7*, 127-138.

McPhail, M. (2002). *The rhetoric of race revisited: Reparations or segregation?* Lanham, MD: Rowman & Littlefield.

Middleton, J. I. (2004). "Both print and oral" and "talking about race:" Transforming Toni Morrison's language issues into teaching issues. In E. B. Richardson & R. L. Jackson (Eds.), *African American rhetoric(s): Interdisciplinary perspectives* (pp. 242-258). Carbondale: Southern Illinois University Press.

Miles, R. (1989). *Racism.* London: Routledge.

Montagu, A. (1997). *Man's most dangerous myth: The fallacy of race* (6th ed.). Walnut Creek, CA: Alta Mira Press.

Moon, D. (1999). White enculturation in bourgeois ideology: The discursive production of "good (white) girls." In T. K. Nakayama & J. N. Martin (Eds.), *Whiteness: The communication of social identity* (pp. 177-197). Thousand Oaks, CA: Sage.

Moon, D., & Flores, L. (2000). Antiracism and the abolition of whiteness: Rhetorical strategies of domination among "race traitors." *Communication Studies, 51,* 97-115.

Moon, D., & Nakayama, T. K. (2005). Strategic social identities and judgments: A murder in Appalachia. *Howard Journal of Communications, 12,* 87-107.

Morris, R., & Wander, P. (1990). Native American rhetoric: Dancing in the shadows of the ghost dance. *Quarterly Journal of Speech, 76,* 154-191.

Morrison, T. (1989). Unspeakable things unspoken: The Afro American presence in American literature. *Michigan Quarterly Review, 28,* 1-34.

Murray, J. W. (1998). Constructing the ordinary: The dialectical development of Nazi ideology. *Quarterly Journal of Speech, 46,* 41-59.

Myrdal, G. (1962). *An American dilemma: The Negro problem and Negro democracy.* New York: Harper & Row. (Original work published 1944)

Nakanishi, D. (1988). Seeking convergence in race relations research. In P. A. Katz & D. A. Taylor (Eds.) *Eliminating racism: profiles in controversy* (pp. 159-180). New York: Plenum Press.

Nakayama, T. K., & Krizek, R. L. (1995). Whiteness: A strategic rhetoric. *Quarterly Journal of Speech, 81,* 291-309.

Ono, K. A., & Sloop, J. M (2002). *Shifting borders: Rhetoric, immigration and California's Proposition 187.* Philadelphia: Temple University Press.

Orbe, M. P., & Strother, K. E. (1996). Signifying the tragic mulatto: A semiotic analysis of Alex Haley's *Queen. The Howard Journal of Communications, 7,* 113-126.

O'Sullivan, J. L. (1845). Annexation. *United States Magazine and Democratic Review, 17,* 5-10.

Pal, M., & Dutta, M. J. (2008). Theorizing resistance in a global context: Processes, strategies, and tactics in communication scholarship. In C. S. Beck (Ed.), *Communication yearbook 32* (pp. 41-87). New York: Routledge.

Pease, D. E. (2003). Ralph Ellison and Kenneth Burke: The nonsymbolizable (trans) action. *boundary, 2,* 65-96.

Perry, S. (1983). Rhetorical functions of the infestation metaphor in Hitler's rhetoric. *Central States Speech Journal, 34,* 229-235.

Pieterse, J. N. (1992). *White on black: Images of Africa and blacks in Western popular culture.* New Haven, CT: Yale University Press.

Pinar, W. (2001). *The gender of racial politics and violence in America: Lynching, prison rape and the crisis of masculinity.* New York: Peter Lang.

Projansky, S., & Ono, K. A. (1999). Strategic whiteness as cinematic racial politics. In T. K. Nakayama & J. N. Martin (Eds.), *Whiteness: The communication of social identity* (pp. 149-174). Thousand Oaks, CA: Sage.

Ramsey, M. E., Achter, P. J., & Condit, C. M. (2001). Genetics, race, and crime: An audience study exploring *The Bell Curve* and book reviews. *Critical Studies in Media Communication, 18,* 1-22.

Riggs, M. T. (Producer and Director), & Salmon, K. (Associate Producer) (1987). *Ethnic notions* [documentary]. San Francisco: California Newsreel.

Rockler, N. R. (2002). Race, whiteness, "lightness," and relevance: African American and European interpretations of *Jump Start* and *The Boondocks. Critical Studies in Media Communication, 19,* 398-418.

Roediger, D. R. (1991). *The wages of whiteness: Race and the making of the American working class.* New York: Routledge.

Roediger, D. R. (1994). *Towards the abolition of whiteness: Essays on race, politics, and working class history.* New York: Routledge.

Roy, A., & Rowland, R. C. (2003). The rhetoric of Hindu nationalism: A narrative of mythic redefinition. *Western Journal of Communication, 67,* 225-248.

Rueckert, W. H. (1982). *Kenneth Burke and the drama of human relations* (2nd ed.). Berkeley: University of California Press.

Ryan, K. (2005). "Humans vs. Orcs": A semiotic analysis of race in massively multiplayer online role-playing games. *Journal of Intergroup Relations, 32,* 29-39.

Said, E. (1978). *Orientalism.* New York: Vintage Press.

Said, E. (1993). Commentary. In S. Jhally (Producer and Director), *On Orientialism* [documentary]. Northhampton, MA: Media Education Foundation.

Shah, H. (1999). Race, nation and citizenship: Asian Indians and the idea of whiteness in the U.S. press, 1906-1923. *Howard Journal of Communication, 10,* 249-267.

Shome, R. (1996). Race and popular cinema: The rhetorical strategies of whiteness in *City of Joy. Communication Quarterly, 4,* 502-518.

Shome, R. (1999). Whiteness and the politics of location: Postcolonial reflection. In T. K. Nakayama & J.N. Martin (Eds.), *Whiteness: The communication of social identity* (pp. 107-128). Thousand Oaks, CA: Sage.

Shome, R. (2000). Outing whiteness. *Critical Studies in Media Communication, 17,* 366-371.

Shufeldt, R. W. (1907). *The Negro a menace to American civilization.* Boston: R. G. Badger.

Smedley, A. (1993). *Race in North America: Origin and evolution of a worldview.* Boulder, CO: Westview Press.

Spickard, P. R. (1992). The illogic of American racial categories. In M. P. P. Root (Ed.), *Racially mixed people in America* (pp. 12-23). Newbury Park, CA: Sage.

Stratton, J. (2005). *Buffy the Vampire Slayer*: What being Jewish has to do with it. *Television & New Media, 6,* 176-199.

Steyn, M. E. (2004). Rehabilitating a whiteness disgraced: Afrikaner white talk in post-Apartheid South Africa. *Communication Quarterly, 52,* 143-169.

Stoler, A. L. (1995). *Race and the education of desire: Foucault's History of Sexuality and the colonial order of things.* Durham, NC: Duke University Press.

Sullivan, P. A. & Goldzwig, S. R. (2004). Autobiography, rhetoric, and Frank McCourt's *Angela's Ashes* and *Tis: A Memoir*. In P. A. Sullivan & S. R. Goldzwig (Eds.) *New approaches to rhetoric* (pp. 267-291). Thousand Oaks, CA: Sage.

Supriya, K. E. (1999). White difference: Cultural constructions of white identity. In T. K. Nakayama & J. N. Martin (Eds.), *Whiteness: The communication of social identity* (pp.149-174). Thousand Oaks, CA: Sage.

Takaki, R. (1993). *Iron cages: Race and culture in 19th century America*. New York: Oxford University Press.

Tierney, S. M. (2006). Themes of whiteness in *Bulletproof Monk, Kill Bill,* and *The Last Samurai*. *Journal of Communication, 56*, 607-624.

Tierney, S., & Jackson, R.L. (2003). Deconstructing whiteness ideology as a set of rhetorical fantasy themes: Implications for interracial alliance building in the United States. In M. J. Collier (Ed.), *International and Intercultural Communication Annual, 2002: Intercultural alliances: Critical transformation* (pp. 81-106). Thousand Oaks, CA: Sage.

Toch, H. H., Deutsch, S. E., & Wilkens, D. M. (1960). The wrath of the bigot: An analysis of protest mail. *Journalism Quarterly, 37*, 173-185.

Toyosaki, S. (2007, March/April). *"I am a recovering client": Autoethnographic metatherapy*. Paper presented at the annual meeting of the Central States Communication Association, Minneapolis, MN.

Trank, D. M. (1970). The Negro and the Mormons: A church in conflict. *Western States Speech Journal, 35*, 220-230.

Trimble, J. E. (1988). Stereotypical images, American Indians, and prejudice. In P. A. Katz & D. A. Taylor (Eds.), *Eliminating racism: profiles in controversy* (pp. 181-202). New York: Plenum Press.

Turner, R. F. (Ed.). (2001). *Jefferson-Hemings Scholars Commission Report on the Jefferson-Hemings matter.* Monticello, VA: Thomas Jefferson Heritage Society.

van Dijk, T. A. (1992). Discourse and the denial of racism. *Discourse & Society, 3*, 87-118.

Waltman, M. S. (2003). Stratagems for heuristics in the recruitment of children into communities of hate: The fabric of our future. *Southern Communication Journal, 69*, 22-36.

Waltman, M. S., & Davis, J. (2004). Deadly humor: How racist cartoons further the ideology of hate and create a symbolic code for ethnoviolence. *Journal of Intergroup Relations, 31*, 3-23.

Waltman, M. S., & Davis, J. (2005). How to be a proper racist: Mythic representations in *The Turner Diaries*. *Journal of Intergroup Relations, 32*, 19-39.

Wander, P. C. (1972). The savage child: The image of the Negro in the pro-slavery movement. *Southern Speech Communication Journal, 37*, 335-360.

Wander, P., Nakayama, T., & Martin, J. (1999). Whiteness and beyond: Sociohistorical foundations of whiteness and contemporary challenges. In T. K. Nakayama & J. N. Martin (Eds.), *Whiteness: The communication of social identity* (pp. 13-26). Beverly Hills, CA: Sage.

Warren, J. T. (2001). Doing whiteness: On performative dimensions of race in the classroom. *Communication Education, 50*, 91-108.

Watts, E. K. (1997). An exploration of spectacular consumption: Gangsta rap as a cultural commodity. *Communication Studies, 48*, 42-58.

Watts, E. K. (2005). Border patrolling and "passing" in Eminem's *8 Mile*. *Critical Studies in Media Communication, 22*, 187-206.

West, C. (1982). *Prophesy deliverance! Toward an Afro American Christianity.* Philadelphia: Westminster Press.

Whillock, D. E. (1995). Symbolism and the representation of hate in visual discourse In R. K. Whillock & D. Slayden (Eds.), *Hate speech* (pp. 122-141). Thousand Oaks, CA: Sage.

Whillock, R. K. (1995). The use of hate as a stratagem for achieving political and social goals. In R. K. Whillock & D. Slayden (Eds.), *Hate speech* (pp. 28-54). Thousand Oaks, CA: Sage.

Wilhelm, S. M. (1980). A little white lie: Institutional divisions of labour and Life. *Contemporary Sociology, 9*, 90-91.

Williamson, L. (2002). Racism, tolerance and perfected redemption: A rhetorical critique of the Dragging Trial. *Southern Communication Journal, 67*, 245-258.

Williamson, L., & Pierson, E. (2003). The rhetoric of hate on the Internet: Hateporn's challenge to modern media ethics. *Journal of Mass Media Ethics, 18*, 250-267.

Wilson, K. H. (2002). *The reconstruction desegregation debate: The politics of equality and the rhetoric of place, 1870-1875.* East Lansing: Michigan State University Press.

Young, L. (1996). *Fear of the dark: 'Race', gender and sexuality in the cinema.* London: Routledge.

Yousman, B. (2003). Blackophilia and blackophobia: White youth, the consumption of rap music, and white supremacy. *Communication Theory, 13*, 366-391.

CHAPTER CONTENTS

8 Mapping Media Literacy

Key Concepts and Future Directions

Judith E. Rosenbaum
Albany State University

Johannes W. J. Beentjes
Radboud University Nijmegen

Ruben P. Konig
Radboud University Nijmegen

This chapter examines how different researchers define media literacy (i.e., what people need to know about the media and their use to be deemed media literate). As opposed to previous reviews, this chapter attempts to structure the multitude of definitions using a schematic representation of media production and use. Such a construction provides a thematic overview of diverse definitions of media literacy. Thus, it specifies key aspects of the media and their use in terms of media literacy and corresponding emphasis in the media literacy literature. This analysis reveals that the vast majority of researchers consider understanding how media content is created to be a central aspect of media literacy. Scholars treat the ability to handle the media in a constructive manner as far less important, and the media literacy literature virtually ignores the fact that media producers are prone to media influence. Furthermore, this chapter indicates that little has changed in the field of media literacy in the last few decades, with the majority of the dimensions of media literacy present in definitions utilized in the 1970s and 1980s. Finally, this chapter also identifies the features of media literacy that require additional investigation, such as the relationship between media literacy and Internet-based technologies.

Correspondence: Judith E. Rosenbaum, Department of English, Modern Languages, and Mass Communication, Albany State University, 504 College Drive, Albany, GA 31705; Phone: 229-430-3684; E-mail: rosenbaumjudith@gmail.com

INTRODUCTION

I f everyday life is a play, then the media are the lead actors. They remain on stage in virtually every act. If people are not actually reading newspapers, listening to the radio, or watching television, they can often be found talking about what they have seen in movies, thinking about what they read in a magazine, or using the knowledge acquired through the media in some other way. This play, however, is not staged by the lead actors only; notably, the media are not in complete control of people's daily lives. Among numerous other actors, media literacy plays opposite the media. Some people "read" the media in a more knowledgeable and critical way (i.e., they are more media literate and, thus, better equipped to deal with the media).

Owing to the large role that the media play in people's daily lives, an enormous diversity of definitions of media literacy exist. Large numbers of scholars have been creating a wide variety of definitions since the 1970s. Because of the size and scope of media literacy scholarship, we should not underestimate the importance of a well-structured and thorough overview. Various scholars have already created overviews that summarize some of the ideas about media literacy, and we discuss those reviews in more detail below. However, while acknowledging that those works do provide interesting and valuable insights into the current ideas held by media literacy scholars, they fall short in one respect. Most reviews merely list who defined media literacy in which way. They concentrate on either a historical account of definitions (e.g., Buckingham, 1998), a description of media curricula (e.g., Bazalgette, Bevort, & Savino, 1992; J. A. Brown, 1991, 1998), or a listing of how researchers have conceptualized media literacy in different countries (e.g., Hart, 1998; Piette & Giroux, 1997). As a result, they do not create a structured view of the field, comparing the various aspects that diverse definitions touch upon and pointing out the possible bias within current definitions of media literacy.

In this chapter, we structure the multitude of opinions about the concept of media literacy according to topical themes. We list who said what about media literacy but, more importantly, we highlight the dominant themes in the media literacy arena. Additionally, we illuminate which areas of the media and their usage receive less attention and which could, thus, be further elaborated. To attain this goal, we utilize a schematic representation of media use and media production to organize what has been written about the concept of media literacy so far. This schematic representation enables us to answer the question—How is media literacy defined? Furthermore, it allows for a description of how the definitions relate to media production and use. In the creation of this review, we decided that each aspect of media literacy had to be mentioned and explicated by at least one publication from a peer-reviewed source.

Within the field of media literacy, we discovered some variation in research depending on three factors—the genre, the medium (i.e., "old" [newspaper, television, and film] or "new" [the Internet]), and the country from which the research originated. This chapter provides insight into whether these differences also lead to diverse approaches to what media literacy should entail. Furthermore, in the past, various researchers have defined so-called key concepts; that is, they presented a list of abilities, skills, or knowledge that they deemed to be the essential aspects of media literacy. Examples of such key concepts include the principles of media education put forward by the British Film Institute in the 1980s (Bazalgette, 1992), the definition of media literacy as advanced during the National Leadership Conference on Media Literacy (Aufderheide, 1997), the principles advocated by the Center for Media Literacy (Thoman, 1999), the theory of media literacy developed by Potter (2004), and, finally, the framework for media literacy recently developed by Primack et al. (2006). This chapter explicates how these key concepts fit into the schematic representation of media literacy.

To collect relevant literature, we searched the databases ERIC and PsycInfo as well as the Social Sciences Citation Index and Communication Abstracts, using the key words "media education" and "media literacy." We conducted these searches at regular intervals between March, 2002, and March, 2007. In addition, we selected relevant literature using the reference lists of articles in the database search. Although each search revealed new contributions to the field of media literacy, after a few years, it became apparent that new contributions generally added little in terms of new insights into what media literacy should entail and that the four databases showed significant overlap, not only in terms of articles but also insights and perspectives on media literacy. Most of the differences between authors tended to arise from a focus on different genres, media, or countries. This chapter describes aspects of media literacy that most authors agree on, as well as those areas that only a few authors deem important. Thus, we incorporate definitions from a wide variety of media and genres as well as ones that originated outside the United States and the United Kingdom, the two leading countries regarding media literacy.

ROOTS OF MEDIA LITERACY AND MEDIA EDUCATION

The field of media literacy is rich and multi-facetted, a feat that will become apparent through this overview. In part, the richness of the field can be attributed to the fact that media literacy has taken root in many different areas, ranging from different scholarly perspectives to individual media practitioners and users. Before we expand on how media literacy has been defined, we discuss the different areas that contribute to the media literacy arena.

Media literacy comprises an important concept from the field of communication that has made the transition into societal discussions. For instance, when discussing the harmful effects of watching R&B videos or playing violent computer games, most people assume that not everyone is media literate enough to handle the messages of sex and violence supposedly mediated through these videos and games. Additionally, when pressure groups try to ban the *Harry Potter* books because of their alleged occult content, they assume that children are not capable of distinguishing between fact and fiction and will, therefore, not be able to judge these books on their own merits and, as a result, go religiously astray. Moreover, parents provide their offspring with a form of media education when they explain why their children cannot watch certain television programs, play specific video games, or read certain books (Means Coleman & Fisherkeller, 2003).

Many people feel, however, that media education is not solely the responsibility of the parents. Proponents argue that professional educators bear some responsibility in this respect as well. Encouraging critical thinking is one of the main aims of education (e.g., Anderson & Ploghoft, 1980; Buckingham, 1993, 2003; Feuerstein, 1999; Thoman, 1999). Hence, advocates stress that schools should endeavor to make their pupils more media literate, to teach them about the production of media messages, media use, and the influence the media may exert on themselves, others, and society (e.g., Bazalgette, 1992; Buckingham & Sefton-Green, 1997; Hobbs, 1998a; Thoman, 1999).

Thus, not surprisingly, the concept of media literacy actually originated in the field of education before communication scholars began their own investigations. Schools, as early as the 1960s (e.g., Hall & Whannel, 1964; Murdock & Phelps, 1973), were concerned with teaching students about the media. Even today, media literacy remains a grassroots concept with schools and other educational settings constantly supplying new initiatives and ideas that enrich the field of media literacy (e.g., Fox, 1995; Gaudard & Theveniaut, 1992; Maness, 2004). When it comes to promoting critical thinking regarding the media or related issues, education plays a primary role. Educators have the privilege of sometimes being the first to introduce children to a new perspective on the media. They can play an important part not only in how children perceive media content such as commercials or violent fiction programs (e.g., Lloyd-Kolkin, Wheeler, & Strand, 1980; Vooijs & van der Voort, 1990) but also in how children use their leisure time (Kline, 2005), feel empowered enough to create their own media content (e.g., D. Lemish & P. Lemish, 1997), or try and influence media stations or networks (e.g., Hobbs, 2005a). Emphasizing the importance of education for media literacy, Dennis (2004) lamented the fact that so little media education opportunities exist for adults and argued that continuing education remains paramount to creating critical media users. The importance of media education also became apparent in Potter's (2004) study of media literacy. Here, Potter observed that "personal locus," or a person's ability to control the media and mindfulness when using the media, is the most important factor when explaining the degree to which a person is media literate. From this perspective, media literacy involves more than just knowledge or skills; it is a state of mind that requires continuous monitoring. Although Potter thus shifted the responsibility of critical media use to the user, he still supported the idea that media education programs are essential when it comes to increasing people's control and mindfulness.

The general concern with media literacy extends beyond the field of education. For several decades now, media literacy has attracted the attention of communication researchers throughout the Western world (e.g., Alvarado & Boyd-Barrett, 1992; Aufderheide, 1997; Court & Criticos, 1998; Masterman, 1983; Quin, 2003; Tufte, 1992). These scholars have focused on defining and measuring media literacy as well as developing media education programs. While doing so, they raised topics such as media production, media effects, and the interpretation of media content. Thus, media education programs play a role in the dispersion of scientific knowledge about the media across society, and the measurement of media literacy shows the extent to which efforts to disperse this knowledge have met with success. Media literacy research reveals the societal relevance of our efforts as communication researchers to come to grips with the myriad aspects of media and communication.

Media literacy implies a critical attitude toward the media, one that is functional in many ways for media literate media consumers and their society. In that respect, media literacy has attained relevance far beyond the field of media literacy and media education studies. For instance, health communication research has revealed that the media play a role in obesity and smoking, while studies into media literacy and health-related issues have shown that media literacy can have a curbing influence on unhealthy attitudes or behaviors (J. D. Brown, 2006). Further, several projects found that media education can play a positive role in reducing the attitudes that could lead to eating disorders (Irving & Berel, 2001; Wilksch, Tiggeman, & Wade, 2006). Moreover, media literate "couch potatoes" are better able to recognize media habits that may lead to obesity; hence, media literacy could decrease the risk of obesity (Kline, 2005). Similarly, more media literate teenagers are better equipped to resist luring images of smoking heroes (Primack et al., 2006).

Another example of the possibly beneficiary functions of being media literate concerns media and politics. The media play a crucial role in the political processes of Western democracies; both voters and politicians depend on the media. However, according to various political communication scholars (Entman, 1989; Keane, 1991), the media serve their own goals, and those goals are not necessarily compatible with democracy's needs, as quality reporting on current events and political developments may not always lead to the high ratings or the large circulation needed by viable media. A media literate populace and a media literate politician are aware of such potential clashes of interests and may, thus, critically circumvent the potential political pitfalls presented by their dependency on the media (Brookfield, 1987; Covington, 2004).

Beyond health and politics, intercultural communication constitutes another area in which media literacy benefits media users. Communication between and within cultures is easily hampered by stereotypes, and those stereotypes may inadvertently be propagated by the media because people rely on the media for their information about other sub-cultures (Ball-Rokeach & DeFleur, 1976; Van Dijk, 1987; see related arguments by del Río, 2006; Keränen & Sanprie, this volume; Lacy, this volume; Pal & Dutta, this volume). Furthermore, communicators always bring their own cultural knowledge—including their prejudices—when they create meanings. Subsequently, this cultural knowledge influences the way in which they "decode" or "encode" the messages that they exchange (see Fiske & Taylor, 1991; Hall, 1980; Lind, 1996). A critical awareness of such intercultural bias in communication dampens the possible detrimental consequences for intercultural communication (e.g., Vargas, 2006).

In short, a large number of diverse scholarly areas have contributed to (and been impacted by) the concept of media literacy. We now expand on how media literacy has been defined over the last few decades and across numerous academic arenas.

MAPPING THE FIELD

Media literacy centers on knowing how stakeholders construct and receive media messages. A quick glance at any of the major contributions to the field of media literacy will confirm this statement (e.g., Bazalgette, 1992; Thoman, 1999). In spite of the large numbers of different definitions of media literacy, all agree on one fact: Media literacy entails an awareness of one or more aspects of the use and production of media messages. Therefore, the best way to structure the wide variety of definitions entails creating a schematic representation of media production and use in which all of these definitions can be classified.

Although the processes of media production and use have been conceptualized in diverse ways, all of these conceptualizations include three players—the producer, the user, and the media (e.g., McQuail, 2000). Therefore, these three participants comprise the central elements of the schematic representation used in this literature review. The "producer" refers to any individual who is involved in the creation of media products, while the "user" refers to any individual using the media. These two elements interact with the media through four different processes, signified by four arrows in Figure 8.1.

The first arrow in the schematic representation refers to how the media influence a producer. It focuses on the manner in which the media can influence the producer's ideas about media production. The second arrow, which runs from the producer to the media, indicates those processes through which stakeholders construct media content. The third arrow denotes how the media influence a media user. Finally, the fourth arrow centers on how people handle the media. When using this schematic representation as a starting point, media literacy can be conceptualized as an understanding of these four arrows, or dimensions, of media production and use.

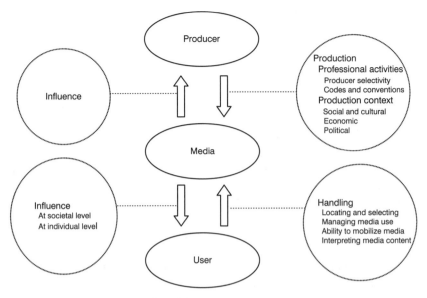

Figure 8.1 Aspects of Media Literacy

LITERATURE OVERVIEW: ASPECTS OF MEDIA LITERACY

In this section of the chapter, we organize diverse conceptualizations of media literacy by connecting them to the arrows of the schematic representation of media literacy delineated in Figure 8.1. For a complete overview of all articles and books considered in this chapter and categorized within the schematic representation, see Appendix 1. It specifies which authors mentioned which aspects of media literacy.

Media Influence on Producers

We begin by exploring media influence on the producers of media content. Media producers not only craft the media but use them, both as professionals and as private individuals, and they can, thus, be affected by the content and style of media representations. For example, a television news producer might see a breaking story on another news channel and consider running the same story. Further, the makeover of a television station could give the producers of another one ideas about how to alter the image of their own station.

Although it is relevant for media users to be aware of this influence, only one author fleetingly refers to it when she described media literacy as including the ability to recognize the complex nature of authorship (Quin, 2003). The notion that media producers themselves also use and are, thus, influenced by other media content appears to be ignored in the field of media literacy.

Researchers do not generally describe producers as anything other than people who construct messages in a certain context. We expand on this important issue in the next section.

Production of Media Content

The schematic representation in Figure 8.1 also depicts media content as a construction. As detailed below, media literacy literature indicates that the way in which producers create media content results from two factors—professional activities and production context. Although most authors discuss either one or both of these factors, some focus solely on the concept of construction in its entirety.

Generally, researchers argue that awareness of the constructed nature of media content is essential to a valid evaluation of media content. Bazalgette (1992), in his description of the key aspects of media education that have been widely adopted across the United Kingdom, noted that media education includes teaching that media content does not mirror reality but, instead, that the media create their own version of reality. During the National Leadership Conference on Media Literacy, scholars from around the world agreed that one of the basic precepts of media literacy involves the notion that "media are constructed and construct reality" (Aufderheide, 1997, p. 80). Thoman (1999), founder of the Center of Media Literacy, affirmed this point, asserting that media literacy encompasses the awareness that media messages are constructed and that "whatever is constructed by just a few people, then becomes 'the way it is' for the rest of us" (p. 51).

Morgan (1998) emphasized that one of the key concepts of media literacy in Canada entails the understanding that all media messages are constructions. Scharrer (2003) stressed that media literacy requires realizing that "the media construct and are constructions of reality" (p. 70). Brookfield (1986) cited various empirical studies when claiming that the news must be regarded as a constructed reality. Thoman and Jolls (2004) framed this same principle a little differently when they posited that people need to grasp that the media are not windows on the world (see also Hobbs, 2005a). Criticos (1997) further expanded on this point by positing that media education should teach people to see the human agency and manufactured nature of the media.

This aspect of the key concepts of media literacy has filtered through to countries besides the United States and the United Kingdom as well. In South Africa, media educators focus on teaching their students to become aware of the representation and construction of reality in the media, particularly in newspapers. Media educators in South Africa maintain that "media education is a potentially liberating force," one that helps students to understand themselves and society and to create critical citizens (Court & Criticos, 1998, p. 100).

Hobbs (1998b) claimed that orienting toward media messages as constructions enables viewers to better appreciate and interpret content. Masterman

(1997, 1998) added that people need to know about production because it enables them to challenge the "naturalness" of media images.

Some authors argue, as will become apparent in the remainder of this paragraph, that the best way to learn about the constructed nature of media content entails being involved in its construction. In the United Kingdom, media education includes the production of media messages (Bazalgette, 1992), and scholars gathered at the National Leadership Conference on Media Literacy concurred (Aufderheide, 1997). Desimoni (1992) described how a Swiss media education program echoed this perspective, and the Israeli Ministry of Education contended that the ability to create and produce a media message should be a part of any media education program (D. Lemish & P. Lemish, 1997). In Denmark, media production constitutes an important part of many media education projects. Tufte (1992) argued that media production aids students in acquiring superior analytical abilities regarding media content as well as helping them to understand that television portrays a transformed and selective part of reality. In Australia, learning how to produce media content comprised the foundation of many media education programs for a long time, and it remains an essential part of media literacy teaching (Quin, 2003). In the United States, Tyner (2003) described how teaching students to create their own interactive multimedia, such as an online digital archive, enables them to improve their general problem solving skills and the complexity of their knowledge structures. As Appendix 1 details, production constitutes an important part of media literacy, and, as such, it has become an integral part of many media education projects. We elaborate this finding in the conclusion.

Within the dimension of media production, scholars described the production of media content as hinging on two factors—professional activities and production context. In the next two sections, we discuss these factors in more detail.

Professional Activities

Professional activities play a central role in constructing media messages. This element refers to all actions undertaken by media producers when creating media content. Buckingham (2003) insisted that media literacy includes an awareness of who the people are that make the messages, while Covington (2004) described how Canadian media education programs strive to make students aware of the creative processes that take place during media production. This research tends to concentrate on the selectivity of the producers and the codes and conventions used during the construction of media content.

Producer Selectivity

Producers make conscious and subconscious decisions about what to include (and how) in fictional and non-fictional media messages. In their framework for media literacy, Primack et al. (2006) claimed that one of the core concepts of media literacy entailed knowing that messages filter reality and omit information. Additionally, this framework affirmed that messages contain values and specific viewpoints, something that media literate people should realize. Several years earlier, Thoman (1999) also asserted that the media "have embedded values and points of view" (p. 52). She argued that the media carry a subtext of who and what is (and is not) important, something that people should be able to "read" to properly interpret media messages. Potter (2004), in his theory of media literacy, concurred when he contended that "much of the information from the media does not reflect the real world very well" (p. 93) and observed that many news programs overemphasize certain events and people, while ignoring others.

Hence, media literacy includes knowing about the selectivity which is part of the nature of a mediated message. As Masterman (1983) suggested, "Every television image is, of course, a selected one" (p. 208). In Israel, the Ministry of Education stressed that media literacy includes the ability to "understand that mass media products are a result of professional and personal activities and not a neutral reflection of reality" (D. Lemish & P. Lemish, 1997, p. 221). Livingstone (2003) described how different British institutions view media literacy, and the British Office of Communications argued that one of the goals of its office should be to increase public understanding of "the processes by which materials are selected and made available" (p. 7). More specifically, Hobbs (2005a) highlighted critical reading and viewing as one of the phases of media literacy, especially the study of "patterns in choice of aesthetic forms, genres and modalities, with an emphasis on choices that shape the representation of social reality" (p. 20). Furthermore, several scholars from around the globe emphasize that media education should teach students that television constructs reality (i.e., that what appears on television may seem like reality but it depicts a selective and transformed part of reality; J. A. Brown, 1991; Lloyd-Kolkin et al., 1980; Tufte, 1992; Vooijs & van der Voort, 1990).

In some cases, media literacy researchers expanded the notion of selectivity by also examining how the selection that takes place during media production can embed certain values and/or points of view in the messages. Thoman and Jolls (2004) noted that "[b]ecause all media messages are constructed, choices have to be made. These choices inevitably reflect the values, attitudes, and points of view of the ones doing the constructing" (p. 26). Brookfield (1986) concurred, claiming that "producers and reporters select from the range of possible interpretations of news events the ideas, beliefs and values that reflect the dominant culture" (p. 158). Brookfield added, "If adults begin to speculate on how and why television emphasizes certain views and messages, they will be more likely to ask why other views and messages were excluded and how apparently 'neutral' events might have been presented from a different perspective" (p. 162).

In Northern Ireland, teachers enable students to understand that newspaper reporters present the news from a certain viewpoint and that the same event can be viewed from a completely different angle, such as a Catholic or a Protestant orientation (Collins, 1998). Anderson (1983) suggested that students of the media should be able to recognize the values presented by a media message as well as to compare them to their own and the ones held by their society.

A large number of media literacy projects also address the notion of producers' motivations, purposes, and viewpoints. These scholars reason that, if media users understand that producers have specific motivations regarding a media message, they will also grasp that this motivation contributes to a certain selectivity regarding the creation of the message. Masterman (1983) observed that people need to realize that a reporter's task "is not to seek out the truth of particular situation, but to seek evidence which supports an angle which will have been pretty well set before the reporter leaves the office" (p. 208). For example, a Swiss media education program emphasized producers' motivations and aims (Desimoni, 1992). This line of thinking appears to be echoed by a study that specifically investigated how teenage girls interpreted weight loss advertisements. Hobbs, Broder, Pope, and Rowe (2006) defined media literacy as encompassing the ability to recognize the author's purpose, goals, motives, and point of view because it increases critical thinking skills regarding media messages that might influence body image, eating disorders, and nutrition. Similarly, Hobbs (2005b) focused on how media literate youngsters regard the news. For Hobbs, media literacy includes awareness of the author's purpose as well as omitted topics, perspectives, and contents from a news broadcast. Alvermann (2004), in a study that explored youngsters and Internet-based technologies, noted that developing critical awareness in relation to new media and Internet-based technologies meant alerting youngsters to the fact that all texts promote or silence certain opinions or perspectives.

Producer selectivity is not the only factor that determines media content. Codes and conventions employed by the producers also help shape the message, and we explore the literature that addresses this factor next.

Codes and Conventions

Anderson (1983) summarized the meaning of "codes" and "conventions" when he mentioned that media literacy should include an understanding of the grammar and syntax of television. During the National Leadership Conference on Media Literacy, scholars agreed that media literacy involves recognizing that "form and content are related in each medium, each of which has a unique aesthetic, codes, and conventions" (Aufderheide, 1997, p. 80). The framework for media literacy by Primack et al. (2006) also indicated that producers use multiple production techniques to create messages. Thoman (1999) linked media literacy with the awareness that media messages utilize their own language. In the United Kingdom, educators encourage students to look at media content and examine codes and conventions that "refer to, symbolize, or summarize particular meanings or sets of ideas" (Bazalgette, 1992, p. 212). Likewise, in the Netherlands, most media education programs incorporate learning about the language used to create media content (Ketzer, Swinkels, & Vooijs, 1989). Similarly, in South Africa, media educators focus on the technical and symbolic codes used to create messages as well as the expression of director intentions (Court & Criticos, 1998). Moreover, in Israel, media education programs teach students to recognize "different forms of expression in the languages of the mass media" and to understand "the connections between contents and form of media products in general" (D. Lemish & P. Lemish, 1997, p. 221). Finally, a number of media education programs that focus on rendering respondents critical toward advertising include teaching how to recognize the persuasive techniques used in commercials. For example, viewers should be able to distinguish a program from a commercial; discern special effects, visual and verbal elements, and symbolism; comprehend the persuasive intent underlying a commercial, and realize the role of actors in advertisements (J. D. Desmond & Jeffries-Fox, 1983; S. Feshbach, N. D. Feshbach, & Cohen, 1982; Hobbs, 2004; Livingstone & Helsper, 2006)

Most media literacy authors distinguish between two types of conventions: (1) production procedures and (2) dramatic and/or narrative codes, such as genre, and we address them below. Anderson (1983) argued that an awareness of these conventions is essential for it decreases the chance that people will make "reality errors in assessing behaviors presented in television content" (p. 307).

Production procedures include, for instance, sound, camera point of view, lighting techniques, framing, special effects, the use of props, and the constraints of time and technology. Bazalgette (1992), in his description of the key aspects utilized in the United Kingdom, claimed that students should know what kinds of technology are used in the production of media messages. Armed with such information, students should be able to recognize the role of technology in shaping the meaning of a text and note which audience members possess the required equipment to access the message. Potter (2004) agreed when he asserted that people should understand the meanings of certain techniques used in the media, such as the close-up and the flashback. Thoman (1999) argued that an awareness of the technical conventions used in a message helps people to be "less susceptible to manipulation" (p. 51; see also, Piette & Giroux, 1997; Thoman & Jolls, 2004). Vande Berg, Wenner, and Gronbeck (2004) suggested that media literacy involves knowing that technical and conventional codes "work to position viewers to 'see' the 'preferred' meanings and to create 'oppositional' meanings" (p. 222). In Switzerland, media education includes gaining knowledge and understanding regarding "images, sounds, media texts, encoding of signs and the production of meaning" (Desimoni, 1992, p. 34).

In addition to these more "visual" production procedures, other production procedures remain less visible but play a role in shaping the message nonetheless. Educators in the United Kingdom stress the constraints of time and technology and how these issues can affect a media message (Bazalgette, 1992). Masterman (1983) agreed, claiming expectations of a certain quality of television images poses constraints. He also argued that media users should be aware that the presence of a camera and a production crew can affect the events on screen.

The second category includes definitions of media literacy that focused on the knowledge of non-technical codes, such as awareness of genre, narrative structures, and the distinction between fiction and fact. Media education programs in the United Kingdom highlight the awareness of different genres in the media. Experts reasoned that the genre of a program influences how viewers interpret programs and that recognizing a genre facilitates the recognition of the codes and conventions that are typical to each genre (Bazalgette, 1992). In addition, in his theory for media literacy, Potter's (2004) definition of media literacy included an understanding of the different formulas usually employed in certain types of programs such as the news and entertainment shows, and Hobbs (2005a) noted the ability to distinguish a commercial from regular programming. McMahon (2003) provided another example of dramatic and/or narrative codes when he argued that media literacy should include the ability to identify narrative elements such as character, plot, and setting. Media education programs in the Netherlands (Ketzer et al.,1989) have historically included teaching about the relationship between audiovisual products and reality, as well as focusing on narrative structures. In Northern Ireland (Collins, 1998), various teachers focus on making students aware of the use of stereotyping and emotive language to convey a message. Emotive language also constitutes a topic of various media education programs in South Africa (Court & Criticos, 1998), where some of the projects also concentrated on perceiving bias in media texts. A project aimed at understanding how teenage girls interpreted weight loss advertisements alleged that media literacy entailed the ability to recognize persuasive claims and other devices used to construct messages (Hobbs et al., 2006). Codes and conventions play a pivotal role in shaping media content. In the next section, we discuss another factor that influences media content—the production context.

Production Context

Besides the professional activities described in the previous section, the second factor that influences media message construction can be best described as the production context. This factor refers to the various institutions that shape the content of media messages. A large amount of media literacy literature mentions an awareness of the institutions that produce mediated messages. J. A. Brown noted:

Critical viewing is one major component of media literacy, referring to the study of media industries and of economic, political and ethical contexts to learn about forces shaping media content, including advertising economics and government regulation and public interest groups. (2001, p. 684)

In Israel, media education programs include the ability to analyze the communication structures to which students are exposed, to know about the historical development of the mass media, and to evaluate expected developments in the media arena (D. Lemish & P. Lemish, 1997). One very practical media education project in Canada (Covington, 2004) actually entailed media producers coming into class and explaining about the various influences that help shape the process of media production. Media literacy scholars generally focus on one or more of the following production contexts: social and cultural, economic, and political aspects. We elaborate each of these aspects in the following three sections.

Social and Cultural Aspects

In his summary of critical viewing skills, J. A. Brown (1991) found that a number of media education projects taught students about the role that social and cultural aspects play in the production of media content, a notion which has been echoed by various others, and which will be expanded below. In Switzerland, media education encompasses an awareness of the social context of media production (Desimoni, 1992), while, in Israel, media education programs integrate instruction about ideological aspects of the media (D. Lemish & P. Lemish, 1997). Masterman (1983), when outlining his definition of television literacy, referred to the conservative nature of media institutions and the middle-class biases of their staff. According to J. A. Brown, the Catholic Education office in Australia claimed that people need to know about the structure of media institutions to become "discriminating truth seekers" (p. 74).

Furthermore, Thoman and Jolls (2004) claimed that media content reflects the values, attitudes, and perspectives of the ones doing the constructing. The ability to identify these values as they are expressed through media content renders people "more tolerant of differences and more astute in our decision making to accept or reject the message" (p. 26). Some authors, when describing the social context of media production, also referred to the social position of the user, seemingly making the point that production and usage are inexorably linked. McMahon (2003), for instance, suggested that media literate people should be able to make "the connection between the construction of texts, their contexts, and the societies in which they are produced and consumed" (p. 12). Alvermann (2004) described the discussion surrounding new media as centered on "the perceived need to develop young people's critical awareness of how all authored texts...situate them as readers, writers, and viewers within particular historical and cultural contexts" (p. 78). Finally, Vande Berg et al. (2004) claimed that one of the goals of television education programs should be to teach students how to evaluate their encounters with television from a social perspective and to assess the social meanings of a television program.

In short, the social and cultural aspects of media production encompass a wide array of phenomena, which range from understanding how the values of the producers can influence the media message to evaluating the social meanings of a television program. An awareness of these aspects should, according to the authors cited above, render media users more critical of media content.

Economic Aspects

Some authors, in their discussion of media literacy, concentrated on the economic aspect of media institutions. The National Leadership Conference on Media Literacy (Aufderheide, 1997) asserted that media literacy entailed an awareness of the economic constraints that surrounded media production as well as of the commercial implications. In their framework for media literacy, Primack et al. (2006) described how media literacy involves realizing that media messages are produced to create a profit, a point echoed by Thoman (1999), who stated that all media messages are created to sell something. In the United Kingdom, the British Film Institute considers power and profit motives, as well as ownership patterns and market forces, essential elements of any media education program (Bazelgette, 1992).

In the United Kingdom, Masterman (1983) explained that, because the media are owned and controlled by rich and powerful corporations, their views most likely reflect the ideas of capitalism and consumerism, and, as such, people need to be aware of the economic factors that shape media production. In the United States, Rapaczynski, D. G. Singer, and J. L. Singer (1982) noted that children should grasp the nature of commercial TV and the purpose of commercials. The notion that knowing about the economic aspects of media production comprises an essential part of media literacy has also been accepted outside the United States and the United Kingdom. Desimoni (1992), for instance, in his description of a Swiss media education program, mentioned that media literacy includes an understanding of the producers of media content, particularly the awareness that "behind the message there exists a socio-economic system with its financial and ideological implications" (p. 34).

In addition, media education includes teaching about how the media aim to identify new audiences, construct them if necessary, then predict their responses and behavior, and use this knowledge for advertising purposes (Bazalgette, 1992). Other scholars argue that a media literate person must understand that the primary function of commercial media is the "packaging" of audiences for sale to advertisers to make a profit, a point advanced by Primack et al. (2006) in their media literacy framework. Dorr, Browne Graves, and Phelps (1980) taught children that programs are broadcast to make money, that money for programs comes from advertisements, and that the audience size determines how much money a station makes.

Vande Berg et al. (2004) also contended that understanding how audience members are packaged, marketed, and positioned by the media industry will help people understand and become more critical of the television industry. Both Branston (1992) and Potter (2004) noted that to be considered media literate, people have to realize that the media tend to objectify their audiences into measurable, predictable identities to predict the success of a show. The definition presented by Hobbs et al. (2006), in a study centered on girls' understanding of weight loss advertisements, took the logical next step by stressing that media literacy requires the ability to describe the intended audience of a media message. Potter, when outlining his theory of media literacy, advanced this idea one step further and made the point that, since media industries are guided by a profit motive, they will turn out only messages that will attract considerable audiences. Furthermore, he added that media users need to realize that mass media market to niche audiences.

Not all mass media exist for the purpose of making a profit, however, and several authors argued that whether or not a channel or station intends to make money should affect how a viewer perceives its messages. For instance, Hobbs and Frost (1999) described how the state of Texas introduced a media education curriculum that equipped students to distinguish between those media that sell audiences to advertisers and those that do not and to recognize how media economics can shape a message. Thoman and Jolls (2004), as well as a few others (Buckingham, 2003; Lewis & Jhally, 1998), were more direct in their line of reasoning and maintained that much of the world's mass media were developed as moneymaking enterprises and that, if one wants to evaluate a message, one has to know whether profit is its purpose. In line with this reasoning, Lewis and Jhally concluded that students needed to know about the mainly commercial nature of media institutions in the United States because only then would they be able to critically approach the media and appreciate alternative, and possibly more diverse, media forms.

Understanding media ownership patterns can also be considered a part of media literacy. More than two decades ago, Masterman (1983) argued that an awareness of ownership patterns comprises one of the ways that viewers can recognize how and why certain values are embedded in television texts. More recently, Dennis (2004) also observed that adult media literacy assumes an awareness of media ownership and how it influences media content. Both authors, however, noted the danger of oversimplifying the relationship between content and ownership and warned that statements such as "bigness is bad and diversity is good" (Dennis, p. 209) do not do justice to the nuances of ownership.

In short, scholars consider the economic aspects of media production from a large variety of perspectives, ranging from the packaging of audiences, to the difference between profit and non-profit, to the awareness of ownership patterns. Next, we discuss the political aspects of the production context.

Political Aspects

Several definitions of media literacy focus on the need to understand the political influences and allegiances that play a role in shaping the media content turned out by production organizations. Vargas (2006) defined it as the ability to understand "the political economics of global conglomerates" (p. 269). The key aspects of media education as advocated in the United Kingdom includes an awareness of the political allegiances of the media and how these allegiances could affect media content (Bazalgette, 1992). Aufderheide (1997), in her description of the National Leadership Conference on Media Literacy, noted that media literacy encompasses an awareness of the bureaucratic and legal constraints of the production of media messages.

In his description of media education projects in various countries, Hart (1998) lamented that few media curricula appear to delve into the relationship between media institutions and the political aspects of society. Recognizing the importance of studying the political aspects of media production, Hobbs (2005a) noted that one of the key aspects of media literacy should be the awareness that media messages have a political purpose. Masterman (1983) argued that the importance of understanding the political values inherent in media messages stems from the fact that most of these values are presented as "go without saying" (i.e., as a part of common sense, or commonly held ideas). McMahon (2003) referred to this sentiment as the implied nature of many ideologies present in media messages that do affect the meaning in media texts.

Different authors gave varying reasons for the importance of recognizing the presence of political allegiances in the media production context. Masterman (1983) argued that, because of the naturalness of many political ideas present in media messages, people likely accept the values presented to them as truth. Therefore, a more critical attitude toward the media requires recognizing the political values and allegiances present in a message. Thoman and Jolls (2004) explained that, "[w]ith democracy at stake almost everywhere around the world, citizens of every country need to be equipped with the ability to determine... ideological spin" (p. 27). On the other hand, according to Alvarado and Boyd-Barrett (1992), if students grasp the political influences on media content, they will be more likely to see how media institutions can be changed for the better.

Moreover, some definitions of media literacy referred to the rules, set up and enforced by the government, that apply to the media. Buckingham (2003), as well as Anderson (1983), alleged that people need to know about the regulations that guide media production. Furthermore, Potter (2004) argued that people should comprehend both the advantages and disadvantages of the regulations that govern the consolidation of media industries. In short, the political aspects of media production refer to a wide array of aspects that can influence media content, including legal and bureaucratic restraints, possible political allegiances, and regulations that govern media broadcasts.

The different ways in which media literacy researchers have addressed media production as a dimension of media literacy reveal that, in this respect, media literacy can be defined as knowledge about the selectivity of the producers, the codes and conventions used by the producers, as well as the social and cultural, economic, and political context of media production. Next, we turn to how media influence on its users has been included in the various definitions of media literacy.

Media Influence on its Users

A third dimension of media production and use indicates that people should be aware of the media's impact on society and individuals. Definitions of media literacy that refer to the influence of media focus on two different levels—societal and individual.

Influence at the Societal Level

Awareness of the fact that the media shape society in many different ways is generally deemed an essential part of media literacy. When talking about "society," a whole array of issues are implied, and, in fact, the literature consulted for this overview, and this section in particular, touches on a large number of issues regarding media influence on society. Some media literacy scholars advocate a general awareness of media influence on society, without any further elaboration. Messaris (1998), for instance, merely mentioned that media literacy encompasses an awareness of social consequences, without providing additional specification.

Cultural Influences

Other media literacy researchers focus on the media's influence on society in terms of culture. The media and, particularly television, have a "cradle to grave presence" (Vande Berg et al., 2004, p. 221), thus playing an important role in shaping a culture, creating a sense of community and consensus about specific topics, and molding perceptions of societal norms and values. Socialization is essential to the survival of any culture, and most definitions of media literacy mention an understanding of the role the media play in this process (e.g., Vargas, 2006). Various media education projects across the world recognize the media's part in crafting cultures and creating consensus as well as a sense of belonging, albeit sometimes in a very generic manner. In Australia, Greenaway (1997) proposed that one of the core concepts of media education involves knowing that the media can influence one's culture. This definition is very general, leaving a great deal of room for interpretation. A similar definition used in Canada sheds a little more light on how Greenaway's definition could be interpreted. Morgan (1998) suggested that an important aim of media education should be to make people aware of how the media shape both culture and values inherent to it. J. A. Brown (1998) concurred, specifying the need to grasp multiple cultural and social roles of the media and the extent to which the media affect values as part of media literacy. Vande Berg et al. further refined the concept of values by asserting that media literacy includes understanding how the media can impact ethical, social, and cultural values.

Impact on Political and Ideological Perspectives

In the field of media literacy, scholars also attend to the influence that the media can have on political and ideological perspectives (e.g., Vande Berg et al., 2004). In her description of the 1992 National Leadership Conference on media literacy, Aufderheide (1997) stressed the awareness that media messages can have ideological and political implications. The Israeli Ministry of Education remained more general when it remarked that media literate students should be able to evaluate the role of the media in a democratic society (D. Lemish & P. Lemish, 1997).

Influencing Societal Activities

Finally, some definitions of media literacy consider "society as a whole" as a collection of activities that define a specific society and/or that are carried out by the majority of the members of that society. Hence, various authors agreed that media literacy requires an awareness of the impact that televised messages could have on society at large—politics, cultural and artistic activities, and social customs (R. Desmond, 1997; Meyrowitz, 1998; Piette & Giroux, 1997).

In summary, the societal effects that have been described by media literacy scholars as detailed above range from the effects that the media could have on a culture, to how the media help socialize people and create a sense of community, to political perspectives, to how it could impact a society's customs. Besides societal effects, media literacy researchers have also discussed the impact that the media can have on individuals. We elaborate on this issue in the next section.

Influence at the Individual Level

Some authors, in their description of what media literacy entails, focused on the impact that mediated messages can have on an individual. This impact has been described in different ways, outlined in the remainder of the section. Various scholars claimed that media literacy mandates knowing how the media can shape people's view of reality. Others argued that media literacy entailed knowing how the media can affect a person's opinions, feelings, and notion of self. Finally, media literacy also involves an understanding of factors that can mediate the influence that the media can have on people.

Shaping Reality

First, various definitions of media literacy suggest that media messages can help to shape perceptions of reality. J. A. Brown (1998) explained that "media experience becomes the framework by which people perceive their world" (p. 51). Rapaczynski et al. (1982) elaborated on this idea by explaining that children need to understand that television "is a source of information (and stereotypes) about other people, countries and occupations" (p. 48), an idea echoed by D. G. Singer and J. L. Singer (1983). Thoman and Jolls (2004) noted that, if people see how the media shape what they know and understand about the world around them, they will also realize that media content is not a window on reality but a carefully crafted construction. This observation implies that the ability to comprehend that the media can influence how one perceives reality is tied to another aspect of media literacy discussed earlier—conceptualizing the media as a construction.

Understanding that the media shape ideas about reality is especially important when it comes to stereotypes since the media possess the capability to impact how people think about various groups of people (Piette & Giroux, 1997; see related reviews by del Río, 2006; Keränen & Sanprie, this volume; Lacy, this volume; Roessler, 2007). Thus, several media education programs teach students about the stereotypes presented in the media and their effects on the media users (Anderson, 1983; Buckingham & Sefton-Green, 1997).

Influencing Behavior, Ideas, and Self-concept

Second, various scholars pointed out that media literacy encompasses an awareness of how the media influence feelings, behavior, ideas, and one's self-concept. The framework for media literacy developed by Primack et al. (2006) acknowledges that messages can affect attitudes and behaviors. Further, Messaris (1998), for instance, discussed psychological effects, while Potter (2004) categorized media effects as either cognitive, attitudinal, emotional, physiological, or behavioral. D. G. Singer, Zuckerman, and J. L. Singer (1980) expanded this list of effects by adding that the media, and television, in particular, can also influence with whom and how children identify. In terms of identity formation, the media play a crucial role, especially in the lives of teenagers and young adults since the media seemingly sets standards for looks, weight, and even clothes. Hence, Irving and Berel (2001) argued that media literacy requires the ability to recognize and critically evaluate the ideals put forth by the media as well as the effects that it might have on a person's own self-perception. When successful, according to Irving and Berel, people can "reduce the credibility and persuasive influence of media messages" and, consequently, be less likely to accept the media's beauty ideals (p. 103).

An education project developed specifically for Latin American teenage girls featured the media's impact on how individuals shape their identity in a media education project (Vargas, 2006). This endeavor equipped participants to recognize the process through which they constituted their own intercultural identity as well as the role played by the media in this process. Most media literacy projects discussed so far emphasize the more "obvious" effects, such as body image or emotional or behavioral consequences (e.g., violent programming causing violent behavior). However, Lloyd-Kolkin et al. (1980) examined an effect that is generally forgotten, namely the ability to discern the influence that media use has on daily life. The media not only impacts topics of conversation but can also influence daily schedules.

Mediating Factors

Third, grasping potential media influence also entails an understanding of possible mediating factors. Potter (2004) claimed that media literacy encompasses alertness to factors that decrease or increase the risk of being influenced by the media. As the only media literacy scholar to raise this consideration, Potter argued that media literacy necessitates being able to control these factors and, thus, "reduce the probability of a negative effect occurring well before it has the chance to manifest itself" (p. 85).

Thus, in addition to recognizing production of media content, media literacy requires realizing how the media can impact individuals as well as society as a whole. So far, the literature overview has covered three out of the four relationships between the media, their users, and producers. Various media literacy scholars also acknowledge the fourth relationship, which centers on people actively using the media. We explore this dimension of media literacy next.

Handling the Media

Although numerous definitions of media literacy affirm that people should be aware of their active role as media users, authors differ in their perspectives on this role. Media literate viewers should be able to locate and select media content, manage their media use, mobilize the media, and possess an awareness that media users may differ in how they interpret the media.

Locating and Selecting

This section demonstrates that a common denominator in many media education programs and media literacy definitions appears to be the ability to find specific information. Scholars often describe it as essential because of the large amounts of information presented to people through the media (see, e.g., Considine, 1997). Potter (2004) went as far as to call the ability to efficiently locate specific information one of the basic skills of media literacy. J. A. Brown (1991) agreed, adding that this skill needs to be honed and perfected. Concurrent with the idea that simply obtaining information from one source is not sufficient, media education programs stress that people should be able to locate more than one source of information (Anderson, 1983; Considine, 1997) and to make a conscious decision about which source that they will use (Alvermann & Hagood, 2000).

When it comes to media literacy research that looks specifically at new media such as the Internet, the ability to locate and select information is key, since these media are much more geared toward searching and browsing. Dennis (2004) noted that people should be able to find information online and to be aware of the new developments in equipment and other information technologies. Also focusing on new media, Tyner (2003) observed that digital media differ from print media owing to the sheer volume and speed with which information can be obtained and, therefore, require special strategies for browsing and searching. She added that, if people are to benefit from the digital media, they must learn how to "creatively...research, and select" (p. 374). To be media literate regarding new media such as the Internet, people need access to these new media (e.g., Livingstone, 2004). However, as Tyner observed, the question has also been raised whether or not access to new media, in fact, guarantees a higher level of digital literacy.

In a few cases, scholars extended this definition to include assessing the quality of the selected information. The quality of media content can be determined in a variety of ways, and different definitions specify varied evaluation skills. J. A. Brown (1991), for instance, contended that people need to be able to decide if and how information relates to their life. Anderson's (1983) definition of media literacy included reflecting on news stories based on the value that they have regarding a person's purpose for viewing the stories.

When discussing how to examine information, some media literacy scholars opt for a more "scientific" approach. Dennis (2004) referred to it as "evaluating their sources, mode of presentation, accuracy and interpretation" (p. 209); whereas, Considine (1997) argued that media literate people should be able to separate "policy from personality, issue from image" (p. 260). People should also be able to verify received information by checking multiple sources, a notion so generally accepted within the field of media literacy that it was included in the key concepts of media literacy as proposed by the Center for Media Literacy (Thoman, 1999). Potter (2004) also stressed the ability to compare and contrast different sources of information, a skill he referred to as *grouping*. Checking sources can be as simple as obtaining information through television news and then comparing it to information obtained elsewhere (Vooijs & van der Voort, 1990). However, according to Dennis, an awareness of different sources of information and the ability to use them if necessary to obtain a greater understanding of certain issues remains paramount to critical viewing. Tyner (2003) extended this notion to the new media. Because of the sheer amount of information and the speed with which information can be provided online, Tyner argued that viewers require particular strategies when evaluating online content and "verifying the authenticity of the sources, and placing specific content within the context of other information sources" (p. 373).

In short, locating and selecting refers to people's ability to find information and assess its value. Many media literacy scholars link this ability with managing media use, which we discuss in the next section.

Managing Media Use

Numerous media literacy scholars characterize an awareness of when one uses the media as part of media literacy. In his summary of critical viewing programs, J. A. Brown (2001) mentioned that some programs focus on people's patterns of media use. Lloyd-Kolkin et al. (1980) were more specific when they stated that media literacy should entail the ability to evaluate one's media use (i.e., to log when one uses the media and compare one's media use to that of others). Logging media use comprises a recurrent theme for several media education programs. For instance, according to some authors, media literacy training included teaching people to evaluate their own television viewing patterns (e.g., asking viewers to assess patterns in their media use during one week). Kline (2005) instructed children to self-monitor and self-report television, videotape, and videogame use. Similarly, J. A. Brown described a media education program in which students created pre-planned viewing schedules. Besides raising awareness regarding media use, such programs also render people more sensitive regarding the extent of their exposure to the media (i.e., for how long they use the media during a given period of time).

Furthermore, scholars contend that people's ability to manage their use of the media in a well-considered manner constitutes a part of media literacy. Vooijs and van der Voort (1990) summarized this principle when they claimed that critical viewing skills involved "strategies for the management of the duration of viewing and program choices" (p. 545). Further, D. G. Singer and J. L. Singer (1983) described a media education curriculum where one of the goals was to teach children how to control their viewing habits. This aspect of media literacy can have very practical uses. Kline (2005) detailed how media education can be employed to curb child obesity by teaching children how to limit their use of the media, since media consumption has been shown to increase the risk of unhealthy eating habits and a sedentary lifestyle.

Other authors mentioned the ability to create a media use schedule in their definition of media literacy (i.e., the ability to make decisions about what to watch on television before turning it on; Hobbs, 1998a; Vooijs & van der Voort,

1989). Managing media use can also be extended to planning leisure time in general. In a Swiss media education program, students learn to better organize their leisure time "through a greater freedom of decision about the proportion of time to be devoted to the media" (Desimoni, 1992, p. 34). Kline (2005) summarized a pilot study in Vancouver that encouraged children to reflect on their media use and consider alternative ways of leisure. Selecting higher quality programs also contributes to managing media use (J. A. Brown, 1991; Vooijs & van der Voort, 1989), although these authors did not describe what would constitute a "higher quality."

An awareness of the motives and purposes that provide the incentive for media use also impacts media literacy. According to Anderson (1983), scholars can no longer view media users as passive, and media education curricula have to be more oriented toward the individual and their needs. In Switzerland, for instance, media education includes rendering students aware of why they use the media (Desimoni, 1992). Additionally, J. A. Brown (1991) described how some media education programs emphasized knowing about motives and purposes for attending to television programs as well as ways of evaluating how one's motives can shape sense-making of media content (see also McMahon, 2003). Piette and Giroux (1997) elaborated on this idea by adding that, if people are more aware of how and why their own television viewing occurs, they are better able to evaluate media content in terms of their expectations and needs.

After discussing the different aspects of media literacy that focus on how, when, and why people use the media, in the next section, we describe two other aspects of handling the media—the ability to mobilize the media and the ability to interpret media content.

The Ability to Mobilize the Media

Some definitions of media literacy highlight a more activist aspect of dealing with the media; they refer to taking action in regard to specific media content but also to attracting media attention (see related arguments by Pal & Dutta, this volume; Zoller & Kline, this volume). As Means Coleman (2003) noted, "[T]he principal goals of media education are to create media consumers who...work to influence and inform media" (p. 413). In her description of media literacy, Hobbs (1998a, 2005a) underscored the ability to use the media to attract press interest, build coalitions, shape policy decision making, and change political practices in regard to certain social issues. Rapaczynski et al. (1982) specifically stressed the ability to influence networks, producers, and television stations. Further, Vande Berg et al. (2004) emphasized that becoming media literate entailed sharing one's insights regarding the meanings of television content with policy makers, program creators, and industry decision makers (p. 222). Although this aspect of handling the media receives less attention from media literacy scholars than do the others, mobilizing the media constitutes an essential part of the relationship between the media and the user since it is the sole one that highlights user agency in terms of influencing the media, instead of vice versa.

Interpreting Media Content

Definitions of media literacy also feature an awareness of how audiences interpret media content. Branston (1992) observed that media literacy must focus on both textual analysis and audiences. Many of those same definitions also claim that people need to understand how and why other people may interpret the same message differently, as we detail in this next section.

First, some descriptions of media literacy concentrate on the extent to which people understand the process through which they give meaning to media content. Media messages do not contain fixed meanings that are simply copied by media users, and media literacy encompasses the awareness that audiences play an active role in creating meaning (Quin, 2003). Thoman (1999) further specified this idea by claiming that media literacy includes asking as many questions about media content as possible. Besides questioning possible meanings, Bazelgette (1992) argued that media literacy also involves realizing how people construct meaning from media texts (see also Aufderheide, 1992).

Individual interpretations of media messages depend on a variety of factors. In their project on teenage girls and weight loss advertising, Hobbs et al. (2006) asserted that media literacy requires understanding how "people make interpretations of media messages based on their prior knowledge and life experience" (p. 721). Furthermore, in Australia, Quin and McMahon (1997) argued that, though textual analysis is essential to media literacy, it will not completely reveal how the user interprets media content, and, therefore, people need to learn that their positions, attitudes, and values influence their interpretations of media texts. J. A. Brown (2001) elaborated on this notion, arguing that interpretation depends on people's individual cognitive processing, which includes psychological and affective considerations and selective perception and interpretation. In short, this aspect of media literacy centers on media users' comprehending their own complex role as receivers of messages and creators of meaning (Desimoni, 1992).

Second, understanding that people from a range of socioeconomic backgrounds may interpret the same media message differently is another aspect of media literacy. In his description of the key aspects of media education in the United Kingdom, Bazalgette asserted that "different classes, races, ages, cultural backgrounds, and personal histories can all affect the interpretation of texts and the kinds of pleasures people may derive from them" (1992, p. 215). Thoman (1999) echoed that "no two people see the same movie" (p. 51), a notion that can also be found in the framework for media literacy presented by Primack et al. (2006).

Several media literacy projects elaborated on why it is important to understand that different people may have different interpretations of the same content. For example, Thoman and Jolls (2004) argued that this kind of knowledge enhances intercultural respect and understanding. Quin and McMahon (1997) noted that students should understand that audiences are not passive recipients of media messages; instead, they each bring their own social positions, race, gender, and age to bear on their interpretation of the media. This understanding is essential if they desire to "make comparisons and judgments about their own and wider community values" (p. 313). Other media literacy researchers maintained that people who are aware that people may interpret the same message differently increase their critical attitude toward the media. Masterman (1997) alleged that, if people understand how audiences respond to texts, they gain a greater critical autonomy when it comes to media content. The media education program developed by WNET in the early 1980s also taught its students to survey the uses that different people have for the media so that students could better "respond autonomously to messages emanating from the television and evaluate them in terms of their own needs and expectations" (Piette & Giroux, 1997, p. 112).

This section concludes the description of the aspects that constitute the arrow (see Figure 8.1) concerned with handling the media. Within this dimension of media literacy, we have categorized the ability to locate and select the media and the ability to mobilize and interpret media content, which can be added to the definition of media literacy. In the next section, we discuss key findings from our review and offer suggestions for future research.

CONCLUSION AND DISCUSSION

The large variety of definitions outlined in this chapter clearly indicates the richness of the field and the concept of media literacy. This chapter comprises the first attempt to create a schematic representation to categorize the realm of media literacy. Since media literacy has been widely identified as the knowledge of media use and production, it seemed a logical step to use a schematic representation of media use and production to review and categorize existing definitions of media literacy. All of the literature that was examined for this review could be placed into one or more of the four arrows that make up the schematic representation (see Figure 8.1). According to this literature review, media literacy entails the awareness of the different aspects of the production of media content, the influence of the media on its users and its producers, and the way in which users deal with the media. Media literacy encompasses critical attitudes and/or behaviors toward the media and any resulting abilities regarding the media that result from such awareness. The categorization constructed in this chapter allows for drawing the following conclusions.

Key Findings

Considering that various overviews of the media literacy field already exist, what conclusions can be drawn from this literature review regarding the field of media literacy and the wider arena of communication studies?

First, this literature review indicates that media literacy research has been utilized in a wide variety of fields and areas of the communication discipline. It originated in the fields of pedagogy, teaching, and learning where, in educational contexts, the cultivation of critical thinking was propagated in general. From there, it spread to more diverse fields, including health communication (e.g., Livingstone & Helsper, 2006), advertising (e.g., Feshbach et al., 1982; Hobbs et al., 2006), political communication (e.g., Court & Criticos, 1998), and intercultural communication (e.g., Vargas, 2006). Therefore, media literacy certainly applies to fields far beyond the realm of education.

Second, this review reveals that every aspect of the schematic representation of media use and production was already considered a part of media literacy some 20 years ago. Thus, the essence of how experts define media literacy has changed very little over the years. Notably, a large majority of media literacy researchers seem to build on one another's work, incorporating previously developed ideas into newly phrased definitions. For example, the Primack et al. (2006) definition of media literacy was based on the two definitions developed by Thoman (1999) and Bazalgette (1992). Moreover, the field of media literacy has a very practical orientation; thus, most research is concerned with the concrete applicability of the concept (i.e., how can media literacy be taught in different settings and with different topics, as opposed to developing new ways to define media literacy)?

However, recently, Potter (2004) added new insights regarding what it takes for a person to be deemed media literate. Besides discussing the awareness of the different aspects of the production and reception of the media, as outlined above, Potter contributed the concept of "personal locus" to the realm of media literacy. This concept refers to people's personal ability and commitment to displaying media literate behavior. Potter argued that media literacy requires personal ability and awareness of and motivation to control exposures to the media and media effects. Instead of adopting the protectionist stance implicit to some media education programs, Potter returned the responsibility of becoming a critical user to media users themselves and even supplied them with activities to improve their personal locus. This line of thinking could alter current media education programs to integrate an emphasis on "what am I going to do with this in my life," which could have interesting effects as far as critical viewing abilities are concerned.

Third, the majority of media literacy definitions focus on the knowledge that people need to have about media use and production (e.g., Bazalgette, 1992). In some cases, such as the production of media messages or the ability to mobilize the media, researchers explicitly refer to skills that people need to possess (e.g., Rapaczynski et al., 1982), but these areas comprise the only aspects of media literacy where scholars discuss skills. Based on this review, most media literacy scholars assume that knowledge forms the starting point for any kind of media literacy skills, which explains why most definitions of media literacy focus on knowledge.

Fourth, the schematic representation specifies which areas of media use and production are deemed important by media literacy scholars and which have received little attention, thus also shedding light on how communication is represented within media literacy research. This literature review revealed, for instance, that the vast majority of media literacy scholars consider understanding the production of media messages to be an essential aspect of media literacy (e.g., Bazalgette, 1992; Thoman, 1999). Furthermore, the vast majority of media education programs address it as well (e.g., Covington, 2004). The definitions of media literacy specify a wide array of production-related issues, ranging from the practical side of media production (e.g., Masterman, 1983; Tyner, 2003) to the more abstract discussion about the different codes in a message and their possible meanings (e.g., Aufderheide, 1997). Thus, the areas within communication where these issues were first investigated are very well represented in the media literacy arena.

Conversely, the arrow (see Figure 8.1) that focuses on how people handle the media receives relatively little attention from media literacy scholars. Considering that many scholars within the communication discipline investigate how people deal with the media (e.g., the uses and gratifications approach), this area presents considerable opportunity for future research.

Moreover, scholars have virtually ignored the influence that the media can have on media producers. The field of studies that focus on the producers as media users (e.g., Breed, 1955; MacManus, 1994) is excluded from all media literacy definitions; no author points out that producers are not isolated from the media surrounding them but, instead, influenced by them in various ways. Considering the heavy focus that many definitions place on the creation of media content, this gap is unexpected; why do not scholars also recognize the influence that the media have on producers? One possible explanation for this omission could be that scholars implicitly include it as part of the context in which the media messages are created.

Furthermore, this chapter reveals that the application of media literacy has shifted over the past few years, with a greater emphasis on health-related issues. A large number of studies have explored the role that media literacy can play in educational programs that focus on curbing obesity, smoking, and improving people's body image (e.g., Hobbs et al., 2006; Irving & Berel, 2001; Kline, 2005; Livingstone & Helsper, 2006; Primack et al., 2006; Wilksch et al., 2006). When teaching about health issues and the media, these studies mainly aim to teach about the possible influence of the media (e.g., Irving & Berel, 2001; Livingstone & Helsper, 2006). This approach would seem to make the role of the arrow that focuses on the influence of the media on the users much more pivotal (see Figure 8.1). However, we have not yet observed a shift in the definition of media literacy. This finding could mainly be attributed to the fact that these studies continue to place a heavy emphasis on understanding how media messages are created as an essential step in improving the health media literacy of the participants. For instance, in their study into media literacy and smoking, Primack et al. included a definition of media literacy that also addressed understanding how media messages are constructed (see also Hobbs et al., 2006).

Suggestions for Future Research

This chapter raises three points for the media literacy research agenda. The first issue that could be addressed by media literacy scholars is the absence of any literature on the influence that the media have on the producers of media content. Research could explore how this line of influence could be further defined and translated into knowledge that people should possess. Furthermore, scholars could examine how this aspect of media literacy could be introduced into the classroom.

A second issue raised by this literature review involves the possibility of developing a measurement instrument for media literacy. The development of a schematic representation of media production and use that encompasses and has been further specified by existing definitions of media literacy may be regarded as a first step on the way to developing an instrument to measure media literacy. The majority of prior attempts at measuring media literacy were always related to specific media education programs and their effectiveness (e.g., Hobbs et al., 2006; Hobbs & Frost, 1999; Primack et al., 2006; Vooijs & van der Voort, 1990), while this schematic representation opens up the opportunity of measuring media literacy independent of any program or curriculum. Additionally, the aspects that make up the four arrows reflect what media literacy scholars over the years have defined as media literacy, and using them to develop an instrument to measure media literacy means this measure will reflect the general opinion of what media literacy should entail.

A final area that requires further research is the intersection of media literacy and Internet-based technologies, or new media. These new media are becoming increasingly dominant, especially in young people's lives; therefore, if media literacy research is to remain up to date and useful, it should examine the new media. Currently, a great deal of literature that addresses new media and media literacy focuses on how new media can be used in different education projects, for instance, in multicultural education projects (e.g., Hammer & Kellner, 2000) and in health education (e.g., Shah, George, & Himburg, 1999; Wyatt, Henwood, Hart, & Smith, 2005). Some research also explored the role that new media play in people's lives (e.g., Livingstone, 2006). As evidenced by the overview, very few researchers actually pursue how media literacy should be (re)defined regarding the new media. Livingstone (2004) is the only one to discuss how the traditional concept of media literacy as developed by the National Leadership Conference on Media Literacy fits new media. She used the four tenets of this definition (access, analyze, evaluate, and produce) to create a research agenda for Internet-based technologies and media literacy. This very interesting undertaking should be further developed. Research should establish what people need to know or be able to do to approach the new media in a critical manner and how this knowledge and/or these abilities could be translated into an education program.

Final Remarks

In conclusion, this literature overview has provided a conceptual structure, in the shape of a schematic representation (see Figure 8.1) through which one can view the wide array of ideas and opinions about media literacy. While providing insight into how the field of media literacy has been defined, this chapter also offers insight into how developments in this field have benefited other areas of communication research.

NOTE

An earlier version of this manuscript was awarded a Top-2 Student Paper Award at the 2003 International Communication Association conference, San Diego, CA.

REFERENCES

Abelman, R., & Courtright, J. (1983). Television literacy: Amplifying the cognitive level effects of television's prosocial fare through curriculum intervention. *Journal of Research and Development in Education, 17*, 46-57.

Alvarado, M., & Boyd-Barrett, O. (Eds.). (1992). *Media education: An introduction.* London: British Film Institute.

Alvermann, D. E. (2004). Media, information communication technologies, and youth literacies. A cultural studies perspective. *American Behavioral Scientist, 48*, 78-83.

Alvermann, D. E., & Hagood, M. C. (2000). Critical media literacy: Research, theory and practice in "new times." *Journal of Education Research, 93*, 193-205.

Anderson, J. A. (1983). Television literacy and the critical viewer. In J. Bryant & D. R. Anderson (Eds.), *Children's understanding of television: Research on attention and comprehension* (pp. 297-330). New York: Academic Press.

Anderson, J. A., & Ploghoft, M. E. (1980). Receivership skills: The television experience. In D. Nimmo (Ed.), *Communication yearbook 4* (pp. 293-309). New Brunswick, NJ: Transaction.

Aufderheide, P. (1992). Media education in the 90s. *Afterimage, 20*(2), 17-18.

Aufderheide, P. (1997). Media literacy: From a report of the national leadership conference on media literacy. In R. Kubey (Ed.), *Current perspectives. Information and behavior: Vol. 6. Media literacy in the information age* (pp. 79-86). New Brunswick, NJ: Transaction.

Ball-Rokeach, S. J., & DeFleur, M. L. (1976). A dependency model of mass-media effects. *Communication Research, 3*, 3-21.

Bazalgette, C. (1992). Key aspects of media education. In M. Alvarado & O. Boyd-Barrett (Eds)., *Media education: An introduction* (pp. 199-219). London: British Film Institute.

Bazalgette, C. (1997). An agenda for the second phase of media literacy development. In R. Kubey (Ed.), *Current perspectives. Information and behavior: Vol. 6. Media literacy in the information age* (pp. 69-78). New Brunswick, NJ: Transaction.

Bazalgette, C., Bevort, E., & Savino, J. (Eds.). (1992). *New directions: Media education worldwide*. London: British Film Institute.

Bouwman, H. (1989). Cultuurpessimisme en de paradox van een kritische mediapedagogie [Cultural pessimism and the paradox of a critical media pedagogy]. *Massacommunicatie, 17*(1), 61-73.

Branston, G. (1992). Turning to audiences: Some suggestions for the classroom audience. In C. Bazalgette, E. Bevort, & J. Savino (Eds.), *New directions: Media education worldwide* (pp. 70-74). London: British Film Institute.

Breed, W. (1955). Social control in the newsroom. A functional analysis. *Social Forces, 33*, 326-355.

Brookfield, S. (1986). Media power and the development of media literacy: An adult educational interpretation. *Harvard Educational Review, 56*, 151-170.

Brookfield, S. D. (1987). *Developing critical thinkers: Challenging adults to explore alternative ways of thinking and acting.* San Francisco: Jossey-Bass.

Brown, J. A. (1991). *"Critical viewing skills" education: Major media literacy projects in the U.S. and selected countries.* Hillsdale, NJ: Erlbaum.

Brown, J. A. (1998). Media literacy perspectives. *Journal of Communication, 48*(1), 44-57.

Brown, J. A. (2001). Media literacy and critical television viewing in education. In D. G. Singer & J. L. Singer (Eds.), *Handbook of children and the media* (pp. 681-697). Thousand Oaks, CA: Sage.

Brown, J. D. (2006). Media literacy has the potential to improve adolescents' health. *Journal of Adolescent Health, 39*, 459-460.

Buckingham, D. (1990). Making it explicit: Towards a theory of media learning. In D. Buckingham (Ed.), *Watching media learning: Making sense of media education* (pp. 215-230). London: Falmer Press.

Buckingham, D. (1993). *Children talking television: The making of television literacy.* London: The Falmer Press.

Buckingham, D. (1998). Media education in the U.K.: Moving beyond protectionism. *Journal of Communication, 48*(1), 33-43.

Buckingham, D. (2003). *Media education: Literacy, learning and contemporary culture.* Cambridge, England: Polity Press.

Buckingham, D., Fraser, P., & Mayman, N. (1990). Stepping into the void: Beginning classroom research in media education. In D. Buckingham (Ed.), *Watching media learning: Making sense of media education* (pp. 19-59). London: Falmer Press.

Buckingham, D., & Sefton-Green, J. (1997). Multimedia education: Media literacy in the age of digital culture. In R. Kubey (Ed.), *Current perspectives. Information and behavior: Vol. 6. Media literacy in the information age* (pp. 285-305). New Brunswick, NJ: Transaction.

Collins, J. (1998). Media education in Northern Ireland. In A. Hart (Ed.), *Teaching the media: International perspectives* (pp. 57-77). Mahwah, NJ: Erlbaum.

Considine, D. (1997). Media literacy: A compelling component of school reform and restructuring. In R. Kubey (Ed.), *Current perspectives. Information and behavior: Vol. 6. Media literacy in the information age* (pp. 243-262). New Brunswick, NJ: Transaction.

Court, S., & Criticos, C. (1998). Media education in an emergent democracy: KwaZulu-Natal, South Africa. In A. Hart (Ed.), *Teaching the media: International perspectives* (pp. 79-105). Mahwah, NJ: Erlbaum.

Covington, W. G. Jr. (2004). Creativity in teaching media literacy. *International Journal of Instructional Media, 31*, 119-124.

Criticos, C. (1997). Media education for a critical citizenry in South Africa. In R. Kubey (Ed.), *Current perspectives. Information and behavior: Vol. 6. Media literacy in the information age* (pp. 229-240). New Brunswick, NJ: Transaction.

Davies, M. M. (1997). Making media literate: Educating future media workers at the undergraduate level. In R. Kubey (Ed.), *Current perspectives. Information and behavior: Vol. 6. Media literacy in the information age* (pp. 263-284). New Brunswick, NJ: Transaction.

Davison, J. (1992). Theory in practice: Learning media concepts through practical work. In C. Bazalgette, E. Bevort, & J. Savino (Eds.), *New directions: Media education worldwide* (pp. 26-30). London: British Film Institute.

del Río, E. (2006). The Latina/o problematic: Categories and questions in media communication research. In C. S. Beck (Ed.), *Communication yearbook 30* (pp. 387-430). Mahwah, NJ: Erlbaum.

Dennis, E. E. (2004). Out of sight and out of mind. The media literacy needs of grown-ups. *American Behavioral Scientist, 48*, 202-211.

Desimoni, C. (1992). Breaking new ground: Experimental work in the canton of Vaud. In C. Bazalgette, E. Bevort, & J. Savino (Eds.), *New directions: Media education worldwide* (pp. 31-41). London: British Film Institute.

Desmond, J. D., & Jeffries-Fox, S. (1983). Elevating children's awareness of television advertising: The effects of a critical viewing program. *Communication Education, 32*, 107-115.

Desmond, R. (1997). Media literacy in the home: Acquisition versus deficit models. In R. Kubey (Ed.), *Current perspectives. Information and behavior: Vol. 6. Media literacy in the information age* (pp. 323-343). New Brunswick, NJ: Transaction.

Dorr, A., Browne Graves, S., & Phelps, E. (1980). Television literacy for young children. *Journal of Communication, 30*(3), 71-83.

Entman, R. M. (1989). *Democracy without citizens: Media and the decay of American politics*. New York: Oxford University Press.

Feshbach, S., Feshbach, N. D., & Cohen, S. E. (1982). Enhancing children's discrimination in response to television advertising: The effects of psychoeducational training in two aspectary school-age groups. *Developmental Review, 2*, 385-403.

Feuerstein, M. (1999). Media literacy in support of critical thinking. *Journal of Educational Media, 24* (1), 43-54.

Fiske, S. T., & Taylor, S. E. (1991). *Social cognition* (2nd ed.). New York: McGraw-Hill.

Fox, R. F. (1995). Manipulated kids: Teens tell how ads influence them. *English Journal, 53*(1), 77-79.

Gaudard, M., & Theveniaut, O. (1992).The Polaroid test: An educational action project with young children. In C. Bazalgette, E. Bevort, & J. Savino (Eds.), *New directions: Media education worldwide* (pp. 10-12). London: British Film Institute.

Gray, J. (2005). Television teaching: Parody, *The Simpsons*, and media literacy education. *Critical Studies in Media Communication, 22,* 223-238.

Greenaway, P. (1997). Media and arts education: A global view from Australia. In R. Kubey (Ed.), *Current perspectives. Information and behavior: Vol. 6. Media literacy in the information age* (pp. 187-198). New Brunswick, NJ: Transaction.

Hall, S. (1980). Encoding/decoding. In S. Hall, D. Hobson, A. Lowe, & P. Willis (Eds.), *Culture, media, language: Working papers in cultural studies, 1972-79* (pp. 128-138). London: Unwin Hyman.

Hall, S., & Whannel, P. (1964). *The popular arts.* London: Hutchinson.

Hammer, R., & Kellner, D. (2000). Multimedia pedagogy and multicultural education for the new millennium. *Religious Education, 95,* 475-489.

Hart, A. (1998). Conclusion: Paradigms revisited. In A. Hart (Ed.), *Teaching the media: International perspectives* (pp.169-196). Mahwah, NJ: Erlbaum.

Hobbs, R. (1997). Expanding the concept of literacy. In R. Kubey (Ed.), *Current perspectives. Information and behavior: Vol. 6. Media literacy in the information age* (pp. 163-183). New Brunswick, NJ: Transaction.

Hobbs, R. (1998a). Democracy at risk: Building citizenship skills through media education. In M. Salvador & P. Sias (Eds.), *The public voice in a democracy at risk* (pp. 57-76). Westport, CT: Praeger.

Hobbs, R. (1998b). Literacy in the information age. In J. Flood, D. Lapp, & S. Brice Heath (Eds.), *Handbook of research on teaching literacy through the communicative and visual arts* (pp. 7-14). New York: Macmillan.

Hobbs, R. (1998c). The seven great debates in the media literacy movement. *Journal of Communication, 48*(1), 9-29.

Hobbs, R. (2004). Does media literacy work? An empirical study of learning how to analyze advertisements. *Advertising and Society Review, 5,* 1-28.

Hobbs, R. (2005a). Strengthening media education in the twenty-first century: Opportunities for the state of Pennsylvania. *Arts Education Policy Review, 106,* 13-23.

Hobbs, R. (2005b). What's news? Students' attraction to news and entertainment media can fuel comprehension and critical thinking. *Educational Leadership, 62,* 58-61.

Hobbs, R., & Frost, R. (1999). Instructional practices in media literacy education and their impact on students' learning. *New Jersey Journal of Communication, 6*(2), 123-148.

Hobbs, R., Frost, R., Davis, A., & Stauffer, J. (1988). How first-time viewers comprehend editing conventions. *Journal of Communication, 38*(4), 50-60.

Hobbs, R. Broder, S., Pope, H., & Rowe, J. (2006). How adolescent girls interpret weight-loss advertising. *Health Education Research, 21,* 719-730.

Irving, L. M., & Berel, S. R. (2001). Comparison of media literacy programs to strengthen college women's resistance to media images. *Psychology of Women Quarterly, 25*(2), 103-111.

Keane, J. (1991). *The media and democracy.* Cambridge, England: Polity Press.

Keränen, L., & Sanprie, V. (2008). "Oxygen of publicity" and "lifeblood of liberty:" Communication scholarship on mass media coverage of terrorism for the twenty-first century. In C. S. Beck (Ed.), *Communication yearbook 32* (pp. 231-275). New York: Routledge.

Ketzer, J.W., Swinkels, H., & Vooijs, M.W. (1989). Media educatie in de Nederlandse praktijk [Media education in Dutch practice]. *Masssacommunicatie, 17*(1), 26-35.

Kline, S. (2005). Countering children's sedentary lifestyles. An evaluative study of a media-risk education approach. *Childhood, 12*, 239-258.

Lacy, M. (2008). Exposing the spectrum of whiteness: Rhetorical conceptions of white absolutism. In C. S. Beck (Ed.), *Communication yearbook 32* (pp. 277-311). New York: Routledge.

Lemish, D., & Lemish, P. (1997). A much debated consensus: Media literacy in Israel. In R. Kubey (Ed.), *Current perspectives. Information and behavior: Vol. 6. Media literacy in the information age* (pp. 213-228). New Brunswick, NJ: Transaction.

Lewis, J., & Jhally, S. (1998). The struggle over media literacy. *Journal of Communication, 48*(1), 109-120.

Lind, R. A. (1996). Diverse interpretations: The "relevance" of race in the construction of meaning in, and the evaluation of, a television story. *Howard Journal of Communications, 7*, 53-74.

Livingstone, S. (2003, March). *Assessing the media literacy of UK adults: A review of academic literature.* London, England: Broadcasting Standards Commission, Independent Television Commission and NIACE.

Livingstone, S. (2004). Media literacy and the challenge of new information and communication technologies. *The Communication Review, 7*, 3-14.

Livingstone, S. (2006). Drawing conclusions from new media research: Reflections and puzzles regarding children's experience of the Internet. *Information Society, 22*, 219-230.

Livingstone, S., & Helsper, E. J. (2006). Does advertising literacy mediate the effects of advertising on children? A critical examination of two linked research literatures in relation to obesity and food choice. *Journal of Communication, 56*, 560-584.

Lloyd-Kolkin, D., Wheeler, P., & Strand, T. (1980). Developing a curriculum for teenagers. *Journal of Communication, 30*, 119-125.

Lund, D. J. (1998). Video production in the English language arts classroom. *English Journal, 87*(1), 78-82.

MacManus, J. H. (1994). *Market-driven journalism: Let the citizen beware?* Thousand Oaks, CA: Sage.

Maness, K. (2004). Teaching media-savvy students about the popular media. *English Journal, 93*(3), 46-51.

Masterman, L. L. (1983). Television literacy and adult education. In M. Tight (Ed.), *Education for adults. Volume II: Education opportunities for adults* (pp. 203-222). London: Croom Helm.

Masterman, L. (1997). A rationale for media education. In R. Kubey (Ed.), *Current perspectives. Information and behavior: Vol. 6. Media literacy in the information age* (pp. 15-68). New Brunswick, NJ: Transaction.

Masterman, L. (1998). The media education revolution. In A. Hart (Ed.), *Teaching the media: International perspectives* (pp. viii-xi). Mahwah, NJ: Erlbaum.

McClure, C. R. (1997). Network literacy in an electronic society: An educational disconnect? In R. Kubey (Ed.), *Current perspectives. Information and behavior:*

Vol. 6. Media literacy in the information age (pp. 403-439). New Brunswick, NJ: Transaction.

McMahon, B. (2003, June). *Relevance and rigour in media education.* Keynote address given at the annual meeting of the National Media Education Association, Baltimore, MD.

McQuail, D. (2000). *McQuail's mass communication theory* (4th ed.). London: Sage.

Means Coleman, R.R. (2003). Bringing diversity and activism to media education through African American-centered pedagogical cases. The mediation of ebonics and the NAACP television networks boycott. *Television & New Media, 4,* 411-438.

Means Coleman, R. R., & Fisherkeller, J. (2003). Introduction. Media education: Dilemmas of perspective, policy, and practice. *Television & New Media, 4,* 345-349.

Messaris, P. (1998). Visual aspects of media literacy. *Journal of Communication, 48*(1), 70-95.

Meyrowitz, J. (1998). Multiple media literacies. *Journal of Communication, 48*(1), 96-108.

Minkkinen, S. (1978). *A general curricular model for mass media education.* Paris, France: Unesco.

Morgan, R. (1998). Media education in Ontario: Generational differences in approach. In A. Hart (Ed.), *Teaching the media: International perspectives* (pp.145-167). Mahwah, NJ: Erlbaum.

Murdock, G., & Phelps, G. (1973). *Mass media and the secondary school.* London: MacMillan.

Pal, M., & Dutta, M. (2008). Theorizing resistance in a global context: Processes, strategies, and tactics in communication scholarship. In C. S. Beck (Ed.), *Communication yearbook 32* (pp. 41-87). New York: Routledge.

Piette, J., & Giroux, L. (1997). The theoretical foundations of media education programs. In R. Kubey (Ed.), *Current perspectives. Information and behavior: Vol. 6. Media literacy in the information age* (pp. 89-134). New Brunswick, NJ: Transaction.

Potter, W. J. (2004). *Theory of media literacy: A cognitive approach.* Thousand Oaks, CA: Sage.

Primack, B. A., Gold, M. A., Switzer, G. E., Hobbs, R., Land, S. R., & Fine, M. J. (2006). Development and validation of a smoking media literacy scale for adolescents. *Archives of Pediatrics and Adolescent Medicine, 160,* 369-374

Quin, R. (2003). Questions of knowledge in Australian media education. *Television & New Media, 4,* 439-460.

Quin, R., & McMahon, B. (1997). Living with the tiger: Media curriculum issues for the future. In R. Kubey (Ed.), *Current perspectives. Information and behavior: Vol. 6. Media literacy in the information age* (pp. 307-321). New Brunswick, NJ: Transaction.

Rapaczynski, W., Singer, D. G., & Singer, J. L. (1982). Teaching television: A curriculum for young children. *Journal of Communication, 32*(2), 46-55.

Roberts, D. F., Christenson, P., Gibson, W. A., Mooser, L., & Goldberg, M. E. (1980). Developing discriminating consumers. *Journal of Communication, 30,* 94-105.

Roessler, P. (2007). Media content diversity: Conceptual issues and future directions for communication research. In C. S. Beck (Ed.), *Communication yearbook 31* (pp. 464-520). Mahwah, NJ: Erlbaum.

Scharrer, E. (2003). "I noticed more violence": The effects of a media literacy program on critical attitudes towards media violence. *Journal of Mass Media Ethics, 21*(1), 69-86.

Scheibe, C. L. (2004). A deeper sense of literacy. Curriculum-driven approaches to media literacy in the K-12 classroom. *American Behavioral Scientist, 48*, 60-68.

Shah, Z., George, V. A., & Himburg, S. P. (1999). Computer-assisted education for dietetics students: A review of literature and selected software. *Journal of Nutrition Education, 31*, 255-261.

Singer, D. G., & Singer, J. L. (1983). Learning how to be intelligent consumers of television. In M. J. A. Howe (Ed.), *Learning from television* (pp. 203-222). London: Academic Press.

Singer, D. G., Zuckerman, D. M., & Singer, J. L. (1980). Helping elementary school children learn about TV. *Journal of Communication, 30*(3), 84-93.

Singer, J. L., & Singer, D. G. (1983). Implications of childhood television viewing for cognition, imagination and emotion. In J. Bryant & D. R. Anderson (Eds.), *Children's understanding of television: Research on attention and comprehension* (pp. 265-295). New York: Academic Press.

Stafford, R. (1990). Redefining creativity: extended project work in GCSE media studies. In D. Buckingham (Ed.), *Watching media learning: Making sense of media education* (pp. 81-100). London: Palmer Press.

Swinkels, H. (1992). Critical viewing: Creating a balance between maker and viewer. In C. Bazalgette, E. Bevort, & J. Savino (Eds.), *New directions: Media education worldwide* (pp. 42-47). London: British Film Institute.

Thoman, E. (1999). Skills and strategies for media education. *Educational Leadership, 56*(5), 50-55.

Thoman, E., & Jolls, T. (2004). Media literacy: A priority for a changing world. *American Behavioral Scientist, 48*, 18-29.

Tufte, B. (1992). Television, taste and teaching: Developments in media education in Denmark and Scandinavia. In C. Bazalgette, E. Bevort, & J. Savino (Eds.), *New directions: Media education worldwide* (pp. 177-184). London: British Film Institute.

Tyner, K. (2003). Beyond boxes and wires. Literacy in transition. *Television & New Media, 4*(4), 371-388.

Vande Berg, L. R., Wenner, L. A., & Gronbeck, B. E. (2004). Media literacy and television criticism. Enabling an informed and engaged citizenry. *American Behavioral Scientist, 48*, 219-228.

Van Dijk, T. A. (1987). *Communicating racism: Ethnic prejudice in thought and talk.* Newbury Park, CA: Sage.

Vargas, L. (2006). Transnational media literacy: Analytic reflections on a program with Latina teens. *Hispanic Journal of Behavioral Sciences, 28*, 267-285.

Vooijs, M.W., & van der Voort, T. H. A. (1989). Teaching critical television viewing skills De Amerikaanse aanpak [Teaching critical television viewing skills: The American approach]. *Massacomunicatie, 17*(1), 48-60.

Vooijs, M.W., & van der Voort, T. H. A. (1990). Teaching television: The effects of critical TV viewing curricula. *Institutional Journal of Educational Research, 14*, 543-552.

Wilksch, S. M., Tiggeman, M., & Wade, T. D. (2006). Impact of interactive school-based media literacy lessons for reducing internalization of media ideals in young adolescents girls and boys. *International Journal of Eating Disorders, 39*, 385-393.

Wyatt, S., Henwood, F., Hart, A., & Smith, J. (2005). The digital divide, health information and everyday life. *New Media & Society, 7*, 199-218.

Zettl, H. (1998). Contextual media aesthetics as the basis for media literacy. *Journal of Communication, 48*(1), 81-95.

Zoller, H., & Kline, K. (2008). Theoretical contributions of interpretive and critical research in health communication. In C. S. Beck (Ed.), *Communication yearbook 32* (pp. 89-135). New York: Routledge.

Appendix Overview of Which Authors Address Which Aspects of Media Literacy

Aspect of Media Literacy	Author
Media Influence on Producers	Quin, 2003
Production of Media Content	
General Discussion	*Media as a Construction* Aufderheide, 1997; Bazalgette, 1992; Brookfield, 1987; Court and Criticos, 1998; Criticos, 1997; Greenaway, 1997; Hobbs, 1997, 1998b, 1998c, 2005a; D. Lemish & P. Lemish, 1997; Masterman, 1997, 1998; Morgan, 1998; Scharrer, 2003; Thoman, 1999; Thoman & Jolls, 2004
	Ability to Produce Media Content Alvermann & Hagood, 2000; Aufderheide, 1997; Bazalgette, 1992; Brookfield, 1986; Collins, 1998; Davison, 1992; Dennis, 2004; Desimoni, 1992; Gaudard & Theveniaut, 1992; Hart, 1998; Hobbs, 1998a, 1998c, 2005a; Ketzer et al., 1989; D. Lemish & P. Lemish, 1997; Livingstone, 2003; Lund, 1998; Minkkinen, 1978; Quin, 2003; Scheibe, 2004; Stafford, 1990; Thoman & Jolls, 2004; Tufte, 1992; Tyner, 2003; Vande Berg et al., 2004; Vargas, 2006
Professional Activities	Buckingham, 2003; Covington, 2004
Producer Selectivity	Alvermann, 2004; Brookfield, 1986; J. A. Brown, 1991; Collins, 1998; Considine, 1997; Covington, 2004; Desimoni, 1992; Greenaway, 1997; Hobbs, 2005a, 2005b; Hobbs et al., 2006; D. Lemish & P. Lemish, 1997; Livingstone, 2003; Lloyd-Kolkin et al., 1980; Masterman, 1983; Potter, 2004; Primack et al., 2006; Thoman, 1999; Thoman & Jolls, 2004; Tufte, 1992; Vooijs & van der Voort, 1990

continued...

Appendix continued

Aspect of Media Literacy	Author
Codes and Conventions	Anderson, 1983; Aufderheide, 1997; Bazalgette, 1992; Court & Criticos, 1998; J. D. Desmond & Jeffries-Fox, 1983; Feshbach et al., 1982; Hobbs, 2004; Ketzer et al., 1989; D. Lemish & P. Lemish, 1997; Livingstone & Helsper, 2006; Primack et al., 2006; Thoman, 1999

Production Procedures

Anderson, 1983; Bazalgette, 1992, 1997; Brookfield, 1986; J. A. Brown, 1991, 2001; Buckingham, 1990, 1993, 1998, 2003; Buckingham, Fraser, & Mayman, 1990; Buckingham & Sefton-Green, 1997; Collins, 1998; Considine, 1997; Davies, 1997; Davison, 1992; Desimoni, 1992; Gray, 2005; Greenaway, 1997; Hobbs, 1997, 1998a, 1998b, 1998c, 2005a; Hobbs et al., 2006; Hobbs & Frost, 1999; Hobbs, Frost, Davis, & Stauffer, 1988; Livingstone, 2003; Lloyd-Kolkin et al., 1980; Masterman, 1983, 1997, 1998; McClure, 1997; McMahon, 2003; Messaris, 1998; Meyrowitz, 1998; Piette & Giroux, 1997; Potter, 2004; Quin & McMahon, 1997; Rapaczynski et al., 1982; Scheibe, 2004; D. G. Singer et al., 1980; D. G. Singer & J. L. Singer, 1983; J. L. Singer & D. G. Singer, 1983; Swinkels, 1992; Thoman, 1999; Thoman & Jolls, 2004; Vande Berg et al., 2004; Vooijs & van der Voort, 1989, 1990; Zettl, 1998

Dramatic and/or Narrative Codes

Abelman & Courtright, 1983; Anderson, 1983; Bazalgette, 1992; Brookfield, 1986; J. A. Brown, 1991, 2001; Buckingham, 1990, 1993, 1998, 2003; Buckingham et al., 1990; Buckingham & Sefton-Green, 1997; Collins, 1998; Considine, 1997; Court & Criticos, 1998; Davies, 1997; Desimoni, 1992; R. Desmond, 1997; Dorr et al., 1980; Greenaway, 1997; Hobbs, 1997, 1998a, 1998b, 1998c, 2005a; Hobbs et al., 2006; Hobbs & Frost, 1999; Hobbs et al., 1988; Ketzer et al., 1989; Livingstone, 2003; Lloyd-Kolkin et al., 1980; Masterman, 1983, 1997; McClure, 1997; McMahon, 2003; Meyrowitz, 1998; Piette & Giroux, 1997; Potter, 2004; Quin & McMahon, 1997; Rapaczynski et al., 1982; Roberts, Christenson, Gibson, Mooser, & Goldberg, 1980; D. G. Singer & J. L. Singer, 1983; D. G. Singer et al., 1980; J. L. Singer & D. G. Singer, 1983; Swinkels, 1992; Vande Berg et al., 2004; Zettl, 1998

continued...

Appendix continued

Aspect of Media Literacy	Author
Production Context General Discussion	J. A. Brown, 2001; Covington, 2004; D. Lemish & P. Lemish, 1997
Social and Cultural Aspects	Alvarado & Boyd-Barrett, 1992; Alvermann, 2004; Anderson, 1983; Bazalgette, 1997; J. A. Brown, 1991, 1998, 2001; Buckingham, 1993, 2003; Considine, 1997; Desimoni, 1992; Hart, 1998; Hobbs, 1998a, 1998c, 2005a; D. Lemish & P. Lemish, 1997; Lewis & Jhally, 1998; Livingstone, 2003; Masterman, 1983; McMahon, 2003; Meyrowitz, 1998; Scheibe, 2004; Thoman & Jolls, 2004; Vande Berg et al., 2004
Economic Aspects	Anderson, 1983; Aufderheide, 1997; Bazalgette, 1992, 1997; Branston, 1992; J. A. Brown, 1991, 1998; Buckingham, 1993, 2003; Dennis, 2004; Desimoni, 1992; J. D. Desmond & Jeffries-Fox, 1983; Dorr et al., 1980; Hart, 1998; Hobbs, 2005a; Hobbs & Frost, 1999; Hobbs et al., 2006; Lewis & Jhally, 1998; Livingstone, 2003; Masterman, 1983, 1998; McMahon, 2003; Messaris, 1998; Meyrowitz, 1998; Piette & Giroux, 1997; Potter, 2004; Primack et al., 2006; Rapaczynski et al., 1982; Thoman, 1999; Vande Berg et al., 2004; Vargas, 2006
Political Aspects	Alvarado & Boyd-Barrett, 1992; Anderson, 1983; Aufderheide, 1997; Bazalgette, 1992; J. A. Brown, 1998; Buckingham, 1993, 2003; Hart, 1998; Hobbs, 2005a; Hobbs et al., 2006; Masterman, 1983; McMahon, 2003; Meyrowitz, 1998; Potter, 2004; Thoman & Jolls, 2004; Vande Berg et al., 2004; Vargas, 2006
Media Influence on Its Users Influence at the Societal Level	Aufderheide, 1997; J. A. Brown, 1991, 1998; Buckingham & Sefton-Green, 1997; R. Desmond, 1997; Greenaway, 1997; D. Lemish & P. Lemish, 1997; Masterman, 1997; Messaris, 1998; Meyrowitz, 1998; Morgan, 1998; Piette & Giroux, 1997; Vande Berg et al., 2004; Vargas, 2006
Influence at the Individual Level	*Media Shape People's Perception of Reality* Alvermann & Hagood, 2000; Anderson, 1983; J. A. Brown, 1998; Buckingham, 2003; Buckingham & Sefton-Green, 1997; R. Desmond, 1997; Piette & Giroux, 1997; Rapaczynski et al., 1982; D. G. Singer & J. L. Singer, 1983; Swinkels, 1992; Thoman & Jolls, 2004

continued…

Appendix continued

Aspect of Media Literacy	*Author*
	Media Influence Feelings, Behavior, Self-concept Anderson, 1983; J. A. Brown, 1991; Buckingham, 2003; R. Desmond, 1997; Irving & Berel, 2001; Lloyd-Kolkin et al., 1980; Messaris, 1998; Potter, 2004; Primack et al., 2006; Rapaczynski et al., 1982; Scharrer, 2003; D. G. Singer et al.,1980; J. L. Singer & D. G. Singer, 1983; Vargas, 2006
	Factors That Mediate Media Influence Potter, 2004
Handling the Media Locating and Selecting	*Finding and Selecting Information* Alvermann & Hagood, 2000; Anderson, 1983; J. A. Brown, 1991, 1998, 2001; Buckingham, 1993, 2003; Considine, 1997; Dennis, 2004; Hobbs, 1997, 1998a; Livingstone, 2004; Lloyd-Kolkin et al., 1980; McClure, 1997; Meyrowitz, 1998; Potter, 2004; Scheibe, 2004; Thoman, 1999; Tyner, 2004; Vooijs & Van der Voort, 1990
	Assessing Quality of Selected Information Anderson, 1983; Aufderheide, 1997; Considine, 1997; Covington, 2004; Dennis, 2004; Hobbs, 1997, 1998a; Potter, 2004; Thoman, 1999; Tyner, 2003
Managing Media Use	*Awareness When One Uses the Media* Anderson, 1983; Branston, 1992; J. A. Brown, 1991, 1998; R. Desmond, 1997; Hobbs, 1998a, 2005a; Hobbs & Frost, 1999; Kline, 2005; Lloyd-Kolkin et al., 1980; Masterman, 1997; McMahon, 2003; Piette & Giroux, 1997; Rapaczynski et al., 1982; D. G. Singer & J. L. Singer, 1983; D. G. Singer et al., 1980; Vargas, 2006; Vooijs & van der Voort, 1989
	Managing Media Use in Well-considered Manner Anderson, 1983; J. A. Brown, 1991; Desimoni, 1992; Hobbs, 1998a; Kline, 2005; Rapaczynski et al., 1982; D. G. Singer & J. L. Singer, 1983; D. G. Singer et al. 1980; J. L. Singer & D. G. Singer, 1983; Vooijs & van der Voort, 1989, 1990
	Awareness of Motives and Purposes Anderson, 1983; J. A. Brown, 1991, 2001; Desimoni, 1992; McMahon, 2003; Piette & Giroux, 1997; Vooijs & van der Voort, 1990

continued...

Appendix continued

Aspect of Media Literacy	*Author*
The Ability to Mobilize the Media	J. A. Brown, 1991, 1998; Criticos, 1997; Hobbs, 1998a, 2005a; Means Coleman, 2003; Rapaczynski et al. 1982; D. G. Singer & J. L. Singer, 1983; D. G. Singer et al., 1980; Vande Berg et al., 2004
Interpreting Media Content	
General Discussion	Branston, 1992
	Understand Process of Meaning-giving Alvarado & Boyd-Barrett, 1992; Alvermann & Hagood, 2000; Anderson, 1983; Aufderheide, 1992; Bazalgette, 1992; Bouwman, 1989; Branston, 1992 J. A. Brown, 1991, 1998, 2001; Buckingham, 1993, 1998, 2003; Buckingham & Sefton-Green, 1997; Davies, 1997; Desimoni, 1992; R. Desmond, 1997; Hobbs, 1998c; Hobbs et al., 2006; Masterman, 1983; McClure, 1997; McMahon, 2003; Quin, 2003; Quin & McMahon, 1997; Thoman, 1999; Thoman & Jolls, 2004; Zettl, 1998
	Different People—Different Interpretations Alvarado & Boyd-Barrett, 1992; Alvermann & Hagood, 2000; Bazalgette, 1992; Branston, 1992; J. A. Brown, 1991, 1998; Buckingham, 1990, 1993, 1998, 2003; Buckingham & Sefton-Green, 1997; Considine, 1997; Criticos, 1997; Dorr et al., 1980; Greenaway, 1997; Hobbs, 1998a, 2005a; Hobbs et al., 2006; Masterman, 1983, 1997; Meyrowitz, 1998; Piette & Giroux, 1997; Primack et al., 2006; Quin & McMahon, 1997; Swinkels, 1992; Thoman, 1999; Thoman & Jolls, 2004; Vande Berg et al., 2004

CHAPTER CONTENTS

9 Explaining Variations in the Effects of Supportive Messages

A Dual-Process Framework

Graham D. Bodie
Purdue University

Brant R. Burleson
Purdue University

Although some recipients benefit from exposure to sophisticated and sensitive support messages, the effects of these messages are moderated (sometimes substantially) by characteristics of the recipient, the helper, and the situation. Thus, enhancing the success of helpers who provide support requires a comprehensive explanation of why support messages are effective in some circumstances but less effective in others. To understand why supportive messages work, we must understand how these messages are *worked on* (i.e., processed) by their recipients. This chapter uses a recently developed dual-process theory of supportive message outcomes to explain how and why multiple variables moderate the effects of supportive messages. We provide a comprehensive review of published research findings concerning the demographic, personality, cognitive, and situational moderators of supportive messages and show that these moderators can be interpreted as (1) factors influencing the message recipient's ability and/or motivation to systematically process these messages or (2) environmental cues that quickly trigger responses to the message.

INTRODUCTION

Supportive communication—"verbal and nonverbal behavior produced with the intention of providing assistance to others perceived as needing that aid" (Burleson & MacGeorge, 2002, p. 374)—is rapidly emerging as a core concern across the communication discipline. Supportive communication

Correspondence: Graham D. Bodie and Brant R. Burleson, Department of Communication, Purdue University, W. Lafayette, IN 47907-2098; Phone: 765-494-3429; E-mail: gbodie@purdue.edu; brantb@purdue.edu comprises a fundamental form of human interaction that plays critical roles in a host of contexts and settings. For example, considerable research indicates that supportive communication serves essential functions in the family (see review by Gardner & Cutrona, 2004) and other close relationships (see review by Burleson & MacGeorge, 2002). Additionally, supportive communication contributes to well-being in the workplace (see review by Apker & Ray, 2003), schools (e.g., Goldsmith & Albrecht, 1993; MacGeorge, Samter, & Gillihan, 2005), and the community (e.g., Albrecht, 1994). Much of the interest in supportive communication has been stimulated by research documenting the effects of social support on health, both physical (see review by Uchino, 2004) and mental (see review by Schwarzer & Leppin, 1992). These findings have motivated researchers to investigate supportive communication processes and outcomes that may enhance the prediction of health-related effects (see reviews by Albrecht & Goldsmith, 2003; Zoller & Kline, this volume). Likewise, scholars with interests in communication technology have probed whether the social and health benefits of supportive communication can be achieved through on-line support groups (e.g., Wright, 2002; Wright & Bell, 2003), while those with interest in gender issues have explored similarities and differences in men's and women's supportive communication practices and preferences (see reviews by Burleson & Kunkel, 2006; Goldsmith & Dun, 1997). Moreover, the study of supportive communication is increasingly a global concern, with researchers exploring cultural similarities and differences in supportive communication practices, preferences, and outcomes (e.g., Burleson, M. Liu, Y. Liu, & Mortenson, 2006; Feng & Burleson, 2006; Mortenson, M. Liu, Burleson, & Y. Liu, 2006; Xu & Burleson, 2004). Clearly, communication researchers have embraced social support as a key communicative phenomenon.

A major feature that differentiates communication-focused scholarship on social support from the extensive sociological and psychological literatures on this topic is the concern with the *messages* through which helpers seek to realize their supportive intentions (Goldsmith, 2004). That is, "from a communication perspective, the study of 'social support' *is the study of supportive communication"* (Burleson & MacGeorge, 2002, p. 384). Although supportive messages may exhibit a variety of help-intended goals, including dispensing information and advice, fostering a sense of belonging or inclusion, and enhancing the recipient's self-esteem (see Cutrona & Suhr, 1992; House, Landis, & Umberson, 1988), perhaps the most common goal pursued in supportive messages is the provision of *emotional support* (Burleson, 2003).

Messages that aim to provide emotional support—those intended to comfort, reduce suffering, and relieve distress—can powerfully affect the feelings, coping behavior, personal relationships, and even physical health of the recipient (Albrecht & Goldsmith, 2003; Goldsmith, 2004; Uchino, 2004; Wills & Fegan, 2001). Several research programs have sought to identify properties of more and less effective emotional support messages (see reviews by Burleson & MacGeorge, 2002; Cunningham & Barbee, 2000; Goldsmith,

2004). In particular, more empathic, person-centered, face-supportive, and solace-oriented messages are especially helpful at reducing the recipient's emotional distress and achieving other desirable outcomes (Burleson, 2003; Burleson & Goldsmith, 1998; Dunkel-Schetter, Blasband, Feinstein, & Herbert, 1992; Goldsmith, 1994).

However, a growing number of studies have concluded that the effects of support messages differ (sometimes substantially) as a function of several characteristics of the recipient, the helper, and the communication situation (see reviews by Lakey & Cohen, 2000; B. R. Sarason, I. G. Sarason, & Gurung, 1997; W. Stroebe & M. Stroebe, 1996). These variations in message outcome are theoretically interesting and pragmatically important. For example, these variations may define boundary conditions for the helpfulness of different support messages (see Helgeson, Cohen, Schulz, & Yasko, 2000) and, thus, indicate that certain support messages are more appropriately used with some recipients and/or contexts than others. Hence, maximally effective supportive practice requires knowing how relevant features of the recipient and context likely qualify the effects of various message options.[1] At the level of theory, variations in outcomes of supportive messages demand explanation: *Why* do certain variables moderate the effects of supportive messages in specific ways and on specific occasions? Answering this question should contribute to theory by generating a richer understanding of how people process supportive messages, how various factors affect message processing in particular ways, and why messages lead to characteristic outcomes. For example, what appear to be inconsistent results for various supportive messages may actually point to the operation of cognitive and affective processes in recipients that influence how they notice, process, and experience messages (e.g., Kaul & Lakey, 2003). Indeed, the research documenting moderators for the effects of support messages underscores what we take to be a fundamental axiom of message reception research—to understand how supportive messages work, we must understand how these messages are *worked on* (i.e., processed) by recipients.

Currently, we lack a comprehensive explanation for the factors that moderate the effects of support messages. Thus, the purpose of this chapter is twofold. First, we offer an integrative explanation for variations in support message outcomes by drawing from a recently developed theory of support message reception. Grounded in a *dual-process* approach to information processing (Chaiken & Trope, 1999; Todorov, Chaiken, & Henderson, 2002), this explanation suggests that many of the variables found to moderate the outcomes of supportive messages do so either through (1) their influence on the recipient's ability and/or motivation to systematically process these messages or (2) serving as cues that quickly trigger responses to the message. Second, the core of the chapter comprehensively reviews extant research findings on the moderators of support messages to determine if these findings can be explained within the dual-process framework. This review provides an evaluation of the integrative power and potential of the dual-process approach for support message processing, and it organizes these findings for future research in this area.

Beyond helping to explain why the effects of supportive messages vary, our analysis contributes to an enhanced understanding of the fundamental, yet understudied, core communication process of *message reception* (see Berger, 2005). By extending the scope of the influential dual-process approach outside the realm of persuasion where it was originally developed, the current analysis explores the general utility of this approach as well as its value for addressing questions such as: Why do particular messages have certain effects with certain people in particular contexts but different effects with different people in other contexts? How do supportive messages influence the feelings, thoughts, and coping behaviors of those that they seek to assist? How and why do these messages work—or fail to work? Further, why do some supportive episodes and interactions have extended, lasting effects on health and well-being while others do not?

To address these and related issues, we begin by offering an overview of the properties of more and less helpful emotional support strategies and discussing some of the factors found to moderate the effects of these messages. We also note some limitations in existing theory and research on supportive messages that need to be addressed.

EFFECTIVE EMOTIONAL SUPPORT STRATEGIES: PROPERTIES AND MODERATORS

Properties of Effective Emotional Support Strategies

Numerous studies have sought to identify helpful forms of supportive behavior, and synthetic reviews of these empirical findings (e.g., Burleson, 2003; Burleson & MacGeorge, 2002; Cunningham & Barbee, 2000; Dunkel-Schetter et al., 1992; Goldsmith, 2004; Wortman, Wolff, & Bonanno, 2004) provide considerable insight about the behavioral features that distinguish the supportive efforts most people find more versus less helpful. We derive the following generalizations about the properties of more and less effective forms of support from these reviews, which offer many more details than the current space permits.[2]

Messages expressing positive helper intent, feeling, and commitment are broadly perceived as helpful. In particular, recipients perceive messages that convey acknowledgement, comprehension, and understanding and those that express sincere sympathy, sorrow, or condolence as sensitive and helpful. Similarly, recipients typically experience statements by helpers that provide legitimacy for feelings (and sometimes actions) as quite helpful, especially when helpers embed such statements in *highly person-centered* (HPC) messages that also encourage the articulation, elaboration, and exploration of those feelings (Burleson, 1994).

Not surprisingly, recipients consider low person-centered (LPC) messages (which deny, criticize, or ignore their feelings and perspectives) as especially unhelpful. Particularly dysfunctional messages include criticism of the recipient's experience and/or expression of negative feelings, statements or implications that the recipient's feelings are unwarranted or illegitimate, and telling the recipient how he or she should feel and think about the upsetting situation (Burleson & Goldsmith, 1998). Recipients also resent an extended focus by the helper on his or her own feelings about the current situation or about a similar situation in the past. Moreover, such responses prove unhelpful at improving recipient affect, although this form of support may be viewed more positively if it comes from someone with genuinely similar experiences (Dakof & Taylor, 1990). Finally, recipients do not benefit from helper "overinvolvement, intrusiveness, oversolicitousness, and overconcern" (Dunkel-Schetter et al., 1992, p. 97).

Several other forms of emotional support elicit mixed reactions. Recipients occasionally perceive reassurance, particularly assertions that "the worst is over" and that "everything will work out," as helpful, but such statements can also be experienced as insensitive and unhelpful. Efforts aimed at distracting the target's attention from the upsetting situation may be helpful in some circumstances (Derlega, Barbee, & Winstead, 1994), but recipients can interpret them as invalidating and unhelpful in other circumstances (Barbee & Cunningham, 1995). Similarly, providing advice about how to manage aspects of the problem comprises a risky enterprise that frequently backfires; advice may be viewed as helpful, but it is also regularly identified as an unhelpful feature of supportive efforts (Goldsmith, 1994). Recent research indicates that individuals more likely perceive advice as helpful if it is contextually appropriate (i.e., solicited by the recipient and appropriately timed; Goldsmith, 2000; Jacobson, 1986), contains sound content (i.e., proposals that appear to be effective, implementable, and without significant disadvantages; MacGeorge, Feng, Butler, & Budarz, 2004), and is presented in a "face-supportive" way (i.e., in a manner that conveys positive regard and respects the target's autonomy; Goldsmith & MacGeorge, 2000; MacGeorge, Lichtman, & Pressey, 2002).

Factors Found to Moderate the Effects of Supportive Messages

Though substantial research indicates that some supportive messages are generally more helpful or effective than others, research increasingly finds that the effects of supportive messages are moderated by several characteristics of the recipient, the helper, and the communication situation (see reviews by Goldsmith, 2004; Lakey & Cohen, 2000; Sarason et al., 1997; W. Stroebe & M. Stroebe, 1996). More specifically, several *demographic factors* have been found to moderate the effects of supportive messages, including the recipient's age, nationality, ethnicity, social class (socioeconomic status), and sex.

Researchers have also determined that individual differences among recipients with respect to *personality traits* and *cognitive factors* moderate the effects of supportive messages, including attachment style, perceived support availability, locus of control orientation, gender schematicity, and interpersonal cognitive complexity. Finally, several features of the *interactional context* moderate the effects of supportive messages, including the recipient's need for support, the sex of the helper, the status of the relationship between the helper and the recipient, and certain features of the supportive message itself.

For example, numerous studies have found that the sex of the support recipient influences the outcomes of supportive messages. Specifically, although both men and women evaluate HPC comforting messages more positively than they do LPC messages, women tend to regard HPC messages more positively and LPC messages less positively than do men (see review by Burleson & Kunkel, 2006). Sex of the support provider also influences outcomes of supportive messages. Several studies (e.g., Glynn, Christenfeld, & Gerin, 1999; Samter, Burleson, & Murphy, 1987) report that recipients experience supportive messages originating from (or attributed to) female sources as more helpful than supportive messages coming from male helpers, even when researchers strictly control message content. Similar patterns of moderation have been detected for a broad range of individual and situational factors. The variable effects of supportive messages constitute a puzzle that we seek to explain through a comprehensive model of how various moderating factors influence the processing and outcomes of supportive messages.

The effects observed for most variables that moderate the impact of supportive messages typically have been rather modest in magnitude and rarely, if ever, completely qualify effects owing to message content. Despite their typically modest effect sizes, these moderators remain pragmatically important and theoretically interesting as indicated above. Currently, no comprehensive explanation exists for the moderating action of these variables on the effects of support messages, nor is it apparent that researchers recognize that the existence of these moderators constitutes a problem. Moreover, we lack agreement about which variables moderate the effects of supportive behaviors. The fragmented character of the literature has led many researchers to treat particular moderators in an isolated fashion, with several recent reviews of putative moderators focusing on largely different sets of variables (e.g., compare Goldsmith, 2004, pp. 16-19; Reis & Collins, 2000, pp. 146-165; Uchino, 2004, pp. 74-80). This practice has led to a complex and often confusing array of explanations for the effects of these moderators. Typically, the action of each moderating variable has been explained by a distinct theoretical mechanism— if researchers explain it at all.

Clearly, researchers concerned with the outcomes of supportive messages need a parsimonious theoretical account that provides a coherent explanation for the moderating effects of different variables on message outcomes. We believe that such an integrative account can be derived from a recently developed theory of support message processing, a theory that is grounded in a dual-process framework.

A DUAL-PROCESS THEORY FOR THE RECEPTION AND OUTCOMES OF SUPPORTIVE MESSAGES

Communication scholars are probably most familiar with dual-process approaches to human information processing in the context of persuasion (e.g., see Gass & Seiter, 2007; O'Keefe, 2002; Perloff, 2003). Approaches such as the Elaboration Likelihood Model of Petty and Cacioppo (1986; Petty, Rucker, Bizer, & Cacioppo, 2004) and Chaiken's Heuristic-Systematic Model (Chaiken, 1980; Todorov et al., 2002) were introduced in the early 1980s in an effort to resolve several problems in the persuasion and attitude-change literatures. In particular, dual-process models offered testable explanations for such puzzling phenomena as the varied (and even contradictory) effects of message, source, receiver, and contextual factors on attitude change; the variable strength and persistence of the attitude change achieved through persuasion, and the variable extent to which attitude change predicted behavioral change.

Bodie and Burleson (2006) suggested the potential of the dual-process approach for resolving similar problems in the supportive communication literature; they advocated this approach could explain (1) differences in the effects of various independent variables (message, source, receiver, and contextual factors) on recipient responses to supportive messages (e.g., message evaluations, changes in affect, coping, and behavior) and (2) differences in the persistence or endurance of changes in affect and coping achieved through supportive communication. The dual-process theory for supportive message outcomes (which we briefly summarize here) provides a detailed analysis of the varied processes through which changes in affect may occur, the processing modes that can be applied to supportive messages, the consequences that follow from particular processing modes for changes in affect and behavior, and determinants of the mode of processing employed by message recipients in particular contexts.[3] Figure 9.1 provides a graphic summary of the essential components of this model.

Processing Modes

Similar to dual-process theories developed for persuasive messages, the dual-process theory for supportive message outcomes assumes that people process supportive messages on an elaboration continuum that ranges from the highly systematic and thoughtful processing of messages to a very low level of thought. *Elaboration* refers to the extent to which an individual thinks with respect to message content. Thus, when processing messages systematically, recipients carefully reflect on the content of the message and the information

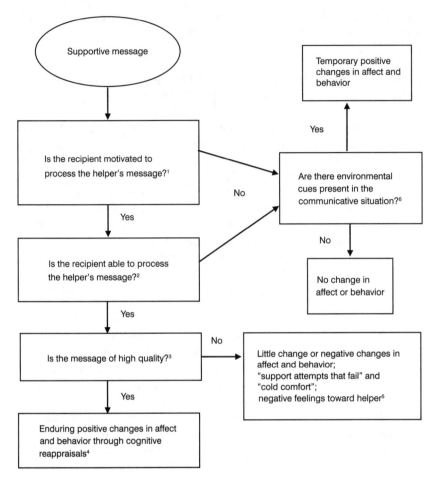

Figure 9.1 A dual process model for supportive communication (after Petty & Cacioppo, 1986)

Notes

1. Motivation to process supportive messages is influenced by both situational factors (e.g., severity of problem, timing of message, message content) and individual-difference factors (e.g., perceived support availability, attachment style, affiliative need, locus of control).

2. Ability to process supportive messages is influenced by both situational factors (e.g., presence/absence of attention distracters) and individual-difference factors (e.g., age, cognitive complexity, communicative competence).

3. Quality of supportive messages is influenced by factors such as the explicit statement of helping intentions, verbal person centeredness, facework or politeness, and nonverbal immediacy, among others.

4. Mechanisms through which cognitive reappraisals effect enduring positive changes in affect and behavior are described by Burleson and Goldsmith (1998).

5. The harmful consequences of poor quality supportive messages that receive thoughtful processing are detailed in Burleson (2003).

6. Environmental cues that can activate low elaboration affect change mechanisms include sex and attractiveness of the helper and type of the relationship between the helper and recipient.

contained within it, thoughtfully consider this information in relation to prior ideas, and give close attention to the full content of a message. In contrast, when engaged in a low level of elaboration, recipients of supportive messages pay comparatively little attention to the content of the message. Instead, environmental cues (e.g., sex of the helper, status of the relationship with the helper) largely influence communication outcomes. These cues may activate mechanisms of affect change that require relatively little thought, including certain cognitive heuristics—tacit interpretive and decisional rules (e.g., "women provide sensitive support;" "friends provide helpful support")—and distraction, refocusing attention away from the cause of upset.[4]

Undoubtedly, people systematically process many of the supportive messages that they receive. Often, individuals explicitly seek support and assistance from others, and, when they do, they appear to attend quite thoughtfully to message content (e.g., Barbee & Cunningham, 1995; Derlega, Winstead, Oldfield, & Barbee, 2003; Larose, Moivin, & Doyle, 2001). However, research also provides convincing evidence that people do, at least on occasion, engage in little elaboration when processing supportive messages. For example, some research indicates that people often report feeling comforted by the mere presence of others and cannot remember (or report) the content of the supportive messages generated by these others (e.g., Lehman, Ellard, & Wortman, 1986; Lehman & Hemphill, 1990). These results suggest that recipients did not attend to or deeply process the content of helpers' supportive messages; rather, the presence of a particular kind of helper served as the basis for recipient response. Further, in certain circumstances, people are affected more by the perception that a helper could be supportive than by whether the helper actually produced a well-crafted supportive message (see Mankowski & Wyer, 1997).

Consequences of Processing Mode

Both low and high elaboration of supportive messages can produce desirable outcomes (e.g., improved affect and coping), especially in the short term (Burleson, in press). Yet, the reasons for these outcomes, as well as their duration and stability, differ. For instance, many cognitive heuristics triggered by various environmental cues in support situations imply to recipients that they *should* feel better about things owing to the presence of these cues (e.g., receiving support from a woman or a friend) and rules associated with these cues (e.g., support from women and friends is helpful). However, the changes in affect and coping generated by such heuristics (and other low-elaboration mechanisms of affect change such as distraction) are likely to be short-lived since affect-change mechanisms activated by environmental cues do not act on the causes of upset, which—along with emotion scholars such as Lazarus (1991)—we assume to be the recipient's *appraisals* of the problematic situation.

In contrast, persuasion research (e.g., Haugtvedt & Petty, 1992; Petty, Haugtvedt, & Smith, 1995) suggests that when recipients elaborately process supportive messages, the content of these messages will have a considerable and lasting effect on outcomes. In particular, under conditions of high elaboration, messages exhibiting high levels of empathy, solace, person centeredness, and face support should yield desirable outcomes; messages exhibiting low levels of these characteristics should yield few or even harmful outcomes. Environmental cues should have comparatively little effect on outcomes when supportive messages are processed systematically; they may add somewhat to the effects of systematically processed message content when consistent with that content (e.g., a female helper using a HPC comforting strategy), but they tend to be discounted when inconsistent with systematically processed message content (see Todorov et al., 2002, for a discussion of the additivity and attenuation hypotheses).

The brief duration of emotional and behavioral changes achieved through low-elaboration affect change mechanisms may not be a cause for concern when recipients experience relatively mild forms of distress (see Endnote 2). In such instances, the recipient's mild distress and the problem underlying that distress likely decay rapidly on their own accord. Simple supportive strategies that rely on mechanisms such as heuristics or distraction might be quite effective in these circumstances (Burleson, in press); helpers may need to provide only a temporary lift in the recipient's affect until the upset dissipates and attention is refocused.[5]

The use of simple supportive strategies that rely on low-elaboration mechanisms of affect change (e.g., heuristics, distraction) are likely to be much less effective when recipients suffer from more intense emotional upsets and consequential problems. Once the cue is absent and the associated change mechanism is no longer active, negative affect and dysfunctional coping likely resurface, especially if the problematic situation is severe (Pennebaker, 1997). More distressed persons may cheer up only briefly when cues activating positive affect are present and then return to ruminating about the upsetting situation (Nolen-Hoeksema & Larson, 1998; Nolen-Hoeksema & Morrow, 1993).

For recipients dealing with a serious upset, lasting changes in affect and coping (as well as related outcomes such as improvements in mental and physical health) usually occur when they systematically process high-quality forms of emotional support (i.e., those providing empathy, solace, face support, and HPC comforting). Burleson and Goldsmith (1998) identified *cognitive reappraisal* as an affect change mechanism that can produce stable improvements in affect and coping; reappraisal involves changing judgments about the meaning and personal significance of events and tends to happen when recipients elaborately process high quality supportive messages. HPC comforting messages and other beneficial forms of support are more likely than their unhelpful counterparts to facilitate a cognitive reappraisal of the problematic situation (Jones & Wirtz, 2006). Because these messages address the underlying causes of emotional states and coping orientations—the recipient's cognitive appraisals of the problematic situation—the systematic processing of these messages has a good chance of yielding enduring changes in the recipient's thoughts, feelings, and behaviors (e.g., Donnelly & Murray, 1991; Lepore & Helgeson, 1998; Lepore, Ragan, & Jones, 2000).

Determinants of Processing Mode

The character of the changes in affect and coping achieved through low versus high elaboration of support messages makes it important to understand the factors that influence recipient processing. Systematic processing of messages most likely occurs (and occurs most extensively) when recipients are *motivated* to attend to the message and posses the *ability* to consider its content thoughtfully (Petty & Cacioppo, 1986). According to Petty and Cacioppo, motivational factors comprise those "that propel and guide people's information processing and [give] it its purposive character" (p. 218); whereas, ability factors "encompass a person's capabilities and opportunities" (Petty & Wegener, 1999, p. 53).

Both qualities of the individual (e.g., personality traits, cognitive capacities, demographic variables) and the situation (e.g., characteristics of the message source, aspects of the topic, features of the interactional setting) influence the motivation and ability to carefully consider message content. For example, situational factors that can increase the recipient's motivation to systematically process supportive messages include the severity of the problematic situation and the intensity of emotional upset experienced. Motivation to systematically process support message content can also be enhanced by several personality dispositions (e.g., need for cognition, perceived support availability). Situational factors likely to decrease the ability to process supportive messages systematically include environmental distractions (e.g., noise) and increased cognitive load (e.g., other tasks demanding cognitive resources). Finally, several social-cognitive capacities (e.g., interpersonal cognitive complexity, emotional intelligence), which reflect individual differences in ability, can promote systematic processing of support message content.

When either the motivation or ability to process supportive messages is low, environmental cues that activate low-elaboration processes more strongly influence responses to supportive behavior. For example, some feature of the message, source, or communication situation (i.e., a cue) may activate a decisional heuristic. The operation of heuristics activated by peripheral cues appears to be governed by three principles (Todorov et al., 2002). Specifically, as Todorov et al. observed, the use of a particular heuristic is most likely to occur when an individual has a heuristic (decision rule) stored in memory (*availability principle*) that recipients can access during the presentation of a message (*accessibility principle*) and apply to the decision making task at hand (*applicability principle*). Factors such as the recency and frequency of the heuristic's use govern principles such as the accessibility of a heuristic (and, thus, the triggering potential of its associated environmental cue). For example, in contemporary American society, many will have available the heuristic that women provide helpful emotional support (see Burleson & Kunkel, 2006); this heuristic may be easily accessible for some owing to its frequent use (e.g., those high in gender schematicity), and it becomes applicable in a particular situation when a female helper seeks to provide comfort.

Summary

In sum, the dual-process theory of supportive message outcomes maintains that the effects of supportive messages vary as a joint function of the way in which individuals process messages (low to high elaboration) and features of the communicative situation (message content versus environmental cues). This theory further maintains that the likelihood of processing supportive messages systematically is influenced by factors that impact the motivation and ability to scrutinize message content in supportive contexts. The next section seeks to apply this theory to explaining moderators of supportive message outcomes.

EXPLAINING MODERATORS OF THE EFFECTS OF SUPPORTIVE MESSAGES: A DUAL-PROCESS APPROACH

The dual-process theory of supportive message outcomes suggests an inclusive, yet parsimonious, framework for organizing and explaining the results of studies showing that numerous source, recipient, message, and contextual factors moderate outcomes of supportive messages. Specifically, this theory suggests that these moderating factors can (1) affect how recipients process supportive messages by influencing their ability and/or motivation to elaborate on message content or (2) serve as cues in low-elaboration processes such as the use of decisional heuristics.[6] In an effort to explain extant findings about moderators of support message effects and evaluate the integrative potential of the dual-process theory of supportive message outcomes, we present a comprehensive review of the various demographic, personality, cognitive, and situational factors found to moderate the effects of supportive messages. For each moderator documented by extant research, we consider whether it can be reasonably viewed as impacting the recipient's processing mode (by influencing the motivation and/or ability to process message content) or cuing the use of quick decisional judgments under low elaboration conditions. In addition, to evaluate the heuristic potential of our dual-process theory, we suggest several as-yet unexamined factors that may moderate the effects of supportive messages by either of the aforementioned processes.

Explaining Demographic Moderators of the Effects of Supportive Messages

Researchers have determined that several demographic characteristics of message recipients moderate the effects of supportive messages. We suggest that the sex, culture, age, and social class of a support recipient affect the motivation and/or the ability to process supportive messages in a systematic manner.

Sex Differences

Sex of the support recipient serves as a reliable moderator of the effect of supportive behavior. Numerous studies (see review by Cutrona, 1996) indicate that women are less satisfied with the support that they receive than are men; this sex difference holds true in marital relationships (Acitelli & Antonucci, 1994) and early adolescence (Shirk, Van Horn, & Leber, 1997). Numerous studies (Burleson & Samter, 1985b; Jones & Burleson, 1997; Kunkel & Burleson, 1999; MacGeorge, Graves, Feng, Gillihan, & Burleson, 2004; Samter, Whaley, Mortenson, & Burleson, 1997) reveal that, although both men and women evaluate and respond more positively to HPC comforting messages than to LPC messages, women respond somewhat more favorably to HPC messages than do men; whereas, men respond more favorably to LPC messages than do women (see review by Burleson & Kunkel, 2006). Other studies (Carels & Baucom, 1999) provide evidence that women's evaluations of supportive interactions with their spouses are more influenced by the content of the interaction (i.e., the messages) than are men's evaluations of supportive interactions with their spouses.

Women, thus, appear to discriminate more critically and carefully than men among the supportive messages that they receive, perhaps because they are more motivated and/or better able to evaluate the supportive messages they receive do than men. Compared to men, women report a stronger desire for support (especially emotional support; e.g., Xu & Burleson, 2001), and they place a greater value on the supportive skills of friends and family members (e.g., Burleson, Kunkel, Samter, & Werking, 1996; MacGeorge, Feng, & Butler, 2003). These findings coincide with the notion that women are more motivated than are men to systematically process the supportive messages they receive. Other findings suggest that women are better able than men to systematically process these messages. For example, women exhibit higher levels of cognitive complexity (e.g., Samter, 2002), empathy (e.g., Trobst, Collins, & Embree, 1994), and emotional intelligence (e.g., Brackett, Mayer, & Warner, 2004) than do men, all of which appear to influence the capacity to systematically process support messages, especially highly sophisticated messages (see Burleson & Caplan, 1998).

Cultural Differences

Ethnicity and nationality of the support recipient also moderate the effects of supportive messages. Members of different ethnicities in contemporary America (African Americans, Asian Americans, European Americans) all evaluate HPC comforting messages more positively than LPC comforting messages. However, European Americans evaluate HPC messages more favorably than do African Americans; whereas, African Americans evaluate LPC messages more favorably than do European Americans (Samter et al., 1997). Somewhat similarly, though highly sensitive comforting messages and coping behaviors are evaluated more positively than less-sensitive support behaviors by both Americans (Burleson & Samter, 1985a) and Chinese (Burleson et al., 2006), Americans respond somewhat more favorably to HPC messages than do Chinese; whereas, Chinese respond much more favorably to LPC messages than do Americans (Burleson & Mortenson, 2003; Mortenson et al., 2006).

One explanation for these cultural differences in responses to supportive messages builds on the distinction between low- and high-context communication. Specifically, European Americans and members of other, more individualist cultures routinely engage in *low-context* communication; whereas, Chinese, Asian Americans, African Americans, and members of other, more collectivist cultures are more inclined to engage in *high-context* communication (Gudykunst & Matsumoto, 1996; Hall, 1976). As Hall explained, in low-context communication, "the mass of information is vested in the explicit code" (p. 70), yet, in high-context communication, "most of the information is either in the physical context or internalized in the person" (p. 79). Thus, when Chinese receive support from in-group members such as friends and family, they probably are less motivated than are Americans to examine the content of these messages and rely less on the specific content of support behaviors to infer the helper's intentions and concerns. Rather, a provider's concerned desire to help can be taken for granted, with these assumed intentions providing the context or interpretive frame for processing and evaluating verbal messages (see Chang & Holt, 1991). Moreover, within a collectivist culture, the distressed person—who probably already feels guilty about disturbing social harmony by sharing unpleasant feelings—may be especially motivated to avoid further upsetting social harmony by critically (i.e., systematically) evaluating what may be less-than-tactful behavior from a friend (Gao, Ting-Toomey, & Gudykunst, 1996).

In contrast, low-context Americans appear more motivated to scrutinize and evaluate what helpers actually say (i.e., systematically process supportive messages). Individualist Americans who experience emotional upset appear to be more focused than are collectivist Chinese on having their personally distressing feelings and problems addressed (Feng, 2006; Taylor et al., 2004); this orientation may motivate them to draw sharper distinctions among various supportive messages. The individualist desire for others to directly address their distressed feelings may also account for Americans viewing highly sensitive support messages as slightly, but significantly, more helpful than Chinese (see Burleson & Mortenson, 2003). In sum, members of distinct groups appear differentially motivated to scrutinize the content of the supportive messages that they receive.

Age Differences

To date, only a few studies have examined how age moderates the effects of support messages. Utilizing a sample that included adults ranging in age from 19 to 85, Segrin (2003) found that age moderated the effect of social support on well-being, with older individuals indicating satisfaction even with decreased levels of social support when compared to their younger counterparts. Some theorists maintain that, as the end of life nears, people become more detached and withdrawn and less interested in social interactions (see review by Blieszner, 2000), all of which may lead to less effort being expended in processing supportive messages. Thus, the moderating effect of age might represent lesser motivation by older adults than by their younger counterparts to systematically process the content of the supportive messages they receive.

Other studies suggest that age influences the ability to understand sophisticated comforting messages (Clinton & Hancock, 1991) and that younger children do not discriminate among supportive messages that vary in sensitivity to the same extent as adolescents and adults (R. A. Clark & MacGeorge, 2006; Denton & Zarbatany, 1996). Thus, age differences in evaluations of supportive messages may reflect differences in recipients' ability to process these messages systematically. According to Clinton and Hancock, younger children, in particular, may not be able to appreciate differences among various support strategies, given their more limited linguistic, cognitive, and social skills. Consistent with this view, research indicates that youngsters generally do not develop the cognitive and social skills needed to produce highly sensitive support strategies until late childhood or early adolescence (Burleson, 1984; Ritter, 1979). Similarly, the oldest of adults, who may have diminished cognitive and social capacities (Antonucci, 1990), may be less able to differentiate among the supportive messages they receive.

Social Class

Very few studies have examined whether social class (socioeconomic status) moderates the effects of supportive messages. Some research suggests that the provision of emotional and esteem support is more salient and relationally significant for the middle class than the working class (Bergin, Talley, & Hamer, 2003). As with sex, the importance placed on certain types of support behaviors by individuals in different socioeconomic classes may speak to the motivation to process supportive messages. R. A. Clark and MacGeorge (2006) found that upper-middle-class children and adolescents viewed simple support messages as less helpful than did working-class children and adolescents; in addition, the message evaluations of the upper-middle-class participants were more sensitive to situational differences than the message evaluations of working-class participants. This finding implies that social class may be a marker of the ability to process supportive messages. Consistent with this interpretation, numerous studies report a positive correlation between socioeconomic status and the social and cognitive abilities needed to produce highly sophisticated supportive messages (e.g., Applegate, Burke, Burleson, Delia, & Kline, 1985; Dekovic & Gerris, 1992). Together, these findings suggest that socioeconomic status may contribute to the motivation and ability to process supportive messages; however, future research should directly assess these proposed associations.

Summary

Demographic variables, including the sex, culture, age, and socioeconomic class of the support recipient, moderate outcomes of support messages. Our review reveals that sex and socioeconomic class may affect either the motivation or the ability to process these messages systematically. Further, studies suggest that culture appears to affect motivation, and age impacts the ability to process these messages. Additional research needs to further specify the precise mechanisms through which these variables impact message outcomes.

Explaining Personality Moderators of the Effects of Supportive Messages

Several aspects of the recipient's personality have been found to moderate the effects of supportive messages, including affiliative need, locus of control orientation, perceived support availability, attachment style, depression, communication values, self-concept, and gender schematicity. As we suggest below, these aspects of personality appear to affect the individual's motivation to process supportive messages.

Affiliative Need

A series of studies by C. A. Hill and his colleagues (C. A. Hill, 1987, 1997; C. A. Hill & Christensen, 1989) indicate that individuals high in affiliative need (the motivation or drive to be close to others during times of stress) report more stress-buffering effects from enacted support than do individuals low in affiliative need. C. A. Hill (1997) suggested that "[greater] dispositional affiliative need is likely to increase the sensitivity of recipients to the interpersonal rewards available from contact with relationship partners" (p. 158). Indeed, research affirms that those with a high level of the affiliative need trait want to receive support (especially emotional support) during stressful times (Manne, Alfieri,

Taylor, & Dougherty, 1999). Thus, individuals with a high level of dispositional affiliative need tend to be more motivated to systematically process the support messages that they receive from others.

Locus of Control

Locus of control (LOC) references the tendency to see events as caused by (or under the control of) either (1) the self and, more generally, individuals (an internal LOC) or (2) external forces, God, powerful others, or luck or chance (an external LOC; Lefcourt, 1982). Internals more often take responsibility for solving problems than do externals and believe that they can alter the circumstances producing their distress (Manne et al., 1999). Thus, internals should be more motivated than externals to attend to the support messages that they receive and to process these messages systematically. Consistent with this view, the stress-buffering effects of social support have been found largely for internals; externals generally do not benefit from the supportive messages that they receive (Cummins, 1988; Lefcourt, Martin, & Saleh, 1984; Sandler & Lakey, 1982).

Perceived Support Availability

A growing body of research reveals that people process and respond to support messages based on their general level of *perceived support availability*, the global perception that support will be accessible to them when needed (see review by Lakey & Lutz, 1996). Specifically, Lakey and Cassady (1990) proposed that perceived support availability "operates in part as a cognitive personality variable that influences how supportive transactions with others will be interpreted and remembered" (p. 341). Several studies indicate that people with high levels of perceived support availability evaluate standard support messages more favorably than do people with low levels of perceived support (Kaul & Lakey, 2003; Lakey, McCabe, Fiscaro, & Drew, 1996; Lakey, Moineau, & Drew, 1992; Mankowski & Wyer, 1996; Pierce, B. R. Sarason, & I. G. Sarason, 1992), especially when these messages exhibit high levels of empathy or person-centeredness (Servaty-Seib & Burleson, 2007). In addition, several studies have discovered that people with high levels of perceived support availability recall the support messages they receive better than do their counterparts with low perceived support availability (e.g., Lakey & Cassady, 1990; Lakey et al., 1992). These findings suggest that those with high levels of perceived support availability are more motivated to systematically process the support messages that they receive. Persons with low levels of perceived support availability generally hold a lower expectation of receiving helpful support from others and, thus, may be less motivated to carefully scrutinize message content. In contrast, those with high levels of perceived support availability have a greater expectation of receiving helpful support from others, which may incline them to thoughtfully consider the support messages that they receive.

Attachment Style

Global perceptions of perceived support availability are closely associated with attachment style.[7] Those who consider support to be generally available more likely have secure attachment styles; whereas, those who see support as less available more likely have anxious and/or avoidant attachment styles (Asendorpf & Wilpers, 2000; Ognibene & Collins, 1998). Thus, not surprisingly, attachment style influences responses to support messages (Collins & Feeney, 2004; Herzberg et al., 1999; Larose et al., 2001; Lemieux & Tighe, 2004), with securely attached persons generally responding more favorably to these messages than those with anxious and/or avoidant attachment styles. Moreover, Jones (2005) found that the influence of attachment style on evaluations of comforting messages varied as a function of the person-centered quality of the messages evaluated. Hence, persons with secure attachment styles seem more motivated (and prone) to systematically process the support messages that they receive than those with non-secure attachment styles. Consistent with this view, Miller (2001) reported that persons with secure attachment styles had better memories for supportive interactions that they observed than did those with non-secure attachment styles; this result implies that a secure attachment style promotes greater attention to and processing of supportive interactions.

Results similar to those obtained for attachment style have been observed for personality traits conceptually linked to particular attachment styles. For example, Lepore (1995) determined that those high in the personality trait of cynical hostility (which constitutes a key component of the avoidant attachment style) did not benefit from social support provided in a stressful situation; whereas, those low in cynicism did benefit from supportive messages (exhibiting lower levels of cardiovascular reactivity than those in a control group who did not receive supportive messages). A plausible explanation for these findings is that those with high levels of cynical hostility (who generally mistrust others) are less motivated to reflect on the supportive messages that they receive and, therefore, process these messages less systematically and gain less from them than do those with low levels of cynicism.

Depression

Depressed individuals often believe that others cannot help them cope with their distressed states or the perceived causes of those states (see reviews by Segrin, 1998; Weary, 1990). Indeed, some research indicates that depression is inversely associated with the perceived availability of support (e.g., Schwarzer & Leppin, 1992; Vinokur, Schul, & Caplan, 1987). Thus, depressed individuals may be less motivated to systematically process the supportive messages that they receive from others, leading them to view such messages as less helpful than do non-depressed individuals. Consistent with this reasoning, studies (Hollander & Hokanson, 1988; Shirk et al., 1997) find that depressed persons evaluate standardized support messages less positively than their non-depressed counterparts. Though these results fit with the notion that depression reduces the motivation to systematically process supportive messages, depression may also reduce the ability to process such messages; Gotlib, Yue, and Joormann (2005) argued that depression negatively affects cognitive performance by reducing the attentional resources available for information processing tasks (see also review by Gotlib, Roberts, & Gilboa, 1996).

Communication Values

Communication values reflect an aspect of personality captured by the importance that individuals place on various communication skills; hence, *supportive communication value* is the importance (i.e., value) that people put on the skill of providing support, especially emotional support. Two recent studies (Burleson, in press; Study 1; Burleson & Mortenson, 2003) found that people who highly value supportive skills evaluate HPC comforting messages more positively, and LPC messages more negatively, than do people who place less value on supportive skills. It seems reasonable to assume that people who prioritize emotional support skills will be more motivated to process supportive messages, and, thus, they should discriminate more sharply between better and worse forms of these messages than people who value emotional support skills to a lesser extent.

A second method of assessing communication values involves identifying the goals that individuals indicate they would be likely to pursue in support situations. Researchers (Barbee & Cunningham, 1995; Burleson & Gilstrap, 2002) have identified several goals that potential helpers might pursue in support situations, including providing solace, solving problems, dismissing problems, and escaping from the other's negative emotional state. People who regard the goal of providing solace as particularly important clearly value the provision of emotional support. Those who value the provision of solace discriminate more sharply between better and worse forms of these messages in comparison to those who place less value on solace and/or greater value on other goals for support situations (Burleson & Mortenson, 2003; Kunkel, 2002; Mortenson et al., 2006). This pattern of results coincides with the notion that those who highly regard solace are comparatively more motivated to systematically process supportive messages.

Self-concept

Responses to supportive messages appear to be influenced by at least two aspects of the self-concept—people's self-definitions as expressive and as instrumental. People who perceive themselves as highly expressive believe themselves to be emotional, kind, warm, gentle, and sensitive to the feelings of others; people who consider themselves to be highly instrumental believe themselves to be independent, active, decisive, confident, and persistent (Spence & Helmreich, 1978). In contemporary American society, individuals often associate an expressive orientation with femininity; an instrumental orientation is typically linked with masculinity (Prentice & Carranza, 2002; Spence & Buckner, 1995), although men and women vary widely in their self-perceived degrees of expressiveness and instrumentality.[8] Given the centrality of affect in their self-definitions, high expressives might be expected to evaluate HPC comforting messages more positively, and LPC messages less positively, than to low expressives. In contrast, given their focus on solving practical problems, high instrumentals might be expected to evaluate MPC messages more favorably than low instrumentals. To date, two studies (Burleson, in press, Study 2; MacGeorge, Graves, et al., 2004) have examined the influence of expressive and instrumental orientations on evaluations of comforting messages that differ in person centeredness. Both of these studies revealed that high instrumentals more positively evaluated MPC comforting messages than did low instrumentals; whereas, high expressives more positively evaluated HPC messages, and more negatively evaluated LPC messages, than did low expressives. These results are consistent with the our predictions that (1) high expressives are more motivated to systematically process LPC and HPC messages than low expressives and (2) that high instrumentals are more motivated to systematically process MPC messages than are low instrumentals.

Gender Schematicity

Some personality variables may moderate the effects of support messages by decreasing the likelihood that these messages receive systematic processing. One such variable is *gender schematicity*, a trait that reflects an individual's reliance on and investment in culturally prevalent (i.e., traditional) conceptions of masculinity and femininity. Gender schematics hold specific, comparatively rigid expectations for men's and women's behavior, readily employ gender-based schemata in the interpretation and evaluation of others' behaviors, and respond negatively to "gender-bending" conduct (e.g., Markus, Smith, & Moreland, 1985). Thus, high gender schematics may often use sex of the helper as a cue that guides the evaluation of supportive behavior.

Consistent with this view, Holmstrom, Burleson, and Jones (2005) reported that highly gender-schematic women responded more favorably to a comforting message when it was attributed to a female helper than when it was attributed to a male helper; in contrast, women low in gender schematicity did not differ in their responses to the message as a function of helper sex. These findings suggest individual differences in reliance on the "women provide good support" heuristic. Highly gender-schematic women appear to be more reliant on it than are less schematic women. In contrast, women low in gender schematicity appear to process comforting messages more systematically; they respond more to the content of the messages used and less to the environmental cue of the helper's sex. Somewhat similarly, W. G. Hill and Donatelle (2005) found that gender-schematic men exhibited a lower capacity to recognize support when it was available to them, thus diminishing their appreciation of the benefits of supportive relationships. These findings coincide with research that indicates certain personality traits (e.g., the need for cognitive closure) reduce the motivation to process messages systematically and increase the likelihood of processing them through less elaborate means (e.g., Webster & Kruglanski, 1994).

Summary

Existing research affirms the notion that several personality traits (including affiliative need, locus of control, perceived support availability, attachment style, communication values, self-concept, and gender schematicity) impact the outcomes of supportive messages by increasing (or decreasing) the motivation to process support messages in a systematic manner. Depression also appears to reduce the motivation to systematically process supportive messages, although this variable potentially impedes the ability to process support messages. Several other personality factors, such as need for cognition (Cacioppo & Petty, 1982) and self-esteem (Nadler, 1986), may also affect the motivation to systematically process supportive messages. These possibilities should be evaluated in future research.

Explaining Cognitive Moderators of the Effects of Supportive Messages

Research demonstrates that several cognitive variables moderate the effects of supportive messages, including interpersonal cognitive complexity and communicative competence. We suggest that these cognitive factors affect the ability to systematically process supportive messages.

Cognitive Complexity

Interpersonal cognitive complexity is a stable, individual difference in the ability to represent and process social information; cognitively complex perceivers have more differentiated, abstract, and organized constructs or schemes for processing social information and, thus, possess more advanced social perception skills than do less complex perceivers (Burleson & Caplan, 1998). Considerable research suggests a positive relationship between cognitive complexity and the ability to generate sophisticated, helpful support messages (see reviews by Applegate, 1990; Burleson & Caplan, 1998; Coopman, 1997). Thus, cognitively complex recipients also should be better able to systematically process the support messages that they receive than less complex recipients. Consistent with this notion, Burleson and Samter (1985b) discovered that cognitively complex perceivers evaluated HPC comforting messages more positively than did less complex perceivers. Similarly, Samter, Burleson, and Basden-Murphy (1989) provided evidence that complex perceivers acquired more information about the message source from comforting messages than less complex perceivers, with the greatest difference between low- and high-complexity perceivers involving those exposed to HPC messages. These findings imply that complex perceivers are able to spontaneously process supportive messages more deeply and, thus, get more from these messages—particularly their more sophisticated forms—than are less complex perceivers.

Communicative Competence

Communicative competence (CC) refers to an individual's general ability to achieve desired communicative goals effectively, efficiently, and appropriately (Parks, 1994; Wilson & Sabee, 2003). As more skilled communicators, those with high levels of CC should be better able to process supportive messages in a systematic manner than are those with lower levels of CC. Anderson, Carson, Darchuk, & Keefe (2004) generated results consistent with this hypothesis. Anderson et al. tested participants for social skill (CC) and subsequently asked them to complete a disclosure task in which they discussed an emotionally painful event with either a highly skilled or low-skilled facilitator. The skill level of the facilitator did not influence the affect of low-CC disclosers; however, high-CC disclosers reported significantly greater positive affect when paired with a high-skill facilitator than when paired with a low-skill facilitator. These results suggest that high-skill disclosers gained more from the support offered by high-skill facilitators than do low-skill disclosers.

Summary

Research indicates that certain cognitive factors, including cognitive complexity and CC, affect a support recipient's ability to process support messages in a systematic manner. Other cognitive factors—such as working memory capacity (Barrett, Tugade, & Engle, 2004), mental retardation (Lunsky & Benson, 2001), and emotional intelligence (Brackett et al., 2004)—may also influence the ability to systematically process supportive messages and, hence, should be explored in future research.

Explaining Situational Moderators of the Effects of Supportive Messages

Several features of the communicative situation moderate the effects of supportive messages, including the recipient's need for support, the status (or quality) of the relationship between the helper and the recipient, the sex of the helper, and features of the helper's message such as its timing and content.

Next, we address how the effects of these contextual features can be explained through our dual-process framework.

Recipient's Need for Support

One set of factors that moderates the effects of supportive messages includes aspects of the recipient's need or desire for support (e.g., severity of the stressor, intensity of negative affect). Theoretically, as stressors or negative affect states become more severe, so should the desire for support and the motivation to systematically process supportive messages received from others. Consistent with this prediction, Hagedoorn and colleagues (2000; also see Kuijer et al., 2000; Kuijer, Buunk, & Ybema, 2001) found that the marital satisfaction of cancer patients was higher when their spouses used more helpful support strategies (i.e., those reflecting active engagement) and lower when spouses employed less helpful support strategies (i.e., those reflecting protective buffering or overprotection). Most important, the effects for type of spousal support strategy on recipient marital satisfaction were stronger for those recipients with a greater need for support (i.e., those in poor psychological and physical condition). This latter finding, in particular, suggests that recipients process supportive messages more deeply when their need for support intensifies.

More recently, Burleson (in press, Study 3) asked participants to assume that they experienced either a mild version of a problem (e.g., receiving a $25 parking ticket) or a more serious version of the problem (e.g., getting one's car towed and having to pay $350 in fines and fees to get the car released); the participants subsequently read and evaluated six comforting messages that varied in level of person-centeredness. Analyses revealed that participants confronting the serious problem discriminated more sharply between LPC and HPC comforting messages than did those confronting a mild problem. These results suggest that problem severity increased the motivation to process the supportive messages systematically.

We suspect that problem severity (and related factors such as stress and emotional intensity) has a curvilinear effect on the motivation to process supportive messages. As Burleson's results (in press) suggest, persons experiencing only a mild degree of irritation or upset may not have much motivation to thoughtfully consider the content of any supportive messages that they happen to receive. In contrast, those experiencing moderate-to-strong upset are likely to be quite motivated to scrutinize supportive messages that they receive for helpful content. However, at extremely high levels of emotional upset, persons may be unmotivated (and unable) to process supportive messages in a systematic fashion; they may be "paralyzed by fear," "overcome with grief," or "consumed by anger." In such cases, supportive messages likely have little impact, at least until the intensity of the recipient's emotional state becomes less extreme. Ethical considerations preclude most experimental assessments of extreme emotional upset on message processing, but evidence relevant to its effects on processing might be obtained from field studies or retrospective self-reports.

Relationship Status

Another set of situational factors that moderates the effects of supportive messages includes the status (e.g., acquaintance versus friend) or quality (i.e., closeness, intimacy, positivity) of the relationship between the support provider and the recipient. For example, R. A. Clark et al. (1998) determined that recipients perceived standard supportive messages as more helpful and comforting when attributed to a close friend than to a casual acquaintance. This finding indicates that relationship status functions as an environmental cue associated with a decisional heuristic for processing messages in support situations (e.g., "close friends provide helpful support in times of need"). Indeed, Fincham, Garnier, Gano-Phillips, and Osborne (1995) demonstrated that, when the status of a relationship is easily accessible from memory, this cue exerts a stronger influence on responses to supportive behavior than when it is less accessible from memory.[9]

Several other studies have reported results consistent with the notion that relationship status constitutes an environmental cue associated with the heuristic processing of supportive messages (e.g., Christenfeld et al., 1997; Knobloch, MacGeorge, & Lucchetti, 2004; Uno, Uchino, & Smith, 2002; Young, 2004). In addition, numerous studies provided evidence that satisfaction with support efforts is greater when messages come from providers that the recipient perceives as particularly intimate or close (Cutrona, Cohen, & Igram, 1990; Dakof & Taylor, 1990; Frazier, Tix, & Barnett, 2003; Hobfoll, Nadler, & Leiberman, 1986).

Pierce, I. G. Sarason, and B. R. Sarason (1991) suggested that individuals "develop sets of expectations about the availability of social support for each of their specific significant relationships" (p. 1028). Thus, a particular person (e.g., one's mother) can act as an environmental cue that activates a heuristic (e.g., "mother cares about me" or "mother doesn't care about me") that guides the individual's response to messages received in support situations. Pierce et al. (1992) reported that daughters' evaluations of standard support messages attributed to their mothers were substantially influenced by the daughters' perceptions of the quality of the mother-daughter relationship. In sum, relationship status can serve as a cue that promotes low-elaboration processing of supportive messages, at least under certain circumstances.

Sex of Helper

Sex of the support provider constitutes another feature of the situation that moderates the outcomes of supportive messages. For example, several experiments using identical, standardized messages (Glynn et al., 1999; Samter et al., 1987; Uno et al., 2002) determined that participants respond more favorably to these messages when they are attributed to female helpers as opposed to male helpers. Burleson (in press, Study 3) found that participants evaluated standard comforting messages attributed to a female helper more positively than those attributed to a male helper but only when participants confronted a mild upset (and, therefore, were presumably engaged in a low level of message elaboration). When participants confronted a more serious upset, Burleson did not find any difference in message evaluations due to the sex of the helper, presumably because the more upsetting situation motivated a high, rather than a low, level of elaboration. Other research has shown that men who use HPC messages when comforting distressed males elicit less favorable reactions than women who employ such messages (Burleson, Holmstrom, & Gilstrap, 2005).

Together, these results suggest that sex of the helper serves as an environmental cue linked to the heuristic "women provide good support" (or "women provide better support than men"). Several lines of evidence affirm the existence of such a heuristic. First, research provides support for a broadly shared cultural expectation that women will be ready and willing providers of warm, nurturing support (Ashton & Fuehrer, 1993; Barbee et al., 1993; Prentice & Carranza, 2002; Wood, 1994). Second, and consistent with this cultural stereotype, many studies have found that, compared to men, women are more nurturing, "tender minded," expressive, and emotionally supportive (Eagly, 1987; Feingold, 1994). Third, numerous studies document that women tend to provide more sophisticated forms of support than men (e.g., solace, face support, HPC comforting) to those in need (e.g., Basow & Rubenfeld, 2003; Goldsmith & Dun, 1997; MacGeorge, Gillihan, Samter, & Clark, 2003; MacGeorge, Graves, et al., 2004, Study 1; Oxley, Dzindolet, & Miller, 2002). Collectively, these findings underscore the existence of the "women provide sensitive support" heuristic; the experimental finding that people respond more favorably to standard support messages from female rather than from male helpers suggests the use of this heuristic when processing supportive messages, at least under certain conditions.

Timing or Sequencing of Support Messages

The effects of supportive messages are moderated by their timing or sequential placement in the supportive interactional episode; as Jacobson (1986) observed, the "same behavior, offered by others and intended to be supportive, may be seen as helpful by the recipient if provided at the right time and as unhelpful if provided at the wrong time" (p. 255). This conclusion holds especially true for messages that give informational support (i.e., advice; Goldsmith & Fitch, 1997). Though recipients often evaluate advice negatively (Dunkel-Schetter et al., 1992), they respond more positively when advice is solicited (Goldsmith & MacGeorge, 2000; MacGeorge, Feng, et al., 2004) or when it is offered following the provision of emotional support (Feng, 2006, Study 3; Jacobson, 1986). One explanation for these results is that recipients are more motivated to attend to advice and, thus, process these messages more systematically at particular points in the support episode (Feng & MacGeorge, 2006; Parkes, 1982). Simply put, extending from Feng (2006), when recipients want advice and are ready to receive it (i.e., they are motivated), they more likely process the advice that they receive in a systematic manner, get more from that advice, and respond more favorably to it, assuming the advice contains good content. This explanation receives support from recent research by Feng (2007), who found that individual differences in the motivation to process message content moderated the effects of the sequential placement of advice in an interaction on judgments of advice quality, implementation intention, and facilitation of coping. In sum, when recipients want advice and are ready to receive it, they more likely process that advice in a systematic manner, get more from that advice, and respond more favorably to it (assuming that advice contains good content; Feng, 2006, 2007; Feng & MacGeorge, 2006; MacGeorge, Feng, et al., 2004).

Message Content

An understudied factor in the support situation that may moderate the effects of support messages includes certain features of these messages. In particular, Burleson and Goldsmith (1998) suggested that the content of a supportive message may itself serve to encourage (or discourage) systematic processing. Specifically, these theorists maintain that HPC comforting messages (and, possibly, other highly sensitive forms of supportive communication) encourage recipients to articulate and elaborate their thoughts and feelings about upsetting situations (i.e., engage in systematic thought about them). According to appraisal theories of emotion (e.g., Lazarus, 1991) and related theories of coping (e.g., L. F. Clark, 1993; Smyth & Pennebaker, 1999), this sort of systematic thinking about the nature and causes of the distressful situation should engender functional reappraisals of these situations and, thereby, result in improved affect. In contrast, LPC comforting messages discourage recipients from expressing and exploring their thoughts and feelings (by telling recipients how they should act and feel) and, thereby, undermine systematic thinking about the upsetting situation.

Recently, Jones and Wirtz (2006) provided direct evidence that exposure to HPC versus LPC comforting messages encourages more thought about an upsetting situation. Jones and Wirtz directed participants to disclose an upsetting experience to confederates who responded with low, moderate, or highly person-centered comforting messages; the interactions between participants and confederates (which generally lasted about five minutes) were recorded and subsequently transcribed. The researchers found that participants exposed to HPC messages utilized more positive emotion words, negative emotion words, and cognitive mechanism (e.g., causal analysis) words during the course of the discussion with the confederate than participants exposed to less person-centered messages. These findings suggest, then, that the content of a supportive message may play an important role in motivating systematic thinking about the support situation, the stressful event, and even support messages themselves.

Summary

As shown above, several aspects of the support situation appear to influence the motivation to process supportive messages, including features of message content, the timing or sequence of the supportive message, and the recipient's need for support. Other situational variables, such as sex of the helper and status of the relationship with the helper, appear to serve as cues that foster reliance on heuristics when processing supportive messages (at least in some circumstances). Additional situational factors that may influence the processing of supportive messages encompass the recipient's mood state (Forgas, 2001; Petty, Schumann, Richman, & Strathman, 1993; Schwarz, Bless, & Bohner, 1991), environmental distracters that disrupt attention (Petty & Brock, 1981), the privacy of the setting (Burleson, Samter, et al., 2005), and the perceived attractiveness or similarity of the helper (Suitor & Pillemer, 2000).

CONCLUSION

Though much research has identified the general characteristics of more and less helpful supportive messages, other research indicates that the effects of these messages are moderated (sometimes substantially) by properties of the recipient, the helper, and the situation. Our review comprises the first comprehensive synthesis of research findings regarding these moderators and provides the first unified explanation for their effects. We argue that a dual-process analysis of message reception provides an integrative framework that explains how and why diverse moderating factors affect the outcomes of supportive messages. As with dual-process approaches to persuasive messages, this theory maintains that support messages receive more or less cognitive elaboration from recipients. The degree of message processing, in conjunction with the qualities of the message and features of the interactional situation, jointly determine the outcomes of the supportive episode. Application of this theory enabled us to explain why numerous demographic, personality, cognitive, and situational factors moderate the effects of supportive messages in the ways that they do. We demonstrated that these moderators can be interpreted as affecting message outcomes either through their influence on the ability and/or motivation to systematically process these messages or by acting as cues that trigger certain low elaboration processes such as heuristics. Table 9.1 summarizes our review, indicating the roles that different moderating variables serve within our dual-process framework.

The dual-process framework enabled us to organize and explain most of the existing findings about moderators of the effects of supportive messages

Table 9.1 Variables Shown to Moderate Effects of Supportive Messages

Individual factors influencing the motivation to process systematically

Variable	Citations
Affiliative need	Hill, 1987, 1997; Hill & Christensen, 1989
Attachment style	Collins & Feeney, 2004; Herzberg et al., 1999; Jones, 2005; Larose et al., 2001; Lemieux & Tighe, 2004; Miller, 2001
Communication values	Burleson, in press; Burleson & Mortenson, 2003; Kunkel, 2002; Mortenson et al., 2006
Culture of support recipient	Burleson et al., 2006; Burleson & Mortenson, 2003; Mortenson et al., 2006; Samter et al., 1997
Depression	Hollander & Hokanson, 1988; Shirk et al., 1997
Gender schematicity	Hill & Donatelle, 2005; Holmstrom et al., 2005
Locus of control	Cummins, 1988; Lefcourt et al., 1984; Sandler & Lakey, 1982
Perceived support availability	Kaul & Lakey, 2003; Lakey & Cassady, 1990; Lakey et al., 1996; Lakey et al., 1992; Mankowski & Wyer, 1996; Pierce et al., 1992; Servaty-Seib & Burleson, 2007
Self-concept	Burleson, in press; MacGeorge, Graves, et al., 2004
Sex of support recipient	Burleson & Samter, 1985b; Carels & Baucom, 1999; Jones & Burleson, 1997; Kunkel & Burleson, 1999; MacGeorge, Graves et al., 2004b; Samter et al., 1997

Situational factors influencing the motivation to process systematically

Message content	Jones & Wirtz, 2006
Message timing or sequential placement	Feng, 2006; Goldsmith & MacGeorge, 2000; MacGeorge, Feng, et al., 2004
Recipient need for support	Burleson, in press; Hagedoorn et al., 2000; Kuijer et al., 2001; Kuijer et al., 2000

Individual factors influencing the ability to process systematically

Cognitive complexity	Burleson & Samter, 1985b; Samter et al., 1989
Communicative competence	Anderson et al., 2004
Social class	Clark & MacGeorge, 2006

Environmental cues tied to decisional heuristics

Cue	Decisional Heuristic and Citations
Relationship status	"Close others provide helpful support in times of need." Christenfeld et al., 1997; R. A. Clark et al., 1998; Fincham et al., 1995; Knobloch et al., 2004; Pierce et al., 1992; Uno et al., 2002; Young, 2004
Sex of helper	"Women provide good support." Burleson, in press; Burleson, Holmstrom, et al., 2005; Glynn et al., 1999; Samter et al., 1987; Uno et al., 2002

within a single, cohesive account. Previously, these findings were diverse and fragmented, mostly explained through a host of unconnected mechanisms. The dual-process theory of supportive message outcomes is more parsimonious, and it exhibits greater integrative power, thereby enhancing our understanding of why support strategies affect particular people as they do on particular occasions. Of course, our framework is not the only possible one for explaining why diverse factors moderate the effects of supportive messages. Indeed, we encourage other scholars to propose alternative explanatory frameworks for these moderators; doing so will only deepen our understanding of why supportive messages work as they do.

In addition to synthesizing and integrating existing findings, the dual-process framework generates a rich set of predictions about other potential moderators of supportive message outcomes. For example, this model proposes that the recipient's motivation to systematically process may be influenced by several additional personality traits (e.g., need for cognition, need for cognitive closure, self-esteem) and several other contextual factors (e.g., physical attractiveness of helper, stage or phase of the recipient's grieving process, privacy of the setting). Similarly, this model suggests that the recipient's ability to systematically process supportive messages may be impacted by additional cognitive variables (e.g., emotional intelligence) and other contextual factors (e.g., attention distraction, information processing demands). Thus, this dual-process approach provides a heuristic theoretical framework for subsequent research on factors that may influence the processing and effects of supportive messages.

Of particular note, the dual-process theory enabled us to treat aspects of supportive message content as moderators of message outcomes. That is, this theory positions message content not only as an object to be processed but as a factor that influences degree of elaboration. This attribute represents an important extension of dual-process approaches—one that stands to have more general applicability (i.e., to persuasive and informative messages as well as supportive messages). More generally, our review reveals the applicability and utility of a dual-process approach for analyzing the outcomes of supportive communication. Up until now, dual-process models have been developed almost exclusively with respect to persuasive communication (see Chaiken & Trope, 1999). By demonstrating the fruitfulness of the dual-process approach with another, quite distinct domain of communication, this review will hopefully contribute to the development of more general theories of message reception and outcome.

Finally, we believe that our review and the dual-process theory that informed it hold considerable pragmatic potential. In particular, this theory has the potential to generate an empirically sound basis for prescribing the types of support strategies to be used on various occasions with various recipients. If this potential is borne out by empirical research, our theory may contribute to improving the training and effectiveness of the laypersons, therapists, counselors, pastors, and other formal and informal helpers who provide support to others. For example, our review suggests when simple, brief support messages may be just as effective (and, perhaps, more effective) than longer, more complex messages that require considerable cognitive processing to yield desirable effects. Our review further indicates that, when longer more complex support messages are needed and simple, brief messages are likely to be ineffective—or even counterproductive. Ultimately, our analysis reiterates that helpers should implement a recipient-centered and contextually sensitive approach to providing support. We believe that the principles guiding this approach to support provision can be incorporated in various forms of clinical practice (e.g., Greenberg, 1993) and professional practice (e.g., Hullett, McMillan, & Rogan, 2000), in the design of community support groups (e.g., Helgeson et al., 2000) and support interventions (e.g., Gottlieb, 2000), and in the development of more helpful and supportive social networks (Cutrona & Cole, 2000).

Several limitations in our explanatory efforts should be noted. For example, we are presently unable to specify whether certain factors that moderate the effects of supportive messages (e.g., recipient sex, recipient depression) do so by affecting processing ability, processing motivation, or both of these. Research designs that employ tests for different sets of potential mediating variables will help reduce this ambiguity. In this context, however, it is important to underscore a fundamental claim of dual process models—many variables may serve multiple roles, sometimes influencing processing mode, sometimes functioning as a cue, and sometimes functioning as an influence on cognitions and behaviors through high-elaboration processes (Petty et al., 2004; Todorov et al., 2002). Hence, future theoretical developments and research need to pinpoint the precise role served by particular variables in particular sets of circumstances. Researchers could accomplish this task by designing studies that incorporate variables hypothesized to impact the ability and motivation to process support messages; they should also test proposed mediators (e.g., elaboration) through the use of hierarchical regression, path analysis, or structural equation modeling. Without careful tests of specific connections and linkages implied by our theory, the powerful dual-process framework will quickly devolve into a morass of non-falsifiable propositions (Stiff, 1994; Stiff & Boster, 1987).

The major limitation with our dual-process analysis of how moderating variables affect the outcomes of supportive messages is that it has not yet been subjected to direct test. We maintain that the moderating effects of demographic, personality, cognitive, and situational factors on supportive message outcomes occur because these factors affect the processing of supportive messages. Thus, direct tests of our claims need to examine the extent to which elaboration or processing depth (as assessed by thought listing, reaction time, or self-reports; see Petty & Cacioppo, 1986) mediates the effects of moderators on supportive messages. We are currently engaged in a program of research designed to provide these tests by examining the mediating effects of processing depth with regard to several moderators, including several potential moderators not previously examined with regard to supportive communication (e.g., need for cognition) and those that have received only limited attention thus far (e.g., cognitive complexity). This empirical work should lead to refinements in our analysis and a better understanding of how supportive messages produce their effects under various conditions with diverse groups of people.

Limitations notwithstanding, the current review offers a heuristic framework for understanding an otherwise fragmented set of findings within an area central to many domains of communication research. Our review also crosses disciplinary boundaries and could potentially influence theory building and practice in counseling, social cognition, message processing, and epidemiology, among other areas. Building a better understanding of supportive processes in everyday life is important for scholars, practitioners, and everyday social actors.

ACKNOWLEDGMENTS

Portions of this chapter are based on a paper by the authors presented at the 2006 meeting of the National Communication Association, San Antonio, TX. The authors thank Amanda Holmstrom and Jessica Rack for collaboration on related projects that contributed to the insights developed in this chapter and thank Susanne Jones, Scott Caplan, and Erina MacGeorge for commenting on previous versions of this manuscript.

NOTES

1. The contingent nature of the effects of supportive messages suggest that, like persuasion, the provision of support is an *art* that would be usefully informed by a theoretically sophisticated and empirically valid *rhetoric of support.*
2. Most studies examining properties of more and less helpful messages have focused on contexts where the recipient is (or appears to be) experiencing moderate to severe emotional upset. Little research to date has examined supportive behavior in the context of mild upset or has sought to determine whether the message forms found helpful in contexts of moderate and severe upsets are equally helpful in coping with mild upsets.
3. A rather different effort to apply the logic of the dual-process approach to therapy and counseling was presented more than 20 years ago by Petty et al. (1984). Little development or extension of this model has occurred in the intervening years.
4. Multiple mechanisms exist through which the communicative effects of helpers can foster affect change in distressed recipients. Here, we focus on one mechanism that requires a high degree of cognitive elaboration—reappraisal—and two mechanisms that generally require low levels of elaboration, distraction and the use of heuristics. In future work, we plan to explore systematically multiple mechanisms of affect change.

5. Of course, it remains important for helpers to avoid using minimization strategies and other invalidating behaviors that have been found to exacerbate the recipient's upset; as numerous studies show, clumsy efforts at providing support can make things worse rather than better (e.g., Barbee et al., 1998; S. L. Clark & Stephens, 1996; Hays et al., 1994).

6. Readers familiar with dual-process theories of persuasive message processing will recognize that variables can serve a third function in these models—they can bias both the valence and outcome of message processing (for details, see Petty et al., 2004; Todorov et al., 2002). We do not discuss this potential function of moderating factors here as, to date, we discovered no efforts directed at examining this function in the context of supportive communication, and few of the extant findings appear consistent with this function. Of course, future research focused on extending the dual-process theory of supportive message outcomes should investigate the possibility that moderators of message effects exert their influence through this biasing function.

7. Attachment theory is generally attributed to Bowlby (1969, 1973) who observed that, when separated from their primary caregiver, infants displayed diverse emotional reactions. Ainsworth and her colleagues (1978) subsequently provided a three-category system for identifying the primary attachment style of an infant based on the consistency with which his or her primary caregiver attended to needs. Applying this theory to adult romantic relationships, Hazan and Shaver (1987) described attachment along these same three dimensions: Individuals with a *secure* attachment style are comfortable with intimate relationships, enjoy becoming somewhat dependent on others, and do not often worry about abandonment. The *avoidant* style refers to difficulty in trusting other people and a general reluctance to get close. Finally, the *anxious/ambivalent* individual desires to be close with others but is apprehensive that others will not share this feeling.

8. Several scholars (e.g., Bem, 1974; Spence & Helmreich, 1978) advocate using items tapping self-perceptions of expressiveness and instrumentality as assessments of gender-role orientation. These measures, however, have often been only moderately correlated with biological sex and other measures of gender (Burleson et al., 2003; MacGeorge, Graves, et al., 2004); thus, they appear to be less measures of gender than of personality traits that may be manifest in members of both sexes.

9. This result was present only for husbands but not for wives, suggesting that some men may use a heuristic pertaining to general relationship satisfaction to judge supportive behaviors of their wives (e.g., "My wife provides good support"). Consistent with research on sex differences in support message evaluations, however, wives may be more motivated or able to process support messages systematically regardless of their relationship attributions.

REFERENCES

Acitelli, L. K., & Antonucci, T. C. (1994). Gender differences in the link between marital support and satisfaction in older couples. *Journal of Personality and Social Psychology, 67,* 688-698.

Ainsworth, M. D. S., Blehar, M. C., Waters, E., & Wall, S. (1978). *Patterns of attachment: A psychological study of the strange situation.* Hillsdale, NJ: Erlbaum.

Albrecht, T. L. (1994). Social support and community: A historical account of the rescue networks in Denmark. In B. R. Burleson, T. L. Albrecht, & I. G. Sarason (Eds.), *Communication of social support: Messages, interactions, relationships, and community* (pp. 267-279). Thousand Oaks, CA: Sage.

Albrecht, T. L., & Goldsmith, D. J. (2003). Social support, social networks, and health. In T. L. Thompson, A. M. Dorsey, K. I. Miller, & R. Parrott (Eds.), *Handbook of health communication* (pp. 263-284). Mahwah, NJ: Erlbaum.

Anderson, T., Carson, K. L., Darchuk, A. J., & Keefe, F. J. (2004). The influence of social skills on private and interpersonal emotional disclosure of negative events. *Journal of Social and Clinical Psychology, 23*, 635-652.

Antonucci, T. C. (1990). Social support and social relationships. In R. H. Binstock & L. K. George (Eds.), *Handbook of aging and the social sciences* (3rd ed., pp. 205-226). Orlando, FL: Academic Press.

Apker, J., & Ray, E. B. (2003). Stress and social support in health care organizations. In T. L. Thompson, A. M. Dorsey, K. I. Miller, & R. Parrott (Eds.), *Handbook of health communication* (pp. 347-368). Mahwah, NJ: Erlbaum.

Applegate, J. L. (1990). Constructs and communication: A pragmatic integration. In G. Neimeyer & R. Neimeyer (Eds.), *Advances in personal construct psychology* (Vol. 1, pp. 203-230). Greenwich, CT: JAI Press.

Applegate, J. L., Burke, J. A., Burleson, B. R., Delia, J. G., & Kline, S. L. (1985). Reflection-enhancing parental communication. In I. E. Sigel (Ed.), *Parental belief systems: The psychological consequences for children* (pp. 107-142). Hillsdale, NJ: Erlbaum.

Asendorpf, J. B., & Wilpers, S. (2000). Attachment security and available support: Closely linked relationship qualities. *Journal of Social and Personal Relationships, 17*, 115-138.

Ashton, W. A., & Fuehrer, A. (1993). Effects of gender and gender role identification of participant and type of social support resource on support seeking. *Sex Roles, 28*, 461-476.

Barbee, A. P., & Cunningham, M. R. (1995). An experimental approach to social support communications: Interactive coping in close relationships. In B. R. Burleson (Ed.), *Communication yearbook 18* (pp. 381-413). Thousand Oaks, CA: Sage.

Barbee, A. P., Cunningham, M. R., Winstead, B. A., Derlega, V. J., Gulley, M. R., Yankeelov, P. A., et al. (1993). Effects of gender role expectations on the social support process. *Journal of Social Issues, 49*(3), 175-190.

Barbee, A. P., Derlega, V. J., Sherburne, S. P., & Grimshaw, A. (1998). Helpful and unhelpful forms of social support for HIV-positive individuals. In V. J. Derlega & A. P. Barbee (Eds.), *HIV and social interaction* (pp. 83-105). Thousand Oaks, CA: Sage.

Barrett, L. F., Tugade, M. M., & Engle, R. W. (2004). Individual differences in working memory capacity and dual-process theories of the mind. *Psychological Bulletin, 130*, 553-573.

Basow, S. A., & Rubenfeld, K. (2003). "Troubles talk": Effects of gender and gender-typing. *Sex Roles, 48*, 183-187.

Bem, S. L. (1974). The measurement of psychological androgyny. *Journal of Consulting and Clinical Psychology, 42*, 155-162.

Berger, C. R. (2005). Interpersonal communication: Theoretical perspectives, future prospects. *Journal of Communication, 55*, 415-447.

Bergin, C., Talley, S., & Hamer, L. (2003). Prosocial behaviors of young adolescents: A focus group study. *Journal of Adolescence, 26*, 13-32.

Blieszner, R. (2000). Close relationships in old age. In C. Hendrick & S. S. Hendrick (Eds.), *Close relationships: A sourcebook* (pp. 84-95). Thousand Oaks, CA: Sage.

Bodie, G. D., & Burleson, B. R. (2006, November). *A dual-process model for the reception and outcomes of supportive messages.* Paper presented at the annual meeting of the National Communication Association, San Antonio, TX.

Bowlby, J. (1969). *Attachment and loss: Vol. 1. Attachment.* New York: Basic Books.

Bowlby, J. (1973). *Attachment and loss: Vol. II: Separation.* New York: Basic Books.

Brackett, M. A., Mayer, J. D., & Warner, R. M. (2004). Emotional intelligence and its relation to everyday behaviour. *Personality and Individual Differences, 36,* 1387-1402.

Burleson, B. R. (1984). Age, social-cognitive development, and the use of comforting strategies. *Communication Monographs, 51,* 140-153.

Burleson, B. R. (1994). Comforting messages: Features, functions, and outcomes. In J. A. Daly & J. M. Wiemann (Eds.), *Strategic interpersonal communication* (pp. 135-161). Hillsdale, NJ: Erlbaum.

Burleson, B. R. (2003). Emotional support skills. In J. O. Greene & B. R. Burleson (Eds.), *Handbook of communication and social interaction skills* (pp. 551-594). Mahwah, NJ: Erlbaum.

Burleson, B. R. (in press). What counts as effective emotional support? Explorations of individual and situation differences. In M. T. Motley (Ed.), *Studies in applied interpersonal communication.* Thousand Oaks, CA: Sage.

Burleson, B. R., & Caplan, S. E. (1998). Cognitive complexity. In J. C. McCroskey, J. A. Daly, M. M. Martin, & M. J. Beatty (Eds.), *Communication and personality: Trait perspectives* (pp. 230-286). Cresskill, NJ: Hampton Press.

Burleson, B. R., & Gilstrap, C. M. (2002). Explaining sex differences in interaction goals in support situations: Some mediating effects of expressivity and instrumentality. *Communication Reports, 15,* 43-55.

Burleson, B. R., & Goldsmith, D. J. (1998). How the comforting process works: Alleviating emotional distress through conversationally induced reappraisals. In P. A. Andersen & L. K. Guerrero (Eds.), *Handbook of communication and emotion: Research, theory, applications, and contexts* (pp. 245-280). San Diego, CA: Academic Press.

Burleson, B. R., Holmstrom, A. J., & Gilstrap, C. M. (2003, November). *Are men unmotivated to use highly person-centered comforting messages? An evaluation of sex and gender differences in liking for highly person-centered helpers.* Paper presented at the annual meeting of the National Communication Association, Miami Beach, FL.

Burleson, B. R., Holmstrom, A. J., & Gilstrap, C. M. (2005). "Guys can't say *that* to guys": Four experiments assessing the normative motivation account for deficiencies in the emotional support provided by men. *Communication Monographs, 72,* 468-501.

Burleson, B. R., & Kunkel, A. W. (2006). Revisiting the different cultures thesis: An assessment of sex differences and similarities in supportive communication. In K. Dindia & D. J. Canary (Eds.), *Sex differences and similarities in communication* (2nd ed., pp. 137-159). Mahwah, NJ: Erlbaum.

Burleson, B. R., Kunkel, A. W., Samter, W., & Werking, K. J. (1996). Men's and women's evaluations of communication skills in personal relationships: When sex differences make a difference—and when they don't. *Journal of Social and Personal Relationships, 13,* 201-224.

Burleson, B. R., Liu, M., Liu, Y., & Mortenson, S. T. (2006). Chinese evaluations of emotional support skills, goals, and behaviors: An assessment of gender-related similarities and differences. *Communication Research, 33*, 38-63.

Burleson, B. R., & MacGeorge, E. L. (2002). Supportive communication. In M. L. Knapp & J. A. Daly (Eds.), *Handbook of interpersonal communication* (3rd ed., pp. 374-424). Thousand Oaks, CA: Sage.

Burleson, B. R., & Mortenson, S. R. (2003). Explaining cultural differences in evaluations of emotional support behaviors: Exploring the mediating influences of value systems and interaction goals. *Communication Research, 30*, 113-146.

Burleson, B. R., & Samter, W. (1985a). Consistencies in theoretical and naive evaluations of comforting messages. *Communication Monographs, 52*, 103-123.

Burleson, B. R., & Samter, W. (1985b). Individual differences in the perception of comforting messages: An exploratory investigation. *Central States Speech Journal, 36*, 39-50.

Burleson, B. R., Samter, W., Jones, S. M., Kunkel, A. W., Holmstrom, A. J., Mortenson, S. T., et al. (2005). Which comforting messages *really* work best? A different perspective on Lemieux and Tighe's "receiver perspective." *Communication Research Reports, 22*, 87-100.

Cacioppo, J. T., & Petty, R. E. (1982). The need for cognition. *Journal of Personality and Social Psychology, 42*, 116-131.

Carels, R. A., & Baucom, D. H. (1999). Support in marriage: Factors associated with on-line perceptions of support helpfulness. *Journal of Family Psychology, 13*, 131-144.

Chaiken, S. (1980). Heuristic versus systematic information processing and the use of source versus message cues in persuasion. *Journal of Personality & Social Psychology, 39*, 752-766.

Chaiken, S., & Trope, Y. (Eds.). (1999). *Dual-process theories in social psychology*. New York: Guilford.

Chang, H., & Holt, R. (1991). More than a relationship: Chinese interaction and the principle of *kuan-hsi*. *Communication Quarterly, 39*, 251-271.

Christenfeld, N., Gerin, W., Linden, W., Sanders, M., Mathur, J., Diech, J. D., et al. (1997). Social support effects on cardiovascular reactivity: Is a stranger as effective as a friend? *Psychosomatic Medicine, 59*, 388-398.

Clark, L. F. (1993). Stress and the cognitive-conversational benefits of social interaction. *Journal of Social and Clinical Psychology, 12*, 25-55.

Clark, R. A., & MacGeorge, E. L. (2006, November). *Evaluations of comforting strategies: Two studies of children and adolescents.* Paper presented at the annual meeting of the National Communication Association, San Antonio, TX.

Clark, R. A., Pierce, A. J., Finn, K., Hsu, K., Toosley, A., & Williams, L. (1998). The impact of alternative approaches to comforting, closeness of relationship, and gender on multiple measures of effectiveness. *Communication Studies, 49*, 224-239.

Clark, S. L., & Stephens, M. A. P. (1996). Stroke patients' well-being as a function of caregiving spouses' helpful and unhelpful actions. *Personal Relationships, 3*, 171-184.

Clinton, B. L., & Hancock, G. R. (1991). The development of an understanding of comforting messages. *Communication Reports, 4*, 54-63.

Collins, N. L., & Feeney, B. C. (2004). Working models of attachment shape perceptions of social support: Evidence from experimental and observational studies. *Journal of Personality and Social Psychology, 87*, 363-383.

Coopman, S. Z. (1997). Personal constructs and communication in interpersonal and organizational contexts. In G. Neimeyer & R. Neimeyer (Eds.), *Advances in personal construct psychology* (Vol. 4, pp. 101-147). Greenwich, CT: JAI Press.

Cummins, R. C. (1988). Perceptions of social support, receipt of supportive behaviors, and locus of control as moderators of the effects of chronic stress. *American Journal of Community Psychology, 16,* 685-700.

Cunningham, M. R., & Barbee, A. P. (2000). Social support. In C. Hendrick & S. S. Hendrick (Eds.), *Close relationships: A sourcebook* (pp. 272-285). Thousand Oaks, CA: Sage.

Cutrona, C. E. (1996). *Social support in couples.* Thousand Oaks, CA: Sage.

Cutrona, C. E., Cohen, B. B., & Igram, S. (1990). Contextual determinants of the perceived helpfulness of helping behaviors. *Journal of Social and Personal Relationships, 7,* 553-562.

Cutrona, C. E., & Cole, V. (2000). Optimizing support in the natural network. In S. Cohen, L. G. Underwood, & B. H. Gottlieb (Eds.), *Social support measurement and intervention: A guide for health and social scientists* (pp. 278-308). New York: Oxford University Press.

Cutrona, C. E., & Suhr, J. A. (1992). Controllability of stressful events and satisfaction with spouse support behaviors. *Communication Research, 19,* 154-174.

Dakof, G. A., & Taylor, S. E. (1990). Victims' perceptions of support attempts: What is helpful from whom? *Journal of Personality and Social Psychology, 58,* 80-89.

Dekovic, M., & Gerris, J. R. M. (1992). Parental reasoning complexity, social class, and child rearing behaviors. *Journal of Marriage and the Family, 54,* 675-685.

Denton, K., & Zarbatany, K. (1996). Age differences in support processes in conversations with friends. *Child Development, 67,* 1360-1373.

Derlega, V. J., Barbee, A. P., & Winstead, B. A. (1994). Friendship, gender, and social support: Laboratory studies of supportive interactions. In B. R. Burleson, T. L. Albrecht, & I. G. Sarason (Eds.), *Communication of social support: Messages, interactions, relationships, and community* (pp. 136-151). Thousand Oaks, CA: Sage.

Derlega, V. J., Winstead, B. A., Oldfield, E. C., III, & Barbee, A. P. (2003). Close relationships and social support in coping with HIV: A test of sensitive interaction systems theory. *AIDS and Behavior, 7,* 119-129.

Donnelly, D. A., & Murray, E. J. (1991). Cognitive and emotional changes in written essays and therapy interviews. *Journal of Social and Clinical Psychology, 10,* 334-350.

Dunkel-Schetter, C., Blasband, D., Feinstein, L., & Herbert, T. (1992). Elements of supportive interactions: When are attempts to help effective? In S. Spacapan & S. Oskamp (Eds.), *Helping and being helped: Naturalistic studies* (pp. 83-114). Newbury Park, CA: Sage.

Eagly, A. H. (1987). *Sex differences in social behavior: A social-role interpretation.* Hillsdale, NJ: Erlbaum.

Feingold, A. (1994). Gender differences in personality: A meta-analysis. *Psychological Bulletin, 116,* 429-456.

Feng, B. (2006). *Assessing features and effects of advice in supportive interactions in two cultures.* Unpublished doctoral dissertation, Purdue University, West Lafayette, IN.

Feng, B. (2007, November). *Testing an integrated model of advice-giving in supportive interactions*. Paper presented at the annual meeting of the National Communication Association, Chicago.

Feng, B., & Burleson, B. R. (2006). Exploring the support-seeking process across cultures: Toward an integrated analysis of similarities and differences. In M. P. Orbe, B. J. Allen, & L. A. Flores (Eds.), *The same and different: Acknowledging the diversity within and between cultural groups* (pp. 243-266). Washington, DC: National Communication Association.

Feng, B., & MacGeorge, E. L. (2006). Predicting receptiveness to advice: Characteristics of the problem, the advice-giver, and the recipient. *Southern Communication Journal, 71,* 67-85.

Fincham, F. D., Garnier, P. C., Gano-Phillips, S., & Osborne, L. N. (1995). Preinteraction expectations, marital satisfaction, and accessibility: A new look at sentiment override. *Journal of Family Psychology, 9,* 3-14.

Forgas, J. (2001). Affect, cognition, and interpersonal behavior: The mediating role of processing strategies. In J. Forgas (Ed.), *Handbook of affect and social cognition* (pp. 293-318). Mahwah, NJ: Erlbaum.

Frazier, P. A., Tix, A. P., & Barnett, C. L. (2003). The relational context of social support: Relationship satisfaction moderates the relations between enacted support and distress. *Personality and Social Psychology Bulletin, 29,* 1133-1146.

Gao, G., Ting-Toomey, S., & Gudykunst, W. B. (1996). Chinese communication processes. In M. H. Bond (Ed.), *The handbook of Chinese psychology* (pp. 280-293). New York: Oxford University Press.

Gardner, K. A., & Cutrona, C. E. (2004). Social support communication in families. In A. L. Vangelisti (Ed.), *Handbook of family communication* (pp. 495-512). Mahwah, NJ: Erlbaum.

Gass, R. H., & Seiter, J. S. (2007). *Persuasion, social influence, and compliance gaining* (3rd ed.). Boston: Allyn & Bacon.

Glynn, L. M., Christenfeld, N., & Gerin, W. (1999). Gender, social support, and cardiovascular responses to stress. *Psychosomatic Medicine, 61,* 234-242.

Goldsmith, D. J. (1994). The role of facework in supportive communication. In B. R. Burleson, T. L. Albrecht, & I. G. Sarason (Eds.), *Communication of social support: Messages, interactions, relationships, and community* (pp. 29-49). Thousand Oaks, CA: Sage.

Goldsmith, D. J. (2000). Soliciting advice: The role of sequential placement in mitigating face threat. *Communication Monographs, 67,* 1-19.

Goldsmith, D. J. (2004). *Communicating social support.* New York: Cambridge University Press.

Goldsmith, D. J., & Albrecht, T. L. (1993). The impact of supportive communication networks on test anxiety and performance. *Communication Education, 42,* 142-158.

Goldsmith, D. J., & Dun, S. A. (1997). Sex differences and similarities in the communication of social support. *Journal of Social and Personal Relationships, 14,* 317-337.

Goldsmith, D. J., & Fitch, K. (1997). The normative context of advice as social support. *Human Communication Research, 23,* 454-476.

Goldsmith, D. J., & MacGeorge, E. L. (2000). The impact of politeness and relationship on perceived quality of advice about a problem. *Human Communication Research, 26,* 234-263.

Gotlib, I. H., Roberts, J. E., & Gilboa, E. (1996). Cognitive interference in depression. In I. G. Sarason, G. R. Pierce, & B. R. Sarason (Eds.), *Cognitive interference: Theories, methods, and findings* (pp. 347-377). Mahwah, NJ: Erlbaum.

Gotlib, I. H., Yue, D. N., & Joormann, J. (2005). Selective attention in dysphoric individuals: The role of affective interference and inhibition. *Cognitive Therapy and Research, 29,* 417-432.

Gottlieb, B. H. (2000). Selecting and planning support interventions. In S. Cohen, L. G. Underwood, & B. H. Gottlieb (Eds.), *Social support measurement and intervention* (pp. 195-220). New York: Oxford University Press.

Greenberg, L. S. (1993). Emotion and change processes in psychotherapy. In M. Lewis & J. M. Haviland (Eds.), *Handbook of emotions* (pp. 499-508). New York: Guilford.

Gudykunst, W. B., & Matsumoto, Y. (1996). Cross-cultural variability of communication in personal relationships. In W. B. Gudykunst, S. Ting-Toomey, & T. Nishida (Eds.), *Communication in personal relationships across cultures* (pp. 19-56). Thousand Oaks, CA: Sage.

Hagedoorn, M., Kuijer, R. G., Buunk, B. P., DeJong, G. M., Wobbes, T., & Sanderman, R. (2000). Marital satisfaction in patients with cancer: Does support from intimate partners benefit those who need it most? *Health Psychology, 19,* 274-282.

Hall, E. T. (1976). *Beyond culture.* New York: Doubleday.

Haugtvedt, C. P., & Petty, R. E. (1992). Personality and persuasion: Need for cognition moderates the persistence and resistance of attitude changes. *Journal of Personality and Social Psychology, 63,* 308-319.

Hays, R. B., Magee, R. H., & Chauncey, S. (1994). Identifying helpful and unhelpful behaviours of loved ones: The PWA's perspective. *AIDS Care, 4,* 379-392.

Hazan, C., & Shaver, P. (1987). Romantic love conceptualized as an attachment process. *Journal of Personality and Social Psychology, 52,* 511-525.

Helgeson, V. S., Cohen, S., Schulz, R., & Yasko, J. (2000). Group support interventions for people with cancer: Who benefits from what? *Health Psychology, 19,* 107-117.

Herzberg, D. S., Hammen, C., Burge, D., Daley, S. E., Davila, J., & Lindberg, N. (1999). Attachment cognitions predict perceived and enacted social support during late adolescence. *Journal of Adolescent Research, 14,* 387-404.

Hill, C. A. (1987). Social support and health: The role of affiliative need as a moderator. *Journal of Research in Personality, 21,* 127-147.

Hill, C. A. (1997). Relationship of expressive and affiliative personality dispositions to perceptions of social support. *Basic and Applied Social Psychology, 19,* 133-161.

Hill, C. A., & Christensen, A. J. (1989). Affiliative need, different types of social support, and physical symptoms. *Journal of Applied Social Psychology, 19,* 1351-1370.

Hill, W. G., & Donatelle, R. J. (2005). The impact of gender role conflict on multidimensional social support in older men. *International Journal of Men's Health, 4,* 267-276.

Hobfoll, S. E., Nadler, A., & Leiberman, J. (1986). Satisfaction with social support during crisis: Intimacy and self-esteem as critical determinants. *Journal of Personality and Social Psychology, 51,* 296-304.

Hollander, G. R., & Hokanson, J. E. (1988). Dysphoria and the perception of incongruent communications. *Cognitive Therapy and Research, 12,* 577-589.

Holmstrom, A. J., Burleson, B. R., & Jones, S. M. (2005). Some consequences for helpers who deliver "cold comfort": Why it's worse for women than men to be inept when providing emotional support. *Sex Roles, 53,* 153-172.

House, J. S., Landis, K. R., & Umberson, D. (1988). Social relationships and health. *Science, 241*, 540-545.

Hullett, C. R., McMillan, J. J., & Rogan, R. G. (2000). Caregivers' predispostions and perceived organizational expectations for the provision of social support to nursing home residents. *Health Communication, 12*, 277-300.

Jacobson, D. E. (1986). Types and timing of social support. *Journal of Health and Social Behavior, 27*, 250-264.

Jones, S. M. (2005). Attachment style differences and similarities in evaluations of affectively oriented communication skills and person-centered comforting messages. *Western Journal of Communication, 69*, 233-249.

Jones, S. M., & Burleson, B. R. (1997). The impact of situational variables on helpers' perceptions of comforting messages: An attributional analysis. *Communication Research, 24*, 530-555.

Jones, S. M., & Wirtz, J. (2006). How *does* the comforting process work?: An empirical test of an appraisal-based model of comforting. *Human Communication Research, 32*, 217-243.

Kaul, M., & Lakey, B. (2003). Where is the support in perceived support? The role of generic relationship satisfaction and enacted support in perceived support's relation to low distress. *Journal of Social and Clinical Psychology, 22*, 59-78.

Knobloch, L., MacGeorge, E. L., & Lucchetti, A. E. (2004, July). *Relationship development and evaluations of supportive messages*. Paper presented at the biennial meeting of the International Association for Relationships Research, Madison, WI.

Kuijer, R. G., Buunk, B. P., & Ybema, J. F. (2001). Justice of give-and-take in the intimate relationship: When one partner of a couple is diagnosed with cancer. *Personal Relationships, 8*, 75-92.

Kuijer, R. G., Ybema, J. F., Buunk, B. P., De Jong, G. M., Thijs-Boer, F., & Sanderman, R. (2000). Active engagement, protective buffering, and overprotection: Three ways of giving support by intimate partners of patients with cancer. *Journal of Social and Clinical Psychology, 19*, 256-275.

Kunkel, A. W. (2002). Explaining sex differences in the evaluation of comforting messages: The mediating role of interaction goals. *Communication Reports, 15*, 29-42.

Kunkel, A. W., & Burleson, B. R. (1999). Assessing explanations for sex differences in emotional support: A test of the different cultures and skill specialization accounts. *Human Communication Research, 25*, 307-340.

Lakey, B., & Cassady, P. B. (1990). Cognitive processes in perceived social support. *Journal of Personality and Social Psychology, 59*, 337-348.

Lakey, B., & Cohen, S. (2000). Social support theory and measurement. In S. Cohen, L. G. Underwood, & B. H. Gottlieb (Eds.), *Social support measurement and intervention* (pp. 29-52). New York: Oxford University Press.

Lakey, B., & Lutz, C. J. (1996). Social support and preventive and therapeutic interventions. In G. R. Pierce, B. R. Sarason, & I. G. Sarason (Eds.), *Handbook of social support and the family* (pp. 435-465). New York: Plenum Press.

Lakey, B., McCabe, K. M., Fiscaro, S., & Drew, J. B. (1996). Environmental and personal determinants of support perceptions: Three generalizability studies. *Journal of Personality and Social Psychology, 70*, 1270-1280.

Lakey, B., Moineau, S., & Drew, J. B. (1992). Perceived social support and individual differences in the interpretation and recall of supportive behavior. *Journal of Social and Clinical Psychology, 11*, 336-348.

Larose, S., Moivin, M., & Doyle, A. B. (2001). Parental representations and attachment style as predictors of support-seeking behaviors and perceptions of support in an academic counseling relationship. *Personal Relationships, 8*, 93-113.

Lazarus, R. S. (1991). *Emotion and adaptation.* New York: Oxford University Press.

Lefcourt, H. M. (1982). *Locus of control: Current trends in theory and research* (2nd ed.). Hillsdale, NJ: Erlbaum.

Lefcourt, H. M., Martin, R. A., & Saleh, W. E. (1984). Locus of control and social support: Interactive moderators of stress. *Journal of Personality and Social Psychology, 47*, 378-389.

Lehman, D. R., Ellard, J. H., & Wortman, C. B. (1986). Social support for the bereaved: Recipients' and providers' perspectives on what is helpful. *Journal of Consulting and Clinical Psychology, 54*, 438-446.

Lehman, D. R., & Hemphill, K. J. (1990). Recipients' perceptions of support attempts and attributions for support attempts that fail. *Journal of Social and Personal Relationships, 7*, 563-574.

Lemieux, R., & Tighe, M. R. (2004). Attachment styles and the evaluation of comforting responses: A receiver perspective. *Communication Research Reports, 21*, 144-153.

Lepore, S. J. (1995). Cynicism, social support, and cardiovascular reactivity. *Health Psychology, 14*, 210-216.

Lepore, S. J., & Helgeson, V. S. (1998). Social constraints, intrusive thoughts, and mental health after prostate cancer. *Journal of Social & Clinical Psychology, 17*, 89-106.

Lepore, S. J., Ragan, J. D., & Jones, S. (2000). Talking facilitates cognitive-emotional processes of adaptation to an acute stressor. *Journal of Personality and Social Psychology, 78*, 499-508.

Lunsky, Y., & Benson, B. A. (2001). Perceived social support and mental retardation: A social-cognitive approach. *Cognitive Therapy and Research, 25*, 77-90.

MacGeorge, E. L., Feng, B., & Butler, G. L. (2003). Gender differences in the communication values of mature adults. *Communication Research Reports, 20*, 191-199.

MacGeorge, E. L., Feng, B., Butler, G. L., & Budarz, S. K. (2004). Understanding advice in supportive interactions: Beyond the facework and message evaluation paradigm. *Human Communication Research, 30*, 42-70.

MacGeorge, E. L., Gillihan, S. J., Samter, W., & Clark, R. A. (2003). Skill deficit or differential motivation? Accounting for sex differences in the provision of emotional support. *Communication Research, 30*, 272-303.

MacGeorge, E. L., Graves, A. R., Feng, B., Gillihan, S. J., & Burleson, B. R. (2004). The myth of gender cultures: Similarities outweigh differences in men's and women's provision of and responses to supportive communication. *Sex Roles, 50*, 143-175.

MacGeorge, E. L., Lichtman, R., & Pressey, L. (2002). The evaluation of advice in supportive interactions: Facework and contextual factors. *Human Communication Research, 28*, 451-463.

MacGeorge, E. L., Samter, W., & Gillihan, S. J. (2005). Academic stress, supportive communication, and health. *Communication Education, 54*, 365-372.

Mankowski, E. S., & Wyer, R. S., Jr. (1996). Cognitive processes in perceptions of social support. *Personality & Social Psychology Bulletin, 22*, 894-905.

Mankowski, E. S., & Wyer, R. S., Jr. (1997). Cognitive causes and consequences of perceived social support. In G. R. Pierce & B. Lakey (Eds.), *Sourcebook of social support and personality. The Plenum series in social/clinical psychology* (pp. 141-165). New York: Plenum Press.

Manne, S., Alfieri, T., Taylor, K., & Dougherty, J. (1999). Preferences for spousal support among individuals with cancer. *Journal of Applied Social Psychology, 29,* 722-749.

Markus, H. M., Smith, J., & Moreland, R. L. (1985). Role of the self-concept in the social perception of others. *Journal of Personality and Social Psychology, 49,* 1494-1512.

Miller, J. B. (2001). Attachment models and memory for conversations. *Journal of Social and Personal Relationships, 18,* 404-422.

Mortenson, S. T., Liu, M., Burleson, B. R., & Liu, Y. (2006). A fluency of feeling: Exploring cultural and individual differences (and similarities) related to skilled emotional support. *Journal of Cross Cultural Psychology, 37,* 366-385.

Nadler, A. (1986). Self-esteem and the seeking and receiving of help: Theoretical and empirical perspectives. In B. Maher & W. Maher (Eds.), *Progress in experimental personality research* (Vol. 14, pp. 115-163). New York: Academic Press.

Nolen-Hoeksema, S., & Larson, J. (1998). *Coping with loss.* Mahwah, NJ: Erlbaum.

Nolen-Hoeksema, S., & Morrow, J. (1993). Effects of rumination and distraction on naturally occurring depressed mood. *Cognition and Emotion, 7,* 561-570.

Ognibene, T. C., & Collins, N. L. (1998). Adult attachment styles, perceived social support, and coping strategies. *Journal of Social and Personal Relationships, 15,* 323-345.

O'Keefe, D. J. (2002). *Persuasion: Theory and research* (2nd ed.). Thousand Oaks, CA: Sage.

Oxley, N. L., Dzindolet, M. T., & Miller, J. L. (2002). Sex differences in communication with close friends: Testing Tannen's claims. *Psychological Reports, 91,* 537-544.

Parkes, C. M. (1982). Role of support systems in loss and psychosocial transitions. In H. C. Schulberg & M. Killilea (Eds.), *The modern practice of community mental health* (pp. 215-229). San Francisco: Jossey-Bass.

Parks, M. R. (1994). Communicative competence and interpersonal control. In M. L. Knapp & G. R. Miller (Eds.), *Handbook of interpersonal communication* (2nd ed., pp. 589-619). Thousand Oaks, CA: Sage.

Pennebaker, J. W. (1997). *Opening up: The healing power of expressing emotions* (Rev. ed.). New York: Guilford.

Perloff, R. M. (2003). *The dynamics of persuasion: Communication and attitudes in the 21st century* (2nd ed.). Mahwah, NJ: Erlbaum.

Petty, R. E., & Brock, T. C. (1981). Thought disruption and persuasion: Assessing the validity of attitude change experiments. In R. E. Petty, T. M. Ostrom, & T. C. Brock (Eds.), *Cognitive responses in persuasion* (pp. 55-79). Hillsdale, NJ: Erlbaum.

Petty, R. E., & Cacioppo, J. T. (1986). *Communication and persuasion: Central and peripheral routes to attitude change.* New York: Springer.

Petty, R. E., Cacioppo, J. T., & Heesacker, M. (1984). Central and peripheral routes to persuasion: Application to counseling. In R. P. McGlynn, J. E. Maddux, C. D. Stoltenberg, & J. H. Harvey (Eds.), *Interfaces in psychology: Social perception in clinical and counseling psychology* (Vol. 2, pp. 59-89). Lubbock: Texas Tech University Press.

Petty, R. E., Haugtvedt, C. P., & Smith, S. M. (1995). Elaboration as a determinant of attitude strength: Creating attitudes that are persistent, resistant, and predictive of behavior. In R. E. Petty & J. A. Krosnick (Eds.), *Attitude strength: Antecendents and consequences* (pp. 93-130). Mahwah, NJ: Erlbaum.

Petty, R. E., Rucker, D. D., Bizer, G. Y., & Cacioppo, J. T. (2004). The elaboration likelihood model of persuasion. In J. S. Seiter & R. H. Gass (Eds.), *Perspectives on persuasion, social influence, and compliance gaining* (pp. 65-89). Boston: Allyn & Bacon.

Petty, R. E., Schumann, D. W., Richman, S. A., & Strathman, A. J. (1993). Positive mood and persuasion: Different roles for affect under high- and low-elaboration conditions. *Journal of Personality and Social Psychology, 64*, 5-20.

Petty, R. E., & Wegener, D. T. (1999). The elaboration likelihood model: Current status and controversies. In S. Chaiken & Y. Trope (Eds.), *Dual-process theories in social psychology* (pp. 41-72). New York: Guilford.

Pierce, G. R., Sarason, B. R., & Sarason, I. G. (1992). General and specific support expectations and stress as predictors of perceived supportiveness: An experimental study. *Journal of Personality and Social Psychology, 63*, 297-307.

Pierce, G. R., Sarason, I. G., & Sarason, B. R. (1991). General and relationship-based perceptions of social support: Are two constructs better than one? *Journal of Personality and Social Psychology, 61*, 1028-1039.

Prentice, D. A., & Carranza, E. (2002). What women and men should be, shouldn't be, are allowed to be, and don't have to be: The contents of prescriptive gender stereotypes. *Psychology of Women Quarterly, 26*, 269-281.

Reis, H. T., & Collins, N. (2000). Measuring relationship properties and interactions relevant to social support. In S. Cohen, L. G. Underwood, & B. H. Gottlieb (Eds.), *Social support measurement and intervention* (pp. 136-192). New York: Oxford University Press.

Ritter, E. M. (1979). Social perspective taking ability, cognitive complexity, and listener adapted communication in early and late adolescence. *Communication Monographs, 46*, 40-51.

Samter, W. (2002). How gender and cognitive complexity influence the provision of emotional support: A study of indirect effects. *Communication Reports, 15*, 5-16.

Samter, W., Burleson, B. R., & Basden-Murphy, L. (1989). Behavioral complexity is in the eye of the beholder: Effects of cognitive complexity and message complexity on impressions of the source of comforting messages. *Human Communication Research, 15*, 612-629.

Samter, W., Burleson, B. R., & Murphy, L. B. (1987). Comforting conversations: Effects of strategy type on evaluations of messages and message producers. *Southern Speech Communication Journal, 52*, 263-284.

Samter, W., Whaley, B. B., Mortenson, S. R., & Burleson, B. R. (1997). Ethnicity and emotional support in same-sex friendship: A comparison of Asian-Americans, African-Americans, and Euro-Americans. *Personal Relationships, 4*, 413-430.

Sandler, I. N., & Lakey, B. (1982). Locus of control as a stress moderator: The role of control perceptions and social support. *American Journal of Community Psychology, 10*, 65-80.

Sarason, B. R., Sarason, I. G., & Gurung, R. A. R. (1997). Close personal relationships and health outcomes: A key to the role of social support. In S. Duck (Ed.), *Handbook of personal relationships* (2nd ed., pp. 547-573). Chichester, England: Wiley.

Schwarz, N., Bless, H., & Bohner, G. (1991). Mood and persuasion: Affective states influence the processing of persuasive communications. In M. P. Zanna (Ed.), *Advances in experimental social psychology* (Vol. 24, pp. 161-199). San Diego, CA: Academic Press.

Schwarzer, R., & Leppin, A. (1992). Social support and mental health: A conceptual and empirical overview. In L. Montada, S. H. Filipp, & M. J. Lerner (Eds.), *Life crises and experiences of loss in adult life* (pp. 435-458). Hillsdale, NJ: Erlbaum.

Segrin, C. (1998). Interpersonal communication problems associated with depression and loneliness. In P. A. Andersen & L. A. Guerrero (Eds.), *Handbook of communication and emotion: Research, theory, applications, and contexts* (pp. 215-242). San Diego, CA: Academic Press.

Segrin, C. (2003). Age moderates the relationship between social support and psychosocial problems. *Human Communication Research, 29*, 317-342.

Servaty-Seib, H. L., & Burleson, B. R. (2007). Bereaved adolescents' evaluations of the helpfulness of support-intended statements: Associations with person centeredness and demographic, personality, and contextual factors. *Journal of Social and Personal Relationships, 24*, 207-223.

Shirk, S. R., Van Horn, M., & Leber, D. (1997). Dysphoria and children's processing of supportive interactions. *Journal of Abnormal Child Psychology, 25*, 239-249.

Smyth, J. M., & Pennebaker, J. W. (1999). Sharing one's story: Translating emotional experiences into words as a coping tool. In C. R. Snyder (Ed.), *Coping: The psychology of what works* (pp. 70-89). New York: Oxford University Press.

Spence, J. T., & Buckner, C. (1995). Masculinity and femininity: Defining the undefinable. In P. J. Kalbfleisch & M. J. Cody (Eds.), *Gender, power, and communication in human relationships* (pp. 105-140). Hillsdale, NJ: Erlbaum.

Spence, J. T., & Helmreich, R. L. (1978). *Masculinity and femininity: Their psychological dimensions, correlates, and antecedents.* Austin: University of Texas Press.

Stiff, J. (1994). *Persuasive communication.* New York: Guilford.

Stiff, J., & Boster, F. J. (1987). Cognitive processing: Additional thoughts, and a reply to Petty, Kasmer, Haugtvedt, and Cacioppo. *Communication Monographs, 54*, 250-256.

Stroebe, W., & Stroebe, M. (1996). The social psychology of social support. In E. T. Higgins & A. W. Kruglanski (Eds.), *Social psychology: Handbook of basic principles* (pp. 597-621). New York: Guilford.

Suitor, J. J., & Pillemer, K. (2000). When experience counts most: Effects of experiential similarity on men's and women's receipt of support during bereavement. *Social Networks, 22*, 299-312.

Taylor, S. E., Sherman, D. K., Kim, H. S., Jarcho, J., Takagi, K., & Dunagan, M. S. (2004). Culture and social support: Who seeks it and why? *Journal of Personality and Social Psychology, 87*, 354-362.

Todorov, A., Chaiken, S., & Henderson, M. D. (2002). The heuristic-systematic model of social information processing. In J. P. Dillard & M. Pfau (Eds.), *The persuasion handbook: Developments in theory and practice* (pp. 195-211). Thousand Oaks, CA: Sage.

Trobst, K. K., Collins, R. L., & Embree, J. J. (1994). The role of emotion in social support provision: Gender, empathy, and expressions of distress. *Journal of Social and Personal Relationships, 11*, 45-62.

Uchino, B. N. (2004). *Social support and physical health: Understanding the health consequences of relationships.* New Haven, CT: Yale University Press.

Uno, D., Uchino, B. N., & Smith, T. W. (2002). Relationship quality moderates the effect of social support given by close friends on cardiovascular reactivity in women. *International Journal of Behavioral Medicine, 9*, 243-262.

Vinokur, A., Schul, Y., & Caplan, R. D. (1987). Determinants of perceived social support: Interpersonal transactions, personal outlook, and transient affect states. *Journal of Personality and Social Psychology, 53*, 1137-1145.

Weary, G. (1990). Depression and sensitivity to social information. In B. S. Moore & A. M. Isen (Eds.), *Affect and social behavior* (pp. 207-230). New York: Cambridge University Press.

Webster, D. M., & Kruglanski, A. W. (1994). Individual differences in need for cognitive closure. *Journal of Personality and Social Psychology, 67*, 261-271.

Wills, T. A., & Fegan, M. F. (2001). Social networks and social support. In A. Baum, T. A. Revenson, & J. E. Singer (Eds.), *Handbook of health psychology* (pp. 209-234). Mahwah, NJ: Erlbaum.

Wilson, S. R., & Sabee, C. M. (2003). Explicating communicative competence as a theoretical term. In J. O. Greene & B. R. Burleson (Eds.), *Handbook of communication and social interaction skills* (pp. 3-50). Mahwah, NJ: Erlbaum.

Wood, J. T. (1994). *Who cares? Women, care, and culture.* Carbondale: Southern Illinois University Press.

Wortman, C. B., Wolff, K., & Bonanno, G. A. (2004). Loss of an intimate partner through death. In D. J. Mashek & A. Aron (Eds.), *Handbook of closeness and intimacy* (pp. 305-320). Mahwah, NJ: Erlbaum.

Wright, K. B. (2002). Social support within an on-line cancer community: An assessment of emotional support, perceptions of advantages and disadvantages, and motives for using the community from a communication perspective. *Journal of Applied Communication Research, 30*, 195-209.

Wright, K. B., & Bell, S. B. (2003). Health-related support groups on the Internet: Linking empirical findings to social support and computer-mediated communication theory. *Journal of Health Psychology, 8*, 39-54.

Xu, Y., & Burleson, B. R. (2001). Effects of sex, culture, and support type on perceptions of spousal social support: An assessment of the "support gap" hypothesis in early marriage. *Human Communication Research, 27*, 535-566.

Xu, Y., & Burleson, B. R. (2004). The association of experienced spousal support with marital satisfaction: Evaluating the moderating effects of sex, ethnic culture, and type of support. *Journal of Family Communication, 4*, 123-145.

Young, S. L. (2004). Factors that influence recipients' appraisals of hurtful communication. *Journal of Social and Personal Relationships, 21*, 291-303.

Zoller, H. & Kline, K. (2008). Interpretive and critical research in health communication. In C. S. Beck (Ed.), *Communication yearbook 32* (pp. 89-135). New York: Routledge.

About the Editor

Christina S. Beck (Ph.D., University of Oklahoma, 1992) is Professor in the School of Communication Studies at Ohio University. In addition to editing *Communication Yearbook*, she contributes to *Journal of Health Communication: International Perspectives* as book review editor and serves on the editorial boards of four communication journals. She has authored or co-authored two award-winning books on health communication, *Communicating for Better Health: A Guide Through the Medical Mazes* (2001) and *Partnership for Health: Building Relationships Between Women and Health Caregivers* (1997, with Sandra Ragan and Athena duPre), and numerous journal articles and invited book chapters. She also co-edited *Narratives, Health, and Healing: Communication Theory, Research, and Practice* (2005) and *The Lynching of Language: Gender, Politics, and Power in the Hill-Thomas Hearings* (1996). Her research interests span the areas of health communication, language and social interaction, and mass communication.

About the Contributors

Sally Abdul Wahab is a doctoral student at the School of Communication, Information, and Library Studies at Rutgers University. She earned a B.A. in languages and translation from the University of Balamand in Lebanon and a master's degree in communication and information studies from Rutgers University. Her research interests focus on communication processes in virtual work teams and the impact of virtuality on the development of teams as effective communication and business entities.

Mariaelena Bartesaghi is an Assistant Professor of Communication at the University of South Florida. Her work in discourse analysis highlights the connections between talk in interaction and the larger institutional and social framework within which talk is situated, enabled, and constrained. Work from her dissertation research (forthcoming) addresses the dynamic of authority in therapy as one of unequal accountability between therapist and client in a conversational, institutional, and social context.

Johannes W. J. Beentjes is Professor of Communication Science at the Radboud University Nijmegen in The Netherlands. He graduated in psychology and wrote a thesis on children's television viewing and reading (Ph.D., Leiden University, 1990). He is a member of the Advisory Board of Sesamstraat, the Dutch version of "Sesame Street." In addition to children and media, his current interests include the production, nature, and effects of persuasive communication.

Graham Bodie (M.A., Auburn University, 2002) is a doctoral candidate at Purdue University and has already achieved distinction as a researcher in the areas of listening, information processing, and communication pedagogy. His work on these topics has been presented at regional, national, and international conferences and have been published in several journals. Graham currently serves as Member-at-Large, Special Projects with the International Listening Association.

Brant R. Burleson (Ph.D., University of Illinois, Urbana-Champaign, 1982) is a Professor of Communication at Purdue University. His research centers on communication skill acquisition and development, the effects of communication skills on relationship outcomes, the role of emotion in communication and relationships, and supportive forms of communication such as comforting. He has authored more than one hundred articles and chapters and has edited several publications, including *The Handbook of Communication* and *Social Interaction Skills, Communication of Social Support*, and *Communication Yearbook*. Recent awards include the Distinguished Scholar Award from the National Communication Association, the Berscheid-Hatfield Award for Distinguished Mid-Career Achievement from the International Association for Relationships Research, the Award for the Analysis of Interpersonal Communication in Applied Settings from the International Communication Association, and the Bernard J. Brommel Award for Outstanding Scholarship in Family Communication from the National Communication Association.

Theresa Castor (Ph.D., University of Washington) is an Associate Professor of Communication at the University of Wisconsin-Parkside. Her main areas of research are social construction, organizational decision making, and discourse analysis. She has examined decision making in the contexts of nonprofit boards, university governance, school boards, and student discussion groups. Her work has been published in *Management Communication Quarterly*, the *Journal of Business Communication,* the *International Encyclopedia of Communication*, and *New Directions for Teaching and Learning*.

George Cheney (Ph.D., Purdue University, 1985) is Professor of Communication at the University of Utah, where he also directs the Barbara and Norman Tanner Human Rights Center in conjunction with Peace and Conflict Studies. In addition, he is Adjunct Professor in Management Communication at The University of Waikato, Hamilton, New Zealand. George has authored, coauthored and coedited six books and more than eighty journal articles and book chapters. His teaching and research interests include identity, power, democracy, dissent, globalization, marketization, economic justice, and the rhetoric of war and peace. George has lectured, taught, and conducted research in Europe and Latin America as well.

Mohan J. Dutta (Ph.D., University of Minnesota) is an Associate Professor in the Department of Communication at Purdue University. He conducts research on critical and postcolonial approaches to health communication, with an emphasis on narratives of resistance in marginalized communities.

Jennifer Gibbs is an Assistant Professor of Communication at Rutgers University. She earned her M.A. and Ph.D. degrees from the Annenberg

School for Communication at the University of Southern California. Her research interests center around the impacts of globalization and new technologies on organizations and teams, and self-presentation and relationship formation in online contexts. Her work has been published in *Administrative Science Quarterly, Communication Research, Journal of Computer-Mediated Communication,* and *The Information Society,* among others.

Svetlana (Yana) Grushina is a Ph.D. candidate in the School of Communication, Information, and Library Studies at Rutgers University. She earned an M.A. in communication studies from Kent State University. She is interested in the nature of communication work in multinational organizations in the context of globalization, with a particular focus on corporate social responsibility as a communication practice and an evolving product of communication design.

Lisa Keränen (Ph.D., University of Pittsburgh, 2003) is an Assistant Professor of Communication and faculty affiliate of the Center for Science & Technology Policy Research at the University of Colorado at Boulder. Her research on the rhetoric of science, medicine, and bioethics appears in publications such as *Academic Medicine, Argumentation & Advocacy, Journal of Medical Humanities,* and the *Quarterly Journal of Speech.* Her review of terrorism and mass media scholarship resulted from a relatively new research foray into the rhetorical formations of bioterrorism and biodefense. She serves on the clinical ethics committee at Boulder Community Hospital and is an active member of the advisory board for the National Communication Association-Forum.

Kimberly N. Kline (Ph.D., University of Georgia, 1996) is an Associate Professor at the University of Texas at San Antonio. She employs rhetorical, narrative, critical-cultural, and feminist theories and methodologies to interrogate contemporary meanings of health, illness and medicine as well as their sociopolitical implications. Her research focuses on the social construction of health, illness, and medicine in popular media especially with regard to women's health issues. Published studies have addressed topics such as the theoretical and methodological issues in the study of health and the mass media, socially constructed understanding of issues associated with pregnancy and childbirth, and the persuasive potential and cultural sensitivity of breast cancer education materials. Her research can be found in such journals as *Health Communication, Journal of Health Communication, Social Science and Medicine,* and *Women & Language,* and in edited volumes including *Evaluating Women's Health Messages, The Handbook of Health Communication* and *Constructing Our Health: The Implications of Narrative for Enacting Illness and Wellness.*

Ruben P. Konig is an Associate Professor of Communication Science at the Radboud University Nijmegen in The Netherlands. He graduated in sociology and wrote a thesis on Christian religion and anti-Semitism (Ph.D, Radboud University, Nijmegen, 1997). His current interests include everyday media use and the use of television news.

Michael G. Lacy (Ph. D. University of Texas at Austin) is a Visiting Associate Professor at DePaul University in Chicago. His research, writing, and teaching interests include race, rhetoric, culture, and politics. He has presented original research at international and national communication conferences, and his work has been published by the Education Communication of the States. He is presently coediting a book volume (with Kent Ono, University of Illinois), *Critical Rhetorics of Race.*

Daniel J. Lair (Ph.D., University of Utah, 2007) is an Assistant Professor in the Department of Human Communication Studies at the University of Denver. His work takes critical-cultural and rhetorical approaches to organizational communication, with a particular emphasis on issues of work and identity and emphases on meaningful work, the ethics of work, work socialization, and the representation of work in popular culture. At the University of Denver, he teaches a seminar on the meaning of work for incoming first-year undergraduate students.

Dina Nekrassova is a Ph.D. candidate in the School of Communication, Information, and Library Studies at Rutgers University. She received a master's degree in communication from University of Alaska, Fairbanks. Her research interests include emotion work and its implications for the processes of identification, power construction, and decision making in co-located and virtual organizations.

Mahuya Pal (M.Sc., Calcutta University) is a doctoral candidate in the Department of Communication at Purdue University specializing in public relations and organizational communication. Her research interests include activism, transnational labour, resistance, globalization, and transformative politics

Sally Planalp (Ph.D., University of Wisconsin-Madison, 1983) is a Professor of Communication at the University of Utah. Her primary area of research is interpersonal communication with emphases in face-to-face interaction, close relationships, emotion and, more recently, end-of-life issues. Her work has appeared in journals such as *Journal of Social and Personal Relationships, Human Communication Research, Communication Monographs, Health Communication, Communication Theory* and in her book, *Communicating Emotion* (Cambridge, 1999). Her reading on emotion prompted her interest in happiness and quality of life, leading to the work represented in this volume. In 2006-2007, she and George Cheney taught a year-long interdisciplinary honors course on quality of life.

Judith E. Rosenbaum (Ph.D., Radboud University Nijmegen, 2007) is Assistant Professor in Mass Communication at Albany State University, Georgia. She graduated with a degree in communication science and wrote her doctoral thesis on media literacy. Her current interests include media education and media literacy.

Virginia Sanprie (M.A., San Diego State University, 2005) is a doctoral student at the University of Colorado at Boulder. Her scholarly interests include feminist rhetorical criticism and digital rhetoric. Her critical exploration of women in combat has appeared in *Feminist Media Studies*. Sanprie's recent work is concerned with the demands of new media texts and the development of critical vocabularies and frameworks to address those demands.

Heather Zoller (Ph.D., Purdue University, 2000) is an Associate Professor of Communication at the University of Cincinnati. Her research focuses on the politics of public health, specifically the influence of corporations, public health organizations, and activists on health discourse and public policy. Her theoretical concerns include power and resistance, dialog and participation, issue management, and identity. She has published in journals that include *Communication Monographs, Communication Theory, Health Communication, Management Communication Quarterly*, and *Journal of Applied Communication Research*, among others.

Ted Zorn (Ph.D., University of Kentucky, 1987) is Professor of Management Communication, University of Waikato, Hamilton, New Zealand. He teaches and conducts research in organizational communication. Current teaching and research interests center on organizational change processes, such as the adoption and implementation of new technologies and change-related communication. Recent publications include articles in the *Journal of Applied Communication Research* on influence processes in focus groups, *Health Communication* on socialization of medical students, *New Media & Society* on older people's experiences with computers, and The *Journal of Communication Management* on the role of emotion in implementing new technologies. He is coauthor of a textbook in organizational communication (*Organizational Communication in an Age of Globalization*) published in 2004 by Waveland Press. Professor Zorn is past chair of the organizational communication division of the National Communication Association (USA) and former editor of *Management Communication Quarterly*. He has extensive experience as a trainer and organizational development consultant.

Author Index

Subject index